MW01050164

Negotiation

*To my mother, Barbara Hames, my late father, Royal Hames,
and my wife, Corrinne Shearer, each of whom has given me
far more than I can ever hope to repay.*

Negotiation

Closing Deals,
Settling Disputes,
and Making
Team Decisions

David S. Hames
University of Nevada, Las Vegas

Los Angeles | London | New Delhi
Singapore | Washington DC

Los Angeles | London | New Delhi
Singapore | Washington DC

FOR INFORMATION:

SAGE Publications, Inc.
2455 Teller Road
Thousand Oaks, California 91320
E-mail: order@sagepub.com

SAGE Publications Ltd.
1 Oliver's Yard
55 City Road
London EC1Y 1SP
United Kingdom

SAGE Publications India Pvt. Ltd.
B 1/I 1 Mohan Cooperative Industrial Area
Mathura Road, New Delhi 110 044
India

SAGE Publications Asia-Pacific Pte. Ltd.
33 Pekin Street #02-01
Far East Square
Singapore 048763

Acquisitions Editor: Lisa Cuevas Shaw
Associate Editor: Eve Oettinger
Editorial Assistant: Mayan White
Typesetter: C & M Digitals (P) Ltd.
Proofreaders: Theresa Kay
                Susan Schon
                Gretchen Treadwell
Indexer: Rick Hurd
Cover Designer: Gail Buschman
Marketing Manager: Helen Salmon

Copyright © 2012 by SAGE Publications, Inc.

All rights reserved. No part of this book may be reproduced or utilized in any form or by any means, electronic or mechanical, including photocopying, recording, or by any information storage and retrieval system, without permission in writing from the publisher.

Printed in the United States of America

Library of Congress Cataloging-in-Publication Data

Hames, David (David S.)

Negotiation: closing deals, settling disputes, and making team decisions/David S. Hames.

p. cm.
Includes bibliographical references and index.

ISBN 978-1-4129-7399-1 (pbk.: acid-free paper)

1. Negotiation. 2. Persuasion (Psychology)
3. Communication. 4. Decision making. 5. Ethics. I. Title.

BF637.N4H35 2012
302.3—dc23   2011031162

This book is printed on acid-free paper.

11 12 13 14 15 10 9 8 7 6 5 4 3 2 1

Brief Contents

Acknowledgments   xvii

Preface   xix

PART I: THE FUNDAMENTALS   1

1 The Nature of Negotiation: What It Is and Why It Matters   3

2 Preparation: Building the Foundation for Negotiating   23

3 Distributive Bargaining: A Strategy for Claiming Value   57

4 Integrative Negotiation: A Strategy for Creating Value   83

5 Closing Deals: Persuading the Other Party to Say Yes   117

PART II: SPECIAL CHALLENGES   157

6 Communication: The Heart of All Negotiations   159

7 Decision Making: Are We Truly Rational?   205

8 Power and Influence: Changing Others' Attitudes and Behaviors   237

9 Ethics: Right and Wrong Do Exist When You Negotiate   267

10 Multiparty Negotiations: Managing the Additional Complexity   297

11 Individual Differences: How Our Unique Qualities Affect Negotiations   323

12 International Negotiations: Managing Culture and Other Complexities   355

13 Difficult Negotiations: Managing Others Who Play Dirty and Saying No to Those Who Play Nice   383

14 Third-Party Intervention: Recourse When Negotiations Sputter or Fail?   409

Appendix   459

Glossary   467

Index   477

About the Author   497

Detailed Contents

Acknowledgments   xvii

Preface   xix

PART I: THE FUNDAMENTALS   1

1 The Nature of Negotiation: What It Is and Why It Matters   3

Intended Benefits of This Chapter   3
The Essence of Negotiation   4
What Is Negotiation?   5
When Do People Negotiate?   6
Why Has Negotiation Become a More Important Skill?   6
     Technology   6
     The Workplace   7
How People Negotiate: The Dual Concerns Model   8
The Pros and Cons of Negotiating   9
What Does a Negotiation Look Like?   10
The Shadow Negotiation   10
Conclusion and Implications for Practice   11

READING 1.1 – ONLINE DISPUTE RESOLUTION: DO YOU
KNOW WHERE YOUR CHILDREN ARE?, BY DAVID A. LARSON   13

READING 1.2 – BALANCING ACT: HOW TO MANAGE NEGOTIATION TENSIONS, BY SUSAN HACKLEY   19

2 Preparation: Building the Foundation for Negotiating   23

Intended Benefits of This Chapter   23
The Essence of Preparation   23
The Preparation Process, or How to Make It All Happen   25
Strategic Planning: Establishing the Framework   25
     Defining the Situation   25
     Setting Goals   29
     Determining Your Strategy   30

Strategy Implementation: Operationalizing the Plan   30
    The Component Parts of the Situation   30
    Best Alternative to a Negotiated Agreement (BATNA)   32
    Reservation Prices or Resistance Points   33
    Bargaining Power   35
    Analyzing the Other Party   35
Rapport Building and Testing Assumptions   36
Where Should You Negotiate?   37
Conclusion and Implications for Practice   38
Appendix I: Preparation Checklist   39

READING 2.1 – HOW TO ANALYZE THAT PROBLEM, BY PERRIN STRYKER   42

READING 2.2 – INVESTIGATIVE NEGOTIATION, BY DEEPAK MALHOTRA AND MAX H. BAZERMAN   51

READING 3.1 – THE DANGERS OF COMPROMISE, BY MAX H. BAZERMAN   75

READING 3.2 – MASTER THE ART AND SCIENCE OF HAGGLING, BY PROGRAM ON NEGOTIATION   78

4 Integrative Negotiation: A Strategy for Creating Value 83

Intended Benefits of This Chapter   83
The Essence of Integrative Negotiation   83
Preparation and Integrative Bargaining   84
Integrative Negotiating Myths   86
Tactics of Integrative Bargaining   87
    Separating the Person From the Problem   87
    Focus on Interests, Not Positions   90
    Invent Options for Mutual Gain   92
    Types of Integrative Solutions   94
Use Objective Criteria to Evaluate Options   96
Fine Tuning Your Efforts to Achieve Integrative
    Solutions   97
    Avoid Focusing on One Issue at a Time   97
    Use Multiple Equivalent Offers   98
    Trust   98
Conclusion and Implications for Practice   99

READING 4.1 – TAKING STEPS TOWARD 'GETTING TO YES' AT
BLUE CROSS AND BLUE SHIELD OF FLORIDA, BY BRIDGET BOOTH AND MATT McCREDIE   103

READING 4.2 – 3-D NEGOTIATION: PLAYING THE WHOLE GAME,
BY DAVID A. LAX AND JAMES K. SEBENIUS   107

5 Closing Deals: Persuading the Other Party to Say Yes 117

Intended Benefits of This Chapter   117
The Essence of Closing Deals   118
The Most Common Objections   118
    It Is Not My Idea   118
    Unmet Interests   119
    The Other Party Is Losing Face   120
    Too Much Information Too Fast   120
    It Is Too Expensive or I Cannot Afford It   121
    It Does Not Work for Me or I Do Not Want It   121
    I Want to Think About It or I Need More Time   122
    I Do Not Believe That You Will Comply   122
Closing Deals   123
    When Should You Attempt to Close?   123

Closing Tactics   124
Ask the Other Party to Agree   124
Split the Difference or Compromise   124
Comparison   124
Cost-Benefit or Balance Sheet   125
Multiple Equivalent Offers   125
Sweeteners   126
Default Options   126
Other Closing Tactics to Consider (If the Relationship Matters Less)   127
Conclusion and Implications for Practice   128

READING 5.1 – GETTING PAST YES: NEGOTIATING AS IF IMPLEMENTATION MATTERED, BY DANNY ERTEL   130

READING 5.2 – CLOSING THE DEAL, BY MICHAEL WHEELER   138

CASE 1 – WHO'S THE BOSS A & B, BY RAYMOND FRIEDMAN   143

CASE 2 – A CUSTOMER TRIES TO SOLVE HER PROBLEM WITH
THE PHONE COMPANY, BY REBECCA GUIDICE   145

PART II: SPECIAL CHALLENGES   157

6 Communication: The Heart of All Negotiations   159

Intended Benefits of This Chapter   159
The Essence of Interpersonal Communication   160
Perceptions   161
Communication Styles   163
Communication and Negotiation   163
What Messages are Exchanged During in Negotiations?   163
Problem Solving and the Questions You Should Ask   166
Active Listening   168
The Channels or Media Used by Negotiators to Exchange Messages   169
Communicating Without Words   172
First Impressions   173
Building Rapport   173
Structuring Conversations   174
Detecting Deception   175
Conclusion and Implications for Practice   176

READING 6.1 – YOU'VE GOT AGREEMENT: NEGOTI@TING VIA EMAIL, BY NOAM
EBNER, ANITA D. BHAPPU, JENNIFER G. BROWN, KIMBERLEE K. KOVACH, AND ANDREA K. SCNEIDER   182

READING 6.2 – THE VIEW FROM THE OTHER SIDE OF THE TABLE,
BY ADAM GALINSKY, WILLIAM MADDUX AND GILLIAN KU   200

7 Decision Making: Are We Truly Rational?   205

Intended Benefits of This Chapter   205
The Essence of Decision Making in Negotiation   206
Decision-Making Errors   207
    Cognitive Biases   208
    Perception Errors   212
    Emotional Biases   218
Conclusion and Implications for Practice   220

READING 7.1 – DECISIONS WITHOUT BLINDERS, BY MAX H. BAZERMAN AND DOLLY CHUGH   225

READING 7.2 – PICKING THE RIGHT FRAME: MAKE YOUR BEST OFFER SEEM BETTER, BY MAX H. BAZERMAN   233

8 Power and Influence: Changing Others' Attitudes and Behaviors   237

Intended Benefits of This Chapter   237
The Essence of Power and Influence   237
    Attitudes   239
    Debunking Some Myths About Power and Influence   239
Where Power Comes From and How I Can Increase My Own   239
Influence: Using Power to Negotiate More Effectively   241
    The Central or Direct Route   241
    Message Content   242
    Message Organization   243
    Message Presentation   244
    The Peripheral or Indirect Route   244
Defending Against Others' Attempts to Influence You   249
    Preparation   249
    Gather Information About Influence Tactics and Decision Biases   250
    Attractiveness and Disclosure of Intentions   250
    Process Influence Attempts Using The Central Route   250
Negotiating With Inferior Power   250
Conclusion and Implications for Practice   251

READING 8.1 – THINK YOU'RE POWERLESS? THINK AGAIN, BY PROGRAM ON NEGOTIATION   256

READING 8.2 – HARNESSING THE SCIENCE OF PERSUASION, BY ROBERT B. CIALDINI   258

9 Ethics: Right and Wrong Do Exist When You Negotiate   267

Intended Benefits of This Chapter   267
The Essence of Ethics in Negotiation   268
    What Is Ethics?   268
What Might Cause Negotiators to Behave Unethically?   269
    Power   269
    Personal Motives   270

How Ethicality Is Assessed   270

Individual Differences   271

What If We Are Unethical or "See Unethical" and Don't Even Know It?   272

Unconscious or Unknowing Ethical Breaches   272

Overlooking the Unethical Behavior of Others   272

Overlooking the Actions of Those Who

Delegate Unethical Tasks   272

Overlooking Indirect Unethical Behavior   273

Overlooking Gradual Unethical Behavior   273

Overlooking Unethical Processes Until the Outcome Is Bad   274

In-Group Favoritism   275

Tactics That Commonly Raise Ethical Questions   275

Determining Whether Negotiating Behavior Is Unethical   277

Utilitarianism   277

Rights and Duties   277

Fairness and Justice   278

Social Contract   279

The Consequences of Unethical Negotiating Behavior   281

Legal Pitfalls When You Negotiate   282

Conclusion and Implications for Practice   282

READING 9.1 – WHY YOUR NEGOTIATING BEHAVIOR MAY BE ETHICALLY
CHALLENGED AND HOW TO FIX IT, BY PROGRAM ON NEGOTIATION   287

READING 9.2 – THREE SCHOOLS OF BARGAINING ETHICS, BY G. RICHARD SHELL   291

10 Multiparty Negotiations: Managing the Additional Complexity   297

Intended Benefits of This Chapter   297

The Essence of Multiparty Negotiations   298

The Challenges of Multiparty Negotiation   298

Why Multiparty Negotiations Are More Complex   298

Informational Complexity   299

Social Complexity   299

Procedural Complexity   299

Strategic Complexity   300

Agents and Representatives   300

When We Should Use Representatives   301

Managing Relationships Between Representatives and Principals   302

Multiparty Negotiations   303

Decision Making   304

Six Thinking Hats   306

Audiences and Audience Effects   309

Coalitions   309

Inter-team Negotiations   311
Conclusion and Implications for Practice   312

READING 10.1 – HOW TO MANAGE YOUR NEGOTIATING TEAM,
BY JEANNE M. BRETT, RAY FRIEDMAN AND KRISTIN BEHFAR   316

READING 10.2 – THE SURPRISING BENEFITS OF CONFLICT IN NEGOTIATING TEAMS,
BY PROGRAM ON NEGOTIATION   320

11 Individual Differences: How Our Unique Qualities Affect Negotiations   323

Intended Benefits of This Chapter   323
The Essence of Individual Differences   323
Gender   324
        Gender Differences and Their Origins   325
Personality   328
        Personality Traits   328
        The Five-Factor Model   329
        Myers-Briggs Type Inventory   330
Negotiation Styles   332
Emotions and Emotional Intelligence   332
        Emotional Intelligence   333
        Addressing Underlying Concerns   333
Conclusion and Implications for Practice   337

READING 11.1 – WHAT HAPPENS WHEN WOMEN DON'T ASK? BY PROGRAM ON NEGOTIATION   342

READING 11.2 – WILL YOUR EMOTIONS GET THE UPPER HAND? BY PROGRAM ON NEGOTIATION   350

12 International Negotiations: Managing Culture and Other Complexities   355

Intended Benefits of This Chapter   355
The Essence of International Negotiations   356
How International and Domestic
    Negotiations Differ   356
        International Monetary Factors   356
        Legal Pluralism   356
        Political Pluralism   357
        Role of Foreign Governments   357
        Instability and Change   358
        Ideological Differences   359
Culture   359
        Cultural Deal Breakers   360
        How Culture Influences Our Conception of a Negotiation   360

What Is Culture?   361
Dimensions of Culture   362
Culture and Negotiated Outcomes   363
Culture and Negotiation Processes   363
Conclusion and Implications for Practice   365

READING 12.1 – THE HIDDEN CHALLENGE OF CROSS-BORDER NEGOTIATIONS, BY JAMES K. SEBENIUS   368

READING 12.2 – NEGOTIATING: THE TOP TEN WAYS THAT CULTURE CAN AFFECT YOUR NEGOTIATION, BY JERALD W. SALACUSE   376

13 Difficult Negotiations: Managing Others Who Play Dirty and Saying No to Those Who Play Nice   383

Intended Benefits of This Chapter   383
The Essence of Difficult Negotiations   384
Impasses   384
  Why They Happen   384
  How to Break Them   385
Dirty Tricks   385
  What Are They?   385
  How to Manage Them   385
Alternative Approaches for Managing Difficult Negotiations   386
  The Shadow Negotiation   386
  Changing the Nature of the Game   392
Managing Difficult Conversations   395
  The Conversations Within a Difficult Conversation   395
  The Feelings Conversation   396
  The Identity Conversation   396
  How to Manage Them   396
Saying 'No' to People Who Are Important to You   397
  How We Usually Say 'No'   397
  Saying 'No' Positively   398
Conclusion and Implications for Practice   398

READING 13.1 – BRING YOUR DEAL BACK FROM THE BRINK, BY PROGRAM ON NEGOTIATION   400

READING 13.2 – WILL YOU NEGOTIATE OR LITIGATE? BY DEEPAK MALHOTRA   404

14 Third-Party Intervention: Recourse When Negotiations Sputter or Fail?   409

Intended Benefits of This Chapter   409
The Essence of Third-Party Intervention   410
Alternative Dispute Resolution (ADR)   410

        Dispute-Wise Organizations   410
        When ADR Is Likely to Be Used   410
    Mediation   411
        When Mediation Is Most Appropriate and Effective   411
        How the Mediation Process Works   412
    Arbitration   415
        When Arbitration Is Most Appropriate and Effective   415
        Problems With Arbitration   416
        Mandatory Arbitration   417
        How the Arbitration Process Works   418
        Interpretation Cases   419
        Terminations for Just Cause   419
    Managers as Third Parties   420
        How Managers Should Intervene   421
        Goals of the Manager   421
        Characteristics of the Conflict   421
        Characteristics of the Parties   421
        Linking the Determinants and the Intervention Strategies   421
    Conclusion and Implications for Practice   422

READING 14.1 – RESOLVE EMPLOYEE CONFLICTS WITH MEDIATION TECHNIQUES,
BY PROGRAM ON NEGOTIATION   426

READING 14.2 – BORROWING FROM BASEBALL: THE SURPRISING BENEFITS OF FINAL-OFFER ARBITRATION,
BY STEPHEN B. GOLDBERG   427

CASE 3 – MUSICAL OPERATING ROOM A & B, BY RAYMOND FRIEDMAN   431

CASE 4 – TAKE THE MONEY – OR RUN, BY JOHN W. MULLINS   433

CASE 5 – COLLECTIVE BARGAINING AT MAGIC CARPET AIRLINES:
A UNION'S PERSPECTIVE, BY PEGGY BRIGGS AND WILLIAM ROSS   442

Appendix   **459**
        Cultural Intelligence Scale (CQS)   459
        Incidents in Negotiation Scale   462
        Communication Style Survey   464

Glossary   **467**

Index   **477**

About the Author   **497**

Acknowledgments

This project has received invaluable support, assistance, and guidance from many people to whom I am forever grateful. Paul McNamara gave me my first opportunity to negotiate collective bargaining agreements. Bill Bigoness, PhD introduced me to the behavioral side of negotiation and encouraged me to pursue my passion for it. More recently, Corrinne Shearer, EdD shared information that is pertinent to important parts of the process, and incredible support and patience throughout the entire process. Rebecca Guidice, PhD shared valuable experiences and insights into how electronic negotiations play out. Janet Runge, PhD also shared valuable information pertaining to important parts of the process, and pushed me when I needed it. Many of my students, mostly from my MBA and Executive MBA classes, deserve special mention for providing me with very useful examples of actual negotiations in a variety of contexts, the successes they most commonly enjoyed and the difficulties they most commonly encountered. My conversations with them provide the basis, either directly or indirectly, for many of the practical examples and insights included in the book.

I'm not sure I can adequately express my appreciation for the assistance, guidance, patience, support, understanding, and encouragement of the people at Sage Publications who enabled me to complete this project. Knowing that this is a wholly inadequate expression of my gratitude, thank you Lisa Shaw, Deya Saoud, Julie Nemer, Eve Oettinger, and MaryAnn Vail.

I also want to thank the many reviewers who provided invaluable insights and suggestionss that helped me improve this book.

For allowing me to use their establishments to accomplish more work than I was able to at school or home on many occasions, and definitely enhancing my enjoyment, I thank Mehdi and his staff (current and former) at Crazy Pita in the District, Melissa and her staff (current and former) at Panera Bread in the District, Jeannie and her staff (current and former) at Saxbys (Maryland Parkway), and Jessie and her staff (current and former) at Saxbys (Black Mountain).

Preface

We begin negotiating when we are very young, and we continue to do so on a daily basis throughout our lives. Since 'practice make perfect', we must all be very effective negotiators. Unfortunately, the evidence suggests that we commonly make mistakes that cause us to 'leave money on the table.' Without sufficient training, perhaps practice reinforces our bad habits instead of making us perfect.

THE GOAL OF THE BOOK

While some people may have stronger aptitudes for negotiating than others, negotiators are not born. It is a competency that must be developed and a process that must be learned. Since we all have experience negotiating, we have developed some skills and learned something about the process. A book, therefore, cannot teach you how to negotiate. The purpose of this book is to help you cultivate your negotiating competency by refining your skills and abilities and enhancing your understanding of the process so that you can achieve more favorable outcomes.

MERGING THEORY, RESEARCH AND PRACTICE

To help you cultivate your negotiation skills and enhance your understanding of the negotiation process, this book merges theory, research, and practice. It draws extensively upon the academic work that has been undertaken in business, communication, economics, public administration, psychology and, of course, negotiation. Conversations with senior and middle managers, government officials, public administrators, human resources and labor-management relations managers, sales professionals, health care professionals, technology experts, communication professionals, commercial lenders, and real estate professionals from China, Hong Kong, Italy, Japan, Korea, Mexico, Norway, Poland, Spain, the United States and other countries have also provided insights that help to bring the theory and research to life and illustrate how the concepts and principles discussed herein really work in practice.

THE STRUCTURE OF THE BOOK

Most of the examples included in this book are drawn from business, health care, government, non-profit and other organizations. Since negotiation is a life skill rather than just a business/organizational skill, however, the concepts and principles discussed in the 14 chapters are applicable to all nego-tiations. The first section of the book discusses the fundamental or basic components of the nego-tiation process. **Chapter 1** introduces you to the nature of the negotiation process. **Chapter 2** discusses what is arguably the most important part of the process—preparation. This builds the foundation upon which the rest of your negotiation rests. The distributive bargaining strategy, a competitive approach that is used to claim value, is examined in **Chapter 3.** The integrative negotia-tion strategy, a collaborative approach that is used to create value before claiming it, is the focus of **Chapter 4. Chapter 5** discusses the remaining fundamental or basic component of the negotiation process—closing deals.

The rest of the chapters examine special challenges that often plague negotiators. Communication, whether it is done face-to-face or electronically, is central to the negotiation process. It is the focus of **Chapter 6**. Though we genuinely try to be rational and logical when we make decisions, the evi-dence demonstrates that we are consistently and predictably irrational. Decision making and the most common decision-making errors made by negotiators are discussed in **Chapter 7**. **Chapter 8** examines power and influence, and how negotiators can persuade others to agree with them. **Chapter 9** discusses ethics in negotiation because people knowingly and unknowingly engage in ethically questionable behavior when they negotiate. This usually involves different degrees of truth telling and withholding information. **Chapter 10** discusses multiparty negotiations because most negotiations involve more than two people—agents, audiences, coalitions, constituents, teams, and perhaps others. The influence of gender, personality, emotions, negotiation styles, and other indi-vidual differences on negotiation processes and outcomes is examined in **Chapter 11. Chapter 12** discusses international negotiations, including culture, because they are becoming increasingly common as the world becomes a smaller place. Difficult negotiations are examined in **Chapter 13.** This includes dealing with impasses, dirty tricks or other difficult tactics, countering misguided approaches used by opposing negotiators, and managing difficult conversations, especially those with people who are important to you. **Chapter 14** investigates difficult negotiations from a different perspective—how to involve third parties when negotiations sputter or fail.

PEDAGOGY

For this book to reflect the most current thinking and information about the negotiation process, it draws extensively from the relevant theoretical and research literatures. As is typical of most text-books, this should enhance your academic understanding of the process. To add practical value so that it can help you enhance your negotiation skills and abilities, it draws heavily from the experi-ences of managers and other practitioners. The practical material should make the book more useful and more enjoyable to read than many textbooks because it brings the theory and research to life and illustrates how the concepts and principles discussed really work. Several other features are included to make the material easier to understand and to facilitate skill development.

- Although the theory and research upon which this book is based reflects current knowledge and thinking, th e book is written informally. Rather than diminishing the book's rigor, the informal-ity makes the material more accessible to readers by making it easier to understand and more enjoy-able to read.

- The **Negotiation in Action** and other examples that are included in each chapter generally reflect true negotiation experiences, or observations of true negotiation experiences. They should enhance your ability to execute pertinent concepts, principles, and tactics when you negotiate.

- This book provides comprehensive coverage of the negotiation process because it includes text, readings, cases, questionnaires, and role-play exercises, all in a single volume. The *text* material introduces the important concepts and principles encompassed by the negotiation process. The *readings* at the end of each chapter provide expanded coverage of important topics, a different perspective than the author's on those topics, or both. The cases illustrate the effective or ineffective conduct of negotiations, or provide a basis for readers to decide how they should negotiate in certain situations. This provides a basis for thinking critically about the material discussed in the book and readings, and applying it. The questionnaires enable readers to engage in some self-analysis to enhance their understanding of their own styles and abilities, and what they think about certain actions. The role-play exercises allow readers to practice executing different parts of the negotiation process. Applying and practicing the material should enhance readers' abilities to execute different parts of the process.

- The conclusion to each chapter includes several **Implications for Practice**. These are behavioral or tactical suggestions for executing important material in that chapter.

- In short, this book is loosely based on the 'behavior modeling' learning process. After learning the relevant concepts and principles (from the text and the readings), readers can see how some of them are actually applied (the cases) and then practice executing them (the role-play exercises). Supplementing the cases with video demonstrations of how these concepts and principles are executed would make this an even more compelling example of behavior modeling.

P A R T I

The Fundamentals

1. The Nature of Negotiation: What It Is and Why It Matters
2. Preparation: Building the Foundation for Negotiating
3. Distributive Bargaining: A Strategy for Claiming Value
4. Integrative Negotiation: A Strategy for Creating Value
5. Closing Deals: Persuading the Other Party to Say Yes

CHAPTER 1

The Nature of Negotiation

What It Is and Why It Matters

Negotiation is an important aspect of our everyday lives, especially because it offers an effective means for resolving conflicts. Whether we like it or not, conflicts—differences that interfere with our efforts to satisfy our interests—are ubiquitous. Sometimes they motivate us to find great solutions that work for everyone involved. Sometimes they frustrate us and make us so angry that we devote all of our energies to "beating" the other side or they might scare us or make us so angry that we avoid them, hoping the problem will go away on its own so that we do not have to deal with it. There are many ways to deal with conflict, and people have tried them all—war, fighting, lawsuits, arguing, blaming, giving up and letting the other side "win" and probably many others. This book presents a comprehensive discussion of negotiation, a technique that people use to resolve their differences, whether these differences are as minor as what to have for dinner or as major as where to draw the line between two countries' borders.

INTENDED BENEFITS OF THIS CHAPTER

When you finish reading this chapter, you should be able to

1. Explain the nature of negotiation, and why it is an increasingly important skill for people to possess.

2. Recognize negotiation opportunities and determine whether you should try to capitalize on these opportunities.

3. Describe the process that most negotiations follow.

THE ESSENCE OF NEGOTIATION

People negotiate every day, often without realizing it. Every time you ask for something you are actually negotiating. The following scenario illustrates a few of the many types of negotiation situations that you may find yourself experiencing on any given day.

NEGOTIATION IN ACTION 1.1

On his way to work one morning, Jay was in a car accident. He was hit by a driver making what he believed was an illegal left turn. The other driver initially refused to give Jay her insurance information. He persisted and she finally relented. When the police officer arrived, nearly an hour later, she investigated and decided that neither driver was at fault so she didn't cite either one. Jay tried to explain that the turn was illegal, but the officer wouldn't listen. Jay's car needed repairs so he went to rent a car. The man behind the counter offered him a car that he had always wanted to drive, but the price was very high. Jay explained that he had been in an accident and would be renting the car for an extended period. After some additional conversation, the agent agreed to drop the price if he kept the car for at least two weeks.

When he finally got to work, more than 2 hours late, Jay's boss jumped all over him for missing an important meeting. Jay tried to explain what happened, and his boss relaxed a little, but he still seemed annoyed. When he finished with his boss, Jay called the director of the MBA program in which he was enrolled. His classes meet every other Friday and Saturday for 4 hours each day, and he is taking two classes. He had heard rumors that the director was instituting an attendance policy that would subject students to removal from the program if they missed more than three classes. He was going to miss all four of his classes the following weekend to attend a meeting at which he would be making a presentation to senior management. He hoped the director would understand that the meeting was a fantastic opportunity for his career and professional development: Jay wanted to ensure that he would not be disciplined, but he knew that one of his classmates had been given a disciplinary warning for missing class for similar reasons.

At home that night, Jay's girlfriend, wanted to go out for a nice dinner to celebrate her promotion. He was happy for his girlfriend, he wanted to support her, and he wanted to help her celebrate her achievements, but he really didn't want to go out. Jay explained to her that he needed to finish a project for work, and then study.

The insurance company called the next morning to arrange an appointment to assess the damage to Jay's car. When the adjuster claimed that he couldn't meet for several days. Jay explained that since he didn't have rental car coverage, he would like to move faster. When the adjuster finally assessed the damage, he told Jay that it would probably take two weeks after the insurance company authorized payment for the body shop to get the parts and repair the car. Two weeks later the company had still not authorized payment. Jay reiterated his concerns about the costs he was incurring for his rental car and asked the company to expedite the process. The adjuster told him it would take another three weeks to complete the repairs. Jay then asked the insurance company to pay his rental car costs since they took so long to authorize payment.

Jay negotiated with the driver of the other car and he, tried, unsuccessfully, to negotiate with the police officer. He then negotiated with the rental car agent, his boss, the MBA director and his girl-friend. He negotiated with the insurance agent several times. Jay's stake in the outcomes of some of these negotiations was greater than in others. So was his success.

We negotiate because we think we can accomplish more with others than we can on our own. We begin negotiating when we are very young (think of the young child in the candy aisle of the grocery store with mom or dad). If we negotiate often and start when we are young, and if practice makes perfect, do we really need to study and learn how it is done, or how it should be done? The answer is yes. While practice can help, it also reinforces bad habits and the empirical evidence demonstrates that negotiators often make mistakes that prevent them from achieving optimal outcomes. Relative to expert negotiators, for example, novices are more likely to think that negotiators' interests are incompatible; negotiation is characterized by sequential issue settlement and it is a competitive activity. Novices are also more likely to believe that impasses and third parties lead to successful negotiations (O'Connor & Adams, 1999). Whether you are an experienced and accomplished negotiator or more of a novice, this book will enhance your understanding of the process and help you refine your skills and abilities, or develop new ones. This will help you avoid the mistakes that often plague negotiators so that you can achieve better outcomes.

WHAT IS NEGOTIATION?

Negotiation is a *social process* by which *interdependent* people with conflicting interests determine how they are going to allocate resources or work together in the future (Brett, 2007). It is a *social process* because people must interact with others to achieve their desired outcomes. This interaction may occur face-to-face, telephonically, by mail or, increasingly, electronically via e-mail, instant messaging, or video conferencing. Reading 1.1 at the end of this chapter demonstrates how technology is changing the face of negotiation. We interact with others because we are *interdependent*—we have something they need or they have something we need. Knowledge, information, skills, abilities, access to important people and, of course, money, are but a few examples. Interdependence often takes a subtler form as well. How we initiate an interaction depends upon the nature of our prior interactions with the other party, and the manner in which we convey information to him or her influences how he or she responds. Cooperation in prior interactions, for instance, begets cooperation in future interactions and, conversely, competition begets competition.

WHEN DO PEOPLE NEGOTIATE?

Traditionally, negotiation was viewed as a combative process—a battle between adversaries. Though some still hold these beliefs, and this approach still exists, attitudes and even the evidence are changing. Negotiation is now viewed widely as a collaborative process that is used to find the best solutions for everyone involved (Babcock & Laschever, 2007). We negotiate when we believe we can achieve more with others than without them. This is true whether we are making deals, settling disputes, making team decisions, solving problems, or trying to capitalize on new opportunities. If we interact with someone because we want him or her to take something from us, or because we want something from him or her, a negotiation opportunity exists. If both sides are willing and able to adjust their differences, a very strong negotiation opportunity exists. If one or both sides is unwilling or unable to adjust their differences, a very poor negotiation opportunity exists. Negotiation in Action 1.2 illustrates a potential negotiation opportunity that was thwarted because one of the parties, the college administrator, was unwilling to adjust his differences with the students who made the request.

NEGOTIATION IN ACTION 1.2

A college administrator announced on a Friday morning that he wanted to meet with a group of graduate students that day at lunch. These students were enrolled in two classes that met for 4 hours each on Fridays and again on Saturdays. The day the administrator wanted to meet with them was the last Friday of these classes. The students had team projects and presentations due the next day and they had planned to meet with their teammates at lunch to coordinate and finalize their projects. The students e-mailed the administrator, explained their dilemma and asked if he would meet with them on Saturday instead. The administrator typed his rejection of their proposal and asked one of his staff members to read it verbatim.

WHY HAS NEGOTIATION BECOME A MORE IMPORTANT SKILL?

The ability to negotiate effectively is becoming increasingly important, especially for those who work or volunteer in business, government, healthcare, or any other type of organization. There are many reasons for this development and they are illustrated in the following examples.

Technology

- The rise of e-commerce, especially online auctions and trading, has created a new realm for buying, selling, and otherwise doing business.

- Technology brings customers much closer to organizations, thus increasing the incidence of negotiating to secure and maintain productive relationships with them.

The Workplace

- Organizations have become less bureaucratic and flatter with fewer layers of managers and employees in their hierarchies. Job responsibilities and reporting lines have become less formalized and command-and-control management styles have been displaced. These changes, coupled with the wide array of other organizational structures that have been adopted, have left employees with fewer and fewer definitive rules to follow about how work should be done. They are now expected to negotiate many aspects of their work.
- People change jobs, and even careers, more often than ever before. This increases the number of employment packages they must negotiate. The growth of customized employment contracts designed to meet employees' unique needs for flexibility also make more elements of an employee's work life negotiable (Babcock & Laschever, 2007).
- Domestically and internationally, organizations are increasingly using team-based work processes, and many of these teams are devoid of formal leaders. Decisions, therefore, must be negotiated by team members.
- The workforces in the U.S. and other countries are becoming more diverse, and demographic trends suggest this will continue. Working with diverse coworkers often requires employees to negotiate their differences. Done well, this produces beneficial outcomes. It appears, however, that this is frequently done poorly or not done at all.
- The decline of union membership in the U.S. (Budd, 2010) means that unions are now negotiating employment packages for far fewer employees. This means that individual employees must now negotiate the terms of their employment for themselves.
- Managers spend a substantial amount of their time at work dealing with employee conflict or helping other managers deal with conflict (Brotheridge & Long, 2007). The ability to negotiate well, and to intervene effectively when necessary, should make them better conflict managers and enhance their work performance.
- Like conflict, organizational change is ubiquitous and must be managed to be successful. Addressing the concerns of those individuals who are affected by the change is one very important component of this process, notably overcoming resistance. Negotiating the change and reaching a mutually acceptable outcome with these people is often far more effective than simply imposing the change on them.
- When businesses expand their operations overseas, they sometimes do so by forming joint ventures or strategic alliances with a company in the host country. This obviously requires the dealmakers to negotiate the terms of the joint venture or alliance and how they will be implemented.
- Generally speaking, we negotiate with others if we need their cooperation and we cannot command them to do something. In organizations, this might include peers or superiors, or coworkers in other departments. Managers might even negotiate with their subordinates because they have their own interests, understandings, sources of support, and areas of discretion (Lax & Sebenius, 1986).

HOW PEOPLE NEGOTIATE: THE DUAL CONCERNS MODEL

Early conflict researchers argued that how people manage conflict depends upon the relative importance they attach to their own outcomes and the other party's outcomes (Thomas, 1976; Blake & Mouton, 1964). This **dual concerns model** posits five different approaches for handling conflict, as depicted in Figure 1.1. People who attach substantially more importance to their own outcomes than they attach to the other party's outcomes adopt a *competitive* or win-lose strategy. *Accommodation* is a lose-win strategy. It is used by those who place greater importance on the other party's outcomes than their own. Those who have little concern for either party's outcomes *avoid* conflict. This is a lose-lose strategy. *Compromising* is what people do if they are only moderately concerned about both parties' outcomes. *Collaboration* is the strategy of choice for people who seek a win-win outcome—they attach great importance to both parties' outcomes.

What does this have to do with how people negotiate? Savage, Blair, and Sorenson (1989) modified the *dual concerns model* by arguing that how people negotiate depends upon the relative importance they place on the *substantive terms* of the outcome at stake, and their relationship with the other party. If concern for the relationship" is equivalent to "concern for the other party's outcome, this framework simply extends the *dual concerns model* to negotiation. Using this framework, there are two dominant strategies.

One is a *competitive* approach reflecting greater concern for the substantive terms of the outcome for him- or herself than for the relationship. This strategy is typically called distributive, positional, zero-sum, or win-lose negotiating. These are different names for the same phenomenon, all of which assume that the negotiation is a zero-sum exercise—if one party gains something the other must lose. This strategy is about *claiming value* and is most appropriately used when the parties' goals are in fundamental conflict, resources are fixed or limited, they attach greater importance to the substantive terms of the outcome than the relationship, and trust and cooperation are lacking.

The other dominant strategy is commonly called integrative, principled, interest-based, mutual gains, or win-win negotiating. Again, these are different labels for the same phenomenon. This is a *collaborative* approach whereby substantial importance is attached to both the relationship and the substantive terms of the outcome for both parties. This strategy is about *creating value* so that both negotiators can benefit from it. It is most appropriately used when the parties' goals are not in fun-

Video 1.1
Win-win negotiations

damental conflict, resources are not fixed or limited, sufficient trust or cooperation exists, and the parties want to find mutually beneficial outcomes.

What about the other three approaches? Some have argued that *compromising* is lazy problem solving involving a half-hearted attempt at satisfying both parties' interests (Pruitt & Olozak, 1995). For the purpose of this book, it will be treated not as a strategy but as an outcome. Suggestions for when and how to compromise or concede will be proffered when the process of claiming value is examined. *Accommodation* is a form of soft distributive bargaining where one is willing to accept less so that the other party can gain more, ostensibly to maintain or improve the relationship. *Avoidance* usually connotes inaction whereas negotiation connotes action. Thus, it is not considered a bargaining strategy. It is possible, however, to avoid conflict aggressively. Some people use *intimidation* to prevent the other party from engaging in the process. This is consistent with the notion of aggressive distributive bargaining.

Which of these approaches is best? The simple answer is that it depends. One of the central tenets of this book is that the aforementioned situational characteristics—goals, resources, relationship,

Figure 1.1 The Dual Concerns Framework

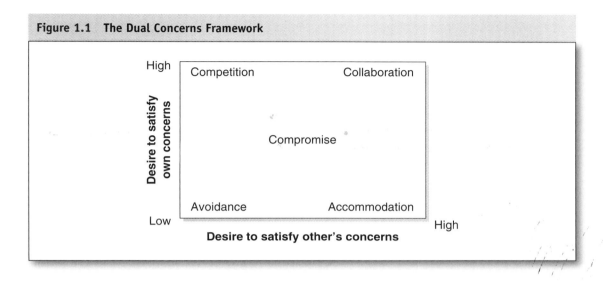

THE PROS AND CONS OF NEGOTIATING

trust—determine which strategy is most appropriate. Moreover, there is rarely such a thing as a purely distributive or integrative negotiation. Although the two dominant strategies will be discussed independently in Chapters 3 and 4, respectively, real negotiations are generally a mixture of these two approaches because they are *mixed-motive* events. Negotiators cooperate to ensure an agreement is reached. They compete to ensure that their needs are satisfied. **Reading** 1.2 at the end of this chapter provides a more detailed discussion of the dilemmas negotiators face because of these mixed motives.

Negotiation holds great promise for realizing net benefits when you are trying to close deals, settle disputes, make team decisions, solve problems, or capitalize on new opportunities. It provides you with a useful tool for satisfying your needs if you and the other party are interdependent, you believe you can persuade him or her to give you more than he or she had planned or more than you can get on your own, and both of you are willing to adjust your differences to reach an agreement (Lewicki, 1992; Rubin & Brown, 1975). Despite its promise, it is not always appropriate to negotiate.

- If you may lose everything by negotiating, you probably should find another way to address the situation.
- If you do not have time, are inadequately prepared, or have no stake in the outcome, it is wiser to find another way to address the situation.
- If waiting will improve your ability to satisfy your needs, you should wait.
- Some also argue that it is inappropriate to negotiate if the other party's demands are unethical or illegal (Levinson, Smith, & Wilson, 1999).

WHAT DOES A NEGOTIATION LOOK LIKE?

It is hard to describe a typical negotiation because no two are identical. Yet there are common themes that emerge, and common flows or patterns that they often follow (Greenhalgh, 2001; Morley & Stephenson, 1977). These flows or patterns are not truly linear. Many negotiations move forward, get stuck, regress, or even move sideways. Nevertheless, they will be described as if they are linear for the sake of clarity. As depicted in Figure 1.2, the *initial stage* of a negotiation typically includes, or should include, pre-negotiation preparation and, when you meet with the other party, rapport building and more information gathering to test your assumptions. As will be discussed in Chapter 2, building rapport enhances preparation because it engenders more information sharing and trust, and reduces the issuance of threats (Nadler, 2004). In addition, your preparation should include an analysis of the other party. Since full disclosure is rare or nonexistent in negotiations, these analyses contain assumptions, estimates or educated guesses about the other party. Testing your assumptions, therefore, is required to verify your hunches about *what* he or she intends to negotiate (the substance), *how* he or she intends to do so (the process), and the relationship.

Figure 1.2	How Negotiations Typically Flow		
Initial Stage →	**Middle Stage** →		**Final Stage**
Pre-negotiation preparation	Formulate arguments & counterarguments		Implement the agreement
Build rapport	Formulate offers & counteroffers		
Test assumptions	Close deals		

Formulating your arguments and counterarguments to persuade the other side to agree with you, exchanging offers and counteroffers, and closing the deal are the focus of the second or *middle stage*. In essence, this is about using the information you gathered during the initial stage to achieve your goals and satisfy your needs.

Agreements are implemented in the third or *final stage*. Your focus should be on ensuring that the terms of the agreement are executed as intended and that the parties comply with them. Including a mediation or arbitration clause to settle disputes pertaining to the agreement might be warranted to ensure that the parties comply with the terms of their agreement.

THE SHADOW NEGOTIATION

The foregoing describes what most people think and talk about when discussing a negotiation—the transaction. Underlying all such transactions, however, is the **shadow negotiation** (Kolb & Williams, 2003). This entails the subtle games people play, often before they even get to the table. It is not about the *what* of the negotiation but the *how*. The shadow negotiation involves jockeying for position. This includes using **strategic moves** to ensure that the other party comes to the table and gives your interests and proposals a fair hearing, using **strategic turns** to reframe the negotiation in your favor if it turns in an unproductive direction, and using **appreciative moves** to build a stronger connection with the other party to develop a shared and complete understanding of the situation and a more productive negotiation (Kolb & Williams, 2003). Although it is present in all negotiations and often precedes negotiating the substantive terms, the shadow negotiation and the various moves and turns it encompasses will be discussed in detail in Chapter 13. It is particularly salient when managing various special challenges that make negotiations quite difficult.

CONCLUSION AND IMPLICATIONS FOR PRACTICE

Negotiation is not always an appropriate way to manage interactions. But it usually is if you want the other person to take something from you or you want to receive something from him or her. Moreover, it holds greater potential for finding mutually beneficial outcomes and preserving or improving relationships than many other techniques that are commonly used. There is no single best way to always execute this process—which way is best depends upon the characteristics of the situation. Nor is it possible to describe what all negotiations look like. They follow common paths, but no two are identical. The remaining chapters discuss effective ways to negotiate in different situations. For now, consider the following suggestions to guide your negotiations.

1.   Think of a negotiation as a life skill, not just a business skill. As indicated in the opening scenario, we negotiate many times a day—at work, home, and elsewhere. Think about your daily interactions. How many of them did you engage in without really considering whether you were negotiating? If the other person wanted to receive ideas or things from you, or if you wanted to collect ideas or things from him or her, you were in a negotiation situation.

2.   Realize that like most skills, the ability to negotiate can be learned. Many people seem to think that some people are born negotiators. Some people do have stronger aptitudes for negotiating than others, just as some people have stronger aptitudes for the sciences or math or technology or music than others. Whether you possess these apparent gifts for negotiating or not, even those people with apparent Change to: gifts for negotiating can learn to be more effective at it. This is critical, especially if you work or interact with others, because more and more situations are negotiable. Traditionally, for example, it has been argued that the core tasks of a manager include planning, directing, leading, and controlling. You might want to add negotiating to this list because it has become a crucial competency for managers.

3.   Although all negotiations are "mixed motives" events that require some cooperation to reach an agreement and some competition to claim sufficient value for yourself, you must determine whether you want to negotiate more competitively or more collaboratively. When making this determination, consider the relative importance of your relationship with the other party and the substantive terms of the outcome for you.

4. However you choose to negotiate, remember that preparation is crucial because it builds the foundation for your negotiation. This is the first stage of successful negotiations. In the middle stage, negotiators generally exchange offers and counteroffers, and close the deal. The final stage of most negotiations is critical but often ignored—the implementation of your agreement. To avoid having your agreement fall apart after you have negotiated it, consider including provisions for ensuring that it is implemented, managed, and enforced properly.

STUDENT STUDY SITE

Visit the Student Study Site at **www.sagepub.com/hames** for additional learning tools.

KEY TERMS

Accommodation approach to negotiation

Appreciative moves

Avoidance approach to negotiation

Collaborative approach to negotiation (a.k.a. integrative, principled, interest-based, mutual gains, and win-win approach)

Competitive approach to negotiation

Compromising approach to negotiation

Distributive negotiating (a.k.a. positional, zero-sum, and win-lose negotiating)

Dual concerns model

Final stage of a negotiation

Initial stage of a negotiation

Integrative approach to negotiation (a.k.a. collaborative, principled, interest-based, mutual gains, or win-win approach)

Interest-based approach to negotiation (a.k.a. collaborative, integrative, principled, mutual gains, or win-win approach)

Lose-win approach to negotiation necessary

Middle stage of a negotiation

Mixed-motive negotiation

Mutual gains approach to negotiation (a.k.a. collaborative, integrative, principled, interest-based, and win-win approach)

Negotiation

Positional negotiation (a.k.a. distributive, zero-sum, and win-lose negotiation)

Principled approach to negotiation (a.k.a. collaborative, integrative, interest-based, mutual gains, and win-win approach)

Shadow negotiation

Strategic moves

Strategic turns

Win-lose (a.k.a. distributive, positional, and zero-sum negotiating)

Win-win approach to negotiation (a.k.a. collaborative, integrative, principled, interest-based, mutual gains approach)

Zero-sum negotiation (a.k.a. distributive, positional, and win-lose negotiation)

REFERENCES

Allred, K. G. (2000). Distinguishing best and strategic practices: A framework for managing the dilemma between creating and claiming value, *Negotiation Journal*, 16(4), 387-397.

Babcock, L. & Laschever, S. (2007). *Women Don't Ask*. New York: Bantam.

Blake, R. R. & Mouton, J. S. (1964). *The managerial grid*. Houston: Gulf Publishing.

Brett, J. M. (2007). *Negotiating globally: How to negotiate deals, resolve disputes and make decisions across cultural boundaries*, 2nd. San Francisco: Jossey-Bass.

Brotheridge, C. M. & Long, S. (2007). "The "real-world" challenges of managers: Implications for management education", *Journal of Management Development*, 26(9), 832-842.

Budd, J. (2010). *Labor Relations: Striking a Balance*. New York: McGraw-Hill/Irwin.

Greenhalgh, L. (2001). *Managing strategic relationships*. New York: The Free Press.

Kolb, D. G. & Williams, J. (2003). *Everyday negotiations: Navigating the hidden agendas in bargaining*. San Francisco: Jossey-Bass.

Larson, D. A. (2003). Online dispute resolution: Do you know where your children are?, *Negotiation Journal*, 19(3), 199-205.

Lax, D. & Sebenius, J. (1986). *The manager as negotiator: Bargaining for cooperation and competitive gain*. New York: The Free Press.

Lewicki, R. J. (1992). Negotiating strategically. In A. Cohen (Ed.), *The portable MBA in management*. New York: John Wiley and Sons, 147-189.

Levinson, J. C, Smith, M. S. A. & Wilson, O. R. (1999). *Guerilla negotiating: Unconventional weapons and tactics to get what you want*. New York: John Wiley.

Morley, L. & Stephenson, G. M. (1977). *The social psychology of bargaining*. London: Allen and Unwin.

Nadler, J. (2004). Rapport in legal negotiations: How small talk can facilitate email dealmaking, *Harvard Negotiation Law Review*, 9, 223-253.

O'Connor, K. M. & Adams, A. A. (1999). What novices think about negotiation: A content analysis of scripts, *Negotiation Journal*, (15(2), 135-147.

Pruitt, D. G. & Olozak, P. V. (1995). Beyond hope: Approaches to resolving seemingly intractable conflicts. In B. B. Bunker & J. Z. Rubin (Eds.), *Conflict, cooperation and justice:Essays inspired by the work of Morton Deutsch*. San Francisco: Jossey-Bass, 59-92.

Rubin, J. & Brown, B. (1975). *The social psychology of bargaining and negotiation*. New York: Academic Press.

Savage, G. T., Blair, J. D. & Sorenson, R. L. (1989). Consider both relationship and substance when negotiating strategically, *Academy of Management Executive*, 3(1), 37-48.

Thomas, K. W. (1976). Conflict and conflict management. In M.D. Dunnette (ED.), *Handbook of industrial & organizational psychology*. Chicago: Rand McNally, 889-935.

READINGS

Reading 1.1

ONLINE DISPUTE RESOLUTION: DO YOU KNOW WHERE YOUR CHILDREN ARE?

David A. Larson

Will we ever see the day when the Internet serves as the primary venue for problem solving and dispute resolution? Social science research suggests that our online communication skills will improve as we learn relational behaviors based upon nonverbal cues available online. Dispute resolution and problem solving will move online, however, whether or not you and I master those skills. Our children already have developed

Source: Larson, D. A. (2003). Online dispute resolution: Do you know where your children are?, *Negotiation Journal*, 19(3), 199–205.

effective online relational behaviors and can establish trust and intimacy online.

Although most of us acknowledge that the Internet is becoming an increasingly important supplemental tool for dispute resolution and problem solving, we cannot imagine ourselves resolving disputes primarily online. Because online communication's distinct limitations include an absence of verbal cues and body language, the online environment does not appear conducive to dispute resolution. We may not have the confidence to make, or help others to make, the honest and private disclosures online that often are essential to effective problem solving[1]. Yet in spite of these reservations, dispute resolution will move online.

Why? Because our kids already have learned to develop close relationships and solve problems using the Internet. Regardless of whether you or I are prepared to take problem solving online, the next generation already has made that move. The only real question is whether the rest of us — generally "over 35" types — will join them.

Consider three possibilities:

(1) The dynamic potential that online dispute resolution offers is almost unimaginable, and some day it will become the preeminent ADR process;

(2) Online exchanges capture neither the essence nor nuance of human communication and, consequently, initial excitement will evaporate quickly and online dispute resolution soon will be relegated to the same lonely space now occupied by monochromatic monitors; or,

(3) Online dispute resolution increasingly will become a valuable, and perhaps ultimately invaluable, complement to ADR processes; but it always will be, shall we say, a side dish and never the main course.

Confused? Then you are not alone. Although online dispute resolution is attracting significant attention from scholars,[2] governments, professional associations,[3] and service providers, the idea of resolving disputes online still is in its infancy. So it is difficult, if not impossible, to predict how valuable online dispute resolution will become.

Some of us are hoping quietly, or declaring dismissively, that the second possible outcome is most likely. Many of us will identify the third outcome as the most plausible. But there is a genuine possibility that the first prediction is the one that will materialize and it may happen more quickly than we ever could have imagined.

Truly fascinating data being collected and analyzed by communication experts suggests that, rather than finding themselves unable to create trust and intimacy online, experienced individuals exchange more intimate questions and disclosures in computer-mediated [assisted] communication than in face-to-face contexts. A growing body of research asserts that personal relationships developed in computer-mediated communication are comparable to those developed face-to-face. Assuming the research is reliable, then as we become more experienced and skilled online communicators, we will create an environment online that encourages disclosure and facilitates effective problem solving. Some will find it not only a workable environment, but also the optimal environment.

The Comfort Factor

Although initial research concerning the creation of personal relationships online suggested that individuals were unable to form impressions of each other in the absence of nonverbal cues, groundbreaking research indicates that online communicators have adapted.[4] Social Informational Processing theory asserts that even without nonverbal cues, parties who

alternative dispute resolution

communicate online can develop effective relational behaviors that rely upon the cues that do exist online, including typographic or chronemic cues as well as content and linguistic strategies.[5] Additional research suggests that when nonverbal cues are lacking, parties using computer-mediated communication focus and narrow their conversations and thus engage in more intimate exchanges. Computer-mediated communication becomes in effect "hyperpersonal." Parties engaged in computer-mediated communication develop more intense, although not broader, impressions.[6]

So will we be able to form the types of impressions online that may be required to participate in an intimate conversation? Studies have shown that by using available uncertainty reduction strategies such as direct questions and self-disclosure (which prompt reciprocal disclosures) more intensely than one would face-to-face, computer-mediated communicators can engage in very personal exchanges.[7] In fact, hyperpersonal relationships thus can be created. A growing body of literature maintains that effective online communicators experience more intimate conversations and offer more personal disclosures than they would in face-to-face situations.[8]

Because computer-mediated communication is characterized by visual anonymity and text-only communications, some researchers have declared that computer-mediated communication inevitably will be task-oriented and lack emotional content." Furthermore, others have argued that computer-mediated communication will encourage anti-normative, aggressive (i.e., "flaming") behavior.[9] More recent studies, however, reveal that visual anonymity and increased private awareness, coupled with a reduced public awareness, result in greater self-disclosure in computer-mediated communication as compared to face-to-face.[10]

Assuming this is true, as we increasingly use computer-mediated communication by e-mailing and posting messages, we will create a comfort zone that will allow us to reveal ourselves online in ways that we are unable to do offline. Once that comfort level is established, online dispute resolution becomes a very plausible option.[11]

You don't buy it? Perhaps you do not believe the research. You may believe that your online communications never can achieve the level of intimacy that can be established face-to-face. If you are right, then in the short term this may slow the evolution of online dispute resolution. But in the long run, it will not make any difference. The fact is that your children already have established that critical level of intimacy online.

The Next Generation Lives Online

The research investigating how teens and preteens communicate online is eye opening, even stunning. Although many of us have not thought critically about how our children communicate online, it now is something that we need to consider. In fact, one could offer a fourth prediction to supplement the three predictions articulated in this article's third paragraph:

(4) The possibilities that online dispute resolution presents are incomprehensible to the current population of ADR professionals, who have neither the technical expertise required nor, frankly, the energy and motivation necessary to employ this powerful tool. Experienced neutrals and facilitators are quickly recognized as ineffective in the online environment and seldom are invited to facilitate conversations or participate in problem solving. Their places are taken by members of a younger generation who understand computer-mediated communication.

Yikes.

The research exploring how teenagers live online is fascinating, exciting, and dynamic. The Pew Internet and American Life Project's Mission Statement explains that its goal is to: ". . . create and fund original, academic-quality research that explores the impact of the Internet on children, families, communities, the workplace, schools, health care and civic/political life. The Project aims to be an authoritative source for timely information on the Internet's growth and societal impact, through research that is scrupulously impartial"[12]

The Project intends to publish 15 to 20 research reports per year of varying size and scope. Among the topics of these reports are: "Cyber-Faith: How Americans Pursue Religion Online" (Larsen 2001); "Getting Serious Online" (Horrigan 2002)[13]; "Use of the Internet at Major Life Moments" (Kommers 2002); and "Online Communities: Networks that Nurture Long-Distance Relationships and Local Ties" (Horrigan 2001). The report that is most relevant to this article, however, is "Teenage Life Online: The Rise of the Instant Message Generation and the Internet's Impact on Friendships and Family Relationships" (Lenhart and Rainie 2001).

Lenhart and Rainie, in the "summary of findings" which introduces the article, deliver a powerful statement. And please keep in mind—this research was published in June 2001. It is reasonable to assume that the statistics are even more compelling today. Seventeen million young people ages 12 through 17 already were using the Internet in 2001, which represents 73 percent of that age group. Not only do 76 percent of the online teens declare that they would miss the Internet if they were not provided access, almost one half (48 percent) say that using the Internet improves their relationships with existing friends. Approximately 56 percent of all 12-through 17-year-olds use instant messaging < JM) and report that this form of communication holds a key place in their lives. In fact, one fifth of this online group asserts that instant messaging is the main way they deal with their friends.

The "main way that they deal with their friends"? Anyone interested in communication, conversation and dispute resolution cannot ignore the dramatic cultural change that is occurring. These online exchanges are not merely superficial. A significant number of teenagers use IM for serious communications, including beginning and ending relationships or relating unpleasant thoughts or feelings. Thirty-seven percent of online teens, according to Lenhart and Rainie, report that they have used IM to communicate something that they would not have said in person. There is a wealth of provocative information in the "Teenage Life Online" report. The "Teens and Their Friends," section, for example, reports that face-to-face and telephone communications are being replaced, at least in part, by e-mail and IM. Some teens believe that the Internet allows them to show their true personalities more easily than they can face-to-face. In a distinctly ageless way, asking someone out on a date can be an unnerving event. Seventeen percent of online teens have used IM to ask someone out.

Other relevant findings can be cited, but the material above is sufficient to make the point. The ways you and I communicate are changing, and those changes have implications for dispute resolution. But the ways in which our kids are communicating will have greater implications.

The next generation is developing an intuitive comfort level online that will elude, if not baffle, many of us. Their electronic interactions may be ill suited by their nature to existing dispute resolution processes or models. Additionally, the technology and language of computer-mediated communication with which kids are so familiar may feel awkward to experienced practitioners. Accordingly, experienced problem solvers and dispute resolvers may be unable to participate effectively online.

The Teenage Life Online report, however, does not present a universal endorsement of online communications. Most teens, for instance, do not believe that the Internet is especially helpful when it comes to making new friends. For instance, 67 percent of online teens believe the Internet helps "a little" or "not at all."

But even among the teens, we can see that age makes a difference. Younger teens can be more comfortable communicating online than teens just a few years older. The responses regarding making new friends are not uniform, for example. Younger children feel more strongly than older children that the Internet helps them make new friends. Thirty-seven percent of younger teens claim that the Internet helps them create new friendships, according to the Lenhart and Rainie study. Younger teens 12-to-l4 years of age are more likely to use IM to break up with someone. Almost one-fifth of that age group has ended a relationship using IM.

In the 21st century, children are being introduced to computers and books simultaneously. My wife and I have a three-year-old who, not unlike many three-year-olds, loves to play on the computer. Our daughter literally is learning computer skills while she is mastering her ABCs. The real question is not whether you and I will be able to help resolve disputes when our teenagers move into adulthood. The real question is whether we will be ready when the next decade of children weaned on computers joins them.

Notes

1. Numerous different processes are available to address disputes (e.g., arbitration, mediation, negotiation, and early neutral evaluation) and each process may have several distinct models. For instance, mediations can be transformative, evaluative, or problem-solving/facilitative. The behavioral evolutions discussed in this article may impact different models to varying degrees. The dramatic changes underway may be so momentous; however, that new ADR processes and models are required.

2. See, for instance, Katsch and Rifkin (2001) and Rule (2002).

3. See, for example, the American Bar Association E-Commerce and ADR Task Force Report at http.//www.law. Washington.edu/ABA-eADR/home.html.

4. See Tidwell and Walther (2002), citing Kiesler (1986); Kiesler, Siegal, and McGuire (1984); Walther (1993); and Walther and Burgoon (1992).

5. The references cited in note four also provide information on this point.

6. For example, see Hancock and Dunham (2001) and Walther (1997). Additionally, social identity and de-individuation theory maintains that the absence of nonverbal cues in computer-mediated communication causes parties to form impressions based on social categories rather than interpersonal cues. See the ABA E-Commerce and ADR Task Force Report (note three), citing Lea and Spears (1992).

7. Information and uncertainty are inversely proportional — the more I know, the less uncertain I feel. White uncertainty reduction strategies may be limited in computer-mediated communication, research indicates that a more intensive use of the available strategies may be sufficient.

8. See Joinson (2001), citing Rice and Love (1987).

9. See Kiesler, Siegal, and McGuire (1984: 1124-1134),

10. Tidwell and Walther (2002: 4, 7, 11, and 19-22).

11. The "disinhibition effect" can be powerful in cyberspace. Psychological barriers are reduced for a variety of reasons. For example, parties engaged in computer-mediated communication may be more open because no one can see them (invisibility); asynchronicity (not having to deal with immediate reactions); "solipsistic introjection" (absence of face-to-face cues combined with online text communication may create the feeling that the online message is a voice originating within [or "introfected" into] one's own psyche); disassociation (these communications are merely a game); and a neutralization of status (Tin equal to him or her"). See Suler (2003).

12. The Pew Internet and American Life Project, http://www.pewinternet.org.

13. "As Americans gain experience, they use the Web more at work, write e-mails with more significant content, perform more online transactions, and pursue more activities online." See Horrigan (2002).

References

Hancock, J.T. and PJ. Dunham. 2001. Impression formation in computer-mediated communication revisited: An analysis of the breadth and intensity of impressions. *Communication Research* 28: 325-347.

Katsh, E, and J, Rifkin. 2001, *Online dispute resolution: Resolving conflicts in cyberspace.* San Francisco: Jossey-Bass.

Horrigan, J.B. 2002. Getting serious on line. The Pew Internet and American Life Project, http://www.pewinternet.org.

——. 2001. Online communities: Networks that nurture long-distance relationships and loyalties. The Pew Internet and American Life Project, http.Y/www.pewintemetofg,

Joinson, A. N. 2001. Self-disclosure in computer-mediated communication: The role of self-awareness and visual anonymity. Institute of Educational Technology, The Open University.

Kiesler, S., J. Siegal, and T. McGuire. 1984. Social psychological aspects of computer-mediated communication, *American Psychologist* 39: 1123-1134.

Kommers, N. 2002. Uses of the Internet at mafor life moments. The Pew Internet and American life Project, http://www.pewinternet.org.

Larsen, E. 2001. CyberFaith: How Americans pursue religion online. The Pew Internet and American Life Project, http://www.pewintemet.org.

Lea, M. and R. Spears. 1992. Paralanguage and social perception in computer-mediated communication. *Journal of Organizational Computing* 2: 321-341.

Lenhart, A. and L. Rainie. 2001. Teenage life online: The rise of the instant message generation and the Internet's impact on friendships and family relationships. The Pew Internet and American Life Project, http://www.pewinternet.org.

Rice, R.E. and G. 1987. Electronic emotion: Socioemotional content in a computer- mediated network. *Communication Research* 14: 85-108.

Kiesler, S. 1986. The hidden messages in computer networks. *Harvard Business Review* January-February l986: 46-54, 58-60.

Rule, C. 2002. *Otiline dispute resolution for business: B2Bt ecommerce, consumer, employtnent, itisurance, and other commercial conflicts.* San Francisco: Jossey-Bass.

Suter, J. 2003. The online disinhibition effect. In *The Psychology of Cyberspace.* Online hypertext book originally published in 1996. http://www.rider .edu/users/suler/psycyber/disinhibitJitml

Tidwell, L.C. and J.B. Walther. 2002, Computer-mediated communication effects on disclosure, impressions, and interpersonal evaluations. *Human Communication Research* 28(3): 318-319.

Walther, J.B. 1993. Impression development in computer-mediated interaction. *Western Journal of Communication* 57: 381-398.

——, 1997. Group and interpersonal effects in international computer-mediated collaboration. *Human Communication Research* 23: 342-369.

Walther, J.B. and J.K. Burgoon. 1992, Relational communication in computer-mediated interaction. *Human Communication Research* 19: 50-58.

Thinking Further 1.1

1. What evidence do you see from your experiences with social media that online dispute resolution is a viable alternative to face-to-face dispute resolution? How comfortable would you feel using face-to-face versus online dispute resolution? Why?

2. Describe situations in which face-to-face dispute resolution might be more effective than online dispute resolution. Explain why. Describe situations in which you believe online dispute resolution might be more effective than face-to-face dispute resolution. Explain why.

Reading 1.2

BALANCING ACT: HOW TO MANAGE NEGOTIATION TENSIONS

Susan Hackley

The more aware you are of the tensions underlying a negotiation, the greater your chances of success.

JUDITH LAWSON DREADED her upcoming meeting with the mayor. As head of the city's environmental department, she had promised her staff that she would confront the mayor with their complaints. Unless her office was given the budget to implement proposals to improve air quality and deal with polluters, several key members of her staff planned to quit. Furthermore, they would have no qualms about airing their grievances publicly.

Lawson knew this would be a tough negotiation, for several reasons. The mayor would be understandably upset that a high-profile department was threatening mutiny. Lawson wanted to represent her staff aggressively, but she also worried that too assertive.! stance might incline the mayor to "shoot the messenger"—which her career couldn't afford

What made I.awson's task so complicated is that it required her to manage three tensions simultaneously:

1. The tension between creating and distributing value.

2. The tension between empathy and assertiveness.

3. The tension between principals and agents.

These three tensions are "inherent in negotiation, whether the goal is to make a deal or settle a dispute," write Robert H. Mnookin, Scott R. Peppet, and Andrew S. Tulumello in *Beyond Winning: Negotiating to Create Value in Deals and Disputes* (Belknap, 2000). Managing them is vital for successful negotiations.

Distributing Value Versus Creating It

Some negotiations are purely *distribute*—the task is to divide a fixed amount of value. When haggling over the price of a suit, you can try to affect the distribution of value (who gets how much), but you're unlikely to create new value. Other negotiations are potentially *value creating:* they offer the opportunity to create value by expanding the universe of what is being negotiated. For example, a celebrity might get a suit for free by agreeing to wear it to a well-publicized event. In a trade negotiation, political face-saving tactics may be as important as the tariffs being decided.

Skillful negotiators make sure they get their fair share while exploring ways to "enlarge the pie," to use a popular negotiation metaphor. It you bargain in a job negotiation for a higher salary but miss opportunities to discuss stock options, merit bonuses, or a more generous retirement package, you may end up with a relatively poor deal. At the same time, you need to protect your core distributive interests, being careful not to share too much information {you're desperate for the job) or give away too much value (you'd take half the salary offered).

Judith Lawson knew there would be value-creating opportunities in her meeting with the mayor. If citizens perceived that the city was handling environmental problems more effectively, both the mayor and the environmental department would score a public relations victory. Moreover, it would be in the mayor's

Source: Hackley, S. (2005). Balancing act: How to manage negotiation tensions, *Program on Negotiation Newsletter,* 7–9.

Note: This article first appeared in *Negotiation*, a monthly newsletter published by the Program on Negotiation at Harvard Law School, www.pon.harvard.edu. Copyright 2006–2011 Harvard University.

interest not to incur the disruption of a protracted dispute with his environmental department.

Lawson also recognized the distributive issues at stake. What additional resources could the mayor give her department? How much time would he be willing to spend on their concerns and projects?

Empathy Versus Assertiveness

In many negotiations, you may find it difficult to truly understand the other side's viewpoint. If you're angry with a supplier who sent you shoddy goods, you won't want to hear his sob story about the poor raw materials with which he had to work. Yet a little empathy could inspire you to help him find ways to solve his problem and in turn, ensure better-quality goods.

Asking open-ended questions, listening closely, and Managing Negotiation Tensions demonstrating an understanding of the other sides position will not only allow you to explain your own perspective but may also give you new and useful information.

On the other hand, you don't want to be overly swayed by another's story. Being assertive means being able to express your own interests with confidence and clarity. Skilled negotiators have learned how to be assertive *and* empathetic. They make it clear what they want and need, and they also are genuinely curious to discover what the other side wants and needs.

Lawson was tired of the mayor's excuses for undercutting her department's initiatives, yet she knew she needed to see the situation from his point of view. Once their meeting got under way, she learned to her surprise that the mayor had greater sympathy for her requests than she'd expected and that he felt frustrated and hamstrung by the city council's budget decisions. He had avoided engaging with her department because he felt helpless. This new knowledge

made it easier for Lawson to engage in creative problem solving that answered her needs as well as the mayor's. What about demonstrating to the council how better air quality would elevate the city's reputation as a desirable place to live, which, in turn, would improve real estate values, public health, and economic development?

Being a Principal Versus Serving as an Agent

In her negotiations with the mayor, Lawson was acting as an *agent* for the members of her department, who depended on her to represent their grievances fairly and effectively. As a *principal* in the negotiation, Lawson also had personal interests that were not perfectly aligned with those of her staff, including concerns for her career and her professional relationship with the mayor.

Lawyers represent clients. Money managers give investment advice. Labor leaders negotiate on behalf of unions, and real estate agents represent sellers and buyers. People "constantly delegate authority to others so they may act in our place" as agents, note Mnookin, Pep-pet, and Tulumello. Unfortunately, the principal-agent relationship is "rife with potential conflicts." Looking for differences in incentives is an important part of preparing for a negotiation. A victim in a car accident suing for damages needs to examine her lawyer's interests. Does he have a financial incentive to either settle the case early or prolong it unnecessarily?

One way to manage the principal-agent tension is to acknowledge it up front and treat it as a "shared problem." Before her meeting with the mayor, Lawson and her staff agreed that she would not have authority to make commitments without their approval. What if the mayor offered her a promotion without addressing her department's needs? Lawson resolved not to he swayed by bribes, while her staff promised to back her up should the mayor make punitive moves.

Recognizing that the "use of agents complicates bargaining by creating a web of relationships in which a variety of actors interact" helped Lawson and her team prepare for the negotiation.

Ten Hard Bargaining Tactics

Don't be caught unprepared by hard bargainers, warn Mnookin, Peppet, and Tulumello in *Beyond Winning*. Here is their Top 10 list of common tactics to watch out for:

1. Extreme claims followed by small, slow concessions. Don't let a strong demand "anchor" your expectations. Be clear going in about your own demands, alternatives, and bottom line—and don't be rattled by an aggressive opponent.

2. Commitment tactics. Your opponent may say that his hands are tied or that he has only limited discretion in negotiating. Make sure that these commitment tactics are for real.

3. Take-it-or-leave-it offers. This game of chicken can be countered by making another offer. But watch out: if both parties play this game, you may not get a deal.

4. Inviting unreciprocated offers. When you make an offer, wait for a counteroffer before reducing your demands. Don't bid against yourself.

5. Trying to make you flinch. Your opponent keeps making demands, waiting for you to reach your breaking point. Don't fall for it.

6. Personal insults and feather ruffling. These personal attacks can feed on your insecurities and make you vulnerable. Grow a thick skin.

7. Bluffing, puffing, and lying. Exaggerating and misrepresenting facts can throw you off-guard. Be polite but skeptical.

8. Threats and warnings. Recognizing threats and oblique warnings as the tactics they are can help you stand up to them.

9. Belittling your alternatives. Have a firm sense of your best alternative to a negotiated agreement *(BATNA)*, and don't let your opponent shake your resolve.

10. Good cop, bad cop. One of your opponents is reasonable; the other is tough. Realize that they are working together, and get your own bad cop if you need one.

Awareness Is Power

Beyond Winnings authors believe you'll be more likely to succeed if you learn to recognize the three tensions that can exist in negotiations. Overlook them, and you may fail to come to agreement, even when an agreement would be better for both sides.

Sometimes the other side is reasonable, and you can still miss opportunities to create value. You might not pursue the necessary in-depth conversation or, if you do, you might not listen well enough to your counterpart. Another pitfall: not working hard enough to establish the strong relationship that would lead to the give-and-take that results in better deals.

When the other side isn't reasonable, it's that much harder to reach agreement. A divorcing couple may find it impossible to listen and empathize with each other, engaging instead in scorched-earth litigation that depletes the very financial resources in dispute. Beware of tough negotiators, who may employ a variety of strategies ranging from the unpleasant to the unethical. (See the sidebar "Ten Hard-Bargaining Tactics")

"Making the right moves or using good technique will not cause these tensions to disappear," observe Mnookin, Peppet, and Tulumello. 'They are present in most negotiations, from beginning to end, and should be consciously and thoughtfully considered." Learn to seek additional sources of value while also ensuring you get your fair share. Empathize with the other side and assert your own interests convincingly. And when you're employing an agent or acting as one yourself, be aware that your interests may not all be shared.

Thinking Further 1.2

1. How appropriate or necessary is balancing each of the three tensions in this article if you are a customer who is negotiating the price of a car? What if you are the car salesperson? Support your responses with information from the article.

2. How appropriate or necessary is balancing each of the three tensions in this article if you are a diplomat charged with negotiating peace between your country and a country with which you are at war? Support your responses with information from the article.

CHAPTER 2

Preparation

Building the Foundation for Negotiating

A negotiation is like a building. Without a strong foundation it will fail. If the negotiation foundation, which is provided by your preparation, is strong, your negotiation is likely to be successful. If it is weak or nonexistent, it is more likely to fail. In fact, if the stakes are substantial and you are unable to prepare adequately, you should consider postponing or canceling the negotiation. The material in this chapter helps you construct the foundation upon which all other parts of the negotiation process rest and points out circumstances in which you should postpone or cancel your negotiation.

INTENDED BENEFITS OF THIS CHAPTER

When you finish reading this chapter, you should be able to

1. Explain why preparation is the key to a successful negotiation.
2. Describe the important elements of the preparation process, and explain how to perform them.
3. Prepare effectively for negotiations.

THE ESSENCE OF PREPARATION

Many negotiators underemphasize the preparation process. This a problem because negotiators sometimes make mistakes or fall victim to a number of biases that cause them to walk away when a desirable agreement is possible, agree to lesser terms than what could have been achieved by pursuing other alternatives, or otherwise preclude them from maximizing their own gain or joint gain. More specifically, inadequate preparation may cause negotiators to miss opportunities to negotiate beneficial outcomes, see weakness even when strength exists, bargain themselves down (lower their demands or objectives) before they meet with the other party, feel overconfident, try to make sure everyone else is happy, or mistake toughness for effectiveness (Kolb & Williams, 2003). Negotiation in Action 2.1 illustrates the consequences of underemphasizing preparations when negotiating employment packages. The short- and long-term costs could be substantial.

NEGOTIATION IN ACTION 2.1

When I finished college, I was hoping to find a job that paid me a decent wage for my first job. I spent a solid 3 months looking for various jobs, hoping I wouldn't have to go back to selling insurance—I sold insurance during most of my undergraduate years. Since every job I found required experience and I only had insurance sales experience, I finally decided to pursue some options doing that. I met with several agents, but most would have required a very long commute—something I didn't want to do every day.

My first interview with the agent I ended up working for included typical questions. The second interview was more of a wage negotiation, and I was not prepared for it. Although I had previous sales experience, my positions and pay had been a reflection of my education and part-time status. I had no idea what a college graduate should be paid right out of college, nor what commission rate I should be getting. The agent, who had been in the business for 8 years and was just opening his own office (I would be his first employee) proceeded to talk up his side of things—all the positives of the position. They were all general ideas with no specific promises. In the end, I agreed to his first offer as far as commission, but he never mentioned an hourly wage and I didn't press him for it. I just trusted I would be treated fairly. That was a big mistake in retrospect. On my first day a few weeks after the interview, he simply told me what the salary would be since I had already accepted the position. The overall outcome of the hiring process included a $12/hour wage, a commission scheme favoring the agent, and no health benefits. I worked for him for almost 2 years, but never felt that I had a fair compensation package during that time. I eventually quit the job for a few reasons, but the major catalyst was the pay (*personal communication*).

Many people assume that employers will offer a fair wage or salary when they are offered a new job. Would preparing for this negotiation have helped him avoid the dissatisfaction that eventually caused him to quit? If so, how should he have prepared?

Thorough preparation enables you to avoid, overcome, or at least minimize many of the aforementioned problems, and those illustrated in Negotiation in Action 2.1. Taking a more positive view, adequate preparation leads to beneficial outcomes by helping you determine whether negotiation is an appropriate tool for managing a given situation, establish appropriate goals and objectives, formulate appropriate strategies, and effectively implement your strategies. Moreover, thorough preparation engenders confidence and positive beliefs about negotiations, both of which help you achieve better outcomes (Elfenbein, Curhan, Eisenkraft, Shirako, & Baccaro, 2008). Preparation is so important that the 80-20 rule applies–about 80% of your efforts should be devoted to preparation while 20% should be devoted to the actual negotiation (Thompson, 2009).

THE PREPARATION PROCESS, OR HOW TO MAKE IT ALL HAPPEN

In general, preparing to negotiate requires you to answer several questions.

- What do you want or need and how do you intend to get it?
- What are your alternatives if you are unable to reach an acceptable outcome negotiating with this party?
- What does the other party want or need and how will he or she attempt to get it?
- What are his or her alternatives if an acceptable agreement cannot be reached with you?

STRATEGIC PLANNING: ESTABLISHING THE FRAMEWORK

Developing a strategic plan for your negotiation should help you capitalize on the benefits of negotiating while minimizing or avoiding the aforementioned problems. Assuming negotiation is an appropriate tool for a given situation (consider the requisite conditions discussed in Chapter 1), a strategic framework will guide your negotiation. This is especially important if the stakes are high. Strategic planning is not about creating a script that you will follow throughout the negotiation because flexibility is essential. Instead, it entails defining the situation, establishing the goals you hope to achieve, formulating your strategy for achieving them, and deciding how you will implement it.

Defining the Situation

Defining the situation can be straightforward and easy. Many, however, are very complex and negotiators end up addressing symptoms rather than the true problem.

Consider the situation depicted in Negotiation in Action 2.2.

NEGOTIATION IN ACTION 2.2

A manufacturer of front quarter panels for automobiles maintains four separate production lines, each of which is headed by a large hydraulic press that stamps the panels out of steel sheets. A problem arose one morning when two of the lines began experiencing a significantly larger number of defects than normal for no apparent reason–eight or nine rejects per hour because of burrs and other rough spots instead of the normal one or two. Two hours later, the third line began experiencing the same problems. The fourth line did not experience problems even though it used the same metal sheets. The plant manager, production chief, quality control manager, industrial relations manager, and four line supervisors were trying to decide what the problem was and how to solve it. Several managers

(Continued)

(Continued)

believed it was deliberate sabotage by the machine operators who were upset that one of their coworkers had been suspended the day before: their "hotheaded, anti-union supervisor" alleged that he was drinking on the job but failed to conduct a reasonable investigation to prove it. These managers also believed that the men working on the line that was devoid of problems were very loyal to their supervisor and would not engage in sabotage or any other actions that would make him look bad.

Other managers were not convinced that it was a labor problem, but they could find no better explanation. Their examination revealed no problems with the hydraulic system and press speed did not explain the problem because the lines ran at different speeds. Nor did the metal sheets appear to be the problem—they looked fine going into the press but came out extremely rough. The plant manager appeared to have two choices: back up the supervisor who had disciplined the employee and risk a strike, or undercut the supervisor by reinstating the employee and asking the rest of the men to help them eliminate the defects. Neither course of action was appealing—or appropriate. In fact, a more productive analysis of the problem (see Reading 2.1 at the end of this chapter) would have revealed that the problem actually involved a change in the composition of the metal sheets (adapted from Stryker, 2001a).

The plant manager hired a consultant to help him define the true problem. How could you have done this without incurring the expense of the consultant, thereby enabling you to negotiate a solution to the true problem?

Accurately defining the situation is necessary to ensure that any outcome that you negotiate satisfies all of your true needs, and perhaps those of the other party. This requires you to thoroughly investigate the situation by *gathering relevant information*. Examining relevant documents and records; interviewing witnesses; talking with constituents and others who may affect or be affected by the negotiation and considering, the bargaining history between the parties, if there is one, to discover past successes and failures are all examples of the elements that may be useful when attempting to define the situation. If the stakes are high (e.g., BHP Billiton's nearly $147.4 billion unsolicited offer to acquire Rio Tinto), extensive and costly preparation are warranted (see the due diligence considerations summarized in Negotiation in Action 2.3). For other negotiations with stakes that are not so high, preparations are essential, though they need not be this rigorous.

NEGOTIATION IN ACTION 2.3

Due diligence is the process of gathering objective and reliable information about the past, present, and predictable future of an organization prior to merging with or acquiring it. It is the name we give to the function of "kicking the tires and looking under the hood." The purpose of due diligence is to determine the benefits that will be gained and the liabilities that will be incurred by completing this transaction. It also provides the basis for negotiating the terms of the deal (Grau, 2005). Examples of the documents and related information that should be reviewed include the following (see, e.g., LaPiana, 2004; DePamphilis, 2003):

1. **Corporate Documents of the Target Company and Its Subsidiaries** (e.g., articles of incorporation, bylaws, minutes of directors meetings and shareholder meetings)

2. **Securities Matters** (e.g., annual, quarterly and special reports to shareholders, the number of shares currently authorized, issued and outstanding)

3. **Intellectual Property Matters** (e.g., patents, trademarks, service marks, trade names and copyrights owned or used by the company, applications pending for each)

4. **Assets, Real Property, and Personal Property Matters** (e.g., domestic and foreign facilities owned, leased or used by the company)

5. **Conduct of Business Information** (e.g., currently marketed products and services, sales records, important customers, important suppliers, key competitors)

6. **Financial and Accounting Matters** (e.g., balance sheets, year-end financial statements, listing of inventories, accrued expenses, accounts receivable and payable)

7. **Tax Information** (e.g., income tax returns, information regarding tax deficiencies and pending tax audits, unemployment tax experience ratings and reserves)

8. **Legal Matters** (e.g., descriptions of current, pending or expected investigations, arbitrations or litigations, policies pertaining to legal and ethical conduct)

9. **Risk Management Information** (e.g., insurance policies, including claims experience, risk management policies and programs, product warranties)

10. **Employment, Labor and Management Information** (e.g., organization chart, compensation and performance data for employees and managers, employment, labor, consulting and retirement agreements, HR policies, salary/wage schedules)

Examining all of the information available can be inefficient and ineffective. Considering only information that is truly relevant to the situation will ensure that the real problem is identified and avoid creating new ones as the managers depicted in Negotiation in Action 2.2 nearly did (Stryker, 2001b). **Reading 2.1** at the end of this chapter demonstrates how you can determine the true problem so that you can negotiate an appropriate solution.

The foregoing should help you define the problem to be solved. Other factors must also be considered to help you understand the situation more thoroughly.

The Nature of the Interaction. Will you be negotiating a deal, settling a dispute, or making a team decision? Will you negotiate with this party once or multiple times? Will you negotiate publicly or privately? These questions matter because they influence the dynamics of your interactions and the importance of your relationships. These interactions also have implications for your reputation. Your reputation clearly matters in ongoing relationships, but it is not unique to them. Many negotiations occur in the context of a social network, so even if you will not be meeting with this particular person again your reputation may precede or follow you. Public and private negotiations also differ. Private negotiations, those without an audience, are usually more rational than those that play out in front of audiences.

Other Negotiations. Will your negotiation be influenced by other negotiations, or influence subsequent negotiations? Historically, for example, some labor unions negotiated pattern contracts–they reached an agreement with one employer in a particular industry and then insisted that other employers in that industry agree to the same terms. This was common in the automobile and oil industries. Likewise, employers may be reluctant to offer salaries or signing bonuses that are too large when negotiating the terms of employment packages with new hires because doing so will set unwanted precedents for future hires.

Obligations to Negotiate With This Party. Are you obligated to negotiate or do you have the luxury of saying no or opting out of it? Must you reach an agreement or do you have the luxury of choosing an alternative to dealing with this party? These influence your ability to walk away and thus, how you negotiate and what you achieve.

Relative Power. If you have more power or even equal power, you are likely to negotiate differently than if you have appreciably less power than the other side. You are likely to use different tactics when negotiating with a peer on a team project, for example, than when you are negotiating with your supervisor.

Resources and Constraints. Parties with substantial resources or few constraints (e.g., information, expertise, alternatives, skills, materials, laws, regulations, procedures, customs, charisma, money) are likely to set more ambitious goals, while those with few resources or tight constraints are likely to be more conservative. Time (deadlines) is a particularly salient resource or constraint because the rate at which negotiators make concessions increases as final deadlines approach (Lim & Murnighan, 1994). Although a deadline for one negotiator is a deadline for all of the negotiators, we often predict the consequences of deadlines incorrectly (Windschitl, Kruger, & Simms, 2003). This will be discussed in greater detail in Chapter 3.

Others Who May Affect or Be Affected By Your Negotiation. This may include direct participants who are at the table with you (e.g., colleagues, attorneys), participants to whom you report or are accountable even though they are not at the table with you (e.g., superiors, other constituents), and indirect participants (e.g., managers of other departments, shareholders, financial analysts, competitors, suppliers, the media). The influence of these parties varies, but they may provide you with resources or impose constraints, or they may clarify your interests. Satisfying a superior or being recognized for a job well done, for instance, may be significant interests for you.

Environment or Context. This includes labor markets, unemployment rates, workforce demographics, market wages and benefits, financial markets, stock prices, interest rates, inflation levels, competition, growth rates, merger/acquisition activity, governmental policies, the degree of globalization, legal developments, and the ethical environment. Negotiation in Action 2.4 demonstrates how the environment, notably the economy, affects negotiations.

NEGOTIATION IN ACTION 2.4

Small businesses are getting hit with another aftershock of the credit crisis: Customers who are delaying payment of their bills for weeks or months. These firms are hugely dependent on their cash flow so they are being forced to either cut costs or find alternative funding if they aren't being paid on time. With money tight and bank loans hard to come by, a cash-strapped company can easily be pushed to the brink. Making the problem worse, big companies typically delay payments to their smaller suppliers—at least in part because small businesses are not likely to have teams of people devoted to chasing down their accounts receivables. Artisan Shutter, which makes custom shutters for high-end residential and commercial buildings, started having problems with late payers as the real estate market tumbled. Half of the company's customers are paying late, up from 5% before the real estate decline started. The biggest blow came when an architectural firm called to say it couldn't pay the last $40,000 of a $180,000 project on a high-end hotel. The hotel's construction depended on financing from Lehman Brothers and building ground to a halt when Lehman filed for bankruptcy protection. Many firms are taking steps to reduce their risk. One is negotiating down payments on services and penalties on late payments. Another is restricting the credit it is willing to extend when deals are negotiated with customers. These turbulent times seem to be changing the way small businesses negotiate deals with their customers and clients (adapted from Spors & Covel, 2008).

Setting Goals

When you have defined the situation, you must determine your goals, that is what you want to accomplish, and what you think the other party wants to accomplish. Most negotiators emphasize goals that are *substantive* in nature. Examples include price and contract language.

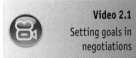

Video 2.1
Setting goals in
negotiations

Relationship goals may also be important. You may want to preserve or change your relationship with the other party because you value a certain type of relationship, or because you believe it will help in future interactions with this party. Finally, goals may pertain to the *process* of negotiating or how the parties attempt to accomplish their substantive and relationship goals. You may prefer to negotiate in a certain manner because you are most comfortable with it, you believe it is the best way to accomplish your other goals, or because it will help you with the other party in the future.

The foregoing suggests that substantive, relationship, party and process goals are interdependent. Parties adopting substantive goals that are more ambitious than the other party's goals tend to secure better outcomes as long as their ambitious goals are not outrageous (Kray, Thompson, & Galinsky, 2001; Thompson, 1995), but they may jeopardize their relationship with the other party (Lewicki, Saunders, Barry, & Minton, 2003). Similarly, negotiators may adopt certain relationship goals because the nature of the bargaining relationship influences the effectiveness with which particular bargaining strategies are implemented. Not surprisingly, adversarial relationships are better suited for competitive bargaining and cooperative relationships are more appropriate for collaborative bargaining (Walton & McKersie, 1965).

Effective goals, those that are clear, specific, measurable, and challenging yet attainable (Mitchell, Thompson, & George-Falvy, 2000; Locke & Latham, 1984), serve several purposes for negotiators.

- They guide behavior. It is easy to get sidetracked in a negotiation. Knowing what your goals are provides direction and enables you to stay the course.
- Goals help you clarify expectations and determine priorities.
- Goals suggest what information is needed.
- Substantive and relationship goals help you determine which strategy and tactics are most appropriate.

Determining Your Strategy

A strategy is the plan or process by which negotiators attempt to achieve their goals. Tactics are the specific, short-term actions that serve to implement the broader strategy. Strategies and tactics are the *how to* component of the negotiation process. As noted earlier when discussing the dual concerns model, how people negotiate depends on the relative importance they attach to their substantive and relationship concerns (Savage, Blair, & Sorenson, 1989; Blake & Mouton, 1964). Negotiators who are highly concerned with achieving their substantive goals but have significantly less concern for the relationship or for the other party's substantive goals are likely to adopt a *competitive* or *distributive* strategy. This strategy works best when resources are fixed and you want to maximize your share of them. It is about claiming value or "dividing the pie in your favor." It will be discussed in detail in Chapter 3.

Negotiators who are highly concerned with achieving their substantive goals and with the relationship or for the other party's substantive goals are likely to adopt a *collaborative* or *integrative* strategy. This strategy works best when resources are not fixed and you want to maximize joint gain. It is about "expanding the pie," or creating value by expanding the pool of available resources. It will be discussed in detail in Chapter 4.

STRATEGY IMPLEMENTATION: OPERATIONALIZING THE PLAN

Once your framework or plan is formulated, it must be operationalized so that you can implement it. This includes identifying and defining the component parts of the plan for yourself and for estimating them for the other party.

The Component Parts of the Situation

Issues

Issues are the specific components or dimensions of the situation that must be addressed. Together, the issues make up the **bargaining mix.** When you negotiate the terms of a job offer, for instance, your bargaining mix may include job title, the duties you will perform, salary, signing bonus, performance bonus, stock options, benefits, relocation allowance, and your start date. If negotiators fail to identify all of the issues, important dimensions of the situation remain hidden and this leads to incomplete agreements or incomplete solutions. Since the importance of the issues may vary, prioritizing them enables you to allocate more effort to the most important parts of your negotiation. It also enables you to add value to the negotiation by crafting beneficial tradeoffs or packages of issues (Lax & Sebenius, 2002, 1986). In the job offer negotiation mentioned earlier, for example, salary may be a higher priority issue for the employer because it wants to avoid setting undesirable precedents. For the applicant, signing bonus or relocation allowance may be higher priority issues because he or she just graduated and has no money in the bank. Recognizing these differences may allow both parties to gain by trading low priority items for high priority items.

Positions

In most negotiations, each person takes a position—commonly an offer or a counteroffer, it is one possible outcome—argues for it and makes concessions to reach a compromise (Fisher, Ury, & Patton, 1991). The basic problem in most negotiations, however, lies not in conflicting positions but in conflicting needs, desires, concerns, or fears—interests.

Interests

Interests are the motives underlying your positions, your reasons for wanting them. These reasons reflect the purposes the stated position will serve for you, not your justification for it. Interests are commonly unmet needs. They may include basic needs like hunger, shelter, safety or security, or higher-level needs for affection, respect, recognition, achievement, or self-fulfillment (Maslow, 1943). Returning once again to the job offer negotiation, assume that you demand a starting salary of $75,000 to accept the position of financial analyst that was offered to you. One *issue* is your salary. Your *position* is the $75,000 starting salary you demanded. Your *interests* are the purposes $75,000 will serve for you. Perhaps it will enable you to gain sufficient respect from your classmates or from other financial analysts in this organization. You may be looking for the hiring executive to recognize your competence and the knowledge you would be bringing to this company. Another possibility is that you may need this amount to support your family. Issues and interests are particularly important because, together, they define the situation. If you know all of the dimensions or components of the situation and the needs associated with each, you have a comprehensive understanding of the problem to be solved or the deal to be made.

Aspiration Levels or Target Points

Aspiration levels or target points are what you realistically hope to achieve for each issue. Unlike the goals developed during the strategic planning process, which are broader, aspiration levels are specific to each issue. To illustrate, when the former chief executive officer (CEO) of Bank of America initiated merger negotiations with the former CEO of NationsBank, his goal was to achieve a merger of equals. One of his targets was for each bank to have an equal number of people on the merged company's board of directors (Zuckerman, 1999).

Determining target points seems pretty straightforward–determine what is required to satisfy your interests and set that as your target. At times, it is this simple. But it can be much more difficult because we make perceptual, cognitive, or emotional errors that hinder this (Neale & Bazerman, 1991). The example in Negotiation in Action 2.5 is illustrative.

NEGOTIATION IN ACTION 2.5

Joseph Bachelder negotiates job contracts for executives. Early in his career, he was representing an experienced grocery executive. After discussing some preliminary matters, he demanded 4.9% of the company for his client. The hiring executive immediately and jubilantly accepted. Bachelder's heart sank because he knew he had set his target too low and asked for too little. He suffered what is called the winner's curse – he got what he asked for but wasn't happy with it (adapted from Anders, 2003).

These and other errors that plague decision makers will be discussed in detail in Chapter 7. When setting target points, it is essential to remember that all parties will simultaneously be trying to satisfy their respective interests. This does not mean you should set your targets in response to your estimate of the other party's targets, and definitely not in response to his or her opening offers. Setting your targets should be based on your research and emphasize your own needs.

Best Alternative to a Negotiated Agreement (BATNA)

Identify your **best alternative to a negotiated agreement** or BATNA (Fisher, Ury, & Patton, 1991). People negotiate because they think they can satisfy their interests more effectively with the other party than

Video 2.2
BATNA

they can without him or her. But what will you do if you are unable to reach an agreement with him or her? Each party's best alternative if an agreement cannot be reached defines the worst acceptable outcome in this negotiation. The basic test of any *proposed* agreement, therefore, should be whether it offers greater value than your best course of action without the other party. If your alternatives are good, you will be able to ask for more and walk away from poor offers. But alternatives, even best alternatives, may not be good. This makes walking away more difficult. When preparing to negotiate, it is important to identify and analyze your best *no-agreement alternatives* because it influences whether you should negotiate and whether you should accept an offer (Lax & Sebenius, 1986).

In some negotiations, alternatives are obvious and well defined. Many employment and commercial contracts require the parties to enlist the aid of a mediator or arbitrator if they are unable to settle disputes on their own. A real estate developer auctioning off plots of land to homebuilders can easily compare bids from different builders. At other times, they are more difficult to define and measure. Among the more salient problems are the following:

• Some negotiators believe that a BATNA is something they can work out with the other party. It is not. By definition, a BATNA is the best that you can do *without* him or her.

• Some negotiators confuse wishful thinking with reality. A BATNA is about objective reality. If, for instance, you are negotiating your starting salary with Your Ideal Employer, Inc., your BATNA is the job offer you already received from The Other Company, Inc. Continuing your job search might be your best alternative if you do not have another job offer. What you think you *should* have been offered, or what you *might* be offered by Yet Another Company, Inc., however, are not BATNAs.

NEGOTIATION IN ACTION 2.6

People were given identical information about the negotiation of a personal injury lawsuit, and then asked to estimate the probability that the plaintiff would win the case and the amount of the judgment for him. Although their information was identical, those who were assigned to the role of plaintiff consistently estimated the probability of winning and the amount of the judgment to be significantly higher than those who were assigned to the role of defendant. Those who were not assigned to either role rendered estimates between those of the plaintiffs and defendants (adapted from Raiffa, 1982).

As demonstrated in Negotiation in Action 2.6, we often misjudge valuations, including the value of alternatives (Lax & Sebenius, 1986). Exercise caution when evaluating your alternatives because accuracy matters.

• BATNAs are not passive or static. Negotiators can and should cultivate additional alternatives, or increase the value of an existing alternative. Securing a different supplier with a more favorable price, another job offer, or a friendly merger with a different firm to counter a hostile takeover attempt are examples. It is also important to recognize that the other party may attempt to diminish the value of your BATNA, typically by presenting new information that casts your BATNA in a negative light, or even a false light. Adequate pre-negotiation preparation, especially if it is based on objective information, makes it easier to resist the other party's efforts to devalue your BATNA.

Reservation Prices or Resistance Points

Knowing your BATNA is beneficial for at least two reasons. First, a BATNA is the basis for determining **reservation prices** (also called **resistance points** or **walk away prices**). A reservation price is your breakeven point or the worst acceptable outcome for each issue. You would rather walk away without an agreement if you cannot achieve terms that are better than or equal to this point. For instance, Ross recently accepted a new job in a different state, so he and Susan, his wife, must sell their house. Their resistance point is the least amount of money they will accept for it. If a buyer is not willing to pay that amount or more, they would rather sell it to a different buyer who is, or keep the house and use it as a rental property.

Reservation prices set limits that preclude us from settling for less than what we could have achieved without negotiating with this party. Likewise, they enable us to avoid rejecting offers that are better than our BATNA. Although these sound like perverse outcomes, they do happen. Resistance points are also important because they are significant drivers of final outcomes. When market price, aspiration level, and reservation price were made available to negotiators, only the latter determined their final outcomes (Blount-White, Valley, Bazerman, Neale, & Peck, 1994).

Quantifying their BATNA is one way negotiators can determine their resistance points. Sometimes this is straightforward because the value of an alternative is given. The scenario described in Negotiation in Action 2.7 illustrates such a straightforward conversion.

NEGOTIATION IN ACTION 2.7

When the IRMAN Printing Company changed its strategy from fine art printing to more remunerative areas, it no longer needed one of its presses. A person who is planning to open a shop that would require this type of press inquired about IRMAN's willingness to sell it. When told the shop owner would consider selling the press, the buyer offered $1,000. Before responding to the buyer, the shop owner did some homework. She knew that the press was exotic and expensive so finding additional buyers was unlikely. She also knew the press cost $10,000 when she bought it and a new one would cost $12,000 today. Then she cultivated alternatives. She called a junk dealer and learned that he would pay her $500 and cart it off as scrap. She also called the art department at a local university and learned that it would be interested in having the press donated. This would be worth $2,500 as a tax deduction for her, and she would rather see it used than scrapped. Quantifying her BATNA established her resistant point as $2,500. She and the buyer agreed to a price of $3,500 (adapted from Lax & Sebenius, 1986).

In other instances, quantifying a BATNA is not this simple. It may be necessary to compute the subjective or expected probabilities of obtaining certain outcomes (Thompson, 2009). Negotiation in Action 2.8 revisits the scenario depicted in Negotiation in Action 2.7, this time assuming that donating the press and selling it as scrap are not viable options. This approach should be viewed as a guide or a rule of thumb. It is better than an arbitrary guess but it is not a perfect measure because it is based on subjective estimates.

NEGOTIATION IN ACTION 2.8

Assume the shop owner determined her target point to be $7,500, the depreciated value of her press. She then estimated the probability she would receive an offer for $6,000 or more to be 15%; she estimated the probability she would receive an offer for $4,500 to be 45%; and she estimated the probability she would receive an offer for $2,500 to be 100%. Thus,

$P_{\text{offer of \$6,000}} = 15\%$

$P_{\text{offer of \$4,500}} = 30\%$ (this is 30% because it includes the 15% probability of selling the press for $6,000)

$P_{\text{offer of \$2,500}} = 55\%$ (this is 55% because it includes the 45% probability of selling it for $4,500)

Her reservation price is: $0.15(\$6,000) + 0.30(\$4,500) + 0.55(\$2,500) = \$3,625$. She should not sell the press for less than $3,625.

If these methods do not apply, resistance points can also be determined by considering how much you can afford to pay, or how much you perceive something to be worth. When assessing worth, it is important to consider the cost of obtaining it, including the cost of negotiating (the value of your time, the resources required, and other tasks you will not be able to perform) in your valuation.

Bargaining Power

The second reason BATNAs are important is because having a good one increases your **bargaining power**. Perhaps the most common conception of this is the ability to bring about desired outcomes (Salancik & Pfeffer, 1977). This suggests power over the other party, which is consistent with the notion of distributive bargaining where you are trying to maximize your share of fixed resources. According to this view, bargaining power is largely a function of relative dependence. The party who needs the other most has the least power. Assume that Sweet Tooth, a bakery, is negotiating a deal to supply its confections to Sammy's Soup & Sandwich. Sammy's has many other suppliers. It is also interested in doing its own baking. Sweet Tooth has few other outlets for selling its product. Under these circumstances, Sammy's needs Sweet Tooth less than Sweet Tooth needs Sammy's. Since Sammy's can walk away more easily, Sammy's has more power.

An it alternative conception of bargaining power is the ability to work effectively with the other party. This "power with" conception (Follett, 1942) implies that negotiators must learn to influence the other party even if they have no formal authority to do so. This is more consistent with the notion of integrative bargaining (Coleman, 2000) where you are trying to find solutions that work well for both parties.

Negotiators are generally concerned with relative bargaining power–how much they have relative to the other party. Having more power enables you to establish more ambitious aspiration levels and reservation prices, and these lead to better outcomes (Kray et al., 2001; Thompson, 1995). Understanding your relative power is also useful because it likely will influence the effectiveness with which you can execute your strategy and tactics. More will be said about power and influence in Chapter 8.

Analyzing the Other Party

The foregoing described elements that help you determine what you want or need and how you will attempt to get it. To prepare effectively, you must also analyze the other party to help you estimate these things for him or her. Estimating the aforementioned elements from the other party's perspective–definition of the situation, goals, strategy, issues, target and resistance points, interests, BATNA, and so on–should help you identify the settlement ranges or zone of possible agreement (ZOPA) (the range between your resistance points). This will shape your determination of appropriate offers and counteroffers. Understanding the other party's perspectives should help you anticipate his or her objections to your proposals, thereby enabling you to craft responses that overcome them. Understanding his or her issues and interests, and how they are prioritized, will also help you find possible tradeoffs or packages that make it easier for you and the other party to agree. Finally, unexpected events are common in negotiations and may derail your plans. Understanding the other party as much as possible should minimize these surprises, make it easier for you to stay on track, and help you achieve beneficial outcomes.

It may be valuable, but is it really possible to determine or accurately estimate the other party's definition of the situation, goals, issues, interests, and so on? Since negotiators rarely, if ever, engage in full disclosure and may even bluff, deceive, or otherwise distort information, it can be difficult. This is why the twin dilemmas of trust and honesty can be so frustrating. The *dilemma* of trust argues that the other party may take advantage of you if you believe too much of what he or she tells you, but you may not be able to reach an agreement if you believe too little. The *dilemma* of honesty argues that the other party may take advantage of you if you share too much information, but you may not be able to reach an agreement if you share too little (Rubin & Brown, 1975).

Despite these difficulties, there are many sources of information that enable you to analyze the other party. If a bargaining relationship exists and is ongoing, both the outcome and the process of prior negotiations may be revealing. The demands made during a previous negotiation that were not satisfied, or only partially satisfied, will probably be raised again. If the other party has complained about how a prior agreement was implemented, those issues are likely to be raised. In a labor-management relationship, for instance, grievances filed typically reflect "hot button" issues. This is particularly true if arbitrators decide these grievances and the other party is unhappy with one or more of the decisions. Examining how a particular policy, practice, or contract provision has evolved over time in ongoing relationships may signal a trend that is problematic for the other party. If it does, he or she will probably attempt to ameliorate it. The bargaining history should also provide information about the strategies and tactics used in previous negotiations. These are likely to be repeated, especially if he or she was satisfied with these prior negotiations.

Whether or not there is a bargaining history between the parties, internal politics are often enlightening. Comments or promises made during interviews or at shareholder meetings, public announcements, reports made by financial analysts or consultants about the organization, publicly traded companies' earnings calls, and media accounts of a situation may all provide useful guidance. Any personal knowledge of the other party (e.g., its financial situation, new products, labor unrest) should also help. Talking with colleagues who have negotiated with the other party may be informative if they are willing to share the issues that were raised, what the other party demanded and conceded, the strategies and tactics used, or at least information about the nature of their interactions.

For intraorganizational negotiations, coworkers and supervisors possess valuable information. They may be aware of problems encountered, comments and complaints made about pertinent matters, or even rumors. For instance, the human resources director for a small unionized hospital routinely engaged employees and supervisors in conversation when they were not treating patients. "Managing by walking around" enabled him to learn about contract provisions, operational issues, or other matters that were confining, costly, contentious, or otherwise problematic. When it was time to begin negotiating a new collective bargaining agreement, this information often proved useful. Finally, the nature of the relationship between the two parties, including the level of trust and personal traits or characteristics of the other party, may suggest how he or she will negotiate. Reading 2.2 at the end of this chapter provides additional insight into why analyzing the other party is necessary, and how to do it.

RAPPORT BUILDING AND TESTING ASSUMPTIONS

Your preparation thus far establishes a solid beginning but there is more work to be done. Building rapport and testing your assumptions will enhance your foundation. Many negotiators in the U.S. ignore these tasks. They view this as a waste of time and choose instead to begin hammering out solutions immediately upon meeting with the other party. *Building rapport* is not a waste of time. Negotiators who chat for just 5 to 10 minutes, even about topics unrelated to their upcoming negotiations, share more information, make fewer threats, and develop more trust and respect than pairs who do not (Nadler, 2004).

Nor is *testing your assumptions* a waste of time. Discussing matters that are indirectly related to the issues you plan to raise will help you complete your foundation more than if you merely exchange social niceties. The agent for a best-selling novelist, for example, might engage the publisher's agent in conversation about general trends in the publishing industry, the success of recently released books of other authors and any difficulties encountered along the way before attempting to reach agreements on each of the issues. This is necessary because your efforts to analyze the other party involve making estimates, assumptions, educated guesses, or even hunches. At some point, we must attempt to validate or verify these. Even if your information is more definitive, testing assumptions may allow for an easier segue into your discussion of the focal issues.

Another reason for doing this is because we are susceptible to making and being influenced by first impressions. In addition, virtually everyone holds unconscious stereotypes based on race, gender, and other traits that most of us would consciously condemn (Greenwald, Nosek, & Banaji, 2003; Greenwald, McGhee, & Schwartz, 1998). Take the "Implicit Association Test" at http://implicit.harvard .edu/implicit if you think you are immune. Negotiation in Action 2.9 demonstrates how this might affect a negotiation.

NEGOTIATION IN ACTION 2.9

Randy is a commercial loan officer and an experienced negotiator. When he entered a negotiation with a bank auditor, he thought he would have an easy time of it because he had observed the auditor in a different setting and concluded that he was soft. Fortunately for Randy, he spent some time testing his assumptions about his counterpart before they got too far into the negotiation. This enabled him to learn that the other negotiator was merely a man of few words and soft spoken. He was clearly not weak or inexperienced. Randy initially underestimated the other party. He caught his mistake before it could do any real damage because he took time to test his assumptions (personal communiction).

Rachel, a brand manager with a health-food company, e-mailed Pete, the owner of an organic market, to set up a meeting at an upcoming industry convention. Rachel wanted to discuss cross-marketing opportunities—a win-win topic she was sure. When they met, Pete greeted her with a big smile. Dressed in denim, he was suntanned and younger than she expected. A laid-back, outdoorsy type, Rachel assessed—agreeable and maybe a bit dim. But Rachel watched Pete's smile fade as soon as she began walking him through her new product line. Soon he looked bored, even hostile. He interrupted her with a tricky pricing question—she was surprised he knew the numbers—and she flubbed her way through it. After 5 minutes had passed, Rachel knew she had bombed. She failed to test her assumptions (adapted from Program on Negotiation, 2007).

The opening minutes of a negotiation between new acquaintances are often critical. What happens can doom an agreement or lay the foundation for a profitable, lasting relationship. Within seconds of meeting Pete, Rachel had absorbed a wealth of visual information and synthesized it into a compact profile—outdoorsy, amiable, dim. This distillation process serves us well when we're making quick decisions. When deliberate thinking is required to reach a high-quality decision, however, mental shortcuts often lead us astray. Rachel's snap judgments caused her to misread Pete and to begin talking down to him. Pete's body language and interruption proved she'd gotten him all wrong (Program on Negotiation, 2007).

WHERE SHOULD YOU NEGOTIATE?

Before you implement your plan, think about *where you are going to negotiate*. Conventional wisdom suggests that you are better off negotiating on your home turf because a familiar setting will put you at ease, make resources readily available, and enhance your confidence. If you travel to the other party's turf, however, you convey a strong desire to make a deal. Moreover, the visual cues and the information they impart about the other side may be valuable. A neutral site is common, but it likely closes off learning opportunities for both sides because it is devoid of all of these qualities and visual cues (Salacuse & Rubin, 1990). Regardless of where you negotiate, the *physical arrangement* of the room may be important. Sitting side-by-side at a round table, for example, connotes more cooperation and may inspire negotiators to take a problem-solving approach. Sitting on opposite sides of the table connotes the opposite (Rubin & Brown, 1975). How you choose to arrange the room should be consistent with your goals and your strategy.

More and more negotiations are being conducted electronically–by e-mail, instant messaging, videoconference, or telephonically–and this renders the location and the physical arrangement moot. Does it impact other elements of your preparation? Clearly, you must have the requisite hardware and software to send and receive e-mails and instant messages, to conduct videoconferences, or to exchange text messages. Electronic negotiations make schmoozing and testing assumptions more difficult. To circumvent this problem, consider meeting with or at least placing a phone call to the other party before the actual negotiation begins to build rapport and test your assumptions (Morris, Nadler, Kurtzberg, & Thompson, 2002). The dynamics of your negotiation will also change, notably the communication process. These changes will be discussed in Chapter 6.

CONCLUSION AND IMPLICATIONS FOR PRACTICE

Preparing to negotiate is about defining the situation, determining your goals, and devising a plan for achieving them. It involves determining the bargaining mix, and the interests, aspiration levels, and reservation prices for each issue in the bargaining mix. It is about determining and cultivating alternatives so that you can more easily walk away if the negotiation does not produce a **wise agreement**–one that satisfies your interests and, perhaps, the other party's (Fisher et al., 1991). Effective preparation also includes analyzing the other party. Simply put, building a good foundation requires you to assess the situation, yourself, and the other party. Before beginning your negotiation, consider the following suggestions.

1. Be prepared. How extensive your preparation must be depends upon the stakes. If they are low, you need not be as thorough. If they are high, rigorous preparation is essential to build a strong foundation to guide the rest of your negotiation and avoid making the mistakes that commonly cause negotiators to settle for suboptimal outcomes. Consider the elements in Appendix I.

2. Fully explore and understand the situation you are negotiating. This will help you achieve beneficial outcomes. Exploring it on your own may reveal additional interests that you want to satisfy (e.g., considering others who will be affected may force you to consider how your supervisor will use this information when evaluating your performance or making promotion decisions). Exploring it with the other party will enable you to ensure that your are both trying to solve the same problem, again helping you achieve a wiser outcome more efficiently.

3. Identify all of the issues. This ensures that the agreement you reach satisfies all of your wants and needs, and perhaps all of the other party's wants and needs. Even single issues can often be broken into component parts and treated as if they are separate issues.

Negotiations may be faster and easier if you address only one or two issues but the outcome will be less beneficial and satisfying.

4. I~~dentify interests for each issue~~. Many negotiators who are familiar with the notion of interests tend to identify them for the negotiation in general. It is usually better for you to identify them for each issue. You may decide to accept or reject an offer based on whether it is better or worse than your BATNA, and that makes sense. Since we negotiate to satisfy our needs, however, you should also consider whether an offer satisfies your interests. Even if it is better than your alternatives, do you really want to accept an offer that fails to satisfy your needs? If you have a choice, you may want to continue looking for solutions with or without this person that do.

5. W~~ork hard to understand and improve your BATNA~~. It is a critical element in negotiations–the better it is, the more satisfied you are likely to be with the outcome you achieve..

6. ~~Take time to get to know the other negotiator~~. It may seem like this will slow you down and be inefficient at a time when efficiency is critically important. In actuality, it should make your negotiation more effective. It will increase trust and respect and allow you to gain the benefits that derive from those qualities - fewer threats to deal with and more information sharing. It will also help you avoid or minimize implicit associations and first impressions, both of which are far more prevalent and influential than most of us imagine.

APPENDIX I: PREPARATION CHECKLIST

Both tables should be completed for each party. The second includes items that pertain to each issue and some that are not unique to each issue.

Strategic Planning/Establishing the Framework

Define the Situation	What is the true problem to be solved, opportunity to be mined, dispute to be settled, team decision to be made?
Establish Goals	What do you want to accomplish, and what do you think the other party wants to accomplish in your negotiation?
Strategy Formulation	Which of the dominant strategies is most appropriate for you and for this situation? How do you think the other side will negotiate?

Implementing Your Plan/Operationalizing Your Framework

Key Elements			
Bargaining Mix	Issue #1	Issue #2	Issue # . . .
Target Points			
BATNA*			
Resistance Points			

*A BATNA is issue-specific if a different party can satisfy each one. If that is not possible, the BATNA applies to the entire negotiation.

(Continued)

(Continued)

Key Elements That Aren't Issue-Specific			
Relative Power			
Build Rapport			
Test Assumptions			

STUDENT STUDY SITE

Visit the Student Study Site at **www.sagepub.com/hames** for additional learning tools.

KEY TERMS

Aspiration levels (a.k.a. target points)

Bargaining mix

Bargaining power

Best alternative to a negotiated agreement (BATNA)

Dilemma of honesty

Dilemma of trust

Goals

Interests

Issues

Position

Relationship goals

Reservation price (a.k.a. resistance point or walk away price)

Resistance point (a.k.a. reservation price or walk away price)

Strategy

Substantive goals

Tactics

Target points (a.k.a. aspiration levels)

Walk away price (a.k.a. reservation price or resistance point)

Wise agreement

Zone of Possible Agreement (ZOPA)

REFERENCES

Anders, G. (2003). Upping the ante: As some decry lavish CEO pay, Joe Bachelder makes it happen, The Wall Street Journal, June 25, A1.

Blake, R. R. & Mouton, J. S. (1964). The managerial grid. Houston: Gulf Publishing. Blount-White, S., Valley, K., Bazerman, M., Neale, M. & Peck, S. (1994). Alternative models of price behavior in dyadic negotiations: Market prices, reservation prices, and negotiator aspirations, Organizational Behavior and Human Decision Processes, 57(3), 430-447.

Coleman, P. (2000). Power and conflict. In M. Deutsch & P. Coleman (Eds.), Handbook of conflict resolution. San Francisco: Jossey-Bass, 108-130.

DePamphilis, D. (2003). Mergers, acquisitions, and other restructuring activities. San Diego, CA: Academic Press.

Elfenbein, H. A., Curhan, J. R., Eisenkraft, N., Shirako, A. & Baccaro, L. (2008). Are some negotiators better than others? Individual differences in bargaining outcomes, Journal of Research in Personality, 42(6), 1463-1475.

Fisher, R., Ury, W. & Patton, B. (1991). Getting to yes: Negotiating agreement without giving in. New York: Penguin Press.

Follett, M. P. (1942). Constructive conflict. In H. C. Metcalf & L. Urwick (Eds.), Dynamic administration: The collected papers of Mary Parker Follett. New York: Harper & Brothers, 30-49.

Grau, D. (2005). Research assignment: When buying or selling an advisory firm, due diligence may be the most important thing you do before signing on the dotted line, Financial Planning, February 1, 1-4.

Greenwald, A. G., Nosek, B. A. & Banaji, M. R. (2003). Understanding and using the Implicit Association Test: An improved scoring algorithm, Journal of Personality and Social Psychology, 85(2), 197-216.

Greenwald, A. G., McGhee, D. E. & Schwartz, J. L. K. (1998). Measuring individual differences in implicit cognition: the Implicit Association Test, Journal of Personality and Social Psychology, 74(6), 1464-1480.

Kolb, D. G. & Williams, J. (2003). Everyday negotiations: Navigating the hidden agendas in bargaining. San Francisco: Jossey-Bass.

Kray, L., Thompson, L. & Galinsky, A. (2001). Battle of the sexes: Gender stereotype confirmation and reactance in negotiations, Journal of Personality and Social Psychology, 80(6), 942-958.

LaPiana Associates (2004). Strategic restructuring: Partnership options for nonprofits, http://www.lapiana.org/resources/faqs/9_16_03b.html

Lax, D. & Sebenius, J. (2002). Dealcrafting: The substance of three-dimensional negotiations, Negotiation Journal, 18(1), 5-28.

_____. (1986). The manager as negotiator: Bargaining for cooperation and competitive gain. New York: The Free Press.

Lewicki, R. J., Saunders, D. M., Barry, B. & Minton, J. (2003). Essentials of Negotiation, New York: McGraw-Hill/Irwin.

Lim, R. G. & Murnighan, J. K. (1994). Phases, deadlines, and the bargaining process, Organizational Behavior and Human Decision Processes, 58, 153-171.

Locke, E. & Latham, G. (1984). Goal setting: A motivational technique that works! Englewood Cliffs, NJ: Prentice-Hall.

Maslow, A. (1943). A theory of human motivation, Psychological Review, 50. 373-396.

Mitchell, T., Thompson, K. & George-Falvy, J. (2000). Goal setting: Theory and practice. In C. Cooper & E. Locke (Eds), Industrial and organizational psychology: Linking theory with practice. Malden, MA: Blackwell Business, 211-249.

Morris, M., Nadler, J., Kurtzberg, T. & Thompson, L. (2002). Schmooze or lose: Social friction and lubrication in e-mail negotiations, Group Dynamics: Theory, Research, & Practice, 6(1), 89-100.

Nadler, J. (2004). Rapport in legal negotiations: How small talk can facilitate email dealmaking, Harvard Negotiation Law Review, 9, 223-253.

Neale, M. A. & Bazerman, M. H. (1991). Cognition and rationality in negotiation. New York: The Free Press.

Program on Negotiation (2007). Negotiation, 10(10), 1-3.

Raiffa, H. (1982). The art and science of negotiation. Cambridge, MA: Belknap Press.

Rubin, J. & Brown, B. (1975). The social psychology of bargaining and negotiation. New York: Academic Press.

Salacuse, J. W. & Rubin, J. Z. (1990). Your place or mine? Site location and negotiation, Negotiation Journal, 6, 5-10.

Salancik, G. R. & Pfeffer, J. (1977). Who gets power and how they hold on to it: A strategic-contingency model of power, Organizational Dynamics, 5, 3-21.

Savage, G. T., Blair, J. D. & Sorenson, R. L. (1989). Consider both relationship and substance when negotiating strategically, Academy of Management Executive, 3(1), 37-48.

Spors, K. K. & Covel, S. (2008). Slow payments squeeze small-business owners, The Wall Street Journal, October 31, B1.

Stryker, P. (2001a). Can you analyze this problem? In HBR on decision making. Boston: HBS Press, 97-111.

_____. (2001b). How to analyze that problem. In HBR on decision making. Boston: HBS Publishing, 113-142.

Thompson, L. L. (2009). The mind and heart of the negotiator. Upper Saddle River, NJ: Pearson.

_____. (1995). They saw a negotiation: Partnership and involvement, Journal of Personality and Social Psychology, 68, 839-853.

Walton, R. E & McKersie, R. B. (1965). A behavioral theory of labor negotiations: An analysis of a social interaction system. New York: McGraw-Hill.

Windschitl, P. D., Kruger, J. & Simms, E. N. (2003). The influence of egocentrism and focalism on people's optimism in competition: When what affects us equally affects me more, Journal of Personality and Social Psychology, 85(3), 389-408.

Zuckerman, S. (1999). Breaking the bank: The untold story of how David Coulter lost BofA, San Francisco Chronicle, September 30, A1.

READINGS

Reading 2.1

HOW TO ANALYZE THAT PROBLEM

Perrin Stryker

The Situation

In a plant making quarter panels and other parts for one or the Rig Three auto companies, the Plant Manager and three of his key subordinates are trying to find out why burrs and rough spots are suddenly appearing on so many panels, causing them to he rejected. They strongly Suspect deliberate sabotage by the men on the production lines, who are reported to be angry over the suspension of worker Joe Valenti by a hotheaded supervisor, who accused him of drinking on the job. The shop steward threatens to call a strike if the supervisor is not reprimanded fur his arbitrary' action and also if Valenti is nut reinstated.

The Plant Manager collects as many facts as he can in a meeting with his key subordinates, and then adjourns the meeting until the next morning. In the meanwhile, he hopes he can decide what to do. He sees two alternatives; back up the supervisor and risk a strike that might be stopped by Injunction; nr avoid a strike by undercutting the supervisor, reinstating Valenti, and asking the men on the line to cooperate in eliminating the excessive rejects. The Plant Manager hopes that he can find another, better alternative, however, before the second meeting with his managers.

The Principals

The following short descriptions of the characters who appear in this second part of the article (the names are disguised) may be useful:

- *Oscar Burger, Want Manager*
- *Robert Polk, Production*
- *Ben Peters, Quality Control*
- *Ralph Coggin, Industrial Relations*
- *Tom Luane, Scheduling*

Problem Analysis

Burger: Before we begin this morning, you notice I've asked Tom Luane, our Scheduling Supervisor, to sit in with us. He's just returned from taking a five-day course in problem solving and decision making, and I thought this would be a good chance to see if he's really learned anything. Now then, Ben, let's hear about those reject rates on the panels. How do they look this morning?

Peters: They're still way over our 2% tolerance on lines #1, #2 and #4. If anything, they're a bit higher than yesterday.

Source: Excerpted from Perrin Stryker, How to analyze that problem. In *Harvard Business Review, July–August 1965,* Harvard Business School Press, 99-104. Used by permission of Harvard Business School Publishing.

Burger: Hasn't Line #3 begun to foul up a lot of panels yet?

Peters: No signs of it, Oscar.

Burger: Bob, did Engineering check out the stamping press on Line #3? You know we wanted to track down that rumor about the stamping job on the Cheetah panels being easier than on the Panther panels.

Polk: Engineering says it's strictly rumor — there's absolutely no difference in the stamping time required on any of the tour lines.

Burger: All tight, then, that settles it. I've made up my mind. Since we've got to avoid a strike at all costs, with Detroit hounding us for all the panels we can ship, we're going to reinstate Volenti, reprimand Farrell, and also jack op the other supervisors so they'll catch any man trying; to produce rejects deliberately. Then we'll ask the men to cooperate in keeping the reject rates within our tolerance. You, Ralph, will tell Patella that if we catch him inciting the men to sabotage the production lines by burring a lot of panels—just in the hope of getting a hot issue for the new contract negotiations—then we'll charge him and his union with this before the NLRB. If they threaten us with a strike, we'll get an injunction to carry us at least over the next two months of maximum output.

Defining the Problem

Let us pause here for a moment and see what these managers have been doing, first, Plant Manager Burger checked on the points of information he'd asked for at the previous meeting, and these satisfied him that he was right in assuming sabotage to be the cause of the high reject rates on the panels, He then made several decisions which he judged capable of taking care, of both the reject problem and the labor difficulties.

Some of Burger's decisions seem tight to Production Chief Polk, who only disputes Burger's handling of Farrell and Valenti.

Then Scheduling Supervisor Tom Luanne begins to ask some permanent questions and finds that each manager is using the word "problem" in a different sense, without realizing it. And they have been repeatedly committing the major error in problem solving — namely, jumping to conclusions about the cause of a problem. For example. Polk says the "basic problem" is lack of discipline in the shop, and he assumes that this problem is the cause of the excessive rejects. Burger views all these failings and assumed causes as part of one big "problem of managing this entire plant."

These confusions in meaning are apparent to Luanne because he has learned to distinguish problems from decisions. He sees any problem us u deviation from some standard or norm of desired performance. And to him a decision is now always a choice among various ways of getting a particular thing done or accomplished. Thus he recognizes that Coggin is really talking about a decision when he says that "our real problem is the need in train supervisors." Similarly, Luanne realizes that Burger's "whole problem" is not a mere collection of failures and causes, but a statement describing his responsibility for making decisions as head of the plant. So Luanne tries to clarify some of this confusion.

Luane: I suggest we agree on what we mean by a problem so we can concentrate on that, and not worry right now about any decisions or any causes. The simplest way to solve a problem is to think of it as something that's wrong, that's out of kilter, something we want to fix. If we identify that for sure, then we can begin to look for what caused it; and when we've found the cause, then we can get into decision making, which is choosing the best way to correct the cause.

Burger: But it isn't that simple, is it? We want to correct a lot of things around here, and they're usually mixed up together.

Luane: Yes, but you can't work on them all at once, and you can't solve a lot of problems by correcting just one of them.

Burger: OK. Let's go along with Tom on this, but I personally think there arc tunes when you can solve a lot of problems by solving one key problem.

Luane: I think you'll find that the key problem is almost always at the end of a chain of other problems and causes. That is, the cause of one problem is itself a problem, and its cause is another problem, and the cause of that other problem is still another problem to be solved, and so on. It's kind of a stair-stepping sentence. Usually, if you correct the cause of the basic problem in such a sequence, the other problems and their causes will automatically disappear. Let's call this reject problem our number one problem. We can list the others, too, but Rive, them less priority right now. Next, we've got to describe this reject problem precisely, and I mean *precisely.*

Polk: Oh, so they taught you to "define the problem first"? Sounds very familiar. Next you'll be telling us to "get all the facts." I've seen a lot of these step-by-step gimmicks, but 1 don't believe they really work.

Luane: Matter of fact, getting all the information would just be a big waste of time. Only some of the facts would he useful to us. That's one reason I want to describe this problem precisely. Another reason is that we're going to use this specification to test any possible causes we find.

Outlining the Specification

Again let us see what these managers have been accomplishing. Luane has stated three basic concepts: a problem is a deviation from some standard of desired performance: a decision is a choice of the best way to correct the. cause of a problem; and every problem has only one cause. He also has pointed out the stair-stepping process of going from one problem to its cause, which, in turn, may be a problem to be solved.

But the managers don't pay much attention to these ideas, and Polk clearly misunderstands stair-stepping, for he clings to the conclusion he earlier jumped to—that lax discipline is the cause, of several problems. Industrial Relations Manager Coggin thinks "people problems" are fundamentally more important, but he accepts the priority his superiors give to the reject problem. At this point, Luane has tried to get the managers to think in terms of the urgency, seriousness.

Luane: We'll have to get more specific. We're trying to describe this exactly. As an overall description, how about "Excessive rejects from Inn ring on quarter panels"? Anyway, let's write that down for a starter, (He *goes to an easel blackboard and writes these words out.)* Now we have to dissect this problem in detail, getting specific facts about it in four different dimensions—*What, Where, When,* and *Extend.* {He writes *these four words down on the left side of the blackboard.)* What's more, we want to get two sets of facts opposite each of these dimension* — those that describe precisely what the problem Is and those that describe precisely what the problem Is Not. *(He writes* Is *and* Is Not *at the top of two columns of blank space.)*

Polk: What's all this for, anyway? Arc we drawing a chart or something?

Luane: Sort of a map. This is the specification worksheet, and the point is to fill the

Is column with only those things directly affected by the problem. In the Is Not column we will put the things that are closely related to the problem but nor affected by it. You'll see why we do this in a few minutes.

Burger: OK, but I hope this doesn't take too long. Sounds kind of detailed to me.

Luane: It's pretty simple, actually. Under *What,* we can first put down "burrs" as the deviation in this Is column, and "any other complaint" in the Is Not column, since, as I understand it, there are no other complaints reported on these panels. But we can be more specific here, too. For instance, what did this deviation, "burrs," appear on? Were they on all kinds of panels?

Luane: The point here is we're trying to sep-arate what the problem Is from everything that Is Nᴏᴛ the problem. We're aiming to draw a tight line around the problem, to describe it precisely, and later you'll see how this gives us the clues to the cause of the problem.

Luane: Now we do the same thing for this *Where* section of the specification, Where was the deviation seen on the objects affected? Obviously, the burrs appeared on the Panther panels, so we put this down under Is. Also, where in the plant were the burrs observed?

Burger: So far only on lines #1, #2, and #4, but with Line #3 expected to go bad any minute.

Luane: Now we come to the *When* part of this specification. Here we ought to be extra careful and get exact times, if possible. Ben, what times did those, reject rates start going up yesterday morning?

Peters: You mean exactly? *(He consults his papers.)* On Lane #2, the first exces-sive rejects showed up at 9:33 a.m.; on Line #1, they appeared at 10:18; and on Line #4, at 11:23 a.m. From those times on, each of these lines turned out rejects that were far above our tolerance of 2%.

Luane: That's nice and precise. Can't tell, it may be important, so well put the exact times down. Now, how about the Is Nᴏᴛ here? There were no burrs at all on lines #1, #2, and #4 before these times, and none at all on Line #3 at any time.

Burger: I think I begin to see why you use those Is and Is Nᴏᴛ columns. It's to put off to one side all the facts you aren't going to think about in solving this problem.

Luane: No. that's not exactly why, but it will be clear as soon as we finish this specification. Tills last section, called *Extent,* covers the size of the problem — how big or serious it is. how many items are involved. We can put down "had burring" and list the percentage of rejects on each line. Now what were those percent-ages, Ben?

Peters *(consulting his papers again):*   *On* Line #2, 11% rejects. On Line #1, 17.5%, and on Line #4, 15%. That's according to final counts last night.

Luane: Thai leaves us only the Is Nᴏᴛ col-umn to fill in here, and this would cover the rejects on Line #3. We can say "Line #3 rejects" here, since they have stayed within the 2% toler-ance. Now we've got the specifica-tion all filled in.

Spotting the Distinction

Here we can briefly review what Luane has done in drawing up this specification. He fallowed a systematic outline to describe precisely both the problem and what lies outside the problem but is closely related to it.

The contrast between the Is and the Is Not not only draws a boundary around the problem, but strictly limits the amount of Information needed for its solution, There is no need to "get all the facts"—only the relevant facts.

Note that Burger, Polk, and Peters all had different ways of describing the reject problem at first. Also, Burger thinks the specification looks too "detailed," while to Polk it sounds "too simple" at one point. The separation of the Is and the Is Nor sounds strange to these man-agers because, like everyone else, they have learned to think In terms of similarities, not differences. This habit will bother them again a little further on in this problem analysis. Both Burger and Polk are Impudent with this specification stage because they haven't yet seen the reasoning behind it.

A precise specification makes possible two logical steps toward finding possible causes of the problem, and after that, as Luane pointed out, it serves as a testing sheet to identify the most likely cause. Luane now turns to the specification on the board and introduces the managers to the most demanding part of this analytical process.

Luane: We're ready now to use those contrasts between the Is and the Is Nor of this specification. Whatever caused this problem produced *only* those effects we have described on the Is side; so if one thing is affected and another related thing is not, then there must he something distinctive or unique about the thing affected to set it apart from the other. If we know what is distinctive. . . .

Burger (interrupting): 1 don't see any contrast between "burrs" and "any other complaint" in this specification, but] do see one between "Panther panels" and "Cheetah panels." I begin to get what you're driving at. The Panther panels are affected by the cause; the Cheetah ones aren't. We want to find out what sets the Panther panels apart from the Cheetahs, isn't that it?

Luane: Yes, you look first for a sharp contrast between the Is and the Is Nor, like the one you've spotted. Then we know there must be something distinctive about those Panther panels.

Burger: Both panels are made from the same steel sheets, so the only way you could distinguish one from die other would be by its shape.

The Panther panels are a deeper draw than the Cheetah panels.

Luane: That's a distinction all right. We'll put down "deep draw" as a distinction in this *What* section of the specification. *(He write the distinction off to one side of the blackboard.)* Now can you see any distinction in the *Where* Section?

Peters: Wait a minute! I've got a hunch those times have something to do with the stacks of blanks delivered to the presses. I remember Adams on Line # I told me late yesterday that the bad burrs began on his line just after using up the Four stacks of blanks his area had been loaded with in the morning. And another thing — maybe those high-speed presses are just right for the shallow-draw panel that Dawson's line is stamping, but not quite right for the deep-draw Panther panels.

Burger: I think Ben has a point there about the stacks of blanks on Line # I being used up just before the bad burring started. How about the other lines?

Peters: I don't know, but we can find out.

Luane: Will it take long?

Peters: No, just a phone call. *(He reaches for the phone, gets his assistant on the line, and asks him to check the times when lines #2 and #4 used up this stacks of blanks they started out with the morning before.)*

Peters *(reading a note his assistant has just brought in to him):* Here are those times we asked for, Line # 2 used up its stacks of Tuesday blanks at 9:30 a.m. yesterday, and Line #4 at 11:20 a.m. That checks out, as I thought. The bad burrs started on all these lines just after they started using stacks of blanks delivered to the floor Wednesday morning.

Luane: Looks like that gives us a distinction for the *When* section. We can call it, "Stacks of Tuesday's blanks used up at these times."

Polk: But how about Line #3? Ben did your man get the time that Dawson's line finished using its supply of Tuesday's "blanks?

Peters: Yes, At 8:30 yesterday morning.

Polk: And no bad burring started on Line #5, so what's the importance of this distinction?

Luane: We can't tell yet, Bob, but we'll just put it down for now. That seems to complete our distinctions, unless anyone sees any more in this specification. If not, we can proceed to look for the possible causes of this problem.

Seeking the Cause

At this point these managers have presumably collected all the relevant information that describes their problem precisely and have dug out those distinctive things in the Is facts that are characteristic marks of the problem. But they had trouble spotting the distinctions, as Luane expected. Also, one of them, Peters, introduced a couple of hunches into the discussion, exhibiting a tendency to "feel" that things are connected somehow or are important.

Note that Luane does not completely discourage such hunches, only recommends they be set aside until later. But note, too, that Peters' reasoning about his first hunch is faulty, as Polk quickly points out, while his second hunch is simply another example of jumping to a conclusion about the cause, as Luane points out. It is Burger who seems to be the sharpest here in spotting a distinction, after stumbling at first. By this time apparently only Industrial Relations Manager Coggin is still interested in the "human side of the problem," as he puts it, but his job is, of course, most directly concerned with this angle.

Luane, by keeping the discussion on the specification, prevents a time-wasting digression. He also warns Polk against prematurely judging the last distinction {about using up Tuesday's blanks) as useless just because it doesn't seem to fit in with another fact in the specification — that is, the absence of serious burrs on Line #3.

Now Luane introduces the managers in a concept that lies at the heart of problem analysis, the concept that the cause of every problem is a change of one kind or another.

Luane: The distinctions we've gotten out of the specification give us the areas where we can look for possible causes of these burred panels. Let's look for any changes we can find in any of the distinctions. What's new or different in these distinctions? We probably won't find many. Maybe only one.

Burger: Do you mean any kind of change?

Luane: No, only those changes which have occurred within one of these areas of distinction, or have had an effect on one of them. We can start with that distinction of "deep draw."

Peters: Well, the shift from Tuesday's blanks to Wednesday morning's blanks would be a change.

Luane: That sounds like a real change to me. Wednesday's stacks are the new blanks the lines started to work on just before the burring started.

Burger: If that's the cause of these rejects, how do you figure it? I can see that if Wednesday's blanks were different in some way from Tuesday's, that might make them the cause of the rejects.

Luane: Let's hold off on possible causes until we're sure there aren't some more changes in these distinctions.

Polk: I can't see any more changes. I say let's get on with it and start looking for possible causes.

Luane: OK, if you want to, but are we sure there's not some change connected with that other distinction in the *Extent* section, which we put down as "rates not proportional to involvement in Valenti conflict"?

Burger: I don't see anything new or different there, unless it's the differences between those rates themselves,

Luane: I can't either, so let's go ahead and check that possible cause you suggested a moment ago, when you said yesterday's blanks might be the cause of the excessive burrs. But we should test this possible cause, not just rationalize ourselves into accepting it. If this possible cause fails to explain all the facts in this specification — that is, both the facts on the Is side and those on the Is NOT side — then we can be sure it's not the actual cause. Because the actual cause would have produced exactly all those things that we put down as Is in the specification, and also would explain those things we put down as Is NOT.

Burger: I assume this is what you meant when you said earlier that the specification would be used in testing the possible causes?

Luane: That's right. We can start testing against the *What* of the specification by asking, "Does the use of yesterday's blanks explain the fact that the excessive burrs appear on the Panther panels and not on the Cheetah panels?"

Polk: No, of course it doesn't. Line #3 started using Wednesday's blanks even before the other lines did, and it still hasn't produced excessive burrs on the Cheetah panels.

Luane: Well then, there goes your possible cause. It doesn't fit the first facts in our specification's Is and Is NOT. We'll have to toss it out.

Burger: You mean we've got to find a possible cause that accounts for every fact in this specification?

Luane: What this means is that our specification isn't really complete. We must have missed something somewhere.

We'll have to go back and sharpen up our facts if we can.

Respecifying the Problem

We can pause briefly here to point out that Luane himself was responsible for the unsatisfactory results of this first search for the cause of the problem. When he accepted the change that Burger suggested — that is, the change to Wednesday's blanks just before the bad burring started — Luane didn't think to ask about the difference between Tuesday's and Wednesday's blanks. A shift from one, days blanks to another's is not a change if the blanks are identical. Polk saw this at once, of course, and torpedoed thin possible cause, as he should have. But this error of Luane's might not have occurred if he had been more careful earlier, as we shall now see.

Luane: We can go back and look over our Is and Is Not facts in the specification, but these look pretty accurate and precise to me. I think we probably missed a distinction or change.

Peters: Hold everything! I think we skipped a point. We talked about yesterday's blanks, but those aren't just yesterday's blanks — they're also blanks from a new supplier, Zenith. I missed this point because we'd made some parts with the Zenith metal before we ever put it in production, and it worked fine. Besides, Zenith's metal met all our specifications. We checked the blanks again when the excessive burring first occurred yesterday, and they looked perfect going through the blanker. So we dropped this as a possibility, especially when the labor trouble looted so hot.

Luane: Then that means we should change, that distinction in the *When* suction of our specification to "Stacks of *Zenith's* blanks began to be used at these times."

Polk: How will that help? Dawson's Line #3 is also using Zenith blanks, and there's no burring there.

Luane: Well, anyway, the new alloy is a change in an area of distinction. What is distinctive about those burring times is that stacks of new metal began being used then, and the change here is that a slightly different metal is going into the presses. We can state the possible cause this way — "A new alloy in Zenith's sheet steel is causing the excessive burring in the presses".

Burger: Ben just said he thinks the alloy change wasn't enough to matter.

Luane: I know he did, but it was a change in an area of distinction, so it's a possible cause. We can test it against the facts in the specification. Could this change — the slightly different alloy — explain the appearance of excessive burrs in the Panther panels, but not in the Cheetah panels?

Coggin: No, it couldn't, because the Cheetah panels aren't having trouble with excessive burrs.

Polk: Hold it a moment! Maybe the alloy could explain it. It just dawned on me that Engineering did say something about those Cheetah panels a couple of months back. Something about how their shallow draw would make it easier to use a tougher alloy in the blanks. That could mean the Panther panels are fouling up on these Zenith blanks with the new alloy! Let's check it! *(He picks up the phone and calls*

Engineering, which immediately confirms his hypothesis.) Engineering says the new alloy in the Zenith sheets makes the Panther panels much more likely to burr than the Cheetah panels.

Luane: Looks like you've found it, Bob. We could go on and test this out against the rest of the specification, but I'd say you've probably discovered the most likely cause of the excessive burrs. I suggest you have Engineering verify this.

Conclusion

In these concluding exchanges we see that the analysis has clearly uncovered a cause which none of the managers were thinking of when they began, and which was actually verified as the cause. Note that the due to the change that caused the trouble did not appear until Luane went back to the specification and sharpened up one of the distinctions. It was the point about Zenith's steel sheets that finally jogged Polk into recalling the possible effects of a deep draw on blanks made of the new alloy. Had Luane been more expert in the Kepner-Tregoe analysis procedure, the respecification might not have been necessary.

As it was, this solution turned out to be one of the more difficult kinds — for it involved, as Luane pointed out, a change *of* distinction *plus* a second distinction. This second distinction was an essential condition (the deep draw) that had to occur before the particular change (the new alloy) could take effect and burr the panels.

Without a precise specification and careful analysis, only time-wasting guesswork and luck could have arrived at the most likely explanation of this problem. More important, this analysis prevented the Plant Manager from taking action that could have produced a more serious problem than the one he was trying to solve. Also, it should be noted that the managers did not automatically became expert problem-analyzers in going through this experience. They are still likely to jump to conclusions, as Polk did toward the end when he quickly prescribed actions to be taken on Coggin's labor problems without knowing their causes. It takes time to change a manager's thinking habits into a systematic approach to problem analysis.

Sherlock Holmes: "It's quite a three-pipe problem."

— Sir Arthur Conan Doyle

Thinking Further 2.1

1. What could Oscar Burger, plant manager, have done to prepare more effectively for his first meeting with the other managers? Consider positioning, goals, interests, strategy, tactics, and issues, as well as any other information that you believe is relevant.

2. The managers in this group were not equally skilled in problem solving. Why might a bargaining group that has members with different problem-solving skill levels negatively affect the negotiation process and outcome? In what ways did it negatively affect these plant managers' ability to resolve their problem? What would you suggest to improve the outcome of a negotiation in which one party's negotiating skills are more sophisticated than the other party's skills?

Reading 2.2

INVESTIGATIVE NEGOTIATION

Deepak Malhotra and Max H. Bazerman

CHRIS, A *FORTUNE* 500 EXECUTIVE, is known in his firm as a gifted negotiator who can break impossible deadlocks. Consider his performance in the following deal.

A few years ago, Chris's company entered into negotiations with a small European firm to buy an ingredient for a new health care product. (Some details have been changed to protect the companies involved.) The two sides settled on a price of $18 a pound for a million pounds of the substance annually. However, a disagreement developed over terms. The European supplier refused to sell the ingredient exclusively to the U.S. firm, and the U.S. firm was unwilling to invest in a product that was based on an ingredient its competitors could easily acquire. With considerable hesitation, the U.S. negotiators sweetened the deal, offering guaranteed minimum orders and a higher price. To their shock, the supplier still balked at providing exclusivity - even though it had no chance of selling anything close to a million pounds a year to anyone else. The negotiation seemed to be at a dead end, with the U.S. negotiators out of ideas for pushing through a deal. Even worse, the relationship had deteriorated so much that neither side trusted the other to continue bargaining in good faith.

At that point the stymied U.S. team brought in Chris to help improve relations. He did more than that. After listening to the facts, he asked the Europeans a simple question: Why? *Why* wouldn't they provide exclusivity to his corporation, which would buy as much of the ingredient as they could produce? The response surprised the Americans. Exclusivity would require the supplier's owner to violate an agreement with his cousin, who bought 250 pounds of the ingredient each year to make a locally sold product. Armed with this new knowledge, Chris proposed a solution that allowed the two firms to quickly wrap up a deal. The European firm would provide exclusivity with the exception of a few hundred pounds annually for the supplier's cousin.

In retrospect, that solution seems obvious. But as we've seen in real-world negotiations, as well as in classroom Simulations with seasoned deal makers, this type of problem solving is exceedingly rare. That's because most negotiators wrongly assume that they understand the other side's motivations and, therefore, don't explore them further. The U.S. team members initially failed because they thought they knew why the supplier was being difficult: Clearly, they assumed, the Europeans were holding out for a higher price or didn't want to lose out on future deals with other customers.

Would you have made the same mistake? We have presented this case to hundreds of experienced executives in negotiation courses at Harvard Business School. When we asked them to strategize on behalf of Chris's team about how to break the impasse, roughly 90% of their answers sounded like these: "Consent to a larger minimum purchase agreement." "Ask for a shorter exclusivity period." "Buy out the suppliers-Increase your offer price." "Threaten to walk away." All those suggestions share the same flaw: They are solutions to a problem that has not been diagnosed. Moreover, even if one of them had been effective in securing exclusivity, it would have been more costly than Chris's solution.

Chris succeeded because he challenged assumptions and gathered critical information regarding the other party's perspective - the first

Source: Deepak Malhotra and Max H. Bazerman, "Getting Information from Distrustful Negotiators, from Investigative *Harvard Business Review*, September 2007, 85(9), 77. Used by permission of Harvard Business School Publishing.

step in what we call "investigative negotiation." This approach, introduced in our new book, *Negotiation Genius,* entails both a mind-set and a methodology. It encourages negotiators to enter talks the same way a detective enters a crime scene: by learning as much as possible about the situation and the people involved.

Though the solution to every negotiation may not be as straightforward as Chris's, his approach can help in even the most complex deals. In this article, we delineate five principles underlying investigative negotiation and show how they apply in myriad situations.

Principle 1 Don't just discuss *what* your counterparts want - find out *why* they want it.

This principle works in fairly straightforward negotiations, like Chris's, and can be applied fruitfully to complex multiparty negotiations as well. Consider the dilemma facing Richard Holbrooke in late 2000, when he was the U.S. ambassador to the United Nations. At the time, the United States was more than $1 billion in arrears to the UN but was unwilling to pay it unless the UN agreed to a variety of reforms. As a result, U.S. representatives were being sidelined in UN committee meetings, and the country faced losing its vote in the General Assembly. Meanwhile, U.S. senators were calling for a withdrawal from the organization.

Why the turmoil? For decades the United States had paid 25% of the regular UN budget Believing that was too large a share, Congress decided to hold the $1 billion hostage until the UN agreed to, among other changes, reduce the U.S. assessment from 25% to 22% of the budget. The other UN member states saw this as a nefarious tactic.

Ambassador Holbrooke faced a tough challenge. According to UN regulations, a change in the allocation of dues needed the approval of all 189 members. What's more, a hard deadline was fast approaching. The Helms-Biden bill, which had appropriated close to $1 billion to cover much of what the United States owed, stipulated that if a deal was not struck by January 1, 2001, the money would disappear from the federal budget.

Holbrooke's team had hoped that Japan and some European countries would absorb most of the U.S. reductions. Unfortunately, the Japanese (who were already the second-highest contributors) rejected that idea outright The Europeans also balked. How could Holbrooke break the impasse?

With the clock ticking, he and his team decided to concentrate less on persuading member states of the need for change and more on better understanding their perspectives. Whenever a member resisted an increase, Holbrooke, instead of arguing, would push further to discover precisely why it could not (or would not) pay more. Soon, one entirely unanticipated reason became salient: Many countries that might otherwise agree to increase their contributions did not have room to do so in their 2001 budgets, because they had already been finalized. The January 1 deadline was making the deal unworkable.

This new understanding of the problem gave rise to a possible solution. Holbrooke's proposal was to immediately reduce U.S. assessments from 25% to 22% to meet Congress's deadline but delay the increase in contributions from other nations until 2002. (The 2001 shortfall was covered by CNN founder and philanthropist Ted Turner, who agreed to make a onetime personal contribution of $34 million to the UN.) The key to resolving the conflict, however, was discovering that the dispute entailed not one issue but two: the timing of assessments as well as their size. Once the negotiators broadened their focus to include the issue of the timing, they could strike a deal that allowed each side to get what it wanted on the issue it cared about most.

Principle 2 Seek to understand and mitigate the other side's constraints.

Outside forces can limit our ability to negotiate effectively. We may be constrained by advice from lawyers, by corporate policies that prohibit making concessions, by fear of setting a dangerous precedent, by obligations to other parties, by time pressure, and so on. Similarly, the other side has constraints that can lead it to act in ways that don't seem rational - and that can destroy value for both sides - but unfortunately, the constraints of the other side are often hidden from (or ignored by) us.

Smart negotiators attempt to discover the other party's constraints - and to help overcome them - rather than dismiss the other side as unreasonable or the deal as unworkable. Above all, investigative negotiators never view the other side's constraints as simply *"their* problem."

The experience of a company we'll call HomeStuff demonstrates why. At Home Stuff, a producer of household appliances, the CEO was negotiating the purchase of mechanical parts from a supplier we'll call Kogs. The two key issues were price and delivery date. Home Stuff wanted to pay a low price and get immediate delivery; Kogs sought a high price and more time to deliver the goods.

Eventually, the parties agreed on a price of $17 million and delivery within three months. "Meeting that deadline will be difficult for me," said the supplier, "but I'll manage." The CEO of HomeStuff was tempted to let the discussion end there - the deal was already done and meeting the deadline was now the supplier's problem - but she decided to explore matters further. Aware that a delivery after three months would cost her company close to $1 million, she offered to accept a delay if Kogs would drop the price by that amount. "I appreciate the offer," the supplier responded, "but I can't accommodate such a large price cut."

Curious, the CEO pressed on. "I'm surprised that a three-month delivery would be so costly to you" she said to the supplier. "Tell me more about your production process so that I can understand why you can't cheaply manufacture the parts in that time frame." "Ah! But that's not the problem "the supplier explained."We can easily manufacture the products in three months. But we have

no way of cheaply shipping the order so it would arrive on time."

When the HomeStuff CEO heard this, she was thrilled. Because her firm often had to transport products quickly, it had arranged favorable terms with a shipping company. Using that service, HomeStuff could have the parts delivered in *less than* three months for a small fraction of what the supplier would have paid.

The CEO made the following offer, which the supplier immediately accepted: HomeStuff would arrange for its own shipper to deliver the parts in two and a half months, the supplier would pay the shipping costs, and the price would drop from $17 million to $16.5 million.

As this story illustrates, the other side's problem can quickly become your own. This is true not only when the other party is quietly accepting its constraints but also when it's being disagreeable. Often, when the other side refuses to meet demands, its intransigence is interpreted as a sure sign it's acting in self-interest, but in fact its hands may be tied. Through investigation, negotiators may find that they can help mitigate the other side's constraints to their own advantage.

Principle 3 Interpret demands as opportunities.

The CEO of a successful construction company was negotiating a deal to build a number of midsize office buildings. After months of talks-but just before the contract was signed - the developer approached the CEO with an entirely new and potentially costly demand: a clause that would require the builder to pay large penalties if the project fell more than one month behind schedule. The CEO, understandably, was irritated by this last-minute attempt to squeeze more concessions from him.

The builder weighed his options. He could accept the new clause and seal the deal, he could reject it and hope the deal would survive, or he could try to negotiate lower penalties. As he thought more deeply, he began to focus less on possible responses and more on what the demand revealed. At the very least, it showed that the developer had a strong interest in timely project completion. But might it also suggest that the developer valued *early* completion? With that in mind, the CEO approached the developer with a new proposal: He would pay even higher penalties than the developer wanted if the project was delayed. If the project was completed earlier than scheduled, however, the developer would give the construction company a bonus. Both sides agreed to that clause and were happier with the new terms. The builder was confident that his company would finish ahead of schedule and receive the bonus, and the developer minimized his downside risk.

Typically, when the other side makes seemingly unreasonable demands, negotiators adopt a defensive mind-set: "How can I avoid having to accept this?" In contrast, investigative negotiators confront difficult demands the same way they confront any statement from the other party: "What can I learn from the other side's insistence on this issue?

What does this demand tell me about this party's needs and interests? How can I use this information to create and capture value?" The construction company CEO's breakthrough came from his ability to shift his efforts away from fighting the other side's demand and toward investigating the opportunities hidden beneath it

Principle 4 Create common ground with adversaries.

Negotiation professors often engage their students in a complex simulation called "The Commodity Purchase," written by Leonard Greenhalgh of Dartmouth's Tuck School of Business. In it, one student plays the role of the seller of 100,000 pheasant eggs, and five other students play potential egg buyers. The buyers have different motives (for example, some want chemicals in the eggs to manufacture health products) and need a variety of quantities, encouraging the formation of coalitions among them. The alliance that will create the most value, however, involves two competing pharmaceutical firms that, by cooperating, have the

potential to outbid the other three buyers. The problem is that one of the firms needs at least 80,000 eggs, the other needs at least 70,000, and it is not obvious how both can get what they want, given that there are only 100,000 eggs. In fact, only about 5% of MBA students and executives that participate in this simulation manage to discover the solution.

To find it the company reps must first realize that the needs of their respective pharmaceutical firms are complementary, not competitive. Specifically, one firm needs the whites of the eggs, and the other needs the yolks. Once they know this, the two firms can split the cost of the eggs and each take what they need from the acquired product. However, few come to this conclusion, because to develop it the parties must adopt an investigative negotiation approach, overcome their reluctance to seek common ground with someone who is considered the enemy, and attempt to understand their competitor's perspective. The naive assumption that other firms in the same industry are strictly competitors typically prevents negotiators from taking an investigative approach.

As professors Adam Brandenburger of New York University and Barry Nalebuff of Yale University demonstrate in their book *Co-opetition,* it is often possible to simultaneously cooperate and compete with others. Investigative negotiators understand this. Those who view their relationship with the other side as one-dimensional - "He is my competitor"- forgo opportunities for value creation, whereas those who appreciate the complexity of relationships and explore areas of mutual interest are able to find common ground.

Principle 5 Continue to investigate even after the deal appears to be lost.

How many times have you tried to close a deal only to have your final offer rejected? If you are like most people, once someone has said no to your best offer, you presume there is nothing left to do. Often, this is the case. Sometimes, however, you are wrong - and you lose the deal not because there was no viable agreement but because you did not negotiate effectively.

A few years ago the chief executive of a specialty-gift-item manufacturer learned that a *Fortune* 500 company she had courted for months had decided to purchase from her competitor. Though she had no further plans for winning the deal, the CEO placed one final call to the prospect's vice president, asking why her offer was rejected and explaining that an answer could help her improve future offerings.

To the CEO's surprise, the VP explained that the competitor, despite charging more, had beaten her offer by including product features that his company valued. Under the false assumption that the prospect cared mostly about price, the CEO had made a final offer that reduced the prospect's cost as much as possible. The CEO thanked the VP for his explanation and added that she had misunderstood his position earlier. "Knowing what I know now," she told him, "I'm confident that 1 could have beaten their offer. Would you consider a revised offer?" The answer was yes. One week later the CEO won over the prospect -and signed the deal.

After being rejected, an investigative negotiator should immediately ask, "What would it have taken for us to reach agreement?" Though it may appear costly to continue negotiating when a "no deal" response appears certain, n you're confused about the *reason* your deal fell through in the first place, it could be even more costly to abandon the discussion.

Even if you find that you cannot win the deal, you may still acquire important information that will help in future negotiations. By staying at the table, you can learn about this customer's future needs, the interests and concerns of similar customers, or the strategies of other players in the industry. Keep in mind that it is often easier to get candid information from the other side when you are not in selling mode and there is little reason to distrust your motives. Next

time you've lost the deal and been asked to leave the room, see if you can stick around and investigate further. You may be surprised by what you find out.

As these five principles demonstrate, successful investigative negotiation requires challenging some time-honored negotiation approaches. Chief among these is the reflex to "sell" your position.

Imagine that you're observing a salesperson at work. What is he doing? Most people picture a smooth talker with a briefcase making a pitch - arguing his case and trying to persuade a potential target to buy what he has to offer. Now imagine that you're observing a negotiator at work. What is he doing? If, once again, you picture a smooth talker with a briefcase making a pitch, you are missing a crucial distinction between selling and negotiating.

Selling involves telling people about the virtues of your products or services, focusing on the strengths of your case, and trying to induce agreement or compliance. While effective negotiating requires some of those activities, as the previous cases demonstrate, it also requires a strong focus on the other side's interests, priorities, and constraints. Investigative negotiators - like truly effective salespeople - keep this focus top of mind. They also understand that constructing a value-maximizing deal often hinges not on their ability to persuade but on their ability to listen.

In the end, negotiation is an information game. Those who know how to obtain information perform better than those who stick with what they know. In the situations described here, the decision to challenge assumptions, probe below the surface, and avoid taking no for an answer helped negotiators improve their options and strike better deals. More generally, the investigative negotiation approach can help you transform competitive negotiations into ones with potential for building trust and cooperation, creating value, and engendering mutual satisfaction.

Thinking Further 2.2

1. In your opinion, are these tips for getting information from distrustful negotiators manipulative or genuine—or a combination of the two? Explain your view with regard to each of the three tips.

2. Would you, personally, feel comfortable sharing information honestly and openly with the other negotiating party? Why or why not? Would you trust the other negotiating party to reciprocate if you did share, openly and honestly? Why or why not?

CHAPTER 3

Distributive Bargaining

A Strategy for Claiming Value

The focus of this chapter is *distributive bargaining*, a competitive or individualistic negotiation strategy. This is what most people think of when someone mentions bargaining or negotiation, and it is how most people negotiate when they buy houses and cars, haggle in open markets, make other deals, settle disputes, or make team decisions (see Reading 3.2 at the end of this chapter). This chapter discusses the essence of distributive bargaining, when it is appropriate to use this strategy, and the tactics that are used to implement it.

INTENDED BENEFITS OF THIS CHAPTER

When you finish reading this chapter, you should be able to

1. Determine when it is appropriate to bargain distributively.
2. Recognize and apply the tactics that can be used to implement this strategy.
3. Negotiate effectively using this strategy.

THE ESSENCE OF DISTRIBUTIVE BARGAINING

Distributive bargaining is a competitive process for determining how to distribute or allocate scarce resources (see Negotiation in Action 3.1 for an illustration). According to the dual concerns model presented in Chapter 1, this is the strategy to use when you want to claim value for yourself but you are not very concerned about the relationship or the other party's outcome. That does not mean you want to harm the relationship. It simply is not a high priority for you. Stated differently, this strategy works best when the parties' goals are in conflict, resources are fixed or limited, your goal is to maximize your share of these scarce resources, and securing favorable substantive terms is more important to you than your relationship with the other party.

NEGOTIATION IN ACTION 3.1

Danny is a commercial loan officer. Al, one of his clients, is a partner in a real estate holding company. Al and his partner bought vacant land for the purpose of selling it at a later date for profit. Danny's bank financed the purchase of this land in September 2005 based on a 65% loan-to-value ratio. The loan was payable in 1 year with an option to extend it for 6 months. After 18 months, the bank extended the loan for an additional 18 months when Al and his partner agreed to reduce the principal owed by 10%. Now 3 years have elapsed and the property still has not been sold. Al approached Danny about extending the loan again.

Al began by demanding a 1 percentage point reduction in the interest rate or elimination of the 1% loan fee. He presented Danny with an appraisal of the property he had secured from a licensed appraiser. It indicated that the value of the property had increased. That, coupled with the reduced principal owed, made the loan-to-value ratio less than 50%. According to Al, he and his partner deserved a lower interest rate than the 7.5% they were currently paying (6.5% interest rate plus the 1% loan fee) – the more favorable loan-to-value ratio made the loan less risky so it shouldn't cost as much. Nor should they have to reduce the principal by another 10%. Danny ignored the appraisal, though he thought it was wrong. Instead, he argued that the bank would not accept anything less than a 10% reduction in the principal balance. Since the purpose of the loan was speculative, regulators must see performance on the loan, meaning a reduction of principal. He also explained that in the current lending environment, the added scrutiny that would come from regulators could harm the bank and management would not tolerate that. Danny argued that he could not reduce the interest rate because the loan had not performed. In fact, the bank would probably want to increase it. Visibly frustrated, Al interrupted Danny and complained loudly that, "You and the bank are cheating us, even though our loan is undoubtedly one of the best in the bank's portfolio." Danny warned Al that management's response to those arguments would likely be, "If you don't like the terms of the loan, pay it off." Claiming that he valued Al's business, Danny said he might be able to convince his superiors to let Al pay a 5% principal reduction now and the other 5% in 6 months. Al agreed, and again demanded a full 1 percentage point reduction in the interest rate or elimination of the loan fee. Danny reiterated that he couldn't touch the interest rate and eliminating the entire 1% loan fee was out of the question. He offered to reduce it by .25 percentage point. Al cussed and demanded a .5 percentage point reduction. Danny said the best he could do was reduce it by .375 percentage point and they agreed (Personal Communication).

Distributive bargaining is the strategy of choice when you want to win. Table 3.1 compares the situational characteristics that determine when this and the other dominant strategy, integrative or collaborative negotiation, are appropriate.

PREPARATION AND DISTRIBUTIVE BARGAINING

All of the elements discussed in Chapter 2 are important and must be considered when preparing to negotiate. Some, though, are more or less important depending upon which strategy you choose. For distributive bargaining, positions, reservation prices, aspiration levels, and alternatives are particularly salient.

Table 3.1   Factors to Consider When Choosing Which Strategy to Use

Condition	Distributive	Integrative
Goals	In Fundamental Conflict	Not in Fundamental Conflict
Relationship	Not a High Priority	Is a High Priority
Resources	Fixed or Limited	Not Fixed or Limited
Trust & Cooperation	Is Lacking	Exists

- *Positions* are the primary focus of distributive bargainers–it is sometimes called positional bargaining for this reason. When you bargain this way, you typically adopt a position such as your opening offer and then try to persuade the other side to accept it. The negotiation described in Negotiation in Action 3.1 illustrates this. Al and Danny stated their positions, argued for them, and made adjustments as needed to find an acceptable compromise.

- *Reservation prices or resistance points* are important because they set limits. Since they are the worst acceptable outcomes for each issue, they define the settlement range or ZOPA–you must settle between your resistance point and the other party's (Lax & Sebenius, 1986). Your goal in distributive bargaining is to maximize your share of fixed resources, so you want to settle as close to the other party's resistance point as possible (Walton & McKersie, 1965). This is why estimating his or her resistance points and then testing your assumptions when the negotiation begins is so crucial. Reservation prices are also important determinants of final outcomes (Blount-White, Valley, Bazerman, Neale, & Peck, 1994).

- *Aspiration levels or target points* are what you realistically hope to achieve. They define your objectives for each issue. Challenging (but not outrageous) and specific targets, like challenging and specific goals, produce better outcomes for negotiators (Northcraft, Neale, & Earley, 1994; Huber & Neale, 1986). Aspiration levels also influence your opening offers–they must be greater than your target points if you hope to achieve them because making some adjustments or concessions is inevitable, and it is generally accepted that negotiators will not follow opening offers with demands that are even more extreme. In other words, distributive bargainers make offers and counteroffers between their opening offers and their reservation prices. Opening offers will be discussed in more detail when the tactics of distributive bargaining are discussed later in this chapter.

The relationship between target and resistance points is depicted graphically in Figures 3a and 3b. Revisiting the loan fee negotiation discussed in Negotiation in Action 3.1, remember that Al's opening offer was for the bank to reduce his interest rate by 1 percentage point or eliminate the entire 1% loan fee. Assume that his target was to have the bank reduce it .5 percentage point and his resistance point was for the bank to reduce it .25 percentage point. Furthermore, assume that Danny's opening offer was to increase the interest rate or loan fee .25 percentage point, his target was to not change the loan fee or the interest rate, and his resistance point was to decrease the loan fee .375 percentage point. As indicated in Figure 3a, the settlement range is positive, meaning that Al and Danny could settle by reducing the loan fee between .375 and .25 percentage point. This also suggests that Al did as well as he could negotiating this issue. Had he insisted that the fee be reduced even more, Danny would have ended the negotiation rather than concede.

Consider a slightly different scenario. What would have happened if Danny's resistance point had been to reduce the loan fee no more than .25 percentage point and Al's resistance point had been to reduce the loan fee or interest rate .375 percentage point as depicted in Figure 3b? Since the settlement range is negative, there could be no settlement unless one of them changed his reservation price.

Figure 3a   The Relationship Between Target and Resistance Points

−1%	−5%	−.375%	−.25%	0%	+.25%
OO-A	T-A	R-D	R-A	T-D	OO-D

Figure 3b   The Relationship Between Target and Resistance Points

−1%	−5%	−.375%	−.25%	0%	+.25%
OO-A	T-A	R-A	R-D	T-D	OO-D

The parties' bargaining ranges overlap in Figure 3a so an agreement is possible. The settlement range or ZOPA is negative in Figure 3b because their bargaining ranges do not overlap. An agreement is not possible unless one of them changes his resistance point.

• *Alternatives* are particularly important when bargaining distributively because they define your resistance points and your power–your ability to walk away. You are less dependent upon the other party if you have a very attractive BATNA. This allows you to realistically set higher aspirations and reservation prices, and end the negotiation if the other negotiator does not offer something at least as valuable to you as your BATNA/resistance point. Conversely, unattractive BATNAs make it much harder to walk away. This is one reason why cultivating alternatives can be so beneficial.

TACTICS OF DISTRIBUTIVE BARGAINING

Most people bargain distributively. They usually adopt a position and then try to persuade the other party to accept it. When executing this strategy, you want to persuade the other negotiator to settle at or near his or her resistance points because this enables you to maximize your share of the scarce resources. The tactics you use should help you achieve this, and help you resist his or her efforts to move you closer to your own resistance points.

Estimate the Other Party's Resistance Points

Estimating the other party's resistance points when you prepare, and then testing your assumptions when you meet with him or her to determine if you are right, will clarify what you want to achieve when you negotiate each issue. This is not a simple task because a negotiator is not likely to reveal them. If he or she does tell you, be wary–they are probably not his or her real resistance points. Parties are more apt to reveal their BATNAs, especially if they are strong. This is both good news and bad. The good news is that you may be able to estimate his or her resistance points by quantifying them (remember the methods discussed in Chapter 2). The bad news is that if they are revealed early, and they are strong, you are likely to make less demanding offers, disclose more truthful information, and settle for less (Parse & Gilin, 2000). If the other party does not disclose his or her BATNA, stand in his or her shoes and consider, "What would I do if I was unable to reach an agreement with me?"

Understand Your BATNA and Improve It

Your BATNA is an important source of your power. A good one helps you move the other party toward his or her resistance points. It also helps you resist his or her efforts to move you toward your own. The tendency to inaccurately value alternatives was discussed in Chapter 2. When this happens, your comparisons of his or her offers to your BATNA will be flawed–a garbage in, garbage out problem. Avoid this if you can by taking the time necessary to determine what your alternatives are really worth.

If your BATNA is weak, if you are not sure of its value, or if you simply want a better one, improve it. Pursue another job opportunity in hopes of being offered a better employment package, or find a different contractor who performs higher quality work for a comparable price, or consider buying a different object. This will increase your power and, if you reveal it early, he or she is likely to make less demanding offers, disclose more truthful information, and settle for less than if you do not disclose it (Parse & Gilin, 2000). Negotiation in Action 3.2 demonstrates what will happen if you play your BATNA and then you discover it is not as strong as the other party's.

NEGOTIATION IN ACTION 3.2

When a large bakery was reorganizing due to financial problems, its service suffered. In fact, its grocery store clients went for weeks, even months, without having their shelves restocked. Heath, a store manager, tried repeatedly calling the salesperson, her boss, and even several levels higher in their corporate chain of command to persuade the bakery to stock his shelves. When these efforts failed, he resorted to threats and ultimatums. This, too, failed so he exercised his BATNA by filling the shelves slotted for the bakery's products with competitors' products. When his former sales representative was hired back by the vendor, she visited Heath's store. She was not happy when she saw what he had done. Heath told her that it wasn't anything personal, but her company had not filled his orders while she was away.

(Continued)

(Continued)

When she asked for the space back, he gave her part of it and told her that he would give her more when she demonstrated that her company could keep the shelves stocked. The bakery responded by sending its legal team to the store and threaten Heath with a breach of contract lawsuit if he didn't honor the contract between the bakery and the store—the contract required the store to allocate a specific amount of shelf space to this bakery's products (Personal Communication).

A good BATNA can enhance your ability to achieve favorable outcomes. For this to happen, however, you must understand the value of the other negotiator's and your own and make wise choices about how and when you use it. Heath obviously did not—because he was unaware of the store's contract with the vendor.

Set Your Targets High: Be Optimistic But Not Outrageous

Negotiators who set their aspirations higher than the other party's aspirations "slice the pie" in their favor (Chen, Mannix & Okumura, 2003). Since specific targets generate better outcomes than nonspecific targets (Northcraft et al., 1994; Huber & Neale, 1986), they should not be set as "target ranges." Nor should they be driven by your reservation prices – we tend to set them too low when we merely adjust from our resistance points. The two points should be established separately because, as noted earlier, setting targets too low often results in the **winner's curse** – getting what you want too easily and being unhappy with it.

If you are able to accurately estimate the other party's resistance points, use them as your targets. If you are unable to estimate them, use your preparation to guide you. Objective data or evidence can be particularly helpful. Remember to be optimistic because higher aspirations pay dividends. But avoid being outrageous because that will not help you and it may hurt by leading to a failed negotiation. Why? Give and take is expected in negotiations, so your opening offer must be more favorable than your target point if you hope to achieve it. If your target is outrageous, your opening offer will also be outrageous. This may lead the other negotiator to believe that you are not serious about reaching an agreement and cause him or her to walk away.

Ask for More Than You Expect to Get: Be Optimistic But Not Outrageous

Optimistic opening offers inform the other party that he or she has underestimated your resolve and that making more concessions than were originally intended will be necessary. It is generally accepted that once you make an opening offer, you will not renege on it and make a subsequent offer that is even more extreme. It is also expected that negotiators will engage in the process of give and take to reach an agreement. As already noted, this means your opening offer must be more favorable to you than your target point so that you have room to make concessions without jeopardizing your target points or your resistance points. The give and take of bargaining also enables you to learn more about the other party's wants, needs, and priorities by observing any patterns in how his or her demands change over time. For all of these reasons, optimistic opening offers help you achieve better outcomes.

While optimism helps, outrageousness does not. Opening offers establish important anchor points. The final outcome of any negotiation is typically the midpoint between the first two offers that fall within the ZOPA (Raiffa, 1982). Extreme offers that fall outside the ZOPA are not likely to have much of an impact on the final outcome. Outrageous opening offers may also cause the other negotiator to simply walk away. That is, your offer may be so extreme that it leads him or her to believe that you are not serious about reaching an agreement.

It is one thing to say that you should make an opening offer that is optimistic but not outrageous. It is quite another to determine what exactly this means in practical terms. What is optimistic? At what point do you cross the line from optimistic to outrageous? If your preparation and testing of assumptions have given you a reasonably clear understanding of the ZOPA, or if the situation you are negotiating is so familiar that you have a reasonable understanding of it, you should be able to make an accurate estimate of the other party's resistance points. Making your opening offer near these points is optimistic because it is the best you can hope for. It is not outrageous because it is acceptable for him or her, or close to it.

If you are negotiating a novel situation for which there is no good basis for estimating the other negotiator's BATNA or reservation prices, and he or she has not been forthcoming when you have tried to explore or test your assumptions, there are no easy answers. The rule of thumb illustrated in Negotiation in Action 3.3 argues that if the other party makes the first offer, your target point should be treated as the midpoint between his or her opening offer and your own.

NEGOTIATION IN ACTION 3.3

Assume you are negotiating the sale price of new generation technology to be purchased by a hospital that is a potential client. The capabilities of this new technology are clearly superior to those of the previous generation, which sold for $70,000 per unit, so you set your target at $80,000 per unit. If the hospital offers you $75,000 per unit, your opening offer should be $85,000 per unit. There does not appear to be any evidence pertaining to this method and it should be used with caution. Since the two initial offers are equidistant from your target (assuming it is based on reasonable cost projections and profit margins), the risk of your offer being deemed outrageous and bringing the negotiation to a premature end is minimal. The bigger risk is that the buyer's offer is so extremely low that you will be leaving money on the table.

Make the First Offer If You Are Prepared

Some argue that you should let the other party make the first offer. Doing so enables you to learn more about his or her expectations before you make a move. The evidence, however, tells us that the party who makes the first offer usually secures a better final outcome. More specifically, first offers anchor the negotiation and these anchors are strongly correlated with final outcomes (Galinsky & Mussweiler, 2001). Allowing the other side to anchor the negotiation may also distort your judgment about what is possible during the negotiation, to your detriment. If the other part opens with an extreme offer, we commonly react by talking ourselves "down." We decide, in haste and without much thought or justification, that our planned offer, target point and resistance point were set too optimistically and we revise them – unfavorably. This means the other party's tactic worked – he or she sucked us in with an extreme opening offer. Making the first offer will protect you against such unfounded revisions. Anchoring and adjustment, and other decision-making errors are discussed in more detail in Chapter 7.

If the other party does make the first offer, respond immediately but thoughtfully. This signals your willingness to negotiate and simultaneously reduces the influence of his or her anchor. Maintaining your focus on other factors such as your own target point or BATNA will also diminish the influence of his or her anchor (Galinsky & Mussweiler, 2001). You want to avoid "being anchored" by his or her offer because negotiators typically adjust from whichever offer anchors the negotiation. Your chances of "winning" are greater if you adjust from your anchor rather than the other negotiator's anchor because yours is favorable and his or hers is not.

An alternative conception of who should make the first offer argues that it depends upon your relative understanding of the ZOPA (Program on Negotiation, 2008).

If Your Understanding Is Inferior. You will have trouble anchoring effectively if the other party knows more about the ZOPA than you do. An applicant negotiating a job offer who is hoping for a salary at the high end of an estimated $70,000-$80,000 pay range, for instance, should open with, "Correct me if I'm wrong but my understanding is that people at my experience level typically earn $90,000." This is an aggressive but flexible effort to introduce an anchor. Since the applicant has an inferior understanding of the ZOPA, an extreme demand would be detrimental (Program on Negotiation, 2008).

If Your Understanding Is Superior. If the converse is true and you have a greater understanding of the ZOPA, take advantage of your superior knowledge by making an optimistic (but not outrageous) first offer. This is likely, for example, when you are extending a job offer to an applicant or when you are selling your home.

If Both Parties Understand the ZOPA Well. If both sides understand the ZOPA well, who makes the opening offer is of little consequence because anchors will not be very influential. Instead, both parties are typically more concerned about how fairly they are being treated (Program on Negotiation, 2008). Using objective standards such as market price or local custom is more appropriate under these circumstances.

If Neither Party Understands the ZOPA Well. If neither side has a clear understanding of the ZOPA, be careful! You run the risk of being too concessionary or too demanding. Consider the scenario in Negotiation in Action 3.4.

Zone of Positive agreement

NEGOTIATION IN ACTION 3.4

A consulting firm was interviewing a candidate to do hourly but high-level work in an emerging field. The interviewer thought $120/hour sounded about right but she wasn't sure. Rather than blurting out an offer, she asked the candidate to name his price. He suggested $60 and they settled on $50 (Program on Negotiation, 2008).

To his detriment, the candidate in Negotiation in Action 3.4 unwittingly dropped a very low anchor. Increasing your understanding of the ZOPA will help you avoid such mistakes. Thorough preparation and testing your assumptions are the best tools available for doing so.

Plan Your Concessions

Opening offers are rarely accepted in negotiations. Instead, each party makes an opening offer and then makes adjustments or reductions in their demands. These adjustments are called **concessions** and this is why opening offers must be greater than your aspiration levels if you hope to achieve them.

Concessions are important for several reasons. They reflect the expected give and take of distributive bargaining and signal that the parties are willing to adjust their differences to reach an agreement. Without them, negotiators would be left with two choices – accepting the opening offer or reaching an impasse. People resent the "take it or leave it" approach and are typically much more satisfied if agreements result from shared concession making (Deutsch, 1958). By making concessions, you also acknowledge the other party and recognize the legitimacy of his or her position (Rubin & Brown, 1975). These intangibles may prove to be very beneficial for future interactions, or even to protect your reputation. Although your goal is to win, this does not mean you want to harm the relationship or have the other party **lose face** – his or her image and status in the eyes of others. Helping the other negotiator save face might make it easier for him or her to say yes, especially if the agreement must be approved by constituents. Patterns of concessions may also be quite revealing. The other party may be nearing his or her resistance point if, for example, he or she begins with a larger concession and then reduces its size each time.

How should you manage this concession-making process?

- It is generally accepted that when one party makes a concession the other will reciprocate. You should not, therefore, make successive concessions – once you concede, wait for the other party to reciprocate. If you make a second concession before he or she reciprocates, you will be giving something away without getting anything in return.
- The amount you concede should be significant, but not so much that you materially change the value of the deal.
- Negotiators who make fewer and smaller concessions fare better than those who make larger and more frequent concessions (Yukl, 1974). That is not surprising. What may be more surprising is that negotiators who begin with a tough stance and make few early concessions, and later make larger concessions, elicit more concessions from the other party than do negotiators who begin with generous concessions and then become tough and unyielding. Negotiators are apparently relieved to no longer be dealing with the tough tactics (Hilty & Carnevale, 1993). **Reading 3.1** at the end of this chapter offers additional suggestions.

Provide Objective Support and Explanations for Your Offers

Objective support is generally more persuasive than no support or emotional appeals. Even if the explanations offer little information of any real value, they tend to be more influential. For example, people who negotiated to cut in line at a copy machine were least successful when they provided no explanation (60% success rate). Those who provided an essentially useless explanation–"I have to cut in line because I have to make copies"–were almost as successful (93% success rate) as those who provided a rational explanation (94% success rate). The word *because* seems to be the key, not the actual explanation (Langer, Blank, & Chanowitz, 1978).

Do Not Say Yes to the Other Party's First Offer

Even if the other party's first offer is near your target point, or better than your target point, do not accept it. What if you set your target incorrectly? Many negotiators do. Moreover, it is highly unlikely that the person is opening at his or her resistance point. That means you can do better. It will also help the other party avoid the winner's curse–the inevitable dissatisfaction that accompanies the realization that he or she unwittingly dropped an anchor that was too low or too high. This dissatisfaction may cause him or her to fight much harder for other issues, some of which may be more important for you. For all of these reasons, the costs you incur by saying yes to his or her firs offer may be greater than the benefits you gain.

Use Silence

You obviously have to talk to move the other side toward your desired outcome, but you should listen at least as much because you cannot learn anything new if you do all of the talking. Successful negotiators ask many open-ended, probing questions. They are always trying to gather additional information that will help them secure a favorable agreement. They also wait for answers after asking their questions. If the other party is not forthcoming with an answer, they wait some more. Silence makes many people uncomfortable. To ease the discomfort, they start talking. Remaining silent may be difficult for you, too, but the pain might pay great dividends if the other party reveals valuable information.

Another way to gain information, or perhaps additional concessions, is to respond to the other negotiator's argument or offer with silence. If he or she shares information, argues a point or extends an offer, do not respond. Simply gazing at him or her expectantly, or staring if you want to be more forceful, may encourage him or her to offer more information, elaborate, or extend another offer–essentially making another concession without gaining anything in return for the previous concession. or to and you want a more favorable one, do not respond verbally. Stated differently, especially if it is used strategically. (This should begin after concession.)

Use Time to Your Advantage

Most agreements are reached in the eleventh hour–as contracts are expiring or other deadlines approach. In fact, negotiators reduce their demands and increase the rate at which they make concessions as they approach final deadlines (de Dreu, 2003; Lim & Murnighan, 1994). Most negotiators do believe their deadlines are a strategic weakness and they hide them to avoid having this weakness exploited (Moore, 2004). Showing up for a negotiation with your suitcase in hand and announcing that you have a plane to catch in an hour, therefore, is probably not a good idea.

This is peculiar because a deadline for one negotiator is a deadline for all negotiators–if you have to complete the negotiation by a specified time or date, so must the other parties. Nor is hiding deadlines supported by the evidence. Rather than helping you achieve better outcomes, hiding your own deadlines may hurt you. This is because being aware of your deadline often causes you to rush and concede to get the deal done on time. The other party, being unaware of the deadline, expects a longer negotiation and concedes at a slower pace (Moore, 2004). The reason hiding deadlines hurts more than it helps is because we focus on the deadline's consequences for ourselves more so than for the other party (Kruger, 1999). If you want to emphasize the other party's deadlines and hide your own, enhance your BATNA to help you avoid making unnecessary concessions too quickly. In addition, enlist others as monitors to help you avoid rushing your own concessions to reach an agreement before your hidden deadline.

Appeal to Norms of Fairness

Like explanations, appeals to fairness tend to be quite persuasive. This is convenient because most people want, and consider themselves, to be fair. Unfortunately, it is not this simple. There are different norms of fairness–equality, need, and equity–and we tend to focus on the norms that serve our own interests (Loewenstein, Thompson & Bazerman, 1989).

If you can determine which norms of fairness guide the other party, you can effectively frame your offers to appeal to them. If you ignore their definition of fairness, your offers may fall on deaf ears. Negotiation in Action 3.5 demonstrates why the indiscriminate use of fairness will not help you. Various factors influence which norm of fairness is likely to be relevant. Table 3.2 summarizes which norms tend to be applied when different situational characteristics are present.

NEGOTIATION IN ACTION 3.5

Shortly after moving into her new home, Connie's bathroom faucets started leaking. After negotiating with the customer service manager for several weeks to have them fixed or replaced, the manager finally made an offer that the manager claimed was, "more than fair." Connie thought about it briefly and then responded, "That depends upon your definition of fairness!" For her, fair meant paying the amount it will cost to buy the faucets and the new ones installed." The manager eventually agreed to pay that amount, which was somewhat greater than her initial "more than fair" offer.

Flinch

Flinching Is about feigning shock or surprise when the other party extends an offer. Without saying anything, this may help you convey that the offer is not acceptable. Consider an insider's account of the negotiation that led to the acquisition of Mirage Resorts by MGM Grand Resorts in 2000 (see Negotiation in Action 3.6).

NEGOTIATION IN ACTION 3.6

When Kirk Kerkorian, MGM's controlling shareholder, and Steve Wynn, the CEO of Mirage Resorts, sat down to talk about the deal, Kerkorian told Wynn that he could go as high as $19/share. During his preparation he had actually learned the company was worth $22–$23/share. Wynn said he wanted $21/share and Kerkorian grimaced. They agreed to a price of $21/share or $6.4 billion. The deal would have cost substantially more at $22–$23/share (Binkley, 2008).

Table 3.2   The Application of Fairness Norms

Situational Determinants	Fairness Norms Applied		
	Equality	Equity	Need
Relationship Goals	X		
Performance or Productivity Goals		X	
Personal Development Goals			X
With Friends, Ongoing Relationships	X		
Nonacquaintances		X	
Allocating Rewards	X		
Allocating Costs		X	

(See, e.g., Thompson, 2009; Ohtsubo & Kameda, 1998; Sondak, Neale, & Pinkley, 1995; Steil & Makowski, 1989; Austin, 1980; Leventhal, 1976; Deutsch, 1953.)

Be Willing to Walk Away

Of course you should enter negotiations committed to reaching an agreement. But some negotiators are so committed to reaching an agreement that they ignore the consequences of doing so. Remember that we negotiate because we think we can satisfy our needs better with this party than we can on our own. If what he or she is offering is less beneficial than what you can gain from others, or otherwise fails to satisfy your needs, why would you agree? Developing the mindset that you will walk away if the negotiation is not progressing well should prove to be very beneficial, especially if your BATNA is strong.

HARDBALL TACTICS AND DIRTY TRICKS

Hardball tactics are used to pressure negotiators into doing things they otherwise would not do (Lewicki, Saunders & Barry, 2006). They are sometimes referred to as dirty tricks because they raise ethical questions when they are used. Think of them as very aggressive distributive bargaining tactics. These tactics are used, but most of the evidence suggests that they do not work very well–and they

Video 3.1
Dirty Tricks

may backfire (Schneider, 2002). Many people find them offensive and seek revenge when they are subjected to them. They may also harm the user's reputation and jeopardize relationships. A brief discussion of some of the more common "dirty tricks" follows.

Bogey

A bogey involves pretending that an issue is very important even though it is not. It is later traded, reluctantly, for a concession from the other side that is more important. This is most effective when an issue is selected that is of great value to the other party but of little value to the negotiator using the bogey. It is considered dirty because it is deceptive–pretending that an unimportant issue is very important. This deception raises ethical questions and may put the user in a very awkward position if the other negotiator calls his or her bluff and offers it instead of what he or she really needs. To counter this tactic, estimate how the other side prioritized his or her issues and test this assumption when you prepare. This should enhance your ability to recognize when it is being used by the other negotiator.

Good Cop–Bad Cop

This is named for the police interrogation technique popularized on television. The bad cop usually opens with a very tough position, often laced with threats. After pressuring the opponent for awhile he or she leaves the room to cool off or for some other contrived reason. The good cop then "plays nice," trying to reach an agreement before the bad cop returns and makes things difficult again. The evidence suggests that this may lead to concessions and agreements but its transparency makes it easy to counter, it often alienates the other party and negotiators may devote more energy to executing this tactic than trying to achieve their goals (Brodt & Tuchinsky, 2000; Hilty & Carnevale, 1993).

Intimidation and Other Aggressive Behavior

Intimidation and other aggressive behaviors are tactics that negotiators use to make themselves appear more powerful so they can impose their offers on the other party. Anger, guilt, threats, personal insults, attacks on your positions, pushiness, impatience, intransigence and hard-nosed demands for justifications or concessions are all examples. Rather than succumbing to such ploys and making decision out of fear, decide to accept or reject offers because they do or do not exceed your BATNA and satisfy your needs.

Lowball–Highball

Negotiators using this tactic begin with an extremely high or low opening offer – to convince the other negotiator to temper his or her demands. Optimistic opening offers serve as powerful anchors and have this effect. For the reasons discussed earlier, outrageous opening offers do not work and may bring the negotiation to a premature end.

Nibble

After negotiating for some time on a major issue, negotiators using this tactic ask for a small concession on an issue that has not yet been discussed to close the deal. The amount of the concession is too small to lose the deal over, but large enough to be upsetting. Not placing this issue on the agenda along with the others earlier in the negotiation suggests deception and raises ethical questions. Identify the issues that you must address, and ask the other party to identify the issues that he or she must

Video 3.2
Ethical questions

address, when you prepare. If one of these issues has not been raised as you progress, expect that it will be before you finish (Lewicki et al., 2006; Cohen, 1980).

Snow Job

This tactic involves inundating the other party with so much information that it is not possible to determine what is accurate or relevant. This may take the form of hundreds or even thousands of pages of documents, much of which is not necessary. Alternatively, it may involve large volumes of highly technical information that is designed to overwhelm or snow the other party. Discerning what information is correct or incorrect, and what information matters and what does not, can be accomplished by thoroughly preparing, asking questions, listening actively, and asking more questions. Digging for more information until it is truly understood, or bringing others to the table who possess the requisite technical expertise, should also help. We tend to employ a variety of shortcuts to simplify information processing, especially when large quantities of information are involved. These shortcuts will be discussed in more detail in Chapters 7 and 8. For now, it is important to remember that they lead to a variety of decision-making errors and they makes us vulnerable to others' influence attempts.

Selective Presentation, Deceiving, Bluffing, Concealing, and Distorting Information

These are common distributive tactics. When negotiating distributively, most experts caution against revealing your resistance points, and perhaps your target points. A negotiator may only present information that supports his or her proposal, while ignoring its drawbacks. Commitments (see the next section) are sometimes used as bluffs. Negotiators may listen to the other party's proposals and then interpret the outcomes for them. The scenario in Negotiation in Action 3.7 provides an example.

NEGOTIATION IN ACTION 3.7

While interviewing for a promotion, an employee tried to persuade the manager that he should be promoted to a particular position. Unconvinced, the manager said he could do that. He then spun it in a very unappealing manner by telling the employee that he would be held accountable for many things. He listed only the ones for which he knew the employee was not ready. The employee soon backed off.

The purpose of these kinds of tactics is to gather information about the other party or to manipulate the other party's perception of what is possible. Questions are sometimes raised about the ethicality of these tactics. This will be discussed in detail in Chapter 9. Reading 3.2 at the end of this chapter presents some interesting findings regarding negotiators' perceived inability to maintain the secrecy of important information.

More will be said about managing difficult negotiations, including dirty tricks, in Chapter 13. For now, thorough preparation is critical. It will help you recognize these tactics when the other party uses them. Consider calling the other negotiator out for using them. Your awareness of what he or she is doing diminishes the effectiveness of the dirty trick and may cause him or her to stop using it. Taking a break to cool off and figure out how you want to proceed, and negotiating the process to find a more productive way to negotiate, should also help.

COMMITMENTS

A **commitment** is a strong position combined with a pledge of a specific course of action. A purchasing agent might argue, "We must have a 5% price decrease or we'll sign with a different vendor." What makes this a strong commitment is that it is clear, specific, and final. Sometimes these are perceived as threats. They might be, but they might simply be intended as strong statements of "this is what I will do if you cannot meet my terms." Commitments are made for a variety of reasons.

- They reduce ambiguity. This purchasing agent left little doubt in the vendor's mind about what is required to reach an agreement.
- They are used to gain advantage. Commitments are powerful statements that limit the other party's choices. They are often taken quite seriously because a negotiator cannot back out of a commitment without losing face.
- They make the other party responsible for making the deal happen. If he or she does not satisfy the terms of the commitment, the deal will collapse.

Despite these advantages, commitments reduce flexibility. As already noted, once you make them you must stand firm or lose face. There may be other ways to satisfy your needs but they are now off the table. In short, commitments back you into a corner. The only way out is if the other negotiator agrees or if the negotiation ends.

There are ways to convey similar messages without limiting your options so drastically. Some of these suggestions may also be useful for helping the other party back out of a commitment he or she made without losing face.

- You can convey a similar message without the same degree of clarity, specificity, or finality. The purchasing agent, for example, could reframe his commitment as, "I need a better price or I'll have to reconsider my options."
- A commitment made publicly is more potent, so it will be easier to abandon if it is made privately.
- You can always ignore it (Raiffa, 1982; Walton & McKersie, 1965). Whether made by you or the other party, proceed as if it was not made.
- If you try to abandon your own commitment and the other party calls you on it, attribute your change to new information or to more compelling interests (Lax & Sebenius, 1986).

Commitments can be powerful tools to use but be cautious. They can be so rigid or threatening that the other side walks away. Perhaps they should be used only when you have good alternatives to fall back on.

At some point in your negotiations, you will reach a point beyond which you are unwilling or unable to go. When you get there, make your **final offer**. This can be as simple as saying, "this is the best I can do," or "I cannot move any farther, so this is my final offer." If the other party continues to push, your attempts to overcome objections and close the deal fail (see Chapter 5) and you really have reached the end, there is no point in continuing so repeat your claim that you cannot move any farther and walk away.

CONCLUSION AND IMPLICATIONS FOR PRACTICE

Negotiations generally involve different combinations of interests, rights, and power. When the parties' goals are in conflict, resources are scarce, the relationship is less important than the substantive terms and sufficient trust is lacking, it is more appropriate to use interests, rights, and power in a distributive manner to help you claim as much value for yourself as possible. You do, however, want to make sure that you do not harm the relationship, because that may harm your reputation or preclude the other negotiator from saving face. Both of these outcomes may hinder your efforts to reach an agreement now and in the future.

Critics of the distributive negotiation strategy argue that it produces unwise agreements because it ignores the parties' interests, it is inefficient, and it often harms relationships (Fisher, Ury, & Patton, 1991). It does, however, help to clarify what each party wants by providing anchors in uncertain situations. It commonly leads to compromises, which may demonstrate empathy and concern for the relationship because you do not insist on a complete win. By ensuring that both parties get something, these compromises may also be better than the typical "no deal" alternative when this strategy is used (Lewicki & Hiam, 2006). The following suggestions can help when you execute this strategy.

1. Estimate the other party's resistance points. Prepare thoroughly, test your assumptions, talk with others who might be willing to share pertinent information with you, stand in the other party's shoes to estimate his or her BATNA, and monitor the concessions that are made to see if they reveal informative patterns.

2. Understand your own BATNA and cultivate other offers to improve it. This will increase your BATNA's value, enhance your power, and make it easier to set optimistic targets and make optimistic opening offers. Like challenging goals, this will help you claim more value. It will also enable you to push the other party harder toward his or her own resistance points, and resist his or her efforts to push you toward your own. Finally, it will make it easier for you to walk away if the negotiation is not progressing satisfactorily.

3. If you have prepared well, make the first offer and support it with objective information and explanations. Maintaining your focus on your anchor will enable you to adjust from it instead of from the other negotiator's unfavorable or less favorable anchor.

4. When the other negotiator makes an offer, remain silent. He or she may think you are opposed to it and extend a counteroffer without making you concede first. Even if this does not happen, it will give you time to think about the offer and how you do want to respond. Also consider flinching or feigning surprise or disappointment with his or her offer. These responses, along with silence, may send a powerful message about your reaction.

5. Avoid using dirty tricks and tactics. Although they can be particularly appealing if you are emotionally engaged in your negotiation, or if you do not care if you harm the relationship, you are better off not using these tactics. They are usually easy for the other party to recognize, which

Best Alternative to a Negotiated Agreement

diminishes their effectiveness. They may also harm your reputation, which could cause the other party to have trouble selling a tentative agreement to his or her constituents.

6. Focus on *positions*, not interests. Focusing on interests is not really part of distributive bargaining. Since we negotiate to satisfy our needs rather than our positions, however, interests should be used to evaluate the other party's offers. When deciding whether to accept an offer, the first hurdle should be whether it provides greater value than your BATNA. If it is better than your BATNA but fails to satisfy your needs, and you can legitimately walk away without an agreement, you must determine whether there is some benefit to be gained by accepting it–now or in the future.

STUDENT STUDY SITE

Visit the Student Study Site at **www.sagepub.com/hames** for additional learning tools.

KEY TERMS

Bogey

Commitment

Concessions

Dirty tricks (a.k.a. hardball tactics)

Distributive bargaining

Distributive tactics

Final offer

Flinching

Good cop–bad cop

Hardball tactics (a.k.a. dirty tricks)

Intimidation

Lose face

Lowball-highball

Nibble

Snow job

Winner's curse

REFERENCES

Austin, (1980). Friendship and fairness: Effects of type of relationship and task performance on choice of distribution rules, *Personality and Social Psychology Bulletin*, 6, 402-408.

Binkley, C. (2008). How Kerkorian won Wynn's Mirage, *The Wall Street Journal*, March 5, B1.

Blount-White, S., Valley, K., Bazerman, M., Neale, M. & Peck, S. (1994). Alternative models of price behavior in dyadic negotiations: Market prices, reservation prices, and negotiator aspirations, *Organizational Behavior and Human Decision Processes*, 57(3), 430-447.

Brodt, S. E. & Tuchinsky, M. (2000). Working together but in opposition: An examination of the "Good-Cop/Bad-Cop" negotiating team tactic, *Organizational Behavior and Human Decision Processes*, 81(2), 155-177.

Chen, Y., Mannix, E. & Okumura, T. (2003). The importance of who you meet: Effects of self-versus other-concerns among negotiators in the United States, the People's Republic of China, and Japan, *Journal of Experimental Social Psychology*, 390, 1-15.

Cohen, H. (1980). *You can negotiate anything*. Secaucus, NJ: Lyle Stuart.

de Dreu, C. K. W. (2003). Time pressure and closing of the mind in negotiation, *Organizational Behavior and Human Decision Processes*, 91, 280-295.

Deutsch, M. (1958). Trust and suspicion, *Journal of Conflict Resolution*, 2, 2565-279.

_____. (1953). The effects of cooperation and competition upon grou processes. In D. Cartwright & A. Zander (Eds.), *Group dynamics*. Evanston, IL: Row, Peterson, 319-353.

Fisher, R., Ury, W. & Patton, B. (1991). *Getting to yes: Negotiating agreement without giving in*. New York: Penguin Press.

Galinsky, A. D. & Mussweiler, T. (2001). First offers as anchors: The role of perspective-taking and negotiator focus, *Journal of Personality and Social Psychology*, 81(4), 657-669.

Hilty, J. A. & Carnevale, P. J. (1993). Black-hat/white-hat strategy in bilateral negotiation, *Organizational Behavior and Human Decision Processes*, 55, 444-469.

Huber, V. & Neale, M. A. (1986). Effects of cognitive heuristics and goals on negotiator performance and subsequent goal setting, *Organizational Behavior and Human Decision Processes*, 40, 342-365.

Kruger, J. (1999). Lake Wobegon be gone! The "below-average effect" and the egocentric nature of comparative ability judgments, *Journal of Personality and Social Psychology*, 77, 221-232.

Langer, E., Blank, A. & Chanowitz, B. (1978). The mindlessness of ostensibly thoughtful action: The role of placebic information in interpersonal interaction, *Journal of Personality and Social Psychology*, 36, 635-642.

Lax, D. & Sebenius, J. (1986). *The manager as negotiator: Bargaining for cooperation and competitive gain*. New York: The Free Press.

Leventhal, H. (1976). The distribution of rewards and resources in groups and organizations. In I. Berkowitz & E. Walster (Eds.), *Advances in experimental social psychology, 9*. New York: Academic Press, 92-133.

Lewicki, R. J. & Hiam, A. (2006). *Mastering business negotiation: A working guide to making deals & resolving conflict*. San Francisco: Josses-Bass.

Lewicki, R. J., Saunders, D. M. & Barry, B. (2006). *Negotiation*, 5th. New York: McGraw-Hill/Irwin.

Lim, R. G. & Murnighan, J. K. (1994). Phases, deadlines, and the bargaining process, *Organizational Behavior and Human Decision Processes*, 58, 153-171.

Lowenstein, G. F., Thompson, L. & Bazerman, M. H. (1989). Social utility and decision making in interpersonal contexts, *Journal of Personality and Social Psychology*, 57(3), 426-441.

Moore, D. A. (2004). The unexpected benefits of final deadlines in negotiation, *Journal of Experimental Social Psychology*, 40, 121-127.

Northcraft, G. B., Neale, M. A. & Earley, C. P. (1994). The joint effects of goals-setting and expertise on negotiator performance, *Human Performance*, 7, 257-272.

Ohtsubo, Y. & Kameda, T. (1998). The function of equality heuristic in distributive bargaining: Negotiated allocation of costs and benefits in a demand revelation context, *Journal of Experimental Social Psychology*, 34, 90-108.

Parse, P. W. & Gilin, D. A. (2000). When an adversary is caught telling the truth: Reciprocal cooperation versus self-interest in distributive bargaining, *Personality and Social Psychology Bulletin*, 26(1), 79-90.

Program on Negotiation (2008). Should you make the first offer?, *Negotiation*, 11(1), 3-4.

Raiffa, H. (1982). *The art and science of negotiation*. Cambridge, MA: Belknap Press.

Rubin, J. & Brown, B. (1975). *The social psychology of bargaining and negotiation*. New York: Academic Press.

Schneider, A. K. (2002). Shattering negotiation myths: Empirical evidence on the effectiveness of negotiation style, *Harvard Law Review*, 7, 143-233.

Sondak, H., Neale, M. A. & Pinkley, R. (1995). The negotiated allocation of benefits and burdens: The impact of outcome valence, contribution and relationship, *Organizational Behavior and Human Decision Processes*, 64(3), 249-260.

Steil, J. M. & Makowski, D. G. (1989), Equity, equality and need: A study of the patterns and outcomes associated with their use in intimate relationships, *Social Justice Research*, 3, 121-137.

Thompson, L. L. (2009). *The mind and heart of the negotiator*. Upper Saddle River, NJ: Pearson.

Walton, R. E & McKersie, R. B. (1965). *A behavioral theory of labor negotiations: An analysis of a social interaction system*. New York: McGraw-Hill.

Yukl, G. (1974). Effects of the opponent's initial offer, concession magnitude, and concession frequency on bargaining behavior, *Journal of Personality and Social Psychology*, 30, 323-335.

Reading 3.1

THE DANGERS OF COMPROMISE

Max H. Bazerman

The tendency in negotiation is to "split the difference." Yet a more creative approach would allow both sides to get more than half of the value under dispute.

IN JULY 2000, Arthur Levitt, then chairman of the U.S. Securities and Exchange Commission (SEC), held hearings on the question of auditor independence. Believing that auditors' close ties to their clients posed a conflict of interest that could endanger U.S. financial markets, the SEC's accounting staff and a number of academics (including me) argued for new. tough standards, such as prohibiting auditors from, "cross-selling" services to their clients and taking jobs with clients.

These changes, which could nave helped to establish true independence, were strongly opposed by the "Big 5" auditing firms. Aware of the need to take some action, the SEC chose to compromise rather than push for significant reform. The SEC required auditing firms to disclose related business relationships and instated a variety of other steps too small to actually solve the problem of independence.

About a year after the SEC hearings, in October 2001. energy-trading firm Enron announced that it had lost $613 million in the third quarter of 2001 and disclosed a $1.2 billion reduction in shareholder equity. Enron's stock price fell through the floor, and the company soon became what was then the largest corporate bankruptcy in U.S. history. Stockholders and former Enron employees left without pensions filed civil lawsuits against both Enron and its auditor, Arthur Andersen, for deceptive practices. Within a year, Andersen was found guilty of obstruction of justice in a federal criminal trial. The Big 5 had become the Final 4.

Arguably, the collapse of Enron and Andersen, as well as the wave of earnings restatements from U.S. corporations that followed in 2001 and 2002, could have been avoided if the SEC had acted more forcefully to institute meaningful auditing reforms in 2000. But reasonable people make compromises, right? While this is often true, with compromise come hidden dangers. Perhaps the most common is the tendency of negotiators to "split the difference" when a more creative solution would have allowed both sides to get more of whatever quantity was in dispute.

Compromise is a useful device for dealing with small items with people you see in an ongoing relationship. But we run into trouble when we split the difference in situations in which a compromise will harm everyone involved, hi this article. I move beyond the problem of compromise as a barrier to mutually beneficial tradeoffs to the even more problematic tendency of parties to compromise instead of debating wiser, bolder strategies.

Compromise as a Social Heuristic

Decision researchers use the term *heuristic* to describe the cognitive shortcuts we use to make quick decisions in life instead of resorting to a full cost benefit analysis of every action. David Messick, Kaplan Professor of Ethics and

Source: Bazerman, M. H. (2005). The dangers of compromise. *Program on Negotiation Newsletter*, 8(2), 1–4.

Note: This article first appeared in *Negotiation*, a monthly newsletter published by the Program on Negotiation at Harvard Law School, www.pon.harvard.edu. Copyright 2006–2011 Harvard University.

Decision in Management at Northwestern University's Kellogg School of Management, uses the term *social heuristics* to refer to the rules of thumb people use to make snap decisions in social environments, in part to reduce conflict. Messick notes that people often divide things—such as a restaurant bill—fifty-fifty, even when one side deserves more.

Similarly, negotiators tend to compromise not because splitting the difference is the best option, but because they have learned that such social heuristics get them through life with less hassle. In a metastudy of how relationships affect negotiation, Kathleen McGinn of Harvard Business School, Margaret Neale of the Stanford Graduate School of Business, and Beta Mannix of the Johnson Graduate School of Management at Cornell found that when people are very close, their concern for the relationship leads them to compromise rather than search for creative gains through tradeoffs. As a result, when you negotiate with someone you're very close to, you are less likely to expand the pie of value than you would be when dealing with an acquaintance.

Should your company continue to sell its old technology or take a gamble on a promising innovation? Either choice may make sense, and a compromise between the two may make sense in some contexts. When the compromise is illogical, however, the tendency to rely on social heuristics can destroy careers and companies. Far too often, in an effort to make sure that all are included, we compromise on the content of a decision. But true respect for the opinions of others should mean that we can debate the merit of alternative actions and make a choice, rather than compromise on a plan that is logically confused.

Financial Scandals: Is Compromise the Answer?

Many experts believe that the fall or Enron and Arthur Andersen was partially due to the obligation the auditors felt to keep their client happy at all costs. After all, in 2000, Enron paid Andersen $25 million in auditing fees and another $27 million in consulting tees.

It's important to note that audits exist to provide stakeholders with an independent assessment of the validity of companies' accounting practices. Without independence, auditors have no reason to exist. Independence requires that auditors have no motivation to view their clients' books with cither too much lenience or skepticism. An array of social psychology studies has shown that when people are motivated to view data in a certain light, they are incapable of true objectivity.

Yet under the current U.S. system, auditors are motivated to be rehired by their clients from year to year. In addition, auditing firms benefit financially by selling consulting and other services to their clients, and individual auditors often take jobs with their clients. Under these structural conditions, can they be independent?

After the wave of accounting scandals, Congress recognized the need to secure investor confidence in U.S. financial markets. Legislators might have debated the left-wing notion of creating true independence through tough regulation or the right-wing proposal of requiring audits to be insured. Instead, under pressure from the accounting industry and U.S. corporations, they compromised. The Sarbanes-Oxley Act put limits on the selling of some consulting services, required assignment rotation of individual auditors (but not of the auditing firms themselves), and limited senior auditors (but not lower-level professionals) from taking jobs with clients.

This compromise solution is not likely to be effective. A better solution would be to debate strong ideas that make conceptual sense rather than watering down elements of various plans. Too often, policymakers and executives make compromise between strategies. While each strategy may be viable, the compromise is generally too weak to be effective.

Questioning Compromises

In my executive-decision-making classes, my students often ask me whether they should monitor their decisions constantly to avoid bias. The answer is no. Social heuristics serve a useful function, allowing our social interactions to run more smoothly. When it comes to minor decisions, go ahead and compromise,

But when your organization is negotiating over important decisions and strategies, you must question the wisdom of compromising and strive to be more cautious, thoughtful, and insightful.

The next time you face a serious negotiation, ask yourself the following questions:

- What should the meeting agenda look like?
- Are two polar opinions likely to develop, such that only a compromise will save face for all?
- Would compromise come at the expense of growing the pie through creative trades?
- Would I be compromising to avoid a tough debate between reasonable alternative proposals?

WHERE HAVE ALL THE FISH GONE?

One of the amazing economic failures over the last 30 years has been the worldwide depletion of fishing basins. Propelled by high-tech equipment and government subsidies, fishers have emptied the oceans of once-plentiful species. Far too many boats are chasing far too few fish, leading to international skirmishes over borders and poaching.

Two viable plans have been promoted to solve the crisis. The political left prefers to regulate and enforce fishing of a given species before depletion occurs. The political right advocates selling or allocating rights to own or fish portions of the ocean at costs that ensure species sustainability.

While one of these plans may appeal to you more than the other, the point is that either plan could solve the crisis. Yet throughout the world, governments and fishing groups too often implement neither plan.

Instead, environmental and fishing groups argue for and against the need to reduce the harvest, and political forces come into play. Decision makers make compromises, slightly restricting harvests to show that they are doing something. The rate of depletion slows a bit hut not enough to keep the fishing basin from becoming commercially' extinct. Compromise slows down the problem rather than solving it.

A better way would be to fight the tough battle between the logical solutions of the political left and the political right.

Leaders often have the opportunity to shape the discussion in their organizations. They can highlight the dangers of compromising to others in their organization and make sure that good ideas are fully debated.

How? By creating an environment where respect is defined as listening to and considering the ideas of others, not by the willingness to compromise on a deficient middle ground.

At a political level, we tend to believe that the term "bipartisan"[1] describes the behavior of responsible, cooperative politicians who drop their biased concerns in the search for value-creating changes for society. When true bipartisanship occurs, we as citizens should support such innovation. But bipartisanship can also be a shortcut to lazy compromises for those eager to reach any deal at all.

Thinking Further 3.1

1. Think about a situation in which you compromised and regretted having done so. Would you handle the situation differently now if you could revisit it? Why or why not?

2. What are the benefits of compromising? What are the drawbacks? Give examples of each.

Reading 3.2

MASTER THE ART AND SCIENCE OF HAGGLING

Program on Negotiation

In our current marketplace, opportunities to negotiate are cropping up in new places.

Imagine you're celebrating a special occasion with friends at an upscale restaurant. Soon after you take your seats, the wine director introduces himself and hands you a list of high-end bottles of wine. You notice that the prices—all in the S200 to $600 range—have been slashed through with a red pen.

"The prices on our reserve list are negotiable tonight," the wine director says. "Would you care to make an offer on a bottle?"

This sales ploy might sound like the daydream of an oenophile. But believe it or not. a fine-dining restaurant in New York City, David Burke Townhouse, was practicing the strategy in May. Chef and restaurateur David Burke has taken unusual steps to navigate the economic downturn, including printing the word *sale* on menus and holding this "wine auction" promotion, writes Katy McLaughlin in the *New York Times.*

Did the gimmick work? The restaurant's wine director reported negotiating the sale of about five bottles of wine per night at prices that met or improved on his *reservation price—the* minimum he would accept to reach a deal. While most upscale Manhattan restaurants were experiencing sales declines of about 15% in 2009 as compared with 2008. Burke told the *Times* that Townhouse was down only about 8% during the recession, perhaps due in part to his flexible pricing strategies.

The story illustrates a larger trend: businesses that never would have considered negotiating with customers last year are now willing, even eager, to make a deal. Just like the prices of houses, cars, and other big-ticket items, the prices of furniture, electronics, wine, jewelry, and other "medium-ticket" goods are now frequently up for discussion. The ancient art of haggling—the back-and-forth dance of offers and concessions between buyer and seller—is making a comeback, and you would do well to brush up on your skills.

Do I *have* to haggle?

In some cultures, a long tradition of haggling in markets and bazaars flows naturally into brick-and-mortar stores. By contrast, in the United States and many other commies, haggling between buyers and sellers is an under-practiced art. typically employed only in negotiations for cars and real estate. As a consequence, many Westerners have an aversion to haggling, especially in contexts where negotiation is not the norm. You might routinely pass up opportunities to haggle because you're afraid of offending the seller or because you feel inexperienced or uncomfortable.

Source: Program on Negotiation (2009). Master the art and science of haggling. *Program on Negotiation Newsletter, 12*(8), 1–4.

Note: This article first appeared in *Negotiation,* a monthly newsletter published by the Program on Negotiation at Harvard Law School, www.pon.harvard.edu. Copyright 2006—2011 Harvard University.

But you're probably passing up chances to save money. A May 2009 *Consumer Reports* poll found that 66% of Americans had tried to negotiate discounts in the previous six months. Of these hagglers, 83% succeeded in. getting lower hotel rates, 81% got better deals on clothing and cell phone service, 71% negotiated cheaper electronics and furniture, and 62% lowered their credit-card fees.

If the potential financial benefits aren't enticing enough, look at haggling as a chance to improve your negotiation skills in a relatively low-risk context. The price cut you negotiate at a chain store for a washing machine could make you feel more confident in your next heavy-hitting workplace negotiation. (And you can haggle on your company's behalf, of course, whether for lower rent, travel expenses, or office supplies.)

In addition, many sellers are hurting these days. When faced with a choice between haggling with you or losing you as a customer, many will gladly accept the challenge. Similarly, lenders and landlords may be willing to renegotiate existing contracts to keep good customers or tenants who are struggling financially due to layoffs and pay cuts.

In today's market, consumers are often the more powerful parties in negotiations with sellers. To claim the most value in your next haggling experience, use the following six strategies.

1. Explore your alternatives.

Sometimes negotiation opportunities pop up on the fly, such as David Burke's "wine auction" or a one-of-a-kind piece of jewelry you stumble across while traveling. You can be forgiven for plunging into such negotiations without doing much, if any. research. But in most haggling situations, thorough preparation is advisable.

Suppose your television breaks and you'd like to get a replacement quickly, but you don't want to pay full price. Before you inarch into the nearest electronics superstore, take time to conduct the same type of research you would if you were in the market for a house or a car. Otherwise, you could sacrifice more value than necessary or pass up a good deal.

Begin with a thorough consideration of your BATNA-or best alternative to a negotiated agreement—the action you'll take if a particular negotiation ends in impasse. In the case of a television, your BATNA might be a low, no-haggle price from an online retailer or it might be to repair your current TV.

Even when a negotiation is impromptu, as in the case of a bargaining wine director, you can still ask for time to think through your BATNA. If your negotiation fails, will your group buy a cheaper bottle of wine off the regular wine list or order wine by the glass?

Knowing what you will do if you can't get a good deal will give you bargaining power during the negotiation that follows. Your BATNA also helps you calculate your reservation price—the highest price you'd be willing to pay for that bottle of wine, television, or washing machine in the current negotiation.

Suppose your neighborhood electronics store is selling the TV you want for about $1,100 and Amazon.com is selling the same TV for $900 as part of an electronics sale that will end the next day. (For simplicity's sake, assume taxes and shipping are included in these prices.) Buying from Amazon.com becomes your BATNA in your negotiation at the electronics store. As for your reservation price, you might decide that ifs $975, or $75 above Amazon.com's price, for the added benefit of taking the TV home that day and not having to worry about shipping it back if you don't like it.

2. Assess their alternatives.

Now it's time to assess the best deal you might get. Figuring out the other party's reservation price is the key to knowing how far you will be able to push him, write Deepak Malhotra and Max H. Bazerman in their book *Negotiation Genius: How to Overcome Obstacles and Achieve*

Brilliant Results at the Bargaining Table and Beyond (Bantam. 2007).

Start by considering the other party's BATNA: What will he do if he can't close the sale with you? Like most retailers, he'll simply have to wait for someone else to walk through the door. You may be able to judge how desperate a business is to make a deal by the amount of foot traffic in the store or by researching its financial standing. Generally, the worse business is, the more willing an organization will be to haggle with you—and to give you a very good price.

To estimate just how low a salesperson will go, you can do online research on the product, just as you would when buying a car. Study store policies concerning discounting, returns, and warranties. You can even do your research in the store: *Consumer Reports* notes that inventory tags often indicate how long an item has been on the shelves. Salespeople may be more willing to haggle over merchandise that has been sitting on the floor a long time.

Sellers: Negotiate more, worry less

Sellers sometimes resist haggling over commodities that in a stronger economy, aren't typically open to negotiation.

It's true you don't want to waste time haggling over inexpensive items or negotiating with buyers who make unreasonable demands. Still, if you're facing money woes, consider being flexible in your pricing of slow-to-move stock. That's what chef David Burke did when he opened up his reserve wine list to negotiation. "It's worth a shot," he told the New York *Times*. "I'm sitting on $200,000 worth of wine anyway, already paid for."

Not only can haggling move unwanted merchandise, but promotions that mention negotiable pricing might draw in new customers who want to try their hand at making a deal.

3. Set the stage for success.

Suppose your research reveals that the TV you want is fairly new on the market. Further research about your local store leads you to believe it may be willing to so as low as Amazon.com's price of $900. Now you have a general sense of the ZOPA, or *zone of possible agreement:* between S900 (your estimate of the store's reservation price) and S975 (your reservation price). Thus, your goal in the upcoming negotiation is to get a deal that's as close to S900 as possible.

Once you've done your homework, it's time to set the stage for success. *Consumer Reports* advises you to negotiate early or late in the day, when stores are often quiet, and late in the mouth, when salespeople may be especially eager to meet quotas. At chain stores, where regular sales staff may not have the power to haggle, you might need to approach a manager. Open negotiations out of earshot of other customers, recommends *Consumer Reports,* as sales staff may not want others to get wind of your haggling. Bring along up-to-date information about competitors' prices (your BATNA) and expect the other side to verify it.

Be polite and cordial throughout the negotiation process, and also be willing to accept no for an answer. Finally, because stores typically pay fees on credit-card purchases, keep in mind that salespeople may be more willing to bargain if you offer to pay in cash.

4. Make the first offer.

After you discuss the pros and cons of your desired item, the salesperson might offer to give you a discount without any prompting. If not. open the negotiation yourself: "I can buy this TV online this weekend at a much lower price. Can we work together toward a more competitive deal?"

If the salesperson is willing to negotiate, and if you have a strong sense of the ZOPA. you are positioned to make an offer: "Can you beat Amazon.com's price? It's $900. I can pay in cash, by the way." Imagine that the salesperson tells you his store has a new policy against matching, let alone beating, Internet deals. Furthermore, he reminds you that your great online deal is about to expire. Even so, by dropping this "anchor," you have likely swayed him away from the previous anchor—the TV's $1,100 list price—and toward your end of the ZOPA. What's more, because you proved you've done your homework, he is likely to view your offer as credible, if not entirely reasonable.

5. Insist on reciprocation.

At this point, you have entered the realm of haggling: the dance of concessions that follows each party's first offer. (In our TV negotiation, the $1,100 list price was the store's first offer.) For some, this is where the real fun begins; for others, it's a time of great anxiety. To manage your stress, keep your BATNA at the forefront of your mind. Knowing that you have a good alternative if the negotiation fails will help you stay calm and rational.

Suppose the salesperson tells you there's no way he can go as low as $900. "I could come down $75 to $1,025, though." Note that this offer is $50 above your $975 reservation price—the maximum you're willing to pay to get a deal.

"I'd like to take the TV home today," you might say, "so I'm willing to go up to $925."

Rather than responding to your offer, the salesperson starts going over the features of the TV with you one more time.

Experienced negotiators sometimes take their time responding to an offer, aware that the other side could grow nervous and make a better offer, according to authors Malhotra and Bazerman. But it would be a serious mistake for you to make an unreciprocated concession. Savvy hagglers wait out their counterpart's stalling tactics and insist on receiving a concession in return. If none is forthcoming, thank the salesperson for his time. The mere suggestion that you are about to walk away could inspire him to come up with a counteroffer.

6. Explore interests further.

One common misconception of haggling is that it must focus only on a single issue: price. Although price might be the most important issue at stake, you could sweeten the deal for both sides by discussing other issues, such as delivery, financing, and the possibility of repeat business. You can open up such opportunities through direct questioning or by making what Malhotra and Bazerman call *contingent concessions*—concessions that you link to specific actions by the other party.

In the TV negotiation, the salesperson might reciprocate your last offer by grudgingly agreeing to come down to $950, a price within the bargaining zone. Or you might agree to pay $975 in exchange for having the store dispose of your old TV. But if the salesperson (or his manager) is still unwilling to make a deal that you prefer to your online option, you should feel comfortable walking away with the knowledge that you did your best.

Sometimes in a negotiation, you can get a better all-around deal by changing the item under discussion. Returning to the wine negotiation at a restaurant, suppose your group has little interest in fine wines, but several of you are tempted by a pricey entrée. "We'll pass on the reserve list," you might say, "but if three of us order the truffles, can you give us a group discount?" It's a negotiating gambit that chef Burke would almost certainly admire.

6 Tips for Novice Hagglers

1. Thoroughly research what you want and where you can get it.

2. Consider what the other side will do if you walk away from a deal.

3. Set a stage for the negotiation that's comfortable for both sides.

4. Anchor talks in your direction by making the first offer.

5. Insist that the other side reciprocate each concession you make.

6. Expand the pie by discussing issues other than price.

Thinking Further 3.2

1. How comfortable are you with negotiating? Which of the six skills do you need to practice most prior to your next negotiation to help you negotiate successfully?

2. Your computer just crashed. It is 5 years old and not worth fixing. You have no more than $1,000 to spend on a new computer, but the lowest price you can find either online or in a local store for the model that you absolutely need is $1,100. What would you say to the salesperson to convince him or her to sell you the computer for $1,000? Consider objections that the sales representative might make and how you would respond to them.

CHAPTER 4

Integrative Negotiation

A Strategy for Creating Value

Imagine that two sisters are vying for the last orange in their refrigerator. How should they decide who gets it? Most people would cut it in half because neither one could convince the other to give up the whole thing. But what if each sister approached the situation by asking the other why she wanted it? If one wanted the peel for baking and the other wanted the fruit for the juice, they both could win (Follett, 1994). This scenario illustrates the classic distinction between distributive and integrative negotiation, the two dominant negotiation strategies. In contrast with distributive negotiation's competitive approach, integrative negotiation is collaborative. "Expanding the pie" allows both parties to create value and satisfy their needs. The following pages discuss the essence of integrative negotiation, when it is appropriate to negotiate this way, and the tactics that are used to implement it.

INTENDED BENEFITS OF THIS CHAPTER

When you finish reading this chapter, you should be able to

1. Determine when it is appropriate to negotiate integratively.
2. Recognize and apply the tactics that are used to implement this strategy.
3. Negotiate effectively using this strategy.

THE ESSENCE OF INTEGRATIVE NEGOTIATION

Integrative negotiation requires a different mindset than distributive bargaining because it is used when

Table 4.1   Factors to Consider When Choosing Which Strategy to Use

Condition	Distributive	Integrative
Goals	In Fundamental Conflict	Not in Fundamental Conflict
Relationship	Not a High Priority	Is a High Priority
Resources	Fixed or Limited	Not Fixed or Limited
Trust & Cooperation	Is Lacking	Exists

you want to solve problems in a way that works for both sides, not merely for yourself. Returning to the Dual Concerns Model presented in Chapter 1, this is the strategy to use when you are highly concerned with your outcomes and those of the other party. Table 4.1 again summarizes and compares the situational characteristics that determine when it is most appropriate to use each of the two dominant strategies.

PREPARATION AND INTEGRATIVE BARGAINING

All elements of the preparation process are important, regardless of which strategy you employ. Chapter 3 explained why positions, target points, resistance points, and alternatives are particularly important when you negotiate distributively. Defining the situation, interests, and rapport building assume greater importance when you negotiate integratively.

Video 4.1

Benefits of Value Creating Model of Negotiation

Defining the situation is always important because it helps you determine what you will be negotiating, your goals, and the issues that must be addressed to produce a complete solution. It assumes greater importance when you negotiate integratively because you and the other party must develop a shared understanding of the situation. It seems obvious, but you must be trying to solve the same problem if you hope to find solutions that help both of you.

Interests are the primary focus of integrative negotiators—is sometimes called interest-based bargaining for this reason. When you negotiate this way, you identify your own interests and those of the other party, and then try to invent solutions that satisfy all of them. Since we negotiate to satisfy our needs, and interests are typically unmet needs, it makes sense to focus on these rather than positions. Viewed differently, there is only one way to satisfy a position—you get it or you do not. There are usually many different ways to satisfy interests so integrative negotiation affords greater opportunities to find mutually beneficial solutions. The negotiation described in Negotiation in Action 4.1 between Allison and her boss illustrates the interest-based focus of the integrative approach. They clarified interests and then invented solutions to satisfy them.

NEGOTIATION IN ACTION 4.1

On Thursday, Allison was summoned to meet with the Chief Executive Officer (CEO) of the nonprofit organization at which she works. When she arrived, they exchanged pleasantries for a few minutes. Since neither of them enjoyed small talk, Allison quickly asked what she could do for him. The CEO told her that he had decided to fill the vacant Chief Operating Officer (COO) position with the current Vice President of

Operations, and he was reorganizing the Institute. The new COO would be responsible for all non-research activities and the CEO would retain responsibility for all research areas. Since the new COO lacks a strong understanding of information technology, he would like to move Allison out of Corporate Information and have her report to the COO as the new Vice President of Clinical Information. She would be responsible for all of the clinical information technology needs of the Institute. In this role, she would retain some of her current duties and assume many new ones. He then handed her an organization chart and told her to determine how the newly formed areas should be structured. Taken aback, Allison pretended to study the chart. After a few minutes, she asked what the new COO thought about how this should be structured. He told her it was up to her to find out and to make it work. She then asked what the current Chief Information Officer (CIO), her immediate boss, thought about it. He explained that the CIO was asked to provide input but took too long. Thus, it was up to Allison to work it out with him. Allison then asked, "So basically you want me to facilitate the reorganization of the whole division because no one else is doing it quickly enough for you?" He laughed and said, "Yes, now get to it." She thanked him for the opportunity and left.

Allison and the new COO met the following morning and quickly created the new organization chart. They also agreed that Allison would initially negotiate the reallocation of responsibilities with the CIO because she had a better relationship with him. The COO would intervene only if it became necessary. On the way back to her office, Allison asked her boss if he wanted to have lunch. Since they ate together nearly every day, this was not a surprise. At lunch, after discussing some work issues, talk turned to the reorganization. Allison confessed that the CEO told her about it. They talked about various aspects of the change, including what they liked and disliked about it. They agreed that it was important to organize the Institute in an efficient and effective manner. They discussed separating Clinical Information from Corporate Information to enable the clinical division to function more effectively. They agreed this was a particularly important concern for both of them and for the organization as a whole.

With this agreement on their shared concern, Allison asked what the CIO thought about two important issues—digitizing patient records and information security. The CIO's position regarding patient records was that they should remain with him. Allison then asked if the clinical division could function effectively without responsibility for patient records. After some discussion, the CIO reconsidered their shared interest in organizational effectiveness and agreed that it should move with Allison to Clinical Information. Regarding information security, the CIO felt strongly that it should remain with Corporate Information because contracts were negotiated for the entire Institute all at once. Although Allison believed patient records posed unique security risks that could be managed more effectively in Clinical Information, she agreed that greater savings could be realized by negotiating all of the security programs at once and that it would serve their mutual interests to leave it in Corporate Information.

Their agreement to move digitizing patient records to Clinical Information and leave information security to Corporate Information was derived by focusing on the interests of the organization, and on each of their personal interests. They agreed that the reorganization promoted efficiency and effectiveness for the Institute, which would enhance its overall success. More personally, the CIO benefited from this because he was now able to spend more time on important projects, thereby enhancing his success with them. It also reduced some of the risk he would have to assume and enhanced his job security, both of which he valued highly. Allison's career would benefit from the promotion and from her new responsibilities. She valued the additional risk she was assuming and the added recognition she would receive if her efforts were successful. In fact, she gained immediate recognition from the CEO when, in less than one day, she and the COO presented him with the new organization chart.

Building rapport also assumes greater importance when using the integrative strategy. It was noted in Chapter 2 that negotiators who engaged in a mere 10 minutes of conversation, even if it is unrelated to the negotiation, share more information, make fewer threats, and develop more respect and trust during talks than pairs who do not do so (Nadler, 2004). These are particularly important when negotiating integratively because trust, cooperation, and information sharing help negotiators develop a shared understanding of the situation, identify interests, and invent solutions that satisfy them. Moreover, trust, information sharing, and the absence of threats enhance relationships, which is one reason we use this strategy.

INTEGRATIVE NEGOTIATING MYTHS

There are a number of myths or misconceptions surrounding this strategy. People seem to think it is about being soft or nice, and that they have negotiated integratively if they *maintain or improve the relationship*. Though the relationship matters and may be an important goal, it is only one piece of the puzzle. It is true that integrative negotiators are soft on the people, but they are not soft on interests or the problem. Trading substance for the relationship is more consistent with accommodation. Even worse, the other side may use this against you when trying to claim value. Like the spouse who claims, "If you really loved me you would go to the store for me," the other party might say, "If you really valued our business relationship you would give me a better price." If you give in once, he or she is likely to use this tactic again and again. To illustrate, Negotiation in Action 4.2 describes a manager who treats dissatisfied customers very nicely and politely.

NEGOTIATION IN ACTION 4.2

A food server at an upscale restaurant incorrectly submitted an order for a vegetarian couple, and their meals were served with chicken mixed into their pasta. The customers demanded to see a manager. After inviting them to discuss the situation in a quieter location where their concerns could be heard more clearly, he listened to their complaints—mostly about how badly lunch tarnished her birthday celebration. When they finished venting their frustrations, they discussed different ways these repeat customers could be compensated for their unsatisfactory experience. The couple finally explained that they did not want a free or discounted meal. What they really wanted was to ensure that situations like this were prevented in the future by properly training employees. The manager proudly informed them of their rigorous training program. He also explained that despite the effectiveness of their training efforts, employees occasionally make mistakes, especially when they are as busy as their server was during the lunch rush. After being informed of this incident, the restaurant's general manager sent the couple a $100 gift certificate and a formal letter of apology for failing to meet their expectations. The letter assured them that experiences like these were atypical of the restaurant and graciously asked them to give the establishment another chance to serve them and exceed their expectations (Personal Communication).

Does this scenario illustrate an integrative negotiation, or did the managers merely accommodate the customers for the server's mistake?

- Aggressiveness is not inappropriate when negotiating integratively. Insisting on digging deeper to find relevant information, ensuring that all of your interests are satisfied, and pointing out problems associated with exercising a BATNA are examples of when it is appropriate and necessary to be aggressive.
- Nor is integrative negotiating about *compromising*. If you compromise your interests you will not achieve a wise agreement. While it is true that value will eventually have to be claimed and compromising may be involved, the integrative part of the negotiation is the value creation component. Be careful not to confuse satisfaction with integrative negotiating. Just because you are satisfied or happy does not necessarily mean that you have created value (Thompson, Valley, & Kramer, 1995).
- The assumption of a fixed pie is another myth that may prevent people from using this strategy properly, or even attempting to use it. Negotiators commonly assume that resources are fixed or that their interests are completely incompatible (Bazerman & Neale, 1983; Fisher, Ury, & Patton, 1991). If this is true, expanding the pie is impossible. While some negotiations truly are zero-sum exercises, most are not—if there are two or more issues and the negotiators prioritize them differently, integrative potential exists.

TACTICS OF INTEGRATIVE BARGAINING

In their book *Getting to Yes*, Fisher et al. (1991) provide an invaluable framework for understanding the tactics that are used to implement this strategy. These include separating the person from the problem, focusing on interests rather than positions, inventing options for mutual gain, and using objective criteria to evaluate options.

Separating the Person From the Problem

This tactic strikes some people as being warm and fuzzy because its central tenets include "be soft on the person" and "attack the problem not the person." Being soft on the person may be the reason some people incorrectly think they have negotiated integratively—because they were nice to each other. This set of tactics is about depersonalizing the problem, but it is much more than merely being nice. It is about emotions, perceptions, and communication and how these help the parties find creative solutions that allow them to maximize joint gain.

This set of tactics strikes others as being odd—why would a negotiator attack the other party when they are trying to satisfy their respective needs? It may be counterintuitive and counterproductive, but negotiations do become quite tense and emotional at times. Imagine that you articulate what you know are very logical and compelling arguments and counterarguments in support of your positions, but they fall on deaf ears. When this happens and when you reach impasses, frustrations mount. You begin to doubt whether the other negotiator would know a good argument if he or she heard one. As your deadline nears you tell the other negotiator that he or she is not negotiating in good faith, or maybe that he or she is not smart enough to understand what you are proposing. Even in simulated role-plays conducted as classroom exercises, participants sometimes react verbally (yelling, swearing), physically (walking away, slamming doors), and physiologically (beet-red faces, exaggerated gestures). What would happen if they truly had a vested interest in the outcomes?

The role of emotions. Actions often beget equal and opposite reactions. If one negotiator attacks the other, he or she is likely to reciprocate. Such an emotional response only serves to escalate the conflict, thereby undermining the process. Negative emotions cause negotiators to pay less attention to the other party's interests, diminish the accuracy of their judgments about these interests, lead to the use of less cooperative strategies and the creation of less favorable outcomes, and less compliance with the terms of the agreements that are reached. These emotions also make negotiators less interested in having future interactions with the other party (Allred, Mallozzi, Matsui, & Raia, 1997; Forgas, 1998). Interestingly, negotiators also cooperate less and are less likely to honor agreements that are reached when the other party experiences negative emotions (Forgas, 1998). Emotion affects electronic negotiations as well. When people negotiating via email believe a relationship is not possible, they issue more threats and ultimatums, and they are more likely to reach an impasse (Moore, Kurtzburg, Thompson, & Morris, 1999).

If negative emotions hinder negotiations, do positive emotions help? They do, to a point. When the aforementioned email negotiators believed that a relationship was possible, they conveyed expressions of positive affect that enhanced rapport and diminished the likelihood of reaching an impasse (Moore et al., 1999). Positive emotions also engender better outcomes and, when the negotiators can see each other, they use fewer contentious tactics (Carnevale & Isen, 1986; Kramer, Newton, & Pomerenke, 1993). Emotions that are extremely positive, however, may distort negotiators' judgments (Ariely & Lowenstein, 2006).

The moral of the story is that emotions must be managed.

- Recognize and understand that emotions are an inevitable part of the bargaining process.
- Do not attack the other side even if you think it might feel good to do so because of the way he or she is behaving. It will not help you maximize joint gain.
- If the other party is very emotional, allow him or her to vent his or her frustrations but do not react to them. Sit back and wait for him or her to cool off, or take a break and resume at a later time or date.
- If your emotions are strong, do the same things.
- If he or she attacks you, recast it as an attack on the problem and not you. This takes confidence, self-control, and perhaps some wordsmithing.

- Taking a short break might help with this as well. You will not produce wise agreements if you continue trying to negotiate while emotions are strong (Fisher et al., 1991; Ury, 1991). Additional suggestions for managing emotions are discussed in Chapter 13.

The role of perceptions. It is well documented that our own point of view makes it very difficult to process and evaluate information objectively (Galinsky & Moskowitz, 2000; Kronzon & Darley, 1999). This is a problem because successful integrative negotiation requires parties to develop a shared and complete understanding of the situation. They may be trying to solve different problems if their perceptions differ. These distortions will be amplified if emotions are strong. Viewing the situation from the other party's perspective is very beneficial because it enhances problem solving and facilitates efforts to achieve integrative agreements (Neale & Bazerman, 1983; Richardson, Hammock, Smith, Gardner, & Signo, 1994). For these reasons, stand in the other party's shoes to view the situation from his or her perspective, and have him or her stand in your shoes to see it from your perspective. After doing so, discuss each of your perceptions explicitly. Asking how he or she views the situation, and sharing your own view, will enable you to make sense of your different viewpoints and reconcile them (Fisher et al., 1991).

Video 4.2

Detecting Anger in a Negotiation

The role of communication. Unfortunately, communication problems are as common as misperceptions. Instead of talking with the other party, negotiators sometimes talk at each other or they stop talking altogether. They may misunderstand or misinterpret the other party because they do not listen well. Negotiation in Action 4.3 illustrates how easily miscommunications might arise.

So what? If the word *rich* engenders such diverse interpretations, what happens when we negotiate issues that are far more complex and important than this?

NEGOTIATION IN ACTION 4.3

Hundreds of students were asked to answer the following question: "How much money does a single person without children have to earn in a year for you to consider him or her to be rich?" Some of the answers weren't about money. Instead, students gave narrative descriptions about achieving goals and being happy in life. For those who did share dollar amounts, they ranged between $20,000 per year and $3 million per year.

In addition to depersonalizing the problem, managing emotions, and clarifying perceptions, "separating the person from the problem" requires negotiators to create a free flowing exchange of information that helps them gain a clearer and deeper understanding of the situation. Several steps will help you achieve this.

- Ask open-ended and probing questions to gather information and to clarify what has been said.
- Engage in active listening. This includes repeating or paraphrasing what was said to check for understanding and to let the other negotiator know that you understand.
- Talk about the impact of the problem on you instead of blaming him or her for what happened to you—so-called I statements. This will diminish his or her defensiveness.
- If you disagree with something that is said, critique its merits, not him or her.

- If the other negotiator does not seem to understand what you are communicating, reframe it—restate your message in a different way.
- Look forward, not back. You cannot change the past so blaming the other party, or allowing him or her to blame you, for what happened will not help. You can influence the future so steer the conversation forward (Fisher et al., 1991).

The scenario described in Negotiation in Action 4.4 illustrates some of these points.

NEGOTIATION IN ACTION 4.4

Don reports directly to Hank. He is older than Hank and has been with the organization much longer. They were tasked with changing the format of a report that is sent to Congress so that it will be easier to read and understand. Hank and Don are both willing to share their thoughts, including concerns and problems, when they arise. Don was comfortable with the existing form and didn't want to change it but Hank thinks the change is needed. He began drafting a new format for the report before he and Don met to talk about it. When they did meet, Hank focused on his own desires and needs. He used his knowledge and experience with different formats that worked very well elsewhere to justify it. He used the power of his position and other tactics to persuade Don to agree with him, but to no avail. Don responded negatively to these tactics and to Hank's perception of what format was best. Each time he disagreed, Hank became frustrated. Don became defensive and his facial expressions displayed just how frustrated and disgruntled he was. In fact, he eventually walked out.

When they met again, Hank changed his tactics. Instead of trying to convince Don that his proposal was the right one, they talked about the importance of the report. They agreed that it was necessary to provide critical financial information to senior leadership and to Congress. He asked Don about his experience with the current format, why he thought it was appropriate, and any problems he had encountered with it. He also asked Don about the problems he expected with the format he proposed during their previous meeting. They generated an honest and open exchange of information about the report and what it should accomplish. This helped each of them understand the other's perception of the situation. It also helped Hank understand Don's resistance to changing the format. Moreover, they eliminated the emotional responses that guided much of their previous meeting (Personal Communication).

During their second meeting, Hank did a better job of managing emotions, clarifying perceptions, and communicating. This helped them employ other integrative tactics that eventually led to the creation of a report format that was acceptable to both of them, their superiors, and Congress.

Focus on Interests, Not Positions

Interests are a negotiator's fears, concerns, and unmet needs. They are the motives underlying stated positions—the purposes they will serve for you, not your justifications for them. Assume that you are negotiating a $5,000 pay increase with your supervisor. The issue to be negotiated is your pay increase, $5,000 is your position, and the reasons you need $5,000 or how it will help you are your interests. These might include raising your status, gaining recognition for your fine work, helping you maintain your standard of living as your family expands, and undoubtedly others. Confusing issues, positions, and interests is problematic because it stifles the creativity needed to invent solutions that work for both parties. If you focus only on your demand for $5,000, there is only one solution. If you focus on the purposes it will serve for you, there are many plausible solutions.

Interests can pertain to the substantive terms of the negotiation, the relationship, the process, or principles. Substantive interests pertain to the tangible issues being negotiated. These might include price, delivery date, or who will handle installation. Relationship interests pertain to the nature of the relationship you want to have with the other party. Process interests are about how a deal is made or how a dispute is settled. Principle interests are intangible. They pertain to strongly held beliefs about, for example, what is right or wrong (Lax & Sebenius, 1986, 2002).

Each of these types of interests can be intrinsic—you value or need something in and of itself. They can also be instrumental—you value or need something because it will help you in the future. For example, some negotiators prefer to negotiate in a strident manner because it helps them feel like they won when an agreement is reached. This is an intrinsic process interest. Others prefer a cooperative approach because they think it will make future interactions with the other party more productive. This is an instrumental process interest. Principle interests are important to consider because negotiators' beliefs about what is right, acceptable, or fair shape what they believe are appropriate outcomes, and appropriate means for achieving them (Lax & Sebenius, 1986, 2002).

Sometimes people make demands or adopt positions and do not really know why. To identify your own interests, ask yourself some questions.

- Why do I want the position I demanded?
- How will it help me?
- What purposes will it serve for me?
- What will happen if the other party says no to my demand?
- What will happen if the other party says yes to my demand?

It is important to identify your interests for each issue. Redundancy will occur if they overlap, but your understanding of the situation will improve if some are unique to a particular issue. This may increase integrative potential by expanding the range of plausible solutions. Unmet needs or unsatisfied interests are also one of the main reasons people object to and reject proposals, so identifying all of them is essential. Since there are usually multiple interests associated with each issue, identifying as many as possible and prioritizing them will help you create value because it is the presence of different priorities pertaining to issues and interests that make valuable tradeoffs possible. Sharing your interests with the other party is also advised—if you do not, he or she is not likely to share interests with you and your negotiation will go nowhere fast (Bazerman & Neale, 1992). In short, sharing your interests and priorities will increase the likelihood of reaching integrative agreements (Thompson, 1991).

Identifying the other party's interests should follow a similar approach—ask the same or similar questions of him or her that you asked of yourself. In addition, when the other party objects to one of your proposals, ask, "Why don't you think it will work for you?," "What do you think I'm asking for?" When you ask these kinds of questions, you are looking for the other negotiator's fears, concerns, needs, and desires, not his or her justifications. Like you, he or she will have multiple interests associated with each issue. For the reasons just mentioned, it will pay dividends to identify as many as you can and to ask about his or her priorities. Negotiators who ask the other party about his or her priorities are more likely to reach integrative agreements than those who do not (Galinsky, Maddux, Gilin, & White, 2008). Will the other party share this information? If you do, he or she is likely to reciprocate. While it is fairly easy to understand why a negotiator might hide, exaggerate, or misrepresent his or her target and resistance points or BATNA, it is not clear what he or she might gain by misrepresenting interests. Nor does it seem likely that a negotiator could exploit the other party by understanding his or her true interests.

It is sometimes difficult to identify and define interests (Provis, 1996). In addition to asking the aforementioned questions, discuss them explicitly with the other party. This should help you gain clarity and ensure that your understanding is shared. Working together to identify all of the issues, the interests associated with them, and how each of you prioritized them will provide you with the information required to find integrative solutions. This is important because shared interests present different opportunities and challenges than interests that are different but compatible. Both of these present different opportunities and challenges than interests that seem to be incompatible.

Invent Options for Mutual Gain

Some people begin a negotiation by identifying the issues and then hammering out solutions for each. You may reach an agreement by following this path, but it is not likely to maximize joint gain, or even your own gain. The issues, and the interests associated with them, define the situation. If these are ignored, the agreement reached will not be complete or wise. Stated differently, it is hard to solve a problem or capitalize on a new opportunity if you do not have a clear and shared understanding of what it is.

Brainstorming

When each party's issues and interests have been identified and clarified, it is possible to begin searching for solutions that satisfy them. Inventing options is essentially a brainstorming task. You are trying to generate a list of options that you can then choose from, or modify to produce even better options. You can do this with your colleagues and then share them with the other party as part of your brainstorming effort, or you can brainstorm with the other party. Either way, having an open mind, and a creative one, enhances brainstorming efforts. Table 4.2 offers suggestions for fostering creativity. "Green Hat" thinking (see Chapter 10) also helps.

Successful brainstorming requires participants to avoid making some common mistakes.

- *Premature judgment* is the tendency to prematurely criticize or evaluate options when they are invented, perhaps because they seem unworkable or too outrageous. They may be unworkable or outrageous, but that is okay at this point. Your purpose now is to generate a substantial list of potential solutions. Generating more ideas increases the probability of generating better ones, and the best are most likely to surface toward the latter part of the activity (Shea, 1983).
- *Separating the inventing and evaluating functions* is essential because creating and critiquing require very different skills, and the latter inhibits the former. Thus, invent first. You will revisit the options you invent later to determine their efficacy.

Table 4.2   Factors That Increase Creativity

Suggestion	Explanation
Clarify goals; Define the situation	Know what you want to accomplish; Explore what you want in place of what you have
Invent	Look for tools (e.g., metaphors) that help you break out of tradition-bound thinking; Use triggers (e.g., force associations between two unlike things, reverse hidden assumptions, propose outrageous ideas, include team members from different disciplines) to move your brainstorming forward
Incubate	Take a break and engage in divergent thinking by working on unrelated tasks
Create an appropriate working environment	Quiet; Alcohol-free; Natural; Relaxed; Unrestrained
Take your time	Originality and flexibility increase later in the process
External evaluation (e.g., by constituents)	Explicitly consider how the idea will be implemented; Delaying evaluation improves idea generation; External evaluations improve decision making, modification, or improvement of ideas more than it improves idea generation
Individual differences	Open-mindedness; Empathy; Emotional intelligence; Intrinsically motivated (e.g., per interest in task, knowledge of subject); Convergent thinkers; Divergent thinkers; Ability to break out of functional fixedness

(See, e.g., Ellwood, Pallier, Snyder, & Gallate, 2009; Ma, 2009; Beeftink, van Erde, & Rutto, 2008; DeYoung, Flanders, & Peterson, 2008; Hemlin, Allwood, & Martin, 2008; Yuan & Zhou, 2008; Weiss, 2001.)

Many negotiators see their task as narrowing the gap between the parties' positions, not broadening the options available. Moreover, they think they know the correct answer when they attempt to settle a dispute—they proceed by trying to convince the other party that their view should prevail. When making deals, they often believe their proposal is reasonable and that it should be adopted (Fisher et al., 1991). It is important to overcome this tendency to *search for the single best answer*. The beauty of focusing on interests is that it expands the number and type of solutions that will help both sides.

- The *mythical fixed pie* or pool of resources was discussed earlier. While some negotiations truly are zero-sum in nature, most are not. This is a problem here because a negotiator who succumbs to the myth will conclude that a gain for the other party is a loss for him or her. This belief inhibits creativity and the process of inventing options.
- *Egocentrism*, or being too self-interested, stifles brainstorming efforts. While it is necessary for negotiators to focus on their own interests, they must also consider those of the other party. Integrative negotiation is about maximizing joint gain, so thinking that "their problem

is their problem" will undermine your efforts. Again, this strategy is used to solve shared or joint problems (Fisher et al., 1991). Consider framing all issues as shared problems—as our issue rather than as my issue or your issue.

Types of Integrative Solutions

Once your brainstorming has produced a generous list of possible solutions, you and the other party must critique and evaluate them. Consider starting with the ones that appear to be the most promising. Perhaps there is one that satisfies both parties' shared interests. More likely, you can combine or otherwise modify options that were invented to create even better ones. It may help to view the options from different perspectives—your own, the other party's, or an outsider's (Butler, 1996). What these solutions might look like is discussed here and in Reading 4.2 at the end of this chapter.

Bridging Solutions

A bridging solution is described in Negotiation in Action 4.5.

NEGOTIATION IN ACTION 4.5

An entrepreneur is negotiating the sale of her company. She is genuinely optimistic about the future prospects of her fast-growing business. The buyer, who truly likes the company, is much more skeptical about its future cash flow. While the two have negotiated earnestly and in good faith, no price is acceptable to both sides. Active listening for each side's real interests, informal meals together, outings to major sporting events, and other actions to build the relationship and trust have been helpful but insufficient. They have been unable to find a solution that bridges the gap between their distinctly different positions.

Although they were unable to find a mutually acceptable solution, this is not the case of a negative settlement range. There is a viable solution, one that might appear valuable to the optimistic seller and not particularly costly to the less optimistic buyer, if they ignore their stated positions and focus instead on their interests. For example, the buyer could pay a fixed price now that is less than his current valuation of the company, and a contingent amount later based upon the performance of the company over a future period. Properly structured with adequate incentives and monitoring mechanisms in place, such a contingent payment might satisfy their respective interests and be more attractive than their no-agreement alternatives (adapted from Lax & Sebenius, 2002).

Logrolling

Logrolling also leads to integrative outcomes. If the parties attach different priorities to different interests and issues, they may be able to maximize joint gain by finding trades that capitalize on these differences. Teresa and Julia planned an evening out to catch up and to see a movie. Teresa did not really care where they ate, but she desperately wanted to see a movie that was just released. Julia, on the other hand, did not really care which movie they saw, but she had been dying to try a trendy new restaurant in her neighborhood. This enabled them to satisfy their respective interests and maximize their gain—they had dinner at the trendy new restaurant and then went to the movie Teresa wanted to see.

Different attitudes toward risk, as demonstrated in the negotiation between Allison and her boss (the CIO) in Negotiation in Action 4.1, often facilitate such tradeoffs. They were able to trade responsibilities in a way that gave the CIO little risk and more security, in return for assuming greater risk with the prospect of greater career advancement. People who value time differently may also benefit from logrolling. If you need a product now but do not have a lot of money, and the seller needs to clear the product out of inventory more than he or she needs immediate payment, you may be able to receive the product now in return for payment over time. *Different capabilities* provide another basis for finding valuable tradeoffs. A manufacturer may enter into an alliance with a marketing firm to sell what it produces. This enables them to capitalize on their distinct competencies (Lax & Sebenius, 2002). Successful logrolling obviously requires you and the other party to identify more than one issue or to divide an issue into separate parts. Negotiators also find tradeoffs among packages of issues and interests, not just two.

Nonspecific Compensation and Cutting the Cost of Compliance

Nonspecific compensation involves allowing one person to obtain his or her objectives and then paying off the other person for accommodating his or her interests. The payoff is unrelated to the substantive terms of the negotiation but of adequate value to that person.

When *cutting the costs for compliance*, one negotiator again satisfies his or her interests. The other party's costs are then minimized for agreeing to go along. The nature of nonspecific compensation and cutting the cost of compliance, are illustrated in respectively, 4.6.

NEGOTIATION IN ACTION 4.6

Early in his career, Benny wanted to establish his credentials as a trainer to supplement his academic work. When the human resources director of the athletic facility on his campus asked him to conduct training programs for her employees, Benny agreed even though she didn't have a budget that would allow her to pay him. From time to time, however, she gave him tickets to sporting events and concerts that he wanted to attend. This nonspecific compensation persuaded him to continue training for her.

Assume that a college basketball or football coach accepts a new position with a different school or a professional team before his or her current employment contract expires. If the current employment contract requires payment of a sum of money to break it, and the new employer pays all or part of this cost, it is cutting the coach's cost of compliance.

Make the other party's decision to say yes an easy one. While viewing the situation from the other negotiator's perspective, you must believe that your proposals satisfy his or her interests, and you must present them in a manner that makes this clear. If they do not, why would you expect him or her to say yes? Would you agree to a proposal that does not satisfy your interests? Furthermore, it is one thing for the other party to say yes. It may be quite another to persuade his or her constituents to say yes.

Make your proposals easy to sell to his or her constituents. This requires you to possess a clear understanding of the other party's perception of the situation (Fisher et al., 1991).

USE OBJECTIVE CRITERIA TO EVALUATE OPTIONS

Once alternative solutions have been identified, you must evaluate them to decide which options to keep and which to eliminate. Using objective criteria that are independent of your will and independent of the other party's will enables you to choose solutions based on their merits or principles of fairness (Fisher et al., 1991). Objective criteria include things like legal requirements, relevant precedents, customs, market prices or wages, professional standards and policies. When discussing the use of appeals to fairness in Chapter 3, Connie's leaky faucets and the customer service manager's "more than fair" offer were discussed. Negotiation in Action 4.7 illustrates the use of objective criteria in her negotiation.

NEGOTIATION IN ACTION 4.7

Before the "more than fair" offer was extended, Connie asked the customer service manager (CSM) to replace the faucets. Her request was denied because the customer service manager claimed the faucets weren't defective. Incredulous, Connie asked her what she meant. She claimed that since water was still coming out of the faucets as it's supposed to, they weren't defective. Ignoring the fact that her staff had just spent two weeks trying to repair her "non-defective" faucets, Connie got out her dictionary, quoted the definition of *defect*, and explained that her faucets matched that definition precisely. She then asked her how she defined *defect*. After a very weak answer and some additional discussion, including a threat to take the company to court, the customer service manager agreed to pay Connie to replace the faucets and made her "more than fair" offer. When Connie asked how that amount was determined, she again got the runaround. Ignoring it, Connie explained that fairness to her was the retail price of the new faucets plus the amount a licensed contractor would charge to install them, and she presented the price and estimate she had acquired. The customer service manager eventually agreed to pay her this amount, which was several hundred dollars more than her initial "more than fair" offer.

The dictionary definition and the retail price/contractor's estimate are both objective criteria, independent of each negotiator's will. The value in using these is that they are very persuasive, much more so than one's belief or opinion about these matters. It was hard for the customer service manager to dispute Connie's claims about the defect and about a fair price because she supported them with objective evidence. As an aside, this was not an integrative negotiation because Connie used this tactic. As noted in Chapter 3, however, objective evidence can be very persuasive no matter which strategy you use.

Merely because you raise an objective criterion does not mean the other side will accept it. It becomes another issue to negotiate. If you search together, you may eliminate some of the difficulty it takes to reach an agreement. The benefit of commencing a joint search for objective criteria is illustrated in Negotiation in Action 4.8.

NEGOTIATION IN ACTION 4.8

It is a common practice to use market rates when negotiating wages and salaries. Whether an applicant is negotiating his or her own salary or a union is negotiating wages for its members, both parties are likely to use market salaries or wages to support their proposals. This makes sense because paying the going rate for a position seems to be meritorious and much more persuasive than either side's opinion about the appropriate salary or wage for different jobs. Management, however, may survey lower paying firms to determine the market or average salary because this would justify a lower rate. The applicant or union, on the other hand, may survey higher paying employers because this would justify a higher salary or wage. It also helps to negotiate these criteria in advance. If options are invented and then you search for criteria, there is an obvious incentive to look for criteria that support preferred options. Selecting criteria in advance prevents this (Fisher et al., 1991).

When determining which objective standards will be used, explanations are helpful in persuading the other side to agree. As noted earlier, even an explanation that offers little or no new information is better than simply saying, "I think that one is best" or "I think we should pick this one!" Also remember that intangibles such as principle interests may be driving or influencing the other party's choices. Make them explicit because they will influence what each party deems appropriate.

Fair standards work well for evaluating substantive options. In some cases, you must find fair procedures or processes to resolve conflicting interests. This might be as simple as flipping a coin or drawing straws to determine, for example, which heir gets to pick first when dividing an estate's assets. Another alternative is to use the age-old means for dividing a piece of cake between two children—one cuts and the other chooses which piece he or she wants. When these approaches are used, there is an inherent fairness in knowing that chances were equal, even if the ultimate division of the resources is not (Fisher et al., 1991).

FINE TUNING YOUR EFFORTS TO ACHIEVE INTEGRATIVE SOLUTIONS

Avoid Focusing on One Issue at a Time

Negotiators often select one issue to begin with and then negotiate until an agreement is reached. If they get stuck, they move to a different issue and return to this one later. They might start with an easy issue to get both parties comfortable with the process, and with agreeing. Alternatively, they might start with the most difficult issue so that when they finish with it the rest will be easier and they can end on a more positive note. These seem logical, but they do not help you create integrative solutions. We are more likely to compromise on each issue if we focus on one at a time because we spend more time arguing for our positions and against the other party's positions (Hyder, Prietula, & Weingart, 2000). Moreover, focusing on one issue at a time precludes finding beneficial tradeoffs based on different priorities. A better approach is to surface all issues and the interests associated with each early on.

Use Multiple Equivalent Offers

Another reason to avoid dealing with one issue at a time is because extending multiple equivalent offers simultaneously may help you overcome the other party's uncooperativeness, reluctance to share information, or unwillingness to even seriously consider your proposals. This approach requires you to simultaneously extend two or three multiple issue offers to the other negotiator that are of equal value to you. This will move you away from the aforementioned tendency to compromise on each issue when they are dealt with sequentially. If you listen carefully and observe the other party, it will also provide you with information about his or her priorities. Negotiators who make multiple equivalent offers find more integrative solutions, achieve more profitable outcomes, and are thought of more favorably by the other party because we like the flexibility that comes with choices (Hyder et al., 2000; Leonardelli, Medvec, Galinsky, & Clausen-Schulz, 2008).

Trust

Trust means you have confident positive expectations regarding another's conduct. *Distrust* means you have confident negative expectations about his or her conduct (Lewicki, McAllister, & Bies, 1998). Trust matters because integrative negotiation requires the parties to honestly and openly share information so they can generate a complete and shared understanding of the situation, including their respective interests. We know that trust begets cooperation, and cooperation begets trust. We also know that greater expectations of trust between negotiators lead to greater information sharing with the other party and, conversely, greater expectations of distrust lead to less information sharing. Since greater information sharing leads to better outcomes, this is beneficial (Butler, 1995, 1999; Olekalns, Lau, & Smith, 2002).

Blind trust is risky because it makes negotiators vulnerable. Nevertheless, many people exhibit surprisingly high levels of trust when they form new relationships with strangers. Despite their lack of information about the other person, most assume he or she can be trusted (Kramer, 1999; Myerson, Weick, & Kramer, 1996). Suggestions for helping you build trust are summarized in Table 4.3. We also tend to be more trusting if we have opportunities to communicate with the other person and if our personalities predispose us to trust. Integrative processes tend to increase trust while distributive processes decrease it (Olekalns & Smith, 2005). Face-to-face negotiations also encourage greater trust development than online negotiations. Parties anticipating an online negotiation expect less trust before the negotiation even begins, are less satisfied with their outcomes, trust the other party less after the negotiation ends, and have less desire for future interactions with him or her (Naquin & Paulson, 2003).

Table 4.3 Suggestions for Increasing or Repairing Trust

Suggestion	Explanation
Build Rapport	Talk and share information; Nonverbally mirror the other party
Relationships	Ongoing interactions must be honest and trustworthy
Promises	Meet others' expectations and honor your promises—this builds credibility; If promises must be broken, find ways to minimize the harm done to the victim
Discuss Explicitly	Explicitly stress the benefits of creating and maintaining trust
Reciprocate	Sharing information and making concessions creates a sense of indebtedness that induces the other to reciprocate—this builds trust
Avoid Attacking	Do not attribute situationally determined behaviors to others
Apologize	When trust is violated, early apologies are better than no apologies; They are most effective when made after the other party has been given a chance to feel heard and understood; Feeling heard suggests the conflict is ready to be managed
Explanations	Apologies and simple explanations are effective at restoring trust
Consequences	Taking penalties is more effective for restoring mutual cooperation than only offering explanations; Accepting penalties that imply acceptance of responsibility for the trust violation are effective
Responsibility	Apologies with internal attributions are more effective than apologies with external attributions because of the willingness to take responsibility rather than shift blame elsewhere; Mere excuses compromise the credibility and character of the offender
Sincerity	Sincerity magnifies the benefits of apologies
Future Violations	A low probability of future trust violations increases victims' willingness to reconcile, especially for minor violations; The probability of future violations is less relevant following serious violations because victims rely more on the quality of the past relationship when deciding whether to reconcile
Deception	Trust can be restored if untrustworthy behavior is not accompanied by deception; Trust harmed by deception never fully recovers

(See, e.g., Frantz & Bennigson, 2005; Schweitzer, 2004; Tomlinson, Dineen, & Lewicki, 2004; Bottom, Gibson, Daniels, & Murnighan, 2002; Lewicki & Weithoff, 2000; Lewicki & Stevenson, 1998; Lewicki & Bunker, 1996, 1995.)

CONCLUSION AND IMPLICATIONS FOR PRACTICE

Done well, this strategy produces wise agreements because it satisfies the parties' interests, it is efficient, and it often preserves or improves relationships (Fisher et al., 1991). These benefits are achievable if you separate the person from the problem, focus on interests instead of positions, invent options for mutual gain, and use objective criteria to evaluate the options you invent. This model is not, however, entirely separable from the distributive strategy. Once you create value by negotiating integratively, you must claim it. Using objective criteria may help with this, but distributive tactics may also be required. The following suggestions should help you create more value that you and the other negotiator can then claim.

1. Manage emotions, clarify perceptions, and communicate clearly once the requisite conditions for integrative negotiations are met. This allows both parties to develop a complete and shared understanding of the situation.

2. Frame each of the issues as shared or joint problems. This fosters cooperation and reinforces that you are working together to find solutions that help both of you.

3. Keep in mind that the pie can be expanded only when you and the other party try to advance the full set of interests—economic or noneconomic, substantive, relational, process, or principle (Lax & Sebenius, 2002).

4. Focus on both dealcrafting and interpersonal processes. Most people think of negotiations as interpersonal processes and focus on a variety of dynamics, including communication, trust building, cultural differences, perceptions, personality, bargaining styles, no-deal options, and various tactics. These are critical, but they are not the whole story. True integrative negotiation also requires **dealcrafting**—tapping the potential value latent in the situation. Identifying and understanding the full set of interests will enable you to look for bridging solutions, find logrolling opportunities, offer nonspecific compensation, reduce the other party's costs of agreeing, or otherwise brainstorm solutions that satisfy these interests. (See **Reading 4.2.**)

5. Use objective criteria rather than engaging in a contest of wills to decide which options are best. This enables you to evaluate criteria based on their merits, which is more consistent with maximizing joint gain and preserving or improving relationships. Searching for objective criteria with the other party, before you invent options, will help both of you avoid the tendency to look for objective criteria that support preferred options that have already been invented.

STUDENT STUDY SITE

Visit the Student Study Site at **www.sagepub.com/hames** for additional learning tools.

KEY TERMS

Bridging solution	Fixed pie
Cutting the costs for compliance	Instrumental interests
Creating value	Intrinsic interests
Dealcrafting	Logrolling
Expanding the pie	Nonspecific compensation

Principle interests

Process interests

Relationship interests

Substantive interests

REFERENCES

Allred, K. G., Mallozzi, J. S., Matsui, E. & Raia, C. P. (1997). The influence of anger and compassion on negotiation performance, Organizational Behavior and Human Decision Processes, 70, 175-187.

Ariely, D. & Lowenstein, G. (2006). The heat of the moment: The effect of sexual arousal on sexual decision-making, Journal of Behavioral Decision-Making 19, 87–98.

Bazerman, M. & Neale, M. (1992). Negotiating rationally. New York: The Free Press.

_____. (1983). Heuristics in negotiation: Limitations to effective dispute resolution. In M. H. Bazerman & R. J. Lewicki (Eds.), Negotiating in organizations. Beverly Hills, CA: Sage, 51–67.

Beeftink, F., van Erde, W. & Rutto, C. G. (2008). The effect of interruptions and breaks on insight and impasses: Do you need a break right now?, Creativity Research Journal, 20(1), 43–53.

Bottom, W. P., Gibson, K., Daniels, S. & Murnighan, J. K. (2002). When talk is not cheap: Substantive penance and expressions of intent in the reestablishment of cooperation, Organization Science, 13, 497–513.

Butler, J. K., Jr. (1999). Trust, expectations, information sharing, climate of trust and negotiation effectiveness and efficiency, Group & Organization Management, 24(2), 217–238.

_____. (1996). Two integrative win-win negotiating strategies, Simulation and Gaming, 27, 387–392.

_____. (1995). Behaviors, trust and goal achievement in a win-win negotiation role play, Group & Organization Management, 20, 486–501.

Carnevale, P. J. and Isen, A. M. (1986). The influence of positive affect and visual access on the discovery of integrative outcomes in bilateral negotiation, Organizational Behavior and Human Decision Processes, 37(1), 1–13.

DeYoung, C. G., Flanders, J. L. & Peterson, J. B. (2008). Cognitive abilities involved in insight problem solving: An individual difference model, Creativity Research Journal, 20(3), 278–290.

Ellwood, S., Pallier, G., Snyder, G. & Galate, J. (2009). The incubation effect: Hatching a solution?, Creativity Research Journal, 21(1`), 6–14.

Fisher, R., Ury, W. & Patton, B. (1991). Getting to yes: Negotiating agreement without giving in. New York: Penguin Press.

Follett, M. (1994). In P. Graham (Ed.), Mary Parker Follett: Prophet of management – A celebration of writings from the 1920s. Boston: Harvard Business School Press.

Forgas, J. P. (1998). On feeling good and getting your way: Mood effects on negotiating strategies and outcomes, Journal of Personality and Social Psychology, 74, 565–577.

Frantz, C. M. & Bennigson, C. (2005). Better late than early: The influence of timing on apology effectiveness, Journal of Experimental Social Psychology, 41(2), 201–207.

Galinsky, A. D., Maddux, W. W., Gilin, D. & White, J. B. (2008). Why it pays to get inside the head of your opponent: The differential effects of perspective taking and empathy on negotiation, Psychological Science, 19(4), 378–384.

Galinsky, A. D. & Moskowitz, G. D. (2000). Perspective-taking: Decreasing stereotype expression, stereotype accessibility and in-group favoritism, Journal of Personality and Social Psychology, 78(4), 708–724.

Hemlin, S., Allwood, C. M. & Martin, B. R. (2008). Creative knowledge environments, Creativity Research Journal, 20(2), 196–210.

Hyder, E. B., Prietula, M. J. & Weingart, L. R. (2000). Getting to best: Efficiency versus optimality in negotiation, Cognitive Science, 24(2), 169–204.

Kramer, R. M. (1999). Trust and distrust in organizations: Emerging perspectives enduring questions, Annual Review of Psychology, 50, 569–598.

Kramer, R. M., Newton, E. & Pommerenke, P. L. (1993). The social context of negotiation: Effects of trust, aspiration and gender on negotiation tactics, Journal of Personality and Social Psychology, 38(1), 9–22.

Kronzon, S. & Darley, J. (1999). Is this tactic ethical? Biased judgments of others in negotiation, Basic and Applied Social Psychology, 21(1), 49–60.

Lax, D. & Sebenius, J. (2002). Dealcrafting: The substance of three-dimensional negotiations, Negotiation Journal, 18(1), 5–28.

_____. (1986). The manager as negotiator: Bargaining for cooperation and competitive gain. New York: The Free Press.

Leonardelli, G. J., Medvec, V., Galinsky, A. D. & Clausen-Schulz, A. (2008). Building interpersonal and economic capital by negotiating with multiple equivalent simultaneous offers, Unpublished Manuscript. Cited in Thompson, L. (2009). The mind and heart of the negotiator. Upper Saddle River, NJ: Pearson, 87.

Lewicki, R. J. & Weithoff, C. (2000). Trust, trust development, and trust repair. In M. Deutsch & P. T. Coleman (Eds.), The Handbook of Conflict Resolution: Theory and Practice. San Francisco: Jossey-Bass, 86–107.

Lewicki, R. J., McAllister, D. & Bies, R. H. (1998). Trust and distrust: New relationships and realities, Academy of Management Review, 23(3), 438–458.

Lewicki, R. J. & Stevenson, M. (1998). Trust development in negotiation: Proposed actions and a research agenda, Journal of Business and Professional Ethics, 16 (1–3), 99–132.

Lewicki, R. J. & Bunker, B. B. (1996). A model of trust development and decline. In R. Kramer & T Tyler (Eds.), Trust in organizations, Newbury Park, CA: Sage, 114–139.

_____. (1995). Trust in relationsips: A model of trust development and decline. In B. B. Bunker & J. Z. Rubin (Eds.), Conflict, cooperation and justice: Essays inspired by the work of Morton Deutsch San Francisco: Jossey-Bass, 133–174.

Ma, H. (2009). The effect size of variables associated with creativity: A meta-analysis, Creativity Research Journal, 21(1), 30–42.

Moore, D. A., Kurtzberg, T. R., Thompson, L. L. & Morris, M. W. (1999). Long and short routes to success in electronically mediated negotiations: Group affiliations and good vibrations, Organizational Behavior and Human Decision Processes, 77, 22–43.

Myerson, D., Weick, K. E. & Kramer, R. M. (1996). Swift trust and temporary groups. In R. M. Kramer & T. R. Tyler (Eds.), Trust in organizations. Thousand Oaks, CA: Sage, 166–195.

Nadler, J. (2004). Rapport in legal negotiations: How small talk can facilitate email dealmaking, Harvard Negotiation Law Review, 9, 223–253.

Naquin, C. E. & Paulson, G. D. (2003). Online bargaining and interpersonal trust, Journal of Applied Psychology, 88(1), 113–120.

Neale, M. A. & Bazerman, M. H. (1983). The role of perspective-taking ability in negotiating under different forms of arbitration, Industrial and Labor Relations Review, 36, 378–388.

Olekalns, M. & Smith, P. (2005). Moments in time: Metacognition, trust and outcomes in dyadic negotiations, Personality and Social Psychology Bulletin, 31(12), 1696–1707.

Olekalns, M., Lau, F. & Smith, P. (2002). The dynamics of trust in negotiation, Melbourne Business School Working Paper Series, #2002–09.

Provis, C. (1996). Interests vs. positions: A critique of the distinction, Negotiation Journal, 12, 305–323.

Richardson, D., Hammock, G., Smith, S., Gardner, W. & Signo, M. (1994). Empathy as a cognitive inhibitor of interpersonal aggression, Aggressive Behavior, 20, 275–289.

Schweitzer, M. E. (2004). Promises and lies: Restoring violated trust, Unpublished manuscript. Cited in Lewicki et al. (2006). Negotiation. New York: McGraw-Hill/Irwin, 293.

Shea, G. F. (1983). Creative negotiating. Boston: CBI Publishing.

Thompson, L. L. (1991). Information exchange in negotiation, Journal of Experimental Social Psychology, 27, 161–179.

Thompson, L., Valley, K. L. & Kramer, R. M. (1995). The bittersweet feeling of success: An examination of social perception in negotiation, Journal of Experimental Social Psychology, 31, 467–492.

Tomlinson, E., Dineen, B. & Lewicki, R. J. (2004). The road to reconciliation: Antecedents of victim willingness to reconcile following a broken promise, Journal of Management, 30(2), 165–187.

Ury, W. (1991). Getting past no: Negotiating with difficult people. New York: Bantam Books.

Walton, R. E & McKersie, R. B. (1965). A behavioral theory of labor negotiations: An analysis of a social interaction system. New York: McGraw-Hill.

Yuan, F. & Zhou, J. (2008). Differential effects of expected external evaluation on different parts of the creative idea production process and on final product creativity, Creativity Research Journal, 20(4), 391–403.

READINGS

Reading 4.1

TAKING STEPS TOWARD "GETTING TO YES" AT BLUE CROSS AND BLUE SHIELD OF FLORIDA

Bridget Booth and Matt McCredie

Never before has there been a more opportune time for Blue Cross and Blue Shield of Florida, Inc. (BCBSF) to benefit from the concepts of principled negotiation outlined in the book *Getting to Yes*.

BCBSF is the industry leader in Florida, providing health benefit plans and health-related services. The company and its subsidiaries serve more than six million people. However, maintaining a market leadership position is difficult in light of the many challenges facing today's healthcare marketplace.

Factors such as rising healthcare costs, increased competition, consumerism, and shifting demographics have caused the company to search for new and different ways of doing business as customers' healthcare needs expand. Inherent in these new and different business models is the need for more collaborative business practices, such as those outlined in *Getting to Yes*.

Different Times Call for Different Approaches

Today's healthcare marketplace is becoming increasingly consumer driven. Consumers expect the same level of service and convenience from health organizations that they receive from other companies, such as online retailers, banks, and investment firms. The Institute of the Future predicts that by the end of 2010, the health market will be an innovative economy demanding nontraditional offerings such as wellness, food, cosmetics, fashion, health information and even biosecurity.[1] Developing alliances with other organizations is one way the company is positioning itself for the health industry of the future. BCBSF's Alliance Group, a small department formed in 2001, enables business areas to develop strategic relationships with other entities.

Capitalizing on business opportunities through alliances enables BCBSF and other companies to pursue the risks and rewards of mutually compatible goals that would be difficult to achieve alone. Alliances include outsourcing partnerships, joint operating agreements, and joint ventures. These alliances provide the companies with access to new markets, capabilities, knowledge, and capital, along with the ability to share development and acquisition costs. Alliances also enable each party to bring products to market quickly in a cost-effective manner, which is critical in today's healthcare industry.

BCBSF's Alliance Group is experiencing positive outcomes by applying concepts outlined in *Getting to Yes* and is helping to move the organization more toward the management concepts of principled negotiation. Historically, however, businesses have not formally practiced or rewarded employees for these types of behaviors. For example, contract negotiations between companies often focus on each individual organization championing its own positions without considering the other's interests. Rewards are often linked to how well an organization's position is defended or "won" without giving thought to what bigger solutions could emerge by focusing on mutual gains.

Source: Friedman, R. A., & Shapiro, D. L. (1995). Deception and mutual gains bargaining: Are they mutually exclusive? *Negotiation Journal, 11*(3), 243–253.

Contract negotiations between companies often focus on each individual organization championing its own positions without considering the other's interests.

To expand beyond this type of traditional mind-set. BCBSF is seeking out ways to indoctrinate the concepts of principled negotiation throughout the entire organization. Principled negotiation, according to *Getting to Yes*, involves looking at issues based on their merits rather than defending stead fast positions. Its goal is to meet the underlying concerns of the parties. Shifting behavior away from a contest of wills toward this type of collaborative mindset can be challenging. To help make the transition, BCBSF is emphasizing three major steps: top-level executive support; a disciplined, programmed approach to alliance management; and reinforcement of desired behaviors and related outcomes.

BCBSF is further embracing the concepts of principled negotiation by working with Vantage Partners, a consulting firm? that partners with leading companies to institutionalize the capability to negotiate, build, and manage critical relationships effectively. Initially, BCBSF was seeking external perspectives for establishing superior alliance management capabilities. As part of that process, the company was introduced to mutual-gains behavior as a necessary component of developing successful alliances and other collaborative relationships. Vantage, founded by *Getting to Yes* coauthor Roger Fisher, helps its clients incorporate concepts from the book into their daily management practices. BCBSF has been working with Vantage Partners for approximately two years and has experienced increased trust and alignment with business associates as a result of implementing *Getting to Yes* concepts.

Putting the Concepts Into Practice

On a daily basis, BCBSF is learning first hand about the benefits of applying principled negotiation concepts in its alliances, as well as the pitfalls of what happens when the concepts are not applied consistently.

The company's movement toward applying *Getting to Yes* concepts is illustrated by the formation and management of a strategic alliance with a key competitor. Availity, L.L.C., a joint venture between subsidiaries of BCBSF and Humana, Inc., was conceived out of a desire to lower health costs, improve efficiencies, and provide more timely service to physicians and hospitals. Humana is one of the nation's leading publicly traded health benefits companies, with approximately seven million medical members in 19 states and Puerto Rico. The company offers coordinated health insurance coverage and related services to employer groups, government-sponsored plans, and individuals. Both Humana and BCBSF were trying to reach the same goal of improving the manner in which hospitals and physicians conducted business with their organizations.

The resulting joint venture, Availity, is an Internet-based solution that streamlines administrative workflow and improves communication between physicians, hospitals, payers, and pharmacies. Through a secure website, physicians can submit requests for payments, check the status of payments for services, verify patients' coverage and eligibility, and receive authorizations for referrals and other medical services online. This streamlined process replaces time-consuming manual interactions such as phone calls and paperwork. Currently, there are more than 9,000 physician offices, 208 hospitals, and more than 27,000 physicians in Florida using the Availity platform to process routine transactions.

The challenges of managing a joint venture with a key competitor could be daunting, if not impossible, without a shift in behavior by both parties to think of the other as a partner. Adding to the complexity is the organizations' differing corporate cultures, due in part to their structures: Humana is a for-profit publicly traded company, while BCBSF is a private, not-for-profit policyholder-owned mutual company. In addition, Humana serves a national market, while BCBSF primarily serves Florida.

The change in mindset to be collaborative vs. competitive in the development of this solution was critical to the formation and ongoing success of the joint venture.

Separating the People From the Problem

Although BCBSF had not yet institutionalized *Getting to Yes* concepts during the early formation of Availity, the company became more deliberate in following the concepts alter the alliance was operational and the organization became more aware of the benefits of principled negotiation. Looking back, despite a lack of formal training in *Getting to Yes* concepts, the company unconsciously implemented some of the concepts during the formation of Availity, which helped greatly in building the alliance.

As outlined in the book, separating the people from the problem requires emphasizing relationships by dealing directly with perceptions. BCBSF looked for ways to demonstrate its desire to collaborate by coming to the table with a sincere intent to build a relationship and determine common interests. Although it was not formally stated that the concepts of principled negotiation would be followed, the negotiators realized that forming a successful joint venture would require a collaborative approach. Both parties approached initial discussions in an open manner by listening rather than trying to debate or persuade. The two parties invested substantial amounts of time at the executive level to build the relationship. As the book says, prevention works best—and building this type of personal relationship "cushioned the people on each side against the knocks of negotiation." A strong relationship at the senior level continues to benefit the alliance today through subsequent governance activities.

Once Availity was established and operational, BCBSF began to interact with Availity as a business associate. This new relationship benefited from additional collaborative negotiation skills.

A significant challenge in implementing the concept of separating the people from the problem was the complex nature of the multiple relationships inherent in the Availity alliance. On the surface, it seemed as though only one relationship existed: the two initial owners. A closer look revealed several different relationships between BCBSF and Availity, ranging from BCBSF having an ownership interest in Availity, to BCBSF being the largest customer of Availity, to BCBSF being a vendor for Availity for technical development. Similarly, Humana has multiple relationships with Availity.

Many of the people involved in the formation had multiple accountabilities reflecting different aspects of the relationship. These multiple relationships and their corresponding accountabilities made it difficult to understand a person's perspective on a given issue. By mapping out the different relationships and corresponding accountabilities, ambiguity was reduced and problem solving improved. The exercise helped the parties understand the various perspectives and clarified accountabilities. Mapping out accountabilities in alliances is an approach that BCBSF is adopting which is starting to result in more favorable outcomes in learning to separate people from problems. In addition, when individuals have several roles, the organization is learning the value of having those individuals clearly communicate which role they are representing.

Focus on *Interests, Not Positions*

During initial discussions, Humana and BCBSF laid the groundwork to understand each other and see the situation from the other's perspective. General discussions about how each party viewed the industry, the future of healthcare, opportunities for collaboration, and anticipated future challenges helped both parties to identify and understand the other's interests regarding electronic connectivity. At later stages, for example, during the testing phase, this exercise served as a strong foundation in helping the parties to separate people from problems because there was an understanding of the other's viewpoints.

One challenge in focusing on interests rather than positions had to do with the two organizations having different approaches to testing the various capabilities of Availity. One party was accustomed to using a prescribed methodology for testing the various capabilities. The other, being a new organization, had processes that were still under development. The "positions" had to do with which organization's testing procedures to follow, but the underlying interests for both parties were identical: for Availity to be up and running error-free.

After holding a number of brainstorming sessions, it became evident that the parties could combine components of their methodologies to create a joint solution. By focusing on interests rather than positions, the parties realized that testing did not have to follow a certain methodology; it just had to result in error-free operations. By shifting the focus to interests rather than the positions, a new solution involving leveraging existing resources in a more effective manner was designed. A joint testing approach was agreed upon to meet mutual interests, and the parties were able to learn from each other in creating the solution.

Inventing Options for Mutual Gain

Getting to Yes says, "Skill at inventing options can be one of your most useful assets." This was especially evident in the formation of Availity. Before Availity was conceived, Humana and BCBSF came together and identified their interests regarding electronic connectivity. Both parties wanted to improve relationships with hospitals and physicians, reduce healthcare industry costs for consumers, and improve workflow for hospitals, physicians, and payers. The solution resulted in the joint venture that became Availity, which mutually benefited both organizations.

Getting to Yes *says, "Skill at inventing options can be one of your most useful assets."*

To assure that options for mutual gain were being sought throughout the development of Availity, relationship manager responsibilities were assigned to individuals to keep the best interests of the alliance in the forefront. Each party had someone who functioned in this capacity, which helped with the overall success of the alliance. Relationship manager roles are now included in many of BCBSF's alliances to serve as objective arbitrators between the parties and to look for options for mutual gain.

Additional Lessons Learned

BCBSF has learned a number of lessons about how to develop collaborative and productive alliance relationships.

In general, the company's experience has been that applying the concepts from *Getting to Yes* came more naturally at the executive/strategic level and required much more deliberation at subsequent levels. When alliance parties moved away from the conceptual level and into daily operations, implementing *Getting to Yes* concepts became more challenging. There are several reasons for this, including the experience levels of those involved, challenges with establishing strategic alignment throughout all levels, and varying reward systems at different levels of the organization. Among the steps that BCBSF is taking to address these challenges are: establishing alliance specialists at the middle-management level, and providing training regarding principled negotiation concepts at all levels of the organization.

Applying the concepts from Getting to Yes *came more naturally at the executive/strategic level and required much more deliberation at subsequent levels.*

Many of the lessons learned involve setting clear expectations in the beginning of the alliance formation. One is the importance of being deliberate in establishing ground rules for interacting with others early in the relationship before negotiation begins. Agreed-upon methods for communicating, making decisions, and handling conflicts, although somewhat awkward to create, are critical in relationship building and can help the parties to separate people from problems, especially when conflicts arise and emotions are high.

Along the same lines, a documented business plan that defines the market opportunity, product or service, sales and promotion approach, and validates financial forecasts can prove beneficial. The business plan is not only an effective tool for guiding the alliance; it also clarifies the interests and expectations of the parties.

In addition to a business plan, the alliance parties have found benefits in clearly defined strategies with supporting organizational goals. In addition, the company is establishing metrics that measure not only the business results of alliances but the quality and strength of the relationships as well.

Thinking Further 4.1

1. In your opinion when, if ever, is the use of deception acceptable in negotiations? Is it possible for deceptive tactics to not hurt the other party? How would you feel if you learned that deceptive tactics were used against you in a negotiation—even if the negotiation resulted in exceeding your target point? How would you have felt if the negotiation resulted in no deal?

2. Do you assume that the other party always uses some degree of deception in a negotiation? How would making that assumption change your tactics compared to assuming that the other party will not use deception?

Establishing early on what each party will contribute in terms of capital, resources, and revenue is also a lesson that the company has learned in forming successful alliances. Without this foundation, the parties may have differing viewpoints of what the other is contributing, which often leads to misunderstanding and can prevent the alliance from progressing smoothly.

Perhaps the biggest reward for implementing the concepts from *Getting to Yes* is being able to see first hand the benefits—meeting business goals, spending less time defending positions, creating a less stressful business environment, and meeting the underlying interests of both parties. The concepts have helped the company discover new ways of doing business—opening a new world of possibilities never imagined before.

Endnote

1. The Emerging Health Economy: A Special Report, SR-787 B. 2003. Menlo Park, CA: Institute for the Future.

Reading 4.2

3-D Negotiation Playing the Whole Game

David A. Lax and James K. Sebenius

WHAT STANDS between you and the yes you want? In our analysis of hundreds of negotiations, we've uncovered barriers in three complementary dimensions; the first is tactics; the second is deal design; and the third is setup.

Source: David A. Lax and James K. Sebenius, "3-D negotiation: Playing the whole game," *Harvard Business Review*, Nov 2003, 81(11), 65–74. Used by permission of Harvard Business School Publishing.

Each dimension is crucial, but many negotiators and much of the negotiation literature fixate on only the first two.

For instance, most negotiation books focus on how executives can master tactics-interactions at the bargaining table. The common barriers to yes in this dimension include a lack of trust between parties, poor communication, and negotiators' "hardball" attitudes. So the books offer useful tips on reading body language, adapting your style to the bargaining situation, listening actively, framing your case persuasively, deciding on offers and counteroffers, managing deadlines, countering dirty tricks, avoiding cross-cultural gaffes, and so on.

The second dimension, that of deal design—or negotiators' ability to draw up a deal at the table that creates lasting value—also receives attention. When a deal does not offer enough value to all sides, or when its structure won't allow for success, effective 2-D negotiators work to diagnose underlying sources of economic and non-economic value and then craft agreements that can unlock that value for the parties. Does some sort of trade between sides make sense and, if so, on what terms? Should it be a staged agreement, perhaps with contingencies and risk-sharing provisions? A deal with a more creative concept and structure? One that meets ego needs as well as economic ones?

Beyond the interpersonal and deal design challenges executives face in l-D and 2-D negotiations the 3-D obstacles—flaws in the negotiating setup itself. Common problems in this often-neglected third dimension include negotiating with the wrong parties or about the wrong set of issues, involving parties in the wrong sequence or at the wrong time, as well as incompatible or unattractive no-deal options. 3-D negotiators, however, reshape the scope and sequence of the game itself to achieve the desired outcome. Acting entrepreneurially, away from the table, they ensure that the right parties are approached in the right order to deal with the right issues, by the right means, at the right

time, under the right set of expectations, and facing the right no-deal options.

Former U.S. trade representative Charlene Barshefsky, who has negotiated with hundreds of companies, governments, and nongovernmental organizations to spearhead deals on goods, services, and intellectual property, characterizes successful 3-D negotiations this way: "Tactics at the table are only the cleanup work. Many people mistake tactics for the underlying substance and the relentless efforts away from the table that are needed to set up the most promising possible situation once you face your counterpart. When you know what you need and you have put a broader strategy in place, then negotiating tactics will flow."

3-D Negotiation in Practice

Even managers who possess superior interpersonal skills in negotiations can fail when the barriers to agreement fall in the 3-D realm. During the 1960s, Kennecott Copper's long-term, low-royalty contract governing its huge El Teniente mine in Chile was at high risk of renegotiation: the political situation in Chile had changed drastically since the contract was originally drawn up, rendering the terms of the deal unstable. Chile had what appeared to be a very attractive walk away option—or in negotiation lingo, a BATNA (best alternative to negotiated agreement). By unilateral action, the Chilean government could radically change the financial terms of the deal or even expropriate the mine. Kennecott's BATNA appeared poor: Submit to new terms or be expropriated.

Imagine that Kennecott had adopted a 1-D strategy focusing primarily on interpersonal actions at the bargaining table. Using that approach, Kennecott's management team would assess the personalities of the ministers with whom it would be negotiating. It would try to be culturally sensitive, and it might choose elegant restaurants in which to meet. Indeed,

Kennecott's team did take such sensible actions. But that approach wasn't promising enough given the threatening realities of the situation. Chile's officials seemed to hold all the cards: They didn't need Kennecott to run the mine; the country had its own experienced managers and engineers. And Kennecott's hands seemed tied: It couldn't move the copper mine, nor did it have a lock on downstream processing or marketing of the valuable metal, nor any realistic prospect, as in a previous era, of calling in the U.S. fleet.

Fortunately for Kennecott. its negotiators adopted a 3-D strategy and set up the impending talks most favorably. The team took six steps and changed the playing field altogether. First, somewhat to the government's surprise, Kennecott offered to sell a majority equity interest in the mine to Chile. Second, to sweeten that offer, the company proposed using the proceeds from the sale of equity, along with money from an Export-Import Rank loan, to finance a large expansion of the mine. Third, it induced the Chilean government to guarantee this loan and make the guarantee subject to New York state law. Fourth. Kennecott insured as much as possible of its assets under a U.S. guarantee against expropriation. Fifth, it arranged for the expanded mine's output to be sold under long-term contracts with North American and European customers. And sixth, the collection rights to these contracts were sold to a consortium of European, U.S., and Japanese financial institutions.

These actions fundamentally changed the negotiations. A larger mine, with Chile as the majority owner, meant a larger and more valuable pie for the host country: The proposal would result in more revenue for Chile and would address the country's interest in maintaining at least nominal sovereignty over its own natural resources.

Moreover, a broad array of customers, governments, and creditors now shared Kennecott's concerns about future political changes in Chile and were highly skeptical of Chile's capacity to run the mine efficiently over time. Instead of facing the original negotiation with Kennecott alone, Chile now effectively faced a multiparty negotiation with players who would have future dealings with that country—not only in the mining sector but also in the financial, industrial, legal, and public sectors. Chile's original BATNA—to unceremoniously eject Kennecott—was now far less attractive than it had been at the outset, since hurting Kennecott put a wider set of Chile's present and future interests at risk.

And finally, the guarantees, insurance, and other contracts improved Kennecott's BATNA. If an agreement were not reached and Chile acted to expropriate the operation, Kennecott would have a host of parties on its side. Though the mine was ultimately nationalized some years later, Chile's worsened alternatives gave Kennecott a better operating position and additional years of cash flow compared with similar companies that did not take such actions.

This case underscores our central message: Don't just skillfully play the negotiating game you are handed; change its underlying design for the better. It is unlikely that 1-D tactical or interpersonal brilliance at the table—whether in the form of steely gazes, culturally sensitive remarks, or careful and considered listening to all parties—could have saved Kennecott from its fundamentally adverse bargaining position. Yet the 3-D moves the company made away from tho table changed the negotiation's setup (the parties involved, the interests they saw at stake, their BATNAs) and ultimately created more value for all involved—much of which Kennecott claimed for itself.

How 3-D Moves Work

Successful 3-D negotiators induce target players to say yes by improving the proposed deal, enhancing their own BATNAs, and worsening those of the other parties. 3-D players intend such moves mainly to *claim* value for themselves but also to *create* value for all sides.

Claiming Value. 3-D negotiators rely on several common practices in order to claim value, including soliciting outside offers or bringing new players into the game, sometimes to create a formal or informal auction. After negotiating a string of alliances and acquisitions that vaulted Millennium Pharmaceuticals from a small startup in ~~1993~~ to a multibillion-dollar company less than a decade later, then-chief business officer Steve Holtzman explained the rationale for adding parties to the negotiations: "Whenever we feel there's a possibility of a deal with someone, we immediately call six other people. It drives you nuts, trying to juggle them all. But number one. It will change the perception on the other side of the table. And number two, it will change your self-perception. If you believe that there are other people who are interested, your bluff is no longer a bluff; it's real. It will come across with a whole other level of conviction." (For more on Millennium, see "Strategic Deal-making at Millennium Pharmaceuticals" HBS case 110.9-800-032.)

While negotiators should generally try to improve their BATNAs, they should also be aware that some of the moves they make might inadvertently worsen their walk away options. For instance, several years ago, we worked with a U.S. manufacturing firm on its joint-venture negotiations in Mexico. The company had already researched possible cultural barriers and ranked its three potential partners according to the competencies it found most desirable in those companies. After approaching the negotiations in a culturally sensitive spirit, and in what had seemed a very logical sequence, the U.S. team had nevertheless come to an impasse with the most attractive partner. The team abandoned those talks and was now deep into the process with the second most desirable candidate—and again, things were going badly. Imagine subsequent negotiations with the third, barely acceptable, partner if the second set of talks had also foundered—in an industry where all would quickly know the results of earlier negotiations.

As each set of negotiations failed, the U.S. firm's BATNA—a deal with another Mexican company or no joint venture at all—became progressively worse. Fortunately, the U.S. company opened exploratory discussions with the third firm in parallel with the second. This helped the U.S. company to discover which potential partner actually made the most business sense, to avoid closing options prematurely, and to take advantage of the competition between the Mexican companies. The U.S. business should have arranged the process so that the prospect of a deal with the most desirable Mexican partner would function as its BATNA in talks with the second most desirable partner, and so on. In short, doing so would have created the equivalent of a simultaneous four-party negotiation (structured as one U.S. firm negotiating in parallel with each of the three Mexican turns) rather than three sequential two-party negotiations. This more promising 3-D setup would have greatly enhanced whatever 1-D cultural insight and tactical ingenuity the U.S. firm could muster.

In addition to strengthening their own position, 3-D negotiators who add parties and issues to a deal can weaken the other side's BATNA. For instance, when Edgar Bronfman, former CEO of Seagram's and head of the World Jewish Congress, first approached Swiss banks asking them to compensate Holocaust survivors whose families' assets had been unjustly held since World War II, he felt stonewalled. Swiss banking executives saw no reason to be forthcoming with Bronfman; they believed they were on strong legal ground because the restitution issue had been settled years ago. But after eight months of lobbying by Bronfman, the World Jewish Congress, and others, the negotiations were dramatically expanded—to the detriment of the Swiss. The bankers faced a de facto coalition of interests that credibly threatened the lucrative Swiss share of the public finance business in states such as California and New York. They faced the divestiture by huge U.S. pension funds of stock in Swiss banks as well as in all

Swiss-based companies; a delay in the merger between Swiss Bank and UBS over the "character fitness" license vital to doing business in New York; expensive and intrusive lawsuits brought by some of the most formidable U.S. class-action attorneys; and the wider displeasure of the U.S. government, which had become active in brokering a settlement.

Given the bleak BATNA the Swiss bankers faced, it's hardly surprising that the parties reached an agreement, including a commitment from the Swiss bankers to pay $1.25 billion to survivors. It was, however, an almost unimaginable outcome at the beginning of the small, initially private game in which the Swiss seemed to hold all the cards.

Another way for negotiators to claim value is to shift the issues under discussion and the interests at stake. Consider how Microsoft won the browser war negotiations. In 1996, AOL was in dire need of a cutting-edge Internet browser, and both Netscape and Microsoft were competing for the deal. The technically superior, market-dominant Netscape Navigator vied with the buggier Internet Explorer, which was then struggling for a market foothold but was considered by Bill Gates to be a strategic priority. A confident, even arrogant, Netscape pushed for a technically based "browser-for-dollars" deal. In the book *aol.com,* Jean Villanueva, a senior AOL executive, observed, "The deal was Netscape's to lose. They were dominant. We needed to get what the market wanted. Most important, we saw ourselves as smaller companies fighting the same foe—Microsoft."

But when all was said and done, it was Microsoft that had etched a deal with AOL. The software giant would provide Explorer to AOL for free and had promised a series of technical adaptations in the future. Microsoft had also agreed that AOL client software would be bundled with the new Windows operating system. Microsoft—a direct competitor to AOL— would place the AOL icon on the Windows desktop right next to the icon for its own on-line

service, the Microsoft Network (MSN). AOL's position on "the most valuable desktop real estate in the world" would permit it to reach an additional 50 million people per year at effectively no cost, compared with its $40 to $80 per-customer acquisition cost incurred by "carpet bombing" the country with AOL disks. In effect, Bill Gates sacrificed the medium-term position of MSN to his larger goal of winning the browser war.

How did 3-D moves swing the negotiations in Microsoft's favor? Microsoft's Web browser was technically inferior to Netscape's, so the chances of Microsoft winning on those grounds were poor, regardless of its negotiating skills and tactics at the table. Instead Microsoft shifted the negotiations from Netscape's technical browser-for-dollars deal toward wider business issues on which it held a decisive edge. Rather than focus on selling to the technologists, Microsoft concentrated on selling to AOL's businesspeople. As AOL's lead negotiator and head of business development, David Colburn, stated in his deposition to the Supreme Court in 1998, "The willingness of Microsoft to bundle AOL in some form with the Windows operating system was a critically important competitive factor that was impossible for Netscape to match." Instead of trying to skillfully play a poor hand when dealing with party X on issues A and B, Microsoft changed the game toward a more compatible counterpart Y, emphasizing issues C, D, and E on which it was strong.

These examples of 3-D value-claiming moves conflict with the standard 1-D interpersonal approach to negotiation. Actions taken away from the table—sharply altering parties and issues, restructuring and resequencing the process, changing BATNAs—are not primarily about 1—D interpersonal skills but rather about enhancing the underlying setup of the negotiation itself.

Creating Value. By adding complementary parties or issues to the negotiating process, 3-D negotiators can not only claim value for themselves but also create more value for all parties involved. In *Co-opetition,* their influential book on business strategy, Adam Brandenburger and Barry Nalebuff explored the concept of the *Value net,* or the collection of players whose potential combination and agreement can create value. 3-D negotiators often facilitate in the development of such value nets. They scan beyond their specific transactions for compatible players with complementary capabilities or valuations, and they craft agreements that profitably incorporate these players.

The world of foreign affairs offers many examples in which potentially valuable bilateral deals can be impossible unless a third party with complementary interests is included. In a 1985 issue of *Negotiation Journal,* University of Toronto professor and international negotiation specialist Janice G. Stein wrote the following about the importance of Henry Kissinger's 3-D role in a crucial Middle East negotiation: "The circular structure of payment was essential to promoting agreement among the parties. Egypt improved the image of the United States in the Arab world, especially among the oil-producing states; the United States gave Israel large amounts of military and financial aid; and Israel supplied Egypt with territory. Indeed, a bilateral exchange between Egypt and Israel would not have succeeded since each did not want what the other could supply."

In an example from the business world, the owners of a niche packaging company with an innovative technology and a novel product were deep in price negotiations to sell the company to one of three potential buyers, all of them larger packaging operations. Instead of mainly working with its bankers to make the case for a higher valuation and to refine its at-the-table tactics with each packaging industry player, the niche player took a 3-D approach. Its broader analysis suggested that one of its major customers, a large consumer goods firm, might particularly value having exclusive access to the niche player's technologies and packaging products, so it brought the consumer goods firm into the deal. The move

uncovered a completely new source of potential value—and a much higher potential selling price. It also increased the pressure on the larger packaging companies: They would face more competition and might not be able offer the same kind of exclusive, customized packaging service to their customers.

The potential elements of a value net are not always obvious at the start of a negotiation. For example, a U.S.-European conservation group wished to preserve the maximum amount of rain-forest habitat in a South American country. From membership contributions and foundation support, the conservation group had U.S. dollars it could use (after converting the dollars to local currency at the official exchange rate) to buy development rights. The owner of the land and the conservation group negotiated hard and tentatively agreed on an amount of rain forest to be protected and a price per hectare based on local currency. But 3-D thinking ultimately improved the deal for all sides.

The host country was indebted in dollar-denominated bonds, which were trading at a 45% discount to their face value (given their perceived default risk). The country had to use scarce dollar-export earnings, needed for many pressing domestic purposes, to keep its debt-service obligations current; of course, interest payments were determined by the face value of the debt, not the bond discount. These facts suggested that more value could have been created by adding two other sets of players to the initial negotiation between the landowner and the conservation group.

In this green variant of a debt-for-equity swap, the conservation group bought country debt from foreign holders at the prevailing 45% discount. It then brought this debt to the country's Central Bank and negotiated its redemption for local currency at a premium between the discounted value of the debt and its full-dollar face value (up to an 82% premium over the discounted value). The conservation group then used this greater quantity of local currency from the Central Bank to buy more development rights from the landowner at a somewhat higher unit price.

This expanded four-party negotiation—sequentially involving the conservation group, international bondholders, the Central Bank, and the landowner—benefited everyone more than the best result possible in the initial negotiation between just the landowner and the conservation group. The bank was able to retire debt and cancel dollar-interest obligations, which were very costly to the country, using cheaper (to it) local currency without exporting more or diverting scarce export earnings. The conservation group was able to save more rain forests at the same dollar cost, and the landowner got a higher price in a currency it was better positioned to use.

To find complementary parties and issues, as the conservation group did, you should ask questions that focus on relative valuation. What uninvolved parties might highly value elements of the present negotiation? What outside issues might be highly valued if they were incorporated into the process? Are there any parties outside the immediate negotiations that can bear part of the risk of the deal more cheaply than the current players?

On the other hand, it is sometimes necessary to shrink—or at least stage—the set of involved issues, interests, and parties in order to create value. For example, rather than enter into a full multiparty process at the outset, an industry association that wants to negotiate a certain set of standards may benefit from first seeking agreement between a few dominant players, which would then serve as the basis for a later deal among the wider group. Or, negotiations to forge a multi-issue strategic alliance between two firms may be dramatically simplified by one side which instead proposes an outright acquisition.

Certainly, the form chosen for a transaction can dramatically affect the complexity of negotiations and the value to be had. The planned merger of equals by Bell Atlantic and Nynex would have required separate negotiations with regulatory authorities in each of the 13 states served by the companies. To avoid having to undergo politically charged negotiations at 13 different tables, the parties changed the game by creating a functionally equivalent structure in which Bell Atlantic was the nominal acquirer.

Indeed, it can be necessary to change the process, rather than the substance, of a negotiation. For example, two partners seeking to terminate their relationship may have difficulty determining exactly who gets what. But they may instead be able to agree to a special mechanism like the "Texas shoot-out" in which one side names a price at which it would be either a buyer (of the other's shares) or a seller (of its own shares) and the other side must respond. Often, changing the form of a negotiation by bringing in a skilled third-party mediator creates value. For example, two intensive mediation efforts by outside parties helped to finally thaw the frozen negotiations between Microsoft and the Justice Department. Many fundamentally different variants of mediation, arbitration, and other special mechanisms exist, but all are options to change the game itself rather than efforts to negotiate more effectively by purely interpersonal means.

Implementing a 3-D Negotiation Strategy

Sophisticated negotiators act in all three dimensions to create and claim value. While 3-D negotiators should play the existing game well, as tacticians and deal designers, they should also act as entrepreneurs, seeking to create a more favorable target game. They can do so by scanning widely to identify possible elements of a more favorable setup; "mapping backward" from the most promising structure for the deal to the current setup; and managing and framing the flow of information to improve their odds of getting to yes.

Scan widely. To act outside the box, one must first look outside the box. By searching beyond the immediate deal on the table for elements of a potential value net, 3-D negotiators can retrain their focus on complementary I capabilities and valuations that other players might add. Useful game-changing questions include: ~~Who outside the existing deal might most value an aspect of it? Who might minimize the costs of production, distribution, risk bearing, and so on?~~ Who might supply a piece missing from the current process? Which issues promise mutual advantage? What devices might bring such potential value-creating parties and issues into the deal? And at what point does complexity or conflict of interest between parties call for shrinking the scope of the negotiation? Scanning beyond the current game to claim value normally focuses on a parallel set of questions: Are there additional bidders or parties who could favorably alter BATNAs in other ways? Can certain issues be linked for leverage?

Such scanning should result in a map of all the actual and potential parties (including other interested groups within an organization, if necessary). You need to assess their actual and potential interests and BATNAs, as well as the difficulty and cost of gaining agreement with each party and the value of having its support. Your map should also identify the crucial relationships among the parties: who influences whom, who tends to defer to whom, who owes what to whom, who would find it costly to oppose an emerging agreement with key parties on board, and so on.

The founders of new ventures almost always need to scan widely in order to construct the most promising sequence of deals that lead to a self-sustaining company. Consider the situation WebTV 1 Networks founder Steve Perlman faced in the early and mid-1990s. He had obtained seed funding, developed the technology to bring the Web to ordinary television sets, created a prototype, and hired his core team. Running desperately low on cash, Perlman scanned widely and discovered an array of potential negotiating partners—ISPs, VCs, angel investors, industrial partners, consumer electronics businesses, content providers, manufacturers, wholesale and retail distribution channels, foreign partners, and the like. He needed to engage in 3-D analysis to determine the right subset of potential partners to create the most promising deals to build his company.

Map backward and sequence. It is helpful to think of the logic of backward mapping as being similar to the logic of project management. In deciding how to undertake a complex project, you start with the end point and work back to the present to develop a time line and critical path. In negotiation, however, the completed "project" should be a set of value-creating, sustainable agreements among a supportive coalition of parties.

For instance, when Perlman's WebTV was almost out of money, it might have seemed obvious that he should approach venture capital firms first. However, because VCs were deeply skeptical of consumer-electronics deals at that time, Perlman mapped backward from his VC target. He reasoned that a VC would find WebTV more appealing if a prominent consumer-electronics company were already on board, so Perlman embarked on a sequential strategy. After his first choice, Sony, turned him down, Perlman kept reasoning backward from his target. Finally, he was able to get Phillips on board. He then used Phillips to reopen and forge a complementary deal with Sony. Next he negotiated new venture money—at a far higher valuation—since both Sony and Phillips had signed on. With new money in the tank, it was fairly straightforward to thread a path of supporting agreements through manufacturers, wholesale and retail distribution channels, content providers, ISPs, and alliance partners abroad.

As the WebTV case suggests, a common problem for a would-be coalition builder is that approaching the most difficult—and perhaps most critical—party offers slim chances for a deal, either at all or on desirable terms. To improve the odds of getting to yes, figure out which partners you would ideally like to have on board when you initiate negotiations with the target party. As the answer to this question becomes clear, you have identified the penultimate stage. Continue mapping backward until you have found the most promising sequence of discussions. Consider the successful sequencing tactics of Bill Daley, President Clinton's strategist for securing congressional approval of the North American Free Trade Agreement as reported in a 1993 *New Yorker* article: "News might arrive that a representative who had been leaning toward yes had come out as a no. 'Weenie,' [Daley would] say. When he heard the bad news, he did not take it personally. . . . He'd take more calls. 'Can we find the guy who can deliver the guy? We have to call the guy who calls the guy who calls the guy.'"

Beyond pure sequencing, the 3-D negotiator can use the scope of the negotiation—how elements are added, subtracted, combined, or separated—to influence the chances of bringing each party on board. Issues can be added to make a deal more attractive (as Microsoft did with AOL) or a BATNA less attractive (as happened to the Swiss banks). And by not bringing on board a party to whom others have antipathy, negotiators can increase the probability of their success. That's what James Baker did when building the first Gulf War coalition; by omitting Israel from explicit membership in the group, he was able to attract moderate Arab states.

Manage the information flow. Some negotiations are best approached by gathering all affected parties together, fully sharing information, and brainstorming a solution to the shared problem. Frequently, however, vital 3-D questions involve deciding which stages of the process should be public or private as well as how information from one stage should spill over to or be framed at other stages.

A wry story illustrates the potential of such choices to set up a linked series of negotiations. A prominent diplomat once decided to help a charming and capable young man of very modest background from Eastern Europe. Approaching the chairman of the state bank, the statesman indicated that "a gifted and ambitious young man, soon to be the son-in-law of Baron Rothschild," was seeking a fast-track position in banking. Shortly thereafter, in a separate conversation with the baron, whom he knew to be searching for a suitable match for his daughter, the statesman enthusiastically described a "handsome, very capable young man who was making a stellar ascent at the state bank." When later introduced to the young swain, the dutiful daughter found him charming, with enviable talents and prospects, and acceptable to her father. When she said yes, the three-way deal allegedly went through—to everyone's ultimate satisfaction.

Setting aside the dubious factual base and ethics of this negotiation, notice how the diplomat's 3-D actions set up the most promising game for his purposes. By separating and sequencing the stages of the process, as well as opportunistically framing his message at each juncture, the statesman created a situation that fostered an otherwise most unlikely outcome. Of course, had the banker, the baron, the daughter, and the young man been initially thrown together in a face-to-face meeting, it is doubtful that even the statesman's suave 1-D approach could have closed the deal.

Analogously, potential investors should be wary of the common tactic of separating deals to close both: for instance, getting investor A to commit funds based on the commitment of "savvy investor" B, when B has indeed committed, but only on the informal (and wrong) understanding that "reputable investor" A has unconditionally agreed to do so.

Negotiations to assemble land for a real estate project offer another good example of the importance of staging the release of information. Early knowledge of a developer's plans can be quite valuable to landowners in the target area. Since landowners may use this knowledge to extract maximum price concessions in later stages of assembly, the need for secrecy and separation of the individual negotiations is usually obvious. Indeed, the choice of which parcel to buy first, second, and so on, may depend on the relative odds that a given purchase will leak the developer's intentions as well as whether the parcels already obtained would permit some version of the project to go ahead, or whether they would be useless without a later acquisition.

Indeed, a 3-D player's ability to determine whether a related negotiation happens before or after his own—as well as whether the results become public—can greatly influence the outcome. For example, according to a 1985 article in *International Studies Quarterly,* while the United States was in separate talks with Japan, Hong Kong, and Korea over textile trade agreements, a Korean negotiator told the U.S. representatives, "We'll ask Hong Kong to go first, then see what they get." The Koreans apparently regarded Hong Kong officials as highly skilled negotiators, with better language skills for dealing with the Americans. An observer reports that, "After waiting for Hong Kong and Japan to go first, Seoul asked for the features they had secured and then also held out for a bit more." In essence, the order chosen by the Americans (as encouraged by the Koreans) revealed information about the U.S. approach that was of great value to the Koreans. One wonders whether the Americans should have rethought the sequence and started with Seoul.

That negotiators should be good listeners, persuaders, and tacticians is a given. But beyond perfecting these 1-D skills, negotiators should also be innovative 2-D deal designers who have mastered the principles for crafting value-creating agreements. And the third, often-missing dimension—actions taken to change the scope and sequence of the game itself—can be crucial to a negotiation that would otherwise be completely out of tactical reach.

Negotiators must take care to keep sophisticated 3-D moves from blurring into the unethical and manipulative. Yet without 3-D actions, coalitions vital to many worthy initiatives could never have been built.

To create and claim value for the long term, great negotiators should be at home in all three dimensions. To do anything less is to risk playing a one- or two-dimensional strategy in a three-dimensional world.

Thinking Further 4.2

1. What are the three dimensions in 3-D negotiation? What implementation strategies do the authors suggest? Would these strategies be helpful in negotiating salary and benefits for a job? Why or why not?

2. Describe one or two personal situations in which you believe knowing how to use 3-D negotiating effectively would be beneficial to you.

CHAPTER 5

Closing Deals

Persuading the Other Party to Say Yes

Preparation builds the foundation for your negotiation. Distributive and integrative strategies provide alternative means for achieving your goals and satisfying interests. The remaining fundamental component of the negotiation process is about closing deals or persuading the other party to say yes. Even if your arguments are very compelling, the other party may be hesitant to agree with you, for a variety of reasons. Closing deals is about overcoming the other party's objections to your proposals and making it easier to accept them. Failing to accomplish these objectives may cause your negotiation to collapse and thereby preclude both parties from achieving a satisfactory outcome.

INTENDED BENEFITS OF THIS CHAPTER

When you finish reading this chapter, you should be able to

1. Explain the nature of closing deals, and why this is an important part of the negotiation process.
2. Discuss the most common objections and explain why they occur and how to overcome them.
3. Recognize various closing tactics, their respective benefits, and describe how to use them to close deals effectively.

THE ESSENCE OF CLOSING DEALS

Negotiators, and disputants in mediation and arbitration cases, often seem to spend most of their time trying to convince the other side that they are right. In arbitration, this makes sense because convincing the arbitrator that you are right likely means that he or she will support your claim. In negotiation and mediation, however, successfully closing a deal or settling a dispute requires you to convince the other party why or how your proposal satisfies his or her interests and warrants acceptance. This may sound like more integrative bargaining, but it is really about human nature. Why would a rational person agree to your proposal if it does not satisfy his or her interests? Clearly, your proposals must satisfy your own interests. You should not extend offers that do not. It is not enough, however, to merely satisfy your own interests. One of the critical ingredients for getting to yes is helping the other party understand why or how your offers satisfy his or her interests. How you close a deal is also important for ensuring that the terms of your agreement are implemented effectively. Reading 5.1 at the end of this chapter demonstrates why this is so.

Closing is the culmination of the negotiation process, but it should not be viewed as a formal stage that only comes at the end of the negotiation (Ingram, LaFarge, Avila, Schwepker, & Williams, 2004). As odd as this may sound, closing begins when you prepare because you are likely to craft at least some of your proposals while you are preparing. You must be convinced that they satisfy the other party's interests—before you make them. If you are not confident that they do, how will you convince the other negotiator that they do?

During the middle stage of a negotiation, when the parties are exchanging offers and counteroffers, objections are likely to arise. You make an offer and the other party rejects it. He or she may claim that your offer is unacceptable for many reasons. Some negotiators get discouraged when this happens, especially if they have devoted substantial effort to formulating the proposal and supporting it. To state the obvious, you would prefer that he or she accept your proposal. Objections, however, are better than having the other party laugh and walk away because your proposal is so far off the mark that it is not even worth discussing. Objections signal that he or she is interested in your offer, though not yet convinced that it is acceptable. View objections as questions for which adequate answers have not been given.

THE MOST COMMON OBJECTIONS

Of the many reasons why a negotiator might object, the following seem to be the most common.

It Is Not My Idea

Your proposal is more likely to be rejected if it was not invented during the negotiation and the other party was not involved in developing it. Negotiation is not merely a technical problem-solving exercise. It is also a political process in which each negotiator must participate in crafting the agreement. Most people do not like to be told what to do or that something is good for them. Nor do they like decisions or solutions imposed upon them without discussing them first. Employees reject change, for example, even that which would benefit them, because they are not involved with identifying problems that would clarify the need to change, they are not involved in designing the change intervention, and they are not involved with implementing the change. Suggestions for overcoming this follow.

- Ask the other negotiators for ideas rather than telling them why your solution is good or right, and then build on those that seem most constructive. This should allow you to move toward a beneficial solution

- Invite constructive criticism of your proposals as you are developing them. Seek the other negotiator's feedback and suggestions for improving the proposal, not a "yes" or "no" decision. After eliciting these suggestions, develop a draft proposal that incorporates these suggestions and run it by him or her again. This should help you build consensus (Ury, 1993).

Unmet Interests

Even if you involve the other negotiator in developing the solution, it may still be rejected because it fails to satisfy all of his or her interests. This should not be surprising because we negotiate to satisfy our needs—the importance of interests was discussed in both Chapters 3 and 4. Negotiation in Action 5.1 presents another example.

Finding out why rejected critical to move forward?

NEGOTIATION IN ACTION 5.1

Campbell Soup Co. was trying to buy a very successful restaurant from its owner-manager because it wanted to create a chain of such restaurants. Campbell's negotiator began by making what he thought was a very fair offer but it was rejected. Over the ensuing six weeks, he made several additional offers that were even more favorable to the owner. They, too, were rejected. He blamed the impasse on the owner's difficult personality. He was close to giving up and walking away unsatisfied. Before he did, he decided to change his approach and give it one last try. In their next meeting, he began asking probing questions and encouraged the owner to discuss his reservations. The owner explained that the restaurant is his baby, it made him famous and he's not sure he wants to work for the Campbell Soup Company after working for himself and running his own show for all of these years.

The offer to have him sell the business and work for Campbell's clearly did not satisfy his very strong interests—autonomy and recognition. Campbell's negotiator thought for a while and then asked him if he would be willing to form a joint venture with the Campbell Soup Company. Acknowledging that this would be a bit unusual, he explained that, "Rather than being an employee, we will both own part of the restaurant. You will be the President of the joint venture. You will stay in charge but we will buy your part of the business at some point in the future. The longer you stay, the more we will pay for your part." The seller reacted positively and they soon reached an agreement (adapted from Ury, 1993).

In addition to the suggestions presented earlier for identifying all of the other negotiator's interests, you must explore his or her perceptions. There is undoubtedly a logical connection between his or her objection ad your proposal.

Needs other than money must also be satisfied. All too often, we get hung up on money or price. Other interests such as recognition, autonomy, affiliation, respect, status, and so on are equally powerful. In a situation like the one described in Negotiation in Action 5.1, you must consider the organization's interests and the negotiator's personal interests. All must be satisfied if you want to reach an agreement. Finally, do not blindly assume that your interests are incompatible or otherwise fall victim to the mythical fixed pie. If there are two or more issues or interests that are prioritized differently, you can find integrative solutions—mutually beneficial tradeoffs, bridging solutions (Ury, 1993).

The Other Party Is Losing Face

Audiences, especially if they are constituents to whom the other negotiator is accountable, make saving face particularly important. Nobody wants their name, image, or reputation damaged by what happens at the table. Making a mistake and being taken advantage of make everyone hesitate before saying yes, and these are both about saving face. Backing down from a strong commitment or merely changing positions may also cause someone to feel like he or she is losing face. Helping him or her save face can be accomplished by offering new information that has not yet been rejected or dismissed, demonstrating how circumstances have changed, securing the opinion of a neutral third party, or presenting a different objective criterion. These should all help you demonstrate the fairness of your offer. You could also help him or her prepare the presentation of the outcome to the constituents or actually help present it. Anticipating critics' arguments and developing persuasive counterarguments or rebuttals, or reframing a retreat as an advance by giving the other side credit for a wise agreement that works for both sides, are examples of how you could help (Ury, 1993).

Too Much Information Too Fast

Presenting the other party with a complex proposal and requiring an answer in a very short period of time may engender objections rather than acceptances because he or she is overwhelmed. Even if the decision is too big and the time allowed is too short, you will overwhelm the other party and probably not reach an agreement. Even if your proposal satisfies all of his or her interests and does not cause him or her to lose face, you simplify the process or the decision to facilitate reaching an agreement. Break the situation into component parts and proceed step by step. Securing tentative agreements on the first step, then the second step, and so on should make it easier to secure an agreement on the whole proposal. Alternatively, propose treating your idea as an experiment that will be tried for a brief period of time or only in one department and then reevaluated. Only if it produces the desired results will it be adopted for a longer time period or implemented more fully throughout the organization. Instead of trying to secure an agreement on each step or part, withhold your request for agreement until the end. This will ease any fear the other party has that you will keep asking for more and more if he or she agrees to one step or part of the proposal (Ury, 1993).

Since the rate of making demands and concessions increases in the last part of a negotiation, another way to simplify the process and the decision is to slow down and make sure your communication, both written and oral, is clear. Instead of rushing and hurrying the other side, back off and give him or her a chance to think and to consult with constituents (Ury, 1993). *Give time to think & commit*

It Is Too Expensive or I Cannot Afford It

This is plausible—what you are proposing may exceed the other party's budget. Alternatively, it may suggest the other party is not yet convinced that the value of your proposal exceeds its cost. One simple suggestion for overcoming or even preempting cost objections involves framing. Framing will be discussed in Chapter 7. For now, think of it as how you present your proposal rather than what you present. Framing or presenting the cost of your proposal as a cost per unit or cost per time period (day or month) instead of the total cost may be more palatable, psychologically. If you have purchased a home, the following example may bring back memories. Imagine that a couple wants to borrow $250,000 at 5% for 30 years. The loan officer could tell them that they will owe $1,342 per month, or that they will owe $483,138. Most people find it easier to say yes to $1,342 per month than $483,138, even though both numbers are accurate. Realtors prepare first-time home buyers for this to avoid panic that could jeopardize the deal.

Another approach for dealing with this type of objection is to focus your counterpart's attention on the value of your proposal relative to its cost. You could emphasize how much the other party will save over time relative to his or her costs rather than simply addressing how much it costs now. Helping the other party visualize the value generated by your proposal once it is implemented might also serve this purpose. This requires you to focus the other party's attention on what it does for him or her rather than on what it costs. This may help you persuade him or her to say yes (Ingram et al., 2004; Zigler, 1984). Negotiation in Action 5.2 demonstrates how this might work.

NEGOTIATION IN ACTION 5.2

Stryker Medical sells beds and stretchers to hospitals and emergency rooms. They are never the lowest cost option and they almost always hear the price objection. They overcome these objections by educating their clients: their products last 25–50% longer than their competitors' products. They demonstrate, with evidence, that their product will still be around 5–10 years after their competitors' products have been discarded. If one of the stretchers costs $1,500 more than their competitors' stretcher, they can break down the price over the entire life of the stretcher and actually show a savings over time (adapted from Ingram et al., 2004).

It Does Not Work for Me or I Do Not Want It

This objection suggests the other party does not yet understand how your proposal solves the problem, capitalizes on the opportunity, or satisfies his or her interests. Overcoming this objection requires you to illustrate or demonstrate how your proposal will help. Drawing diagrams or providing word pictures that demonstrate the positive outcomes that the other party will realize when your proposal is implemented will help him or her visualize how it helps. Likewise, demonstrating what these positive outcomes will look like once your proposal is operational will clarify how it serves his or her purposes (Girard,1989; Ingram et al., 2004).

I Want to Think About It or I Need More Time

If your proposal is complex, the other party may need time to think it over. But how many times do we say this to salespeople even when the decision is simple? Perhaps we do not want to make a snap decision or we want him or her to leave us alone for a while. Whatever the reason, it will be much harder to persuade someone to accept your offer if he or she walks away to think about it. Conversely, it is easier to overcome objections, including this one, if you have an opportunity to influence the other negotiator's thinking. This will not happen if he or she leaves. This objection suggests that your counterpart is not clear, or confident, about the merits of your proposal (Ingram et al., 2004). You can overcome this by asking if he or she has all of the information that is required or needed to make a decision. If the answer is no, provide whatever information is needed to clarify the efficacy of your proposal. If, on the other hand, the answer is yes, ask, "Why won't you decide now? If you have all of the information you need, how will more time help you make a better decision?" The scenario described in Negotiation in Action 5.3 is illustrative.

NEGOTIATION IN ACTION 5.3

John Marcum is a financial planner for Merrill Lynch. He works with many individuals who have different needs and concerns. When John hears clients say "I need to think about it for awhile," he responds with, "What part do you need to think about?" He then follows this up with, "What information do you need that will help you make your decision?" He may follow this up with additional probing questions. John also reassures his clients that they are making a wise decision. "I never ask for an order until I'm sure they are comfortable with all of the information I've presented" (adapted from Ingram et al., 2004).

Overcoming this objection might be even easier if delaying the decision will impose an additional cost. If your proposal satisfies his or her interests, emphasizing the costs that will be incurred or the decrease in value that will be gained if the decision is delayed should introduce a sense of urgency into his or her decision making. Explaining that a price increase is coming soon, and that he or she will lose the current price if an agreement is not signed by then, may clarify the value that will be lost if the decision is delayed.

I Do Not Believe You Will Comply

Negotiators sometimes hesitate to accept your offer because they question your willingness or ability to follow through on what you have promised. This suggests a lack of trust or questions about your ability to deliver. If you encounter such skepticism you can share past experiences that demonstrate your trustworthiness and your capabilities. Recounting similar deals or disputes and how you satisfactorily honored those commitments should enhance the other party's confidence that you are willing and able to comply. Securing testimonials from your satisfied clients detailing how you helped them solve similar problems will be even more compelling (Girard, 1989; Ingram et al., 2004; Zigler, 1984). Box 5.4 demonstrates how testimonials can help.

The root cause of most objections is fear—negotiators are afraid of making a mistake or that the other side is taking advantage of them. As noted earlier, these are about losing face. To overcome these

NEGOTIATION IN ACTION 5.4

Fanny owns and operates The Bistro, a small restaurant and catering company. One of her biggest clients, a tour company for which The Bistro provides lunches every day, is now planning a large banquet. When this client rejected Fanny's bid to cater it, she asked, "Why?" The client claimed, "The Bistro's operation is too small to handle an event of this size." Instead of accepting this argument, Fanny recounted a number of events of similar size that The Bistro had catered. She also explained that several of these clients had asked her to cater subsequent events. She then provided the names and phone numbers of these satisfied clients and encouraged the tour company to contact them. After reconsidering, the tour company accepted The Bistro's bid to cater the banquet.

fears and help him or her save face and avoid looking foolish, you must also persuade the other party that your proposals satisfy his or her interests. Even if you satisfactorily address and overcome these objections, he or she may still need an excuse to say yes or a nudge to finally accept the deal. Closing tactics provide the nudge or the incentive to take that final step.

CLOSING DEALS

As indicated in Reading 5.2 at the end of this chapter, even perfectly executed negotiations sometimes get stuck at "maybe" instead of "yes." Closing the deal is required to overcome this by persuading the other negotiator to say yes.

When Should You Attempt to Close?

It is appropriate to close the deal when you are confident the other party understands that the value of your offer exceeds its cost (Girard, 1989). Different signals may provide useful guidance.

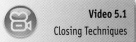

Video 5.1
Closing Techniques

- Asking open-ended questions about your proposal, or more specific questions about particular features of your proposal, will help you discern where he or she stands.

- A decrease in the number or intensity of objections provides more insight. If he or she initially had many objections but now has few, it is time to think about closing.

- If he or she acknowledges that your proposal has potential after initially indicating it would be impossible to accept it, you are moving in the right direction.

- If the nature of the other party's questions changes from concerns about whether your proposal will satisfy his or her interests to how it will actually work when it is operational, it may be possible to close the deal. Examples include questions pertaining to how the equipment actually works or how to operate it, how or when it might be delivered, when it will be ready for pick up, or how it should be implemented.

- Comments such as, "I like that size," or "That will get the job done," or "The price is lower than I thought it would be," or "I did not realize you delivered every day" are all signals that the other party may be ready to close (Ingram et al., 2004).

CLOSING TACTICS

If the aforementioned responses or comments suggest that he or she is ready close, there are a variety of tactics available for persuading the other party to say yes.

Ask the Other Party to Agree

This straightforward tactic requires you to ask the other party to agree because negotiators sometimes fail to do so.

Split the Difference or Compromise

Splitting the difference or *compromising* may be the most comment closing tactic. As the names imply, this is about dividing in half the difference between each of your last offers. Assume that you have been negotiating for some time. Each side has made some concessions and you find yourselves quite close to an agreement, but you and the other party are both reluctant to take the final step and accept the offer. To avoid walking away without a deal, you might say something like, "We have been at this for a while and we are very close. It would be a shame to spend this much time and get this close and still not agree. "Why don't we split the difference and call it a deal?" If his or her final offer is $120/unit and your final offer is $130/unit, this would let you walk away with a deal of $125/unit. Consider one modification to this approach. If the other party tries to split the difference first, try to split it again. If you are successful, you will claim more value for yourself. If you are unsuccessful, you allow him or her to leave feeling like the winner, or at least like he or she got a better deal (Dawson, 1995). This may prove to be very beneficial for compliance purposes or for future deals that you negotiate with him or her.

Video 5.2
Compromise impacts
the negotiation outcome

Negotiators must exercise caution when using this tactic. Splitting the difference between the last two offers made is not necessarily an even split if opening offers were not equidistant from some theoretically correct settlement point, or if the concessions made by both parties were not equal. Assume you are selling a piece of property. The theoretically correct price is $75,000, your opening offer was $85,000 and the buyer's opening offer was $60,000. If you each made concessions totaling $10,000 before you split the remaining $5,000 difference, you would settle on a price of $72,500. Alternatively, assume your opening offer was $85,000 and the buyer's was $65,000, you conceded $10,000 while the buyer conceded only $5,000. If you agreed to split the remaining $5,000 difference, you would again settle on a price of $72,500. In both cases, splitting the difference would cause you to "lose" by settling for less than the "correct" price. Making matters worse, the theoretically correct price is rarely known, if it even exists. The point is simply that the chances of making mistakes by splitting the difference must be considered.

Comparison

This closing tactic requires you to delineate the benefits the other party will derive from your proposal and from his or her own proposal, and compare them. Alternatively, you can compare the likely costs that will be incurred if each proposal is accepted. Making these benefits or costs explicit and comparing them should demonstrate the advantages, for the other side, of your proposal. Obviously, you only want to make these comparisons if you are confident that the benefits of your proposal are greater, or that the costs of your proposal are lower. The cost-benefit.

Cost-Benefit or Balance Sheet

This modifies the comparison close. It entails explicitly and jointly listing the benefits of your proposal on one side of a piece of paper and then asking the other party to list the costs on the other side. Obviously, the benefit side must clearly outweigh the cost side for this to work (Girard, 1989; Ingram et al., 2004; Zigler, 1984).

Multiple Equivalent Offers

As noted in Chapter 4, providing the other party with choices may also be an effective way to close the deal. Since most people prefer to have choices, offering alternatives, or extending multiple equivalent offers simultaneously, should help you close. An example is included in Negotiation in Action 5.5.

NEGOTIATION IN ACTION 5.5

A software company presented three equivalent software packages to its clients at once: a $1 million package with payment due in 30 days, the same software for $1.5 million with payment due in 120 days, or an enhanced package for $1.35 million with a 30-day payment window. Customers responded well to this strategy and the company's profits grew (Medvec & Galinsky, 2005).

Some limits are necessary, however, because too many choices can cause decision paralysis. Many people claim to want as much information as possible before they make a decision and this includes as many choices as possible. The example presented in Negotiation in Action 5.6, however, demonstrates that too many choices can be overwhelming. Simply put, if too many options are presented, deciding not to make any decision at all may be a relief.

NEGOTIATION IN ACTION 5.6

A tasting booth of high-quality jams was set up in a gourmet food store. On one weekend, shoppers were able to taste six different jams. The following weekend, twenty-four different jams were available for tasting. All of the jams were available for purchase on both weekends. The larger selection attracted more people to the tasting table, though the number of jams people tasted was about the same on both weekends. Interestingly, 30% of the shoppers exposed to six different jams bought a jar, but only 3% of those exposed to 24 jams did so. The moral of the story is that some choices, say two or three, are beneficial. But too many choices may overwhelm or irritate the other party, thus preventing him or her from saying yes (Iyengar & Lepper, 2000).

Sweeteners

Using sweeteners is, in a sense, akin to reverse nibbling (nibbling was discussed in Chapter 3). Offering a final concession if the other party accepts your offer is intended to "sweeten" the deal enough to give him or her an excuse to say yes. To illustrate, a couple went to their favorite furniture store to buy a dining room table and chairs. They found one they liked but it cost more than they had planned to spend. While thinking about it, the owner of the store offered to include a vase the couple liked, at no charge, if they agreed to buy the table that day. They now own the table, six chairs, and a vase. When using this tactic, be careful not to offer something that is so costly to you that it diminishes the total value of the deal too much. A sweetener should be of sufficient value to persuade the other party to agree without materially reducing the value of the deal for you.

Default Options

Negotiators should have an easier time persuading the other party to agree when their proposals happen to be the default option. Sometimes called the status quo bias, default outcomes are persuasive because they favor the status quo. Simply put, people are more likely to be concerned about the risk of change than they are about the risk of failing to change—they are motivated to preserve the status quo even if they regard the consequences of the change to be an improvement (Baron & Jurney, 1993; Ritov & Baron, 1990). Examples of the default option abound. When car rental agencies include insurance unless you decline it, and software vendors include recommendations to click "next" to install, they are using defaults to persuade you to say yes. Negotiation in Action 5.7 provides another example—how defaults work with organ donations.

NEGOTIATION IN ACTION 5.7

In some European countries, the default option is to donate organs—you will donate unless you take the necessary steps to opt out. Donation rates in these countries range from 86% to 99%. In other European countries, the default option is to not donate—you will not donate unless you take the necessary steps to do so—donation rates range from 4% to 28% (Johnson & Goldstein, 2003). Similar effects have been found when employees invest in retirement savings programs at work (Goldstein, Johnson, Herrmann, & Heitmann, 2008; Samuelson & Zeckhauser, 1988).

Designing defaults can be complex. Finding solutions or outcomes that satisfy your interests and those of the other party requires careful thought and preparation. Consider developing them in ways that adapt to the initial decisions made by the other negotiator. When customers use automobile websites to configure the vehicle they want to purchase, for example, early decisions often inform later ones. The customer's initial choices indicate his or her preferences and the site responds by presenting subsequent choices that "fit" with the early ones. Computer manufacturers/retailers also utilize defaults. Customers of Dell, for instance, may initially choose a protection package such as DellCare Premium, Plus, or Value. This choice then results in several pre-selected defaults for the subsequent choices. This approach avoids alienating price-sensitive consumers with the sticker shock of high initial prices, and it spares price-insensitive business customers the hassle of upgrading numerous options to get the comprehensive support they need.

OTHER CLOSING TACTICS TO CONSIDER (IF THE RELATIONSHIP MATTERS LESS)

Other closing tactics may be inappropriate if the relationship matters. People typically like to buy, but they do not like to be sold, and these tactics may create the impression that you are selling them (Ingram et al., 2004).

Assume the Close

Many of us have experienced salespeople assuming the close. Here, you literally assume that the other side has agreed even though he or she has not. Writing a purchase order before the other side has explicitly accepted your last offer is an example. You might also suggest that, "Once we have implemented the new program, we can fine tune it to correct any bugs that exist," again before he or she has explicitly accepted your proposal (Zigler, 1984).

Sometimes this tactic is augmented with an assumptive question. Imagine that you are negotiating disciplinary action with an employee's union officer. Before he has actually agreed to a two-day suspension for the employee's infraction, you might ask, "Should we begin the two-day suspension Monday or Thursday?" Alternatively, if you and the union officer are negotiating an overtime pay adjustment, he might ask you, "Will the overtime adjustment be included in this paycheck or the next one?" before you have explicitly agreed to it.

Exploding Offers

These use deadlines and time pressure to close deals. More specifically, offers are made that must be accepted quickly or they will explode. If, for example, an employer extends an attractive job offer to a candidate today that must be accepted by tomorrow at noon, it is extending an exploding offer. If the candidate does not capitulate and accept it by then, it expires. They are used to limit the recipient's choices, preclude him or her from cultivating alternatives, and comparing or "shopping" the offer. These offers are usually made when there are considerable power asymmetries. They harm relationships because the short deadline is often arbitrarily imposed and many find them disrespectful (Robinson, 1995).

If you are subjected to an exploding offer, you may be able to avoid the dilemma of simply capitulating or rejecting the offer. Even if your efforts to refocus the negotiation on interests fails, consider accepting the offer, provisionally. The provision must be reasonable, but it can be anything that will extend the negotiation beyond the deadline. The recipient of the aforementioned job offer might accept the offer, for example, "provided I get to meet the person I will be working for and my coworkers and they proved to be satisfactory." This is about withdrawing from the agreement if a satisfactory outcome is not forthcoming, not about wiggling out of an agreement made in good faith (Robinson, 1995).

Sequential Questions

A negotiator using the sequential questions close asks a series of related questions. The first one is very simple and assuredly will be answered in the affirmative. Subsequent questions lead logically and incrementally from this point to the negotiator's desired end. These questions must also be answered affirmatively, given the answer to the first question and our very strong desire to be consistent. Consistency will be discussed in more detail in Chapters 7 and 8. For now, suffice it to say that it is a manipulative tactic and risks harming the relationship.

CONCLUSION AND IMPLICATIONS FOR PRACTICE

It is obviously preferable for you to have the other party accept your offer. Objections, however, should not cause undue angst, as long as the other party stays at the table. Their reluctance to agree can emanate from various sources – insufficient involvement in developing the solution; loss of face; your offer does not solve their problem or satisfy all of their interests; they need more time to think about it; the solution appears too expensive; and others. Your task is to understand and overcome these objections and persuade the other party to say yes. Some think this is something that only happens at the end of the negotiation, and the way to close effectively is to use the best closing tactic. A more accurate view is that closing requires you to orchestrate adequate preparation, the effective execution of the appropriate strategy, and overcome objections by demonstrating that the value of your proposal is greater than its cost, and that it satisfies the other party's interests. Closing tactics are a very small piece of the negotiation puzzle and are required mainly when the other party needs to be persuaded to say yes. The following suggestions should help you close effectively.

1. View objections objectively. Ask open-ended questions to enhance your understanding of the other party's perspectives about and attitudes toward all or key parts of your proposal. When the other negotiators continue to engage in the process after objecting to your offer, it suggests that they are still interested but not yet convinced of your offer's merits. Interpreting objections in this way is more appropriate and effective than attributing blame to the other negotiators' personality, tactics, or lack of intelligence.

2. Learn to identify the signals to close. They include a decrease in the number or intensity of the other party's objections or a change in the nature of their comments and questions (from whether your offer will satisfy their interests to how it can be delivered or implemented, how it will work, or how it must be operated).

3. Educate the other party to clarify how the value of your proposal exceeds its costs, and how or why it satisfies his or her interests. Research shows that salespeople and negotiators are more successful when they find good matches between the product or service they are offering and the client's needs (Sharma, Levy, & Evanschetzky, 2007; Sharma, Levy, & Kumar, 2000).

4. Reframe your offer in different ways if the other party is hesitant to accept. There are several ways to convey the value of your proposal. Examples include discussing cost per unit or time period rather than total cost; savings to be realized relative to a competitive product or service because yours service will last longer or is more productive. Using diagrams or word pictures to convey how your solution will look like when it is operational and how it will solve the other party's problems.

5. Know when to give an extra push and when to back off. Once you have overcome the other party's objections, it may still be necessary to give them a push to say yes, perhaps to overcome their fears of losing face, being taken advantage of, or making a mistake. But sometimes you need to back off. Some evidence suggests that "closing early and often" actually hinders efforts to close (Brashear,

Bellenger, Barksdale, & Ingram, 1997; Hawes, Strong & Winick, 1996). While there is no one best closing tactic, you are more likely to benefit from using tactics that avoid alienating the other party and that preserve the relationship.

6. Ensure that the terms agreed upon are practical, and that they can be implemented easily and effectively. Despite the care and creativity with which negotiations are crafted, implementation can fail miserably unless effective implementation strategies are part of the deal.

STUDENT STUDY SITE

Visit the Student Study Site at **www.sagepub.com/hames** for additional learning tools.

KEY TERMS

Alternatives

Assuming the close

Assumptive question

Balance sheet (aka cost-benefit) closing tactic

Closing tactics

Comparison closing tactic

Compromise (aka split the difference) closing tactic

Cost-benefit (aka balance sheet) closing tactic

Default option

Exploding offers

Multiple equivalent offers

Sequential questions

Split the difference (aka compromise) closing tactic

Status quo bias

Sweeteners

REFERENCES

Baron, J. & Jurney, J (1993). Norms against voting for coerced reform, *Journal of Personality and Social Psychology*, 64(3), 347-355.

Bashear, T. G., Bellenger, D. N., Barksdale, H. C & Ingram, T. N. (1997). Salesperson behavior: Antecedents and links to performance, *Journal of Business & Industrial Marketing*, 12(3/4), 177-184.

Dawson, R. (1995). *Secrets of power negotiating.* Franklin Lakes, NJ: Career Press.

Girard, J. (1989). How to close every sale. New York: Warner Books.

Goldstein, D. G., Johnson, E. J., Herrmann, A. & Heirtmann, M. (2008). Nudge your customers toward better choices, *Harvard Business Review*, 86(12), 99-105.

Hawes, J. M., Strong, J. T., & Winick, R. S. (1996). Do closing techniques diminish prospect trust?, *Industrial Marketing Management*, 25(5), 349-360.

Ingram, T. N., La Farge, R. W., Avila, R. A., Schwepker, C. H., Jr. & Williams, M. R. (2004). *Professional selling: A trust-based approach*, 2nd., Mason, OH: Thompson/Southwestern.

Iyengar, S. S. & Lepper, M. R. (2000). When choice is demotivating: Can one desire too much of a good thing?, *Journal of Personality and Social Psychology*, 79(6), 995-1006.

Johnson, E. J. & Goldstein, D. (2003). Do defaults save lives?, *Science*, 302, 1338-1339.

Medvec, V. H. & Galinsky, A. D. (2005). Putting more on the table: How making multiple offers can increase the final value of the deal, *Negotiation*, April, 3-5.

Ritov, I. & Baron, J. (1990). Reluctance to vaccinate: Omission bias and ambiguity, *Journal of Behavioral Decision Making*, 3(4), 263-277.

Robinson, R. J. (1995). Defusing the exploding offer: The Farpoint gambit, *Negotiation Journal*, 11(3), 277-285.

Samuelson, W. F. & Zeckhauser, R. (1988). Status quo bias in decision making, *Journal of risk and uncertainty*, 1, 7-59.

Sharma, A., Levy, M. & Evanschitzky, H. (2007). The variance in sales performance explained by the knowledge structures of salespeople, *Journal of Personal Selling & Sales Management*, 27(2), 169-181.

Sharma, A., Levy, M. & Kumar, A. (2000). Knowledge structures and retail sales performance: An empirical examination, *Journal of Retailing*, 76(1), 53-69.

Ury, W. (1993). *Getting past no: Negotiating your way from confrontation to cooperation.* New York: Bantam Books.

Zigler, Z. (1984). Zig Ziglar's secrets of closing the sale. Grand Rapids, MI: Fleming H. Revell.

READINGS

Reading 5.1

GETTING PAST YES: NEGOTIATING AS IF IMPLEMENTATION MATTERED

Danny Ertel

In July 1998, AT&T AND BT ANNOUNCED a new 50/50 joint venture that promised to bring global interconnectivity to multinational customers. Concert, as the venture was called, was launched with great fanfare and even greater expectations: The $10 billion start-up would pool assets, talent, and relationships and was expected to jog $1 billion in profits from day one. Just three years later, Concert was out of business. It had laid off 2,300 employees, announced $7 billion in charges, and returned its infrastructure assets to the parent companies. To be sure, the weak market played a role in Concert's demise, but the way the deal was put together certainly hammered a few nails into the coffin.

For example, AT&T's deal makers scored what they probably considered a valuable win when they negotiated a way for AT&T Solution to retain key multinational customers for itself. As a result, AT&T and BT ended up in direct competition for business—exactly what the Concert venture was supposed to help prevent. For its part, BT seemingly out negotiated AT&T by refusing to contribute to AT&T's purchase of the IBM Global Network. That move saved BT money, but it muddied Concert's strategy, leaving the start-up to contend with overlapping products. In 2000, Concert announced a complex new arrangement that was supposed to clarify its strategy, but many questions about account ownership, revenue recognition, and competing offerings went unanswered. Ultimately, the two parent companies pulled the plug on the venture.

Concert is hardly the only alliance that began with a signed contract and a champagne toast but ended in bitter disappointment. Examples abound of deals that look terrific on paper but never materialize into effective, value-creating endeavors. And it's not just alliances that can go bad during implementation.

Source: Danny Ertel, "Getting past yes: Negotiating as if implementation mattered," *Harvard Business Review*, November 2004, 82(11), 61–64, 66–68. Used by permission of Harvard Business School Publishing.

Misfortune can befall a whole range of agreements that involve two or more parties—mergers, acquisitions, outsourcing contracts, even internal projects that require the cooperation of more than one department. Although the problem often masquerades as one of execution, its roots are anchored in the deal's inception, when negotiators act as if their main objective were to sign the deal. To be successful, negotiators must recognize that signing a contract is just the beginning of the process of creating value.

During the past 20 years, I've analyzed or assisted in hundreds of complex negotiations, both through my research at the Harvard Negotiation Project and through my consulting practice. And I've seen countless deals that were signed with optimism fall apart during implementation, despite the care and creativity with which their terms were crafted. The crux of the problem is that the very person everyone thinks is central to the deal—the negotiator—is often the one who undermines the partnership's ability to succeed. The real challenge lies not in hammering out little victories on the way to signing on the dotted line but in designing a deal that works in practice.

The Danger of Deal Makers

It's easy to see where the deal maker mind-set comes from. The media glorifies big-name deal makers like Donald Trump, Michael Ovitz, and Bruce Wasserstein. Books like *You Can Negotiate Anything, Trump: The Art of the Deal,* and even my own partners' *Getting to Yes* all position the end of the negotiation as the destination. And most companies evaluate and compensate negotiators based on the size of the deals they're signing.

But what kind of behavior does this approach create? People who view the contract as the conclusion and see themselves as solely responsible

for getting there behave very differently from those who see the agreement as just the beginning and believe their role is to ensure that the parties involved actually realize the value they are trying to create. These two camps have conflicting opinions about the use of surprise and the sharing of information. They also differ in how much attention they pay to whether the parties' commitments are realistic, whether their stakeholders are sufficiently aligned, and whether those who must implement the deal can establish a suitable working relationship with one another.

This isn't to say deal makers are sleazy, dishonest, or unethical. Being a deal maker means being a good closer. The deal maker mind-set is the ideal approach in certain circumstances. For example, when negotiating the sale of an asset in which title will simply be transferred and the parties will have little or no need to work together, getting the signatures on the page really does define success.

But frequently a signed contract represents a commitment to work together to create value. When that's the case, the manner in which the parties "get to yes" matters a great deal. Unfortunately, many organizations structure their negotiation teams and manage the flow of information in ways that actually hurt a deal's chances of being implemented well.

An organization that embraces the deal maker approach, for instance, tends to structure its business development teams in a way that drives an ever growing stream of new deals. These dedicated teams, responsible for keeping negotiations on track and getting deals done, build tactical expertise, enquire knowledge of useful contract terms, and go on to sign more deals. But they also become detached from implementation and are likely to focus more on the agreement than on its business impact. Just think about the language deal-making teams use ("close" a deal, putting a deal "to bed") and how their performance is measured and rewarded (in terms of the number and size of deals closed and the time required to close them). These teams want to sign a piece of paper and book the expected value; they couldn't care less about launching a relationship.

The much talked about Business Affairs engine at AOL under David Colburn is one extreme example. The group became so focused on doing deals—the larger and more lopsided the better—that it lost sight of the need to have its business partners actually remain in business or to have its deals produce more than paper value. In 2002, following internal investigations and probes by the SEC and the Department of Justice, AOL Time Warner concluded it needed to restate financial results to account for the real value (or lack thereof) created by some of those deals.

The deal maker mentality also fosters the take-no-prisoners attitude common in procurement organizations. The aim: Squeeze your counterpart for the best possible deal you can get. Instead of focusing on deal volume as business development engines do, these groups concentrate on how many concessions they can get. The desire to win outweighs the costs of signing a deal that cannot work in practice because the supplier will never be able to make enough money.

Think about how companies handle negotiations with outsourcing providers. Few organizations contract out enough of their work to have as much expertise as the providers themselves in negotiating deal structures, terms and conditions, metrics, pricing, and the like, so they frequently engage a third-party adviser to help level the playing field as they select an outsourcer and hammer out a contract. Some advisers actually trumpet their role in commoditizing the providers' solutions so they can create "apples to apples" comparison charts, engender competitive bidding, and drive down prices. To maximize competitive tension, they

exert tight control, blocking virtually all communications between would-be customers and service providers. That means the outsourcers have almost no opportunity to design solutions tailored to the customer's unique business drivers.

The results are fairly predictable. The deal structure that both customer and provider teams are left to implement is the one that was easiest to compare with other bids, not the one that would have created the most value. Worse yet, when the negotiators on each side exit the process, the people responsible for making the deal work are virtual strangers and lack a nuanced understanding of why issues were handled the way they were. Furthermore, neither side has earned the trust of its partner during negotiations. The hard feelings created by the hired guns can linger for years.

The fact is, organizations that depend on negotiations for growth can't afford to abdicate management responsibility for the process. It would be foolhardy to leave negotiations entirely up to the individual wits and skills of those sitting at the table on any given day. That's why some corporations have taken steps to make negotiation an organizational competence. They have made the process more structured by, for instance, applying Six Sigma discipline or community of practice principles to improve outcomes and learn from past experiences.

Sarbanes-Oxley and an emphasis on greater management accountability will only reinforce this trend. As more companies (and their auditors) recognize the need to move to a controls-based approach for their deal-making processes—be they in sales, sourcing, or business development—they will need to implement metrics, tools and process disciplines that preserve creativity and let managers truly manage negotiators. How they do so, and how they define the role of the negotiator, will determine whether deals end up creating or destroying value.

Negotiating for Implementation

Making the leap to an implementation mind-set requires five shifts.

1. Start with the end in mind. For the involved parties to reap the benefits outline in the agreement, goodwill and collaboration are needed during implementation. That's why negotiation teams should carry out a simple "benefit of hindsight" exercise as part of their preparation. Imagine that it is 12 months into the deal, and ask yourself:

Is the deal working? What metrics are we using? If quantitative metrics metrics are too hard to define, what other indications of success can we use?

What has gone wrong so far? What have we done to put things back on course? What were some early warning signals that the deal may not meet its objectives?

What capabilities are necessary to accomplish our objectives? What processes and tools must be in place? What skills must the implementation teams have? What attitudes or assumptions are required of those who must implement the deal? Who has tried to block implementation, and how have we responded?

If negotiators are required to answer those kinds of questions before the deal is finalized, they cannot help but behave differently. For example, if the negotiators of the Concert joint venture had followed that line of questioning before closing the deal, they might have asked themselves, "What good is winning the right to keep customers out of the deal if doing so leads to competition between the alliance's parents? And if we have to take that risk, can we put in mechanisms now to help mitigate it?" Raising those tough questions probably wouldn't have

made a negotiator popular, but it might have led to different terms in the deal and certainly to different processes and metrics in the implementation plan.

Most organizations with experience in negotiating complex deals know that some terms have a tendency to come back and bite them during implementation. For example, in 50/50 ventures, the partner with greater leverage often secures the right to break ties if the new venture's steering committee should ever come to an impasse on an issue. In practice, though, that means executives from the dominant party who go into negotiations to resolve such impasses don't really have to engage with the other side. At the end of the day, they know they can simply impose their decision. But when that happens, the relationship is frequently broken beyond repair.

Tom Finn, vice president of strategic planning and alliances at Procter & Gamble Pharmaceuticals, has made it his mission to incorporate tough lessons like that into the negotiation process itself. Although Finn's alliance management responsibilities technically don't start until after a deal has been negotiated by the P&G Pharmaceuticals business development organization, Finn jumps into the negotiation process to ensure negotiators do not bargain for terms that will cause trouble down the road. "It's not just a matter of a win-win philosophy," he says. "It's about incorporating our alliance managers' hard-won experience with terms that cause implementation problems and not letting those terms into our deals."

Finn and his team avoid things like step-down royalties and unequal profit splits with 50/50 expense sharing, to name just a few. "It's important that the partners be provided (with) incentives to do the right thing," Finn says. "When those incentives shift, you tend to end up (with) difficulties." Step-down royalties, for instance, are a common structure in the industry. They're predicated on the assumption that a brand is made or lost in the first three years, so that thereafter, payments to the originator should go down. But P&G Pharmaceuticals believes it is important to provide incentives to the partner to continue to work hard over time. As for concerns about overpaying for the licensed compound in the latter years of contract, Finn asserts that "leaving some money on the table is OK if you realize that the most expensive deal is one that fails."

2. **Help them prepare, too.** If implementation is the name of the game, then coming to the table well prepared is necessary—but not sufficient. Your counterpart must also be prepared to negotiate a workable deal. Some negotiators believe they can gain advantage by surprising the other side. But surprise confers advantage only because the counterpart has failed to think through all the implications of a proposal and might mistakenly commit to something it wouldn't have if it had been better prepared. While that kind of an advantage might pay off in a simple buy-sell transaction, it fails miserable—for both sides—in any situation that requires a long-term working relationships.

That's why it's in your best interest to engage with your counterpart before negotiations start. Encourage the other party to do its homework and consult with its internals stakeholders before and throughout the negotiation process. Let the team know who you think the key players are, who should be involved early on, how you hope to build implementation planning into the negotiation process, and what key questions you are asking yourself.

Take the example of Equitas, a major reinsurer in the London market. When preparing for commutations negotiations—whereby two reinsurers settle their mutual book of business—the company sends its counterpart a thorough kickoff package, which is used as the agenda for the negotiation launch meeting. This "commutations action pack" describes how the reinsure's own commutations department is organized, what its preferred approach to commutations negotiation is, and what stages it follows. It also includes a suggested approach to policy reconciliation and due diligence and explains what data the reinsurer has available—even acknowledging its imperfections and gaps.

The kickoff meeting thus offers a structured environment in which the parties can educate each other on their decision-making processes and their expectations for the deal. The language of the commutations action pack and the collaborative spirit of the kickoff meeting are designed to help the parties get to know each other and settle on a way of working together before they start making the difficult trade-offs that will be required of them. By establishing an agreed-upon process for how and when to communicate with brokers about the deal, the two sides are better able to manage the tension between the need to include stakeholders who are critical to implementation and the need to maintain confidentiality before the deal is signed.

Aventis Pharma is another example of how measured disclosure of background and other information can pave the way to smoother negotiation and stronger implementation. Like many of its peers, the British pharmaceutical giant wants potential biotech partners to see it as a partner of choice and value a relationship with the company for more than the size of the royalty check involved. To that end, Aventis has developed and piloted a "negotiation launch" process, which it describes as a meeting during which parties about to enter into formal negotiations plan together for those negotiations. Such collaboration allows both sides to identify potential issues and set up an agreed upon process and time line. The company asserts that while "formally launching negotiations with a counterpart may seem unorthodox to some," the entire negotiation process runs more efficiently and effectively when partners "take the time to discuss how they will negotiate before beginning."

3. **Treat alignment as a shared responsibility.** If their interests are not aligned, and they cannot deliver fully, that's not just their problem—it's your problem, too.

Unfortunately, deal makers often rely on secrecy to achieve their goals (after all, a stakeholder who doesn't know about a deal can't object). But leaving internal stakeholders in the dark about a potential deal can have negative consequences. Individuals and departments that will be directly affected don't have a chance to weigh in with suggestions to mitigate risks or improve the outcome. And people with relevant information about the deal don't share it, because they have no idea it's needed. Instead, the typical reaction managers have when confronted late in the game with news of a deal that will affect their department is "Not with my FTEs, you don't."

Turing a blind eye to likely alignment problems on the other side of the table is one of the leading reasons alliances break down and one of the major sources of conflict in outsourcing deals. Many companies, for instance, have outsourced some of their human resource or finance and accounting processes. Service providers, for their part, often move labor-intensive to Web-based self-service systems to gain process efficiencies. If users find the new self-service system frustrating or intimidating, though, they make repeated (and expensive) calls to service centers or fax in handwritten forms. As a result, processing costs jump from pennies per transaction to tens of dollars per transaction.

But during the initial negotiation, buyers routinely fail to disclose just how undisciplined their processes are and how resistant to change their cultures might be. After all, they think, those problems will be the provider's headache once the deal is signed. Meanwhile, to make requested price concessions, providers often drop line items from their proposals intended to educate employees and support the new process. In exchange for such concessions, with a wink and a nod, negotiators assure the provider that the buyers will dedicate internal resources to change-management and communication efforts. No one asks whether business unit managers support the deal or whether function leaders are prepared to make the transition from managing the actual work to managing the relationship with an external provider. Everyone simply agrees, the deal is signed, and the frustration begins.

As managers and employees work around the new self-service system, the provider's costs increase, the service levels fall (because the provider was not staffed for the high level of calls and faxes), and customer satisfaction plummets. Finger-pointing ensues, which must then be addressed through expensive additions to the contract, costly modifications to processes and technology, and additional burdens on a communication and change effort already laden with baggage from the initial failure.

Building alignment is among negotiators' least favorite activities. The deal makers often feel as if they are wasting precious time "negotiating internally" instead of working their magic on the other side. But without acceptance of the deal by those who are essential to its implementation (or who can place obstacles in the way), proceeding with the deal is even more wasteful. Alignment is a classic "pay me now or pay me later" problem. To understand whether the deal will work in practice, the negotiation process must encompass not only subject matter experts of those with bargaining authority but also those who will actually have to take critical actions or refrain from pursuing conflicting avenues later.

Because significant deals often require both parties to preserve some degree of confidentiality, the matter of involving the right stakeholders at the right time is more effectively addressed jointly than unilaterally. With an understanding of who the different stakeholders are—including those who have necessary information, those who hold critical budgets, those who manage important third-party relationships, and so on—a joint communications subteam can then map how, when, and with whom different inputs will be solicited and different categories of information might be shared. For example, some stakeholders may need to know that the negotiations are taking place but not the identity of the counterpart. Others may need only to be aware that the organization is seeking to form a partnership so they can prepare for the potential effects of an eventual deal. And while some must remain in the dark, suitable proxies should be identified to ensure that their perspectives (and the roles they will play during implementation) are considered at the table.

4. Send one message. Complex deals require the participation of many people during implementation, so once the agreement is in place, it's essential that the team that created it get everyone up to speed on the terms of the deal, on the mind-set under which it was negotiated, and on the trade-offs that were made in crafting the final contract. When each implementation team is given the contract in a vacuum and then is left to interpret it separately, each develops a different picture of what the deal is meant to accomplish, of the negotiators' intentions and of what wasn't actually written in the document but each had imagined would be true in practice.

"If your objective is to have a deal you can implement, then you want the actual people who will be there, after the negotiators move on, up front and listening to the dialogue and the give-and-take during the negotiation so they understand how you got to the agreed solution," says Steve Finn, vice president for retail industry and former VP for global business development at IBM Global Services. "But we can't always have the delivery executive at the table, and our customer doesn't always know who from their side is going to be around to lead the relationship." To address this challenge, Finn uses joint had-off meetings, at which he and his counterpart brief both sides of the delivery equation. "We tell them what's in the contract, what is different or non-standard, what the schedules cover. But more important, we clarify the intent of the deal: Here's what we had difficulty with, and here's what we ended up with and why. We don't try to reinterpret the language of the contract but (we do try) to discuss openly the spirit of the contract." These meeting are usually attended by the individual who developed the statement of work, the person who priced the deal, the contracts and negotiation lead, and occasionally legal counsel. This team briefs the project executive in charge of the implementation effort and the executive's direct reports. Participation on the customer side varies, because the early days in an outsourcing relationship are often hectic and full of turn-over. But Finn works with the project executive and the sales team to identify the key customer representatives who should be invited to the hand-off briefing.

Negotiators who know they have to brief the implementation team with their counterparts after the deal is signed will approach the entire negotiation differently. They'll start asking the sort of tough questions at the negotiating table that they imagine they'll have to field during the post deal briefings. And as they think about how they will explain the deal to the delivery team, they will begin to marshal defensible precedents, norms, industry practices, and objective criteria. Such standards of legitimacy strengthen the relationship because they emphasize persuasion rather than coercion. Ultimately, this practice make a deal more viable because attention shifts from the individual negotiators and their personalities toward the merits of the arrangement.

5. **Manage negotiation like a business process.** Negotiating as if implementation mattered isn't a simple task. You must worry about the costs and challenges of execution rather than just getting the other side to say yes. You must carry out all the internal consultations necessary to build alignment. And you must make sure your counterparts are as prepared as you are. Each of these actions can feel like a big time sink. Deal makers don't want to spend time negotiating with their own people to build alignment or risk having their counterparts pull out once they know all the details. If a company wants its negotiators to sign deals that create real value, though, it has to weed out that deal maker mentality from its ranks. Fortunately, it can be done with simple processes and control.

More and more outsourcing and procurement firms are adopting a disciplined negotiation preparation process. Some even require a manager to review the output of the process before authorizing the negotiator to proceed with the deal. KLA-Tencor, a semiconductor production equipment maker, uses the electronic tools available through its supplier-management Web site for this purpose, for example. Its managers can capture valuable information about negotiators' practices, including the issues they are coming up against, the options they are proposing, the standards of legitimacy they are relying on,

and the walk away alternatives they are considering. Coupled with simple post negotiation reviews, this information can yield powerful organizational insights.

Preparing for successful implementation is hard work, and it has a lot less sizzle than the brinksmanship characteristic of the negotiation process itself. To overcome the natural tendency to ignore feasibility questions, it's important for management to send a clear message about the value of post deal implementation. It must reward individuals, at least in part, based on the delivered success of the deals they negotiate, not on how those deals look on paper. This practice is fairly standard among outsourcing service providers; it's one that should be adopted more broadly.

Improving the implementability of deals is not just about layering controls or capturing data. After all, a manager's strength has much to do with the skills she chooses to build and reward and the example she sets with her own questions and actions. In the health care arena, where payer-provider contentions are legion, forward-thinking payers and innovative providers are among those trying to change the dynamics of deals and develop agreements that work better. Blue Cross and Blue Shield of Florida, for example, has been working to institutionalize an approach to payer-provider negotiations that strengthens the working relationship and supports implementation. Training in collaborative negotiation tools and techniques has been rolled down from the senior executives to the negotiators to the support and analysis teams. Even more important, those who manage relationships with providers and are responsible for implementing the agreements are given the same training and tools. In other words, the entire process of putting the deal together, making it work, and feeding the lessons learned through implementation back into the negotiation process has been tightly integrated.

Most competitive runners will tell you that if you train to get to the finish line, you will lose the race. To win, you have to envision your goal as just beyond the finish line so you will blow right past it at full speed. The same is true for a negotiator: If signing the document is your ultimate goal, you will fall short of a winning deal.

The product of a negotiation isn't a document; it's the value produced once the parties have done what they agreed to do. Negotiators who understand that prepare differently than deal makers do. They don't ask, "What might they be willing to accept?" but rather, "How do we create value together?" They also negotiate differently, recognizing that value comes not from a signature but from real work performed long after the ink had dried.

Thinking Further 5.1

1. Is "negotiating for implementation" more comparable to a mutual gains or distributive negotiation philosophy? Describe the similarities.

2. Under what circumstance might "negotiating for implementation" not be the best negotiating strategy? Explain why.

Reading 5.2

CLOSING THE DEAL

Michael Wheeler

What to do when you've done everything right, but you still don't have agreement

You've followed the negotiation guidebooks to a T, uncovered the parties' key interests, brainstormed creative solutions, and even developed good rapport with your counterpart. You've done everything right . . . but you still don't have agreement.

How do you turn the other side's maybe into a yes? More concessions are seldom the right answer. If the other side faces a choice between accepting the deal you've put on the table and continuing to negotiate further, you may be unwittingly teaching him to hold out for even more each time you sweeten your proposal. At some point, before you reach your own walkaway point, you have to force him to choose between the deal on the table or no deal at all.

Your goal shouldn't be to create a take-it-or-leave-it ultimatum but to orchestrate the entire negotiation so that it sets up the right end game. Ideally, everything you do and say should deepen both your understanding of what the other side needs and his appreciation of the value you're offering. The following five rules of thumb can help you maintain the right balance of patience and realism, and help close the deal.

Source: Wheeler, M. (2006). Closing the deal, *Program on Negotiation Newsletter, 9*(4), 1–4.

Note: This article first appeared in *Negotiation*, a monthly newsletter published by the Program on Negotiation at Harvard Law School, www.pon.harvard.edu. Copyright 2006—2011 Harvard University.

1. Diagnose the barrier

When you've made progress on certain issues but remain stymied on others, it's time to take a hard look at what's standing between you and a mutually acceptable deal. Professor Robert Mnookin of Harvard Law School and his colleagues at Stanford University have created a catalog of common barriers to agreement, including strategic behavior, reactive devaluation, and authority issues.

If you think strategic behavior—the unwillingness of one or both sides to make a best offer—may be the problem, enlist a trusted, unbiased third party for help. The negotiators can then disclose their respective bottom lines privately to the "neutral," who will tell them if there's an overlap. If so, the negotiators should be able to hammer out a deal quickly within the zone of agreement. If not, it may be wise to abandon talks and pursue other alternatives. (Online mediation has become a growth industry for negotiators who've reached an impasse. Cybersettle [www.cybersettle.com], for instance, has serviced more than 100,000 insurance claims in this fashion.)

Psychological factors can block agreement, too. Professor Lee Ross of Stanford University demonstrated the all-too-human tendency to *reactively devalue* what other people offer us. "If that were truly important to them," we tell ourselves, "they wouldn't have made that concession." We need to avoid that trap in our own thinking and be careful not to trigger that reaction from others. Rather than trying to wrap things up by putting a reasonable number on the table, for instance, wait for the other side to make a specific request. In this manner, you may increase the perceived value of your concession—and your counterpart's satisfaction.

Sometimes a tag-team approach is needed to reach closure. The first cohort of negotiators may settle some important issues but run out of gas when it comes to others. A fresh team may bring a new perspective without the burden of personality problems that their predecessors developed. Changing the lineup maybe especially useful if early negotiators have limited authority. This is common practice in diplomatic negotiations; foreign-service specialists often do much of the groundwork before heads of state meet to resolve any remaining issues.

2. Use the clock

Negotiations expand to fill the time available. We may not like to make important decisions under the gun, but deadlines can provide a healthy incentive to come to agreement. It's no accident that lawsuits settle on the courthouse steps and that strikes often are averted at the eleventh hour. Until that point, the daily costs of protracted negotiation may not seem high (though, clearly, they mount over time). Only when the judge is about to be seated or the contract is due to expire are people jolted out of the relative comfort of the status quo. If you anticipate these moments, recognize your priorities and keep channels of communication clear, you'll be able to move quickly and wisely when you have to.

To avoid getting bogged down in never-ending talks, it pays to impose a deadline at the outset of negotiation. You also can put a fuse on the proposals you make, though exploding offers can backfire if the other party resents being put under artificial pressure.

3. Count your change

Even if you've done everything right, you have to be alert for gambits and tricks as the negotiation winds down. A classic bargaining tactic among lawyers advises, "After agreement has been reached, have your client reject it and raise his demands." It's a common gambit for car salespeople, too, as they return from conferring with the manager. The news is never good: "You've got to offer $1,000 more—but he'll toss in the floor mats for free."

Shame on those who resort to such tired old ploys. Shame on you, too, if you're not ready for them. When you reach agreement, confirm that all the key provisions have been covered so there will be no surprises. Even after you've gotten a sincere handshake, your counterpart may come back with further demands if she is having a tough time selling the deal internally. (You'll sometimes be in that position yourself.) From the outside, of course, its impossible to know when you're being taken for a ride and when the need for revisions is legitimate. How the negotiation has gone up until that point may offer an important clue.

Either way, however, you should be leery about making any unreciprocated concessions. If your counterpart asks for new terms, even if you can afford them, you should get a favorable adjustment in return. Otherwise, you're simply encouraging further requests.

4. Sign here

Most important deals require a written contract. Whatever you've gained through artful negotiation will go down the drain if the understanding you reached is poorly reflected in formal documents.

The technical side of executing an agreement isn't glamorous, but it's where many battles are won or lost. Even if you're weary, resist the temptation to let the other side "write it all up." It's smarter to have your own lawyers and specialists get the language right than to seek their help later in rewriting a draft that the other side has mangled. Because you have control over your own lawyers, you can tell them what risks you're willing to take and where you need protection.

Your attorneys must know the limits of their responsibility, of course. While it's their job to protect your rights and identify potential trouble spots, it ultimately falls to you to determine which risks you're willing to assume. After all, in business (as in life) there are few certainties. As a practical matter, it may be sensible to leave some items unresolved and others ambiguous. For example, if you have retained a corporate trainer to present a program for your company, you will likely want to include a clause allowing for rescheduling if a conflict arises. If that seems unlikely, it may be sufficient to stipulate that the new date will be at "a mutually agreeable time," rather than creating cumbersome procedures and policies that you'll probably never need.

Instead of getting bogged down arguing tedious technical points, consider addressing them globally. A straightforward dispute-resolution clause, crafted while everyone is enthusiastic about the deal, can reduce the cost of unexpected problems and keep you out of court.

At the end of the negotiation, boiler-plate clauses governing renewal options and the like may not seem like deal makers or deal breakers, but they determine who is holding the cards when it comes time to renew the agreement. For this reason, take special care to get the language of exit clauses right so that you'll be in a good position to renegotiate down the road. Parties often are preoccupied with immediate dollars and cents when they execute a deal, but, in the long-term, the option to extend or terminate a deal may have much more financial value.

Finally, be ultra-careful about casually signing a "memorandum of understanding" or an "agreement to purchase." These documents may entail real commitments and limit your ability to win any further benefits, ending the negotiation before you even realized it had begun.

5. Let them brag

You may not have liked your counterpart much at the outset, and after marathon haggling sessions, you may like him even less. It's hard to be civil in such situations, yet grace is most important at the finish hue.

To get a deal ratified, you may have to make your counterpart look good to his constituents. This is not just a question of virtue. If the other side loses face, he may be tempted to retaliate and spurn a deal that, by all rights, he should accept. If someone's agreement comes grudgingly, getting him to deliver on his promises may be like pulling teeth.

To make the other party look good, you may need to orchestrate the concluding moves in the negotiation. In collective bargaining, for example, management often prefers it when the union makes an offer that the company can accept, rather than vice versa. (Appearing weak is less of a concern for management than it is for the union's elected bargaining agents.) Union officials can then say to their membership, "We got the company to accept our proposal," rather than, "Here's what we finally accepted."

Enhancing Your Deal

Not all contracts are created equal. Some maximize joint value through creative trades, while others are barely satisfactory. Strategic wariness causes many people to leave untapped value on the bargaining table. Of course, agreements based on incomplete and distorted information aren't likely to be efficient.

Twenty years ago. as a remedy to this dilemma, Howard Raiffa, author of *The Art and Science of Negotiation: How to Resolve Conflicts and Get the Best out of Bargaining* (Belknap Press, 1985), floated a novel idea: people should continue to negotiate after coming to agreement. Specifically, Raiffa proposed that negotiators consider *postsettlement settlements* in which their current deal is simply the foundation for further value creation. A signed deal would become the bird in the hand; negotiators would entertain revision if—and only if—it were to everyone's advantage. With this assurance, people should be more open to revealing their priorities.

After agreeing on the purchase and sale of a home, for example, the parties might talk over the closing date. If the buyer would like to move in soon (or the seller remain longer), a price adjustment coupled with a date change might leave everyone better off. Other postdeal topics for discussion might include seller financing, furnishings, and, in the case of a vacation property, maybe even some future share. Even if few of these options proved feasible, one or two might offer thousands of dollars of extra value to both sides.

Postsettlement settlements should work in any setting, yet they rarely are attempted. In hard-bargaining cases, it can be difficult to shift gears to a more collaborative approach: even people who have been cooperative throughout the process may simply run out of steam. But consider that it takes little effort to say, "Great! We've got a deal that we both can live with. But it might make sense to roll up our sleeves and see if we can do better."

Bill Ury, author of *Getting Past No: Negotiating Your Way from Confrontation to Cooperation* (rev. ed., Bantam, 1993), calls this strategy "building a golden bridge." It involves allowing the other side to make a graceful exit—and practicing the diplomatic art of letting others have your way.

Michael Wheeler is the Class of 1952 Professor of Management Practice at Harvard Business School and editor of the *Negotiation Journal*. He can be reached at negotiation@hbsp.harvard.edu.

Thinking Further 5.2

1. According to this article, what steps can you take to prepare to close a deal with a hesitant party? Why will these steps help influence the other side to close?

2. Have you ever tried to close a deal with a hesitant party? What tactics did you use? Why did they work/not work?

Part I Cases

CASE 1

"Who's the Boss A+B"

Questions

1. What is the conflict about?

2. Why is there a conflict over these issues?

3. How is Doctor Jordan doing so far at managing this conflict?

4. How is the nursing director, Ms. Brady, doing so far? What is her approach to conflict?

5. Now, as Mary Jones on the board of directors, what would you do to resolve this dispute?

Who's the Boss (A)

"'Dr. Jordan on line three for you, Mary." When Mary Jones pressed the blinking button, she knew Dr. Alex Jordan was not calling to set up their next tee time. As Chief of Surgery, Dr. Jordan had a full access to the Board of Directors and Mary, the Chairperson of the Board, noticed he took full advantage of it. Lately, Dr. Jordan's calls were mostly about Harriet Briggs, the hospital's administrator. Today was no different.

"Mary, as Chief of Surgery, I have authority over all issues that affect the quality of patient care. When something or someone is compromising that quality it is my prerogative, not the prerogative of some layman [Dr. Jordan's word for anyone not

holding an MD] to do what I deem necessary to correct the situation. Don't you agree?"

Mary mentally ran through job descriptions and the hospital's charter and she could remember no clause that explicitly gave the Chief of Surgery this authority. Implicitly, though, his stance was probably correct. "I'll reserve comment on that, Alex, until you tell me the specific situation that has you this upset."

The problem that concerned Dr. Jordan involved the nursing supervisor, Judith Brady, R.N. Ms. Brady schedules the hospital's surgical nurses according to her interpretation of established hospital policy. Surgeons were frustrated with her attitude that maximum utilization must be made of the hospital's operating time for training purposes. She therefore scheduled in such a way that nurses were often assigned to procedures they had not seen before. Surgeons complained that this scheduling method often added to the time it took to perform an operation. This caused problems because the OR was run at full capacity. Surgeons already felt they must hurry to complete a procedure because another procedure was scheduled directly following theirs. Having to wait because a nurse did not automatically know what instrument is needed next only exacerbated this problem and did not permit them sufficient time to complete a surgical procedure in the proper manner. The surgical staff was concerned that this scheduling

Source: Raymond Friedman, "Who's the Boss A & B" and "Musical Operating Room A & B" from "Musical Operating Rooms: Mini-Cases of Health Care Disputes," *The International Journal of Conflict Management,* 2002, 13(4), pp. 417–418, 419–423. © Emerald Group Publishing Limited all rights reserved.

system was impacting quality of care. Furthermore, some of the surgeons had complained that Ms. Brady clearly favored some doctors over others and tended to assign more experienced nurses to their procedures.

The situation came to crisis earlier in the morning when Dr. Jordan, following a confrontation with Ms. Brady, told her she was fired. Ms. Brady then made an appeal to the Harriet Briggs, the hospital administrator. Harriet overturned Ms. Brady's dismissal and then instructed Dr. Jordan that discharge of nurses was the purview of the hospital administrator and only she had the authority to do so. Dr. Jordan vehemently disagreed. The conversation ended with Dr. Jordan yelling, "This is clearly a medical problem and I am sure the Board of Directors will agree with me." Dr. Jordan then called Mary.

After listening to Dr. Jordan, Mary decided to call Harriet Briggs to get her side of the story. Harriet told Mary, "I cannot be responsible for improving patient care if the board will not support me, I must be able to make decisions and develop policies and procedures without worrying whether or not the board will always side with the physicians. As you already know, Mary, I am legally responsible for the care that patients receive here at the hospital. And another thing, the next time Dr. Jordan tells me that I should restrict my activities to fund raising, maintenance, and housekeeping, I will not be responsible for my actions!"

The severity of the problem was obvious but the answers were not. All Mary knew was she needed to fix the situation quickly.

What is this conflict about? How would you assess the actions of Dr. Jordan and Ms. Brady so far? What should Mary Jones do?

Who's the Boss (B)

After some reflection, Mary understood that this was really a conflict within a conflict—an immediate situation that needed to be rectified that was driven by a larger struggle over authority and power. Mary dealt with the immediate issues first.

Judith Brady was re-instated as nursing supervisor. After a long discussion with her, Mary saw that the hospital policy was ambiguous regarding assignment of nurses to the OR and subject to interpretation. Mary ordered Briggs to review these policies with nurses and surgeons and re-write them to better balance the need for training with the needs of the surgeons. Mary next addressed the serious charge that surgeons did not have enough time to complete procedures properly. She directed Briggs to work with the surgical department to investigate and document any indications that patient care was being compromised.

The larger issue of turf battles was more difficult to overcome. Mary was concerned Harriet allowed this power struggle to get this out of control without bringing it to anyone's attention. She was equally concerned with the physicians' attitude that the administrator's job was largely one of maintenance and fund raising. Mary thought perhaps that Harriet had allowed herself to be seen in that role and had not taken enough initiative early on to clarify her authority with all parties involved.

Mary was pleasantly surprised when within a week of the Brady incident, Harriet sent the Board of Directors her proposal that outlined those areas she clearly saw as her purview and those areas she agreed were better controlled by either Dr. Young as Chief of Surgery or Dr. Chet Matthews, Chief of Staff. Harriet also listed those gray areas in which she was unclear exactly who should be in charge. Harriet made it clear to Mary that she was making every effort to work things through with Dr. Young and Dr. Matthews and that if she were unable to do so she would resign. When Mary offered to step in, Harriet declined her help because she believed that unless she could come to an agreement on her own, any dictate from the Board would command no respect from Dr. Young and therefore the physician staff.

The meetings were effective in bringing clarity to the authority issues that had plagued the hospital. There was much give and take before all parties arrived at role descriptions that they could live with. Although not all issues could be resolved completely,

they were resolved to the point where all could live with the authority lines that had been drawn.

Thinking Further—Case 1

Who's the Boss? (A)

1. What is the conflict about? Why is there a conflict over these issues?

2. How are Dr. Jordan and Ms. Brady doing so far at managing this conflict? What are their respective approaches to managing it?

Who's the Boss? (B)

1. Do you believe Mary Jones's handling of the conflict was appropriate? Effective? Why, or why not?

2. What would you have done to resolve the conflict if you were Mary Jones? Explain why.

CASE 2

After several telephone calls, I decided it was time to send an e-mail to explain my problems and concerns with STVZ Telecommunication's network and coverage services. For the most part, my dispute with STVZ was addressed electronically.

The Beginning

For more than six months, I have continually been losing calls when talking from my home (see any one of my monthly statements for verification of the on-going dropped call issue). I went by the local STVZ store a few months ago and the rep seemed quite familiar with my problem. He said that people in the vicinity of Bermuda and Pollock Streets frequently complain. Of course, he had no solution and did not anticipate a solution would be forthcoming. Approximately two months ago I purchased a new phone, hoping maybe reception might improve. No luck. It's just as bad. It is absolutely ridiculous that I can live in the middle of a large metropolitan city and have to stand in designated spots in my house to avoid dropping calls. Does ST have any intention of solving this apparently well known problem, or can I get a refund on my new phone and get out of my two-year contract without penalty so that I can go to a provider that offers constant service in my area? Please advise. Thank you.

STVZ

Rebecca, I am sorry to hear you are unable to use your phone while inside your home. We encourage you to contact us from a landline telephone whenever a problem is encountered. We then pass this information on to our System Performance Team so that we may investigate and resolve the issue within our abilities. I attempted to contact you to assist in getting you to our System Performance Team and to verify the last four digits of your Social Security Number, but I was unable to reach you. My name is Nikki, and it is my personal goal to deliver world class service to you. I have provided more information below.

- At STVZ, we make every effort to meet and exceed your expectations.
- The difficulties you have encountered can be the result of many factors, including the area traveled, structural restrictions, network service issues, or the wireless phone itself. Our System Performance Team continuously monitors our network; however, the valuable feedback we receive from customers such as you often leads to improvements you will see in the future. Should the outcome of the Trouble Ticket be that it is a network or coverage issue,

we will waive the Early Termination Fees should you decide to cancel your service.

- To file a Trouble Ticket to be submitted for your area, please call us from a landline phone at 800-XXX-XXXX and have the following information available:
  - Brief description of the problem
  - Most recent date the problem occurred
  - Approximate time the problem occurred
  - Nearest cross street/intersection of where the problem occurred
  - Recordings you hear
- Please have your wireless phone fully charged and available when you call, for trouble shooting purposes.
- For your protection, I am obligated to ensure that the last four digits of your Social Security Number (SSN) have been verified before I can discuss any account-specific information or process any service changes. I apologize for any inconvenience this may cause.

In order to ensure secure transmission of your information, please do not reply directly to this e-mail. Instead, because our website is a much more secure method for you to transmit sensitive data, please send a new e-mail through our website and include the last four (4) digits of your Social Security Number (SSN) and we will be glad to assist you with your original request.

Rebecca, I hope the information I have provided is helpful to you. We appreciate your business and thank you for using STVZ. Should you have additional questions or concerns, please reply to this e-mail.

Rebecca

Nikki, I don't have a land line phone in my home. So, to call and report this ongoing issue I would need to drive approximately 10 miles to my office (where I don't have reception problems). I can tell you exactly what I hear when I lose a call—I hear two or three beeps and on the screen of my phone it says "call lost." I also know that when I drive out of my neighborhood I have four bars, but when I'm in my neighborhood and home, I have two bars if I'm lucky. I also know it isn't a problem with another carrier because the calls dropped are typically with other STVZ users.

As mentioned in my previous e-mail, I just purchased a new phone and it still drop calls so the recommendation below that it may be due to the phone itself seems unlikely. Moreover, my boyfriend, who also uses STVZ, has the same problems with reception when he's at my house, but not when he's at his own home. This leaves me hard pressed to believe that it's a poorly manufactured phone issue. Instead it seems to be a neighborhood reception issue.

I don't know why you didn't reach me when you called because we have been home the entire day and my phone does not show any missed calls. I'd say it is probably because of the reception (or lack thereof) that we get in this area.

It just seems like STVZ must have some solution besides suggesting it's the customer's equipment or building structure that is the issue. If STVZ representatives at our local store know about it and can tell customers street coordinates where the trouble frequently lies, then it seems that STVZ would do what it takes to fix the problem. Just a thought.

STVZ

Thank you for contacting STVZ through our website. My name is Larry and I am sorry to know you do not have an alternate phone or number to call from. Unfortunately, we still need you to find an alternate phone. Please know, the issue(s) you have described may need to be duplicated with a live representative, as troubleshooting equipment via e-mail is extremely difficult. Typically, when a wireless phone is not fully operating while inside of a home or building, it is because of the interference with our cellular towers.

You may not be receiving a full signal when trying to connect your calls because a wireless signal is limited when it tries to pass through brick, steel, or other material. You can usually make a call with a minimal amount of signal strength; however, receiving a call requires approximately full signal strength.

It is important to us that you understand the potential cause of the low signal strength in and around your residence. If you would like our Technicians to look into your area, please call our Customer Service Department at 800-XXX-XXXX from a landline phone. We ask that you call so we can ask you specific questions regarding the surrounding area where the problem is occurring.

We hope you can find a way to contact us by phone as it is difficult to assess by e-mail. We appreciate your business and thank you for using STVZ. Again, my name is Larry and should you have additional questions or concerns, please reply to this e-mail.

Rebecca

Larry, Nikki, or whoever reads this, While I am apparently slow in understanding, I get it now. The poor reception I receive using my STVZ-provided phone, under a STVZ contract, in the middle of suburb of Las Vegas where a STVZ sales associate said there should be clear reception but is known not to, is my problem and not yours. After I purchase a land line so I can call STVZ from the location my calls continually get dropped, I suppose I should anticipate then being asked to purchase and install a cell tower on my property for STVZ too? Lovely. Customer service is apparently as spotty as reception.

Note

At this point I took a week off to cool down as I felt that my concerns were being dismissed. On November 6 I physically visited a local STVZ store.

The sales associate I worked with spent over 45 minutes with me. She contacted the trouble shooting/technical issues department to explain why I couldn't call using a land line from my home and why she was making arrangements for me. I received a voice mail from one of the technicians approximately a week later while I was out of town. Below are the next round of e-mails based on what the technician said in the voice mail.

Rebecca

I am writing in regards to an on-going service issue I have been having with my wireless coverage. I have been a STVZ customer living in the same residence since August of 2004. I have now been experiencing ongoing dropped calls in and around my home for approximately the past nine months. As is noted in my records, I have contacted STVZ by e-mail and in person. On November 6 my local sales representative made arrangements to have technical support come out to my neighborhood to assess the cause of incessant dropped calls. I was out of town when technicians pursued my report. Below is a direct quote of the message left on my phone:

> Good afternoon my name is Mike, I'm calling from STVZ regarding the problems you reported to us with the poor service in your area. Our technicians for that location did get back to us and basically, the dropped calls you are experiencing are due just to the support coverage that we have at the address. The good news is that we do have a new cell site planned that will be built and be brought on line that should improve coverage there. But at this point we are not certain when that site will be completed. So in the short term the issues you are experiencing will probably persist from our network. We apologize for this. The only thing we could offer as a short-term solution is our network extender. The network extender is a devise that would

serve as a personal cell cite that will bypass the network issues we are having there.

Based on the finding of the technicians (trouble ticket 3274xxx), I would like to move forward with Mike's offer to provide me with a network extender as a short-term solution until the cell site is put into place. As a long-term customer, this complementary offer seems to be a reasonable, albeit temporary solution to the dropped calls I've experienced. Please advise me on how I should proceed in acquiring the aforementioned network extender. Thank you.

STVZ

The STVZ Network Extender enhances indoor voice and data coverage in areas with minimum or no in-building coverage, allowing customers to get the most of their plan minutes while indoors. My name is June and I will be glad to give you more information about the Network Extender.

This indoor coverage solution operates with existing STVZ-branded devices and installation is simple—just "plug and play." For additional information regarding the Network Extender visit the following website: www.stvz.com/networkextender

The cost of the network extender is $249.99. It does require an Internet Connection with a minimum connection speed of 300 Kbps (kilobits per second) upload/download: which includes FiOS, DSL, Cable, Other broadband ISP (Internet Service Provider) but Satellite broadband, MiFi, EVDO are not supported. You must have one available Ethernet Port.

Thank you for giving me the opportunity to let you know about our Network Extender. We appreciate having you as a valued STVZ customer since 2006 and are glad to know our Network Extender is available as a temporary solution for you until the new cell tower can be installed. Should you have additional questions or concerns, please reply to this e-mail.

Rebecca

Thank you for your response, June. Please note, however, that I am not paying $250 for a problem attributable to STVZ. As noted in previous communications, I have had STVZ service since 2004. For four years, I did not have a dropped call issue in my neighborhood. It is only in the recent months that this has occurred and the voice mail from Mike confirms what a representative in my local store stated over two months ago—there is a known coverage problem in my neighborhood. So why should I, as a loyal customer, be expected to pick up the expense? As Mike stated in his voice mail to me, the coverage problem should be rectified in the near future, but he is unsure exactly when. Because of this, he (Mike) *OFFERED* the extender to me as a short term solution.

Is it possible to have a person with decision making authority contact me and explain the above? To avoid confusion, my specific questions include: (1) Why should a long-term customer be required to pick up an expense for a company problem that is in line to be fixed? It just doesn't make sense. (2) Isn't it fair to conclude that if STVZ were truly interested in retaining long-term customers, it would provide the extender on a temporary basis until the acknowledged and known problem is solved?

STVZ

I am sorry for any of the frustration that you have experienced regarding coverage in your area. I tried to call you at 1:41 P.M. Mountain time, but was unable to reach you. I am unable to provide the Network Extend to you on a temporary basis until the cell tower isinstalled in this area. However, I would be able to offer you a $50.00 discount off the price of the Network Extender. The cost of the network extender is $249.99. It does require an Internet Connection with a minimum connection speed of 300 Kbps (kilobits per second) upload/download: which includes FiOS, DSL, Cable, Other broadband

ISP (Internet Service Provider) but Satellite broadband, MiFi, EVDO are not supported. You must have one available Ethernet Port. Thank you for contacting STVZ, my name is Ann and I would be happy to assist you today.

It is my goal to assist you in a timely resolution by providing prompt and courteous information. I hope that I have been able to do that for you. Again, my name is Ann and I make it my personal goal to provide the best customer service in the industry. I hope that I have done that for you today. We appreciate your business and thank you for using STVZ. Should you have additional questions or concerns regarding your service or the Network Extender offer, please reply to this e-mail.

Rebecca

How ironic that you tried to call but couldn't reach me. I was at my home working right next to my phone when you called. As often happens of late, my phone doesn't ring and I'm notified of a quasi "missed call" when the voice mail alert comes through. I tried to call you back but the computerized voice that answered at 505-XXX-XXXX said that I needed the four digit extension of the person I was trying to reach. Unfortunately, that information wasn't included in the voice mail so the system hung up on me rather than redirecting the call to an operator.

In any event and as is likely to be anticipated (assuming it is Ann that reads this), I am not satisfied with the option provided in the message below. Both you and I know that STVZ's cost for the extender is no where near the $250 retail price advertised. Asking me to accept a mere $50 off is therefore inappropriate on more than one front.

Given that I've been a customer for over five years now and would continue to be one for at least the remainder of my recently signed two-year contract, how about agreeing to one of the following three options:

1. Give me the extender as Mike graciously offered in his voice mail last week and I continue to fulfill my service contract for the next two years.

2. Give me a $250 credit on my Verizon wireless account and I'll purchase the extender as well as fulfill my service contract for the next two years.

3. In addition to letting me out of my contract with no financial penalty, reimburse me for both the new phone I was advised by a STVZ representative to purchase in August ($60 after sale discount and rebate) as well as the insurance I was told was a "must purchase" with touch screen phones ($54). That is, agree to pay me $114 out of pocket expenses and let me out of the two year contract I was hoodwinked into in August. Rest assured that had STVZ representatives been honest and told me that the dropped call problem was purely a coverage issue and not a phone issue, I would neither have purchased a new phone nor renewed my contract. I would have gone to a different wireless provider.

As a professor of strategic management, I can not see how either option 1 or 2 puts STVZ at a competitive disadvantage. Indeed the outcome is the opposite since STVZ would recoup its internal cost for the extender in a mere matter of months through the revenue provided with me remaining a loyal customer. Hence, my first question is this—please explain what is strategically illogical about accommodating an existing customer rather than sending him/her to a competitor?

I have two additional questions I'd also appreciate a response to. Given that I've been a customer of STVZ, living in the same residence for five years, why is it that dropped calls were not an issue for the first four years of my contract? Finally, I notice that I never get to communicate with the same person more than once when contacting customer service … is there a person with decision making authority (perhaps Ann) that I can have an on-going dialogue with?

I anxiously await your response to my multiple questions above as well as discussion on which one of the three options above STVZ is willing to agree to.

Note

That evening I received a phone call from Cynthia (Internet response coordinator) who then put me on a conference call with Rusty (technician). The funny thing is that in the process we were disconnected due to the poor coverage in my area. It was dinner time, but I eventually had to put my son into the car and we drove out of my neighborhood so we could safely complete the call.

The conversation lasted approximately 30 minutes. Cynthia said they wanted to "sweeten the deal" by offering an additional $50 off the extender. We went round and round for some time as I struggled to get them to acknowledge that they were expecting me to make myself "whole again," apparently on behalf of STVZ. I said that all I can conclude is that I am just a number to them and not valued. Rusty replied by saying that they were doing everything they could and that they couldn't reduce the price anymore; otherwise they would lose money.

Rebecca

Well you can only imagine my thoughts upon hearing that one. I said back, "interesting that you'll lose sleep if STVZ loses money, but you don't seem to have a problem with me losing money in the process of fixing your company's problem." I then said the whole situation was comparable to the following analogy:

Assume STVZ is Amtrak and their train just broke down. I ride that train daily to and from work

and have a prepaid annual pass to do so. Amtrak knows the breakdown is their responsibility but say that I have to purchase a car to get myself to and from work until they fix the train. Amtrak also says that they know they will be fixing the train sometime in the not-so-distant future, but they can't give an exact date. Because I need to get to and from work, I go ahead and buy the car. Shortly thereafter the train is fixed and I can ride it again. But what am I supposed to do with the car I was forced to purchase?

Finally, Rusty seemed to get it as he correctly vocalized my frustration. Unfortunately, all I could get were a bunch of apologies, but no more taken off the price of the extender. In the end, I asked Cynthia to send me the offer in writing via e-mail and I would think about it for a couple days.

STVZ (A Few Days Later)

Good Evening! I am so glad that I was able to reach you to discuss the coverage issues. Again, my name is Cynthia, and it is my personal goal to deliver great service to you.

Here are the two offers: I am glad that we could discuss your concerns and options with Rusty from our data support department.

1. We would be able to offer you a $100.00 discount off the price of the Network Extender. The original cost of the network extender is $249.99. It does require an Internet Connection with a minimum connection speed of 300 Kbps (kilobits per second) upload/download: which includes FiOS, DSL, Cable, Other broadband ISP (Internet Service Provider) but Satellite broadband, MiFi, EVDO are not supported. You must have one available Ethernet Port.

2. Since you are in an area that is not serviced by STVZ, you may choose to cancel your service

prior to fulfilling your Customer Agreement(s), which ends on 9/03/2011. Please be aware that pursuant to your Customer Agreement, canceling your service prior to your agreement end date would result in your being billed an Early Termination Fee of up to $175.00. However, we will credit this fee since you are in an area with no to low coverage. Your STVZ service will be terminated, and any early termination fee waived. We will submit a disconnect order for the last day of your current billing cycle on 12/04/09.

Please contact Customer Service by telephone at (800) 922-0204 with your decision. We are available from 6 am to 11 pm Pacific Time, seven days a week for your convenience. Rebecca, I do hope you will choose to continue service with us and I also wanted to thank you: You have been a customer for years, and that is appreciated. We value and appreciate your business and thank you for using STVZ products and services. Should you have questions and concerns, please reply to this e-mail.

Rebecca

Cynthia, thank you for taking the time to speak with me the other night. As you experienced, given the two times that you had to call me back, the coverage in my area is frustrating at best when trying to address important issues via my wireless service. Thank goodness my family hasn't required 911 emergency services.

Before I make a final decision on the most recent offer extended, I need to gather more information to better understand the network extender. As Rusty mentioned during our conference call, STVZ doesn't know when the anticipated cell tower will be put in place in my neighborhood. All that is known is that it is scheduled to occur in the near future, which he said could occur in anywhere from a matter of months to a year. So, let's assume (glass half full

rather than half empty) that STVZ takes care of this known and acknowledged issue in the next three to six months. Let's also assume that I accept the offer to buy the network extender next week and it works in improving my reception in and around my house. My question is then, what can I do with the extender that I was required to purchase but is no longer necessary? As I reflect back on our conference call, I don't believe this question was thoroughly answered. I had asked if I was supposed to sell the equipment on eBay to recoup my loss. Rusty said something to the effect that I could. This would suggest that I could also use the extender in a different residence should I ever move or that I could give the extender to a family member in another state to use once it is not needed in my current residence. Can you please describe to me in detail if the extender, once used, can be transferred without complication or cost to another residence and/or another STVZ user (on a contract separate from mine) as well as how this task would be completed (i.e., is it the same setup procedure as I'd use when I install it in my home for my wireless account)? Thank you in advance for the clarification.

STVZ

I am sorry that all of your concerns were not addressed in your most recent conversation with Cynthia. In review of the requirements for the Network Extender, should you choose to purchase a device, this will not require you to agree to a new Contract, nor will there be cost incurred when it is no longer needed and a new user activates it for their needs. My name is Nikki, and it is my personal goal to deliver world class service to you. I have provided more information below.

- The STVZ Network Extender enhances indoor voice and data coverage in areas with minimum or no in-building coverage, allowing customers to get the most of their plan minutes while indoors. This indoor coverage solution operates with existing STVZ-branded devices and installation is simple—just "plug and play."

- Once the coverage in your home area is improved, you do have the ability to transfer this device to another user's account without cost to you or the new user. Once you purchase this device, it is yours to do with as you wish. If you would like to sell this product, you are more than welcome to do so.
- For additional information regarding the STVZ Network Extender visit the following website: www.stvz.com/networkextender

The steps to set up your Network Extender will be included with your order, but I have provided more information below including a link for step by step setup.

1. You can connect the Network Extender to your existing high-speed Internet connection. The Network Extender is compatible with STVZ and other broadband Internet services like fiber optic, DSL, and Cable. Simply connect the Network Extender to your broadband router using the Ethernet cable provided with purchase.

2. Your Network Extender needs to be placed near a window that has a clear view to the sky to be able to access a GPS signal. If you cannot place the Network Extender near a window, an optional external antenna extender is included with purchase.

3. There is no activation required on any STVZ wireless phone within the Network Extender network range.
   - Place your STVZ wireless phone within 15 feet of the Network Extender to register your phone. Dial #48 to confirm registration and set up completion.

- Network Extender has an approximate range of up to 40 feet from the Network Extender device, which translates to a 5,000 square foot area.
- Up to three STVZ wireless phones can automatically access the Network Extender network at one time with no extra charge per minute. A fourth channel is always reserved for emergency (E911) calls.

4. The Network Extender allows all STVZ wireless phones to enjoy the benefits of enhanced coverage. You can manage your settings online by signing in to My STVZ. You also have the ability to prioritize access to your Network Extender to up to 50 STVZ wireless callers you select. Where a compatible cell tower is unavailable, callers that do not appear on your managed access list may access the Network Extender when not in use by priority callers. All callers may access the Network Extender for emergency (E911) calls. It's simple and easy.

The web address to view these setup instructions is: http://www.stvzwireless.com/b2b/store/accessory?action=gotosetup

Rebecca, I hope the information I have provided regarding the Network Extender is helpful to you. We appreciate your business since 2004 and thank you for using STVZ. Should you have additional questions or concerns, please reply to this e-mail.

Rebecca

Thank you for the beneficial information. I believe I have just three more questions before I finalize my decision.

1. I understand that "up to three STVZ wireless phones can automatically access the Network Extender network at one time with no extra

charge per minute"; however, how does a person prevent four or more people accessing the network at one time? Is a three limit control mechanism built into the device? I don't want any surprise charges added to my bill.

2. If/when I no longer need the extender I understand that I can give or sell the extender to a STVZ user should I choose. If this ever occurs, would the new user follow the same activation steps I'm supposed to use (i.e., do they also dial #48 to register) and do I have to do something in particular to unregister my phone and delete my "managed access list"?

3. Can I use the $15 gift card sent to me by STVZ in September to purchase the extender? On the back of the gift card it says, *"Visit us at any of our participating locations and use this $15 gift card towards any purchase. Card has no cash value and cannot be redeemed for cash or applied towards payment to your account."* I don't need any other STVZ products; I just need to get the cell coverage I had for over four years in my residence back and, according to various STVZ representatives, the extender is the short term solution.

Thank you in advance for your willingness to answer the three questions above.

STVZ

The network extender has a built in device that only allows so many to access at a time, so it is self controlled. My name is Genesis, and I am happy to assist you with your inquiries.

If you do decide to give the extender away, it would then need to be re-registered to their specific area. You have the option to bill the network extender to your account, and at that time you may use the $15.00 gift card toward the balance as requested. The STVZ wireless Network Extender

enhances indoor voice and data coverage in areas with minimum or no in-building coverage, allowing customers to get the most of their plan minutes while indoors. This indoor coverage solution operates with existing STVZ-branded devices and installation is simple—just "plug and play."

For additional information regarding the STVZ wireless Network Extender visit the following website: www.stvzwireless.com/networkextender

In closing, I want to thank you for giving me the opportunity to assist you with more information on the network extender today. I really appreciate your business and thank you for using STVZ. If you have additional questions or concerns, please reply to this e-mail.

Rebecca

I appreciate the quick response to the e-mail I sent yesterday, but there wasn't enough detail to fully answer my questions. Let me explain and hopefully you can elaborate.

- My first question was whether there was a three limit control mechanism built into the device so that I do not have to worry about any surprise charges. Genesis said that the network extender has a built in device that allows only "so many" to access at a time, but what exact number is "so many"?

- My second question was about the process of transferring the extender if I no longer needed it. Specifically, I asked, whether the new user would follow the same activation steps I will use (i.e., do they also dial #48 to register) AND what do I need to do to unregister my phone and delete my managed access list? Genesis answered my question by saying that if I gave my extender to someone they would have to re-register in the new area. She didn't, however, describe the process for doing this.

Would the exact same steps I used be used again? She also didn't answer the second half of my question regarding what I should to unregister my phone and delete all existing prioritized users.

- My final question was whether I could use the $15 gift card sent to me by STVZ to purchase the extender. Genesis replied that the purchase of the extender would be billed to my account and that I could "use the $15.00 gift card toward the balance as requested." Does this mean that the terms written on the back of the gift card are being overruled? As noted yesterday, the card says the card "cannot be redeemed for cash or applied towards payment to your account." I believe a better option is to have the $15 credit applied at the time of purchase, not after I receive a bill. I can give the sales associate the gift card SCU number printed on the back of the card. Thank you.

STVZ

I will be happy to go over your additional concerns. My name is Mario, and to start, the Network Extender can support up to 3 active calls at the same time, with a 4th line open for emergency purposes (i e 911 calls). In regards to the designated numbers set up for the Network Extender, those are managed and maintained on the user's online My STVZ Account, so if you were to stop using the Extender and give it to someone else, they would have to register it under their account, register it under their names and with their numbers. Gift Cards can be redeemed at STVZ stores and kiosks for the purchase of phones, accessories, prepay replenishment or starter cards and technical services. They can also be accepted for new activations requiring security deposits, online purchases, and for paying your bill at a store location. But they cannot be used to pay the bill, when remitted by mail.

I believe that covers your additional concerns, Rebecca. I hope I was able to resolve them. I appreciate your time and for choosing STVZ. And if you have any other questions, concerns or if this e-mail did not answer your question please feel free to reply to this e-mail for hope I was able to resolve them.

Rebecca

I appreciate Mario's elaboration on my concerns. I think we are close to a mutual understanding. I just need a little bit more with the third question I had asked regarding the gift card. It sounds like if I purchase the extender it will be done on-line and the extender will be mailed to me and my account charged $150. So how will I go about applying the $15 gift card to this purchase? Neither the card nor Mario provided unambiguous instructions.

One more thought came to mind as I wrote this note, please confirm that there are no shipping costs or additional costs besides the $150 to purchase the extender.

STVZ

Great questions. Thank you for requesting the details that we missed in our last e-mail regarding the gift card and the Network Extender price. Please see below for that information. My name is Nikkie. It is my personal goal to deliver world class service to you. Thank you for taking the time to e-mail me here at STVZ Customer Service.

I read Mario's e-mail to you, and I understand why you might still be a little confused about the gift card. I'm sorry that he was not more clear about that. To use your gift card for online purchases, you would process it as a credit card. You would need to process a $15.00 payment on the gift card, and the rest on a different credit card. Basically the gift card is like a coupon for $15.00 worth of free stuff from us, so if you need any accessories, cases, ear pieces, screen protectors or bluetooth items, you can use the card for that as well.

If you still wish to use the card to help pay for the extender, and you have trouble processing the payment online, please call us so we can help you through that process. I am unsure why you think that the Network Extender is only $150.00. The website that Genesis provided has it listed at $249.99, which is the correct price. June also quoted you a price of $249.99 in her reply to your first e-mail to us.

When you order your extender, the shipping is free unless you see an option to upgrade the shipping for an extra charge. Some areas do not offer this option. You will see on the checkout screen that there is no charge for shipping, unless you order upgraded shipping options. Taxes must be charged on everything that we sell, by law. You will see your tax summary on the checkout screen as well, and depending on which state you are in, the taxes may vary a little. Because of this, I cannot quote you an exact final price, but taxes are usually around 15% in most states. Wireless phones and accessories are considered luxury items in most states, so taxes are a bit more than some other items may be. Either way, you will have a chance to review each charge and the total amount before you commit to the purchase online.

Rebecca, thank you for e-mailing me today to clarify how to use your gift card online and the correct price of the Network Extender. If you have any further questions or concerns, please reply to this email, and I will be delighted to assist you further. Thank you for choosing STVZ for all your wireless needs.

Rebecca

Augh! I don't know how many countless hours I've spent trying to resolve this issue only to be back nearly to square one again since Nikkie just told me that the extender will now cost me $250. Will the person who reads this e-mail please look at the ongoing record I have with STVZ. Doing so should

reveal that during a conference call I had with Cynthia and Rusty on November 18, as well as a follow-up e-mail from Cynthia on the same date, that I was quoted a price of $150 for the extender. As I argued then and on other occasions, it is inappropriate and unfair to make loyal customers bear the expense for a problem acknowledged by STVZ to be short-term in nature, especially given the fact that I have been a loyal customer since 2004 and did not have a problem with coverage in my residence until 2009.

Please, please, please . . . would the person who gets this e-mail check my records and verify that the $150 is still in my records. I have a copy of the e-mail and will send it if necessary. Given the new confusion, I need to know in detail how it is that I'll go about purchasing the extender for the $150 I was quoted. It appears that doing so on-line is likely going to be difficult at best. I would suggest that we complete the transaction over the phone. Is this possible?

STVZ

My name is Sue, and I am so sorry over our confusion on the price you were offered for the Network Extender. After review of your account, I indeed see we offered you an additional $100.00 discount off of the $249.99 cost of the Network Extender. As this was a special offer, I will have to order the Network Extender for you. If you can provide a physical address where you would like the Network Extender shipped, I would be delighted to order it at the cost of $149.99, plus tax. It does ship via Federal Express, so someone will need to be available to sign for it. Rebecca, I look forward to hearing from you so we can order the Network Extender. As a loyal customer since 2006, we appreciate your business and thank you for using STVZ. If you have any further questions or concerns, please reply to this email.

Rebecca

I do want to order the extender. Given that using e-mail does not, despite repeated requests, allow me to communicate with the same person more than once, I want to do the rest of this transaction over the phone. In other words, I would like a customer retention person **knowledgeable** **with my record** to call me to process both my purchase and corresponding gift card. I await your call.

I ended up purchasing the extender with an additional $15 taken off because the representative couldn't get the gift card number I have to be accepted on her system.

Thinking Further—Case 2

1. If you were in Rebecca's shoes, would you have continued to use e-mail for as long a time as she did to try to resolve your complaint? What other form(s) of communication might you have tried?

2. What types of strategies and/or tactics does STVZ Telecommunication apparently use in order to keep the upper hand in a customer dispute? What other strategies and/or tactics might Rebecca have used that would have resulted more favorably for her? For example, did Rebecca negotiate with the appropriate level of management? Could she have sought support from a third party that could have negotiated more effectively for her?

P A R T   I I

Special Challenges

6. Communication: The Heart of All Negotiations

7. Decision Making: Are We Truly Rational?

8. Power and Influence: Changing Others' Attitudes and Behaviors

9. Ethics: Right and Wrong Do Exist When You Negotiate

10. Multiparty Negotiations: Managing the Additional Complexity

11. Individual Differences: How Our Unique Qualities Affect Negotiations

12. International Negotiations: Managing Culture and Other Complexities

13. Difficult Negotiations: Managing Others Who play
    Dirty and Saying No to Those Who Play Nice

14. Third-Party Intervention: Recourse When Negotiations Sputter or Fail?

CHAPTER 6

Communication

The Heart of All Negotiations

At the heart of a negotiation is interpersonal communication. Negotiators communicate face to face, electronically, or through the mail. They exchange information to help reach agreements that are beneficial to themselves, and perhaps to the other party. Communication is so central to the negotiation process that it could be viewed as one of the fundamentals of negotiation. It is treated, instead, as a special challenge, because it can be a complex process, wrought with many challenges that must be overcome for negotiators to be successful. This chapter discusses the elements of the communication process, the types of messages that are typically communicated, the channels through which they are exchanged, and the impact of these messages and channels on negotiation processes and outcomes. Suggestions for enhancing communication effectiveness are also included.

INTENDED BENEFITS OF THIS CHAPTER

When you finish reading this chapter, you should be able to

1. Describe the important elements of the communication process.
2. Explain the challenges that sometimes cause negotiators to communicate ineffectively.
3. Describe the tools that are available for managing these challenges and how to use them to communicate effectively when negotiating.

THE ESSENCE OF INTERPERSONAL COMMUNICATION

The goal of communication is for the person who receives the message to attach the same meaning to it that is intended by the sender. This is important for negotiators to ensure they are discussing the same problems, opportunities, issues, interests, and so on. Communication seems like a simple process: one person sends a message to another person. But it is actually quite complex because there are the many variables that influence how messages are interpreted—both when they are sent and when they are received. These are illustrated in Figure 6.1.

Figure 6.1   The Elements of Communication

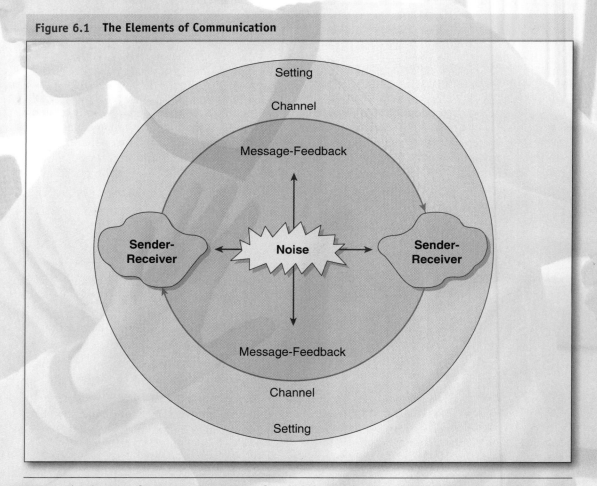

Source: "The Elements of Communication," Figure from Hybels, S. and Weaver, II, RIL., *Communicating Effectively, 8e,* McGraw-Hill, 2007. Used by permission.

Message encoding. Messages are encoded by the sender. One's attitudes, beliefs, values, work experiences, culture, desires, needs, and knowledge all influence what the sender says and how he or she says it. A negotiator with competitive attitudes and beliefs who works for an equally competitive boss, for example, is likely frame his or her offers and arguments very aggressively.

Message decoding. The same forces that influence how the sender encodes messages determine how the receiver *decodes* them—how he or she interprets the message that is received. A negotiator who wants to improve everybody's welfare is more likely to interpret aggressive behavior as a vigorous attempt to achieve a beneficial outcome and respond to it by sending messages that are intended to calm the aggressor down and alter his or her approach.

Feedback. Feedback messages are exchanged in conjunction with the focal message. They can be positive or negative, person-focused or message-focused, immediate or delayed, spontaneous or carefully constructed, and supportive or critical (DeVito, 2009). The absence of feedback also influences how messages are interpreted. Whatever form it takes, this feedback tells the sender how his or her message affected the receiver and this may lead to modifications. Negotiators might respond to an offer, for example, by accepting it, proposing a different alternative, laughing and rejecting it, or with silence. Each of these feedback messages will tell the initial sender something different. For example, the sender may suffer the "winner's curse" if his or her initial offer is accepted. He or she might attempt to clarify the offer if it is met with laughter and was rejected.

The communication channel. This is the medium through which messages are sent. It often affects the effectiveness of communication. Messages exchanged in face-to-face interactions, for instance, are quite different than those exchanged via the telephone or e-mail. Moreover, face-to-face communication implicates multiple channels simultaneously. In addition to the verbal message, facial expressions, gestures, intonation, and touch send messages. How these different channels influence negotiations will be discussed in more detail later in this chapter and in Reading 6.1.

Noise. Noise is any disturbance that interferes with the transmission of a message, is multifaceted and prevalent in all interpersonal communication, including negotiation.

Different types of noise are summarized in Table 6.1.

Perceptions

Perceptions are a source of noise, and more. Noise exists when you and the other negotiator perceive people or things differently. Perceptions also influence all of our communication choices—the messages we send, the channels through which we send them, what messages we listen to, and how we interpret them. They are triggered when something in our environment activates one or more of our senses—we hear, see, smell, taste, or touch something.

We are constantly bombarded by these stimuli, so we do not attend to all of them. Instead, we are quite selective. We usually attend to those that are most useful, meaningful, relevant, novel, familiar, moving, or intense. Our brains then organize or categorize these stimuli, and they seem to do so

Table 6.1   Sources of Noise in Communication and Negotiation

Source of Noise	Description/Examples
Physical Distractions	People walking by; Loud noises that make it difficult to hear; Telephones ringing at the table; Physical interruptions
Language Barriers	People speaking different languages or with heavy accents; Excessive communication (think of the people you know who take forever to make even a simple point); Choice of words and jargon
Cultural Differences	Ethnocentrism; Individualism-collectivism, low context–high context and power distance and other aspects, all of which are discussed in Chapter 12
Status Differences	These affect what messages are sent and how; People are often timid or unwilling to confront others who are more powerful or of higher status—employees may tell their manager only what they think he or she wants to hear, or stay mum about bad news
Perceptions	Derived from our attitudes, beliefs, values, work experiences, culture, desires, needs, and knowledge—the same factors that determine how we encode and decode messages, these affect the process by which we select, organize, interpret, retrieve, and respond to the information around us
Communication Styles	How people communicate varies along two dimensions: direct versus indirect and task-oriented versus relationship-oriented
Nonverbals/ Body Language	Examined in more detail later in this chapter, these reflect anything that transfers meaning other than the spoken word—facial expressions, gestures, touch, how people use physical space and time, pitch, volume, the use of vocal fillers ("ums" and "ahs"), clothes, tattoos, and piercings
Context	An office, a nice restaurant, a golf course, a Final Four basketball game; We may or may not even notice or be affected by it

Source: DeVito, 2009; Dobkin & Pace, 2006; Douglas, 1998.

instantaneously. We may place messages that follow in rapid succession or are similar in the same category because of their close proximity or similarity, respectively. Stereotyping and prototyping are examples. Schemata or mental models are mental structures or frameworks that organize information, ideas, thoughts, and behaviors. Scripts are schemata that tell us how to perform certain actions or procedures. They tell us, for example, what to expect and how to conduct ourselves when we begin a negotiation. Whichever form they take, these organizing rules, schemata, mental models, and scripts are information processing shortcuts that help us understand, remember, and recall information about people and events. Without them, every experience we have would be new and unrelated to anything we have done before (Dobkin & Pace, 2006).

How we organize this information influences how we interpret it. These interpretations are then stored in our memories until we encounter relevant or seemingly relevant stimuli that activate them. In actuality, we may recall information that is consistent with our schemata instead of the specific information for which we are looking. We may also fail to recall information that is relevant but inconsistent with our schemata, or we may recall information that forces us to think about or rethink our schemata (Dobkin & Pace, 2006). These schemata can be very beneficial, but they can also introduce noise that leads to biased, inaccurate, or otherwise inappropriate interpretations and decisions. If your negotiation script is competitive, for example, the integrative approach will be harder for you to wrap your head around. **Reading 6.2** at the end of this chapter provides additional guidance for understanding the other negotiator's perceptions.

Communication Styles

Communication styles are also a source of noise, and more. Noise results when the four different *communication styles* interact. **Directors** are direct and task-oriented communicators. They avoid small talk, focus on outcomes, and make quick decisions. **Expressers** are direct and relationship-oriented communicators. They are animated and emotional storytellers who think out loud and their ideas often flow unedited. **Thinkers** are task-oriented and indirect communicators. They are detail-oriented problem solvers. They ask lots of questions and often postpone decisions until all information, data, and angles are considered. **Harmonizers** avoid conflict and try to please others. They are quiet, and their indirect, relationship-oriented communication style is designed to keep people working happily together (Douglas, 1998). Serious distortions may result if directors, expressers, thinkers, and harmonizers fail to manage these differences when they communicate with each other. An employee who is an expresser and attempts to persuade his or her boss to accept a proposal by telling stories that illustrate its advantages and disadvantages will fail if the boss is a director because he or she is persuaded most by succinct explanations.

COMMUNICATION AND NEGOTIATION

What Messages Are Exchanged During Negotiations?

Some of what is communicated during a negotiation is obvious, but it pays to look beyond the surface to understand the implications of these messages.

Offers and Counteroffers

Opening offers anchor the negotiation, thus defining the bargaining range. The exchange of subsequent offers and counteroffers is a dynamic and interactive process that reflects reciprocal influences—the offer you extend influences the counteroffer (or lack thereof) extended by the other party (Tutzauer, 1992). The sequencing of offers and counteroffers also reflects the expected give and take (concession-making) that is necessary for reaching agreement.

Video 6.1
Offers and Counteroffers

Preferences

The messages negotiators exchange often reveal their *preferences*. Negotiators with strong affiliation motives send messages reflecting their concern for close, friendly relations. As illustrated by Haley's approach in Negotiation in Action 6.5, they prefer cooperative bargaining strategies, and they make and accept more concessions (Langner & Winter, 2001). Verbally aggressive negotiators possess strong power motives and their primary concerns involve impact, prestige, and reputation. They prefer competitive bargaining strategies and resist making or accepting concessions. The scenario in Negotiation in Action 6.1 illustrates Heath's preference for aggressive distributive bargaining. It appears that these preferences emanated from the negotiators' frustrations with the other side.

NEGOTIATION IN ACTION 6.1

When a large bakery was reorganizing due to financial problems, its service suffered. In fact, its grocery store clients went for weeks, even months, without having their shelves restocked. Heath, a store manager, tried repeatedly calling the salesperson, her boss, and even several levels higher in their corporate chain of command to persuade the bakery to stock his shelves. When these efforts failed, he resorted to threats and ultimatums. This, too, failed so he began filling the shelves slotted for the bakery's products with competitors' products. The bakery responded by sending its legal team to the store and threatened Heath with a breach of contract lawsuit if he didn't honor the contract between the bakery and the store—the contract required the store to allocate a specific amount of shelf space to this bakery's products (Personal Communication).

Some argue that Heath's approach reflects the demands of the situation rather than his preference. Do you agree?

This is not an easy question because Heath needed to maintain sales to the extent possible to satisfy his bosses—they told him only that he should do what he thought was necessary to use the space and generate sales. Since he was not told what he must do (he was not even told about the store's contract with the bakery), he did have choices. They may not have been easy ones, but he could have chosen to resolve this problem in whatever manner he thought was appropriate. We almost always have choices about how we negotiate deals, disputes, and team decisions, and our choices reflect our preferences.

Concessions and Other Tactical Choices

A negotiator's willingness to offer or accept concessions depends upon the balance of power and affiliation motives contained in the messages he or she receives, whether these messages contain explicit concessions, and his or her own balance of power and affiliation motives. The other negotiator, therefore, will make fewer concessions if you issue threats or ultimatums and refuse to offer concessions. Likewise, you will make fewer concessions if he or she issues threats or ultimatums and refuses to offer concessions (Langner & Winter, 2001).

What is communicated also reflects a negotiator's tactical choices in other ways. Asking for information about priorities is consistent with integrative negotiation because it leads to tradeoffs that produce larger joint gains. Reciprocating information about priorities and continuing to search for additional information, even if the other negotiator reacts negatively, also leads to larger joint gains. Conversely, proposing tradeoffs based on the available, albeit incomplete, information rather than searching for additional information leads to smaller joint gains (Weingart & Olekalns, 2004; Weingart, Thompson, Bazerman, & Carroll, 1990). Exchanging information about positions is consistent with distributive bargaining because it highlights differences, and this produces smaller joint gains. When this information is communicated contentiously, more impasses result (Hyder, Prietula, & Weingart, 2000; Olekalns & Smith, 2000).

Alternatives

Negotiators with attractive *alternatives* tend to establish stronger aspirations and reservation prices, and they achieve better outcomes. A negotiator who knows you have an attractive BATNA is likely to lower his or her aspirations and reservation prices, make less demanding offers, disclose more truthful information and settle for lesser outcomes (Parse & Gilin, 2000; Pinkley, 1995; Pinkley, Neale, & Bennett, 1994). If you have a strong BATNA, therefore, you should communicate it to the other party. Subtlety is warranted, however, if you want to avoid alienating him or her.

Explanations

Explanations, also called **social accounts**, are often communicated in negotiations. They are particularly important if you must communicate bad news or negative consequences. Some explanations imply that the situation left the negotiator with no choice but to engage in the chosen action. Explaining that the poor economy forced our company to impose a hiring freeze so I will not be able to extend you a job offer, for example, elicits less disapproval and fewer attributions of blame toward the wrongdoer, and more willingness to collaborate with him or her, by the people who were harmed by the decision (Baron, 1990; Bies & Shapiro, 1987, 1988).

Other explanations attempt to persuade the other party that the negative consequences were derived from actions undertaken with legitimate motives. Negotiators deceived by their counterpart, for example, are less punitive and less likely to retaliate if the deceiver gives altruistic rather than selfish reasons for the actions—"I deceived you to help both of us get more money" rather than, "I deceived you to help me get more money" (Shapiro, 1991; Sitkin & Bies, 1993).

Less punishment and fewer negative attributions are also incurred when explanations minimize the perceived undesirability of unfavorable consequences by comparing them to others who received even less favorable outcomes. Telling a subordinate that his negative performance rating was higher than his coworker's rating, or telling a new manager that this year's budget is not as bad as it was last year, are examples (Bies, 1982; Greenberg, 1988).

Explanations work best when they are adequate or sufficient. Job applicants are more accepting of rejections that are logical. Attributing refusals to grant budget separate requests and to requests to company norms, formal company policy, and budget constraints is more compelling than attributing them to subordinates' behavior, upper management, or company politics.

Attributing negative consequences to unintentional or unavoidable causes is better than attributing them to intentional or avoidable causes (Bies, Shapiro, & Cummings, 1988; Shapiro, 1991; Shapiro & Buttner, 1988).

Negotiation in Action 6.2 illustrates another way that explanations enter negotiations.

NEGOTIATION IN ACTION 6.2

When eBay transactions are disputed, the language used by the disputants influences the likelihood that they will settle. Settlements are 2.5 times more likely when respondents provide explanations (e.g., the delivery company made a mistake that caused the delay) or apologies. The chances of a settlement decrease by two-thirds if the complainant tells the respondent what he should or must do to fix the problem. The chances of reaching an agreement are cut in half if the complainant directs negative emotions at the respondent.

Explanations and apologies imply that a negotiator is willing to resolve the problem, and this helps the other party save face. In other words, they communicate respect and acknowledge that a valid social norm such as politeness has been violated. Giving commands and communicating negative emotions, on the other hand, attack face. Commands impugn the other party's reputation by implying blame. Negative emotions violate social norms such as politeness. This causes the other party to lose face and, even worse, these messages harden positions, escalate conflict, and trigger retaliation, thus reducing the likelihood that agreements will be reached (Brett, Olekalns, Friedman, Goates, Anderson, & Lisco, 2007).

Patterns of Communication

The first half of a negotiation is a better predictor of outcomes than the second half because issues are commonly defined during these early discussions. If the words used by a negotiator are reasonably balanced between people and things, he or she is more likely to discover integrative outcomes because this balance reflects variable-sum perceptions—the strong concern for both the substance of the negotiation and the relationship reflects the collaborative approach in the Dual Concerns model. If the definitions of the issues reflect fixed-sum perceptions, distributive outcomes should be expected. Words that focus mostly on things suggest a strong task orientation so competitive tactics should be expected. Accommodation is more likely if; most of his or her words are about people (Simons, 1993; Thompson & Hastie, 1990).

Problem Solving and the Questions You Should Ask

Negotiators are generally advised to ask questions, but they are rarely told what to ask or how—other than, perhaps, to ask open-ended questions. The substance of your questions must obviously pertain to the subject matter you are negotiating, but asking the right questions will prompt responses that move your negotiation forward.

Ask Why. We seem to believe that asking the other negotiator what he or she wants will enable us to frame a deal that he or she will find acceptable. Asking why he or she wants it is wiser because this will help you identify his or her interests.

Craft Your Open-Ended Questions Neutrally. Remaining neutral when you ask your open-ended questions will enhance your understanding. Negotiation in Action 6.3 is illustrative.

NEGOTIATION IN ACTION 6.3

Assume that you and your business partner have just interviewed representatives from two different public relations (PR) firms with the intention of giving your business to one of them. You have a strong preference for one firm and your partner prefers the other. "Don't you think Firm A has more connections in our industry?" you ask. "Maybe, but can't you see that Firm B would devote more attention to us because it's hungrier for business?" your partner responds. Taken aback, you ask, "Do you really want to hire an inexperienced firm to do this critical work for us?" Your partner pauses and asks, "Do you think we can afford to spend the fortune Firm A would demand?"

Now assume that you approached this differently. You begin by asking, "It seems we had very different initial reactions to the two PR firms, and I'm interested in hearing your opinion. What impressed you about Firm B? Why do you think it would be a better fit for us than Firm A?" (adapted from Program on Negotiation, 2010).

In the first paragraph, both parties asked questions to argue their points of view—they were not trying to enhance their understanding. This results in an attack and defend pattern that increases tensions and stalls the negotiation. The leading questions advocated particular positions; the loaded questions were designed to corner the other party. Both types of questions can trigger defensiveness and negative emotional reactions. They also prompt yes or no answers, or no responses at all. To secure reflective and thoughtful responses, ask questions that are open-ended and neutral rather than closed and opinionated. This requires you to look beyond your own biases and open yourself up to being persuaded by the other negotiator. This should turn your conversation from an exchange of demands to a discussion of interests (Program on Negotiation, 2010).

Ask Targeted Questions. The other party may respond guardedly to your questions about his or her interests—because they are difficult to express openly or because they are complex. After asking your open-ended questions, neutrally, you must ask more *targeted questions* that probe and explore important parts of his or her initial answer (see Negotiation in Action 6.4).

NEGOTIATION IN ACTION 6.4

Jacob was concerned that Lucy, a talented assistant, was being underutilized in her current position, so he approached her and said, "You're doing a great job, but I'm wondering if you're bored. Have you thought about what else you might like to do?" The question struck fear in her heart. She wondered if she hadn't been working hard enough, if he was encouraging her to quit or if he was going to fire her. In response, she lied and explained that she was very satisfied in her job. Jacob walked away, confused, and Lucy missed out on a potential career opportunity. After breaking the ice with his initial question

(Continued)

(Continued)

about her job satisfaction, Jacob should have followed with targeted questions. He could have asked, "What are your favorite aspects of your job? What tasks would you rather delegate to someone else if you could? He also could have explained—"I'm asking because I'd like to find a way to put your skills to better use in the company." This would help her let down her guard and engage in an honest, open discussion about her career aspirations (adapted from Program on Negotiation, 2010).

Ask for Advice. Instead of using questions coercively, as illustrated in Negotiation in Action 6.3, consider using them as persuasion tools. When you ask the other negotiator for *advice*, you convey humility rather than arrogance. Moreover, most people like giving advice and are likely to volunteer their ideas. Calling on the other party's expertise and enlisting his or her help in finding a workable solution should help you produce a good outcome that is acceptable to both of you (Program on Negotiation, 2010).

Active Listening

Perhaps the single most important tool available for ensuring effective communication to listen well. Active listening includes listening constructively to ensure you understand what is being said; empathizing; verbally and nonverbally encouraging the person to continue talking with silent pauses, nodding your head and making comments such as, "Okay" or "I see"; restating and paraphrasing for clarification and to demonstrate your understanding; asking "Do I understand you to mean that. . . .?" or "Are you suggesting that . . . ?," and open-ended questions that seek clarification or encourage the other negotiator to expand upon what he or she has already said. To listen actively and effectively, you must focus on the speaker, assume that he or she has something useful to say, be willing to subject your biases and preconceptions to contradictory information, suspend judgments about what is being said until your exchange is complete, and think about how the content of his or her message relates to the bigger picture, not just to yourself (Devito, 2009). In short, active listening entails three steps.

Paraphrase. This entails restating what the other negotiator said, usually in your own words.

Inquire. Ask the other negotiator to elaborate to enhance your understanding. This is particularly helpful when his or her assertions seem confusing, illogical, or inconsistent. You are looking for clarification, detail, and perhaps the reasoning behind his or her positions or arguments. You should then paraphrase or restate and ask if your understanding is correct.

Acknowledge. This is about letting the other negotiator know that you understand his or her message. This is important because many problems arise when people do not feel like they are being heard or understood (Bordone, 2007). This is also about acknowledging his or her feelings. Empathizing will help you manage his or her emotions, which is sometimes necessary before you can effectively negotiate the substantive issues. Simply noting that, for example, his or her experience must have been difficult or frustrating can be very helpful with the rest of your negotiation.

Some people think that listening for too long will make them look weak. Enhancing your understanding is never a weakness—information is an important source of power (see Chapter 8).

Moreover, you will make more progress listening than you will arguing a certain point over and over again. Others believe that active listening will seem contrived. Done poorly, it may. If, on the other hand, you are truly interested in what the other negotiator is saying and you are genuinely trying to learn, your active listening will be appreciated (Bordone, 2007).

THE CHANNELS OR MEDIA USED BY NEGOTIATORS TO EXCHANGE MESSAGES

The "how" of communication is about the channel or medium through which your message is sent. Many negotiations involve face-to-face interactions. Increasingly, however, negotiations are taking place electronically. Which medium is used matters because it influences your social awareness—the degree to which you are conscious of and attend to the other party or parties (McGinn & Croson, 2004). Social awareness influences the way you make sense of social interactions—how you perceive information, the attributions you make about the other party, and the behavior you deem appropriate (Kiesler & Sproull, 1992; Orbell, Van de Kragt, & Dawes, 1988).

Communication media differ in terms of their synchronicity, the number of different channels involved, and efficacy. *Synchronicity* involves the extent to which the parties communicate together in real time as opposed to independently at different times. Whether negotiators experience each other visually, aurally, by touch, or in other ways is a function of the number of different *channels* involved. *Efficacy* refers to whether negotiators convey factual, emotional, and other types of messages or only one type of message (McGinn & Croson, 2004). Face-to-face interactions are highly synchronous, involve multiple channels, and have high efficacy. E-mail involves low synchronicity, a text-only channel, and low efficacy.

Table 6.2 compares face-to-face and text-only media and their implications for social awareness during negotiations. Since electronic negotiations are becoming more common, other implications are noteworthy.

- Electronic media afford greater convenience for parties who are not located in close proximity.
- The parties may be communicating *synchronously or asynchronously*.
- Information conveyed in face-to-face negotiations is *richer* than information conveyed via e-mail or other text-only formats (Daft & Lengel, 1984).
- In e-negotiations, opportunities for informal communication, including informal feedback, may be lost. This includes schmoozing and other rapport-building activities that are essential for successful negotiations (Morris, Nadler, Kurtzberg, & Thompson, 2002).
- The logical sequencing of offers and counteroffers is often disrupted when communicating through text-only media. This interferes with turn taking or the "negotiation dance" (Raiffa, 1982), hinders efforts to build rapport and trust, and delays or delimits opportunities to correct misinterpretations (Higgins, 1999; Morris et al., 2002).
- E-communicators, thus e-negotiators, are less polite, employ more aggressive tactics, and attribute more malevolent motives to their counterparts than face-to-face negotiators (Sproull & Kiesler, 1991; Thompson & Nadler, 2002).

Reading 6.1 at the end of this chapter provides a more detailed discussion of these issues and how they can be managed to enhance e-negotiations.

Table 6.2 The Influence of Text-Only and Face-to-Face Media on Negotiations

Text-Only Communications	Face-to-Face Communications
Little mutual disclosure; it increases when audio and visual signals are added	Greater mutual disclosure, mutual understanding, and mutual construction of rules for the interaction
Less reciprocity and cooperation	Greater reciprocity and cooperation than audio-only (telephone) or text-only (e-mail) media
Bolder, less polite, more emotional outbursts because social norms are less compelling	Greater awareness of the complexity of the other party's position and of his potential response; this awareness also helps to temper boldness
Less trust seeking and fewer norms of caring are established	More positive interpersonal perceptions and trust seeking; more norms of caring are established
Less accurate information processing and fewer insights are gained because only one channel is involved	More accurate information processing; more accurate insights into the other party's situation
Building rapport is enhanced if the parties meet in person or speak on the telephone before the negotiation begins	More small talk and rapport building

(See, e.g., McGinn & Croson, 2004; Nadler, 2004; McGinn & Keros, 2003; McGinn, Thompson, & Bazerman, 2003; de Dreu, Weingart, & Kwon, 2000; Fehr & Gachter, 2000; Valley, Moag, & Bazerman, 1998; Sproull & Kiesler, 1986; Kiesler, Zubrow, & Moses, 1985.)

Haley's experience, as depicted in Negotiation in Action 6.5, illustrates many of the communication problems that often plague negotiators, including the added complexity that exists when more people are added to the negotiation. It also illustrates the benefits of active listening.

NEGOTIATION IN ACTION 6.5

A physician's group (Group) recently invited Haley's firm, a rehabilitation service provider (Rehab), to lease space in its new office building. Before Haley became involved, Group's business manager, Neil, and Rehab's real estate manager, Cora, were having difficulties reaching an acceptable agreement. Haley stepped in when the physicians told her that Neil was rude and unhelpful. Haley found Neil to be very pushy and a poor listener. He didn't seem to care about the reasoning behind some of Cora's requests regarding the lease language. Haley assured Neil that she wanted to proceed as quickly as possible. She also made it clear that both parties must proceed with caution because of the serious conflict of interest questions that could be raised—Group happens to be a major referral source for this future tenant (Rehab), and both entities take federally funded insurance payments for their services. Neil's attitude improved when Haley clarified these concerns and the implications for Group.

Nevertheless, Haley decided to communicate directly with the physicians to avoid more communication problems with Neil and others that typically arise when many people are involved with the transmission of messages. She was not willing to risk derailing the project because of poor communication.

When Haley met with the physicians, she took some time to build rapport and explain why she wanted to speak with them directly rather than through Neil. She told them, " . . . it is important that I understand your perspective of the situation, that you have a clear understanding of the situation from our perspective, and that I am able to answer any questions you might have directly. At the end of the day, the relationship between us is what will make this and any future projects successful, and having an open and honest line of communication is essential." The physicians acknowledged their appreciation. By asking open-ended questions and listening actively, Haley learned that the available square footage, which was larger than Rehab wanted, was nonnegotiable because the permits had been approved. She also learned that Group had terminated discussions with a different rehabilitation service provider because its corporate office took too long to approve the request and make important decisions about the lease arrangements, it planned to open similar facilities in 2–3 more locations in the near future and it wanted similar arrangements with Rehab in these facilities, and it wanted a 5-year lease agreement with Rehab to ensure stability.

Rehab's CEO initially gave Haley the green light to negotiate the best deal she could. Late in the negotiation process, however, he reneged: he told her that she must get the square footage reduced and she must reduce the length of the lease. Knowing that the rent already agreed to was competitive, that it would be impossible to redesign the physical layout to give some square footage back, and that it would be impossible to find a different tenant to whom the extra square footage could be leased, she asked more questions and listened actively to clarify her boss's true interests. She learned that since Rehab had not included this in the budget for the current year, he was worried about the negative financial consequences of the project—especially in the near future.

Fearing that asking for a lower rental rate and less square footage would blow this deal and future deals, and possibly harm what had been a very productive business relationship, Haley didn't ask for these changes. Instead, she told Group that she needed their help with two issues to ease her finance team's concerns about the numbers. She explained that her company had no problem making this large investment, but "we have not budgeted for the project this year. As you know, there will be a ramp up time for the business when it first opens. If we can defer the first three months of rent, it will allow us to work this into next year's budget and make the project look better financially, faster. And a successful track record will facilitate the approval of future projects with you." Group acknowledged her concerns, gave her the 3-month rent abatement she proposed, and spread that amount over the remaining term of the lease. She then explained that making such a large monetary commitment necessitated some protection in the event the project didn't perform. "Your group could split up, for example, or major insurance changes might happen with the new administration in Washington. Consequently, we must have an option to exit the lease at the end of the third year." Group agreed if Rehab was willing to pay for this option and the deal was signed (Personal Communication).

1. What did Haley do that made her communication with Neil and the physicians so effective?

2. What could she do that might make it even more effective now or in the future?

COMMUNICATING WITHOUT WORDS

Nonverbal communication or **body language** (these terms are used interchangeably) pertains to the transfer of messages using any means other than the spoken word. Table 6.3 identifies various ways in which we communicate nonverbally. We attach meaning to all of them, but we need to remain conscious of context. For example, if an attractive woman points her crossed legs at a man and tilts her head slightly to the side when smiling at him, this is likely to mean something very different if it happens at the bargaining table than if it happens at a club.

Video 6.2
How to prevent
information leakage

Nonverbal communication is important for negotiators for many reasons.

- The evidence suggests that 80–95% of messages are communicated nonverbally (Burgoon, 1980; Pease & Pease, 2004).
- Many people believe that nonverbal messages are more spontaneous and harder to fake than verbal messages. Thus, they are more believable (Burgoon, 1980; Mehrabian, 1972).
- Women are better than men at sending nonverbal messages because they are generally more expressive and more actively involved in social interactions (DePaulo & Friedman, 1998; Hall, 1984).
- Women are better at decoding nonverbal messages than men, especially facial cues (Hall, 1978; Rosenthal & DePaulo, 1979)
- Women are not better than men at detecting deception. In fact, men and women are both ineffective at detecting deception (DePaulo, Epstein, & Wyer, 1993; DePaulo, Rosenthal, Eisenstat, Rogers, & Finkelstein, 1978).

Table 6.3   Types of Nonverbal Communication

Types of Nonverbal Communication	Examples of What Is Included
Artifacts/Symbolic	Our cars, clothes, eyeglasses, jewelry, makeup, tattoos, piercings, where we live
Chromatics	Use of color
Chronemics	Use of time (e.g., linear or nonlinear, one thing at a time or multitask)
Context/Environment	Architectural style, decorations, furniture, lighting, smells, temperature, noises
Haptics	Bodily contact, touching
Kinesics	Eye movement, facial expressions, posture, gestures, movement of legs, hands, feet
Paralanguage	How things are said (e.g., accents, ahs & ums, fluency, pitch, volume)
Proxemics	Use of physical space (e.g., personal space bubble, seating arrangements)

Source: Adapted from DeVito, 2009; Reiman, 2007; Knapp & Hall, 2006; Pease & Pease, 2004.

- Body language is a constant. If someone else is present, we are communicating nonverbally.
- Nonverbal messages may repeat, contradict, complement, or substitute for verbal messages. *Repetition* happens, for example, when a person points toward your desired destination after giving verbal directions. Your manager's nonverbal message *contradicts* the verbal message if he or she smiles while delivering negative feedback. When the emotional content of a verbal message increases, it may serve to emphasize the importance of that message. The nonverbal message thereby *complements* the verbal message. If a person walks into his house after work with a very angry facial expression, his significant other does not have to ask if he or she had a bad day. The nonverbal message *substitutes* for the verbal message (Knapp & Hall, 2006).
- When visual and auditory nonverbal messages conflict, we generally rely more on the visual cues because they seem harder to fake (DePaulo, Rosenthal, Eisenstat, Rogers, & Finkelstein, 1978).

Since communication is central to the negotiation process, the influence of body language is quite robust. Perhaps its most important implications for negotiators involve first impressions, rapport building, coordinating or structuring conversation, and deception.

First Impressions

First impressions are closely related to the "implicit assumptions" (discussed in Chapter 2) that we make about people almost instantaneously upon meeting them, or even before we meet them. Within 1/10th of a second after seeing you, even before a word has been spoken, the person with whom you are interacting for the first time has made a judgment about how attractive, trustworthy, competent, and likable you are. Moreover, these judgments influence the quality of your subsequent interactions with him or her (Reiman, 2007). We appear to be this superficial because our initial observations of others trigger our brain to make comparisons and match them to other people we have encountered, in actuality or vicariously. If the match found elicits positive feelings, our first impression of the other person will be positive. If it elicits negative feelings, our first impression will be negative.

First impressions are formed so quickly that we do not have time to adjust after meeting someone. Nor can we control others instant comparisons that are made because we cannot control his or her memory or database. But we can influence the other person's search by using body language that generally triggers positive qualities. Table 6.4 summarizes the behaviors that typically influence the formation of our first impressions. These help or hinder our efforts to convey confidence, credibility, status, sincerity, interest, and rapport. Gathering information about the person with whom you will be negotiating and the context within which you will do so should also help you eliminate those awkward and telling surprises that may send undesirable messages (e.g., appearing surprised or shocked by an executive's extremely lavish office).

Building Rapport

As noted in Chapter 2, building rapport engenders more information sharing, trust, and respect, and it reduces threats (Nadler, 2004). It also helps to create positive first impressions. Building rapport is about creating the sense that you and the other party are in sync—positive, attentive, and well coordinated (Tickle-Degnen & Rosenthal, 1990). To achieve this, your verbal and nonverbal communication should both say, "Tell me more about you," and reinforce your interest in what he or she is saying. Share your appreciation for his or her successes, and acknowledge the difficulties

Table 6.4   Determinants of Positive and Negative First Impressions

Favorable	Unfavorable
Dress appropriately; Good grooming	Exhibiting jewelry, tattoos, or piercings that don't fit the situation or are in poor taste
Genuine smiles	Fake smiles
Good posture	Slouching
Purposeful walk	Shuffling; Walking aimlessly
Lean forward	Invading the other party's personal space
Good eye contact; Attentive	Tapping your feet; Drumming your fingers on the table; Clicking your pen and other fidgeting; Nervously biting your lips; Acting or looking distracted
Keep your arms at your sides	Keeping your hands in your pockets
Firm handshake	Limp handshake

Source: Adapted from Reiman, 2007; Knapp & Hall, 2006; Pease & Pease, 2004.

he or she is experiencing. Maintain soft eye contact (3–5 seconds) because it demonstrates sincerity, but avoid staring. Listen actively and attentively by, again, maintaining soft eye contact, occasionally tilting your head to the side, and nodding at appropriate times. Smiles and other positive facial expressions are better indicators of rapport than vocal cues such as pitch or volume (Grahe & Bernieri, 1999). Avoid fidgeting because it leads to negative first impressions and may detract from your rapport building. It can also be annoying.

Mirroring the other party's behavior—matching his or her pitch, rate of speech, gestures and facial expressions, postural congruence, and well coordinated conversations are among the most useful steps you can take to build rapport (Cappella, 1997; LaFrance, 1985, 1979; Lakin & Chartrand, 2003). Two cautions, however, are warranted. First, mirroring the other negotiator's aggressive behavior will escalate the conflict so it should be avoided. Second, mirroring must be subtle to avoid creating the impression that you are mocking him or her.

Structuring Conversations

Body language is part of a system of cues that help us with structuring conversations—who speaks, when, to whom, and for how long. Think about the conversations you have had with different people. Are some choppy and uncoordinated? Do the two of you always start talking at the same time? Do some people interrupt you when you try to speak? Are other conversations smooth and well coordinated? Is it clear when you should talk and when it is the other person's turn?

The smoothest transitions are achieved when consistent vocal cues, facial expressions, and gestures (samples are included in Table 6.5) are sent simultaneously (Duncan & Fiske, 1977).

Although this may seem like an innate ability we have, successful structuring can often be attributed to nonverbal communication. We use body language to indicate when we want to talk (turn requesting), when we want to continue talking (turn maintaining), when we want the other person to talk (turn yielding), and when we do not want to talk (turn denying). How well a conversation is structured may have as much to do with how it is perceived as does the actual verbal content (Duncan, 1973; Weim & Knapp, 1975).

Table 6.5 Typical Turn Taking Behaviors

Activity	Coordinating Behavior
Turn Requesting	Rapid head nodding to speed up the speaker; Interrupting; Attempting to speak at the same time, louder and with gestures; Vocal stuttering and other vocalizations such as I . . . , Ah . . . ; Raising your index finger (like raising your hand)
Turn Maintaining	Increase volume and speech rate when you sense the other person is requesting a turn; Decrease the frequency and duration of silent pauses and fill those that do occur; Continue using gestures to fill pauses; Touching the other's forearm seems to say, "hold on"
Turn Yielding	Ask questions; Raise your pitch at the end of a comment; Extended unfilled pauses; Fill pauses with, e.g., "you know"; Reduce illustrative gestures; Gaze at the listener; Raise your eyebrows in expectation; Increase eye contact with the listener
Turn Denying	Nod slowly to reinforce what's been said; Relaxed listening pose; Intently gaze at something in the environment other than the speaker; Demonstrate continuing interest in what he or she is saying (e.g., by smiling, nodding, shaking your head); Briefly restate what the speaker just said, ask for clarification; Show approval with "uh hmms," "yeahs"

Source: Adapted from Knapp, Cody, & Reardon, 1987; Bavelas, Black, Lemery, & Mullett, 1986; Duncan & Fiske, 1977; Krivonos & Knapp, 1975; Weimann & Knapp, 1975.

Conversations that are well coordinated help to build rapport and create the perception that you and the other person have hit it off. Rough transitions engender perceptions that the other party is rude, dominating, and frustrating (Knapp & Hall, 2006).

Detecting Deception

The most significant ethical concerns negotiators face involve truth telling, the withholding of information, and **deception**. There are many reasons a negotiator might not tell the truth—competition, greed, retaliation, face saving and others. You are likely to be more successful, therefore, if you can determine when the other side is lying about, or misrepresenting, information. This is not easy—accuracy rates are less than 50% (Zuckerman et al., 1981). Before discussing how we can improve at this, it helps to examine why we are generally not as good as we think we are at detecting deception.

It is widely believed that the face is an honest window into one's true feelings. While the face is our primary medium for communicating emotions, facial expressions are easy to disguise or fake. Moreover, people are least successful in detecting deception when they are able to see the face of the person they are judging (Zuckerman, DePaulo, & Rosenthal, 1981). This means we are vulnerable to manipulation by others' faces. Equally problematic, facial expressions are only loosely coupled with emotions. In response to the same stimulus, we smile more when we are interacting with others than when we are alone, and we tend to display different expressions in response to the same emotion (Ruiz-Belda, Fernandez-Dols, Carrera, & Barchard, 2003). We also display expressions reflecting what someone else is feeling. Men wince, for instance, when a hockey player they are watching on television gets hit in the groin by the puck (Bavelas, Black, Lemery, & Mullett, 1986). Simply put, facial expressions can be and often do reflect our emotions, but they are not purely emotional because the face is a tool of self presentation and social influence. We manage our facial expressions to create a desirable image of ourselves in the eyes of others and to produce desirable behaviors in others.

To illustrate, consider the following findings.

- People who cooperate or who want to cooperate extend longer gazes than those who do not.
- People seek mutual gazes to signal trust, liking, and honesty, and to facilitate the coordination of verbal exchanges.
- Competitors use frequent, short gazes to assess the other party's intentions without giving away their own.
- Listeners judge people who gaze longer to be more persuasive, truthful, informed, sincere, and credible.
- Compliance increases if the requester gazes more (Foddy, 1978; Hemsley & Doob, 1978; Mehrabian & Williams, 1969).

Gazing patterns can be faked. So-called High Machiavellians—people who are opportunistic and seek only to achieve desirable outcomes for themselves (see Chapter 11)—continue gazing longer than Low Machiavellians after being accused of cheating to convince others of their innocence. Deceivers, however, must be careful. Those who are less proficient may stare instead of merely gazing, or avoid visual contact altogether (Exline, Thibaut, Hickey, & Gumpert, 1970).

A negotiator's voice may also be misleading. People with attractive sounding voices—resonant, less monotonous, less nasal, lower pitch for males—are believed to have personalities that are less neurotic, more extraverted, warm, open, agreeable, powerful, honest, and conscientious than people with less attractive sounding voices (Berry, 1992; Zuckerman & Miyake, 1993).

There is no single sign of deceit—no gesture, facial expression, or muscle twitch – that necessarily means the other negotiator is lying (Ekman, 1992). Some verbal and nonverbal tendencies, however, suggest deceit. These are highlighted in Table 6.6.

CONCLUSION AND IMPLICATIONS FOR PRACTICE

Communication is central to all negotiations. We typically communicate quite clearly, but not always. Perceptions were discussed because they directly influence all communication choices. In fact, they are inextricably linked to the communication process. In addition to being aware of how complex this process is, the following suggestions should help you overcome many of the problems that plague your communications, thereby enhancing your effectiveness when you negotiate.

Table 6.6   Behavioral Cues Suggesting Deceit

Cognitive and Emotional Process	Behavioral Cues Suggesting Deceit
Facial Expressions	Excessive blinking; Pupils dilate more and for longer periods of time; Less smiling; Smiling at inappropriate times; Less gazing or even the covering of eyes; Gazes turn to stares if one is overcompensating
Speech & Vocal Cues	Stammering; Speech errors; Higher pitch; Excessive responses; Extreme and offensive language; Curt language; Shorter responses; Appearing to withhold information; Less forthcoming; Slower speaking rates; Incongruous verbal and nonverbal messages; Less cooperative; More negative statements; More words denoting anger, anxiety, and fear; More complaining; More defensive
Gestures	More fidgeting; Tense; Anxious; Phrases presented with fewer gestures
Cognitive Difficulties	Stories seem less plausible, with fewer details and more discrepancies; Fewer spontaneous corrections while telling stories; Less likely to admit when they can't remember something; Speech appears rehearsed; Less engaging because words and phrases are often repeated and presented with fewer gestures; Less direct; More uncertain; More hesitations, errors, and pauses; Fewer direct references; Fewer self-references

Source: Adapted from Knapp & Hall, 2006; Ekman, 1992; Knapp et al., 1987; Exline et al., 1979.

It behooves negotiators to be aware of these problems and to take steps to avoid or correct them to ensure that the messages exchanged are interpreted as intended. Failing to do so may undermine your efforts to achieve beneficial outcomes, or any outcomes.

1. Minimize noise to ensure that communication is effective. This includes finding a secluded place to negotiate where you will not have people walking by, telephones ringing (agree to turn off mobile phones), or other interruptions. It also includes suspending judgments based on extraneous factors such as cultural and language differences, including accents, because they engender stereotypes. It requires learning about and adapting your communication style to fit the other party's preferences. For example, if the other party prefers detailed explanations and strong justifications, communicate in that manner rather than conveying bullet points, sound bites, or telling stories.

2. Remember that meaning is influenced by context and that schemata can result in inaccurate interpretations of messages. By itself, a single behavior could mean many different things. A person who crosses his arms while talking might be deceitful, uncomfortable, uptight, or cold. Clustered together, three or four nonverbal cues send a potentially clearer and more powerful message. Since

individual differences and culture also influence how people sit or stand, what they do with their hands, how much they blink, and so on, it is wise to determine behavioral norms or baselines for that person before interpreting his or her nonverbal cues.

3. Keep in mind that individuals differ in how much they believe verbal and nonverbal messages. We often rely on nonverbal messages more than verbal messages when the two are incongruous because we think nonverbals are more spontaneous and harder to fake. People who are familiar with the language, however, rely on nonverbal cues more than verbal content, while verbal messages are more believable for those who are less familiar with the language. Verbal messages that are logical and supported by objective-appearing evidence are also more believable than nonverbal messages because they are credible.

4. When you are not sure if the other person is telling the truth, look for the signals in Table 6.5 and ask questions. Questions demanding yes or no or other one-word answers help to eliminate lies of omission but may increase lies of commission (Schweitzer & Croson, 1999). Asking different questions throughout your negotiation that address the same topic should help you determine the truth—if the other party gives similar answers each time, they are likely to be telling the truth. Asking for and receiving objective evidence that supports their assertions will also make them more credible and believable (Knapp & Hall, 2006). Finally, look for congruence between his or her verbal and nonverbal messages. When they are closely aligned and convey the same meaning, the other party is probably telling the truth.

5. Listen actively. Active listening is perhapshe or she is probably telling the truth. (I don't know what this sentence means or why it's here.)

6. Listen actively. This includes paraphrasing or restating what you hear and checking for understanding after you do so. This will help you clarify the meaning of what the other negotiator is saying, and you will acknowledge that you hear and understand his or her message. This is valuable because not feeling heard or understood underlies many conflicts and difficulties in negotiation. In addition to using the active listening skills mentioned earlier in this chapter, remember to focus on the speaker, assume that he or she has something useful to say, be willing to subject your biases and preconceptions to contradictory information, suspend judgments about what is being said until your exchange is complete, and think about how the content of the other party's message.

STUDENT STUDY SITE

Visit the Student Study Site at www.sagepub.com/hames for additional learning tools.

KEY TERMS

Active listening

Body language (aka nonverbal communications)

Building rapport

Communication channel

Deception

Director

Explanations (aka social accounts)

Expresser

Feedback

First impressions

Harmonizer

Message decoding

Message encoding

Noise

Nonverbal communication
(aka body language)

Social accounts (a.k.a. explanations)

Status Differences

Structuring conversations

Thinker

REFERENCES

Baron, R. A. (1990). Environmentally induced positive affect: Its impact on self efficacy and task performance, negotiation and conflict, *Journal of Applied Social Psychology*, 20, 368-384.

Bavelas, J. B., Black, A., Lemery, C. R. & Mullett, J. (1986). "I show how you feel": Motor mimicry as a communicative act, *Journal of Personality and Social Psychology*, 50, 322-329.

Berry, D. S. (1992). Vocal types and stereotypes: Joint effects of vocal attractiveness and vocal maturity on person perception, *Journal of Nonverbal Behavior*, 16, 41-54.

Bies, R. J. (1982). The delivery of bad news in organizations: A social information perspective, Paper presented at the National Meeting of the Academy of Management, New York, NY.

Bies, R. J. & Shapiro, D. (1988). Voice and justification: Their influence on procedural fairness judgments, *Academy of Management Journal,* 31, 676-685.

_____. (1987). Interactional justice judgments: The influence of causal accounts, *Social Justice Research*, 1(2), 199-218.

Bies, R. J., Shapiro, D. & Cummings, L. L. (1988). Causal accounts and managing organizational conflict: Is it enough to say it's my fault? *Communication Research*, 14, 381-399.

Bordone, R. C. (2007). Listen up! Your talks may depend on it, *Program on Negotiation Newsletter*, 10(5), 9-11.

Brett, J. M., Olekalns, M., Friedman, R., Goates, N., Anderson, C. & Lisco, C. C. (2007). Sticks and stones: Language, face and online dispute resolution, *Academy of Management Journal*, 50(1), 85-99.

Burgoon, J. K. (1980). Nonverbal communication research in the 1970s: An overview. In D. Nimmo (Ed.), *Communication yearbook 4*, New Brunswick, NJ: Transaction, 179-197.

Cappella, J. N. (1997). Behavioral and judged coordination in adult informal social interaction: Vocal and kinesic indicators, *Journal of Personality and Social Psychology*, 72, 119-131.

Daft, R. & Lengel, R. (1984). Organizational information requirements, media richness and structural design, *Management Science*, 35, 554-571.

de Dreu, C., Weingart, L. R. & Kwon, S. (2000). Influence of social motives on integrative negotiation: A meta-analytic review and test of two theories, *Journal of Personality and Social Psychology*, 78, 889-905.

DePaulo, B. M. & Friedman, H. S. (1998). Nonverbal communication. In D. T. Gilbert, S. T. Fiske & G. Lindzey (Eds.), *The handbook of social psychology, 4th., volume 2*. New York: McGraw-Hill, 3-40.

DePaulo, B.M., Epstein, J.A. & Wyer, M.M. (1993). Sex differences in lying: How women and men deal with the dilemma of deceit. In M. Lewis & C. Sarrni (Eds.), *Lying and deception in everyday life*. New York: Guilford Press, 126-147.

DePaulo, B. M., Rosenthal, R., Eisenstat, R., Rogers, P. L. & Finkelstein, S. (1978). Decoding discrepant nonverbal cues, *Journal of Personality and Social Psychology*, 36, 313-323.

Devito, J. A. (2009). *Human communication: The basic course, 11th*. Boston: Pearson.

Dobkin, B. A. & Pace, R. C. (2006). *Communication in a changing world*. New York: McGraw-Hill.

Douglas, E. (1998). *Straight talk: Turning communication upside down for strategic results.* Davies-Black Publishing: Palo Alto, CA.

Duncan, S. (1973). Toward a grammar for dyadic conversation, *Semiotica*, 9, 24-46.

Duncan, S. & Fiske, D. W. (1977). *Face-to-face interaction.* Hillsdale, NJ: Erlbaum.

Ebner, N., Bhappu, A. D., Brown, J. G., Kovach, K. K. & Schneider, A. K. (2009). You've got agreement: Negoti@ting via Email. In C. Honeyman, J. Coben & G.

De Palo (Eds.), *Rethinking negotiation teaching: Innovations for context and culture.* Downloaded from Marquette University Law School Legal Studies Research Paper Series, No. 09-16, http://ssrn.com/abstract = 1392474.

Ekman, P. (1992). *Telling Lies, 2nd.* New York: Norton.

Exline, R. V., Thibaut, J., Hickey, C. B. & Gumpert, P (1970). Visual interaction in relation to Machiavellianism and an unethical act. In P. Christie & F. Geis (Eds.), *Studies in Machiavellianism*, Ney York: Academic Press, 53-75.

Fehr, E. & Gachter, S. (2000). Fairness and retaliation: The economics of reciprocity, Journal of Economic Perspectives, 14, 159-181.

Foddy, M. (1978). Patterns of gaze in cooperative and competitive negotiation, *Human Relations*, 31, 925-938.

Grahe, J. E. & Bernieri, F. J. (1999). The importance of nonverbal cues in judging rapport, *Journal of Nonverbal Behavior*, 23, 253-269.

Greenberg, J. (1990). Employee theft as a reaction to underpayment inequity: The hidden costs of pay cuts, Journal of Applied Psychology, 75, 561-568.

Greenberg, J. (1988). Using social accounts to manage impressions of performance appraisal fairness, Paper presented at the National Meeting of the Academy of Management, Anaheim, CA.

Hall, J. A. (1984). *Nonverbal sex differences: Communication accuracy and expressive style.* Baltimore: Johns Hopkins University Press.

_____. (1978). Gender effects in decoding nonverbal cues, *Psychological Bulletin*, 85, 845-857.

Hemsley, G. D. & Doob, A. N. (1978). The effect of looking behavior on perceptions of a communicator's credibility, *Journal of Applied Psychology*, 8, 136-144.

Higgins, E. T. (1999). "Saying is believing" effects: When sharing reality about something biases knowledge and evaluations. In L. Thompson, J. M. Levine & D. M. Messick (Eds.), *Shared cognition in organizations: The management of knowledge.* Mahwah, NJ: Erlbaum, 33-48.

Hybels, S. & Weaver, II, R. L. (2007). *Communicating Effectively, 8th.* New York: McGraw-Hill.

Hyder, E. B., Prietula, M. J. & Weingart, L. R., (2000). Getting to best: Efficiency versus optimality in negotiation, *Cognitive Science*, 24(2), 169-204.

Kiesler, S. & Sproull, L. (1992). Group decision-making and communication technology, *Organizational Behavior and Human Decision Processes*, 52(1), 96-123.

Kiesler, S., Zubrow, D. & Moses, A. M. (1985). Affect in computer- mediated communication: An experiment in synchronous terminal-to-terminal discussion, *Human-Computer Interaction*, 1, 77-104.

Knapp, M. L. & Hall, J. A. (2006). *Nonverbal communication in human interaction*, 6th. Belmont, CA: Thomson.

Knapp, M. L., Cody, M. J. & Reardon, K. K. (1987). Nonverbal signals. In C. R. Berger & S. H. Chaffee (Eds.), *Handbook of communication science.* Beverly Hills, CA: Sage, 385-418.

Krivonos, P. D. & Knapp, M. L. (1975). Initiating communication: What do you say when you say hello? *Central States Speech Journal*, 26, 115-125.

LaFrance, M. (1985). Postural mirroring and intergroup relations, *Personality and Social Psychology Bulletin*, 11, 207-217.

_____. (1979). Non-verbal synchrony and rapport: Analysis by the cross-lag panel technique, *Social Psychology Quarterly*, 42, 66-70.

Lakin, J. L. & Chartrand, T. L. (2003). Using nonconscious behavioral mimicry to create affiliation and rapport, *Psychological Science*, 14, 334-339.

Langner, C. A. & Winter, D. G (2001). The motivational basis of concessions and compromising: Archival and laboratory studies, *Journal of Personality and Social Psychology*, 81, 711-727.

McGinn, K. L. & Croson, R. (2004). What do communication media mean for negotiation? A question of social awareness. In M. J. Gelfand & J. M. Brett (Eds.), *The handbook of negotiation and culture.* Stanford, CA: Stanford Business Books, 334-349.

McGinn, K. L. & Keros, A. (2003). Improvisation and the logic of exchange in embedded negotiations, *Administrative Science Quarterly*, 47, 442-473.

McGinn, K. L., Thompson, L. & Bazerman, M. H. (2003). Dyadic processes of disclosure and reciprocity in bargaining with communication, *Journal of Behavioral Decision Making*, 16, 17-34.

Mehrabian, A. (1972). *Nonverbal communication.* Chicago: Aldine-Atherton.

Mehrabian, A. & Williams, M. (1969). Nonverbal concomitants of perceived and intended persuasiveness, *Journal of Personality and Social Psychology*, 13, 37- 58.

Morris, M. W., Nadler, J., Kurtzberg, T. & Thompson, L. (2002). Schmooze or lose: Social friction and lubrication in e-mail negotiations, *Group Dynamics: Theory, Research, and Practice*, 6(1), 89-100.

Nadler, J. (2004). Rapport in legal negotiations: How small talk can facilitate email dealmaking, *Harvard Negotiation Law Review*, 9, 223-253.

Olekalns, M. & Smith, P. (2000). Negotiating optimal outcomes: The role of strategic sequences in competitive negotiations, *Human Communication Research*, 24, 528-560.

Orbel, J. Van de Kragt, A. & Dawes, R. (1988). Explaining discussion-induced cooperation, *Journal of Personality and Social Psychology*, 54, 811-819.

Parse, P. W. & Gilin, D. A. (2000). When an adversary is caught telling the truth: Reciprocal cooperation versus self-interest in distributive bargaining, *Personality and Social Psychology Bulletin*, 26(1), 79-90.

Pease, A. & Pease, B. (2004). *The definitive book of body language.* New York: Bantam.

Pinkley, R. L. (1995). The impact of knowledge regarding alternatives to settlement in dyadic negotiations: Whose knowledge counts? *Journal of Applied Psychology*, 80(3), 403-417.

Pinkley, R. L., Neale, M. A. & Bennett, R. J. (1994) The impact of alternatives to settlement in dyadic negotiation, *Organizational Behavior and Human Decision Processes*, 57, 97-116.

Program on Negotiation (2010). Are you asking the right questions?, *Negotiation*, 13(2), 1-3.

Raiffa, H. (1982). *The art and science of negotiation.* Cambridge, MA: Belknap Press.

Reiman, T. (2007). *The power of body language: How to succeed in every business and social encounter.* New York: Pocket Books.

Rosenthal, R & DePaulo, B. M. (1979). Sex differences in accommodation in nonverbal communication. In R. Rosenthal, (Ed.), *Skill in nonverbal communication:*

Individual differences. Cambridge, MA: Oelgeschlager, Gunn & Hain, 68-103.

Ruiz-Belda, M., Fernandez-Dols, J, Carrera, P & Barchard, K. (2003). Spontaneous facial expressions of happy bowlers and soccer fans, *Cognition and Emotion*, 17, 315- 326.

Schweitzer, M. & Croson, R. (1999). Curtailing deception: The impact of direct questions on lies and omissions, *International Journal of Conflict Management*, 10, 225- 248.

Shapiro, D. (1991). The effects of explanations on negative reactions to deceit, *Administrative Science Quarterly*, 36, 614-630.

Shapiro, D. & Buttner, E. H. (1988). Adequate explanations: What are they, and do they enhance procedural justice under severe outcome circumstances? Paper presented at the National Meeting of the Academy of Management, Anaheim, CA.

Simons, T. (1993). Speech patterns and the concept of utility in cognitive maps: The case of integrative bargaining, *Academy of Management Journal*, 36(1), 139-156.

Sitkin, S. B. & Bies, R. J. (1993). Social accounts in conflict situations: Using explanations to manage conflict, *Human Relations*, 46(3), 349-370.

Sproull, L. & Kiesler, S. (1991). *Connections: New ways of working in the networked organization.* Cambridge, MA: MIT Press.

_____. (1986). Reducing social context cues: Electronic mail in organizational communication, *Management Science*, 32, 1492-1512.

Thompson, L. & Nadler, J. (2002). Negotiating via information technology: Theory and application, *Journal of Social Issues*, 58(1), 109-124.

Thompson, L. & Hastie, R. (1990). Social perception in negotiation, *Organizational Behavior and Human Decision Processes*, 47, 98-123.

Tickle-Degnen, L. & Rosenthal, R. (1990). The nature of rapport and its nonverbal correlates, *Psychological Inquiry*, 1, 285-293.

Tutzauer, F. (1992). The communication of offers in dyadic bargaining. In L Putnam & M. Roloff (Eds.), *Communication and negotiation.* Newbury Park, CA: Sage, 67- 82.

Valley, K. L., Moag, J. & Bazerman, M. H. (1998). A matter of trust: Effects of communication on the efficiency and distribution of outcomes, *Journal of Economic Behavior and Organization*, 34, 211-238.

Weimann, J. M. & Knapp, M. L. (1975). Turn-taking in conversations, *Journal of Communication*, 25, 75-92.

Weingart, L. R. & Olekalns, M. (2004). Communication processes in negotiation: Frequencies, sequences, and phases. In M. J. Gelfand & J. M. Brett (Eds.), *The handbook of negotiation and culture*. Stanford, CA: Stanford Business Books, 143-157.

Weingart, L. R., Thompson, L. L., Bazerman, M. H. & Carroll, J. S. (1990). Tactical behaviors and negotiation outcomes, *International Journal of Conflict Management*, 1, 7-31.

Zuckerman, M. & Miyake, K. (1993). The attractive voice: What makes it so? *Journal of Nonverbal Behavior*, 17, 119-135.

Zuckerman, M., DePaulo, B.M.& Rosenthal, R. (1981). Verbal and nonverbal communication of deception. In L. Berkowitz (Ed.), *Advances in experimental social psychology, volume 14*. New York: Academic Press, 1-60.

READINGS

Reading 6.1

YOU'VE GOT AGREEMENT: NEGOTI@TING VIA EMAIL

Noam Ebner, Anita D. Bhappu, Jennifer Gerarda Brown, Kimberly K. Kovach, & Andrea Kupfer Schneider

Introduction

Negotiation teaching has, in most instances, attempted to prepare students for multi-contextual encounters. Students of negotiation in business schools are trained to recognize and take part in a wide range of negotiation settings, including their own salary and benefits negotiations, intra-organizational negotiations (such as a negotiation over resources with the manager of a competing unit within the same organization), inter-organizational negotiations (such as discussing a joint venture or partaking in a sales/purchasing bar gaining session), and others. Similarly, we expect the negotiation training we give law students to facilitate their interactions with a variety of people, including clients, other counsel, judges, and juries. In fact, participants in negotiation courses are usually invited and encouraged to use their new insights and skills in just about any context: at work, with their families, in their own transactions (e.g., buying a house or a car), in their social relationships, and in casual encounters. In taking this omni-contextual approach, however, teachers must manage a tension between the general and the specific, building general skills applicable to a variety of situations but also fostering sensitivity to the more particularized ways those skills will be used in specific contexts.

Our concern in this chapter is with one contextual element that receives inadequate attention: physical proximity versus distance. Too often, teachers of negotiation assume one or both of the following propositions: 1) people negotiate with others who are physically present "at the table" or "in the room," and 2) when people negotiate with others who are *not* physically present, negotiation skills and strategies do not significantly differ from the "normal" condition of physical proximity.

Ebner, N., Bhappu, A. D., Brown, J. G., Kovach, K. K., & Schneider, A. K. (2009). You've got agreement: Negoti@ting via email. In C. Honeyman, J. Coben, & G. De Palo (Eds.), *Rethinking Negotiation Teaching: Innovations for Context and Culture*. St. Paul, MN: DRI Press.

Editor's Note: Astonishing amounts of negotiation are now conducted by e-mail—often with scant regard for underlying strategy, or even, common courtesy. The authors unpack why this happens, and propose methods that will better prepare students for the realities of future business.

This does not reflect the reality of most negotiators' work. Factors such as the proliferation of low- to no-cost communication tools, along with increasing numbers of technologically adept workers, have made e-communication an ever-increasing alternative to face-to-face meetings. We have all seen the proliferation of wireless handheld devices ("crackberrys" for the truly addicted); email is ubiquitous. According to David Shipley and Will Schwalbe, "trillions of emails are sent every week" and "office workers in the U.S. spend at least 25 per cent of the day on email" (Shipley and Schwalbe 2007). As an illustration of this in the U.S., Shipley and Schwalbe note the roughly three-fold increase in the number of emails produced by the Bush administration over the number created by the Clinton administration (100 million expected under Bush by 2009 compared to 32 million turned over to the National Archives by Clinton in 2001). Clearly, email is a fact of life for any negotiator, and we ignore its potentials and pitfalls at our peril.

In this chapter, we will focus on the use of email, the most common form, of online interaction in professional contexts, and acknowledge the clear advantages of this mode of communication. First, we present research showing how the medium may affect the message. We outline a framework for understanding the specific elements of communication that are most altered in the shift from in-person conversation to exchange of email messages. The next part of the chapter delineates five major implications of these differences for negotiating via email and suggests four basic skill sets that email negotiators need to acquire in order to cope with these implications. The chapter concludes by addressing negotiation teachers and trainers. We suggest effective ways to familiarize students with email negotiation's benefits and challenges and then to equip them with the tools necessary to navigate the online medium.

PART I: NEGOTIATION VIA EMAIL: YES, IT *IS* DIFFERENT!

In negotiation, communication media influence not only what information is shared and how that information is communicated (Carnevale and Probst 1997; Valley et al. 1998; Friedman and Currall 2001), but also how information is received and interpreted. Some information may be easy to communicate face-to-face, but difficult to convey in an email. Other information might be laid out clearly in an email message but misconstrued in a face-to-face setting. We can understand these differences more clearly by comparing face-to-face and email negotiations with reference to two dimensions of communication media: *media richness* and *interactivity* (Barsness and Bhappu 2004). Media richness is the capacity of the medium to transmit visual and verbal cues, thus providing more immediate feedback and facilitating communication of personal information (Daft and Lengel 1984). Interactivity is the potential of the medium to sustain a seamless flow of information between two or more negotiators (Kraut et al. 1992). Both characteristics account for differences across media in the structure of information exchanged (Daft and Lengel 1984), the number of social context cues transmitted (Sproull and Kjesler 1986; Kiesler and Sproull 1992), and the social presence of negotiators (Short, Williams, and Christie 1976).

Media Richness

Email is considered a "lean" medium because it transmits neither visual nor verbal cues. Face-to-face communication is considered a "rich" medium because it transmits both. In face-to-face communication, a significant proportion of a message's meaning comes from its associated visual cues (such as facial expressions and body language) and verbal cues (such as tone of voice) (DePaulo and Friedman 1998). Because these contextual cues are absent in email, negotiators both transmit and receive information differently than they would in person. For example, even in "high context" cultures, where communication tends to draw upon pre-existing knowledge or indirect signals rather than rely upon the explicit content of the message itself (Hall 1976; Ting-Toomey 1988), email may pull participants into communication patterns that resemble (and therefore potentially privilege) "low-context" cultures, where meaning is primarily found in the explicit message conveyed. The absence of contextual cues affects the way negotiators present their information. Email negotiators rely more heavily on logical argumentation and the presentation of facts, rather than emotional or personal appeals (Barsness and Bhappu 2004). The communication medium also affects the *content* of the information negotiators share, as a result of its affecting their communication. Research suggests, for instance, that communication styles in email are more task-oriented and depersonalized than in face-to-face interactions (Kemp and Ratter 1982). This results in less small talk and rapport building, and a more "down to business" approach, as will be discussed below.

Reduced contextual information may also affect the way negotiators receive and interpret email messages. Information exchanged in email tends to be less nuanced than information exchanged face-to-face in the same situation (Valley et al. 1998; Friedman and Currall 2001). Back channel and clarifying information such as speech acknowledgements (e.g., "mmm" or "huh?") and reactive body language such as head nods are eliminated (O'Connaill et al. 1993). Another interesting outcome of the elimination of contextual cues is that negotiators are more likely to focus on the *content* of messages when using lean media (Ocker and Yaverbaum 1999). Although technology is evolving to permit negotiators to include additional visual cues through color, font, and pictures (such as emoticons), these cues are far cruder than the nuanced signaling available in face-to-face

encounters. Additionally, use of these cues is not widespread in professional communication, inhibiting the development of a shared culture or code as to their intent and significance. Indeed, the ambiguity of such text and graphics-based signals can give rise to potential problems in email negotiation, as we shall discuss below.

Interactivity

Interactivity has two dimensions. The first, a temporal dimension, captures the synchronicity of interactions. Face-to-face communication is synchronous and co-temporal. Each party receives an utterance just as it is produced; as a result, speaking "turns" tend to occur sequentially. Email is typically asynchronous: negotiators can read and respond to others' messages whenever they desire and not necessarily sequentially. Minutes, hours, or even weeks can pass between the time a negotiator "sends" a message and the time the recipient reads it (Friedman and Curtail 2001. Because email messages usually appear in recipients' inboxes with most recent messages above the older ones, recipients may read messages out of order, even responding to later messages *before* they have read the antecedent message.

The second dimension of interactivity is parallel processing, which describes a medium's ability to allow two or more negotiators to simultaneously submit messages. Email certainly permits the simultaneous exchange of messages, but negotiators will not necessarily know that this simultaneous submission is occurring—in contrast to face-to-face communication, where the parallel processing will be patent. As we shall see below, the "turn taking" required by email can facilitate communication *by* preventing one party from interrupting the other, giving both parties the chance to express their views fully before relinquishing the floor; however, the same quality that prevents interruption also prevents the parties from engaging in the kind of conscious parallel processing that is possible when face-to-face.

These two characteristics of email - that it requires asynchronicity but allows parallel processing—have profound effects on the way messages are transmitted and the way they are received. On the transmission side, the use of asynchronous media may accentuate analytical-rational expression of information by negotiators. Previous research suggests that there are at least two distinct information-processing modes: an *analytical-rational mode* and an *intuitive-experiential mode* (Epstein et al. 1996). Individuals who adopt an analytical-rational mode rely more heavily on logic and deductive thinking and their associated tactics (e.g., development of positions and limits, use of logical argumentation, and the presentation of facts), while individuals who adopt an intuitive-experiential mode rely more heavily on intuition and experience and their associated tactics (e.g., appeals to emotion, the presentation of concrete personal stories, and the use of metaphors) (Gelfand and Dyer 2000). Email does not lend itself equally to these contrasting information-processing styles.

On the receiving side, email imposes high "understanding costs" on negotiators because it provides little "grounding" to participants in the communication exchange (Clark and Brennan 1991; Friedman and Cutrall 2001). Grounding is the process by which two parties in an interaction develop a shared sense of understanding about a communication and a shared sense of participation in the conversation (Clark and Brennan 1991). Without the clues provided by shared surroundings, non-verbal behavior, tone of voice, or the timing and sequence of the information exchange, negotiators may find it challenging to accurately decode the messages that they receive electronically (Clark and Brennan 1991). In addition, the tendency of email negotiators to "bundle" multiple arguments and issues together in one email message (Adair et al. 2001; Friedman and Currall 2001; Rosette et al. 2001) can place high demands on the receiver's information processing capabilities.

PART II: MEDIA EFFECTS: IMPLICATIONS OF EMAIL COMMUNICATION FOR NEGOTIATION

The foregoing comparison of face-to-face negotiation and email negotiation gives rise to five major implications—incorporating both challenges and opportunities for parties negotiating by email:

1) Increased contentiousness

2) Diminished information sharing

3) Diminished process cooperation

4) Diminished trust

5) Increased effects of negative attribution

1) Increased Contentiousness

Even before the advent of Internet-based e-communication, research showed that communication at a distance via technological means is more susceptible to disruption than face-to-face dialogue. Aimee Drolet and Michael Morris, for example, have found that whereas face-to-face interactions foster rapport and cooperation, telephone communication was prone to more distrust, competition, and contentious behavior (Drolet and Morris 2000).

In Internet-based communication, these findings not only hold true, they are intensified. Communication in cyberspace tends to be less inhibited; parties ignore the possible adverse consequences of negative online interactions because of physical distance, reduced social presence, reduced accountability and a sense of anonymity (Griffith and Northcraft 1994; Wallace 1999; Thompson 2004). The lack of social cues in e-communication causes people to act more contentiously than they do in face-to-face encounters, resulting in more frequent occurrences of swearing, name calling, insults, and hostile behavior (Kiesler and Sproull 1992).

Research shows that these findings on e-communication also hold true in e-negotiation. Early research showed that negotiators are apt to act tough and choose contentious tactics when negotiating with people at a distance (Raiffa 1982). As researchers began to focus on e-negotiation, they discovered the effects of diminished media richness in e-negotiation: the social presence of others is reduced (Short, Williams, and Christie 1976; Weisband and Atwater 1999) and the perceived social distance among negotiators increases (Sproull and Kiesler 1986; Jessup and Tansik 1991). Thus, negotiators' social awareness of each other may be seriously diminished (Valley and Croson 2004) when communicating through email. This might explain why e-negotiators feel less bound by normatively appropriate behavior than face-to-face negotiators apparently do. This weakening of the normative fabric translates into an increased tendency to make threats and issue ultimata (Moms et al. 2002), to adopt contentious, "squeaky wheel" behavior, to lie or deceive (Naquin, Kurtzberg, and Belkin, forthcoming), to confront each other negatively, and to engage in flaming (Thompson and Nadler 2002).

Hence, email negotiators are contending on a much rougher playing field than face-to-face negotiators. Still, the better we understand the nature of email as described in the previous section, the greater our abilities to turn the potentially hazardous characteristics of email to good use—i.e., *reducing* contentiousness. Used properly, lean media may facilitate better *processing* of social conflict exactly because these media do not transmit visual and verbal cues (Carnevale, Pruitt, and Seilheimer 1981; Bhappu and Crews 2005). First, the visible, physical presence of an opponent can induce arousal (Zajonc 1965), which leads to more aggressive behavioral responses. Therefore, the absence of visual and verbal cues in email may defuse such triggers. Second, email may also reduce the

salience of group differences. By masking or deemphasizing gender, race, accent, or national origin, to name just a few, email may actually reduce the impact of unconscious bias (Greenwald, McGhee, and Schwartz 1998) on negotiation. Deemphasizing group membership may also suppress coalition formation. In addition, because negotiators are physically isolated and the social presence of others is diminished, they can take time to "step out" of the discussion and thoughtfully respond rather than merely react to the other party's behavior, potentially limiting escalation of social conflict even further (Harasim 1993; Bhappu and Crews 2005).

2) Diminished Inter-party Cooperation

Experiments in email negotiation have explored two connected concepts: the measure of inter-party cooperation throughout the negotiation process, and the degree to which resulting outcomes are integrative at the end of the negotiation. The connection between the two is obvious: the potential for integrative outcomes grows as parties become more aware of each other's needs and capabilities, and areas of potential joint gain emerge.

Email negotiations make information exchange likely to be constrained, analytical, and contentious. This diminishes negotiators' ability to accurately assess differential preferences and identify potential joint gains. Indeed, one comparison of face-to-face and computer-mediated negotiations revealed that negotiators interacting electronically were less accurate in judging the other party's interests (Arunachalam and Dilla 1995). Reduced social awareness in lean media causes parties to engage more heavily in self-interested behavior when negotiating by email. As a result, they may simply ignore or fail to elicit important information about the other party's interests and priorities. The use of email may,. therefore, accentuate competitive behavior in negotiations (Barsness and Bhappu 2004).

However, when used properly, email could increase information exchange. Lean media may work to promote more equal participation among negotiators. Diminished social context cues (Sproull and Kiesler 1991) and resulting reduction in the salience of social group differences (Bhappu et al. 1997) and encourage lower-status individuals to participate more (Siegel et al. 1936). Rather than discounting or ignoring information provided by lower-status individuals, as they might in face-to-face encounters, negotiators may be receptive to this additional information when using email. Attention to this "new" information may subsequently enable negotiators to identify optimal trades and create more integrative agreements.

The nature of email interactivity reinforces this tendency toward increased participation and more diverse information. As discussed above, the parallel processing allowed by email frees negotiators from sequential turn-taking, prevents interruptions, and allows negotiators to voice their different perspectives simultaneously (Lam and Schaubroeck 2000). Parallel processing can also undermine existing power dynamics and encourage direct confrontation because it stops one individual from seizing control of the discussion and suppressing the views of another (Nunamaker et al. 1991). Thus, in a sense, email exchange can tame and discipline the free-for-all form of parallel processing that can occur in face-to-face encounters. By making parallel processing more coherent, email may further support the simultaneous consideration of multiple issues during negotiation. Coupled with the greater diversity of information produced when social groups are deemphasized and power differentials are reduced, parallel processing in email is likely to promote the search for joint gains (Barsness and Bhappu 2004).

3) Reduction in Integrative Outcomes

As previously mentioned, reduced process cooperation is expected to result in a lower level of integrative agreements. Many experiments measuring these two indicators—cooperative behavior and integrative outcomes - have shown that in e-negotiation, as opposed to face-to-face negotiation, one is less likely to encounter cooperation in the process, and less likely to achieve integrative outcomes (Arunachalam and Dilla 1995; Valley et al. 1998; see also Nadler and Shestowsky 2006). Additionally, the potential for impasse appears to be greater than in face-to-face negotiation (Croson 1999). Conversely, other researchers have found no difference in rates of impasse and frequency of integrative outcomes when comparing email and face-to-face negotiations (Nanquin and Paulson 2003; see also Nadler and Shestowsky 2006).[1]

Why, we might ask, should email bargaining be less integrative than face-to-face encounters (if in fact the trend goes in this direction) We believe that a reduction in the likelihood and degree of integrative solutions could result from lower levels of process cooperation and the difficulty of building rapport in email negotiation. If email somehow encourages negotiators to become more contentious and confrontational in the way they communicate (Kiesler and Sproull 1992), this can lead to spiraling conflict and the hardening of positions. This problem is made even more severe by the difficulty of establishing rapport in email (Drolet and Morris 2000), which we will expand on below. The development of rapport has been shown to foster more mutually beneficial settlements (Drolet and Morris 2000), especially in lean media contexts (Moore et al. 1999) perhaps because it engenders greater social awareness among negotiators (Valley and Croson 2004).

On the other hand, the media effects of email negotiation include one feature that might promote integrative thinking and outcomes. As we have seen, negotiators tend to exchange long messages that include multiple points all in one "bundle" when using asynchronous media like email (Adair et al. 2001; Friedman and Currall 2001; Rosette et al. 2001). Argument-bundling may facilitate integrative agreements by encouraging negotiators to link issues together and consider them simultaneously rather than sequentially (Rosette et al. 2001). This can promote log-rolling, a classic tool for reaching integrative outcomes. However, negotiators should avoid "over-bundling": too many issues and too much information delivered at one time can place higher demands on the receiver's information processing capabilities. Negotiators may, therefore, have more difficulty establishing meaning and managing feedback in asynchronous media (DeSanctis and Monge 1999), further hindering their efforts to successfully elicit and integrate the information that is required to construct a mutually beneficial agreement.

4) Diminished Degreed Interparty Trust

Trust between negotiating parties has been identified as playing a key role in enabling cooperation (Deutsch 1962), problem solving (Pruitt, Rubin, and Kim 1994), achieving integrative solutions (Lewicki and Litterer 1985; Lax and Sebenius 1986), effectiveness (Schneider 2002) and resolving disputes (Moore 2003). Negotiators are trained and advised to seek out and create opportunities for trust-building whenever possible, and as early as possible in the course of a negotiation process (Lewicki and Litterer 1985).

Communication via email, however, is fraught with threats to trust that are inherent in the medium and in the way parties approach and employ it (Ebner 2007). It has been suggested that lack of trust in online opposites is the factor responsible for the low levels of process cooperation and of integrative outcomes reported above (Nadler and Shestowsky 2006). Low levels of inter-party trust in email negotiation have been

measured not only through indirect indicators, such as low process cooperation and infrequently integrative outcomes, but also directly: when questioned about the degree of trust they felt in negotiation processes, e-negotiators reported lower levels of trust than face-to-face negotiators did (Naquin and Paulson 2003). Email negotiators enter the process with a lower level of pre-negotiation trust in their counterparts than do participants in face-to-face negotiations (Naquin and Paulson 2003). This initially low expectation regarding interpersonal trust may exacerbate the fundamental attribution error by reinforcing the tendency to seek out reasons to distrust rather than to recognize trustworthy actions. This becomes a self-fulfilling prophecy: expecting to find counterparts untrustworthy, email negotiators share less information; this reinforces their counterparts' expectations. As a result, participants m email negotiation also experience lower levels of *post*-negotiation trust than do participants in face-to-face negotiations (Naquin and Paulson 2003).

5) Increased Tendency Towards Sinister Attribution

The media effects of email negotiation exacerbate the tendency toward the sinister attribution error: the bias toward seeing negative events as the outgrowth of others' negative intentions rather than unintended results or conditions beyond their control. The lack of social presence and of contextual cues lends a sense of distance and of vagueness to the interaction. The asynchronous dynamic of email negotiations adds to this challenge. Research shows that e-negotiators ask fewer clarifying questions than face-to-face negotiators do. Instead of gathering information from their counterparts, email negotiators may be more likely to make assumptions (Thompson and Nadler 2002); if those assumptions later prove unfounded, the negotiators may perceive the other's inconsistent actions or preferences as a breaking of trust. The power of the sinister attribution error in e-negotiation is clearly demonstrated by experiments showing that e-negotiators are more likely to suspect their opposite of lying than are face-to-face negotiators, even when no actual deception has taken place (Thompson and Nadler 2002). Analysis of failed email negotiations shows that they tend to include unclear messages, irrelevant points, and long general statements (Thompson 2004), each of which provides ample breeding ground for the sinister attribution error.

Summary

In this section, we have described five important implications of the unique characteristics of email communication for negotiation. Highlighting these particular media effects is particularly important in order to understand the challenges posed by the media to negotiators trained to conduct face-to-face interactions. Next, we turn to recommending skill-sets that negotiators need to be equipped with in order to cope with these implications.

PART III: REPACKING THE NEGOTIATOR'S TOOLBOX: RECOMMENDED SKILL-SETS FOR EMAIL NEGOTIATORS

In this section, we will briefly introduce four basic skill-sets that email negotiators need to acquire in order to cope with the media effects of email discussed in the last section. These four skills are discussed as initial proposals, and are certainly not suggested as an exhaustive list; no doubt, others will emerge.

Skill-Set #1: Writing Ability

A central skill that may seem both so obvious and so crucial that we need not address it is the ability to write—clearly, persuasively, and (at times) movingly. For most lawyers, fortunately,

writing is a skill used and developed daily. Much of their legal training has been devoted to developing clear, effective writing. For some lawyers as well as other professionals, however, writing is not considered a central activity in their* employment. Skills become rusty from lack of use. or a particular style of writing (marketing, for example, in the management context; brief writing in the legal context) may not lend itself well to email. Particularly when it comes time to establish rapport, defuse tension, or even apologize, some email negotiators may find that their writing skills are simply not up to the task at hand. Thus, a central skill set for effective email negotiation may be to improve the clarity and emotional power of writing. And when writing skills fall short of the task's requirements, email negotiators need the wisdom to discern then own limitations, pick up a phone, or make an appointment to meet in person with their negotiation counterparts.

Skill Set #2: Message Management

Managing Our Own Anxiety

The art of negotiating solely by exchanging written messages through postal mail is a long-forgotten one. We have become accustomed to exchanging opinions through synchronous communication, either face-to-face or over the telephone. Email negotiators need to relearn the art of asynchronous communication. This may not be intuitive, for one of the Internet's promises is instant access to anything and anyone. Our synchronous-communication upbringing, combined with our expectations of instant access, clash with the basic nature of asynchronous communication. As a result, email communication often involves an anxiety that blends distrust of the channel with distrust of the other. When we send messages and do not receive responses promptly, not only do we question whether our counterparts received the messages, we begin to wonder why (if indeed they *have* received them) they are taking so long to respond (Thompson and Nadler

2002). To manage this anxiety and prevent a downward spiral of distrust, e-negotiators need to understand and bear in mind the limitations of the medium they are using. They also need to develop gentle but effective ways to follow up when counterparts do not respond in what seems to be an appropriate period of time, generously calculated. Shipley and Schwalbe suggest that when a response is not forthcoming, email users can resend the original email, but if they do this, they should "acknowledge that this is the second time around, and apologize (I know how busy you are . . . ')" (Shipley and Schwalbe 2007: 152–53). They warn against simply resending the old message without comment or with "blaming language," such as "Why haven't you responded to this?"

Managing the Other's Anxiety

Research has shown that frequent message exchanges, as opposed to communication broken by intervals, are conducive to trust-building within groups (Wallace 1999; Walther and Bunz 2005). This is also true for the dyadic group formed by two people negotiating. Responding to an email within 24 hours, even if only to say that we are considering what a negotiation counterpart has written, might be a useful standard (Katsh and Rifkin 2001). On the other hand, delivering a strongly negative response or a total rejection of the counterpart's proposal should not be done too hastily. Negotiation counterparts want to know that we have carefully read and processed their proposals to us. But when a negotiator realizes that she has taken an inexcusably long tune to respond in an email negotiation exchange, she should usually acknowledge that fact in the interests of preserving the relationship. Shipley and Schwalbe suggest phrases such as "I have the awful feeling that I've neglected to respond to your email . . ." or "My profuse apologies for the slowness of my reply. . . ." (Shipley and Schwalbe 2007).Thus, in order to manage the other's anxiety, a good email negotiator needs sufficient empathy to sense how the other may be feeling about the negotiator's behavior and the emotional vocabulary to put the other at ease by signaling that understanding.

Utilizing Asynchronicity

Once we become aware of and overcome the challenging characteristics of asynchronous communication, we can focus on the potential it offers for unproved communication dynamics. It can be a very conducive channel for reasoned discussion, careful responses, and trust-building moves. It can help control our response time—to our own advantage. Asynchronous communication allows us to avoid knee-jerk reactions or escalatory cycles of contentious behavior, and to think proactively. The slower pace allows us to fashion and frame our response thoughtfully and productively. It enables us to verify details instead of giving off-the-cuff responses that may later turn out to be inaccurate—providing for more exact information-sharing. Email creates a searchable thread of exchanged email messages so that we can hold others accountable for representations and commitments. And. we can check our own past communications if they over-claim something we have allegedly promised. We can read a received message twice, or ask a colleague to take a look at it and tell us what she thinks, before we reply to it, lowering the effect of sinister attribution. We can do the same with a message we have written, before sending it. By learning when not to click "Reply," and when to delay clicking "Send," email negotiators can use the medium to maximum effect.

Skill-Set #3: Relationship Management

Setting the Stage: Unmasking

As we have seen, the mutual invisibility inherent in email negotiation facilitates adversarial, contentious, and trust-breaking behavior. It is easier to cause damage to a faceless other, particularly when we feel protected by a shield of anonymity and physical distance. The sense of anonymity and distance created between email negotiators leads both to assumptions that one can get away with aggressive or trust-breaking behavior, and to a lowering of moral inhibitions against doing so (Nadler and Shestowsky 2006). This necessitates that negotiators consciously adopt a proactive agenda of unmasking themselves *toward* the other. The more negotiation counterparts perceive us as *people the know* rather than anonymous, faceless email addresses, the more likely they are to share information, rely on us, and trust in us (Nadlerand Shestowsky 2006).

Building Rapport

The concept of using pre-negotiation social interaction to create a positive and unmasked environment for an upcoming negotiation process is widely discussed and advocated in the negotiation literature that focuses on face-to-face interactions. Negotiators are advised to create "instant relationships" absent a past relationship with their negotiating partners. This process has been dubbed "bonding" (Shapiro and Jankowski 1998) or "building rapport" (Drolet and Morris 2000; Thompson and Nadler 2002). Holding preliminary face-to-face meetings has proven to be a highly effective means for building trust that carries over into subsequent e-negotiations (Rocco 1998); indeed, it may be *the* most effective means (Zheng et al. 2002). Supporting an ongoing email negotiation with a face-to-face meeting in the middle of the process has also been advocated (Cellich and Jain 2003). However, notwithstanding the value of incorporating a face-to-face meeting into an email negotiation, this will often prove to be impossible or impractical; sometimes any rapport that will be achieved must be built online.

In face-to-face encounters, introductions and light, social conversations come naturally; in e-negotiation, this tendency diminishes. As we

have discussed, negotiators tend to remain on topic, task-oriented, and analytic, leaving little room for social lubrication. As a result, e-negotiators need to consciously dedicate time and effort to the unmasking process. Experiments have indicated that even minimal pre-negotiation contact, at the most basic level of "schmoozing" via preliminary email introductory messages or brief telephone exchanges, has the potential for building trust, improving mutual impressions, and facilitating integrative outcomes (Morris et al. 2002; Nadler and Shestowsky 2006). By inviting the other to reply, we are initiating a cycle of unmasking which not only transcends physical distance but also reshapes the process into one allowing for recognition and empathy, which can continue to develop as the negotiation progresses.

We would suggest building rapport through words rather than emoticons. A negotiator could write the business part of the email first—working for absolute clarity and thoroughness—and then go back to insert the schmooze factor at the beginning of the email, e.g., "lovely to see you last week," "thanks much for getting back to me," etc. We habitually begin in-person conversation with some ice breaking or small talk, but often forget to include it when using the medium that needs it the most. Exceptions to this guideline exist, of course. When negotiators are engaged in rapid-fire exchange of short, clarifying emails, it could become quite annoying to wade repeatedly through a paragraph of schmooze before reading the point of the email.

Because email lends itself to informal communication, negotiators should be urged to think carefully about the level of formality they want to establish when negotiating by email. Though e-negotiators need to establish rapport and unmask their own humanity, it would be a mistake to open informally, e.g., using the counterpart's first name or simply opening with "Hey Bill!" for many negotiations. For some email recipients, a greater level of formality will actually increase rapport and trust. A good way for negotiators to manage this is to note their counterpart's tone and formality level, and reflect this in their next message, taking care to err on the side of caution.

Showing E-empathy

Demonstrating empathy is universally described as a powerful tool and important skill for any negotiator (Ury 1991; Mnookin, Peppet, and Tulumello 2000; Schneider 2002). This has been found to hold true in online communication as well: e-negotiators who show empathy are trusted by their negotiation opposites more than those who do not (Feng, Lazar, and Preece 2004). This trust might cause the empathic negotiator's actions and intentions to be construed more positively, diminishing the tendency towards sinister attribution. Negotiators will be more likely to share information with a trusted counterpart, opening the door for more integrative agreements (Lewicki and Litterer 1985; Lax and Sebenius 1986).

Showing empathy toward another person via a communication channel characterized by limited contextual cues and by low interactivity is quite a challenge. Unable to smile, nod understandingly, or lay a supportive hand on the arms of their counterparts, email negotiators need to learn new methods for showing e-empathy.

In teaching students to convey empathy in email exchanges, teachers might explain ways to adapt face-to-face methods to the online venue, beginning with the use of communication tools. Many of the most basic communication tools negotiators are advised to employ facilitate the showing of empathy to one's negotiation opposite. Three examples might be active listening, reflecting (or summarizing, and asking questions focusing on the counterparts' needs and concerns (Ury 1991). While some aspects of these tools might appear to be difficult to transfer to the online medium, this does not mean that showing e-empathy is impossible or prohibitively clumsy. All of these communication tools can be adapted for online use. Additionally, mindful use of

specific elements or characteristics of email communication can actually serve to *enhance* our ability to convey empathy at-a-distance (Ebner 2007). For example, word processing makes reflecting a relatively simple process. The ability to ask multiple questions in a single e-mail without the other breaking in to respond or stopping the flow facilitates a show of interest and engagement.

Skill-Set #4: Content Management

The absence of contextual cues focuses email negotiators on the actual *content* of messages (Ocker and Yaverbaum 1999). This necessitates particular skills with regard to three issues:

Clarity

As we have seen, message clarity helps avoid sinister attribution and allows for precise information sharing. Clear messages allow e-negotiators to focus on what their* counterparts have written, reply to their points and consider their proposals. Clarity in reply creates a virtuous cycle.

To achieve such clarity, e-negotiators should avoid unnecessary length. "In summary" sentences might be useful. Negotiators should always remember that, in contrast to a telephone or face-to-face conversation, email creates a searchable file of information. The downside is that this can give rise to "gotcha" opportunities; the upside is that searchability disciplines both sides to stay honest about their representations and commitments. Perhaps because instant messaging does not use subject fields, some e-communicators leave this field blank when sending emails. This, we believe, is a mistake that negotiation students should be urged to avoid. Mindful use of the subject field helps with searchability and message clarity, and also presents a valuable opportunity for framing. Further, even before drafting the text of an email, negotiators should think carefully about each field. To whom should the email be sent? Should anyone appear in the "cc" or disappear in the "bcc" field? Is the negotiator inadvertently offending someone by leaving them out of the exchange or relegating them to the "cc" field when they ought to appear in the "to" field (Shipley and Schwalbe 2007)?

Bundling

Email negotiators tend to bundle multiple points and multiple arguments in a single message. While on the one hand we have noted how this tendency might potentially facilitate the identification of integrative agreements by encouraging negotiators to link issues together and consider them simultaneously rather than sequentially, it might also clash with basic message clarity. Additionally, even if clearly written, an excessive amount of data might send the message recipient into an information overload. Email negotiators need to learn and practice balanced bundling. Judicious use of the "subject" line in an email helps both negotiators and their counterparts to search for and to frame the content of emails they receive. Thus, negotiators should craft subject lines that are sufficiently general that a broad search will produce a list that includes them (e.g., "Smith v. Jones") but also specific enough that they alert the recipient to what they contain and facilitate targeted searches (e.g., "Smith v. Jones—concerns about Smith deposition").

Framing

With the bulk of a message's impact shifted to its content, language and wording become paramount. This is especially important in the framing of issues and discussion topics. Asynchronous communication allows for careful framing of issues and well thought-out revision of frames proposed by the other party. As we have noted, opportunities for using an email message to frame an issue begin with the wording of the subject field.

Part of framing is also thinking about the formatting of the email, which affects the perceptual frame through which the other recipient takes in the message content. In the body of the email, negotiators should alter default settings for style and font with caution and only for good reason. Wallpaper might be too informal for business contexts, including negotiations. Colored fonts should be used only for distinguishing comments written into an earlier document; some email programs will do this automatically when replying or forwarding. Most of the time, however, a simple black typeface is most appropriate. Times Roman, Arial, or other default fonts are preferable to the more exotic options; as Shipley and Schwalbe hilariously point out, some fonts (such as "Chalkboard") "create a homey effect," while others (such as "Blachmoor") "indicate to the reader that a necklace of garlic, a silver bullet, and a wooden cross should be kept close at hand" (Shipley and Schwalbe 2007). A negotiator should also think carefully about using all caps—IT IS THE EQUIVALENT OF SCREAMING in email. Finally, we would suggest not using too many !!! to make a point or too many ☺ to try and lend "tone" to a particular comment - unless negotiators are certain that the relationships they have with their opposites make this suitable.

PART V: PEDAGOGY: TEACHING EMAIL NEGOTIATION

In the previous section, we made suggestions regarding what a negotiator needs to know about negotiating via email. In this section, we suggest some ways that this content might be effectively taught—and learned.

One preliminary question is that of venue: should the art of email negotiation be taught in the classroom, or online? On the one hand, the majority of negotiation courses are taught in traditional face-to-face settings, and we are suggesting that these courses should all incorporate the topic of email negotiation. On the other hand, by interacting in an online classroom of some sort, students have the opportunity to experience firsthand the dynamics of online communication much in the way that the dynamics of a face-to-face negotiation classroom serve to mirror dynamics of negotiation interaction.

For the majority of negotiation courses, an engagement in online exercises is optimal, even if the face-to-face setting is retained for transferring the content. However, we encourage teachers to consider using new methods for teaching the subject, allowing the pedagogical change to mirror and emphasize the departure from the traditional content.

Based on our experience teaching this subject in settings including online, face-to-face, and hybrid formats, here are some suggestions for exercises that can be used to demonstrate and emphasize the major points discussed in this article:

Conducting Negotiation Simulations via Email

An obvious method for teaching the pluses and minuses of email negotiation is to have the participants engage in email negotiations. In a longer course, it would be relatively easy to find time for this exercise—outside of classroom time for the email exchanges to occur, and in class to debrief. Almost any preexisting role play exercise could be adapted simply by requiring that students come to agreement *without* meeting face-to face or speaking on the phone. Alternatively, in order to avoid artificial situations and to enhance learning through using realistic scenarios, teachers might prefer to use simulations in which the need to avoid face-to-face communication is imparted as part of the storyline and makes internal sense in the simulation environment (see Ebner and Efron 2005). Of course, teachers could also allow some conversations in person or by telephone in order to sensitize students to differences in communication media. In large classes, professors could

secretly divide the negotiating dyads into three groups: some would meet in person before initiating email negotiation, some would speak by telephone, and others would move directly to online interaction; during debriefing, students could compare their experiences and possibly then outcomes. Professors might consider running an email negotiation early in the semester to best replicate the lack of preexisting personal relationship that characterizes many email negotiations; later in the semester, students will already know each other too well to experience the conditions of blank anonymity in which email negotiation often occurs. Teachers wishing to replicate these conditions of zero prior familiarity or relationship might also consider partnering with teachers in other universities, pairing up students in their respecting classes as negotiating opposites.

In a shorter course or an executive 1–2 day training, the time and opportunity to conduct email negotiations would be more limited. Still, exchanges that occur via email can be simulated in the classroom in a very short period of time to demonstrate some of the issues. For example, the teacher could project sample exchanges (real or fictional) for critique, group editing, or other discussion.

Conducting "Semi-synchronous" Simulations Via Email

In this type of exercise, students are divided into pairs. Each is assigned a role in a negotiation simulation, and they are positioned in rooms or seated on different sides of a room. Participants, each equipped with a computer, negotiate via email exchanges. As this is in real time, a "semi-synchronous" type of interaction occurs: parties need to reply to each other fairly quickly in order to keep the ball rolling, but can still take a little time to deliberate, frame and fine-tune their messages. One could also divide the class and have some students conduct the role-play face-to-face while others would conduct the same role-play over email. Debriefing this approach provides increased richness in terms of demonstrating the issues outlined earlier.

Fishbowl Back-to-Back

In this type of exercise, two students with laptop computers sit with their backs to each other and negotiate through email or instant messaging. This semi-synchronous interaction is observed by the rest of the class by having the email messages projected on a screen. In this way, all students can observe (silently) what is going on between the negotiators. A trainer could also "tag-team" other participants to step in if they have a better idea for how to conduct the negotiation or to try out different responses.

Real-Time Negotiation Simulation

In this type of exercise, students are put into a situation developing in real time (in other words, it is a synchronous situation), in which the only means they have to communicate with each other is via email. Students are in separate rooms (or cities, for that matter), and the only way for a student to get a clear picture of what is going on is by communicating quickly and effectively *by* email with multiple other parties. Fact patterns that present a crisis situation are particularly well suited to this sort of exercise.

Designing Simulation-Games of Online Negotiation Scenarios

Beyond participation in the various types of simulation discussed above, teachers might assign students the task of envisaging online negotiation situations, and writing them up in the format of a simulation game (in design-styles similar to face-to-face or online simulation- games they have previously participated in).In creating their scenarios with an eye towards triggering online negotiation dynamics (if these simulations were to be play out),

students need to integrate their understanding of these dynamics into their design and storyline. This has been shown to trigger both understanding of discrete concepts as well as an appreciation for how different elements interact with each other when they play out in reality. In addition to these educational benefits, designing exercises enjoy high degrees of student interest, enjoyment and motivation (Druckman and Ebner 2008).

Bringing Real Email Negotiations Into the Classroom

Another method for discussing email, particularly useful in executive trainings, is to ask participants in advance to bring their "favorite" emails—sent or received. What are examples of awful communication? How can we fix these? How can we avoid these mistakes in the future? The trainer can project the emails onto a screen or hand them out and engage the whole class in discussions about how to respond—and how to avoid the more unfortunate examples.

Integrating Email Into the Negotiation Process

A final way to think about teaching email negotiation is to consider integrating it as part of the lessons focusing on communication skills in any negotiation training. When teaching about active listening, rapport, or empathy- or trust-building, after covering basic theory that assumes face-to-face negotiations, teachers could pose questions about the ways email technology might change best practices. In an executive training, almost everyone will already have good (or bad) stories about email communication gone awry. How do our basic guidelines change when eye contact and vocal tone are not available to send signals? What do we assume about motives and intentions? Knowing all of the research available to us (and outlined above), what other advice can we give? To build empathy and communication-related skills, negotiation teachers and trainers could require their students to respond, in writing, to a series of written assertions, complaints, laments, or other emotionally charged messages. Putting other considerations aside, teachers might instruct the students to then write three to four sentences that demonstrate an understanding of what the other person has expressed. These responses could be projected by PowerPoint, enabling students to critique and edit them to improve the empathetic power of the responses.

Conclusion

Negotiating via email is a day-to-day activity for businesspeople, lawyers, and many other negotiators. However, negotiation education has not yet assimilated this fact, and the need to equip negotiators with an updated toolbox of knowledge and skills is vital. In this chapter, we have stressed this, with an eye to bringing about change in the fundamental content of any course or workshop on negotiation: all negotiators need to be prepared to engage in online encounters. By providing not only this prescription but also suggestions for what negotiators need to know and how this might be taught, we hope not only to trigger this change, but also to facilitate it.

Notes

The authors wish to thank Melissa Manwaring and participants in the Quinnipiac Law School Faculty Colloquium for thoughtful comments on drafts of this chapter. Also, our thanks to Ranse Howell and Habib Chamoun-Nicolas for providing suggestions on reference material.

1. Reading through much of the literature on this topic, one might get the sense that most practitioners and researchers have adopted the *assumption* that e-negotiation, as a rule, involves diminished inter-party trust and results in fewer—and less integrative—agreements. The intuitive strength of this assumption notwithstanding, the best one can say about the research exploring it is that it is inconclusive. Several authors have noted experiences and experiments challenging this assumption (Nadler and Shestowsky 2006; Conley, Tyler, and Raines 2006; Chamoun-Nicholas 2007), indicating that more careful examination needs to be done, which might differentiate between different e-communication platforms (only some of the experiments were conducted via email), or examine e-negotiation's suitability to specific types of disputes (Conley, Tyler, and Raines 2006).

2. While this tendency for trust-diminishment in online communication holds true for those brought up in a predominantly face-to-face relational environment, it might not be as strong regarding people for whom the online environment has always been a primary meeting place. The more reflective experience and familiarity people have with online communication, the more they will develop new senses for receiving and assessing new types of contextual cues. This would suggest that people born and raised after the internet revolution may need to put less time and effort into be coming adept at trust-building and trust-assessment than might older communicators, who might be more prone to apply reception, transmission and assessment processes not suitable or not attuned to the medium. On the other hand, familiarity with the medium might lead younger users to being less careful in its use, causing them to send off-the-cuff or excessively informal messages that undermine their goals. The greater care and formality characterizing many older, less experienced users might be helpful in avoiding this. A negotiator's generational affiliation notwithstanding, understanding the differences between face-to-face and email negotiation, and conscious practice at developing new senses and sharpening old senses to new types of nuance, will result in a degree of medium-familiarity conducive to improved

decision-making and negotiation results. For more discussion of this issue see Larson (2003) and Ebner (2007).

3. Exercises involving email negotiation should be considered as a potential vehicle for teaching not only about the process differences of email, but also about substantive issues that permeate multiple communications media, including face-to-face interactions. For example, a teacher focusing on face-to-face negotiation skills could show students an exchange of emails that contain strong indicators of anchoring or attribution bias. The class could discuss that barrier to agreement and then think about the ways the negotiation might proceed to overcome the barrier. This will enable them to facilitate their recognition of these issues in face-to-face situations. Email negotiation exercises also provide an opportunity to practice some of the primary skills imparted in negotiation courses—at a slower rate than do face-to-face exercises. Example of such skills might include reframing and the use of I-messages. Often counter-intuitive, these tools may be difficult for a novice to use effectively in face-to-face simulations. At the reduced pace of an email negotiation simulation, however, these communication tools may be easier to incorporate and perfect.

References

Adair, W., T. Okumura, and J. Brett. 2001. Negotiation behavior when cultures collide: The United States and Japan. *Journal of Applied Psychology* 86(3): 371-385.

Arunachalam, V. and W. Dilla. 1995. Judgment accuracy and outcomes in negotiation: A causal modelling analysis of decision-aiding effects. *Organizational Behavior and Human Decision Processes* 61(3): 289-304.

Barsness, Z. I. and A. D. Bhappu. 2004. At the crossroads of technology and culture: Social influence, information sharing, and sense-making processes during negotiations. In *The handbook of negotiation and culture* edited by M. J. Gelfand and J. M. Brett. Stanford: Stanford University Press.

Bhappu, A. D., T. L. Griffith, and G. B. Northcraft. 1997. Media effects and communication bias in diverse groups. *Organizational Behavior and Human Decision Processes* 70(3): 199-205.

Bhappu, A. D. and J. M. Crews. 2005. The effects of communication media and conflict on team identification in diverse groups. Proceedings of the 38th Hawaii International Conference on System Sciences, Los *Alamitos, California.*

Carnevale, P. J. and T. M. Probst. 1997. *Conflict on the internet. In Culture of the internet,* edited by S. Kiesler. Mahwah, NJ: Lawrence Erlbaum Associates.

Carnevale, P. J., D. G. Pruitt, and S. D. Seilheimer. 1981. Looking and competing: Accountability and visual access in integrative bargaining. *Journal of Personality and Social Psychology* 40(1): 111 -20.

Cellich, C. and S. C. Jain. 2003. *Global business negotiations: A practical guide.* Mason, OH: Thomson/South-Western.

Chamoun-Nicolas, H. and R. D. Hazlett. 2007. *Negotiate like a Phoenician.* Kingwood, TX: Keynegotiations.

Clark, H. and S. Brennan. 1991. Grounding in communication. In *Perspectives on socially shared cognition,* edited by L. Resnick, J. Levine, and S. *Teasley. Washington, DC: American Psychological Association,*

Conley Tyler, M. and S. Raines. 2006. The human face of online dispute resolution. *Conflict Resolution Quarterly* 23(3): 333-342.

Croson, R. 1999. Look at me when you say that: An electronic negotiation *simulation. Simulation & Gaming* 30(1): 23-27.

Daft, R. L. and R. H. Lengel. 1984. Information richness: A new approach to managerial behavior and organizational design. *Research in Organizational Behavior* 6: 191-233.

DePaulo, B. M. and H. S. Friedman. 1998. Nonverbal communication. In The handbook of social psychology, 4th edn., edited by D. T. Gilbert, S. T. Fiske, and G. Lindzey. Boston: McGraw Hill.

DeSanctis, G. and P. Monge. 1999. Introduction to the special issues: Communication processes for virtual organizations. *Organization Science* 10(6): 693-703.

Deutsch, M. 1962. Cooperation and trust: Some theoretical notes. In *Nebraska Symposium on Motivation,* Vol. 10, edited by M. R. Jones, pp. 275-318. Lincoln, NE: University of Nebraska Press.

Drolet, A. L. and M. W. Morris. 2000. Rapport in conflict resolution: Accounting for how face-to-face contact fosters mutual cooperation in mixed-motive conflicts. *Journal of Experimental Social Psychology* 36(1): 26–50.

Druckman, D. and N. Ebner. 2008. Onstage, or behind the scenes? Relative learning benefits of simulation role-play and design. *Simulation & Gaming 39(4): 465-497.*

Ebner, N. 2007. Trust-building in e-negotiation. In Computer-mediated relationships and trust: Managerial and organizational effects, edited by L. Brennan and V. Johnson. Hershey, PA: Idea Group Reference.

Ebner, N. and Y. Efron. 2005. Using tomorrow's headlines for today's training: Creating pseudo-reality in conflict resolution simulation-games. *Negotiation Journal* 21(3): 377-394.

Epstein, S., R. Pacini, V. Denes-Raj, and H. Heier. 1996. Individual differences in intuitive-experimental and analytical-rational thinking styles. *Journal of Personality and Social Psychology* 71(2): 390-405.

Feng, J., P. J. Lazar, and J. Preece. 2004. Empathy and online interpersonal trust: A fragile relationship. *Behavior & Information Technology* 23(2): 97-106.

Friedman, R. A. and S. C. Currall. 2001. E-mail escalation: Dispute exacerbating elements of electronic communication. Working Paper, Owen Graduate School of Management, Vanderbilt University.

Gelfand, M. J. and N. Dyer. 2000. A cultural perspective on negotiation: Progress, pitfalls, and prospects. *Applied Psychology: An International Review* 49: 62-99.

Greenwald, A. G., D. E. McGhee, and J. L. K. Schwartz. 1998. Measuring individual differences in implicit cognition: The implicit association test. *Journal of Personality and Social Psychology* 74(6): 1464-1480.

Griffith, T. L. and G. B. Northcraft. 1994. Distinguishing between the forest and the trees: Media, features, and methodology in electronic communication research. *Organization Science* 5(2): 272–285.

Hall, E. T. 1976. *Beyond culture* New York: Anchor Press.

Harasim, L. M. 1993. Networlds: Networks as a social space. In Global networks: Computers and international communication, edited by L. M. Harasim. *Cambridge, MA: MIT Press.*

Jessup, L. M. and D. A. Tansik. 1991. Decision making in an automated environment: The effects of anonymity and proximity with a group decision support system. *Decision Sciences* 22(2): 266-279.

Katsh, E. and J. Rifkin. 2001. *Online dispute resolution: Resolving conflicts in cyberspace.* San Francisco: Jossey Bass.

Kemp, N. J. and D. R. Rutter. 1982. Cuelessness and the content and style of conversation. *British Journal of Social Psychology* 21 (1): 43-9.

Kiesler, S. and L. Sproull. 1992. Group decision making and communication technology. *Organizational Behavior and Human Decision Processes* 52(1): 96-123.

Kraut, R., J. Galegher, R. Fish, and B. Chalfonte. 1992. Task requirements *and media choice in collaborative writing. Human-Computer Interaction* 7(4): 375-408.

Lam, S. S. K. and J. Schaubroeck. 2000. Improving group decisions by better pooling information: A comparative advantage of group decision support systems. *Journal of Applied Psychology* 85(4): 565-573.

Larson, D. A. 2003. Online dispute resolution: Do you know where your *children are? Negotiation Journal* 19(3): 199-205.

Lax, D. A. and J. K. Sebenius. 1986. *The manager as negotiator: Bargaining for cooperation and competitive gain.* New York: Free Press.

Lewicki, R. J. and J. Litterer. 1985. *Negotiation: Readings, exercises and cases.* Boston: Irwin.

Mnookin, R. H., S. R. Peppet, and A. S. Tulumello. 2000. *Beyond winning: Negotiating to create value in deals and disputes.* Cambridge, MA: Belknap Press.

Moore, C. 2003. *The mediation process: Practical strategies for resolving conflict,* 3rd edn. San Francisco: Jossey Bass.

Moore, D. A., T. R. Kurtzberg, L. Thompson, and M. W. Morris. 1999. *Long* and short routes to success in electronically mediated negotiations: Group affiliations and good vibrations. *Organizational Behavior and Human Decision Processes* 77(1): 22-43.

Morris, M., J. Nadler, T. R. Kurtzberg, and L. Thompson. 2002. Schmooze or lose: Social friction and lubrication in e-mail negotiations. *Group Dynamics* 6(1): 89-100.

Nadler, J. and D. Shestowsky. 2006. Negotiation, information technology and the problem of the faceless other. In *Negotiation theory and research,* edited by L. Thompson. New York: Psychology Press.

Naquin, C, T. R. Kurtzberg, and L. Belkin. (forthcoming). Being honest online: The finer points of lying in online ultimatum bargaining. Reported by the Academy of Management. Available at http://login.aomonline.org/aom.asp?ID = 251&page_ID = 224&pr_id = 39 9 (last accessed Mar. 26, 2009).

Naquin, C. E. and G. D. Paulson. 2003. Online bargaining and interpersonal trust. *Journal of Applied Psychology 8S(* 1): 113-120.

Nunamaker, J. F., A. R. Dennis, J. S. Valacich, and D. R. Vogel. 1991. *Information* technology for negotiating groups: Generating options for mutual gain. *Management Science* 37(10): 1325-1346.

O'Connaill, B., S. Whittaker, and S. Wilbur. 1993. Conversations over video conferences: An evaluation of the spoken aspects of video-mediated communication. *Human-Computer Interaction* 8: 389-428.

Ocker, R. J. and G. J. Yaverbaum. 1999. Asynchronous computer-mediated communication versus face-to-face collaboration: Results on student learning, quality and satisfaction. *Group Decision and Negotiations* 8(5): 427-40.

Pruitt, D., J. Rubin and S. Kim. 2004. *Social conflict: Escalation, stalemate, and settlement,* 3rd edn. New York: McGraw Hill.

Raiffa, H. 1982. *The art and science of negotiation,* Cambridge, MA: Belknap Press.

Rocco, E. 1998. Trust breaks down in electronic contexts but can be repaired by some initial face-to-face contact. In *Proceedings of the SIGCHI conference on human factors in computing systems* [Electronic version], pp. 496-502. Los Angeles: ACM Press.

Rosette, A. S., J. M. Brett, Z. Barsness, and A. Lytle. 2001. The influence of e-mail on Hong Kong and U.S. intra-cultural negotiations. Paper delivered at the Annual Meeting of the International Association for Conflict Management, Paris, France, June 23-27, 2001.

Schneider, A. K. 2002. Shattering negotiation myths: Empirical evidence on the effectiveness of negotiation style, *Harvard Negotiation Law Review* 7(1): 143-233.

Shapiro, R. M. and M. A. Jankowski. 1998. *The power of nice: How to negotiate so everyone wins - especially you!* New York: John Wiley.

Shipley, D. and W. Schwalbe. 2007. *Send: The essential guide to email for office and home.* New York: Knopf.

Short, J., E. Williams, and E Christie. 1976. *The social psychology of telecommunications.* Chichester, England: John Wiley and Sons Ltd.

Siegel, J., V. Dubrovsky. S. Kiesler, and T. W. McGuire. 1986. Group processes in computer-mediated communication. *Organizational Behavior and Human Decision Processes* 37(2): 157-187.

Sproull. L. and S. Kiesler. 1986. Reducing social contest cues: Electronic mail in organizational communications. *Management Science 32(11)'.* 1492-1512.

Sproull. L. and S Kiesler. 1991. *Connections: New ways of working in the net-worked organization.* Cambridge, MA.: MIT Press.

Thompson, L 2004. *The mind and heart of the negotiator,* 3rd edn. Upper Saddle River, NJ: Prentice Hall.

Thompson, L and J. Nadler. 2002. Negotiating via information technology: Theory and application. *Journal of Social Issues* 58(LJ: 109-124.

Ting-Toomey. S. 1980. Intercultural conflict styles: A face negotiation theory. In *Theories in intercultural communication,* edited by Y. Y. Kim and W.B. Gudykunst. Newbury Park, CA: Sage.

Ury, W. 1991. *Getting past no: Negotiating your way from confrontation to cooperation.* New York Bantam Books.

Valley, K. L. and R. Croson. 2004. What do communication media mean for negotiations? A question of social awareness. In *The handbook of negotiation & culture,* edited by M. J. Gelfand and J. M. Brett. Stanford: Stanford University Press.

Valley, K. L, J. Moage, and M. H. Bazerman. 1998. A matter of trust': Effects of communication on the efficiency and distribution of outcomes. *Journal of Economic Behavior and Organization* 34(2): 211-238.

Wallace, P. 1999. *The psychology of the internet* New York: Cambridge University Press.

Walther, J. B. and U. Bunz. 2005. The rules of virtual groups: Trust, liking and performance in computer-mediated communication. *Journal of Communication* 55(4): 828-46.

Weisband, S. and L Atwater. 1999. Evaluating self and others in electronic and face-to-face groups. *Journal of Applied Psychology* 84(4): $32-639,

Zajonc, R. B. 1965. Social facilitation. *Science* 149: 269-74.

Zheng. J. E. Veinott, N. Bos. J. S. Olson, and G. M. Olson. 2002. Trust without touch: Jumpstarting long-distance trust with initial social activities. In *Proceedings of the SIGCHI conference or, human factors in computing systems* [Electronic version], pp. 141-6. New York. NY:" ACM Press.

Thinking Further 6.1

1. Would you prefer to negotiate face to face or via email? Why?

2. Compare and contrast the benefits and drawbacks to negotiating face to face versus negotiating electronically.

Reading 6.2

THE VIEW FROM THE OTHER SIDE OF THE TABLE

Adam Galinsky, William Maddux and Gillian Ku

Getting inside your counterpart's head can increase the value of the deal you walk away with. Here's how to do it.

When you begin negotiating the terms of a deal, do you have a strong sense of what your counterpart is thinking and what strategies he is likely to use? If you don't, you may soon find yourself in trouble.

Consider what happened when undefeated world chess champion Gary Kasparov faced off against an IBM super-computer dubbed Deep Blue in a series of matches in 1997. Kasparov typically prepared for a match by studying his opponent's earlier matches move by move. But IBM refused to give Kasparov information about Deep Blue's previous games, so he entered the match knowing little about Deep Blue's strengths and weaknesses as a chess strategist.

During the match, Kasparov encountered few problems until well into the second game, when Deep Blue made an unusual move that Kasparov was convinced only a human would make. Surprised and confused, Kasparov lost his focus. After losing the game, Kasparov demanded to see the computer's log files, suspecting human interference. IBM again refused. From then on, Kasparov was unsure who his inscrutable opponent was—a person, a computer, or some amalgam of both. He eventually lost the six-game match.

The event was a triumph for IBM and its shareholders. Locked in a struggle for market share against up-and-comers Microsoft and Intel, IBM's stock and computer sales skyrocketed following Deep Blue's victory.

There have been many explanations for Kasparov's defeat, but his inability to "get inside the head" of his opponent deserves particular attention. For experienced negotiators, the questions that confounded Kasparov are all too familiar: "What are they thinking? How did they come up with the move? Why would they do that?" And although few business executives expect to find themselves face-to-face with electronic machines (at least not anytime soon), human adversaries often prove every bit as bewildering.

How do you deal with a negotiator whose moves make no sense to you? By focusing your efforts on understanding where the other side is coming from. In this article, we show you how to use perspective taking—the active

Source: Galinsky, A. D., Maddux, W. W., & Ku, G. (2006). The view from the other side of the table. *Program on Negotiation Newsletter*, 9(3), 1–4.

Note: This article first appeared in *Negotiation*, a monthly newsletter published by the Program on Negotiation at Harvard Law School, www.pon.harvard.edu. Copyright 2006–2011 Harvard University.

consideration and appreciation of another person's viewpoint, role, and underlying motivations—to better understand your counterpart and improve the quality of your deals. The better able you are to "get inside the head" of your opponent, the better your negotiated outcomes are likely to be.

How Perspective Taking Pays Off

Effective perspective taking is often associated with successful leaders who understand their employees' needs as well as external competitive forces. The ability to understand one's adversaries is also crucial in securing power and has been credited with settling seemingly intransigent negotiation standoffs. The successful resolution of the Cuban Missile Crisis, as compared with the failure of the Bay of Pigs invasion, has been attributed to President John F. Kennedy's improved ability to get inside an opponent's head.

Perspective taking achieves these positive effects by leading us to appreciate others' interests without forfeiting our own claims and concerns. Focusing only on oneself leads to aggressive, obstinate behavior, whereas focusing only on others encourages self-destructive concession making, according to SUNY Buffalo emeritus professor Dean Pruitt's dual concern model of effective negotiation. By contrast, a balance of concern for both oneself and other fosters creative problem solving. For this reason, active perspective taking helps deals get done, expands the pie of value, and allows you to claim more value as well. It is important to note that perspective taking is not the same as feeling sympathy for someone else. In fact, being too sy—pathetic often leads negotiators to concede too readily.

Putting Perspective Taking to Work

Some people are born with the ability to effectively take the perspective of others. Luckily for the rest of us, it's also a strategy that can be learned. By asking three simple questions—what, how, and why—both before and during your negotiations, you can improve your negotiation performance.

What are Her Underlying Interests, Motivations, and Needs?

What has brought the other side to the negotiating table? A better understanding of your counterpart's point of view can inspire you to offer novel proposals that also satisfy your own interests.

Imagine a negotiation over the sale of a restaurant, in which a deal based solely on sale price would lead to an impasse because the buyer's reservation price (the maximum she's willing to pay) is substantially lower than the seller's reservation price (the minimum he's willing to accept). However, the underlying interests of the parties are fundamentally compatible. The buyer is interested in hiring a chef with both managerial and culinary experience to oversee the menu of an upscale restaurant chain, and the seller is selling his restaurant to finance a year of culinary school. Armed with this knowledge, the parties can agree to a sale price below the seller's reservation price, with the stipulation that the buyer will help finance culinary school and the seller will take over as culinary manager upon graduation.

In our research using a similar simulation, negotiators who were instructed to take the other side's perspective by asking our series of questions were more likely to avoid an impasse and to arrive at an innovative solution that met both parties' needs.

Perspective taking also helps negotiators create value through an appreciation of counterparts' priorities among the issues. For example, by inquiring about priorities, a recruiter trained in the art of perspective taking may learn that a potential in the art of perspective taking may learn that a potential candidate is very concerned about his job assignment but less concerned about location, an issue of great importance to the recruiter. The recruiter can then offer an efficient tradeoff—the recruiter's preferred location in exchange for the candidate's preferred assignment—that pleases them both.

How Can She Meet Her Needs Elsewhere?

Effective negotiators strive not only to expand the pie of value but also to claim a larger share of the pie for themselves. Our research with psychologist Thomas Mussweiler of the University of Cologne has shown that asking how else your opponent can meet her needs—in other words, by considering her BATNA, or best alternative to a negotiated agreement—you can gain strategic and distributive advantages. When you understand that your opponent's alternatives are not as good as she is implying, you will push for more for yourself.

By considering how your opponent might otherwise meet her needs, you can also defend yourself against her first offer. Usually, whichever party makes the first offer anchors the negotiation and secures the larger share of the overall pie. (For more on this, see Adam Galinsky's article "Should You Make the First Offer?" in our July 2004 issue, Reprint # N0407A.) Perspective takers can eliminate this advantage by reechoing the negotiation.

Suppose that the seller of a custom-built manufacturing plant receives a low first offer from a potential buyer. The seller may focus his attention on the plant's flaws, thereby justifying the first offer in his own mind. But when he considers the buyer's alternatives, the seller will recognize just how much it would cost to build a similar plant from scratch. This knowledge steels him to counter with an offer closer to the plant's true value. Perspective taking helps you avoid the tunnel vision that an opponent's first offer can inspire.

Why Is She Behaving That Way?

Answering this question is the key to overcoming sinister attributions—harsh interpretations of your opponent's negotiating behaviors and intentions that can fuel a cycle of mistrust. By appreciating another person's vantage point, the perspective taker is more likely to see the other side's underlying—and oftentimes benevolent—intentions. Thus, perspective taking is as valuable in resolving disputes as it is in forming deals.

Imagine yourself in the following situation, which is based on the experience of one of the authors. You move to Chicago and have hardwood floors installers accidentally puncture some underground heating pipes, a mistake that you discover only months later when winter comes. The installers deny any responsibility. Feeling cheated, you instinctively consider a lawsuit. But at this point, a good perspective taker would ask the installers why they're so reluctant to accept responsibility; what is motivating their resistance? You may discover that their apparent greed is rooted in a concern about insurance premiums. The installers might be willing to repair the damaged pipes as long as you agree not to file a claim that would raise their premiums.

Perspective Taking and Diverse Experiences

Strategically considering our three what, how, and why questions may be the simplest way to cultivate experiences with different types of people and situations. Do you work with or manage people and situations? Do you work with or manage people who have a variety of interests, abilities, and backgrounds? Does your company encourage the expression of novel ideas and opinions? Have you lived and worked in a foreign country? If so, you're likely to be a good perspective taker simply because you're used to managing diversity.

In our own research, we've found that negotiators who have lived abroad are better perspective takers and are thus more likely to obtain an interest-based deal in a simulated buyer-seller negotiation than are those who have not. Additionally, negotiators who have lived abroad show enhanced performance on creative tasks.

One caveat: there seems to be a critical amount and depth of exposure to foreign cultures that only comes from living abroad for at least six months, not merely from traveling overseas. Job transfers or lengthy sabbaticals can increase perspective-taking ability, but a two-week European vacation likely will not.

Why do diverse experiences encourage perspective taking? Imagine that you're having an important business dinner in the home of an international client. In some cultures (such as China and Jordan), leaving food on your plate at a host's house is a sign of appreciation, implying that the host has given you enough to eat. In other countries (including Indonesia and France), the same behavior may be taken as an insult—a condemnation of the meal. Those with experience living in foreign countries are likely to become sensitive to these different cultural practices. Diverse experiences give you a thorough appreciation for disparate needs, thereby enabling you to understand a counterpart's motives and interests.

Thinking Further 6.2

1. According to this article, is it preferable to assume positive intentions or make sinister attributions regarding the other negotiating party? Explain why.

2. Describe a negotiating situation in which it might be more advantageous to make sinister attributions regarding the other negotiating party. Describe a situation in which it might be more advantageous to assume positive intentions regarding the other negotiating party.

CHAPTER 7

Decision Making

Are We Truly Rational?

Along with interpersonal communication, decision making is an inescapable component of the negotiation process. We make a multitude of decisions prior to, during, and after each negotiation. Whether to negotiate in a particular situation, what information to communicate and through which medium, how high to set target and resistance points, who should make the first offer, which alternative is best, and whether to comply with the terms of the agreement are examples. While it is not surprising that negotiators make many decisions, what is surprising, and problematic, is that these decisions are often flawed. This chapter examines the nature of these flaws, illustrates them, and offers suggestions for avoiding or correcting them.

INTENDED BENEFITS OF THIS CHAPTER

When you finish reading this chapter, you should be able to

1. Recognize decision-making errors that sometimes plague negotiators.

2. Explain why these errors are made.

3. Describe how to avoid these errors when negotiating.

THE ESSENCE OF DECISION MAKING IN NEGOTIATION

What kinds of mistakes are included when we talk about negotiators' decision-making errors? Consider the situation involving Matt Harrington described in Negotiation in Action 7.1.

NEGOTIATION IN ACTION 7.1

In 2000, Matt Harrington was an 18-year-old high-school senior whose picture was on the cover of *USA Today* and *Baseball America*. He was being favorably compared with Josh Beckett who, at the age of 23, was the M.V.P. of the 2003 World Series. After the Colorado Rockies drafted Harrington #7 in the first round of the draft, he turned down offers of $5.3 million over eight years and $4 million over two years, with a $500,000 signing bonus. Although he comes from a family without a lot of money, he was insulted by these offers: he believed they showed a lack of respect by the Rockies. In actuality, the numbers were in the range of what a #7 pick should expect. Acrimonious negotiations eventually fell apart. The following year, Harrington was drafted in the second round, #58 overall, by the San Diego Padres. The Padres offered him $1.25 million over four years with a $300,000 signing bonus. He turned it down. In 2002, Tampa Bay drafted him #374 in the 13th round and offered him less than $100,000. Serious negotiations didn't take place. The next year, the Cincinnati Reds made him pick #711 in the 24th round, but nothing came of it. In 2004, the New York Yankees made Harrington pick #1,089 in the 36th round of the free-agent draft. They weren't in a hurry to sign him (adapted from Jordan, 2004).

This does not appear to be the case of a greedy agent because he has successfully negotiated deals for all but one of the first round picks he represented. Nor does it appear to be the case of a greedy owner because the Rockies have successfully negotiated deals with all but one of their first round picks. The lone exception in both cases is Harrington who, in 2004, was making $800/month pitching for the Fort Worth Cats in the independent Central Baseball League. The independent leagues are home to players rehabilitating from injuries or drug/alcohol abuse, trying to resuscitate a fading talent, or trying to prove they have enough talent to be signed by a major-league team. These are the players on the fringe who, for one reason or another, have been excluded from organized baseball. Like Harrington, except that he excluded himself (Jordan, 2004).

What might possess Matt Harrington or other decision makers to make such seemingly irrational decisions?

Widely accepted economic theory assumes that people are rational. We are supposed to have an accurate concept of the worth of all goods and services, and of the amount of happiness our decisions will produce. Further, we try to maximize profits or happiness and optimize our experiences. This does not seem to describe Matt Harrington's decisions very well. How many of us, especially if we grew up without much money, would walk away from $5.3 million—at the age of 18 or now? Perhaps this is simply a case of a greedy or cocky young man. Trained businesspeople surely would not engage in such irrational behavior. Or would they? Consider the multi-billion dollar acquisition described in Negotiation in Action 7.2 before you answer.

NEGOTIATION IN ACTION 7.2

Robert Campeau, one of *Fortune*'s "Fifty Most Interesting Business People," wanted to acquire Bloomingdale's, the upscale retailer, for its value and for its power to draw people to the shopping malls he planned to build. To accomplish this, he initiated a hostile takeover of Bloomingdale's parent, Federated Department Stores. In the months that followed, a highly public bidding war developed between Campeau and Macy's over what was to become the largest and most visible retail merger in history. As the bidders continued to up the ante, the value of Federated decreased because managers defected and confusion mounted regarding purchases of fall merchandise and expenditures for seasonal promotions. Campeau even told Federated's board that the price for the retailer was too high. But a week later, with Macy's on the verge of winning, he topped Macy's already excessive offer by roughly $500 million and he "won." Or did he? He declared bankruptcy a year later (Bazerman & Neale, 1992).

Are these two scenarios the exception? Or are the economists' aforementioned assumptions about people being rational decision makers wrong? The evidence suggests that it is likely the latter. In the aftermath of the "massive earthquake that reduced the financial world to rubble," one economist noted:

> We're painfully blinking awake to the falsity of standard economic theory—that human beings are capable of always making rational decisions. . . . We are beginning to understand that irrationality is the real invisible hand that drives human decision making. . . . Armed with the knowledge that human beings are motivated by cognitive biases of which they are largely unaware (a true invisible hand if there ever was one), businesses can start to better defend against foolishness and waste. (Ariely, 2009, p. 1)

Taking this a step further, he argued that we are not merely irrational—we are predictably irrational (Ariely, 2008). If negotiators were rational, they would never reach an agreement with a negative ZOPA and they would always reach an agreement with a positive ZOPA (Bazerman & Neale, 1983). Unfortunately, this does not describe reality.

DECISION-MAKING ERRORS

Good information is an essential ingredient in decision making. As discussed in **Reading 7.1** at the end of this chapter, negotiators sometimes use irrelevant or bad information and ignore critical information when they make decisions. This chapter discusses the kinds of decision making errors that sometimes plague negotiators. Some, such as the one demonstrated by Harrington and Campeau, are **cognitive** in nature: they involve deviations from some normative "correct" or "best" outcome. They are usually caused by the use of faulty information-processing shortcuts.

Others are **perceptual**. These biases are interpersonal in nature and have their roots in our faulty perceptions of social entities and situations, including ourselves and those with whom we interact.

Still others are **emotional** in nature. These biases grow out of inconsistencies between feelings and actions, feelings and the judgments made about them, and feelings that arise at different times during a negotiation. Most of us believe that emotions predict behavior and that we can monitor our own and other's feelings. Truth be told, we are often mistaken about what we are feeling, not to mention what others are feeling. This leads to flawed predictions of subsequent behavior (Thompson, Neale, & Sinaceur, 2004; Thompson, Medvec, Seiden, & Kopelman, 2001; Wilson, 1985).

Cognitive Biases

Irrational Escalation of Commitment

The **irrational escalation of commitment**, illustrated by Harrington and Campeau, perhaps entails continuing a previously selected course of action beyond what rational analysis would recommend. Automobile manufacturers' use of rebates and discount financing to help dealerships negotiate deals with customers is an example of this. The evidence demonstrating that managers who make hiring decisions subsequently evaluate these employees more favorably than do managers who were not involved in the hiring process is another example (Bazerman, Beekun, & Schoorman, 1982; Bazerman & Neale, 1992; Schoorman, 1988). The manager who hired, the MBA Program Director who has been discussed elsewhere in the book, is illustrative. Despite receiving ample information from students, faculty, and staff demonstrating the harm he was inflicting on this program, the manager continued to support him and make excuses for him. He defended Morton arguing that those who complained are resistant to change and uncomfortable with his "East Coast" style. Interestingly, Morton's highly respected predecessor is from Boston!

One reason we commit this error is that we seem to be unable to *ignore sunk or unrecoverable costs*. We are afraid to cut our losses for the simple reason that they are losses. We would obviously like to avoid them, but continuing a failing course of action engenders even larger losses. The **confirmation trap** and **selective attention** also contribute. After formulating hypotheses or making even tentative decisions, we look for information that supports or justifies them. When we encounter information that conflicts with or disconfirms our hypotheses or decisions, we ignore or distort it. Perhaps Matt Harrington read media accounts or was told by friends and family members that he was worth more than the Rockies or Padres were offering. That may explain why he concluded the Rockies and Padres were disrespecting him.

Impression management, our desire to manage others' impressions of us, also contributes. Perhaps we refuse to admit failure to defend our reputations. It may also reflect our strong desire to be *consistent*. Consistency is a central motivator for many people and inconsistency is viewed negatively—we call people wishy-washy or fickle if they change their minds. Abandoning a course of action that you previously espoused would certainly make people question your abilities and perhaps your motives. Campeau (see Negotiation in Action 7.1) undoubtedly had to convince his advisors or lenders that Bloomingdale's was necessary for his malls to be successful. If he backed out, they might have questioned his judgment—if it was so important before, why is it not anymore?

How to Manage This Problem

There are several steps you can take to combat this problem.

- *Be Aware*. Knowing that people tend to irrationally escalate commitment, and why it happens, should help you avoid doing so.
- *Cultivate Alternatives and Set Limits*. Having alternatives, and understanding their value, enables you to walk away when your chosen course of action is no longer more valuable

than your alternatives. Cultivating even better alternatives allows you to set more favorable limits, and this makes it even easier to walk away.

- *Reevaluate Your Course of Action.* When you reach your limits, reevaluate the situation assessing the future benefits relative to the future costs. If the future holds no greater promise for positive outcomes, it would be prudent to abandon this course of action now.
- *Establish a Monitoring System.* Involve others who can check your perceptions and judgments before you go too far. When choosing these advisors, be sure they are people you trust and respect enough to truly heed their warnings.
- As described in Chapter 3, and will be described again in Chapter 13, help the other negotiator back out of any commitments he or she makes without losing face.

Framing

Framing is about how we say something, not what we say. It reflects our conception or definition of the situation. *Cognitive frames* are about the heuristics or shortcuts we use to simplify decision making. Perhaps the most significant impact of cognitive frames can be seen when we examine negotiators' risk propensities. The scenario depicted in Negotiation in Action 7.3 is illustrative.

NEGOTIATION IN ACTION 7.3

Assume the United States is preparing for the outbreak of an unusual disease that is expected to kill 600 people. Two preventive programs are being negotiated. If Program A is adopted, 200 people will be saved; if Program B is adopted, there is a one-third probability that all will be saved and a two-thirds probability that none will be saved. Of the people receiving these choices, 76% opted for Program A.

A second group was also told that two preventive programs were being considered, but they were presented differently. If Program A is adopted, 400 people will die; if Program B is adopted there is a one-third probability that no one will die and a two-thirds probability that all will die. Of this group, 87% chose Program B (Tversky & Kahneman, 1981).

Although the expected value of Programs A and B was identical in all cases, these groups reversed their choices because the options were presented to the first group as a certain gain versus an uncertain gain, and they were presented to the second group as a certain loss versus an uncertain loss. Simply put, most people prefer certain gains to uncertain gains, and uncertain losses to certain losses. Reading 7.2 examines frames in more detail.

Implications of This Problem

The implications for negotiators are that positive frames (gains) lead to less risky bargaining strategies because agreements are preferred to holding out for a better, albeit more uncertain, settlement. Positively framed negotiators, in other words, make more concessions, reach more agreements, achieve higher overall profitability (but lower average profits across transactions) and are more satisfied with their agreements than negatively framed negotiators. Whether proposals provide us with a gain or a loss is more determinative of our decisions than their expected utility or value (Bazerman, Magliozzi, & Neale, 1985; Neale, Huber, & Northcraft, 1987).

Whether a negotiator views a proposal as a gain or a loss is a function of his or her reference point, and reference points can be influenced. For instance, Wilma's current annual salary is $70,000. A prospective employer offered her $75,000/year but her initial demand was for $80,000/year. She is more likely to accept the offer if she views it as $5,000 more than her current salary than if she views it as $5,000 less than her initial demand. A negotiator who is trying to persuade Wilma to accept the offer, therefore, should focus her attention on the offer relative to her current salary—the amount she will gain—and divert her attention away from her initial demand because this reflects what she will lose. It is important to remember that both your frame and the other party's frame will shape your evaluation of a proposal and whether you view it as a gain or a loss. Moreover, loss frames appear to be more potent than gain frames—if you are positively framed and the other is negatively framed, you are likely to change your frame (de Dreu, Emans, & van de Vliert, 1992).

Availability of Information

Information that is vivid, concrete, familiar, and emotionally rich is more easily retrieved from memory, and more influential, than pallid, abstract, unfamiliar, and emotionally bland information, even if it is less relevant—it influences our evaluations of proposals and alternatives, how we attempt to persuade others, and our ability to be persuaded. Opportunity costs, for example, are less likely to enter into one's financial analysis of a proposal than out-of-pocket costs. Similarly, if you ask the executives at a large firm to identify the most important problem facing their company, each will likely define it in terms of his or her own functional area of expertise. The VP of Human Resources will define it in terms of human resources, the VP of Marketing will define it in terms of marketing, the VP of Operations will define it operationally, and so on. This is not surprising since an accountant, who has little experience with marketing, is not likely to think in those terms when making decisions or solving problems (Bazerman & Neale, 1992; Borgida & Nisbett, 1977; Northcraft & Neale, 1986). We also tend to overestimate the probability that unlikely events will occur if our memories of them are vivid because things that are easier to remember seem more prevalent and more important to us. Think about our expectation that a terrorist attack will occur now compared with our expectation before 9/11!

Rather than considering information that is relevant and necessary for making high quality decisions, this bias also limits our search to information that is easily recalled from memory. Even if we search outside our memories, we may only focus on that which is consistent with the information that is easily recalled from memory because of the confirmation trap. These tendencies can be managed.

How to Manage This Problem

- Consider your past experiences with what the other side is proposing and remember that this information will unduly influence your decisions if you let it.
- Since information in our memories is differentially recallable, secure help with recalling information that is not so readily available by consulting others who may have new or different information that is relevant and objective. This will be particularly helpful if it contradicts your preliminary assessment.
- Differentiate information that is emotionally available from that which is reliable and relevant. This is not always easy, but it is essential for good decision making.

Anchoring and Adjustment

Many positions can and do in *anchor* negotiations—they define at least one end of the bargaining range and may be the point from which negotiators concede or adjust when issuing their subsequent offers and counteroffers. Opening offers are perhaps the most common, but prior offers, target points, and resistance points also serve as anchors. If we set anchors rationally, making adjustments from these positions would make sense. Unfortunately, we often estimate the value of uncertain objects or events using information that is irrelevant. It may simply be easily recallable because of the availability bias (Bazerman & Neale, 1992; Northcraft & Neale, 1987).

Imagine that someone asks you to write the last 2 digits of your social security number, and then whether you would pay that number of dollars for certain products. Would the mere suggestion of that amount influence how much you would pay, say, for a bottle of wine or a cordless keyboard? If you think this sounds crazy, you are not alone. But such anchoring is not uncommon. Even arbitrary prices, once they have been established in our minds, shape the prices we would pay now and in the future. A group of MBA students were asked to write the last two digits of their social security numbers on a piece of paper and to indicate whether they would pay this amount in dollars for certain products. They were then asked to actually bid on these items in an auction. The average bids for these products, and the statistically significant correlations between the last two digits of students' social security numbers and their bids, are shown in Table 7.1.

Table 7.1 An Illustration of How Even Arbitrary Anchors Influence Behavior

Product	Last 2 Digits of Social Security #					Correlations
	00–19	20–39	40–59	60–79	80–99	
Cordless Trackball	$8.64	$11.82	$13.45	$21.18	$26.18	0.42
Cordless Keyboard	$16.09	$26.82	$29.27	$34.55	$55.64	0.52
1998 Cotes du Rhone (wine)	$8.64	$14.45	$12.55	$15.45	$27.91	0.33
1996 Hermitage (wine)	$11.73	$22.45	$18.09	$24.55	$37.55	0.33

Source: Adapted from Ariely, Lowenstein, & Prelec, 2003.

Similar findings have been found with professional auditors estimating the incidence of management-level fraud, professional real estate agents or Realtors estimating real estate values, and even the amount of money one would demand for listening to unappealing noises for which there are no market prices. Just as first impressions are formed very quickly and influence subsequent interactions, anchors, even those set arbitrarily, are very influential and quite persistent. They do change, but not easily or quickly (Ariely et al, 2003).

Video 7.1

Example of the Endowment Effect

Whether due to inadequate preparation, the use of "bad" information, or the lack of confidence, some negotiators set their anchors too low (think of the Joseph Bachelder scenario recounted in Negotiation in Action 2.5). Others set them too aggressively because they are poorly prepared, overconfident, or over-optimistic (this bias is discussed next). Either way, anchoring and adjustment is likely to produce outcomes that are nonoptimal. The endowment effect also contributes to this problem. This entails artificially inflating the value of things that belong to us because, in addition to market value, we add a premium for our emotional attachment to them. Thus, if we are negotiating the sale of our car, we are likely to overvalue it relative to what the buyer or an objective observer would consider reasonable. This means we set our anchors too high. The following suggestions should help you manage this bias.

How to Manage This Problem

Preparation is critical because it helps you determine realistic values for the various components of your negotiation—goals, target and resistance points, opening offers. As discussed in Chapters 2 and 3, an opening offer near the other's resistance point is optimistic but not outrageous—it is the best outcome you can achieve.

Refraining from giving the other party's anchors too much credence is essential. If you legitimize his or her opening offer as an important parameter, you are likely to adjust from that point, thus hindering your efforts to achieve optimal outcomes.

Overconfidence/Overoptimism

Overconfident negotiators exaggerate the likelihood that the other party will accept their offers and other positive events, their own abilities, and the degree to which they can control events. They underestimate the occurrence of negative events. They also tend to ignore the other party's needs and concerns, are less concessionary, and achieve lesser outcomes than realistically confident negotiators (Lovallo & Kahneman, 2003; Neale & Bazerman, 1985). This suggests that overconfident negotiators are likely to set their own aspiration levels and reservation prices too high, make unrealistically high opening offers, and exaggerate the value of their own BATNA. Conversely, they may undervalue the other party's BATNA and underestimate his or her aspiration levels and reservation prices.

The overconfidence bias may result from personality traits, insufficient information, our tendency to exaggerate our own talents, prior successes, or a combination of the aforementioned biases and others that will soon be discussed.

The tendency toward optimism is unavoidable for most people. Moreover, it is desirable and should be encouraged, at least to a point.

How to Manage This Problem

Understanding the causes of this bias can help negotiators challenge assumptions, bring in alternative perspectives, and, in general, take a balanced view of the future. Thorough preparation, training, and consulting, a qualified advisor should also enhance negotiators' understanding, help them overcome or minimize this bias, and counter its negative effects (Bazerman & Neale, 1992; Lovallo & Kahneman, 2003). This bias is so prevalent and potentially damaging that a more complete discussion is presented in Reading 7.1.

Perception Errors

Framing

While some frames are cognitive in nature, others are perceptual. Negotiators define situations along one of three dimensions: relationship versus task; emotional versus intellectual; and compromise versus winning (Pinkley, 1990). These *perceptual frames* affect negotiators' behaviors and outcomes. When both negotiators adopt task as opposed to relationship frames, they achieve higher individual

Table 7.2 A Summary of Cognitive Decision-Making Errors

Cognitive Error	Definition	Causes
Irrational Escalation of Commitment	Pursuit of an objective beyond what rational analysis would recommend	Ignoring sunk costs; Confirmation trap; Competition; Selective attention; Impression management; Need for consistency
Framing	How a negotiator defines the situation	Negotiators determine whether a proposal provides a gain or a loss rather than assessing its value or utility
Availability of Information	Information that's easily retrieved from memory is more influential	Vivid, emotionally rich, concrete, and familiar information is more easily retrieved and deemed more important than that which is pallid, emotionally poor, abstracts, and unfamiliar; Search patterns established through experience make certain information more prominent and easier to recall
Anchoring and Adjustment	Opening offers and other positions set anchors from which adjustments or concessions are made	Availability bias; Inadequate preparation; Lack of confidence; Overconfidence
Overconfidence/ Overoptimism	Negotiators overestimate their abilities or the occurrence of positive events, and underestimate the occurrence of negative events	Personality traits; Inadequate preparation; Prior successes; Exaggerated talents and abilities; A combination of other cognitive and perceptual errors

and joint gains (Pinkley & Northcraft, 1994). Negotiators who frame negotiations in emotional terms tend to make apologies or talk about how negative feelings should be handled (Pinkley, 1990). Viewed somewhat differently, a negotiator who adopts a power-based frame and issues threats, makes ultimatums, and uses other aggressive tactics is likely to elicit different responses than a negotiator who adopts an interest-based frame. And both of these frames are likely to elicit different responses than a negotiator who adopts a rights-based frame. Perceptual frames might also reflect, for example, a negotiator's predisposition to achieve a certain outcome—an outcome frame.

Mythical Fixed Pie

At times, resources truly are fixed—there is no way to avoid a zero-sum negotiation whereby one party gains and the other loses. If, however, there are two or more issues and the negotiators' preferences differ, integrative potential exists. Even in these situations, however, most negotiators assume resources are fixed or that their interests and positions are incompatible with those of the other party (Bazerman & Neale, 1983; Thompson, 1991). This is why the mythical fixed pie assumption is so prevalent. Fixed pie perceptions are problematic because they lead to lower individual and joint profits (Thompson & Hastie, 1990).

This assumption is common, especially in the United States, because our culture is so competitive. We compete in sports, for admission to good schools, for scarce resources, for market share, and so on. This contributes to our assumption that negotiations, too, will be competitive. We also have trouble putting our initial assumptions or perspectives aside. This compounds the problem because it causes us to search for and process information in a biased manner (Pinkley, Griffith, & Northcraft, 1995). Most negotiators also focus on one issue at a time. Some start with an easy issue to get the parties comfortable working with each other and agreeing. Others begin with the most difficult issue. They assume that once this issue is settled, the rest of the negotiation will be relatively simple. Both of these approaches are flawed. Focusing on one issue at a time engenders more justification, substantiation, and defending of one's position on each issue, and this produces more compromising on each issue. It also precludes negotiators from searching for and finding mutually beneficial tradeoffs (Hyder, Prietula, & Weingart, 2000).

Expectations

If we believe beforehand that something will be good, chances are it will be. If we think it will be bad, it usually is. This is why placebos work. People who believe they are being medicated feel better, even though they did not really take any medication. Higher prices work in the same way. We believe that we get what we pay for, so if it costs more it must be better (Waber, Shiv, Carmon, & Ariely, 2008). Consider another example. Students who were given a beer and told it was laced with balsamic vinegar before they drank it generally did not like it. Of those who were not told about the vinegar before they drank it, some reported that they liked it and even added more vinegar to their beer (Lee, Frederick, & Ariely, 2006). If knowledge alone informed our decisions and judgments, telling us before or after we drank the beer would not affect our evaluations of it. Nor would price or placebos influence our efficacy assessments.

For negotiators, this means that detailed descriptions, explanations, or presentations of proposals and how they will help the other party should induce positive expectations, thus a better chance that they will be accepted. If the other party provides such explanations, be sure to evaluate them objectively. Accepting a proposal based largely or solely on positive expectations is as unappetizing as drinking beer laced with balsamic vinegar.

Stereotypes

Every time we encounter a new situation, we draw on our past experiences to understand how we are supposed to behave. These mental models, schemata, or scripts simplify information processing and decision making. Similarly, when we encounter a new person at the bargaining table, we draw on our stereotypes, a form of a schema, to help us understand him or her. Although they command negative attention, stereotypes are not intrinsically malevolent. They are simply information-processing shortcuts. Like many of these shortcuts, however, they often derail effective decision-making because they provide us with specific expectations about members of a group and these may unfavorably influence our perceptions and our behavior. In short, he or she may not fit the stereotype.

An interesting feature of stereotypes is that people can be primed to behave consistently with them. Consider two stereotypes: Asians are good at math and women are not good at math. If you ask some Asian American women questions about their ethnicity, and ask other Asian American women questions about their gender, the women who were primed with information about their ethnicity performed much better on a math project than those who were primed with information about their gender (Shin, Pittinsky, & Ambady, 1999). Priming can even affect people who are not members of the stereotypic group. When undergraduate students were primed with stereotypic information about the elderly, for example, they took significantly longer to exit the building than those who were not primed. Similarly, when people were primed with information about being polite or rude, they behaved more politely or rudely (Bargh, Chen, & Burrows, 1996).

Fundamental Attribution Error

Video 7.2
FAE as it applies to business

According to the fundamental attribution error, we tend to attribute our own behaviors and others' behaviors to different causes. Generally, we attribute our own positive behaviors, including our successes, to internal causes such as skill or effort. We attribute our own negative behaviors to situational causes such as inadequate resources or others' difficult personalities. When explaining others' behaviors, however, we do the opposite. We attribute their positive behaviors and successes to situational causes and their negative behaviors and failures to dispositional causes (Ross, 1977). These differential attributions have been observed in negotiations. For example, we erroneously attribute others' tough bargaining behaviors to their difficult personalities. Moreover, the aforementioned tendency to exaggerate our talents is amplified by this bias (Lovallo & Kahneman, 2003).

Perspective Taking

Perspective taking refers to our ability to consider the situation from another person's point of view. It is well documented that our own position or point of view strongly influences our ability to process information objectively. People who identify with perpetrators rather than victims, for example, evaluate perpetrators' behavior more favorably. The converse is true for people who identify with victims (Kronzon & Darley, 1999).

Some people are better than others at understanding others' perspectives. Those who find it more difficult must work harder to put their own perspectives aside, but it is worth the effort for negotiators.

- Perspective takers stereotype less (Galinsky & Moskowitz, 2000; Jones & Nisbett, 1987).
- Perspective takers are better at coordination, problem solving, and creating integrative agreements (Galinsky, Ku, & Wang, 2005; Galinsky, Wang, & Ku, 2008; Richardson, Hammock, Smith, Gardner, & Signo, 1994).
- Perspective takers react more effectively to the other party's attempts to anchor, and claim more resources (Bazerman & Neale, 1982; Galinsky & Mussweiler, 2001).

Ignoring Others' Cognitions

Rather than trying to understand them, many negotiators *ignore the other party's cognitions* (Neale & Bazerman, 1991). This may reflect one's inability to assess the other party's perspectives, his or her unwillingness to do so, or, perhaps, his or her egocentrism—the tendency to focus on ourselves. Alternatively, we sometimes fail to incorporate valuable information about the decisions made by the other party because we develop strategies to simplify decision making (Carroll, Bazerman, & Maury, 1988; Samuelson & Bazerman, 1985). When negotiating tasks that require the use of information about future contingent events, for instance, we make simplifying assumptions to make decision making under uncertainty easier. As with the perspective taking bias, ignoring others' cognitions such as their interests makes it very difficult to achieve integrative outcomes that maximize joint gain.

Illusion of Transparency

Egocentrism, failing to understand the other party's perspective and ignoring his or her cognitions, may explain yet another decision-making error—the illusion of transparency. This entails our tendency to overestimate the extent to which others can discern our thoughts and objectives (Gilovich, Savitsky, & Medvec, 1998). Liars overestimate the ability of others to detect their lies. Negotiators believe their opponents have access to their confidential information (Keysar, Ginzel, & Bazerman, 1995). Others overestimate the transparency of their objectives—we presume our objectives are more readily apparent to others than they actually are (Vorauer & Claude, 1998).

Reactive Devaluation

Reactive devaluation is the tendency for negotiators to discount or dismiss proposals or concessions merely because of who offered them. Assume, for example, that a union negotiator offers to reduce his wage demand by 25 cents/hour. His management counterpart rejects it as insufficient. After reaching a stalemate, a mediator is called in. The mediator speaks with both sides and then advises the management negotiator that he has persuaded the union negotiator to reduce his wage demand by 25 cents per hour. After briefly discussing the proposal, the management negotiator agrees that this is acceptable. Negotiation in Action 7.4 provides an additional illustration of reactive devaluation at work.

NEGOTIATION IN ACTION 7.4

People were asked to assess the value of various options regarding U.S.–Soviet Union disarmament during the so-called Cold War. The options presented to everyone were identical except for who authored them. The evaluations were strongly determined by the author, not by the content of the proposals. Americans evaluated the proposals much more favorably when informed that they were offered by the United States than when they were offered by the Soviet Union (Oskamp, 1965).

Extremism

We believe that our own perceptions reflect objective reality. When we learn that the other side's perceptions differ, we initially try to correct his or her "mistake." If this does not work, we regard him as an extremist. The extremism bias also causes us to believe that his or her interests are more opposed to our own than they actually are, thus exacerbating the mythical fixed pie assumption (Robinson, Keltner, Ward, & Ross, 1995). In face-to-face negotiations, these exaggerated differences escalate conflict and partisan perceivers ascribe more negative qualities to the other negotiator. This reduces the probability that agreements, especially integrative agreements, will be reached (Keltner & Robinson, 1993; Robinson & Kray, 2001).

Managing Perceptual Errors

Avoiding or minimizing the negative consequences of perceptual biases can be accomplished by gathering accurate and objective information about ourselves, others, and the situation (Morris, Larrick, & Su, 1999). Thus, thorough preparation, including analyzing the other party, asking open-ended questions, testing assumptions, active listening, standing in his or her shoes to learn and clarify perceptions, and the other suggestions proffered in Chapter 2 should enhance your understanding of his or her perceptions and cognitions. Understanding and clarifying all of the issues, the interests associated with each to, and their priorities should make it clear to each party that there are a variety of solutions available that will work for all of you. Some people may hold tightly to unfounded assumptions and refuse to engage in creative problem solving with you. Making multiple-issue offers reduces negotiators' tendency to defend and justify proposals for individual issues. This will help you avoid the typical result—inferior outcomes or impasses.

Table 7.3   Perceptual Decision-Making Errors

Perceptual Error	Definition	Causes
Mythical Fixed Pie	Erroneous belief that the other's interests are directly opposed to our own	Competitive culture; Inability to put initial assumptions aside; Negotiate one issue at a time
Expectations	If we think something will be good or bad, it usually is	Experiencing objects or events using biased sensory lenses; Information processing shortcuts; Inability to take the other's perspective
Stereotypes	Expectations about members of a particular group	Inability to take the other's perspective; Information processing shortcuts
Attribution Error	Tendency to attribute others' successes externally and failures internally, and our own successes internally and failures externally	Fixed pie perceptions; Egocentrism; Faulty assumptions about the credibility of information
Perspective Taking	Ability to consider the situation from another's point of view	Personality trait; Egocentrism
Ignoring Other's Cognitions	Inability or unwillingness to assess another's thoughts, concerns, perspectives	Inability/unwillingness to ask about or consider the other's perceptions; Egocentrism; Information processing shortcuts
Illusion of Transparency	Overestimating the extent to which others can discern our internal states	Egocentrism; Perspective taking; Ignoring others' cognitions
Reactive Devaluation	Discounting offers or concessions because of who made them	Distrust; Emotions; Poor preparations
Extremism	We believe our own perceptions map onto objective reality—when others differ, they are viewed as extremists	Fixed pie perceptions; Egocentrism

Emotional Biases

Mood

Mood or affect engenders emotional biases because it influences the quality and depth of our information processing. For example, people demonstrate better information processing abilities when the information they are processing is affectively consistent with their mood (Thompson et al., 2004). More prosocial (see Chapter 11) behaviors are executed when people are in a good mood, and more antisocial behaviors are executed when they are in a bad mood (Bower, 1991; Forgas, 1998; Isen, 1993). Good moods also foster more creativity and increase the likelihood that innovative solutions will be negotiated (Isen, Daubman, & Nowicki, 1987). Finally, negotiators who are in a good mood make more concessions when negotiating face-to-face (Baron, 1990). For obvious reasons, this may not be a good thing.

Anger

Mood refers to low intensity, diffuse affect, and it may derive from factors outside the negotiation (Fiske & Taylor, 1991). Emotion, on the other hand, suggests more intense feelings that arise during the negotiation and are directed at the other party. These feelings may be particularly influential because they can be contagious. That is, emotions can even affect the judgment of uninvolved observers (Thompson & Kim, 2000).

Negotiators who are angry with each other achieve smaller joint gains and have less desire to work together in the future than do negotiators who have more positive emotional regard for the other side (Allred, Mallozzi, Matsui, & Raia, 1997). This happens because angry negotiators' assessments of the other party's interests are less accurate and their preferences are more self-centered. Such preferences make it harder to reach an agreement (Allred et al., 1997; Thompson & Lowenstein, 1992). Anger may actually engender retaliatory actions toward the other party if we believe he or she is responsible for some harm to the negotiator (Allred, 1999).

Competitive Arousal

Competitive arousal is an adrenaline-fueled emotional state. It occurs too often in business and often leads to costly mistakes (Malhotra, Ku, & Murnighan, 2008). The consequences of this error are similar to those of the irrational escalation of commitment error. The causes, however, differ. The irrational escalation of commitment stems from our inability to ignore sunk costs, while competitive arousal grows out of rivalry, time pressures, and audience effects (Ku, Malhotra, & Murnighan, 2005).

When rivals and time pressures exist, or negotiations enter the public realm, logic and reason exit and emotion takes over. Rather than engaging in a concerted effort to find the best solution for everyone involved, dealcrafting becomes a fierce competition where each party seeks victory and destruction or humiliation of the other party. (Welch & Welch, 2007). Examples abound in professional athletics, labor negotiations, and in other industries. Joe Torre's negotiation to continue managing the New York Yankees was conducted under the hot glare of media scrutiny and rationality departed. The National Hockey League's lockout of its players resulted in the cancellation of the 2004–2005 season. Eastern Airlines shut down, in significant part because of the destructive negotiations that were conducted with its labor unions. Logic and reason are also replaced by emotions when rivalries exist. When airlines shop for new planes, for example, they are masters of pitting companies against each other and emotions boil. Any time an acquisition fight falls under the public eye, competing buyers can get a little wacky. These deals are transformed from buying a company at a reasonable price into who will be declared the winner and who the loser. It's unusual for companies to take their private disputes public to break impasses. Hours before ABC's telecast of the Academy Award show in 2010 (its biggest broadcast day of the year), the Walt Disney Company (the owner of the ABC network) pulled the signal on its top-rated affiliate serving 3 million homes. It had been unable to extract a larger fee per month per cable subscriber from Cablevision, so it turned to the public for help. Engaged in a pricing dispute with Coca Cola, Costco removed Coke products from its shelves for several weeks and informed shoppers it was demanding lower prices from the soda company. Amazon temporarily removed the buy button from Macmillan books on its website in 2010 to protest the publisher's demands for new terms for the sale of its e-books. In these and other cases, companies seem to be willing to take a short-term financial hit to further their longer-term negotiation goals. As will be discussed in Chapter 10, audiences make negotiating more difficult so negotiate privately and avoid public scrutiny if you can. If you exhaust your private efforts and believe that you must take your negotiation public, issue advance warning to the other party. Catching the other party off guard will not help and this will afford him or her an opportunity to respond to your requests and demands. So that your customers will tolerate any inconveniences that arise, inform them of your behavior and why you think it is necessary. When you settle your differences, issue a joint statement indicating your renewed commitment to working together on behalf of your customers (Program on Negotiation, 2010; Welch & Welch, 2007).

Impact Bias/Miswanting

People are generally quite adept at predicting whether future events are likely to be pleasant or unpleasant. But we routinely mispredict how much pleasure or displeasure these events will bring, and how long it will last. Sometimes we underestimate intensity and duration. More often, we exaggerate our emotional reactions to future events. As a consequence, we sometimes work to achieve things that do not maximize our happiness (Wilson & Gilbert, 2005). This impact bias often causes us to miswant.

This error suggests that negotiators may have trouble deciding what they are negotiating for, and how hard to push for it. If we think something will bring us great pleasure, we are likely to pursue it vigorously. If we think it will bring us great displeasure, we are likely to fight it vigorously. The predicament seems obvious—if we do not really understand how much pleasure we will gain or how much pain we will suffer, should we work really hard to get or resist it? Moreover, the impact bias may cause us to distort the value of our BATNA and set our resistance points incorrectly. It may also cause us to set our targets too high or too low. It may even cause confusion when we determine our own interests.

Why are we often mistaken about how happy or unhappy events will make us? One reason involves focalism–our tendency to overestimate how much we will think about this event in the future and to underestimate the extent to which other events will influence our thoughts and feelings (Schkade & Kahneman, 1998; Wilson, Wheatley, Meyers, Gilbert, & Axsom, 2000).

A second reason involves the sophisticated *sense-making* capabilities that we possess and use, often unconsciously, when novel or unexpected events happen. We are motivated to recover from negative events using coping, rationalizing, and psychological defense mechanisms. Just as our physiological immune system fights threats to our physical health, these mechanisms fight threats to our emotional well-being. Unexpected or novel positive events initially cause us to attend, emotionally, to those that are self-relevant but poorly understood. We then try to explain or make sense of them until they become more "normal" (Wilson & Gilbert, 2005; Wilson et al., 2000).

Managing Emotional Biases

These coping mechanisms are not very surprising. What is surprising is that they are largely unconscious and work more effectively when they remain unconscious. They work quickly and we generally do not recognize, beforehand, that they will occur. Nor do we recognize that they are occurring while they are helping us. For these reasons, we persist in miswanting (Gilbert, Pinel, Wilson, Blumberg, & Wheatley, 1998; Wilson & Gilbert, 2005).

Focalism can be corrected, or at least mitigated somewhat. When forecasting our affective response to a particular event, we can remind ourselves, or ask others to remind us, to consider the many other events that will demand our attention in the future (Wilson et al., 2000). As demonstrated in Negotiation in Action 7.5, framing options to induce optimal decisions may help with the sense-making process.

NEGOTIATION IN ACTION 7.5

Assume that Ricardo, a very difficult tenured faculty member at a large university, is suing his employer for national origin discrimination. His attorney is an experienced litigator. Ricardo has never been involved in a lawsuit and knows little about the law. The employer offered a settlement package that included a sizable sum of money if Ricardo agreed to terminate his employment at the university. Ricardo, in his emotional state, thinks he can do better at trial. Knowing that a better outcome at trial is unlikely, his attorney could frame the settlement as a certain gain and trial as an uncertain gain to help Ricardo make a wiser decision (Guthrie & Sally, 2004).

Cooling off periods may also help. Making the final decision away from the bargaining table offers two potential benefits. First, it may reduce the cognitive load on the decision maker and this can increase the accuracy of his or her affective forecasts. Second, stepping away may help the decision maker manage his or her own emotions more effectively (Guthrie & Sally, 2004).

CONCLUSION AND IMPLICATIONS FOR PRACTICE

Decision making is an inescapable component of the negotiation process. We usually make good decisions, but they can be and often are plagued by various problems. Many of these biases and errors are subtle and we may not realize that we are making them. Being aware of these problems and taking steps to avoid or correct them should help us make decisions that are rational and optimal. Understanding them is also important for another reason. The other negotiator may attempt to capitalize on the "unconscious" nature of many of these errors and leverage them to influence us.

Table 7.4 Emotional Decision-Making Errors

Emotional Error	Definition	Cause
Mood	Low intensity, diffuse affect	Positive or negative factors outside the negotiation
Anger	Intense feelings arising during the negotiation that are directed at the other party	Negative factors inside the negotiation
Competitive Arousal	Adrenaline-fueled emotional state	Rivalry; Time pressure; Audiences
Impact Bias/Miswanting	Mispredicting the intensity or duration of the pleasure or pain that future events will bring	Focalism; Sense-making capabilities

Likewise, we might be able to leverage them to influence him or her. If this sounds manipulative and raises ethical problems for you, remember that the distinction between "influence" and "manipulation" is subtle. Moreover, the intent behind all bargaining tactics is to influence the other side to agree to solutions that we find attractive and beneficial for ourselves, and perhaps for him or her as well. The following suggestions should help you avoid or minimize these errors when you are negotiating.

1. Be thorough in your preparation. Thorough preparation, especially cultivating alternatives, setting limits (resistance points), analyzing the other negotiator, and testing these assumptions, is the best defense available to you for avoiding these errors. "Standing in the other negotiator's shoes" will also enhance your understanding of the situation from his or her perspective, and of his or her other perceptions. For example, learning the other negotiator's reference point will enable you to frame your offers as certain rather than uncertain gains or as uncertain rather than certain losses, both of which should make his or her decision easier to make. Understanding these biases is also essential. They should be considered when you prepare, or at least before you make important decisions. Taking your time before you make a decision, and walking away from the stresses and pressures of the negotiation, even for a few minutes, will help you make better decisions.

2. Gather additional information, including that which is contrary to your existing thoughts and beliefs, evaluate it carefully, and use it to guide your decision making. Consult with colleagues, associates, and others you trust and respect to gather and evaluate the information. Also ask them to monitor your decisions to ensure that you are not inappropriately exceeding your limits or otherwise making bad choices.

3. Reevaluate your chosen course of action when you reach your pre-set limits or resistance points. Ignore what you have already lost—your sunk costs—and determine whether the future benefits outweigh the future costs. If so, it may be okay to continue. If not, you should probably change course. This may require you to put your ego aside. If changing course will hinder your efforts to manage others' impressions of you, consider whether holding firm to a failing course

of action is better or worse than enduring others' questions and criticisms because you changed your mind.

4. Keep in mind, information and explanations that are vivid, familiar, and emotionally rich unduly influence our decisions. Attributions, stereotypes, and other shortcuts simplify information processing. These qualities all lead to decision-making errors, often the unconscious variety. They also make us more vulnerable to the other negotiator's influence attempts. Use them to your advantage, but beware when they are used against you.

5. Maintain your focus on your own anchor so that you adjust from the favorable end of the bargaining range. If the other negotiator anchors you, refocus your attention on your target point or opening offer to limit the chances that you will adjust from his or her unfavorable end of the range and make bad decisions.

6. Avoid rivals, intense time pressures, and audiences when you negotiate. Doing so will help make your decisions more rational.

STUDENT STUDY SITE

Visit the Student Study Site at **www.sagepub.com/hames** for additional learning tools.

KEY TERMS

Affect (aka mood)

Anchoring

Anger

Attribution error

Availability bias

Availability of information

Cognitive decision-making errors

Competitive arousal

Confirmation trap

Egocentrism

Emotional decision-making errors

Endowment effect

Expectations

Extremism bias

Focalism

Framing error

Fundamental attribution error

Ignoring other's cognitions

Illusion of transparency

Impact bias

Impression management

Irrational escalation of commitment

Miswanting

Mood (aka affect)

Overconfidence bias

Perceptual decision-making errors

Perspective taking

Reactive devaluation

Selective attention

Stereotypes

REFERENCES

Allred, K. G. (1999). Anger-driven retaliation: Toward an understanding of impassioned conflict in organizations. In R. J. Bies, R. J. Lewicki & B. H. Sheppard (Eds.), *Research on negotiation in organizations*, 7, Stamford, CT: JAI Press, 27-58.

Allred, K. G., Mallozzi, J. S., Matsui, F. & Raia, C. P. (1997). The influence of anger and compassion on negotiation performance, *Organizational Behavior and Human Decision Processes*, 70, 175-187.

Ariely, D. (2009). The end of rational economics, *Harvard Business Review*, July-August, 78-84.

Ariely, D. (2008). Predictably irrational: The hidden forces that shape our decisions. New York: HarperCollins.

Ariely, D., Loernstein, G. & Prelec, D. (2003). Coherent arbitrariness: Stable demand curves without stable preferences, *Quarterly Journal of Economics*, 118, 73-105.

Bargh, J., Chen, M. & Burrows, L. (1996). Automaticity of social behavior: direct effects of trait construct and stereotype activation on action, *Journal of Personality and Social Psychology*, 71, 230-244.

Baron, R. A. (1990). Environmentally induced positive affect: Its impact on self efficacy and task performance, negotiation and conflict, *Journal of Applied Social Psychology*, 20, 368-384.

Bazerman, M. H. & Neale, M. A. (1992). *Negotiating rationally*. New York: The Free Press.

_____. (1983). Heuristics in negotiation: Limitations to effective dispute resolution. In M. H. Bazerman & R. J. Lewicki (Eds.), *Negotiating in organizations*, Beverly Hills: Sage, 51-67.

Bazerman, M. H., Magliozzi, T & Neale, M. A. (1985). Integrative bargaining in a ompetitive market, *Organizational Behavior and Human Performance*, 35, 294-313.

Bazerman, M. H., Beekun, R. & Schoorman, F. (1982). Performance evaluation in a dynamic context: The impact of prior commitment to the taree, *Journal of Applied Psycholgy*, 67, 873-876.

Borgida, E. & Nisbett, R. E. (1977). The differential impact of abstract vs. concrete information on decisions, *Journal of Applied Social Psychology*, 7, 258-271.

Bower, E. G. (Ed.), (1991). The psychology of learning and motivation: Advances in research and theory, 27. San Diego: Academic Press.

Carroll, J., Bazerman, M. & Maury, R. (1988). Negotiator cognitions: A descriptive approach to negotiators' understanding of their opponents, *Organizational Behavior and Human Decision Processes*, 41, 352-370.

de Dreu, C. K. W, Emans, B. J. M. & van de Vliert, E. (1992). The influence of own cognitive and other's communicated gain or loss frame on negotiation behavior, *International Journal of Conflict Management*, 3(2), 115-132.

Fiske, S. T. & Taylor, S. W. E. (1991). Social cognition. Reading, MA: Addison-Wesley.

Forgas, J. P. (1998). On feeling good and getting your way: Mood effects on negotiator cognition and bargaining strategies, *Journal of Personality and Social Psychology*, 74, 565-577.

Galinsky, A. D., Wang, C. S. & Ku, G. (2008). Perspective-takers behave more stereotypically, *Journal of Personality and Social Psychology*, 95(2), 404-419.

Galinsky, A. D., Ku, G. & Wang, C. S. (2005). Perspective-taking: Fostering social bonds and facilitating coordination, *Group Processes and Intergroup Relations*, 8, 109-125.

Galinsky, A. D. & Mussweiler, T. (2001). First offers as anchors: The role of perspective-taking and negotiator focus, *Journal of Personality and Social Psychology*, 81(4), 657-669.

Gilbert, D. T., Pinel, E. C., Wilson, T. D., Blumberg, S. J. & Wheatley, T. P. (1998). Immune neglect: A source of durability bias in affective forecasting, *Journal of Personality and Social Psychology*, 75(3), 617-638.

Gilovich, T., Savitsky, K. & Medvec, V. H. (1998). The illusion of transparency: Biased asesssments of others' ability to read one's emotional states, *Journal of Personality and Social Psychology*, 75, 332-346.

Guthrie, C. & Sally, D. (2004). The impact of the impact bias on negotiation, *Marquette aw Review*, 87, 817-828

Hyder, E. B., Prietula, M. J. & Weingart, L. R., (2000). Getting to best: Efficiency versus optimality in negotiation, *Cognitive Science*, 24(2), 169-204.

Isen, A. M. (1993). Positive affect and decision making. In M. Lewis and J. Haviland (Eds.), *Handbook of emotion*. New York: Guilford, 261-277.

Isen, A. M., Daubman, K. A. & Nowicki, G. P. (1987). Positive affect facilitates creative problem solving, *Journal of Personality and Social Psychology*, 52, 1122-1131.

Jordan, P. (2004). The holdout, *New York Times*, July 18, www.nytimes.com/2004/07/18/magazine/the-holdout.html

Keltner, D. & Robinson, D. J. (1993). Imagined ideological differences in conflict escalation and resolution, *International Journal of Conflict Management*, 4, 249-262.

Keysar, B., Ginzel, L. E. & Bazerman, M. H. (1995). States of affairs and states of mind: The effect of knowledge about beliefs, *Organizational Behavior and Human Decision Processes*, 64, 283-293.

Kronzon, S. & Darley, J. (1999). Is this tactic ethical? Biased judgments of ethics in negotiation, *Basic and Applied Social Psychology*, 21(1), 49-60.

Ku, G., Malhotra, D. & Murnighan, J. K. (2005). Towards a competitive arousal model of decision-making: A study of auction fever in live and Internet auctions, *Organizational Behavior and Human Decision Processes*, 96, 89-103.

Lee, L., Frederick, S. & Ariely, D (2006). Try it, you'll like it: The influence of expectation, consumption, and revelation on preferences for beer, *PsychologicalScience*, 17(12), 1054-1058.

Lovallo, D. & Kahneman, D. (2003). Delusions of success, Harvard Business Review, July, 56-63.

Malhotra, D., Ku, G. & Murnighan, J. K. (2008). When winning is everything, *Harvard Business Review*, May, 78-86.

Morris, M. W., Larrick, R. P. & Su, S. K. (1999). Misperceiving negotiation counterparts: When situationally determined bargaining behaviors are attributed to personality traits, *Journal of Personality and Social Psychology*, 77, 52-67.

Neale, M. A. & Bazerman, M. H. (1991). *Cognition and rationality in negotiation*. New York: The Free Press.

_____. (1985). The effect of externally set goals on reaching integrative agreements in competitive markets, *Journal of Occupational Behavior*, 6, 19-32.

Neale, M. A., Huber, V. L. & Northcraft, G. B. (1987). The framing of negotiations: Contextual versus task frames, *Organizational Behavior and Human Decision Processes*, 39(2), 228-241.

Northcraft, G. B. & Neale, M. A. (1987). Experts, amateurs, and real estate: An anchoring-and-adjustment perspective on property pricing decisions, *Organizational Behavior and Human Decision Processes*, 39, 84-97.

_____. (1986). Opportunity costs and the framing of resource allocation decisions, *Organizational Behavior and Human Decision Processes*, 37, 348-356.

Oskamp, S. (1965). Attitudes toward U.S. and Russian actions: A double standard, *Psycholgical Reports*, 16, 43-46.

Pinkley, R. (1990). Dimensions of conflict frame: Disputant interpretations of conflict, *Journal of Applied Psychology*, 75, 117-126.

Pinkley, R. & Northcraft, G. B. (1994). Conflict frames of reference: Implications for dispute processes and outcomes. *Academy of Management Journal*, 37(1)193-205.

Pinkley, R., Griffith, T. L., & Northcraft, G. B. (1995). "Fixed pie" a la mode: Information availability, information processing, and the negotiation of suboptimal agreements, *Organizational Behavior and Human Decision Processes*, 62, 101-112.

Richardson, D., Hammock, G., Smith, S., Gardner, W. & Signo, M. (1994). Empathy as a cognitive inhibitor of interpersonal aggression, *Aggressive Behavior*, 20, 275-289.

Robinson, R. J., Keltner, D., Ward, A. & Ross, L. (1995). Actual versus assumed differences in construal: "Naïve realism" in intergroup perception and conflict, *Journal of Personality and Social Psychology*, 68, 404-417.

Robinson, R. J. & Kray, L. (2001). Status versus quo: Naïve realism and the search for social change and perceived legitimacy. In J. T. Jost & B. Major (Eds.), *The psychology of legitimacy: Emerging perspectives on ideology, justice, and intergroup relations*. New York: Cambridge University Press, 135-154.

Ross, L. (1977). The intuitive psychologist and his shortcomings: Distortion in the attribution Process. In L. Berkowitz (E.), *Advances in experimental social psychology*, 10. Orlando, FL: Academic Press, 173-220.

Samuelson, W. F. & Bazerman, M. H. (1985). The winner's curse in bilateral negotiations. In V. L. Smith (Ed.), *Research in experimental economics*. Greenwich, CT: JAI Press, 105-137.

Schkade, D. A. & Kahneman, D. (1998). Does living in California make people happy? A focusing illusion in judgments of life satisfaction, *Psychological Science*, 9, 340-346.

Schoorman, F. (1988). Escalation bias in performance appraisals: An unintended consequence of supervisor participation in hiring decisions, *Journal of Applied Psychology*, 73, 58-62.

Shin, M., Pittinsky, T. L. & Ambady, N. (1999). Stereotype susceptibility: Identity salience and shifts in quantitative performance, *Psychological Science*, 10(1), 80-83.

Thompson, L. (1991). Information exchange in negotiation, *Journal of Experimental Social Psychology*, 27, 161-179.

Thompson, L, Neale, M. & Sinaceur, M. (2004. The evolution of cognition and biases in negotiation research: An examination of cognition, social perception, motivation and emotion. In M. J. Gelfand & J. M. Brett (Eds.). The handbook of negotiation and culture. Stanford, CA: Stanford University Press, 7-44.

Thompson, L. Medvec, V. H., Seiden, V & Kipelman, S. (2001). Poker face, smiley face, and rant and rave: Mythis and realities about emoition in negotiation. In M. Hogg & S. Tindale (Eds.), Blackwell handbook in social psychology: Vol 3-Group processes. Oxford, England: Blackwell, 139-163.

Thompson, L. L. & Kim, P. H. (2000). How the quality of third parties' settlement solutions is affected by the relationship between the negotiators,

Journal of Experimental Psychology: Applied, 6(1), 3-14.

Thompson, L. L. & Lowenstein, G. (1992). Egocentric interpretations of fairness and interpersonal conflict, *Organizational Behavior and Human Decision Processes*, 51, 176-197.

Thompson, L. & Hastie, (1990). Social perceptions in negotiation, *Organizational Behavior and Human Decision Processes*, 47, 98-123.

Tversky, A. & Kahneman, D. (1981). The framing of decisions and the psychology of choice, *Science*, 40, 453-463.

Vorauer, J. D. & Claude, S. (1998). Perceived versus actual transparency of goals in negotiation, *Personality and Social Psychology Bulletin*, 24, 371-385.

Waber, R., Shiv, B., Carmon, Z. & Ariely, D. (2008). Commercial features of placebo and therapeutic efficacy, *Journal of the American Medical Association*, 299(9), 1016-1017.

Welch, J. & Welch, S. (2007). Negotiate in a cool, dark place; Lessons from the very public breakup of Joe Torre and the New York Yankees, *BusinessWeek*, November 5, 94-95.

Wilson, T. D. & Gilbert, D. T. (2005). Affective forecasting: Knowing what to want, *Current Directions in Psychological Science*, 14(3), 131-134.

Wilson, T. D., Wheatley, T. P., Meyers, J. M., Gilbert, D. T. & Axsom, D. (2000). Focalism: A source of durability bias in affective forecasting, *Journal of Personality and Social Psychology*, 78, 821-836.

READINGS

Reading 7.1

DECISIONS WITHOUT BLINDERS

Max H. Bazerman and Dolly Chugh

The "bounded awareness" phenomenon causes people to ignore critical information when making decisions. Learning to expand the limits of your awareness before you make an important

choice will save you from asking "How did I miss that?" after the fact.

BY THE TIME MERCK WITHDREW VIOXX from the market in September 2004 out of concern that the pain relief drug was causing heart attacks and strokes, more than 100 million prescriptions for it had been filled in the United

Source: Max H. Bazerman and Dolly Chugh, "Decisions Without Blinders," Harvard Business Review, Jan 2006, pp. 88–97. Used by permission of Harvard Business School Publishing.

States alone. Researchers now estimate that Vioxx may have been associated with as many as 25,000 heart attacks and strokes. And more than 1,000 claims have been filed against the company. Evidence of the drug's hazards was publicly available as early as November 2000, when the *New England Journal of Medicine* reported that four times as many patients taking Vioxx experienced myocardial infarctions as did those taking naproxen. In 2001, Merck's own report to federal regulation showed that 14.6% of Vioxx patients suffered from cardiovascular troubles while taking the drug; 2.5% developed serious problems, including heart attacks. So why, if the drug's risks had been published in 2000 and 2001, did so many doctors choose to prescribe it?

Social science research has shown that without realizing it, decision makers ignore certain critical information. Doctors, like the rest of us, are imperfect information processors. They face tremendous demands on their time and must make life-and-death decision under highly ambiguous circumstances. In the case of Vioxx, doctors more often than not received positive feedback from patients taking the drug. And, as we now know, the Merck sales force took unethical steps to make Vioxx appear safer than it was. So despite having access to information about the risks, doctors—even those who had read the *New England Journal of Medicine* article—may have been blinded to the actual extent of those risks.

Most people fail to bring the right information into their conscious awareness at the right time. And why did Merck's senior executives allow the product to stay on the market for so long? Evidence points to intentional misrepresentation by the sales force, but it is quite possible that some members of Merck's top management team did not fully understand how harmful the drug was. In fact, many respected individuals have vouched for the ethics of former chairman and CEO Raymond Gilmartin, insisting that he would have pulled Vioxx from the market earlier if he had believed that it was killing people. Although senior executives are, ultimately, responsible for what happens in their organizations, the lapse here may have been more in the quality of their decision making than in any intentional unethical behavior.

In this article, we'll examine the phenomenon of *bounded awareness*—when cognitive blinders prevent a person from seeing, seeking, using, or sharing highly relevant, easily accessible, and readily perceivable information during the decision-making process. "The information that life seves is not necessarily the information that one would order from the menu," notes Dan Gilbert of Harvard University's psychology department, "but like polite dinner guests and other victims of circumstance, people generally seem to accept what is offered rather than banging their flatware and demanding carrot."

Most executives are not aware of the specific ways in which their awareness is limited. And failure to recognize those limitations can have grave consequences, as the Vioxx example demonstrates. Simply put, pain relief and profits may well have been within doctors' and executives' bounds of awareness, whereas the risks of Vioxx may have fallen outside these bounds.

It's important to note that bounded awareness differs from information overload, or having to make decisions with too much information and too little time. Even when spared a deluge of information and given sufficient time to make decisions, most individuals still fail to bring the right information into their conscious awareness at the right time.

Bounded awareness can occur at various points in the decision-making process. First, executives may fail to see or seek out key information needed to make a sound decision. Second, they may fail to use the information that they do see because they aren't aware of its relevance. Finally, executives may fail to share information with others, thereby bounding the organization's awareness.

Failure to See Information

The ability to focus on one task is undoubtedly useful, but focus also limits awareness. Consider a study by Cornell psychologist Ulric Neisser, for instance. Neisser had participants watch a videotape of two teams (wearing different-colored jerseys) passing basketballs and asked everyone to count the number of passes between players on one of the teams. The assignment was more difficult than it might sound, because each team had played at different times but their footage was superimposed onto one video. So focused were the subjects on their task that only 21% of them reported seeing a woman walking with an open umbrella among the players. But anyone who watches the video without an assignment notices the woman there for a significant part of the video. When we use this tape in the executive classroom, even fewer than 21% of executives spot the woman.

That's cause for concern, since executives need to stay alert to peripheral threats and opportunities as well as concentrate on the job at hand. Failure to notice regulatory, political, or market-oriented changes in their environment will keep them from adapting their strategies so that their organizations can thrive.

People overlook more than just the information they aren't expecting, as Jeremy Wolfe and Todd Horowitz of Harvard Medical School and Naomi Kenner of Brigham and Women's Hospital in Boston have shown. These researchers replicated in a lab the process of screening for weapons at airports. Study participants screened bags for dangerous objects after having been told how often those objects would appear. When they were told that the objects would appear 50% of the time, participants had a 7% error rate. But when they were told that the objects would appear only 1% of the time, the error rate jumped to 30%. Since people didn't expect to see the objects, they gave up looking for them—or as Wolfe explains, "If you don't see it often, you often don't see it."

Another area of perceptual blindness has to do with gradual change, as demonstrated in a study by Harvard Business School's Francesca Gino with Max Bazerman. Participants were divided into two groups: one charged with estimating the amount of money in jars filled with pennies, the other with "auditing" the estimations of others. The estimators were rewarded not when they were accurate but when their high estimates were approved by the auditor. The auditors were rewarded for approving the estimates but penalized if caught accepting an extreme overestimate. When the first group gradually increased its numbers in comparison with the true value, the auditors were less likely to see the estimates as inflated and unethical than if the estimators suddenly moved to the same exaggerated member. In practice, this helps explain how the Enron and WorldCom scandals grew so huge. Small ethical transgressions that were originally overlooked snowballed into larger and larger crimes.

Fortunately, people can learn to be more observant of changes in their environment, which will help to remove their decision-making blinders. U.S. Secret Service agents, for instance, are trained to scan a crowd and notice when someone reaches into his coat or moves to the front of a pack, things most of us would be oblivious to. Similarly, executives can cultivate an awareness of what kind of information could directly affect their organizations. They should also assign responsibility to others for this task. Since different people will have different bounds of awareness, getting multiple views will be more apt to yield all the relevant data necessary for a fully informed decision. Psychologists Dan Lovallo and Daniel Dahneman discussed the wisdom of developing—or buying —an outsider's perspective in "Delusions of Success: How Optimism Undermines Executives' Decisions" (HBR July 2003). We second their advice because an outside view might help you see critical information that you could easily overlook when immersed in day-to-day activities.

Failure to Seek Information

The *Challenger* space shuttle disaster has been well reviewed through many analytic lenses, but for our purposes, let's consider the decisions leading up to the launch. *Challenger* blasted off at the lowest temperature in the history of the shuttle program, a factor that led to the failure of the O-rings and, ultimately, to the death of all seven astronauts on board. The day before the disaster, executives at NASA argued about whether the combination of low temperature and O-ring failure would be a problem. But because no clear connection emerged between low temperatures and the O-rings in the seven prior launches when O-ring damage had occurred, they chose to continue on schedule.

The most worrisome version of the failure to seek information occurs when decision makers are motivated to favor a particular outcome.

Tragically, the decision makers did not seek out the temperatures for the 17 shuttle launches in which there was no O-ring failure. The data set of all 24 launches would have unambiguously pointed to the need to delay *Challenger*. Later analyses suggest that, given the low temperature, the probability of disaster exceeded 99%. Like many well-meaning executives, the scientists at NASA and Morton Thiokol limited their analysis to the data at hand—they failed to seek out the most relevant data.

The most worrisome decision makers are motivated to favor a particular outcome. Many people believe the Bush administration's decision to invade Iraq was a mistake. We will not argue the general case here, but we do contend that the process leading up to the decision was flawed. Senior U.S. government officials were caught up in their own bounded awareness and did not search for information that would argue against an invasion. Specifically, they failed to notice signs that their assessment of the situation

in Iraq was wrong, particularly regarding the existence of weapons of mass destruction.

The most disturbing evidence comes from Richard Clarke's account of the events of September 11 and 12, 2001. Clarke, the antiterrorism czar at the time, claims in his book *Against All Enemies* that on the night of September 11, he was directed by then-National Security Advisor Condoleezza Rice to go home for a few hours of sleep. When he returned to work the next morning, Clarke reports, Vice President Dick Cheney, Defense Secretary Donald Rumsfeld, and Deputy Secretary of Defense Paul Wolfowitz were discussing the role that Iraq must have played in the attack. We now know that this overly narrow assessment was wrong, but in the months that followed, the Bush administration conducted a motivated search to tie Iraq to 9/11 and terrorism. With such a confirmatory effort, information inconsistent with the preferred viewpoint lay outside the bounds of awareness.

How can we be expected to seek out information that lies beyond our very awareness? The key is vigilance in considering what information actually addresses the decision you must reach. Imagine, for instance, that you are in a classroom and the professor gives you the sequence "2-4-6." She then asks you to identify the specific rule she is thinking of that is consistent with the 2-4-6 sequence. In order to guess the rule, you can call out other sequences of three numbers, and the professor will tell you whether or not each sequence you offer follows her rule. You can query as many sequences as you like, but you have only one chance to guess the rule.

We use this exercise, adapted from psychologist P.C. Wason, in our executive education classes. We write 2-4-6 on the board and have a volunteer guess other sequences to determine the rule. The volunteer usually offers only a few sequences before making his final—and always incorrect —guess (most commonly, "numbers that go up by two" or "the difference between the last two numbers"). We then ask for another hypothesis, tries sequences that are consistent with that hypothesis, and then guesses a rule — again, incorrectly. At this stage, it is rare that we will have answered no to a sequence proposed by either executive, because the rule is "any three ascending numbers."

Solving this problem requires participants to accumulate contradictory, rather than confirming, evidence. Thus, if your mind places the bounds of "numbers that go up two" on the problem, you must try sequences that do not conform to find the actual rule. Trying 1-3-5, 10-12-14-124-126, and so on will lead you to "confirm" that going up by two is correct, though it is not. Seeking disconfirming information is a powerful problem-solving approach, but it is rarely a part of our intuitive strategies.

That exercise had one correct answer, but it the real world, few decisions are so cut-and-dried. And yet, by the time information reaches an executive's desk, it is often framed as a recommendation and supported by considerable data. While it's true that executives must rely on others to streamline the data flow for them, they must also be skeptical of the absence of contradictory evidence; it is a red flag indicating highly bounded awareness. When an executive sees it, he should send team members back to search for and articulate the missing contradictory evidence.

Take, for example, the legendary flop of New Coke in 1985. In the mid-1980s, Pepsi was gaining ground on Coke, largely by shifting consumers' attention to taste through the Pepsi Challenge taste tests. The success of Pepsi's campaign also persuaded Coca-Cola executives to focus on the taste dimension—and to devote a massive amount of research and development to the reformulation of the 99-year-old Coke recipe.

Let's put this situation in the context of the 2-4-6 puzzle. Pepsi's focus on taste became the hypothesis at Coke's headquarters. All the focus groups, taste tests, and reformulations that followed seemed to confirm that taste was the problem. However, executives didn't attempt to collect contradictory evidence. Sergio Zyman, Coke's chief marketing officer at the time, reflects, "We didn't ask . . . 'If we took away Coca-Cola and gave you New Coke, would you accept it?'" That question could have proved the taste theory wrong. Just as the way to test the "increase by 2 hypotheses" is to test worse-tasting Coke recipes against Pepsi to see if Coke drinkers remain loyal.

Generating contradictory evidence should be part of everyone's job. But one way to integrate this form of thinking is to assign a "devil's inquisitor" role to a member of the group. This is not the same as a devil's advocate, who argues against the status quo. By asking questions instead of arguing an alternate point of view, the devil's inquisitor pushes people to look for evidence outside their bounds of awareness. Moreover, this role can be comfortably worn by those who are reluctant to take on the majority; it gives them a safe way to contribute.

Failure to Use Information

Although it may be hard to believe, many executives simply disregard accessible and valuable information when they are making an important decision. Consider the case of Citibank in Japan. According to Insead's Mark Hunter, soon after the Financial Services Agency (FSA) was created in 1998, it undertook inspections of Japan's 19 major banks. Foreign banks came under intense scrutiny, and the license of the Tokyo branch of Credit Suisse Financial Products, the derivatives arm of Credit Suisse First Boston, was revoked in November 1999. The FSA's message was clear: many formerly gray areas in banking were now unacceptable, such as cross selling financial products across corporate units. Even so, cross selling remained a core strategy for Citibank.

The FSA also made it clear that transactions aimed at concealing losses were illegal. In May 2000, it suspended Deutsche Bank's Tokyo securities unit from selling equity derivatives products for six months because the unit had sold securities designed to conceal the losses of corporate clients. That was one of many similar punishments levied against banks. In sum, the FSA sent unambiguous signals that hard-selling tactics and practices that would be tolerated elsewhere would lead to punishment in Japan.

Team members frequently discuss the information that they are all aware of and fail to share unique information with one another.

In 2001, under pressure from the FSA, Citibank reported that it had offered products to about 40 companies that would let them transfer book losses on securities holdings and foreign exchange losses to later reporting periods. Obviously, upper-level managers at Citibank had seen newspaper accounts of the punishments of their competitors for this sort of behavior. Yet Citibank executives played aggressively and publicly in the gray areas of the Japanese marketplace. In 2003, to take one example, when a Tokyo fashion school sought a $6.7 million loan, other bankers who saw the school's books turned it down. But Citibank's private bank found a solution: Six of its customers bought three buildings from the school. The school then bought them back a year later, for the same price plus rent and transaction fees, which added 26% to the cost. Citibank kept 11% for itself; its customers got the rest of the profit. Citibank's bounded awareness led it to miss warning signals from the Japanese government and to engage in many other inappropriate behaviors.

Eventually, Citibank paid for its poor decisions. The FSA revoked the licenses of the company's four private banking offices in September 2004. The FSA also damaged Citibank's reputation by claiming that the bank had cheated customers by tacking excessively high margins onto financial products. Why, in the face of mounting evidence of the FSA's enforcement practices, hadn't Citibank executives protected their own interests by stopping this questionable behavior in their Japanese offices? The information about FSA activities was available to Citibank executives, but their focus appeared to have been primarily on financial performance, and marginal violations of Japanese law outside their bounds of awareness.

It seems that success itself can create bounds that prevent executives from using readily available information. Swiss watchmaker invented quartz technology, but as Michael Tushman of Harvard Business School and his colleagues have shown, their dominance in mechanical watches prevented the Swiss from recognizing the future path of the entire watch industry. They essentially gave the quartz technology away and, as a result, lost most of the global watch market to U.S. and Japanese firms. More broadly, Tushman documents a common pattern: Success in a given technical area impairs firms from using new technologies outside that area, even when they are available in-house.

Another common pattern of bounded awareness is not using information about competitors. Don Moore of Carnegie Mellon University and his colleagues have found that decision makers may succeed at focusing on how well they can perform a task but tend to ignore how well the competition can do the same task. As a result, individuals are much more likely to compete on easy tasks, even when facing a great deal of competition, than to compete on harder tasks, despite the fact that it will also be harder for the competition. According to Moore, this tendency often leads firms to enter product domains that have easy access and to enter more difficult product domains too infrequently.

One way to decide if the information at your disposal is useful is to think about the actions of other parties involved and the rules governing their actions. For instance, imagine that you are thinking about acquiring a small firm with a great new product that fits your portfolio. The firm could be worth as little as $5 million or as much as $10 million in the hands of current management, depending on valuation assumptions. Under your ownership, you believe, it would be worth roughly $20 million because of the unique synergies that your company can create. You know that the other firm's founders hold three equal shares and that they have different opinions about the worth of their firm. How much do you offer?

If you learned that the founders have an agreement that they will sell the firm only if all three accept an offer, would your offer change? Or if instead you learned that any one of the three founders can force the sale of the firm (unless the other two buy her shares at an equivalent price, which you are fairly certain the other cannot afford), would that change your offer?

Once you realize that the other players' decision will probably vary, the decision rule about the seller's reservation value (that is, the minimum price that the seller will accept) becomes very important. Imagine that the three founders place their reservation values for selling the firm at $6 million, $7 million, and $9 million. Clearly, if one founder can force the sale, you can offer a much lower price than you could if all sellers must be in agreement.

For most negotiators, however, the decisions of other parties and the rules of the game lie outside their bounds of awareness. When we present this scenario to executives in our classes, they typically disregard the decision rule in effect, and they don't consider the likelihood that the founders would vary in their reservation values.

Executives can take steps to gain access to similarly critical information. One method is to "unpack" a situation, or make the full context of the relevant information clear. Individuals asked to predict how happy or unhappy they would be a few days after their favorite football team won or lost a game, or instance, tend to expect that their happiness will rely heavily on the game's outcome. But when Tim Wilson of the University of Virginia and his colleagues asked participants to list a dozen other things that were happening on the days following the game, they predicted that their happiness would depend far less on the outcome of the game. In other words, they "unpacked" the situation to bring easily available, but previously unused, information into awareness.

Research by Nick Epley of the University of Chicago and Eugene Caruso and Max Bazerman of Harvard University shows that people tend to take more credit than they deserve for a group's accomplishments. When four group members are each asked, "What percentage of the group's accomplishments is due to your ideas and work?" the sum of the four percentages typically far exceeds 100% (this finding applies to academic coauthors). But when they are asked instead, "What percentage of the group's accomplishments can be attributed to each of the four group members?" the degree of self-serving bias declines dramatically. Essentially, the latter question "unpacks" the contributions of the other members, bringing their contributions into the respondent's bounds of awareness.

Other questions that are likely to bring useful information within the bounds of awareness include: What information do we already know in our organization? What information is relevant to the problem at hand? Is it rational to ignore the information that we have not been using? Obviously, the more important the problem, the more care you should take to use the most appropriate inputs.

Executives must rely on others to streamline the data flow for them, but they must be skeptical of the absence of contradictory evidence: It's a red flag indicating highly bounded awareness.

Failure to Share Information

Executives work in teams because, as the saying goes, two heads are better then one. Members are chosen to represent different parts of the organization so that the group can access different sources of information when making decisions and setting strategy. Yet research suggests that most groups have cognitive boundaries to sharing information. Team members frequently discuss the information that they are all aware of, and they typically fail to share unique information with the one another. Why? Because it's much easier to discuss common information and because common information is more positively rewarded as others chime in with their support. Cognitively, individual executives don't realize the importance of sharing their own unique information and fail to seek unique information from others. That dysfunctional pattern undermines the very reason that organizations form diverse teams.

As an example, consider "hidden profile" tasks, developed by Gerald Stasser at the University of Ohio and now a common element of executive courses on group decision making. In a typical hidden profile task, group members are asked to identify the best choice from a number of options, such as the best person for a key executive position. When all group members are given all the information available about all the candidates, the vast majority of groups identify one specific candidate as the best choice. But in one version of the study, excellent information about the best candidate is distributed to only a few group members, while good (but not excellent) information about another candidate is common knowledge to everyone on the team. In that case, most groups choose the lesser candidate because members keep the information about the best candidate to themselves.

The failure to share unique information is a likely factor in the United States' inability to prevent the 9/11 attacks. According to the report of the 9/11 Commission, the U.S. government had access to plenty of information that, collectively, should have been used to protect the nation. The White House, the CIA, the FBI, the Federal Aviation Administration, Congress, and many other parts of the government had some of the information needed to head off the attack. Both the Clinton/Gore and the Bush/Cheney administrations failed to adequately improve aviation security and antiterrorism

intelligence; they passed up opportunities to mandate a system that would have allowed agencies to share available information. Although we cannot be sure that better information sharing would have prevented 9/11, we are certain that if we could replay history, wise individuals would opt for far better communications among the various organizations.

There are many ways to approach the integration of diverse knowledge in group. Meetings should have agendas, and the agendas should specifically request individual reports, rather than assuming individuals who have unique information will speak up as needed. If accountability for critical issues lies in multiple areas, then one person or department can be held responsible for ensuring that individuals or groups share information. But before executives can consider the proper structural responses to a situation, they must first recognize the hidden profile effect. Only then can they bring unique information into the bounds of the group decision-making process.

Breaking Through Your Bounds

Focus is a good thing. Indeed, many executives have achieved their success because of their ability to focus intently on particular information. But when making important decisions, executives would be well advised to consider whether key information remains out of focus because of their bounded awareness. When executives at major U.S. airlines concentrated on aggressively pursuing market share, for instance, they lost sight of other critical strategic considerations and compromised profitability, customer satisfaction, and aviation security.

Of course, not every decision requires a person to consciously broaden his focus. In fact, one risk of describing the problem of bounded awareness is that executives could become hyperaware of their own limitations and, as a result, collect too much information for every choice they face. That would waste time and other valuable resources. But when something large is at stake—such as emergency preparedness or downsizing or marketing a potentially danger-ous product—executives should be mindful of their natural bounds of awareness. In short, if an error would generate almost irrecoverable dam-age, then they should insist on getting all the information they need to make a wise decision. In this regard, executives would do well to learn from high-level diplomats. Ambassadors tend to think intuitively about how negotiations with one country will affect neighboring countries. And diplomats seem to have developed a tendency to expand their bounds of awareness by collecting more information rather than less—a goal that might benefit corporate executives.

In their book *Why Not?*, Barry Nalebuff and Ian Ayres of Yale University provide another clear strategy for expanding the cognitive bounds of executives. They argue that people too often take the status quo as a given; by contrast, creative solutions emerge when we question common assumptions about how things work. Nalebuff and Ayres tell many stories of corporate success that have resulted from asking,"Why not?"—including the discovery that ketchup bottles would be more functional if they rested on their tops. To put that in our terms, you can learn to locate useful information outside your bounds of awareness by asking a simple question: Why not?

Thinking Further 7.1

1. According to this article, is a narrow *focus* beneficial or harmful to making decisions? Explain why.

2. In what ways might a narrow focus be advantageous when negotiating? In what ways might it result in a poorer outcome?

Reading 7.2

PICKING THE RIGHT FRAME: MAKE YOUR BEST OFFER SEEM BETTER

Max H. Bazerman

They say perspective is everything. In negotia-tions, this might literally be true.

Learn how to frame your position so that your opponent is inclined to be in your favor.

Imagine that you bought a house in 2000 for $400,000. Your have just put it on the market for $499,000, with a real target of $470,000—your estimation of the house's true market value. An offer comes in for $460,000. Does this offer represent a $60,000 gain in comparison

with the original purchase price or a $10,000 loss relative to your current target?

Obviously, both are true. Yet some people view the glass as half full (a $60,000 gain), while others see it as half empty (a $10,000 loss). Important individual differences arise in response to choices framed in terms of either gains or losses. These differences affect our decisions. In this case, ample research predicts that the seller will be more likely to accept the $460,000 offer if he frames it as a $60,000 gain rather than as a $10,000 loss.

We are easily swayed by the systematic way in which information is presented. Unfortunately, we also tend to be unaware of the impact of such frames on our decisions. In this article, I will show you how frames affect

Source: Bazerman, M. H. (2004). Picking the right frame: Making your best offer seem better. *Program on Negotiation Newsletter, 7*(10), 9–11.

Note: This article first appeared in *Negotiation,* a monthly newsletter published by the Program on Negotiation at Harvard Law School, www.pon.harvard.edu. Copyright 2006–2011 Harvard University.

your own risk—related decisions as well as others'. I also will advise you how to use frames to your advantage in three areas of negotiation: (1) softening "must have" positions, (2) increasing acceptance of negative outcomes, and (3) mediating disputes among others.

How Frames Influence Risk

Consider the following hypothetical problem, based on the work of researchers Amos Tversky and Daniel Kahneman, from my book *Judgment in Managerial Decision Making* (Wiley, 2002):

Problem: A large car manufacturer has recently been hit with a number of economic difficulties, and it appears as if three plants need to be closed and 6,000 employees laid off. The vice president of production has been exploring alternative ways to avoid this crisis. She has developed two plans:

Plan A: This plan will save one of the three plants and 2,000 jobs.

Plan B: This plan has a one-third probability of saving all three plants and all 6,000 jobs but has a two-thirds probability of saving no plants and no jobs.

Which Plan Would You Select?

Many factors might influence your choice. How would each plan affect the union, as well as the motivation and morale of the retained employees? How would the community be affected? While these questions are important, the way the choices are framed may affect your answer far more than you might expect. Now reconsider the problem, changing the recovery options to those that follow:

Plan C: This plan will result in the loss of two of the three plants and 4,000 jobs.

Plan D: This plan has a two-third probability of resulting in the loss of all three

plants and all 6,000 jobs but has a one-third probability of losing no plants and no jobs.

Which Plan Would You Select?

The two pairs of plans are objectively the same. Saving one of the three plants and 2,000 of 6,000 jobs (Plan A) offers the same outcome as losing two of the three plants and 4,000 of 6,000 jobs (Plan C). Plans B and D also have identical results. Yet research shows that more than 80% of individuals choose Plan A in the first set and Plan D in the second set. The framing of outcomes—jobs and plants saved versus jobs and plants lost—strongly affects our choices.

People Respond to Risks Concerning Gains Differently From Risks Concerning Losses.

People respond to risks concerning gains (saving jobs and plants—Plans A and B) differently from risks concerning losses (losing jobs and plants—Plans C and D). When the expected value between options is equal, most of us are risk seeking when the problem is framed in terms of losses and risk averse when a problem is framed in terms of gains.

Thus, when the choice is framed in terms of *losing jobs* and plants (Plans C and D), we generally are risk seeking; that is, we tend not to perceive the negative value of a loss of three plants and 6,000 jobs as three times as negative as losing one plant and 2,000 jobs. In contrast, then a choice is framed in terms of *saving jobs* and plants (Plans A and B), the potential risk of losing everything becomes salient. In this case, most people do not view the gain of saving three plants and 6,000 jobs as three times as great as saving one plant and 2,000 jobs.

Using Frames in Negotiation

Framing has important implications for negotiators. To avoid the adverse effects of framing, you must be aware of the presence of frames and consider the possibility of adopting alternatives.

Specifically, you can use frames to motivate the other side to more seriously consider viable options, to enhance the appeal of negative outcomes, and to mediate agreements between other parties—a common task for managers.

1. Softening "Must Have" Positions.

Negotiators' frames can mean the difference between agreement and impasse. In a negotiation, both sides typically will name a certain wage or price they "must" get—setting a high reference point against which gains and losses are measured. When this happens, any compromise away from the reference point will be viewed as a loss. This perceived loss leads negotiators to adopt a negative frame toward all compromise proposals, to exhibit risk-seeking behavior, and to be less likely to reach settlement.

Two decades ago, Tom Magliozzi (now the cohost of National Public Radio's *Car Talk*), Margaret Neale (now a professor at Stanford University), and I found that minor changes in framing could dramatically affect the negotiation behavior of buyers and sellers. Participants viewed transactions as either net profit (gains) or expenses (losses) away from their gross profit. Both frames yielded the same objective profit outcome, yet only positively framed negotiators experienced the risk aversion necessary to motivate them to search harder for mutually acceptable agreements. This desire to reach agreement led positively framed negotiators to complete more transactions and obtain greater overall profits than negotiators with a negative frame.

Consider the following recruitment story. Corporation A is trying to hire away an employee from Corporation B. That employee is currently earning $150,000 annually. When Corporation A asks her what it will take to convince her to move to their organization, she tells them that $200,000 would be acceptable. This figure is more than Corporation A is willing to pay. How should the company respond? Consider the following two options:

Option 1: The best we can offer is a $30,000 increase over your current salary.

Option 2: You will have to shave $20,000 off of your demands for us to reach agreement.

Both options effectively offer the woman a $180,000 salary. But Option 1 creates a positive frame, which is likely to lead to risk aversion and acceptance of the offer. In contrast, Option 2 imposes a negative frame, thereby increasing the likelihood that the employee will engage in risk-seeking behavior and hold out for an even higher offer.

To induce concessionary behavior in your fellow negotiator, frame your proposals positively by stressing what he has to gain, thereby increasing opportunities for tradeoffs and compromise. In addition, when you recognize that your counterpart has a negative frame, encourage him to recognize that he has adopted a risky strategy in a situation where a sure gain is possible.

2. Increasing Acceptance of Negative Outcomes.

Consider the following two possible questions that an acquirer might ask the target of a hostile takeover:

Option 1: What's the lowest price you'll take for your lousy firm?

Option 2: I want to do everything possible to make you a more attractive offer, so if you don't mind my asking, what will you do if you don't sell your firm to us?

We can all intuit that the second option is more likely to be effective. It is certainly more pleasant. But notice that the content of the two options is fairly similar—it's the frame that's dramatically different.

3. Mediating Disputes Among Others.

Framing also has important implications for managers who are trying to resolve others' disputes. When striving to reach a mutually beneficial agreement, you should try to convince both parties to view the negotiation with a positive frame. This is tricky, however, since the anchor that will lead to a positive frame for one negotiator is likely to lead to a negative frame for the other. This suggests that when mediators meet with each party separately, they need to present different frames to create risk aversion in each party.

Imagine that a mediator is trying to get two disputants to reach an agreement on a legal action. The plaintiff's attorney is demanding $2 million, while the defendant's attorney is offering $1 million. One side would view a $1.5 million settlement as a gain and the other side would view it as a loss. The wise mediator will frame this amount to the plaintiff as a sure gain of $500,000 over the defendant's last offer, while encouraging the defendant to view it as a $500,000 gain over the plaintiff's last offer—rather than mentioning to either that $1.5 million is $500,000 worse than their own last offer.

To affect the frame, managers and other mediators must emphasize the situation's realistic risks, thus calling attention to its uncertainty and leading both sides to prefer a sure gain through settlement. With your new understanding of the science and tools of framing, you'll be able to significantly increase your negotiation effectiveness.

Thinking Further 7.2

1. How does framing influence both setting and accepting target levels in negotiations? Explain.

2. You borrowed your parents' car to go to a concert. When you returned to their car after the concert, you noticed a sizeable dent in the rear fender that was not there before the concert. What could you say to your parents to frame what happened to their car positively?

CHAPTER 8

Power and Influence

Changing Others' Attitudes and Behaviors

Any discussion of bargaining power and influence is about changing the other party's attitudes and behaviors so that he or she will accept our desired outcomes. This is why negotiators usually want power but do not want the other party to have any. For those who believe that power corrupts, and that changing the other party's attitudes and behaviors suggests manipulation, this topic also raises ethical questions. For these and perhaps other reasons, power and influence are a controversial part of the negotiation process. This chapter discusses the essence of power and its sources, how it can be used to help you negotiate successfully, how to counter the other party's attempts to change your attitudes and behaviors, and how to negotiate effectively when you have less power than the other party.

INTENDED BENEFITS OF THIS CHAPTER

When you finish reading this chapter, you should be able to:

1. Explain what bargaining power is and how it can be increased.
2. Describe the direct and indirect routes for influencing the other party, and the tactics associated with each.
3. Use these tactics to improve both the process and outcome of your negotiations, including situations in which you have less power than the other side.

THE ESSENCE OF POWER AND INFLUENCE

The presence or absence of power, whether it is real or merely perceived, is an important experience in our lives because it influences our assumptions about human

nature and interpersonal relations. Our understanding of power is often filtered through and derived from our personal experiences. The ability to effect desired outcomes is perhaps the most common definition of power (Salancik & Pfeffer, 1977). This suggests "power over" the other party, which is consistent with a competitive or distributive view of negotiation. This form of power is largely a function of relative dependence – the party who needs the other most has the least power. If, for instance, you possess resources or information that the other party needs to achieve a desired outcome, you have power over him or her. The converse is true if he or she possesses resources or information that you need. The scenario presented in Negotiation in Action 8.1 is illustrative of this type of power. It may also raise ethical questions.

NEGOTIATION IN ACTION 8.1

Bob was a supervisor in the Human Resource Management (HRM) department of a division of a large energy company. He reported to Ralph, the Director of HRM. Tim, the Vice President of Exploration & Production, was Bob's mentor and Ralph's boss. He didn't like Ralph. In fact, he eventually got support from his superiors at corporate headquarters to have him transferred to a different division in a different location, and to have Bob succeed him. Many staff members in the division's HRM department liked Bob but didn't think he was ready for this promotion because he was too inexperienced. For nearly two years, Bob and Tim worked well together, mostly because Bob said 'yes' to all of Tim's requests and ideas. Then, when the economy turned bad and layoffs became economically necessary, Tim told Bob to change certain employees' performance ratings to justify keeping them instead of others. Bob explained why he thought this was inappropriate, and he refused Tim's order. Tim didn't care what Bob thought. When his repeated efforts failed to persuade him to change the ratings, Tim again used his influence to have Bob removed from this position. Tim's superiors persuaded the corporate HRM department to offer Bob a choice – take a demotion and return to corporate headquarters or leave the company. He left the company, even though he had done the right thing. He and his wife didn't want to move. Nor did he have sufficient power or support from corporate HRM, or from his staff, to fight Tim and win.

Although Bob had some power, given his position and the relationships he had cultivated over the years, he did not have enough to prevent Tim from changing employees' performance ratings or to keep his own job. Tim's superiors owed him political favors, and he used this to have Ralph transferred and Bob replace him, and later to have Bob removed. Bob did not have allies or supporters in corporate HRM or on his staff because he had been promoted into this position without their support. Later in this chapter, suggestions for negotiating when you have less power than the other party will be discussed. Some of these might have helped Bob.

A different conception of power argues that it is the ability to work effectively with the other party. This "power with" or mutual empowerment conception implies that power can be developed jointly and used to enhance or advance all parties' interests (Follett, 1942). This is more consistent with a collaborative or integrative view of negotiating.

Attitudes

Attitudes are general evaluations people hold about themselves, others, objects and issues. They are often important determinants of how we behave. **Influence** is about changing these attitudes, beliefs and behaviors. Negotiators are generally concerned with the amount of power they have relative to the other party, not with some absolute measure of power – if that even exists. This is important because how much power we amass relative to the other party will probably influence our choice of which strategy to use and how effectively we can execute it. Having more power, for example, enables you to establish more ambitious aspiration levels and reservations prices, both of which lead to better outcomes (Kray, Thompson & Galinsky, 2001). A competitive approach, though, is probably ill-advised if you are negotiating with someone such as your supervisor who has substantially more power than you do.

Debunking Some Myths About Power and Influence

- Many people assume that power is fixed and concentrated in some physical location such as a boardroom, an executive suite or behind the lectern of a classroom.

While some sources of power do, in fact, reside in these locations, additional sources exist. Nor is the amount of power we have fixed or finite. Negotiators can increase their power by, for example, gathering resources or cultivating alternatives to improve their BATNA.

- In organizations, power flows from the top down through the chain of command.

Formal authority in organizations may flow in this manner, but additional sources of power such as unique expertise or the possession of needed resources also exist. These sources disperse power in a variety of different directions to a variety of different people who may or may not be highly placed in the chain of command. Secretarial employees, for example, often have substantial power because they control access to key managers and executives, and the dissemination of important information throughout their organizations. This gives them an advantage when negotiating with people who want to meet or communicate with their bosses.

- Power should be thought of in competitive terms.

This is common, and most people believe that those who have more power gain by using it against others who have less (Coleman, 2000). As already noted, "power with" is an equally legitimate and compelling conception of power.

WHERE POWER COMES FROM AND HOW I CAN INCREASE MY OWN

Power is derived from the combination of characteristics of the negotiators and characteristics of the environment or context in which the negotiation takes place, not by either one independently (Deutsch, 1973). These sources are summarized in Table 8.1. For clarification, professors are authorized to use their **reward** power by granting more points to students when they negotiate grade disputes on assignments. Supervisors negotiating disciplinary action for employees who fail to meet their expectations use their **coercive power** to mete out disciplinary penalties. When executive secretaries negotiate with those who want to see their bosses, they exercise **legitimate power** when authorizing or denying access. One conception of a mentor involves upwardly mobile people who have achieved a position to which you aspire. When negotiating with the individual over an assignment or task that you do not want to perform, you may comply because of his or her connections, interpersonal style, credibility, competence and other qualities – different sources of **referent power**

Video 8.1

Eight power techniques

(Chaiken, 1986; Berscheid & Walster, 1974). When negotiating deals with clients, they may agree because you possess *information* or other resources they require.

Perhaps the most salient situational source of power is the quality of your alternatives. A strong BATNA decreases your dependence on the other party by making it easier for you to walk away if a good outcome cannot be reached.

Table 8.1   Sources of Power

Personal Sources	Explanation
Reward Power	The ability to give the other negotiator items that he or she values, or to credibly promise these items – money, information, tangible resources, approval or other items that he or she wants or needs
Coercive Power	The ability to punish, to credibly threaten to punish, or to withhold rewards or other positive outcomes that the other negotiator wants or needs – declining offers, withholding coveted offers, disapproval
Legitimate Power	Authority derived from a negotiator's age, social status, caste, or rights derived from his or her position, role or title in an organization
Expert Power	Power derived from a negotiator's special expertise, knowledge, understanding, skills or competencies or technical know-how
Referent Power	Power derived from being liked, because the other negotiator can identify with you or because he or she wants to be like you – all because you have integrity, because of your personality, or because you are attractive, charismatic, credible and trustworthy
Informational Power	Grounded in substantial differences in the knowledge of two individuals on particular subjects, this reflects the negotiator's ability to control the availability and accuracy of information
Situational Sources	
BATNA	The ability to influence others because of the quality of your BATNA; this also makes it easier for you to set ambitious target and resistance points, which often causes others to reduce their demands or walk away if good outcomes are not forthcoming
Allies	The ability to influence others because your supporters are respected by them or possess resources (money, information, expertise, etc.) that are needed by them; This is sometimes considered a form of referent power

(Adapted from Fisher, Ury & Patton, 1991; French & Raven, 1959.)

This is why job hunters who are currently employed are likely to negotiate better employment packages with prospective employers – they can fall back on their current job rather than feeling anxious or even desperate about having to accept an offer so that they can eat and pay rent. Having other offers "in hand" will similarly enable job hunters to negotiate better employment packages with their desired employer.

Allies or supporters who are respected by the other negotiator or who possess resources (e.g., money, information, expertise, materials) that he or she needs enhance your power by speaking or acting on your behalf. Negotiation in Action 8.2 illustrates how this might work.

NEGOTIATION IN ACTION 8.2

Dave was a recent college graduate who was looking for his first professional job, preferably in hospital administration. Tom, a radiologist who thought highly of him, told Paul, the administrator of the small hospital where he often worked, about Dave. Paul had great respect and appreciation for Tom, so he arranged for Dave to interview for a position he was thinking about creating. Dave was eventually hired as the Human Resources Director at this hospital, in large part because of Tom's confidence in him. Tom went well beyond merely opening the door for him. He used his credibility, reputation and relationship with Paul to actively sponsor Dave for this position.

INFLUENCE: USING POWER TO NEGOTIATE MORE EFFECTIVELY

Having power is important because it gives negotiators the potential to change the other party's attitudes, beliefs and behaviors. Sometimes, the power we have is real, coming from one of the aforementioned sources. At other times, it is perceived. Even if we don't have much real power, the other side may think we do. The notion of power, therefore, is highly abstract and ambiguous, though its consequences are very real (Coleman, 2000). The important question for negotiators is: How do we use power to ensure favorable outcomes? In other words, how do we influence the other party to seriously consider the information and arguments we present, accept our proposals or invent better ones, and ensure that the solutions that are adopted are implemented successfully? The following pages, and Reading 8.2, provide some useful guidance.

We are inundated every day with messages that attempt to influence us. Think of all the commercials, billboards, pop-up ads, junk mail and so on that you encounter that are trying to get you to buy or do something. Negotiations also involve many influence attempts, but not all of them are successful. We do not even attend to most of them. What makes a message influential? Contemporary thinking about influence and persuasion suggests that people are influenced in two fundamentally different ways.

The Central or Direct Route

Some influence happens because people consciously and actively think about the messages they receive and integrate them into their existing thoughts, schemata or mental models. For this to happen, recipients must be willing and able to expend the mental effort required to identify the issues, consider supporting evidence, gather additional information, identify alternatives and perform cost-benefit analyses (Petty & Cacioppo, 1986). The factors that determine whether a person is motivated and able to process influence attempts along this central route are summarized in Table 8.2.

Table 8.2 Determinants of Negotiators' Motivation and Ability to Evaluate Messages

Motivation	Ability
Personal relevance of messages is high	Noise is absent
Personal responsibility for evaluating the messages is high	Repetition of messages is moderate
The recipient's need for cognition is high	Messages are comprehensible
Information is provided by multiple, independent sources	Messages are transmitted in print, not via videotape, television or audio mechanisms

Motivation to evaluate messages is high if the messages are emotionally rich and important to the recipient, he or she is accountable for evaluating them, thinking and deliberating about various topics is enjoyable, and the information is provided by multiple independent sources (Petty & Cacioppo, 1986). A firm's labor negotiators, for example, are likely to be more motivated to evaluate the contract language proposed by the union if the cost implications are high, the firm's ability to function efficiently and effectively will be affected, and they are accountable for the results achieved at the negotiating table.

Though necessary, motivation is not sufficient – negotiators must also possess the *ability* to evaluate messages. Any kind of noise that diverts our attention away from the message (see the discussion of noise in Chapter 6) inhibits our ability to evaluate messages. Our ability to evaluate messages is also diminished if they are not comprehensible, or if they are repeated too many times or not at all. Print messages, for example, are usually evaluated more thoroughly because we are able to process them at our own pace. If they are complex and proceed too quickly, we are not able to evaluate them carefully (Petty & Cacioppo, 1986).

When messages are processed along the central route, many factors determine how influential they will be. These include the content of your messages, how your messages are organized and how you present them.

Message Content

Personal Relevance. In addition to enhancing a negotiator's motivation to evaluate messages, personally relevant, important and interesting messages are more influential. This is particularly true if they demonstrate how a proposal will satisfy his or her interests – substantive, relationship, process and principle. Framing proposals in a manner that clarifies how they satisfy management's cost, operational and other interests, for example, would enhance the persuasiveness of a labor union negotiator's messages.

Fear. Fear-arousing messages or threats are more persuasive, but only if they are coupled with efficacious recommendations for dealing with them. These messages induce attitude, belief and behavior changes if the threat is real and personally relevant to the target, he or she believes your proposal will eliminate the threat, and he or she can execute your recommendation. This works because people seek rewarding situations and shun uncomfortable ones (Witte & Allen, 2000; Mongeau, 1998). Efficacious proposals for avoiding discomfort that are credible and executable present a rewarding alternative. If you must negotiate the adoption of new work methods with employees who are reluctant to adopt them, for example, informing them that layoffs are likely if productivity does not increase and that you will train them how to execute these new methods will be persuasive if they think the information is credible and that they are capable of performing their redesigned jobs.

Message Organization

Message Sidedness. Two-sided messages that recognize the opposing viewpoint and refute it are more persuasive and produce more favorable responses from the other party than one-sided messages. This means that negotiators who send two-sided messages are more influential and viewed as having more credibility than those who send one-sided messages. Merely acknowledging an opposing view, without refuting it, is not effective (Allen, 1998). Two-sided messages are most appropriate when the goal is to present an accurate assessment of something. For example, if you are trying to convince a purchasing agent to buy your product rather than comparable ones from a different supplier, acknowledge the positive qualities of the other supplier's product and then refute them by explaining why your product is more appropriate for the buyer. If your arguments are credible, they should be influential (Chaiken, Wood & Eagly, 1996).

Message scope and complexity. The scope or complexity of a proposal or message may be too difficult for people to fully grasp. If they are unable to "get their heads around the idea," they will not be able to evaluate it so it will not be persuasive. Breaking the proposal into its component parts and sharing them one at a time is more influential. When a corporate trainer recognized that the middle managers she was working with were unreceptive to their company's new management-by-objectives initiative because they did not understand how it would work, she began talking about how they fit in to different parts of the overall plan. Their interest was piqued, so she continued by talking about things like why coding their employees' time spent on different tasks was so important and how it would benefit them. This approach enhanced their understanding of the initiative and its personal relevance. Soon, they began to accept responsibility for making it work.

Repetition. *Moderate repetition* (usually 2-3 times) of credible messages is more influential than only stating them once or stating them too many times. Some repetition affords recipients greater opportunities to objectively and thoroughly scrutinize the messages. Such scrutiny should enhance recipients' understanding and make the messages more persuasive. Extensive repetition, even if the messages are credible, does not enhance influence more than moderate repetition, and it may diminish it. Perhaps people are annoyed by hearing the same message too many times. Moderate or extensive repetition of weak messages will probably backfire because careful scrutiny of messages that lack credibility will enhance their weakness and diminish their persuasiveness (Petty & Cacioppo, 1986; Cacioppo & Petty, 1985).

Distractions. If your messages are credible, you would like the other side to thoroughly and carefully evaluate them. *Distractions*, like noise, inhibit a negotiator's ability to do so. They hinder influence attempts the most, therefore, when people would normally be processing information along the central route. They may be the least problematic, or even beneficial, if the other negotiator is unlikely to process messages along the central route, or if your offers or arguments supporting them are weak. In short, distractions reduce the influence of strong arguments and increase the influence of weak ones because they decrease the likelihood that others will evaluate them along the central route.

Message Presentation

Powerful Language. Powerful language is likely to be processed along the central route because it creates perceptions that messages are credible and that the speaker is more competent, composed and attractive (Burrell & Koper, 1998; Hosman, 1989). Examples of powerful language include bottom-line arguments such as, "That is as low/high as I can go." Asking for permission to ask questions (Do you mind if I ask you . . . ?); hedges (I sort of . . . or I kind of. . . .); tag questions (It is, isn't it?) and other expressions of uncertainty or timidity (Petty & Cacioppo, 1986; O'Barr & Atkins, 1980) are examples of language that is not powerful. Credible messages presented using powerful language, therefore, should enhance your persuasiveness when you negotiate.

Language Intensity. *Language intensity* is conveyed through emotionality and specificity, and reflects an attitude toward the subject that is not neutral (Hamilton & Hunter, 1998; Bowers, 1963). Threats and expressions of anger are examples of intense language. Implicit threats issued early in a negotiation (e.g., I would prefer to find a mutually acceptable solution with you, but I'll have to consider other options if we cannot), and explicit threats made later in a negotiation (e.g., My BATNA is very strong and I will exercise it if we do not find a good outcome soon) elicit more concessions than explicit threats made early and implicit threats made late (Sinaceur & Neale, 2005). Expressions of anger also elicit more concessions if the negotiator expressing it is perceived as being tough and the negotiator at whom they are directed has poor alternatives (Sinaceur & Tiedens, 2006). Reactions to intense language depend, in part, on the recipient's intentions. If he or she already intends to engage in such behavior, compliance increases, but negative reactions are likely if these intentions are absent. Nor will intense language induce attitude or behavior change if the message, or the person communicating it, lack credibility (Buller, Borland & Burgoon, 1998).

Dialogue. People are more willing to concede when a request is preceded by a pleasant *dialogue* rather than a monologue. This is because dialogue suggests that people are interacting with acquaintances rather than confronting strangers, and requests from the former are received more favorably. This suggests that you will be more persuasive if you actively engage the other side in conversation (Dolinski, Nawrat & Rudak, 2001; Johnson & Eagly, 1990; 1989).

The Peripheral or Indirect Route

If negotiators are not motivated or able to expend the mental effort required to process information along the central route, influencing them is still possible. Subtle cues and content often change our attitudes, beliefs and behaviors. Influence along this peripheral route, like some of the decision-making errors discussed in Chapter 7, is nearly automatic – we change our attitudes, beliefs and behaviors without realizing why, just as we unknowingly make decision errors. This happens because of the mental shortcuts that we commonly take when processing information and making decisions. These heuristics or rules of thumb simplify or expedite these tasks by triggering our schemata or scripts (Cialdini, 1993; Petty & Cacioppo, 1986). Since these messages are not integrated into our knowledge structures, their impact is usually less durable and pronounced than those processed along the central route (Wegener, Petty & Smith, 1995).

It seems odd that negotiators might not be motivated or able to thoroughly evaluate messages from the other party, especially if the stakes are high. Maybe it is because information processing is made so much easier with these mental shortcuts. Alternatively, the qualities that enhance motivation and ability to thoroughly evaluate messages may be absent (see Table 8.2). Whatever the reason, influence is still possible, albeit along the peripheral route.

Explanations. When we ask people to do something for us, they are more likely to comply if we provide them with a reason. This is true even if the explanation provides little information of true value. It is the word "because" that seems to make the difference, not the whole series of words (Cialdini, 1993; Langer, Blank & Chanowitz, 1978).

You Get What You Pay For. As illustrated in Negotiation in Action 8.3, many people assume that if things cost more they are better.

NEGOTIATION IN ACTION 8.3

A jewelry store owner in Arizona was struggling to sell her inventory of turquoise jewelry. On her way out of town on a buying trip, she left a note instructing her head saleswoman to cut the prices on these items in half. When she returned a few days later, she was not surprised to find that every item had been sold. She was shocked, however, to learn that the employee misread the note and doubled the prices instead of cutting them in half. Higher prices increased sales dramatically because they became a trigger for 'good quality' (Cialdini, 1993).

Contrast Principle or Relativity. Exaggerating the difference between offers or objects often influences others' choices. This is the idea behind the **contrast principle** or **relativity**. Realtors, for example, may intentionally show their clients houses that do not satisfy their needs in the beginning. When they get to the ones that do meet clients' needs, the houses look even better than they otherwise would have because of the contrast. Similarly, a supplier may begin by showing manufacturers parts that are expensive and barely serve their needs, and then show them parts that are less expensive and work much better. By contrast, the first set of parts will make the second set appear to be much more affordable, and much more suitable, than they really are (Cialdini, 1993).

Video 8.2
Contrast Principle
to make product
look great

People often do not know what they really want unless they see it in context. They may be particularly vulnerable to the contrast principle because of this. For example, most people will not buy the most expensive item on a restaurant menu, but including it helps the restaurant make money – because they will buy the second most expensive item, which may have a high profit margin. Similarly, if people are given three choices, most will take the middle one (Ariely, 2008). Negotiation in Action 8.4, illustrates how negotiators who issue multiple offers simultaneously can capitalize on the contrast principle by inserting a decoy as one of the options.

NEGOTIATION IN ACTION 8.4

The publisher of *The Economist,* a magazine, placed an ad on the Internet offering three subscription choices – an online-only subscription for $59 per year, a print-only subscription for $125 per year, and a print and online subscription for $125 per year. When these were offered to one group, 16% selected the online-only option, nobody selected the print-only option and 84% selected the online and print option. When the online-only and print and online subscriptions were the only two choices presented to a second group, 68% chose the online-only option and 32% chose the print and online option. This seems odd since the only choice that was deleted was the one that nobody in the first group selected. We generally look at things in relation to others, whether they are objects, experiences or even ephemeral items like attitudes and emotions.

We are quite good at comparing items that are alike. We are not so good at comparing items that lack comparability (adapted from Ariely, 2008).

The simplest way negotiators can capitalize on this when they issue multiple offers simultaneously is to place the option they want the other party to accept in the middle. Alternatively, they could make one of the choices a decoy - similar to the one the negotiator wants the other party to choose but slightly less attractive.

Reciprocity. It is socially acceptable in most cultures to return favors. This is the basis of what we call **reciprocity**. We often reciprocate the acts of others even if it is contrary to our self-interest to do so (Pillutla, Malhotra & Murnighan, 2003; Ortman, Fitzgerald & Boeing, 2000). If you do something for another person, even something that was not invited or wanted, he or she is likely to return the favor. One reason this happens is because we will be viewed more favorably and we prefer this. A second reason is that many people do not like to be indebted to others. The *reciprocity* principle is why concessions usually work in negotiations – if you make one, the other side typically reciprocates (Cialdini, 1993). This may involve exchanging substantive terms, information or even something as small as compliments or being polite.

Reject then Retreat. If you make an extreme demand, the other party is likely to reject it. If you then ask for something smaller, he or she is more likely to accept it. This happens because of the contrast and reciprocity principles. The second demand will be perceived as even smaller than if you had opened with it because of the contrast principle. You also made what appears to be a concession from your first demand, so the reciprocity principle suggests that he or she will agree, or at least make a concession (Cialdini, 1993). Negotiation in Action 8.5 is illustrative.

NEGOTIATION IN ACTION 8.5

When a negotiator asked a group of strangers to volunteer as chaperones for some juvenile delinquents on a two-hour trip to the local zoo, 17% agreed to do so. When a second group was asked to serve as unpaid counselors for juvenile delinquents for two years, nobody accepted. When this request was followed by the request to chaperone the juvenile delinquents on a two-hour trip to the local zoo, 50% accepted. The second request seemed much smaller than it would have if it were the only request made due to the contrast principle, and there was the appearance of a concession because the second request was much smaller than the first (adapted from Cialdini, 1993).

Social Comparisons or Social Proof. When we encounter novel situations and are not sure how to behave in them, we often look to others to determine what we should do. We seem to believe we will make fewer mistakes if we emulate others' behavior. Laugh tracks, as stupid as most of us think they are, serve this purpose. If others are laughing, we should, too. A minor change in the wording of an infomercial also illustrates this principle. When the wording of the initial script was changed from "Operators are standing by, please call now" to "If operators are busy, please call again," the number of people who called to purchase the item for sale reportedly skyrocketed. The first message suggested that nobody was calling so the appropriate course of action for those who were unsure about what they should do was to not call. The second message suggested that many people were calling so others should, too. In short, the change introduced social proof indicating that people should call and purchase the product, and they did (Cialdini & Goldstein, 2004).

Social proof is why testimonials are persuasive (Reinard, 1998). The persuasiveness of your own prior successes, especially if they are acknowledged by others; support from respected experts, allies and celebrities; and other testimonials all increase the credibility and influence of your proposals and messages because they capitalize on social proof.

Scarcity. We equate quality with scarcity, and we believe that scarcity limits our freedom of choice. Messages informing us that what we are being offered is in short supply, therefore, will pique our interest and make us want the scarce items, as well as the items associated with them, significantly more than we previously did. If we believe that someone or something interferes with our access to an item, we will react against the interference and try even harder to possess it (Brehm & Brehm, 1981).

Commitment and Consistency. Consistency is a central motivator for most of us. We even call people names like fickle or wishy-washy if they change their minds or otherwise act inconsistently. Once we make a decision or act in a certain way, we are motivated to behave consistently with that decision or action. If you secure an agreement or commitment from the other side on some minor but relevant point, you can then ask a series of questions or make a series of requests that require responses that are consistent with his or her responses to the previous questions or offers, all of which lead progressively to the desired outcome. Securing the initial commitment or answer is essential. Providing small rewards for these will help, but it is essential to keep the rewards small and inconsequential to ensure that the other negotiator does not attribute his or her commitment to the reward, thereby jeopardizing the larger objective. Commitments are also more effective if they are written, made publicly and owned by the individual. Ownership, again, is why the rewards must be small and inconsequential. Some caution is warranted if you use this influence technique because it can lead to the irrational escalation of commitment discussed in Chapter 7. Those who are influenced using this tactic may also feel like they are being manipulated. Used properly, however, it can work well for you as illustrated in Negotiation in Action 8.6.

NEGOTIATION IN ACTION 8.6

A bartender identified students who were regulars at his bar near a college campus. Half of these "regulars" were asked to sign a petition against drunk driving. The same request was not made of the other "regulars." Over the ensuing six weeks, the bartender monitored when any of the identified "regulars" became intoxicated. Once identified, he asked, "May I call a taxi to take you home?" For those who had not been asked to sign the petition, only 10% agreed to wait for the taxi. For those who did sign the petition, 38% agreed to wait (Taylor & Booth-Butterfield, 1993).

When allocating research and development funds to one of two operating divisions of a company, one group of participants was told that their investment had been successful or unsuccessful and that now, three years later, they must make a second allocation decision. A different group was told that the decision made by someone else in the firm three years earlier had been successful or unsuccessful, and that now the second allocation decision must be made by them. When the first allocation proved to be unsuccessful, those who believed they were responsible allocated significantly more funds to the same operating division the second time than those who were told they were not responsible for the initial allocation (Malhotra & Bazerman, 2008; Staw, 1976).

These examples demonstrate that compliance with a request can be increased by leveraging commitment or consistency.

Gains and Losses. People are motivated to avoid losses more than they are to accrue gains (Kahneman & Tversky, 1979). This means that negotiators will weigh information about losses more heavily than they will weigh information about gains, even if the gains and losses are of the same magnitude. This means that negotiators who frame the exact same set of information as a loss will be more influential than those who frame it as a gain (Tversky & Kahneman, 1991). Examples are discussed in Negotiation in Action 8.7.

NEGOTIATION IN ACTION 8.7

In a medical clinic, women were shown videos aimed at promoting HIV testing. When the videos framed the information in terms of the costs and risks associated with not being tested, 63% agreed to be tested within 2 weeks. When the information was framed in terms of the benefits to be gained from testing, only 23% agreed to be tested within 2 weeks (Malhotra & Bazerman, 2008; Kalichman & Coley, 1995).

A representative of a power company went door to door offering free energy audits to the homeowners. After the audits, he offered products and services that could help insulate the home and lower energy costs. Half of these homeowners were told, "If you insulate your home, you will save X cents per day." The other half were told, "If you fail to insulate your home, you will lose X cents per day." Although the information was identical in all cases, except for the value of X (the value of X depended on the results of the audit), those who were told how much they would lose were significantly more likely to purchase the insulation (Malhotra & Bazerman, 2008; Cialdini, 1993).

Reference Points. Determining how much people value their time and other interests is not as easy and straightforward as it seems. In fact, it is something you can influence. Imagine that a salesperson selling a $50 calculator informs a customer that he or she could save money by driving twenty minutes to another store where it is on sale. Imagine also that a salesperson selling a $2000 computer informs a customer that he or she could save money by driving twenty minutes to another store where it is on sale. In essence, these customers were being asked how much twenty minutes of their time was worth. On average, they said they must save $20 to drive to buy the calculator, but $200 to buy the computer. It seems like twenty minutes should be worth the same amount regardless of what a person is buying. Apparently, it is not. **Rather than objectively evaluating the cost of an item or an issue, we seem to evaluate them relative to important reference points.** And reference points can be influenced. Encouraging the other negotiator to focus on a favorable reference point, or the value of the concession you are demanding relative to the value of the entire deal, may be particularly influential (Kahneman & Tversky, 1981).

DEFENDING AGAINST OTHERS' ATTEMPTS TO INFLUENCE YOU

The foregoing suggests that there are many tactics that you can use to persuade the other party to help you satisfy your interests. It should be evident that other negotiators may attempt to use these tactics to influence you. This begs the question – How do we defend against these efforts and protect ourselves from being persuaded to do something we do not want to do?

Preparation

The importance of thorough preparation was discussed in Chapter 2 and in other chapters. Another reason it is essential is because it protects us against being influenced when we do not want to be. We are most susceptible to the other party's influence attempts when we lack objective information about the value of an idea or proposal. Thorough pre-negotiation preparation, therefore, affords us the best defense we have against unwanted influence because it provides us with this objective information. Several components are particularly important.

- Know what you truly want or need and what it is worth to you.
- Know your BATNA and its value, cultivate a better one, and express your willingness to exercise it.

- Set limits (resistance points) to determine how much you are willing to concede.
- Establish a monitoring system - people you trust and respect who will stop you if you are persuaded to agree to what are unacceptable demands. This is important because responses to influence attempts are nearly automatic (Malhotra & Bazerman, 2008).

Gather Information About Influence Tactics and Decision Biases

Understanding how the other party may attempt to influence you, including the decision-making errors discussed in Chapter 7 and again in this chapter, will help because they make us susceptible to others' influence attempts. Recognizing influence tactics and when they are being used enables you to avoid falling victim to them. If you are not comfortable with your understanding of these tactics, further training may be valuable to inoculate yourself against them (Bazerman & Moore, 2008).

Attractiveness and Disclosure of Intentions

Research suggests that attractive negotiators (salespeople) are more effective at influencing the other party when they disclose their intention to do so. Unattractive negotiators (salespeople) are more persuasive when they keep their intention to do so hidden. This suggests that you should be very careful if the other party is attractive and honest about his or her intentions, and if he or she is unattractive and claims to have your best interests in mind (Reinhard, Messner & Sporer, 2006).

Process Influence Attempts Using the Central Route

One way to avoid the nearly automatic response we direct toward many of these influence attempts, including the other party's ability to use our decision biases "against" us, is to force ourselves to process them along the central route. This requires us to slow down and take the time required to evaluate the other party's ideas. It also requires us to ask for help if we are not willing or able to thoroughly evaluate them. The monitoring system discussed earlier in this section should help with this, especially if the monitors possess varied expertise (Cialdini, 1993).

NEGOTIATING WITH INFERIOR POWER

Even if we want to use it to work effectively with the other party rather than to exploit him or her, we would obviously prefer to have a power advantage because negotiating with less power is challenging. It is not, however, uncommon. When we negotiate employment packages with prospective employers or with our boss, we almost always have less power. If you find yourself negotiating with inferior power, there are several steps you can take to increase it and "level the playing field."

- Improve your BATNA by cultivating alternatives that are appealing and satisfy your interests. If you are negotiating your employment package with a prospective employer, secure other job offers that are also appealing and satisfy your most important interests. If you must negotiate with a preferred supplier, cultivate offers from other suppliers first. In short, try to avoid falling in love with one job opportunity, part, car or whatever else you are negotiating because that will diminish your power even further.

- Acquire resources, information or expertise that is required or valued by the other party. In addition to making him or her more dependent on you, this may enhance the perceived value of your BATNA or reduce the perceived value of the other party's.

- If you can get yourself promoted, you may increase your reward, coercive and legitimate power.

- Forming or joining a coalition may also help. Coalitions are discussed in more detail in Chapter 10. For now, a coalition is a group of two or more parties within a larger social setting who merge their resources and work together to achieve mutually desirable goals (Murnighan, 1986). There may be strength in numbers, or the coalition members may possess expertise, information or other resources that force the other party to pay more attention to your ideas.

- If you have done everything possible to increase your power and you still have less, it is possible to negotiate successfully, albeit maybe not with the same approach you had hoped or planned to use. For example, adopting a very competitive or aggressive approach with a supervisor who has substantially more power than you do is ill-advised.

- Preparation is critical because it will help you understand your own situation and that of the other negotiator. When you analyze the other party, you should learn about his or her interests and priorities because they should become the focus of your negotiation.

- Communicating information in the manner that he or she wishes to receive it is also essential because it will be more appealing and make more sense. At the very least, this will help you build positive affect (mood), reduce noise and enhance your influence attempts along the central route. Active listening is always an essential part of effective communication. It is particularly important when you have less power because it demonstrates your concern for the other negotiator, informs him or her that you heard the information that was conveyed, and allows you gather valuable information.

- Adopting an integrative strategy should be valuable. Inventing creative proposals that satisfy the other party's interests, and your own, will be hard for him or her to reject. If you want your supervisor to accept your project, demonstrate how it will satisfy his or her interests, make him or her look good or otherwise help him or her.

- Present strong and credible arguments and encourage him or her to evaluate them carefully (along the central route) and observe the qualities that enhance your persuasiveness. Asking questions and talking about them more during your negotiation should serve this purpose. Executing the tactics that increase your influence along the peripheral route should also help. Readings 8.1 and 8.2 at the end of the chapter provide some additional guidance for negotiating with less power.

CONCLUSION AND IMPLICATIONS FOR PRACTICE

Negotiators spend a great deal of time and energy trying to persuade each other to agree to their desired outcome. For this reason, power and influence are critical components of the negotiation process – the negotiator with the least to lose if an agreement is not reached can afford to push the hardest for important outcomes. How important is it? Negotiation in Action 8.8 illustrates that it can be very important.

NEGOTIATION IN ACTION 8.8

When college athletic conferences began reconfiguring themselves in the summer of 2010, the Big 12 was in trouble. Two schools defected to other conferences, and five of the remaining ten members were being pursued, vigorously, by other conferences. The Commissioner of the Big 12 knew that The University of Texas was the key because the other four were likely to follow if it left. Following negotiations with the television networks, he promised all members greater television revenues, with Texas getting the most – it was allowed to launch its own network. The five schools that would have been left behind offered their share of the $32 million in departure penalties owed by the two defecting schools to those contemplating invitations from other conferences – if they stayed. Despite its power within the Big-12, however, The University of Texas lacked sufficient power when their primary suitor, the Pac-10, refused to accede to its demand for a sweetener in revenue sharing and its demand to establish its own television network (Program on Negotiation, 2010).

Suggestions for increasing power and capitalizing on it when you negotiate follow.

1. Increase your power so you can enjoy the benefits. Take advantage of increasing your power, even if you do not want to exploit the other party. It will increase your confidence and allow you to set more optimistic target and resistance points, both of which will help you achieve a better outcome. Cultivating alternatives to improve your BATNA, building relationships with respected allies, acquiring resources that are needed or valued by the other negotiator and cultivating referent, legitimate, expert, informational, reward, and coercive power should all make it easier for you to persuade the other party to consider your information and proposals more favorably, and to walk away if they do not (Program on Negotiation, 2009).

2. Change the other party's attitude toward your interests, ideas and proposals to help you create and claim value. Your influence will be stronger and more durable if your messages are credible and the other party evaluates them along the central route. This is more likely to happen if your messages are relevant to the other negotiator and derived from multiple independent sources. They should also be presented in print, comprehensible and repeated two or three times in a location that is devoid of noise, interruptions and other distractions.

3. Try to discern the other party's interests. Include interests that belong both to the other party and his or her constituents. Begin to identify these interests during your pre-negotiation preparations and continue when you initially meet with the other party. If you can determine things like career goals, how the person is compensated, length of service for the principal, and, items more closely related to the substance of your negotiation, you may gain insight into what really matters to this person. Whether you have more or less power, learning the other party's interests will help you determine what is personally relevant and the kinds of proposals that might be acceptable.

4. Use your understanding of the nature of power and influence and of influence, tactics, as a defense maneuver. It should enhance your ability to change the other party's attitudes toward your information and proposals and your ability to recognize when these tactics are being used to persuade you to accept his or her unacceptable proposals. As perverse as this might sound, we do it. This awareness is particularly important because so much influence happens unconsciously.

5. Prepare thoroughly prior to the negotiation. In addition to being aware of influence tactics, thorough preparation is essential. Just as it is a critical way to avoid decision-making errors, preparation is a critical way to minimize the effectiveness of the other negotiator's influence attempts. Knowing the elements of the preparation process (see Chapter 2) is essential.

6. If you find yourself negotiating from a position of weakness, do not despair. Taking steps to increase your power and assess the other negotiator's BATNA will help. If you still have less power, adapt your communication style, understand the other party's interests, extend offers that satisfy all of his or her interests, and your own, and follow the other steps discussed in this chapter and those presented in Reading 8.1 to help you achieve acceptable outcomes despite your inferior power (Program on Negotiation, 2009).

STUDENT STUDY SITE

Visit the Student Study Site at **www.sagepub.com/hames** for additional learning tools.

KEY TERMS

Allies	Power
Attitudes	Reciprocity
Coercive power	Reference points
Contrast principle (a.k.a. relativity)	Referent power
Expert power	Reject then retreat
Influence	Relativity (a.k.a. contrast principle)
Informational power	Reward power
Legitimate power	Two-sided messages

REFERENCES

Allen, M. (1998). Comparing the persuasive effectiveness one- and two-sided message. In *Persuasion: Advances through meta-analysis.* M. Allen & R. W. Preiss (Eds.), Cresskill, NJ: Hampton Press, 87-98.

Ariely, D. (2008). *Predictably irrational: The hidden forces that shape our decisions.* New York: HarperCollins.

Bazerman, M. H. & Moore, D. (2008). *Judgment in managerial decision making, 7th.* New York: John Wiley & Sons.

Berscheid, E. & Walster, E. (1974). Physical attractiveness. In L. Berkowitz (Ed.), *Advances in experimental social psychology, Vol. 7,* New York Academic Press, 157-215.

Bowers, J. (1963). Language intensity, social introversion and attitude change, *Speech monographs,* 30, 345-352.

Brehm, S. S. & Brehm, J. W. (1981). *Psychological Reactance.* New York: Academic Press.

Buller, D. B., Borland, R. & Burgoon, M. (1998). Impact of behavioral intention on effectiveness of message features: Evidence from the family sun safety project, *Human Communication Research,* 24, 433-453.

Buller, S. B. & Hall, J. R. (1998). The effects of distraction during persuasion. In *Persuasion: Advances through meta-analysis.* M. Allen & R. W. Preiss (Eds.), Cresskill, NJ: Hampton Press, 155-173.

Burrell, N. A. & Koper, R. J. (1998). The efficacy of powerful/powerless language on attitudes and source credibility. In *Persuasion: Advances through meta-analysis.* M. Allen & R. W. Preiss (Eds.), Cresskill, NJ: Hampton Press, 203-215.

Cacioppo, J. T. & Petty, R. E. (1985). Central and peripheral routes to persuasion: The role of message repetition. In L. F. Alwitt & A. A. Mitchell (Eds.), *Psychological processes and advertising efforts.* Hillsdale, NJ: Erlbaum, 91-111.

Chaiken, S. (1986). Physical appearance and social influence. In C. P. Herman, M. P. Zanna & E. T. Higgins (Eds.), *Physical appearance, stigma, and social behavior: The Ontario symposium, Vol. 3.* Hillsdale, NJ: Lawrence Erlbaum, 143-177.

Chaiken, S., Wood, W. & Eagly, A. H. (1996). Principles of persuasion. In E. T. Higgins & A. W. Kruglanski (Eds.), *Social psychology: Handbook of basic principles.* New York: Guilford Press, 702-742.

Cialdini, R. B. (1993). *Influence: The Psychology of Persuasion.* New York: Quill/Morrow.

Cialdini, R. B. & Goldstein, N. J. (2004). Social influence: Compliance and conformity, *Annual Review of Psychology,* 55, 591-621.

Coleman, P. (2000). Power and conflict. In M. Deutsch & P. Coleman (Eds.), *Handbook of conflict resolution.* San Francisco: Jossey-Bass, 108-130.

Conger, J. A. (1998). The necessary art of persuasion, *Harvard Business Review,* 76(3), 84-95.

Deutsch, M. (1973). *The resolution of conflict.* New Haven, CT: Yale University Press.

Dolinski, D., Nawrat, M. & Rudak, I. (2001). Dialogue involvement as a social influence technique, *Personality and Social Psychology Bulletin,* 27, 1395-1406.

Fisher, R., Ury, W. & Patton, B. (1991). *Getting to yes: Negotiating agreement without giving in.* New York: Penguin Press.

Follett, M. P. (1942). Constructive conflict. In H. C. Metcalf & L. Urwick (Eds.), *Dynamic administration: The collected papers of Mary Parker Follett.* New York: Harper & Brothers, 30-49.

French, J. R. P., Jr. & Raven, B. H. (1959).The bases of social power. In D. Cartwright, (Ed.), *Studies in social power.* Ann Arbor: University of Michigan Press, 151-157.

Hamilton, M. A. & Hunter, J. E. (1998). The effect of language intensity on receiver evaluations of message, source, and topic. In *Persuasion: Advances through meta-analysis.* M. Allen & R. W. Preiss (Eds.), Cresskill, NJ: Hampton Press, 99-138.

Hosman, L. A. (1989). The evaluative consequences of hedges, hesitations and intensifiers: Powerful and powerless speech styles, *Human Communication Research,* 15, 383-406.

Johnson, B. T. & Eagly, A. H. (1990). Involvement and persuasion: Types, traditions, and the evidence, *Psychological Bulletin,* 107, 375-384.

Johnson, B. & Eagly, A. H. (1989). Effects of involvement on persuasion: A meta-analysis, *Psychological Bulletin,* 106, 290-314.

Johnson, E. J. & Goldstein, D. (2003). Do defaults save lives? *Science,* 302, 1338-1339.

Kahneman, D., & Tversky, A. (1979). Prospect theory: An analysis of decisions under risk, *Econometrica*, 47, 263-291.

Kahneman, D. & Tversky, A. (1981). The framing of decisions and the psychology of choice, *Science*, 211, 453-458.

Kalichman, S. C. & Coley, B. (1995). Context framing to enhance HIV-antibody-testing messages targeted to African American women, *Health Psychology*, 14(3), 247-254.

Kray, L., Thompson, L. & Galinsky, A. (2001). Battle of the sexes: Gender stereotype confirmation and reactance in negotiations, *Journal of Personality and Social Psychology*, 80(6), 942-958.

Langer, E., Blank, F. & Chanowitz, B. (1978). The mindlessness of ostensibly thoughtful action: The role of placebo information in interpersonal interaction, *Journal of Personality and Social Psychology*, 36, 635-642.

Malhotra, D. & Bazerman, M. H. (2008). Psychological influence in negotiation: An introduction long overdue, *Journal of Management*, 34, 509-531.

Mongeau, P. A. (1998). Another look at fear-arousing persuasive appeals. In *Persuasion: Advances through meta-analysis*. M. Allen & R. W. Preiss (Eds.), Cresskill, NJ: Hampton Press, 53-68.

Murnighan, J. K. (1986). Organizational coalitions: Structured contingencies and the formation process. In R. J. Lewicki, B. H. Sheppard & M. H. Bazerman (Eds.). *Research on negotiations in organizations, Vol 1.* Greenwich, CT: JAI Press, 155-173.

O'Barr, W. M. & Atkins, B. K. (1980). "Women's language" or "powerless language?" In S. McConnell-Ginet, R. Borker & N. Furman (Eds.). *Women and language in literature and society*. New York: Praeger, 170-185.

Ortman, A., Fitzgerald, J. & Boeing, C. (2000). Trust, reciprocity, and social history: A re-examination, *Experimental Economics*, 3, 81-100.

Petty, R. E. & Cacioppo, J. T. (1986). *Communication and persuasion: Central and peripheral routes to attitude change.* New York: Springer-Verlag.

Pillutla, M., Malhotra, D. & Murnighan, J. K. (2003). Attributions of trust and the calculus of reciprocity, *Journal of Experimental Social Psychology*, 39, 448-455.

Program on Negotiation (2009). Think you're powerless? Think again, *Negotiation*, February, 1-3.

Program on Negotiation (2010). September 2010, The near collapse of the Big 12: Holding a winning team together, *Negotiation*, 7.

Reinard, J. C. (1998). The persuasive effects of testimonial assertion evidence. In *Persuasion: Advances through meta-analysis*. M. Allen & R. W. Preiss (Eds.), Cresskill, NJ: Hampton Press, 69-86.

Reinhard, M., Messner, M. & Sporer, S. L. (2006). Explicit persuasive intent and its impact on success at persuasion: The determining roles of attractiveness and likeableness, *Journal of Consumer Psychology*, 16(3), 249-259.

Salancik, G. R. & Pfeffer, J. (1977). Who gets power and how they hold on to it: A strategic-contingency model of power, *Organizational Dynamics*, 5, 3-21.

Samuelson, W. F. & Zeckhauser, R. (1988). Status quo bias in decision making, *Journal of Risk and Uncertainty*, 1, 7-59.

Sinaceur, M. & Neale, M. A. (2005). Not all threats are created equal: How implicitness and timing affect the effectiveness of threats in negotiations, *Group Decision and Negotiation*, 14, 63-85.

Sinaceur, M. & Tiedens, L. Z. (2006). Get mad and get more than even: When and why anger expression is effective in negotiations, *Journal of Experimental Social Psychology*, 42, 314-322.

Staw, B. M. (1976). Knee deep in the big muddy: A study of escalating commitment to a chosen course of action, *Organizational Behavior and Human Performance*, 16(1), 27-44.

Taylor, T., & Booth-Butterfield, S. (1993). Getting a foot in the door with drinking and driving: A field study of healthy influence, *Communication Research Reports*, 10, 95-101.

Tversky, A. & Kahneman, D. (1991). Loss aversion in riskless choice: A reference-dependent model, *Quarterly Journal of Economics*, 106(4), 1039-1061.

Wegener, D., Petty, R. E. & Smith, S. M. (1995). Positive mood can increase or decrease message scrutiny: The hedonic contingency view of mood and message processing, *Journal of Personality and Social Psychology*, 69, 5-15.

Witte, K. & Allen, M. (2000). A meta-analysis of fear appeals: Implications for effective public health campaigns, *Health Education and Behavior*, 27, 591-615.

Reading 8.1

THINK YOU'RE POWERLESS? THINK AGAIN

Program on Negotiation

Tap into these sources of bargaining power during your next negotiation.

So, you've communicated your interests, probed your counterpart about his needs, and attempted to uncover hidden sources of value – and you're still feeling as if the other side has all the power. Maybe an important customer insisting that price is the only issue she cares about, and you've gone as low as you can go. Or you've only got one job offer in a shaky economy, and you don't want to risk pressing too hard for the flextime you need to take care of your kids.

When your options to the current negotiation are limited, it's common to assume you have no choice but to accept the unappealing deal on the table. Before you cave in, though, consider whether any of the following five strategies could boost your bargaining power.

1. Closely Examine Your BATNA.

You probably understand the importance of cultivating your BATNA, or *best alternative to a negotiated agreement.* In a job negotiation, your BATNA might be a promising lead or, worse, the prospect of going on unemployment and waiting for other opportunities to arise. The more you can do to build a strong outside alternative, the more power you will have in your current negotiation.

In addition to cultivating a strong BATNA, you also need to assess your best alternative as carefully as possible, according to Harvard Business School and Harvard Law School professor Guhan

Subramanian. This means translating your BATNA to the current deal; prospects that look similar on the surface may differ quite a bit in the details. For example, two job offers might be comparable in terms of salary, but when you weigh one job's flextime opportunities against the other job's limited vacation days, you may discover that one offer is far superior to the other.

The bottom line: Before you accept or reject an offer, make sure you've compared it closely to your best outside alternative.

2. Assess the Other Side's BATNA.

Negotiators often err in assuming that the other side is in a much stronger bargaining position than they are. Subramanian tells the story of a Mississippi farmer who was approached by an entrepreneur who wanted to buy and develop the farmer's riverfront properly commercially, as riverfront gambling had just been legalized in the region. The farmer hired an agriculture professor to take soil samples and assess the value of the land; the professor deemed it to be worth $3 million. No surprise, then, that the farmer was thrilled to walk away with $9.5 million from the entrepreneur.

Now consider what would have happened if the farmer had hired an expert in commercial development and gaming instead of an agriculture professor. He probably would have learned that the potential profits from a casino in a prime location would cause the entrepreneur to value the farmer's land at far more than $9.5 million.

In negotiation, it pays to spend as much time thinking about and researching the other side's bargaining position and BATNA as you spend assessing you own options. You may be

Source: Program on Negotiation (2009). Think you're powerless? Think again, *Program on Negotiation Newsletter*, 12(2), 1–3.

Note: This article first appeared in *Negotiation*, a monthly newsletter published by the Program on Negotiation at Harvard Law School, www.pon.harvard.edu. Copyright 2006–2011 Harvard University.

pleasantly surprised to discover that your counterpart needs you even more than you need her.

3. Change the Game.

If your organization regularly bids for business, you may be accustomed to feeling like the weaker party, write Deepak Malhotra and Max H. Bazerman in their book *Negotiation Genius: How to Overcome Obstacles and Achieve Brilliant Results at the Bargaining Table and Beyond* (Harvard Business School, 2007). Those facing auctions that are won or lost based solely on price may find they're constantly fighting an uphill battle for coveted contracts.

In such cases, your best option may be to change the game. Instead of accepting that you've got to compete on price, find ways to show your desired partner that you offer better all-around value than your competitors. If you have a highly reliable product, a stellar reputation, or impeccable service, it's up to you to convince other parties that they would benefit from working with you.

How can you educate an individual or organization that's fixated on short-term pricing (or another single issue) that they'd get a better long-term deal from you? First, write Malhotra and Bazerman, submit two or equivalent bids simultaneously, such as one that's low on price and service and another that's higher on both.

Second, even if you lose an auction, reach out to the potential customer with a multi-issue package. Assuming your bid was in the low range, the customer may be tempted to work with you instead of the rock-bottom bidder.

Finally, reach out to potential customers *between* auctions. Encourage them to discuss their needs and then show how you can meet those needs. By doing so, you may lock up a deal before it has a chance to go to auction.

4. Examine Your Portfolio.

In the heat of an important negotiation, it's tempting to assume that your entire career hinges on your ability to seal this particular deal, especially in the midst of an economic downturn. Needless to say, this approach to negotiation is counterproductive. When you're stressed, you are likely to be less creative and more concessionary than when you're feeling stronger and calmer.

One way to feel more powerful is to consider your entire portfolio of negotiations advise, Malhotra and Bazerman. They describe the case of a firm that was negotiating in an industry where heightened competition had driven profit margins from 20% to less than 5%. Firm leaders were tired of scraping by on minuscule profits, but because business was slow, they felt they had no choice but to bid as low as possible on each and every contract.

Taking a closer look at the numbers, the firm's leaders realized they would lose about 25% of their business if they held out for 10% profit margins. Simple arithmetic revealed that even if they lost 49% of their business (which was unlikely), they would achieve higher overall profits if they doubled their margins from 5% to 10%. Armed with this new understanding of the finances, firm negotiators were empowered to take the risk of refusing to accept less than a 10% profit margin.

By creating a broad strategy for your entire portfolio of negotiations, you take the pressure off each individual negotiation and gain the strength you need to pass up a bad deal.

5. Acknowledge Your Weakness.

Experts usually advise negotiators to conceal weak BATNAs from their counterparts. After all, if someone knows you have nowhere else to go, he could take advantage of your weakness.

In some instances, however, you may be in a position of such extreme weakness that it's impossible to hide. If so, don't assume you have nothing to offer. It could be that your counterpart has a strong incentive to help keep you afloat. The $700 billion government bailout of the U.S. banking industry in October 2008 stands as one dramatic instance of this type of scenario. As banks teetered on the brink of collapse, Congress decided that some were simply too big to fail. For similar reasons, banks are often willing to negotiate new terms with borrowers facing mortgage defaults. A bank may prefer to refinance an existing mortgage than to sell a property at a loss.

With any luck, you and your organization will never have to appeal for help to avoid a ruinous financial collapse. But there are instances in which you can call on your counterpart's sense of fairness to get a better deal. Malhotra and Bazerman offer the common scenario of an MBA student who is graduating with only one slightly disappointing job offer in hand. The student might choose to accept the offer and only *then* ask her new boss to reexamine whether the salary offered is fair—a tactic that's often surprisingly successful at generating a higher offer.

When you've been unable to improve your bargaining power through the other means we've described, appealing to your counterpart's sense of fairness may be the best strategy you have.

5 Tips for Building Bargaining Power

- Closely compare the specifics of the deal on the table to your BATNA.
- Study your counterpart's outside alternatives as closely as your own.
- If the rules aren't working in your favor, try to change the game.
- Consider each negotiation in light of your broader portfolio of deals.
- When all else fails, appeal to the other side's sense of fairness.

Thinking Further 8.1

1. What type(s) of power (reward, coercive, legitimate, expert, referent or information) do you use when you: 1) closely examine your BATNA; 2) assess the other side's BATNA; 3) change the game; 4) examine your portfolio; and 5) acknowledge your weakness? Explain your reasoning.

2. Which of the article's five tips for building power are related to direct influence? Which are related to indirect influence? Explain your reasoning.

Reading 8.2

HARNESSING THE SCIENCE OF PERSUASION

Robert B. Cialdini

Lucky few have it; most of us do not. A handful of gifted "naturals" simply know how to capture an audience, sway the undecided, and convert the opposition. Watching these masters of persuasion work their magic is at once impressive and frustrating. What's impressive is not just the easy way they use charisma and

eloquence to convince others to do as they ask. It's also how eager those others are to do what's requested of them, as if the persuasion itself were a favor they couldn't wait to repay.

The frustrating part of the experience is these born persuaders are often unable to account for their remarkable skill or pass it on to others. Their way with people is an art, and artists as a rule are far better at doing than at explaining. Most of them can't offer much help to those of us who

Source: Robert B. Cialdini, "Harnessing the Science of Persuasion," Harvard Business Review, October 2001, 72, 74–79. Used by permission of Harvard Business School Publishing.

possess no more than the ordinary quotient of charisma and eloquence but who still have to wrestle with leadership's fundamental challenge: Getting things done through others. That challenge is painfully familiar to corporate executives, who every day have to figure out how to motivate and direct a highly individualistic work force. Playing the "Because I'm the boss" card is out. Even if it weren't demeaning and demoralizing for all concerned, it would be out of place in a world where cross-functional teams, joint ventures, and intercompany partnerships have blurred the lines of authority. In such an environment, persuasion skills exert far greater influence over others' behavior than formal power structures do.

Which brings us back to where we started. Persuasion skills may be more necessary than ever, but how can executives acquire them if the most talented practitioners can't pass them along? By looking to science. For the past five decades, behavioral scientists have conducted experiments that shed considerable light on the way certain interactions lead people to concede, comply, or change. This research shows that persuasion works by appealing to a limited set of deeply rooted human drives and needs, and it does so in predictable ways. Persuasion, in other words, is governed by basic principles that can be taught, learned, and applied. By mastering these principles, executives can bring scientific rigor to the business of securing consensus, cutting deals, and winning concessions. In the pages that follow, I describe six fundamental principles of persuasion and suggest a few ways that executives can apply them in their own organizations.

THE PRINCIPLE OF LIKING:

People like those who like them.

THE APPLICATION:

Uncover real similarities and offer genuine praise.

The retailing phenomenon known as the Tupperware party is a vivid illustration of this principle in action. The demonstration party for Tupperware products is hosted by an individual, almost always a woman, who invites to her home an array of friends, neighbors, and relatives. The guests' affection for their hostess predisposes them to buy from her, a dynamic that was confirmed by a 1990 study of purchase decisions made at demonstration parties. The researchers, Jonathan Frenzen and Harry Davis, writing in the *Journal of Consumer Research,* found that the guests' fondness for their hostess weighed twice as heavily in their purchase decisions as their regard for the products they bought. So when guests at a Tupperware party buy something, they aren't just buying to please themselves. They're buying to please their hostess as well.

What's true at Tupperware parties is true for business in general: If you want to influence people, win friends. How? Controlled research has identified several factors that reliably increase liking, but two stand out as especially compelling—similarity and praise. Similarity literally draws people together. In one experiment, reported in a 1968 article in the *Journal of Personality,* participants stood physically closer to one another after learning that they shared political beliefs and social values. And in a 1963 article in *American Behavioral Scientists*, researcher E. B. Evans used demographic data from insurance company records to demonstrate that prospects were more willing to purchase a policy from a salesperson who was akin to them in age, religion, politics or even cigarette smoking habits.

Managers can use similarities to create bonds with a recent hire, the head of another department, or even a new boss. Informal conversations during the workday create an ideal opportunity to discover at least one common area of enjoyment, be it a hobby, a college basketball team, or reruns of *Seinfeld*. The important thing is to establish the bond early because it creates a presumption of goodwill and trustworthiness in every subsequent encounter. It's much easier to build support for a new project when the people you're trying to persuade are already inclined in your favor.

Praise, the other reliable generator of affection, both charms and disarms. Sometimes the praise doesn't even have to be merited. Researchers at the University of North Carolina writing in the *Journal of Experimental Social Psychology* found that men felt the greatest regard for an individual who flattered them unstintingly even if the comments were untrue. And in their book *Interpersonal Attraction* (Addison-Wesley, 1978), Ellen Berscheid and Elaine Harfield Walster presented experimental data showing that position remarks about another person's traits, attitude, or performance reliably generates liking in return, as well as willing compliance with the wishes of the person offering the praise.

Along with cultivating a fruitful relationship, adroit managers can also praise to repair one that's damaged or unproductive. Imagine you're the manager of a good sized unit within your organization. Your work frequently brings you into contact with another manager—call him Dan—whom you have come to dislike. No matter how much you do for him, it's not enough. Worse, he never seems to believe that you're doing the best you can for him. Resenting his attitude and his obvious lack of trust in your abilities and in your good faith, you don't spend as much time with him as you know you should; in consequence, the performance of both his unit and yours is deteriorating.

The research on praise points toward a strategy for fixing the relationship. It may be hard to find, but there has to be something about Dan you can sincerely admire, whether it's his concern for the people in his department, his devotion to his family, or simply his work ethic. In your next encounter with him, make an appreciative comment about that trait. Make it clear that in this case at least, you value what he values. I predict that Dan will relax his relentless negativity and give you an opening to convince him of your competence and good intentions.

THE PRINCIPLE OF RECIPROCITY:

People repay in kind.

THE APPLICATION:

Give what you want to receive.

Praise is likely to have a warming and softening effect on Dan because, ornery as he is, he is still human and subject to the universal human tendency to treat people the way they treat him. If you have ever caught yourself smiling at a coworker just because he or she smiled first, you know this principle works.

Charities rely on reciprocity to help them raise funds. For years, for instance, the Disabled American Veterans organization, using only a well-crafted fund-raising letter, garnered a very respectable 18% rate of response to its appeals. But when the groups started enclosing a small gift in the envelope, the response rate nearly doubled to 35%. The gift—personalized address labels—was extremely modest, but it wasn't what prospective donors received that made the difference. It was that they had gotten anything at all.

What works in that letter works at the office, too. It's more than an effusion of seasonal spirit, of course, that impels suppliers to shower gifts on purchasing departments at holiday time. In 1996, purchasing managers admitted to an interviewer from *Inc.* magazine that after having accepted a gift from a supplier, they were willing to purchase products and services they would have otherwise declined. Gifts also have a startling effect on retention. I have encouraged readers of my book to send me examples of principles of influence at work in their own lives. One reader, an employee of the State of Oregon, sent a letter in which she offered these reasons for her commitment to her supervisor:

He gives me and my son gifts for Christmas and gives me presents on my birthday. There is no promotion for the type of job I have, and my only choice for one is to move to another department. But I find myself resisting trying to move. My boss is reaching retirement age, and I am thinking I will be able to move out after he retires. . . . [F]or now, I feel obligated to stay since he has been so nice to me.

Ultimately, though, gift giving is one of the cruder applications of the rule of reciprocity. In its more sophisticated uses, it confers a genuine first-mover advantage on any manager who is trying to foster positive attitudes and productive personal relationships in the office: Managers can elicit the desired behavior from coworkers and employees by displaying it first. Whether it's a sense of trust, a spirit of cooperation, or a pleasant demeanor, leaders should model the behavior they want to see from others.

The same holds true for managers faced with issues of information delivery and resource allocation. If you lend a member of your staff to a colleague who is shorthanded and staring at a fast-approaching deadline, you will significantly increase your chances of getting help when you need it. Your odds will improve even more if you say, when your colleague thanks you for the assistance, something like, "Sure, glad to help. I know how important it is for me to count on your help when I need it."

THE PRINCIPLE OF SOCIAL PROOF:

People follow the lead of similar others.

THE APPLICATION:

Use peer power whenever it's available.

Social creatures that they are, human beings rely heavily on the people around them for cues on how to think, feel, and act. We know this intuitively, but intuition has also been confirmed by experiments, such as the one first described in 1982 in the *Journal of Applied Psychology.* A group of researchers went door-to-door in Columbia, South Carolina, soliciting donations for a charity campaign and displaying a list of neighborhood residents who had already donated to the cause. The researchers found that the longer the donor list was, the more likely those solicited would be to donate as well.

To the people being solicited, the friends' and neighbors' names on the list were a form of social evidence about how they should respond. But the evidence would not have been nearly as compelling had the names been those of random strangers. In an experiment from the 1960s, first described in the *Journal of Personality Social Psychology,* residents of New York City were asked to return a lost wallet to its owner. They were highly likely to attempt to do so. But learning that someone from a foreign country had tried to return the wallet didn't sway their decision one way or the other.

The lesson for executives from these two experiments is that persuasion can be extremely effective when it comes from peers. The science supports what most sales professionals already know: Testimonials from satisfied customers work best when the satisfied customer and the prospective customer share similar circumstances. That lesson can help a manager faced with the task of selling a new corporate initiative. Imagine that you're trying to streamline your department's work processes. A group of veteran employees is resisting. Rather than try to convince the employees of the move's merits yourself, ask an old-timer who supports the initiative to speak up for it at a team meeting. The compatriot's testimony stands much better chance of convincing the group than yet another speech from the boss. Stated simply, influence is often best exerted horizontally rather than vertically.

THE PRINCIPLE FOR CONSISTENCY:

People align with their clear commitments.

THE APPLICATION:

Make their commitments active, public, and voluntary.

Linking is a powerful force, but the work of persuasion involves more than simply making people feel warmly toward you, your idea, or your product. People need not only to like you but to feel committed to what you want them to do. Good turns are one reliable way to make people feel obligated to you. Another is to win a public commitment from them.

My own research has demonstrated that most people, once they take a stand or go on record in favor of a position, prefer to stick to it. Other studies reinforce that finding and go on to show how even a small, seemingly trivial commitment can have a powerful effect on future actions. Israeli researchers writing in 1983 in the *Personality and Social Psychology Bulletin* recounted how they asked half the residents of a large apartment complex to sign a petition favoring the establishment of a recreation center for the handicapped. The cause was good and the request was small, so almost everyone who was asked agreed to sign. Two weeks later, on National Collection Day for the Handicapped, all residents of the complex were approached at home and asked to give to the cause. A little more than half of those who were not asked to sign the petition made a contribution. But an astounding sing the petition made a contribution. But an astounding 92% of those who did sign donated money. The residents of the apartment complex felt obligated to live up to their commitments because those commitments were active, public, and voluntary. These three features are worth considering separately.

There's strong empirical evidence to show that a choice made actively—one that's spoken out loud or written down or otherwise made explicit—is considerably more likely to direct someone's future conduct than the same choice left unspoken. Writing in 1996 in the *Personality and Social Psychology Bulletin,* Delia Cioffi and Randy Garner described an experiment in which college students in one group were asked to fill out a printed form saying they wished to volunteer for an AIDS education project in the public schools. Students in another group volunteered for the same project by leaving blank a form stating that they didn't want to participate. A few days later, when the volunteers

reported for duty, 74% of those who showed up were students from the group that signaled their commitment by filling out the form.

The implications are clear for a manager who wants to persuade a subordinate to follow some particular course of action: Get it in writing. Let's suppose you want your employee to submit reports in a more timely fashion. Once you believe you've won agreement, ask him to summarize the decision in a memo and send it to you. By doing so, you'll have greatly increased the odds that he'll fulfill the commitment because, as a rule, people live up to what they have written down.

Research into the social dimensions of commitment suggests that written statements become even more powerful when they're made public. In a classic experiment, described in 1955 in the *Journal of Abnormal and Social Psychology,* college students were asked to estimate the length of lines projected on a screen. Some students were asked to write down their choices on a piece of paper, sign it, and hand the paper to the experimenter. Others wrote their choices on an erasable slate, then erased the slate immediately. Still others were instructed to keep their decisions to themselves.

The experimenters then presented all three groups with evidence that their initial choices may have been wrong. Those who had merely kept their decisions in their heads were the most likely to reconsider their original estimates. More loyal to their first guesses were the students in the group that had written them down and immediately erased them. But by a wide margin, the ones most reluctant to shift from their original choices were those who had signed and handed them to the researcher.

This experiment highlights how much most people wish to appear consistent to others. Consider again the matter of the employee who has been submitting late reports. Recognizing the power of this desire, you should, once you've successfully convinced him of the need to be more timely, reinforce the commitment by making sure it gets a public airing. One way to do that would be to send the employee an e-mail that reads. "I think your plan is just what we need. I showed it to Diane in manufacturing and Phil in shipping, and they thought it was right on target, too." Whatever way such commitments are formalized, they should never be like the New Year's resolutions people privately make and then abandon with no one the wiser. They should be publicly made and visibly posted.

More than 300 years ago, Samuel Butler wrote a couplet that explains succinctly why commitments must be voluntary to be lasting and effective: "He that complies against his will/ Is of his own opinion still." If an undertaking is forced, coerced, or imposed from the outside, it's not a commitment; it's an unwelcome burden. Think how you would react if your boss pressured you to donate to the campaign of a political candidate. Would that make you more apt to opt for that candidate in the privacy of a voting booth? Not likely. In fact, in their 1981 book *Psychological Reactance* (Academic Press), Sharon S. Brehm and Jack W. Brehm present data that suggest you'd vote the opposite way just to express your resentment of the boss's coercion.

This kind of backlash can occur in the office, too. Let's return again to that tardy employee. If you want to produce an enduring change in his behavior, you should avoid using threats or pressure tactics to gain his compliance. He'd likely view any change in his behavior as the result of intimidation rather than a personal commitment to change. A better approach would be to identify something that the employee genuinely values in the work place—high-quality workmanship, perhaps, or team spirit—and then describe how timely reports are consistent with those values. That gives the employee reasons for improvement that he can own. And because he owns them, they'll continue to guide his behavior even when you're not watching.

THE PRINCIPLE OF AUTHORITY:

People defer to experts.

THE APPLICATION:

Expose your expertise; don't assume it's self-evident.

Two thousand years ago, the Roman poet Virgil offered this simple counsel to those seeking to choose correctly: "Believe an expert." That may or may not be good advice, but as a description of what people actually do, it can't be beaten. For instance, when the news media present an acknowledged expert's views on a topic, the effect on public opinion is dramatic. A single expert-opinion news story in the New York Times is associated with a 2% shift in public opinion nationwide, according to a 1993 study described in the *Public Opinion Quarterly.* And researchers writing in the *American Political Science Review* in 1987 found that when the expert's view was aired on national television, public opinion shifted as much as 4%. A cynic might argue that these findings only illustrate the docile submissiveness of the public. But a fairer explanation is that, amid the teeming complexity of contemporary life, a well-selected expert offers a valuable and efficient shortcut to good decisions. Indeed, some questions, be they legal, financial, medical, or technological, require so much specialized knowledge to answer, we have no choice but to rely on experts.

Since there's good reason to defer to experts, executives should take pains to ensure that they establish their own expertise before they attempt to exert influence. Surprisingly often, people mistakenly assume that others recognize and appreciate their experience. That's what happened at a hospital where some colleagues and I were consulting. The physical therapy staffers were frustrated because so many of their stroke patients abandoned their exercise routines as soon as they left the hospital. No matter how often the staff emphasized the importance of regular home exercise—it is, in fact, crucial to the process of regaining independent function—the message just didn't sink in.

Interviews with some of the patients helped us pinpoint the problem. They were familiar with the background and training of their physicians, but the patients knew little about the credentials of the physical therapists who were urging them to exercise. It was a simple matter to remedy that lack of information: we merely asked the therapists' director to display all the awards, diplomas, and certifications of her staff on the walls of the therapy rooms. The result was startling: Exercise compliance jumped 34% and has never dropped since.

What we found immensely gratifying was not just how much we increased compliance, but how. We didn't fool or browbeat any of the patients. We informed them into compliance. Nothing had to be invented; no time or resources had to be spent in the process. The staff's expertise was real—all we had to do was make it more visible.

The task for managers who want to establish their claims to expertise is somewhat more difficult. They can't simply nail their diplomas to the wall and wait for everyone to notice. A little subtlety is called for. Outside the United States, it is customary for people to spend time interacting socially before getting down to business for the first time. Frequently they gather for dinner the night before their meeting or negotiation. These get-togethers can make discussions easier and help blunt disagreements—remember the finding about liking and similarity—and they can also provide an opportunity to establish expertise. Perhaps it's a matter of telling an anecdote about successfully solving a problem similar to the one that's on the agenda at the next day's meeting. Or perhaps dinner is the time to describe years spent mastering a complex discipline—not in a boastful way but as part of the ordinary give-and-take of conversation.

Granted, there's not always time for lengthy introductory sessions. But even in the course of the preliminary conversation that precedes most meetings, there is almost always an opportunity to touch lightly on your relevant background and experience as a natural part of a sociable exchange. This initial disclosure of personal information gives you a chance to establish expertise early in the game, so that when the discussion turns to the business at hand, what you have to say will be accorded the respect it deserves.

THE PRINCIPLE OF SCARCITY:

People want more of what they can have less of.

THE APPLICATION:

Highlight unique benefits and exclusive information.

Study after study shows that items and opportunities are seen to be more valuable as they become less available. That's a tremendously useful piece of information for managers. They can harness the scarcity principle with the organizational equivalents of limited-time, limited-supply, and one-of-a-kind offers. Honestly informing a coworker of a closing window of opportunity—the chance to get the boss's ear before she leaves for an extended vacation, perhaps—can mobilize action dramatically.

Managers can learn from retailers how to frame their offers not in terms of what people stand to gain but in terms of what they stand to lose if they don't act on the information. The power of "loss language" was demonstrated in a 1988 study of California home owners written up in the *Journal of Applied Psychology.* Half were told that if they fully insulated their homes, they would save a certain amount of money each day. The other half were told that if they failed to insulate, they would lose that amount each day. Significantly more people insulated their homes when exposed to the loss language. The same phenomenon occurs in business. According to a 1994 study in the journal *Organizational Behavior and Human Decision Processes,* potential losses figure far more heavily in managers' decision making than potential gains.

In framing their offers, executives should also remember that exclusive information is more persuasive than widely available data. A doctoral student of mine, Amram Kinshinsky, wrote his 1982 dissertation on the purchase decisions of wholesale beef buyers. He observed that they more than doubled their orders when they were told that, because of certain weather conditions overseas, there was likely to be a scarcity of foreign beef in the near future. But their orders increased 600% when they were informed that no one else had that information yet.

The persuasive power of exclusivity can be harnessed by any manager who comes into possession of information that's not broadly available and that supports an idea or initiative he or she would like the organization to adopt. The next time that kind of information crosses your desk, round up your organization's key players. The information itself may seem dull, but exclusivity will give it a special sheen. Push it across your desk and say, "I just got this report today. It won't be distributed until next week, but I want to give you an early look at what it a shows." Then watch your listeners lean forward.

Allow me to stress here a point that should be obvious. No offer of exclusive information, exhortation to act now or miss this opportunity forever should be made unless it is genuine. Deceiving colleagues into compliance is not only ethically objectionable, it's foolhardy. If the deception is detected, and it certainly will be, it will snuff out any enthusiasm the offer originally kindled. It will also invite dishonesty toward the deceiver. Remember the rule of reciprocity.

Putting It All Together

There's nothing abstruse about these six principles of persuasion. Indeed, they codify our intuitive understanding of the ways people evaluate information and form decisions. As a result, the principles are easy for most people to grasp, even those with no formal education in psychology. But in the seminars and workshops I conduct, I have learned that two points bear repeated emphasis.

First, although the six principles and their applications can be discussed separately for the sake of clarity, they should be applied in combination to compound their impact. For instance, in discussing the importance of expertise, I suggested that managers use informal, social conversations to establish their credentials. But that conversation affords an opportunity to gain information as well as convey it. While you're showing your dinner companion that you have the skills and experience your business problem demands, you can also learn about your companion's background, likes, and dislikes that will help you locate genuine similarities and give sincere compliments. By letting your expertise surface and also establishing rapport, you double your persuasive power. And if you succeed in bringing your dinner partner on board, you may encourage other people to sign on as well, thanks to the persuasive power of social evidence.

The other point I wish to emphasize is that the rules of ethics apply to the science of influence just as they do to any other technology; not only is it ethically wrong to trick or trap others into assent, it's ill-advised in practical terms. Dishonest or high-pressure tactics work only in the short run, if at all. Their long-term effects are malignant, especially within an organization which can't function properly without a bedrock level of trust and cooperation.

That point is made vividly in the following account, which a department head for a large textile manufacturer related at a training workshop I conducted. She described a vice president in her company who wrung public commitments from department heads in a highly manipulative manner. Instead of giving his subordinates time to talk or think through his proposals carefully, he would approach them individually at the busiest moment of their workday and describe the benefits of his plan in exhaustive, patience-straining detail.

Then he would move in for the kill. "It's very important for me to see you as being on my team on this," he would say. "Can I count on your support?" Intimidated, frazzled, eager to chase the man from their offices so they could get back to work, the department heads would invariably go along with his request. But because the commitments never felt voluntary, the department heads never followed through, and as a result the vice president's initiatives all blew up or petered out.

This story had a deep impact on the other participants in the workshop. Some gulped in shock as they recognized their own manipulative behavior. But what stopped everyone cold was the expression on the department head's face as she recounted the damaging collapse of her superior's proposals. She was smiling.

Nothing I could say would more effectively make the point that the deceptive or coercive use of the principles of social influence is ethically wrong and pragmatically wrongheaded. Yet the same principles, if applied appropriately, can steer decisions correctly. Legitimate expertise, genuine obligation, authentic similarities, real social proof, exclusive news, and freely made commitments can produce choices that are likely to benefit both parties. And any approach that works to everyone's mutual benefit is good business, don't you think? Of course, I don't want to press you into it, but, if you agree, I would love it if you could just jot me a memo to that effect.

Thinking Further 8.2

1. Is using *persuasion* a form of "power over" or "power with"? Does it depend on the context? Or is persuasion not a form of power? Explain your reasoning. Give some examples.

2. Which of the five types of persuasion discussed in this article might be considered deceptive, or ethically questionable in some respect? Explain your reasoning. Give some examples.

CHAPTER 9

Ethics

Right and Wrong Do Exist When You Negotiate

Trust and integrity are important components of both ethical business practices and ethical negotiations. A variety of tactics, including the hardball tactics and dirty tricks introduced in Chapter 3, often raise ethical questions because they involve deception. Some of our unethical negotiating behavior, however, is unconscious – we are not aware that what we or the other party are doing is unethical. This chapter examines the nature of ethics in negotiation, why negotiators might knowingly or unknowingly behave unethically, tactics that commonly raise ethical questions, how we can determine whether our own actions and those of other negotiators are unethical, and the consequences typically associated with unethical negotiating behavior.

INTENDED BENEFITS OF THIS CHAPTER

When you finish reading this chapter, you should be able to:

1. Explain why negotiators might act unethically and describe the kinds of actions that often raise ethical questions.

2. Apply the different frameworks for assessing the ethicality of various bargaining tactics to explain why these tactics are or are not unethical.

267

3. Avoid ethical lapses when you negotiate, and explain why this will help you achieve better outcomes.

THE ESSENCE OF ETHICS IN NEGOTIATION

Ethics in negotiation is a difficult topic. Compared to our self-assessments, we tend to be more critical of others' ethics, more suspicious of others' motives for their good deeds, and we believe they are more motivated by self-interest and money (Epley & Dunning, 2000). We also believe that we are more honest and trustworthy than others and that we try harder to do good (Messick & Bazerman, 1996). Despite these negative perceptions of others' ethics, we are not always eager to criticize them. Nor are our own ethics beyond reproach. New evidence demonstrates that even the most well-intentioned negotiators routinely and unconsciously commit ethical lapses and tolerate such lapses in others (Gino, Moore & Bazerman, 2009).

What Is Ethics?

Negotiation is a process of *potentially opportunistic* interaction by which two or more parties with some apparent conflict seek to do better through joint action than they could otherwise (Lax & Sebenius, 1986). How negotiators translate this 'potential opportunism' into real advantages or gains often raises ethical concerns because it implies control or manipulation of information. Since **ethics** is the study of interpersonal or social values and the rules of conduct that derive from them, manipulation, truth telling and withholding information are at the core of what is or is not ethical in negotiation (Robinson, Lewicki & Donahue, 2000).

For many, ethics and morals differ – the former reflect societal values while the latter reflect our personal values. How important this distinction is for negotiators is unclear. What matters most is that if we want to negotiate ethically, we must determine whether our intentions, tactics, actions and decisions are right or wrong, and these are rarely easy to define. Some make this determination by assuming that it is ethical if it is legal, and unethical if it is not. This might simplify the process of making these assessments, but the law and ethics are not synonymous. It is true that unlawful behavior is usually unethical, but lawful behavior is not necessarily ethical. Many negotiators, for example, consider lies and other misrepresentations to be unethical (Robinson et al., 2000). They are generally illegal, however, only if they involve perjury (lying while on a witness stand in a legal trial) or fraud (a knowing misrepresenting of a material fact upon which the other party relies to his or her detriment). An employee who tries to avoid disciplinary action for excessive tardiness by lying to his or her boss about why it is happening might be behaving unethically, but such lies are not illegal unless they rise to the level of defrauding the employer for money or other benefits. Many actions or decisions in negotiations do not even raise legal questions.

Negotiation in Action 9.1 illustrates a transaction that might raise ethical questions.

NEGOTIATION IN ACTION 9.1

The Sony Corporation was negotiating a $5 billion purchase of Columbia Pictures. In a $200 million side deal, Sony opened talks with two film producers about running its new film division. The producers desperately wanted the job, but they were tied up in an ongoing contract with Warner Brothers and desperately needed time to negotiate their release. Rather than informing Sony of this, they muddied the waters by adding two issues they didn't really care about to the discussion. An all-night negotiation on the three issues followed. In the morning, the producers conceded on the two phony issues and asked Sony to concede on the timing issue. Sony took the bait, allowing the producers a month to negotiate with Warner (Program on Negotiation, 2010).

Video 9.1
Ethics in Negotiations

Were the producers' tactics unethical?

WHAT MIGHT CAUSE NEGOTIATORS TO BEHAVE UNETHICALLY?

The ethicality of our bargaining behavior is probably determined long before we begin preparing for a negotiation. How much we value our personal integrity will influence the ethicality of the tactics we use. If we value it highly, we will consistently be guided by a thoughtful set of personal values that we can readily explain, justify and defend to others (Shell, 1999). Moreover, these values will influence how we frame our arguments, the tactics we use and how we execute them. Simply put, our choices will be constrained or limited. If we do not place much value on our personal integrity, unethical behavior is more likely. We will have more latitude when choosing which tactics to use. Since we do not like to have our choices limited, this seems desirable. But the cost of using unethical tactics may be substantial – compromising your values and tarnishing your reputation. You must reconcile your tactical choices with your ethical beliefs and decide if the gains you are seeking are worth the risks.

If the other party values personal integrity highly, the cost to you will be lower because his or her values will limit the array of tactics that are usable. If he or she does not value personal integrity highly, you will be required to spend more time, energy and prudence protecting yourself and your interests against his or her wider array of tactics (Shell, 1999).

Most ethically questionable behavior in negotiation is about withholding information and truth telling. Negotiators might engage in these behaviors to profit or win, because they are greedy, or to retaliate against being treated unfairly. It also appears that people are more or less predisposed to use these tactics.

Power

Information is one source of bargaining power and how it is used affects perceptions of how much power a negotiator possesses. Deceptive or other ethically questionable tactics, therefore, may enhance a negotiator's power. Some evidence suggests that negotiators are more willing to use deceptive tactics when the other party is less powerful – less knowledgeable or less informed about the situation. That more powerful negotiators bluff more often and communicate less with the other party than those negotiators who have less power seems counterintuitive. Why would negotiators use ethically questionable tactics when they already have a power advantage? Simply put, power is intoxicating. Those who have it want more because it will increase their chances of profiting or winning even more (Boles, Croson & Murnighan, 2000; Crott, Kayser & Lamm, 1980).

The evidence also suggests that negotiators who have more to gain by lying are more likely to do so, and those with less power use more deceptive tactics and lie. This appears to be a defensive move, or an attempt to help themselves avoid excessively large losses (Olekalns & Smith, 2007; Tenbrunsel & Diekmann, 2007).

Personal Motives

Negotiators with a competitive orientation are more likely to misrepresent information. They also believe it is appropriate to do so if they think the other party negotiates competitively. This is consistent with the fundamental attribution error discussed in Chapter 7 because negotiators are attributing their use of such tactics to external causes – the other party's behavior is used to justify their own (O'Connor & Carnevale, 1997; Lewicki & Spencer, 1991). It may also suggest that social proof is involved (see Chapter 8) because the negotiators are using the other party's behavior to decide how they should behave.

Personal motives influence negotiators' behavior in other ways as well.

- Negotiators misrepresent or omit information more if the other party appears to be trustworthy because the chances of being caught are small, and the costs if they are caught are low.
- Those who have failed in prior negotiations will use whatever means are available, including deception, to redeem themselves.
- Negotiators who have been victimized by the other party's use of unethical tactics will be disappointed with the loss, angry and embarrassed at being duped. They are likely to retaliate or seek revenge, unlikely to trust the unethical negotiator again, and perhaps generalize their distrust to future negotiators – even those who were not responsible for victimizing them.
- The prospect of positive reinforcement probably explains why negotiators who expect to be rewarded for using unethical tactics do so (Olekalns & Smith, 2007; Schweitzer, Ordonez & Douma, 2004; Bies & Moag, 1986; Hegarty & Sims, 1978).

How Ethicality Is Assessed

Tendencies toward engaging or not engaging in ethically questionable behavior seem to be influenced by how people assess ethicality. Four ethical reasoning frameworks will be discussed in greater detail later in this chapter. For now, utilitarianism (Mill, 1989) argues that an action is ethical if it produces the greatest good (happiness) for the greatest number of people affected by it. Social contract ethics (Rousseau, 1947) argues that an action is ethical if it is consistent with or is grounded in the community's social norms that govern the interaction. Advocates of these two frameworks are more likely to use ethically questionable tactics. The rights and duties framework (Kant, 1989) argues that people

Video 9.2

Essentials of Utilitarianism

are governed by certain universal rights, and these rights impose upon themselves and others a corresponding duty. *B*reaching these rights and duties is unethical. The **fairness and justice** framework (Rawls, 1989) argues that similarly situated people should be treated similarly in terms of the allocation of rewards and burdens, and in terms of the process that is used to determine the allocation. Advocates of these more rule-based frameworks are less comfortable with, and less likely to use, ethically questionable tactics (Perry & Nixon, 2005).

Individual Differences

The evidence suggests that age, gender and nationality help us predict who will use, or have more favorable attitudes toward using, ethically questionable negotiating behaviors. These findings are summarized in Table 9.1. These are presented with some trepidation because extreme caution is essential. These are generalizations and many members of these groups will not "fit" into these categories or support these findings. Negotiators must refrain from acting on these assumptions without first attempting to verify them.

Table 9.1 Individual Differences and Ethically Questionable Negotiating Behavior

Characteristics	Findings
Age	People behave more ethically as they get older; Older people rate unethical tactics as less acceptable than younger people
Gender	Men and women are equally willing to exaggerate opening offers and stall for time; Men are more willing to deceive
Nationality	Americans and Asians are more likely to bluff than are Eastern Europeans; Managers from the U.S. and Brazil both rate traditional competitive bargaining tactics (e.g., bluffing) as acceptable, but U.S. managers are less likely to rate deception or subterfuge as acceptable; U.S. managers view the same ethically questionable tactics as more appropriate than Mexican managers; People in individualistic cultures (e.g., the U.S.) are more likely to use deception for personal gain than are people from collectivist cultures (e.g., Israel); Ethically questionable tactics are more acceptable for people when negotiating with someone from a different country than with someone from their own country
Personality	Negotiators who think they are *aggressive* or *competitive* are more likely to use ethically questionable tactics (e.g., bluffing, misrepresentation) than those who think they are *cooperative*; Cooperative negotiators are more ethical than competitive negotiators when dealing with other cooperative individuals, but use more deceptive tactics than others when negotiating with competitive opponents; High Machiavellians (a personality trait characterized by opportunism) use whatever tools are available and necessary – they lie more and are more persuasive when they do because they aren't anxious when they lie to achieve desired gains

(See, e.g., Elahee & Brooks, 2004; Steinel & de Dreu, 2004; Sims, 2002; Volkema & Fleury, 2002; Robinson et al., 2000; Volkema, 1997, 1998, 1999; Lewicki & Robinson, 1998; Anton, 1990; Christie & Geis, 1970.)

WHAT IF WE ARE UNETHICAL OR "SEE UNETHICAL" AND DON'T EVEN KNOW IT?

Unconscious or Unknowing Ethical Breaches

As noted earlier, you may have to rethink your self-assessment if you think your ethics are beyond reproach. Few professionals consciously set out to violate the law or their own moral standards. In the context of negotiation, however, a range of common cognitive patterns can lead us to engage in or condone 'ordinary unethical behaviors' that we would otherwise condemn. We overlook others' unethical behavior that serves our own interests, and managers routinely delegate unethical duties to subordinates in their organizations. People also seem to become comfortable with behavior that gradually becomes less and less ethical, and they ignore unethical process choices if the resultant outcomes are good.

One reason for these unconscious lapses emanates from evidence pertaining to our flawed decision making. We engage in systematic patterns of thinking that prevent us from noticing or focusing on useful, observable and relevant data. (Bazerman & Chugh, 2005). We also engage in behaviors that are inconsistent with our own ethical values. These decisions not only harm others but are inconsistent with our own consciously espoused beliefs and preferences. In fact, we would condemn them upon further reflection or awareness (Bazerman & Moore, 2008).

Overlooking the Unethical Behavior of Others

Accurately assessing the ethicality of the other party's behavior is difficult if you have an incentive to see him or her in a favorable light. In 2000, for example, Enron paid Arthur Andersen $25 million in auditing fees and $27 million in consulting fees. A clear conflict of interest existed between Andersen's responsibility to conduct unbiased, impartial audits and its motivation to gain increasingly lucrative consulting contracts from Enron (Bazerman, Moore, Tetlock & Tanlu, 2006; Moore, Tetlock, Tanlu & Bazerman, 2006). The end result for these two companies is painfully obvious. Moreover, this conflict of interest persists in the auditing industry. Similar conflicts of interest are common in industries that rely extensively on agents (e.g., real estate, law) because it is very difficult to perfectly align an agent's interests with those of his or her client.

Overlooking the Actions of Those Who Delegate Unethical Tasks

This happens commonly in organizations. Managers may tell their subordinates to 'do whatever it takes' to achieve sales or production goals. They also negotiate agreements with subcontractors in other countries to manufacture their products because they are less expensive—labor costs and environmental standards are lower (Gino et al., 2009). Head coaches in college sports may tell their assistant coaches to, "Do whatever it takes to recruit coveted athletes, but do not tell me how you did it." A very public example of a professional sports coach delegating unethical tasks to an assistant coach involves Bill Belichick, the head coach of the New England Patriots professional football team. It is discussed in Negotiation in Action 9.2.

NEGOTIATION IN ACTION 9.2

During the Patriots' game against the Green Bay Packers in 2006, and again against the New York Jets in 2007, Belichick had the same assistant coach film the Packers' and Jets' private defensive signals. Belichick and the Patriots were punished for the second offense, but not the first. The owners of the Patriots, who hired Belichick and encouraged him to win, did not publicly criticize or discipline him either time. Their silence seemed to sanction his conduct. Nor were the ethics of the owners questioned by the league, fans or media (Gino et al., 2009).

These examples illustrate powerful exceptions to our tendency to question and criticize others' ethics more than our own.

Overlooking Indirect Unethical Behavior

As with the previous examples, we do not hold people very accountable for indirect unethical behavior, even when the unethical intent is clear. We apparently do not view indirect harm to be as problematic as direct harm (Royzman & Baron, 2002). This is illustrated in Negotiation in Action 9.3.

NEGOTIATION IN ACTION 9.3

Merck, the pharmaceutical company, sold two cancer drugs to Ovation, a smaller pharmaceutical company. Since these were drugs with limited sales potential, this seemed fairly ordinary. Curiously, though, Merck continued to manufacture these drugs after the sale was completed. Shortly after the deal was closed, Ovation raised the wholesale price of one of the drugs tenfold and the price of the another one even more. Why would Merck do this? Ovation is in the business of buying small-market drugs from large firms that have public relations concerns. If Merck was aware that Ovation would do this, it may have preferred the headline, "Merck sells two drugs to Ovation" to "Merck increases cancer drug prices by 1000%" (adapted from Gino et al., 2009; Berenson, 2006).

The evidence suggests that this strategy works – we do not condemn those who use others to do their dirty work. The only exception that has been discovered is when people explicitly compare the direct and indirect actions and the harm they cause (Paharia, Kassam, Greene & Bazerman, 2009; Royzman & Baron, 2002).

Overlooking Gradual Unethical Behavior

As depicted in Negotiation in Action 9.4, others' unethical behavior that occurs in small increments rather than suddenly is not likely to be noticed (Gino et al., 2009; Tenbrunsel & Messick, 2004).

NEGOTIATION IN ACTION 9.4

Suppose an accountant with a large auditing firm is in charge of the audit of a company with a strong reputation. For three years in a row, the client's financial statements were extremely ethical and of high quality. The auditor, therefore, certified the statements and maintained an excellent relationship with the client. This year, though, the client committed some clear errors in its financial statements – one broke the law.

Alternatively, suppose the same company had stretched but not broken the law in a few areas one year, stretched the ethicality of its financial statements a bit more and committed a minor infraction of federal accounting standards the next year, stretched the ethicality of its financial statements even more severely the next year, and then committed the same violation that broke the law in the first paragraph this year. (Gino et al., 2009).

The evidence suggests that the auditor would be much less likely to refuse certification in the second paragraph than with the abrupt change described in the first paragraph.

Overlooking Unethical Processes Until the Outcome Is Bad

People are much more critical of behavior that inflicts harm – they often judge the ethicality of actions based on whether harm follows rather than on the ethicality of the choice per se. Even when people have rated the ethicality of a decision prior to learning its outcome, their opinions change when they learn the outcome. Simply put, they conclude that decisions with negative outcomes are unethical even if they did not think so before. This may mean that we ignore unethical acts if we do not know the outcome, and we may blame people too much for making sensible choices that have unlucky outcomes. An example of this outcome bias (Baron & Hershey, 1988) is presented in Negotiation in Action 9.5.

NEGOTIATION IN ACTION 9.5

A risk management consultant examines a strategic initiative being contemplated by a client that buys lucrative advisory services. The consultant notices clearly fraudulent elements in the initiative and discussed them with the client who insists there is nothing wrong with the initiative. The client also threatens to withhold future business if the consultant refuses to sanction the initiative. The consultant agrees to let it go for one year and no problems result (adapted from Gino et al., 2009).

Most people would conclude that both parties acted ethically in this case, unless six months later the company had been busted by the authorities for fraud, causing the company to go bankrupt and its 1200 employees to lose their jobs and their life savings that were 'tied up' in what is now worthless company stock.

In-Group Favoritism

Another arena in which our blindness to unethical behavior exists involves in-group favoritism and stereotyping. Our evaluations favor, and we give preference to, those who belong to the same groups as we do. Although we believe we treat everyone we encounter equally and fairly, ample evidence demonstrates that our underlying attitudes toward race, gender and other traits are more biased than we thought. As illustrated in Negotiation in Action 9.6 and again in Reading 9.1 at the end of this chapter, stereotyping, in-group favoritism and other ethical lapses unknowingly affect negotiators' judgments.

NEGOTIATION IN ACTION 9.6

In May 2009, the *Chicago Tribune* reported a special admissions program at the University of Illinois known as 'Category I.' From 2005 to 2009, approximately 800 applicants were granted admission to the school after being recommended by state lawmakers, university trustees and other powerful individuals. On average, despite their lower qualifications, the patronage applicants were admitted at higher rates than others. In what is perhaps the most notable example, a relative of Antoin "Tony" Rezko, a political fundraiser later convicted of influence peddling on behalf of disgraced former Illinois Governor Rod Blagojevich, was admitted because of the intervention of University President B. Joseph White. The Rezko relative had weak credentials and was on the verge of being rejected until the request came from White and the decision was reversed. In the uproar that followed, White resigned and the university created a "firewall" to protect the admissions process from outside influence.

Since people commonly request or provide recommendations for admission to schools, scholarships, jobs, loans and other pursuits, why is this unethical? People tend to help others who are like themselves—the same race, sex, economic background and so on rather than those who differ. In addition, recommenders tend to focus on those they are helping. They do not consider those who are disadvantaged even though they have better qualifications. When resources are limited, this "helping" behavior harms those who are more deserving (Bazerman & Tenbrunsel, 2011; Program on Negotiation, 2011; Cohen, St. Clair, & Malone, 2009).

TACTICS THAT COMMONLY RAISE ETHICAL QUESTIONS

The dilemmas of honesty and trust are at the heart of ethics discussions in negotiation because we must decide how much information to disclose and how honest or accurate it should be. We must also judge the believability of the information received from the other party and how much to rely on it. A controversial article published in 1968 enhanced the importance of these dilemmas. The author argued that bluffing, exaggeration, conscious misstatements and the concealment of important facts, all of which are used to persuade others to agree, should be expected in business negotiations. If an executive or negotiator fails to use these tactics or feels compelled to tell the whole truth, he or she is probably ignorant (Carr, 1968). This conception of negotiation has been criticized (Allhoff, 2003; Koehn, 1997), but it raises an important question – what is or is not ethical? Table 9.2 summarizes the kinds of tactics that often raise ethical questions.

Most negotiators accept traditional competitive bargaining tactics as ethical. They also believe that emotional deception such as faking anger, disappointment and satisfaction is more ethical than distorting information, lies of commission and other verbal misrepresentations. Insincere threats or promises and other bluffing, corrupting the other party's reputation by misrepresenting information to his or her peers, bribing the other side to share information, spying and other inappropriate information gathering ploys are commonly deemed unethical and inappropriate (Fulmer, Barry & Long, 2009; Robinson et al., 2000; O'Connor & Carnevale, 1997).

Table 9.2 Categories of Ethically Questionable Tactics

Category	Examples
Traditional Competitive Bargaining	Exaggerating opening offers; Conveying a false impression regarding your sense of urgency; Lies of omission such as not disclosing target and resistance points
Attacking Opponent's Network	Attempting to get your opponent fired so that he or she is replaced; Threatening to make your opponent look weak or foolish in front of others to whom he or she is accountable; Talking directly to the people to whom your opponent reports to undermine their confidence in him or her as a negotiator
False Promises	Promising that good things will happen to your opponent if he or she gives you what you want, even if you know that you can't or won't deliver these things; Offering future concessions that you don't intend to make in return for immediate concessions; Guaranteeing that your constituents will agree with the terms of your settlement even though you know they probably won't
Misrepresentation	Intentionally misrepresenting information to your opponent to strengthen your arguments or positions; Denying the validity of that information presented by the other party that weakens your position, though you know it to be true and valid
Inappropriate Information Gathering	Paying your friends, associates and contacts to gain information about an opponent's negotiating position; Cultivating the other party's friendship with expensive gifts, entertainment or personal favors to gain information about his or her negotiating position; Recruiting or hiring one of your opponent's teammates to gain confidential information about his or her negotiating position

(Adapted from Robinson et al., 2000.)

DETERMINING WHETHER NEGOTIATING BEHAVIOR IS UNETHICAL

Some people assess the ethicality of negotiation behavior by memorizing lists of actions that are unethical. While some 'universal rights' may exist, this approach is impractical. It is not possible to anticipate all actions or tactics that may be used during a negotiation that will raise ethical questions. Moreover, the availability bias discussed in Chapter 7 unduly influences our ability to accurately recall the relevant actions included on our lists.

Others have adopted simple rules for assessing ethicality. These typically involve asking basic questions before making a decision or using a particular tactic. Examples include: How would I feel if my family found out I made this decision or used this particular tactic?, or How would I feel if my decision or use of this tactic were printed in the local newspaper or aired on the 6:00 p.m. TV newscast?

A more systematic approach is provided by the four widely accepted ethical reasoning frameworks introduced earlier. These are not perfect, and they may produce conflicting results when they are all used to assess the ethicality of a particular action or decision. They do, however, provide useful guidance for thinking about questionable behavior and assessing it – if we are aware of it. They also provide a sound basis for discussing your own negotiating behavior or that of the other party if that becomes necessary.

Utilitarianism

An advocate of **utilitarianism** believes that actions *per se* are not right or wrong. Instead, they are ethical only if they produce more happiness than unhappiness for everyone affected by them – actions are ethical if they provide the greatest good for the greatest number of people. Happiness is pleasure and the avoidance of pain, and unhappiness is pain and the privation of pleasure (Mill, 1989).

Though intuitively appealing, this framework poses some difficulties. Even if your preparation enables you to identify everyone who may affect or be affected by your negotiation, assessing the happiness and unhappiness they experience may not be possible. Moreover, happiness and unhappiness are considered in the aggregate. The group as a whole may benefit, but one or more of the individuals may be unfairly disadvantaged by a particular decision or action. Many people may also care about the process that is used to produce the outcome. For them, the ends do not justify the means used to achieve them (DeGeorge, 1995).

Rights and Duties

Kant (1989) argued that only those actions undertaken from a sense of duty dictated by reason are ethical, and these duties hold for every rational being in all situations. Simply put, our actions are governed by certain universal rights, and these rights impose a corresponding duty. If, for example, you have a right to be told the truth, you have a corresponding duty to be honest with others. Breaching these rights and duties is unethical. Unlike Utilitarianism, what is right and wrong is determined by a negotiator's intentions, actions and decisions, not by their consequences (Beauchamp & Bowie, 1997).

Like Utilitarianism, this framework is not perfect. Who makes the rules and determines our universal rights and duties? Can we really be expected to know and remember them when we negotiate? How do we adapt rules or rights to fit different situations? For example, is it really unethical to lie if doing so will protect an innocent party from egregious harm? The following three-pronged test will help with these questions, but the answers are not always easy ones. To be ethical, actions must:

- Be respectful of others;
- Not preclude others from engaging in the same act; and
- Be acceptable to rational people who are acting rationally (DeGeorge, 1995).

Consider the situation described in Negotiation in Action 9.7.

NEGOTIATION IN ACTION 9.7

The CEO of a struggling business is negotiating to secure a $1.5 billion contract with a foreign government. He believes his business will fail if it does not receive the contract. He also knows the government official who will be deciding which bidder receives the contract has a substantial gambling debt that he is struggling to repay. To ensure that the contract is awarded to his firm, the CEO informs this government official that he will be paid $1 million if his firm is awarded the contract.

Is this ethical under either the *Utilitarian* or *Rights & Duties* frameworks?

A Utilitarian would argue that the CEO and all of his constituents – employees, managers, suppliers, shareholders, customers and the government official could be happy. The other bidders and their constituents, however, would be unhappy. It is not clear whether the government official's constituents would find happiness if they knew that he was interfering with the competitive bidding process. It is difficult to quantify the happiness and unhappiness experienced by these people, but many could be unhappy.

An advocate of the *Rights and Duties* approach would not find this respectful of others because the person offering the bribe does not care what happens to others over whom he gains this special advantage. Moreover, an action is not respectful if the target of the action is treated as a means to an end rather than as an end per se. The government official herein was treated as a means to an end. Whether the bribe precludes others from engaging in the same activity can be viewed in different ways. If the CEO receives the contract because of the bribe, no other firms bidding for it can receive the contract. Viewing this differently yields the same result. The CEO is using the bribe to gain a special advantage. If everyone bribes, though, no one can gain a special advantage. Thus, engaging in bribery will eventually preclude others from gaining a special advantage via bribery. Finally, bribery is not acceptable to rational people acting rationally because we may be disadvantaged and angry about it if others do it (DeGeorge, 1995).

Fairness and Justice

This framework argues that similarly situated people should be treated similarly but dissimilarly situated people should be treated dissimilarly (Rawls, 1989) This is true when determining how rewards and burdens are allocated and for the allocation itself. When deciding how to allocate rewards or burdens, we should evaluate what is fair and just from behind a 'veil of ignorance' – if we knew nothing about a person's social status, economic position, occupation and the like, how would we distribute the resources or burdens in question? The consequences matter, as they do under Utilitarianism, but for different reasons. Whether an allocation is just depends on the fairness of the distribution and the fairness of the procedures used to determine it.

Like its predecessors, this framework is not perfect. Who determines whether people are similarly situated? Who determines whether treatment is similar? Another problem involves timing – the fairness of procedures can usually be determined immediately. Since outcomes may be delayed, however, it may not be possible to assess their fairness when we make a decision.

The scenario depicted in Negotiation in Action 9.8 illustrates how this framework might be applied.

NEGOTIATION IN ACTION 9.8

Linda was removed from a graduate business program for excessive absenteeism, allegedly in violation of the College's attendance policy. According to the Director of MBA Programs, the attendance policy was adopted to "encourage participation in classroom exercises, in-class case analyses and discussions." Linda attempted to negotiate her reinstatement with the Director. According to the professors teaching these classes, participation was essential to the success of some classes, but it was not essential or even required in others. The policy was not published anywhere. Nor had it been communicated to Linda or any of the other students. Thus, she did not know, or have any basis for knowing, that absences were grounds for removal. Linda was removed for missing classes because she had to make a presentation to her employer's senior management team. Some of her classmates were allowed to miss classes because of previously scheduled family vacations. Finally, the number of absences that could be missed without incurring disciplinary action was set arbitrarily. There was no basis for the number of classes – 3 – that students could miss without incurring disciplinary penalties. When Linda presented this evidence while attempting to negotiate her reinstatement with the Director, he refused to change his decision. Nor did he offer any evidence, or even an explanation, to support his decision or counter Linda's evidence.

Was the decision to remove Linda from this program ethical under the fairness and justice framework?

The process and the decision were deemed unfair by a hearing officer because the policy did not effectively serve a legitimate educational purpose, it was not published or communicated to Linda or to any other student, it was inconsistently enforced, and it was based on an arbitrarily determined standard – the number of absences that would warrant removal from the program. For this reason, the Director's decision to remove Linda was unethical under the *Fairness and Justice* framework and it was overturned. From behind the veil of ignorance, the burdens were allocated unfairly, and the procedures used to determine them were unfair.

Social Contract

Unlike Kant's (1989) contention that there are universal rights and duties with which we must comply, the *Social Contract* framework argues that the ethicality of actions or decisions must be judged in accordance with the customs and norms of the community in which the negotiation takes place.

What is best for the common good determines what is right, and only members of the community can determine what constitutes the common good and whether particular actions are consistent with it. These customs and norms are important because they reflect the general will of the community and help to ensure order by providing the ground rules that bind an individual and the community (Rousseau, 1947).

To illustrate, both law and custom in the United States prohibit bribery. If the firm discussed in Negotiation in Action 9.7 is a U.S. company, it would be in violation of the *social contract* framework – whether it was operating domestically or internationally. In other parts of the world, however, bribery is viewed more positively and even expected. Managers in the mining, textile and information technology industries report that bribes are widely expected in their dealings with firms in countries that make up the Indian Ocean rim (Pedigo & Marshall, 2009). Bribery in this region, therefore, would not run afoul of the social contract framework.

This framework is also plagued by several imperfections. Sometimes it is difficult to determine the meaning of 'community.' Is it the nation, state, city or neighborhood? Or, is it now the world because of globalization? Others might argue that it should be defined occupationally. Are we concerned with the common good of engineers or lawyers or medical professionals? Are we concerned with all business transactions, or should we define what is customary or normal more narrowly, for example, in terms of labor negotiations? How do we define the 'general will' and 'common good' of the people as our communities change and become more diverse? What do we do with independent thinkers – were people like Martin Luther King, Jr. unethical because they dared to challenge the status quo? These and other questions must be answered to transform this from a fairly abstract notion to one that is more pragmatic (Hitt, 1990).

Table 9.3 summarizes these four major frameworks, their key proponents and the tests recommended for applying each of them to actions or decisions. The negotiation described in Negotiation in Action 9.9 between Ben and Sammy provides a useful tool for comparing the conclusions that are drawn when each of these frameworks is applied.

Table 9.3   Frameworks for Assessing the Ethicality of Negotiation Tactics

Framework	An Ethical Tactic is:	Proponent	Test
Utilitarianism	One that produces the greatest good for the greatest number of people	Bentham, Mill	They are ethical if those who are affected by them experience more happiness than unhappiness
Rights & Duties	One that conforms to universal rights and duties	Kant	They must be respectful of others, not preclude others from using them and be accepted by rational people acting rationally
Fairness & Justice	One that treats people equitably	Rawls	From behind the veil of ignorance, similarly situated people must be treated similarly
Social Contract	One that conforms to the community's social norms/customs	Rousseau	They must comply with the customs & social norms of the community in which the negotiation occurs

---

NEGOTIATION IN ACTION 9.9

A Negotiation Between the State and Sammy

Ben is the Deputy Director of Information Technology (IT) for his state. In this capacity, he had to find a site to locate radio towers to be used by law enforcement personnel to improve communications. The best site he found was on an Indian reservation. He secured a meeting with Sammy, the "Head of State" of this Indian tribe, to discuss this matter.

Sammy showed up for their meeting more than an hour late. When he finally entered the room, he asked, "Are you the governor?" Ben, of course, replied that he was not. Stating in no uncertain terms that he would discuss this with nobody but the governor, Sammy walked out. Ben went back to his office and shared his experience with Bob, the Director of IT, and the governor. The governor was unwilling to meet with Sammy. He sent Ben and Bob back to meet with him, along with a letter authorizing them to negotiate on his behalf. When Sammy arrived, this time more than five hours late, he acknowledged Ben and asked Bob, "Are you the governor? Bob said, "Yes I am" and they proceeded to negotiate. Sammy agreed to allow the state to use the site. Bob and Ben agreed to grant Sammy and another tribe in the state access to radio frequencies. All parties were satisfied with this outcome (Personal Communication).

1. Using each of the four major frameworks, did Ben and Bob behave ethically or unethically in this situation? Why?

2. How could they have achieved an equally positive outcome without raising ethical questions?

An alternative framework for assessing the ethicality of negotiating behavior is discussed in Reading 9.2 at the end of this chapter.

THE CONSEQUENCES OF UNETHICAL NEGOTIATING BEHAVIOR

As noted previously, negotiators use unethical tactics to help them profit or win, because they are greedy or to retaliate against others for negotiating unethically. Do unethical negotiators fare better than ethical ones and accomplish these things? In other words, do unethical tactics help us achieve more favorable outcomes? The evidence generally suggests that they do not, and they often hurt us. Personally, unethical behavior may harm your reputation. Negotiators tend to operate in a fairly tight network and word spreads quickly, especially in this era of electronic communication. If your reputation as an unethical negotiator precedes you, subsequent negotiations will probably be quite difficult. The other party may bargain more competitively, and this will make it harder for you to create and claim value. In fact, negotiators who discover they have been duped by the other party's unethical behavior seek retribution, even if it is costly to do so. Experienced negotiators are usually able to claim more value than others, but not when they have reputations for being unethical (Schweitzer, Ordonez & Douma, 2004; Croson, Boles & Murnighan, 2003; Tinsley, O'Connor & Sullivan, 2002).

LEGAL PITFALLS WHEN YOU NEGOTIATE

Even if we win, most of us do not enjoy being sued. Misrepresentations of material facts or lies about them may raise allegations of fraud if the other party relies on them to his or her detriment. More than a decade ago, Shell (1999) argued that concerns about fraud in negotiation are raised most commonly when people lie or misrepresent information about their BATNAs, or about the condition of the object for which they are negotiating. A BATNA is an objective state of affairs. It is material and subject to litigation. If the other party relies on your knowingly misrepresenting BATNA to his or her detriment, you have committed fraud. Finally, knowingly misrepresenting the condition of the object you are trying to sell, or the nature or quality of the services you will provide, raises legal questions because they are material facts.

Lies or misrepresentations about positions, interests, priorities and preferences, however, are generally not illegal. There are, of course, exceptions to this generalization but there is no legal obligation to be truthful about positions such as opening offers, demands, target points and resistance points, priorities, preferences, or the value or importance of items in negotiation. These are traditional competitive tactics and usually not material facts under the common law. If someone relies on these misrepresentations to his or her detriment, it is not actionable fraud. While it is not clear what a negotiator would hope to gain by misrepresenting his or her interests, this does not appear to raise serious ethical or legal questions. Since negotiators are motivated by self-interest, there is generally no legal duty of good faith when it comes to communicating your interests. In support of this contention about misrepresenting positions and interests, Shell (1999) cited the court's ruling in *Feldman v. Allegheny International* (1988):

In a business transaction, both sides presumably try to get the best deal. That is the essence of bargaining and the free market. . . . So, one cannot characterize self-interest as bad faith. No particular demand in negotiations could be termed dishonest, even if it seemed outrageous to the other party. The proper recourse is to walk away from the bargaining table, not sue for 'bad faith' negotiations.

More recently, the courts have demonstrated more interest in the negotiation process. For example, negotiators who make explicit claims about better offers that do not exist, or fail to follow through on promises made about the negotiation process (e.g., continuing to "shop" an offer to others after promising the person with whom they have reached a tentative agreement that they would not do so), may be liable for damages. In addition, bidders who collude in a manner that creates value for themselves and for the seller may be running afoul of the law if their collusion inhibits competition or efficiency. Finally, it is acceptable for an agent to represent an undisclosed principal if the other party has no reason to exclude him or her from the negotiation. It is not legally acceptable, however, for an agent to represent an undisclosed principal if, for example, a seller has a reasonable suspicion that the principal has paid others not to bid for the object you are trying to sell at auction (Subramanian, 2010).

CONCLUSION AND IMPLICATIONS FOR PRACTICE

Negotiations are complex, dynamic processes where multiple stakeholders, interests and values are in conflict or unknown, and the laws are often unclear. This uncertainty and ambiguity, the availability of deception and other variants of untruthfulness, and the perceptions that these tactics will help negotiators profit, win or retaliate, make ethically questionable negotiating behavior common. Ethics are about what is right and wrong, so adhering to what is "right" should trump self-interest. This sounds easy but it is challenging because definitions of what is right and wrong vary, and negotiators are generally motivated by self-interest. Moreover, we may fail to recognize unethical behavior because of the decision-making errors discussed in Chapter 7 and in this chapter. Since unethical behavior at the table leads to lesser outcomes and more difficult processes, now and in the future, it should be avoided. That, however, is often easier said than done. The following suggestions should help.

1. Engage in self-assessment. To determine whether your behavior is ethical, refer to the SINS Scale and Reading 9.1 at the end of this chapter. Ask others for their assessments of your approach before you implement and execute it. Consider the four frameworks discussed in this chapter or the three discussed in Reading 9.2. Ask yourself: *Is it legal? It is right? Who will be affected, and how? Does it fit my values and those of the people I'm representing? How will it reflect on me and the people I'm representing? How will I feel if my family knows what tactics I used or if my behavior appears in the news? Would I be comfortable if the other negotiator used these tactics against me?*

2. Create an honest negotiating environment. Prepare well, build rapport, test your assumptions, share your true interests, preferences and priorities, and inquire about the other party's true interests, preferences and priorities. This should help you manage the dilemmas of honesty and trust by helping you create value without subjecting yourself to any appreciable risks.

3. Frame arguments ethically. Consult Table 9.4 for some alternative ways to frame the kinds of potentially unethical arguments that are commonly made in a negotiation. Some of these suggestions are identical to those recommended for avoiding decision-making errors.

4. Detect and call out the other negotiator's deception. This should protect you against his or her efforts to take advantage of you. We tend not to be very good at recognizing deception, but there are some signals you can learn (see Table 6.5). If the other side insists on using deception or other unethical tactics, do not ignore them, because that may sanction his or her conduct. Nor should you respond in kind because that will escalate the conflict, or at least the use of these tactics. Instead, name them. Calling out such behavior lets the other side know you are aware of what they are doing. This inhibits further use of these tactics because your awareness diminishes their effectiveness. If this does not work adequately, stop the negotiation and negotiate the *process*. If you and the other party realize that your exchange is unproductive, and you both want to achieve a beneficial outcome, talk about how you want to negotiate. At the very least, set some ground rules to restore ethicality to your negotiation.

5. Do not stoop to another negotiator's level when the negotiator uses unethical tactics. As desirable as it may seem to retaliate against other negotiators for trying to dupe you with unethical tactics, the benefits you realize from meting out this punishment will likely be fleeting and far less beneficial than creating value and claiming most of it for yourself. Unethical negotiating behavior generally harms reputations, and it makes future negotiations more difficult because you will encounter others who will negotiate more aggressively against you. If you choose to negotiate unethically anyway, you may achieve greater outcomes if the other party will also benefit from this approach because he or she is likely to turn a blind eye to it. If you choose to negotiate unethically, you may achieve greater outcomes if the other party will also benefit from this approach, because he or she will turn a blind

eye to it. But keep in mind the harm you may suffer and how others will negotiate against you if you develop a reputation as an unethical negotiator.

Table 9.4   Alternatives to Lying

Instead of Lying About	Try This
Bottom Line	Blocking maneuvers: Ask about their bottom line; Say, "I'm not free to disclose that"; Tell the truth about your goal; Focus on your problems or needs
Lack of Authority	Obtain only limited authority so that you don't have to lie; Require ratification by your constituents
Availability of Alternatives	Initiate efforts to improve your alternatives; Stress opportunities and uncertainties; Be satisfied with the status quo
Commitment to Positions	Commit to general goals; Commit to standards; Commit to addressing the other side's interests
Phony Issues	Inject new issues with real value; Make a true wish list
Threats	Use cooling-off periods; Suggest third-party help; Discuss the use of a formula or objective standards
Intentions	Make only promises that you can and will keep
Facts	Focus on uncertainty regarding the facts; Use language carefully; Express your opinions

(Adapted from Shell, 1999.)

6. Beware of waiting to see the results of decisions or actions to decide if they were ethical. Due to outcome bias we generally do not believe choices are unethical unless they instill harmful outcomes on others. Nor do we think others are behaving unethically if their actions benefit us or gradually (rather than abruptly) become unethical. Using actions that indirectly harm others and delegating unethical behavior to others may afford you temporary insulation from criticism and enable you to defer other negative attributions for a while, but these options do not make your choice ethical. To avoid these ethical lapses, consider multiple options simultaneously. In addition to the other suggestions in this chapter, compare an ethical option to a more visceral choice in order to highlight the ethical implications of the decision (Program on Negotiation, 2011).

STUDENT STUDY SITE

Visit the Student Study Site at **www.sagepub.com/hames** for additional learning tools.

KEY TERMS

Delegating unethical tasks

Fairness and justice

Gradual unethical behavior

Inappropriate information gathering

Indirect unethical behavior

In-group favoritism

Misrepresentation

Outcome bias

Rights and duties

Social contract

Utilitarianism

REFERENCES

Allhoff, F. (2003). Business bluffing reconsidered, *Journal of Business Ethics*, 45, 283-289.

Anton, R. J. (1990). Drawing the line: An exploratory test of ethical behavior in negotiation, *The International Journal of Conflict Management*, 1, 265-280.

Banaji, M. R., Bazerman, M. H. & Chugh, D. (2003). How (un)ethical are you? *Harvard Business Review,* December, 2003, 56-64.

Baron, J., & Hershey, J. C. (1988). Outcome bias in decision evaluation. *Journal of Personality and Social Psychology*, 54, 569-579.

Bazerman, M., & Chugh, D. (2005). Bounded Awareness: Focusing Problems in Negotiation. In L. Thompson (Ed.), *Frontiers of Social Psychology: Negotiations*. College Park, MD: Psychology Press, 7-26.

Bazerman, M. H. & Moore, D. A. (2008). *Judgment in managerial decision making, 7th*. New York: Wiley.

Bazerman, M. H., Moore, D. A., Tetlock, P. E., & Tanlu, L. (2006). Reports of solving the conflicts of interest in auditing are highly exaggerated. *Academy of Management Review*, 31(1), 1-7.

Bazerman, M. H. & Tenbrunsel, A. E. (2011). *Blind spots: Why we fail to do what's right and what to do about it*. Princeton, NJ: Princeton University Press.

Beauchamp, T. L. & Bowie, N. E. (1997). *Ethical Theory and Business, 5th*. Upper Saddle River, NJ: Prentice Hall.

Berenson, A. (2006). A cancer drug's big price rise is cause for concern. *NYTimes.com*, March 12.

Bies, R. & Moag, J. (1986). Interactional justice: Communication criteria of fairness. In R. J. Lewicki, B. H. Sheppard & M. H. Bazerman (Eds.), *Research on negotiation in organizations*, 1. Greenwich, CT: JAI Press, 43-55.

Boles, T. L., Croson, R. T. A. & Murnighan, J. K. (2000). Deception and retribution in repeated ultimatum bargaining, *Organizational Behavior and Human Decision Processes*, 83, 235-259.

Carr, A. Z. (1968). Is business bluffing ethical? *Harvard Business Review*, 46, 143-153.

Christie, R. & Geis, G. L. (Eds). (1970). *Studies in Machiavellianism*, New York: Academic Press.

Cohen, J. S., St. Clair, S. & Malone, T. (2009). Clout goes to college: Rezko relative is among those admitted to U. of I. in shadow system influenced by trustees and other insiders, *Chicago Tribune*. May 29, 1.

Croson, R., Boles, T. L. & Murnighan, J. K. (2003). Cheap talk in bargaining experiments: Lying and threats in ultimatum games, *Journal of Economic Behavior & Organization*, 51, 143-159

Crott, H., Kayser, E. & Lamm, H. (1980). The effects of information exchange and communication in an asymmetrical negotiation situation, *European Journal of Social Psychology*, 10, 149-163.

DeGeorge, R. T. (1995). *Business ethics, 4th*. Englewood Cliffs, NJ: Prentice Hall.

Elahee, M. N. & Brooks, C. M. (2004). Trust and negotiation tactics: Perceptions about business-to-business negotiations in Mexico, *The Journal of Business & Industrial Marketing*, 19(6), 397-404.

Epley, N. & Dunning, D. (2000). Feeling "holier than thou": Are self-serving assessments produced by errors in self- or social prediction? *Journal of Personality and Social Psychology,* 79(6), 861-875.

Feldman v. Allegheny International, Inc. 850 F.2d 1217 (7th. Cir., 1988).

Fulmer, I. S., Barry, B. & Long, D. A. (2009). Lying and smiling: Informational and emotional deception in negotiation, *Journal of Business Ethics*, 88, 691-709.

Gino, F., Moore, D. A. & Bazerman, M. H. (2009). See no evil: When we overlook other people's unethical behavior. In R. M. Kramer, A. E. Tenbrunsel & M. H. Bazerman (Eds.), *Social decision making: Social dilemmas, social values, and ethical judgments*. New York: Psychology Press, 241-263.

Hegarty, W. & Sims, H. P. (1978). Some determinants of unethical decision behavior: An experiment, *Journal of Applied Psychology*, 63, 451-457.

Hitt, W. (1990). *Ethics and leadership: Putting theory into practice*. Columbus, OH: Battelle Press.

Kant, I. (1989). The foundations of the metaphysics of morals. In L. P. Pojman (Ed.), *Ethical theory: Classical and contemporary readings*. Belmont, CA: Wadsworth, 161-180.

Koehn, D. (1997). Business and game playing: The false analogy, *Journal of Business Ethics*, 16, 1447-14452.

Lax, D. A. & Sebenius, J. K. (1986). *The manager as negotiator: Bargaining for cooperation and competitive gain*. New York: The Free Press.

Lewicki, R. J. & Robinson, R. J. (1998). Ethical and unethical bargaining tactics: An empirical study, *Journal of Business Ethics*, 17, 665-682.

Lewicki, R. J. & Spencer, G. (1991). *Ethical relativism and negotiating tactics: Factors affecting their perceived ethicality,* Paper presented at the annual meeting of the *Academy of Management*, August, Miami, FL.

Messick, D. M., & Bazerman, M. H. (1996). Ethical leadership and the psychology of decision making, *Sloan Management Review*, Winter, 9-22.

Mill, J. S. (1989). Utilitarianism. In L. P. Pojman (Ed.), *Ethical theory: Classical and contemporary readings*. Belmont, CA: Wadsworth, 161-180.

Moore, D., Tetlock, P. E., Tanlu, L., & Bazerman, M. H. (2006). Conflicts of interest and the case of auditor independence: Moral seduction and strategic issue cycling. *Academy of Management Review*, 31, 10-29.

O'Connor, K. M. & Carnevale, P. J. (1997). A nasty but effective negotiation strategy: Misrepresentation of a common-value issue, *Personality and Social Psychology Bulletin*, 23, 504-515.

Olekalns, M. & Smith, P. L. (2007). Loose with the truth: Predicting deception in negotiation, *Journal of Business Ethics*, 76, 225-238.

Paharia, N., Kassam, K. S., Greene, J. D. & Bazerman, M. H. (2009). Dirty work, clean hands: The moral psychology of indirect agency, *Organizational Behavior and Human Decision Processes*, 109(2), 134-141.

Pedigo, K. L. & Marshall, V. (2009). Bribery: Australian managers' experiences and responses when operating in international markets, *Journal of Business Ethics*, 87, 59-74.

Perry, G. M. & Nixon, C. J. (2005). The influence of role models on negotiation ethics of college students, *Journal of Business Ethics*, 62, 25-40.

Program on Negotiation. (2010). Are you prepared for dirty tricks, *Negotiation*, 13(8), August, 1-4.

Program on Negotiation (2011). Our ethical "blind spots" in negotiation, *Negotiation,* 14(4), 1-5.

Rawls, J. (1989). A liberal theory of justice. L. P. Pojman (Ed.), *Ethical theory: Classical and contemporary readings*. Belmont, CA: Wadsworth, 161-180.

Robinson, R., Lewicki, R. J. & Donahue, E. (2000). Extending and testing a five factor model of ethical and unethical bargaining tactics: The SINS scale, *Journal of Organizational Behavior*, 21, 649-664.

Rousseau, J. J. (1947). *The social contract*. New York: Hafner Publishing Commune.

Royzman, E. B., & Baron, J. (2002). The preference for indirect harm. *Social Justice Research*, 15, 165-184.

Schweitzer, M., Ordonez, L. & Douma, B. (2004). Goal setting as a motivator of unethical behavior, *Academy of Management Journal*, 47, 422-432.

Shell, G. R. (1999). *Bargaining for advantage: Negotiation strategies for reasonable people*. New York: Viking.

Sims, R. L. (2002). Support of the use of deception within the work environment: A comparison of Israeli and United States employee attitudes, *Journal of Business Ethics*, 35, 27-34.

Steinel, W. & de Dreu, C. K. W. (2004). Social motives and strategic misrepresentation in social decision making, *Journal of Personality and Social Psychology*, 86, 419- 434.

Subramanian, G. (2010). *Negotiauctions: New Dealmaking Strategies for a competitive marketplace*. New York: Norton.

Tenbrunsel, A. & Diekmann, K. (2007). When you're tempted to deceive, *Negotiation*, 10, 9-11.

Tenbrunsel, A.E. & Messick, D.M. (2004). Ethical fading: The role of self deception in unethical behavior. *Social Justice Research, 17*(2),223-236.

Tinsley, C. H., O'Connor, K. M. & Sullivan, B. A. (2002). Tough guys finish last: The perils of a distributive reputation, *Organizational Behavior and Human Decision Processes*, 88, 621-642.

Volkema, R. (1997). Perceptual differences in appropriateness and likelihood of use of negotiation behaviors: A cross-cultural analysis, *The International Executive*, 39(3), 335-350.

Volkema, R. (1998). A comparison of perceptions of ethical negotiation behavior in Mexico and the United States, *International Journal of Conflict Management*, 9(3), 218-233.

Volkema, R. (1999). Ethicality in negotiation: An analysis of perceptual similarities and differences between Brazil and the United States, *Journal of Business Research*, 45, 49-67.

Volkema, R. & Fleury, M. T. L. (2002). Alternative negotiation conditions and the choice of negotiation tactics: A cross-cultural comparison, *Journal of Business Ethics*, 36, 381-398.

READINGS

Reading 9.1

WHY YOUR NEGOTIATING BEHAVIOR MAY BE ETHICALLY CHALLENGED AND HOW TO FIX IT

Program on Negotiation

Negotiators sometimes make decisions that clash with their ethical standards. Identify pitfalls that could endanger your organization and your reputation.

Financial improprieties destroy energy-trading firm Enron and accounting firm Arthur Andersen. A steroids scandal is exposed in Major League Baseball. Two pharmaceutical companies quietly negotiate a deal that causes the prices of certain cancer drugs to skyrocket.

News stories such as these suggest that a few "bad apples" are capable of tainting entire industries with their greed and twisted motives. But recent psychological research by Harvard Business School professor Max H. Bazerman and his colleagues paints a more nuanced portrait of ethics violations—both those that make headlines and those that do not.

You may think your ethics are beyond reproach, but new research offers evidence that the most well-intentioned negotiators routinely and unconsciously commit ethical lapses and tolerate such lapses in others. Few professionals consciously set out to violate the law or their own moral standards, according to Bazerman. Rather, in the context of negotiation, a range of common cognitive patterns can lead us to engage in or condone "ordinary unethical behaviors" that we would otherwise condemn.

Identify Your Own Ethical Lapses

Here are three types of ordinary unethical behavior that you might be tempted to engage in during a negotiation:

1. Creating Value at the Expense of Outsiders.

In the late 1990s, pharmaceutical company Schering-Plough filed a patent-infringement lawsuit to prevent rival Upsher-Smith from introducing a generic version of one of Schering-Plough's products. The two companies reached an out-of-court settlement: Upsher-Smith agreed to delay its generic drug, and Schering-Plough agreed to pay Upsher-Smith $60 million for five unrelated products.

Source: Banaji, M. R., Bazerman, M. H. & Chugh, D. (2003). How (Un)Ethical are you?, *Harvard Business Review*, 81(12), 56–64.

Note: This article first appeared in *Negotiation,* a monthly newsletter published by the Program on Negotiation at Harvard Law School, www.pon.harvard.edu. Copyright 2006–2011 Harvard University.

The U.S. Federal Trade Commission (FTC) filed a complaint against the two companies, arguing that Schering-Plough made the payment to keep Upsher-Smith's generic product off the market. Bazerman, an expert witness for the FTC in the case, viewed the agreement as an attempt by the companies to create value at the expense of consumers. The administrative law judge in the case ruled in favor of the firms, arguing that the FTC had not offered evidence linking the market delay to the $60 million payment. Ultimately, the FTC commissioners overruled the judge, insisting that the firms would not have arrived at the two agreements independently.

Scholars at the Program on Negotiation at Harvard Law School encourage negotiators to work together to create value. Whether it leads to higher sales, better products, or more efficient services, value creation typically benefits not only the parties involved but also society at large.

Unfortunately, we sometimes focus so narrowly on creating value for those at the bargaining table that we overlook the effects of our agreements on our customers, our community, and our society. Such "parasitic value creation" is most likely in small markets with only two or three major players, according to Bazerman. Future generations also can be the victims of parasitic value creation.

Rather than scrapping any agreement that might have a negative impact on some, Bazerman advises you and your counterpart to consider how the value you're creating for yourselves compares to the impact of your agreement on parties not at the table. If the agreement would achieve a net increase in value to society, you should be able to proceed with a clean conscience.

2. Stereotyping Some, Favoring Others.

Have you ever felt annoyed at a female negotiator who was acting assertively? Have you ever jumped to conclusions about a counterpart after hearing his accent or learning of his religious beliefs?

We like to think we treat everyone we encounter equally and fairly. Yet most people who take a simple online test are surprised to discover that their underlying attitudes toward race, gender, and other traits are more biased than they thought. If you believe you're immune to pernicious stereotypes, try the Implicit Association Test (IAT) for yourself at http://implicit.harvard.edu/implicit. The test, developed by researchers Anthony Greenwald of the University of Washington, Mahzarin R. Banaji of Harvard University, and Brian Nosek of the University of Virginia, reveals deeply rooted attitudes that can influence our judgments. For example, test takers who think they are free of racial bias nonetheless often have more difficulty associating the word "good" with "Black" than with "White."

In negotiation, such unconscious stereotypes can be compounded by *in-group favoritism,* or the tendency to evaluate positively and give preference to those who belong to the same groups you do. When you have favors to award, such as a job or a construction contract, it can feel good to grant a neighbor or a relative special access. Unfortunately, members of privileged groups tend to benefit from such perks at the expense of the less privileged.

3. Ignoring a Conflict of Interest.

What led to the downfall of Enron auditor Arthur Andersen in 2002? A desire to keep the client happy, says Bazerman. In 2000, Enron paid Andersen $25 million in auditing fees and $27 million in consulting fees. A clear conflict of interest existed between Andersen's responsibility to conduct unbiased, impartial audits and its motivation to gain increasingly lucrative consulting contracts from Enron.

Psychological research shows that when decision makers have a motivation to interpret data in a certain way, they are incapable of being truly objective. Yet years after the fall of Enron and Arthur Andersen, a conflict of interest persists in the auditing industry.

Because it's impossible to perfectly align an agent's interests with those of the client, conflicts of interest are particularly common in industries where agents play a role, such as real estate, law, and banking. Whenever you're negotiating on another party's behalf, recognize that it will be difficult for you to offer unbiased advice. Work with your client to structure incentives that will meet her goals, back up your advice with objective analyses, and allow the client to monitor your decisions. Though such measures may sacrifice a bit of short-term profit, they'll pay off in the form of repeat business and a reputation for honesty.

Identify the Ethical Lapses of Others

By overlooking or forgiving unethical behavior that other people commit, we become complicit in their actions. Here are three ways in which observers contribute to unethical practices, as described in a new paper, entitled "See No Evil: When We Overlook Other People's Unethical Behavior," by Francesca Gino and Don A. Moore of Carnegie Mellon University and Bazerman:

1. **Overlooking behavior that would harm us if exposed.** This past December, a report issued by former senator George Mitchell revealed the names of 80 baseball players, representing all 30 major league teams, who allegedly used steroids and growth hormones. The rampant use of performance-enhancing drugs was an open secret in baseball for years, yet when negotiating players' contracts, Major League Baseball (MLB) and the players' union apparently never questioned dramatic changes in certain players' physique and power.

Why did officials look the other way? According to Gino, Moore, and Bazerman, MLB leaders succumbed to *motivated blindness,* or the common tendency to overlook others' ethical lapses when confronting the behavior would harm us. Artificially pumped-up players were breaking performance records, boosting ticket sales and TV viewership. Addressing their steroid use would have jeopardized revenues.

As noted earlier, it's virtually impossible for people to view information without bias when they have a stake in the outcome. That's why broad policy changes are generally the only solution to motivated blindness. Once MLB instituted a strict policy of random drug testing, steroid use fell among players.

2. **Excusing those who delegate unethical behavior.** When powerful people and organizations cause harm, they sometimes do so indirectly through negotiations with others. Companies outsource production to countries where environmental and labor standards are lax. Managers tell their subordinates to "do whatever it takes" to close a deal.

Here's one possible real-world example of a company delegating unethical behavior. In 2005, pharmaceutical giant Merck sold the rights to two slow-selling cancer drugs, Mustargen and Cosmegen, to lesser-known Ovation Pharmaceuticals. To the shock of doctors and patients, Ovation then raised the wholesale price of Mustargen roughly tenfold and the price of Cosmegen even higher. Meanwhile, Merck continued to manufacture the drugs and supply them to Ovation, according to Alex Berenson of the *New York Times.*

If producing the drugs was a distraction, why did Merck continue to manufacture them after the sale? Why not retain ownership and simply raise prices?

By selling the rights to the drugs to Ovation, Merck was able to increase profits without incurring the negative publicity of significantly raising the prices of cancer drugs, write Gino, Moore, and Bazerman. Ovation has a history of buying small-market drugs from large firms and dramatically raising the drugs' prices. Merck may have anticipated Ovation's price increase and shared indirectly in the resulting profits.

In a recent experimental study that attempted to mirror the Merck-Ovation case, Harvard researchers Neeru Paharia, Karim S. Kassam, Joshua D. Green, and Bazerman found that participants did indeed view indirect harmful actions more favorably than equivalent harmful actions carried out directly. When you see negotiators delegating unethical behaviors to others, hold them accountable.

6 Guidelines for More Ethical Negotiations:

1. Weigh benefits achieved at the table against harms inflicted on outsiders.

2. Accept that we're all susceptible to stereotypes, and don't give favors to insiders.

3. Speak up against policies that implicitly promote or condone unethical behavior.

4. When negotiating as an agent, try to align your incentives with your client's.

5. Don't excuse unethical behavior that's been delegated to another party.

6. Hold negotiators accountable for their decisions, not just their results.

Judging outcomes rather than processes. Consider these two scenarios:

A. A toy company contracts with a firm in another country to manufacture some of its products. The toy company does not test the products for lead before selling them, as the expensive testing is not required by U.S. law. A number of children become gravely ill after playing with the toys, which are found to contain lead.

B. A toy company contracts with a firm in another country to manufacture some of its products. Before selling the products, the company discovers that

they contain lead. The company sells the products anyway and makes a profit. No children are injured by the lead.

How would you judge the ethics of the toy company in each scenario? In a recent experiment, Gino, Moore, and Bazerman presented some participants with a scenario resembling A and others with a scenario resembling B. Participants were more critical of the company's actions when children were harmed by the toys than when no children were harmed—although the company's behavior clearly was more unethical in the latter case.

When we focus on outcomes rather than processes in this manner, we allow problematic decisions to slide until they produce predictable bad outcomes. On the flip side, we may condemn negotiators too harshly for making careful decisions that have unlucky outcomes. Organizations can curb this bias by holding negotiators accountable not only for results but also for decisions made along the way.

Addressing Ethical Lapses

Learning that all negotiators are susceptible to the unconscious biases we've discussed should spur you to examine your own decisions more critically. In addition, awareness of these errors should motivate you to probe other negotiators' decisions and behaviors.

Because cognitive biases are so deeply ingrained, however, awareness is not a cure-all. When a conflict of interest exists, we can never completely cleanse our decisions of self-interest. When someone delegates unethical behavior, the behavior may go undetected. To reduce the harmful effects of individual decisions, Bazerman and his colleagues argue, leaders must make structural changes within their organizations and industries to reduce opportunities to behave unethically—or else be held responsible for the ethical lapses that occur on their watch.

Thinking Further 9.1

1. Do you agree that it is unethical to create value at the expense of others or to favor some people over others? Why or why not?

2. Do we overlook unethical behavior intentionally or is it really unconscious behavior? Why?

Reading 9.2

THREE SCHOOLS OF BARGAINING ETHICS

G. Richard Shell

The three schools of bargaining ethics I want to introduce for your consideration are (1) the "It's a game" Poker School, (2) the "Do the right thing even if it hurts" Idealist School, and (3) the "What goes around, comes around" Pragmatist School.

Let's look at each one in turn. As I describe these schools, try to decide which aspects of them best reflect your own attitudes. After you figure out where you stand today, take a moment and see if that is where you ought to be. My advice is to aim as high as you can, consistent with your genuinely held beliefs about bargaining. In the pressured world of practice, people tend to slide down rather than climb up when it comes to ethical standards.

The "It's a Game" Poker School

The Poker School of ethics sees negotiation as a "game" with certain "rules." The rules are defined by the law. Conduct within the rules is ethical. Conduct outside the rules is unethical.

The modern founder of the Poker School was Albert Z. Carr, a former Special Consultant to President Harry Truman. Carr wrote a book in the 1960s called, appropriately enough, *Business as a Game.* In a related article that appeared in the *Harvard Business Review,* Carr argued that bluffing and other misleading but lawful negotiating tactics are "an integral part of the bargaining game and the executive who does not master { and } techniques is not likely to accumulate much money or power."

People who adhere to the Poker School readily admit that bargaining and poker are not exactly the same. But they point out that deception is essential to effective play in both arenas. Moreover, skilled players in both poker and bargaining exhibit a robust and realistic distrust of the other fellow. Carr argues that good players should ignore the "claims of friendship" and engage in "cunning deception and concealment" in fair, hard bargaining encounters. When the game is over, members of the Poker School do not think less of a fellow player just because that person successfully deceived them. In fact, assuming the tactic was legal, they may admire the deceiver and vow to be better prepared (and less trusting) next time.

We know how to play poker, but how exactly does one play the bargaining "game"? Stripped to its core, it looks like this: Someone opens, and then people take turns proposing terms to each other. Arguments supporting your preferred

Source: "Bargaining with the Devil without Losing Your Soul", from BARGAINING FOR ADVANTAGE, 2/E by G. Richard Shell, copyright © 1999, 2006 by G. Richard Shell. Used by permission of Viking Penguin, a division of Penguin Group (USA) Inc.

terms are allowed. You can play or pass in each round. The goal is to get the other side to agree to terms that are as close as possible to your last proposal.

In the bargaining game, it is understood that both sides might be bluffing. Bluffs disguise a weak bargaining hand, that is, the limited or unattractive alternatives you have away from the table, your inability to affect the other side's alternatives, and the arguments you have to support your demands. Unlike poker players, negotiators always attempt to disclose a good hand if they have one in the bargaining game. So the most effective bluffs are realistic, attractive, difficult-to-check (but false) alternatives or authoritative (but false) supporting standards. Experienced players know this, so one of the key skills in the bargaining game is judging when the other party's alternatives or arguments are really as good as he or she says. If the other side calls you on your bargaining bluff by walking away or giving you a credible ultimatum, you lose. Either there will be no deal when there should have been one, or the final price will be nearer to their last offer than to yours.

As mentioned above, the Poker School believes in the rule of law. In Poker, you are not allowed to hide cards, collude with other players, or renege on your bets. But you are expected to deceive others about your hand. The best plays come when you win the pot with a weak hand or fool the other players into betting heavily when your hand is strong. In bargaining, you must not commit outright, actionable fraud, but negotiators must be on guard for anything short of fraud.

The Poker School has three main problems as I see it. First, the Poker School presumes that everyone treats bargaining as a game. Unfortunately, it is an empirical fact that people disagree on this. For a start, neither the idealists nor the pragmatists (more on these below) think bargaining is a game. This problem does not deter the Poker School, which holds that the rules permit its members to play even when the other party disagrees about this premise.

Second, everyone is supposed to know the rules cold. But this is impossible, given that legal rules are applied differently in different industries and regions of the world.

Finally, the law is far from certain even within a single jurisdiction. So you often need a sharp lawyer to help you decide what to do.

The "Do the Right Thing Even If It Hurts" Idealist School

The Idealist School says that bargaining is an aspect of social life, not a special activity with its own unique set of rules. The same ethics that apply in the home should carry over directly into the realm of negotiation. If it is wrong to lie or mislead in normal social encounters, it is wrong to do so in negotiations. If it is OK to lie in special situations (such as to protect another person's feelings), it is also OK to lie in negotiations when those special conditions apply.

Idealists do not entirely rule out deception in negotiation. For example, if the other party assumes you have a lot of leverage and never asks you directly about the situation as you see it, you do not necessarily have to volunteer information weakening your position. And the idealist can decline to answer questions. But such exceptions are uncomfortable moments. Members of the Idealist School prefer to be candid and honest at the bargaining table even if it means giving up a certain amount of strategic advantage.

The Idealist School draws its strength from philosophy and religion. For example, Immanuel Kant said that we should all follow the ethical rules that we would wish others to follow. Kant argued that if everyone lied all the time, social life would be chaos. Hence, you should not lie. Kant also disapproved of treating other people merely as the means to achieve your own personal ends. Lies in negotiation are selfish acts designed to achieve personal gain. This form of conduct is therefore unethical. Period. Many religions also teach adherents not to lie for personal advantage.

Idealists admit that deception in negotiation rarely arouses moral indignation unless the lies breach a trust between friends, violate a fiduciary responsibility, or exploit people such as the sick or elderly, who lack the ability to protect themselves. And if the only way you can prevent some terrible harm like a murder is by lying, go ahead and lie. But the lack of moral outrage and the fact that sometimes lying can be defended does not make deception in negotiations right.

Idealists strongly reject the idea that negotiations should be viewed as "games." Negotiations, they feel, are serious, consequential communication acts. People negotiate to resolve their differences so social life will work for the benefit of all. People must be held responsible for all their actions, including the way they negotiate, under universal standards.

Idealists think that the members of the Poker School are predatory and selfish. For its part, the Poker School thinks that idealists are naive and even a little silly. When members of the two schools meet at the bargaining table, tempers can flare.

Some members of the Idealist School have recently been trying to find a philosophical justification for bluffs about bottom lines. There is no agreement yet on whether these efforts have succeeded in ethical terms. But it is clear that outright lies such as fictitious other offers and better prices are unethical practices under idealist principles.

The big problem for the idealists is obvious: Their standards sometimes make it difficult to proceed in a realistic way at the bargaining table. Also, unless adherence to the Idealist School is coupled with a healthy skepticism about the way other people will negotiate, idealism leaves its members open to exploitation by people with standards other than their own. These limitations are especially troublesome when idealists must represent others' interests at the bargaining table.

Despite its limitations, I like the Idealist School. Perhaps because I am an academic, I genuinely believe that the different parts of my life are, in fact, a whole. I aspire to ethical standards that I can apply consistently. I will admit that I sometimes fall short of idealism's strict code, but by aiming high I hope I am leaving myself somewhere to fall that maintains my basic sense of personal integrity.

I confess my preference for the Idealist School so you will know where I am coming from in this discussion. But I realize that your experience and work environment may preclude idealism as an ethical option. That's OK. As I hope I am making clear, idealism is not the only way to think about negotiation in ethical terms.

The "What Goes Around Comes Around" Pragmatist School

The final school of bargaining ethics, the Pragmatist School, includes some original elements as well as some attributes of the previous two. In common with the Poker School, this approach views deception as a necessary part of the negotiation process. Unlike the Poker School, however, it prefers not to use misleading statements and overt lies if there is a serviceable, practical alternative. Uniquely, the Pragmatist School displays concern for the potential negative effects of deceptive conduct on present and future relationships. Thus, lying and other questionable tactics are bad not so much because they are "wrong" as because they cost the user more in the long run than they gain in the short run.

As my last comment suggests, people adhere to this school more for prudential than idealistic reasons. Lies and misleading conduct can cause serious injury to one's credibility. And credibility is an important asset for effective negotiators both to preserve working relationships and to protect one's reputation in a market or community. This latter concern is summed up in what I would call the pragmatist's credo: What goes around comes around. The Poker School is less mindful of reputation and more focused on winning each bargaining encounter within the rules of the "game."

What separates the Pragmatist School from the Idealist School? To put it bluntly, a pragmatist will lie a bit more often than will an idealist. For example, pragmatists sometimes draw fine distinctions between lies about hard-core facts of a transaction, which are always imprudent (and often illegal), and misleading statements about such things as the rationales used to justify a position. A pragmatic car salesman considers it highly unethical to lie about anything large or small relating to the mechanical condition of a used car he is selling. But this same salesman might not have a problem saying "My manager won't let me sell this car for less than $10,000 even though he knows the manager would sell the car for $9500. False justification and rationales are marginally acceptable because they are usually less important to the transaction and much harder to detect as falsehoods than are core facts about the object being bought and sold.

Pragmatists are also somewhat looser with the truth when using so-called blocking techniques—tactics to avoid answering questions that threaten to expose a weak bargaining position. For example, can you ethically answer "I don't know" when asked about something you do know that hurts your position? An idealist would refuse to answer the question or try to change the subject, not lie by saying "I don't know." A pragmatist would go ahead and say "I don't know" if his actual state of knowledge is hard to trace and the lie poses little risk to his relationships.

The Ethical Schools in Action

As a test of ethical thinking, let's take a simple example. Assume you are negotiating to sell a commercial building and the other party asks you whether you have another offer. In fact, you do not have any such offers. What would the three schools recommend you do?

A Poker School adherent might suggest a lie. Both parties are sophisticated businesspeople in this deal, so a lie about alternatives is probably legally "immaterial." But a member of the Poker School would want to know the answer to two questions before making this move.

First, could the lie be easily found out? If so, it would be a bad play because it wouldn't work and might put the other side on guard with respect to other lies he might want to tell. Second, is a lie about alternatives the best way to leverage the buyer into making a bid? Perhaps a lie about something else—a deadline, for example—might be a better choice.

Assuming the lie is undetectable and will work, how might the conversations sound?

Buyer:	Do you have another offer?
Poker School Seller:	Yes. A Saudi Arabian firm presented us with an offer for $___ this morning, and we have only forty-eight hours to get back to it with an answer.
	Confidentiality forbids us from showing you the Saudi offer, but rest assured that it is real. What would you like to do?

How would an idealist handle this situation? There are several idealist responses, but none would involve a lie. One response would be the following.

Buyer:	Do you have another offer?
Idealist Seller 1:	An interesting question—and one I refuse to answer.

Of course, that refusal speaks volumes to the buyer. Another approach would be to adopt a policy on "other buyer" questions.

Buyer:	Do you have another offer?
Idealist Seller 2:	An interesting question, and one I receive quite often. Let me answer you this way. The property's value to you is something for you to decide based on your needs and your own sense of the market. However, I treat all offers with the greatest confidence. I will not discuss an offer you make to me with another buyer, and I would not discuss any offer I received from someone else with you. Will you be bidding?

Of course, this will work for an idealist only if he or she really and truly has such a policy—a costly one when there is another attractive offer he or she would like to reveal.

A final idealist approach would be to offer an honest, straightforward answer. An idealist cannot lie or deliberately mislead, but he is allowed to put the best face he can on the situation that is consistent with plain truth.

Buyer:	Do you have another offer?
Idealistic Seller 3:	To be honest, we have no offers at this time. However, we are hopeful that we will receive other offers soon. It might be in your interest to bid now and take the property before competition drives the price up.

How about the pragmatists? They would suggest using blocking techniques. These techniques would protect their leverage in ways that were consistent with maintaining working relationships. Once again, assume that the buyer has asked the "other offer" question and there are no other offers. Here are five ways a pragmatist might suggest you block this question to avoid an out-and-out factual lie about other offers while minimizing the damage to your leverage. Some of these blocking techniques would work for idealists, too.

- Declare the question out of bounds. ("Company policy forbids any discussion of other offers in situations like this"—note that, if untrue, this is a lie, but it is one that carries less risk to your reputation because it is hard to confirm. If there really is such a company policy, an idealist could also use this move to block the question.)
- Answer a different question. ("We will not be keeping the property on the market much longer because the market is moving and our plans are changing." Again, if untrue, this statement is a mere lie about a "rationale" that troubles pragmatists less than idealists.)
- Dodge the question. ("The more important question is whether we are going to get an offer from you—and when.")
- Ask a question of your own. ("What alternatives are you examining at this time?")
- Change the subject. ("We are late for our next meeting already. Are you bidding today or not?")

Blocking techniques of this sort serve a utilitarian purpose. They preserve some leverage (though not as much as the Poker School) while reducing the risk of acquiring a reputation for deception. Relationships and reputations matter. If there is even a remote chance of a lie coming back to haunt you in a future negotiation with either the person you lie to or someone he may interact with, the pragmatists argue that you should not do it.

So which school do you belong to? Or do you belong to a school of your own such as "pragmatic idealism"? To repeat: My advice is to aim high. The pressure of real bargaining often makes ethical compromisers of us all. When you fall below the standard of the Poker School, you are at serious risk of legal and even criminal liability. (Adapted from Shell, 1999.)

Thinking Further 9.2

1. Think of times when you used the Poker School or Pragmatist School in a negotiation. How successful were you? How much more/less successful do you believe you would have been if you had used the Idealist School? Why?

2. Consider each of the following schools in a negotiation between heads of state to settle a border dispute: Poker School, Pragmatist School and Idealist School. Which school, in your view, would have the greatest potential to succeed in settling the dispute peacefully? Which school, in your opinion, would have the greatest potential of ending in an escalation of the dispute? Explain your reasoning.

C H A P T E R 1 0

Multiparty Negotiations

Managing the Additional Complexity

Many negotiations include more than one negotiator and numerous people who will be affected by the outcome. You may have other negotiators at the table to negotiate with you, or you may select an agent to negotiate for you. You may have constituents (parties for whom you or your agent will negotiate). Some parties are bystanders – they are not at the table but they are indirectly affected by the outcome. This chapter examines the additional complexity that exists when more than two parties are involved, the role of agents or representatives and how they should be managed, and the nature of multiparty and inter-team negotiations.

INTENDED BENEFITS OF THIS CHAPTER

When you finish reading this chapter, you should be able to:

1. Explain the added complexity that exists in multiparty, negotiations, how to manage them and how to negotiate effectively in these situations.

2. Describe the role of agents or representatives in negotiations, when they should be used to negotiate on your behalf, and how you should manage your relationship with them.

3. Explain the influence of audiences and audience effects on negotiations and how they should be managed.

4. Discuss the role of coalitions in negotiations, how they are formed and how they can be managed to improve the process and outcome of a negotiation.

THE ESSENCE OF MULTIPARTY NEGOTIATIONS

Most negotiations are not dyadic – they may involve multiparty, intra-team and inter-team interactions, multiple negotiators on each side of the table, agents, representatives, audiences and coalitions. This matters because additional parties make negotiating more complex.

The Challenges of Multiparty Negotiations

- Many people and many organizations select or hire someone to negotiate for them. Attorneys, for example, commonly negotiate out-of-court settlements for their clients.
- Many companies have implemented team-based work processes to perform certain tasks or to produce the goods and services they sell. These teams are often devoid of formal leaders with decision-making authority so the members make decisions by negotiating. Self-managed work teams, task forces, committees and perhaps the group projects you have been required to complete for your classes are examples.
- If multiple parties have a vested interest in a negotiation and they want to influence the outcome, each of them may participate in the negotiation. When the Big Ten and Pac-10 conferences decided to expand in 2010, for example, representatives from each of the member universities initially negotiated whether their conferences would expand. They then negotiated to determine which universities they would invite to join their respective conferences.
- Those people who are not negotiating but who are affected by it may watch the negotiation carefully. These audiences affect the processes and outcomes of negotiations.
- Participants in multiparty negotiations may believe they lack sufficient power to influence the decision being made. To enhance their effectiveness in these negotiations, they may join with some of the other participants to form coalitions. Joining together and acting in concert enhances their ability to ensure that the decision negotiated is favorable. During the Big Ten and Pac-10 conference negotiations, for example, several member universities may have banded together to influence the decision to expand and the determination of which universities would be invited to join.
- Inter-team negotiations are also common. In the Big Ten and Pac-10 negotiations, each university sent teams of representatives to negotiate. Labor unions and companies send teams of representatives to negotiate new labor contracts. Two companies that are forming a strategic alliance or merging send teams of representatives to negotiate the terms of these arrangements.

WHY MULTIPARTY NEGOTIATIONS ARE MORE COMPLEX

Multiparty negotiations are more complex and take more time to complete for many reasons.

Informational Complexity

Complex issues usually involve many facts, arguments and other data, even if there are only two negotiators. But the volume of information that must be processed increases dramatically when more than two people are involved. Even if a team has a single goal, and a single set of issues, interests and preferences, each individual has his or her own issues, interests, preferences, perspectives, values and beliefs, and any differences that exist must be managed. As the amount of information increases, the complexity increases. As noted in Chapters 7 and 8, we often use shortcuts to help us process information. The likelihood that we will use these shortcuts increases as the amount of information that must be processes increased. Though easier, this usually results in more decision-making errors and it makes us more vulnerable to others' influence attempts.

Social Complexity

Multiparty negotiations involve multiple relationships, conversations and motives, all of which must be managed. For example, if only two negotiators are involved, one relationship, one conversation and, at most, two motives (usually to cooperate or compete) exist. You do not have to worry about which role the other person assumes because he or she must assume all that are required to secure an agreement. Nor do you have to worry about coalitions or subgroups forming to support or oppose you. If only one person is added to the dyad, there are now three relationships, conversations and motives to manage. Participants change roles and coalitions may form that support or oppose you. At times, adding people will change the nature of your interaction and your behavior only marginally and you may not even be aware of it. At other times, the dynamics of your interaction change dramatically.

Why does this make negotiations more complex? If the negotiators possess a cooperative orientation, they are likely to be more trusting, engage in less argumentation and achieve higher-quality outcomes. If they are looking out only for themselves or if they all have different orientations, however, they will be less trusting, engage in more argumentation and achieve lesser outcomes (Weingart, Bennett & Brett, 1993). It may be difficult to change one negotiator's motivational orientation (e.g., from competitive to cooperative), but it is possible (see Chapter 13). Changing multiple negotiators' orientations is significantly harder. Roles also change when more people are involved in the negotiation. In an inter-team negotiation, for example, one team member may be the primary spokesperson for one issue because he or she possesses the requisite expertise. On another issue, the same person may become an observer because a teammate, who served as an observer and note taker on the first issue, has the most expertise. Monitoring who assumes which role and when, and adapting to these changes, influences negotiation processes and outcomes. Finally, social pressures assume greater importance when multiple negotiators are involved. Pressures for conformity are often prominent in multiparty negotiations. When they work, they unify the negotiators. When they do not work, they are more apt to escalate the conflict. This precludes negotiators from working through their differences, accepting solutions and implementing them successfully.

Procedural Complexity

Two negotiators simply take turns presenting offers, counteroffers, supporting arguments and counterarguments, challenging the other side's contentions or asking questions. When more parties are added, they must determine who goes first, second, third and so on to communicate these ideas. They must also structure the processes for building rapport and testing assumptions.

Strategic Complexity

Negotiators must attend to the strategies and tactics of each person at the table and decide how to respond. You must decide, for example, whether to deal with each negotiator separately or all of them as a group. Even if they are all using the same strategy, each negotiator will undoubtedly execute it differently and use different tactics. These negotiations may even turn into multiple one-on-one negotiations, with the other individuals watching. This means that you must deal with audiences and audience effects (discussed in the next section). Negotiating the process is often beneficial, but it is essential when multiple parties are involved because it enables them to effectively coordinate and manage the additional challenges. This includes agreeing how to handle the larger volume of information, clarifying how information will be communicated and who will be assuming which role, and whether the negotiation will be conducted integratively or distributively.

Strategically, most people choose to negotiate one issue at a time. As noted earlier, this generally results in lower-quality outcomes because it engenders more justifying, defending and compromising. This is particularly true if multiple parties are involved. Higher quality outcomes are commonly achieved if multiple issues are raised and negotiated at the same time. This leads to higher-quality outcomes because it enables the parties to find integrative tradeoffs or other solutions that create value for everyone (Weingart et al., 1993). Despite the advantages of this approach, it is more complicated and time-consuming when multiple parties are involved because they must juggle more issues.

The aforementioned complexities make multiparty negotiations more difficult than dyadic negotiations, but they are only part of the story. Whether they are observing your negotiation directly or indirectly, audiences and audience effects must be managed. If you are serving as an *agent* or otherwise representing others, you must manage your relationship with them. *Coalitions* often form in multiparty negotiations and influence negotiation processes and outcomes. You must determine how to coordinate and mobilize those that are supportive and how to counter those that oppose your efforts. If you are negotiating decisions or solutions with others who have a vested interest in the outcome, or if you are part of a team negotiating against another team, the dynamics of your interactions may change even further. The remainder of this chapter examines each of these challenges.

AGENTS AND REPRESENTATIVES

In theory, agents represent only the interests of their principals. In practice, however, this may not be possible. Even if they have good information about their principals' interests when they begin negotiating, it may not be good information for long. Interests change, or perceptions of them change, as new information is acquired. Agents also represent the interests of people other than their principals. Managers who represent their companies in labor negotiations, for example, must represent the interests of the employees who are not represented by the union, other managers and the company. Agents also have legitimate personal interests that are independent of their principals' interests. Finally, principals do not have immediate access to the information that is exchanged at the table, so it is impossible for them to perfectly observe or control the actions of their agents (Cutcher-Gershenfeld & Watkins, 1999). Despite these difficulties, agents or representatives are commonly used.

When We Should Use Representatives

To Achieve Better Outcomes. We use representatives because we think they are better negotiators. When selecting someone to negotiate for us, therefore, we should select someone who has better negotiation skills and abilities, is more familiar with the norms and expectations that govern the interaction and has more subject matter expertise. Beyond this, the choice of who should be selected is a vexing one. Choosing someone who is "similar" to you and has similar interests is common, and it makes sense because he or she will be a perfect extension of you (Ross, 1973). If achieving an excellent outcome is important, however, it may be wise to use someone who is dissimilar and takes a different approach. This is particularly true if he or she is known as a firm negotiator or wants to be, and maintaining that reputation is important.

To Preserve Relationships. Negotiators sometimes want to preserve or improve their relationships with the other party. These relationship concerns, however, may conflict or interfere with other important interests, including substantive concerns. They may also limit the array of tactics you can use in a particular situation. Using representatives eliminates these concerns (Rubin & Sander, 1988; Lax & Sebenius, 1986). To illustrate, imagine that a professional athlete negotiates against his or her coach for a new contract and their tactics become very aggressive, in part because they want to claim as much value as they can. What happens when the season begins and the two of them must work together? For similar reasons, senior executives rarely negotiate their own employment packages with the chief executive officer or boards of directors. Simply put, a representative may damage his or her relationship with the other representative, but not the relationship between the principals. Having more tactical flexibility may also enable them to achieve better outcomes.

To Separate the Person from the Problem. Using representatives may help if you are so emotionally involved or close to the situation that you cannot see the big picture and how your issues fit into it, consider other perspectives, make even wise concessions to facilitate reaching an agreement or separate the person from the problem to facilitate integrative negotiations.

Despite these advantages, using representatives does introduce some concerns.

• Representatives may be so committed to reaching an agreement that they forget about its contents. They might even withhold information from the principal that, if shared, would impede a deal.

• If you give representatives too much authority and your risk preferences are not aligned, they may use tactics that you do not like or take chances that you are not comfortable with to achieve a better outcome. They may not try hard enough to understand your interests and preferences and, even if they do understand them, they may attempt to satisfy their own interests rather than yours. They might even stop trying to improve the terms of the agreement once a minimally acceptable outcome has been achieved.

• The incentive system created for the representative may exacerbate some of the aforementioned concerns or create new ones. Pay the representative an hourly rate, for instance, and he or she may consciously or unconsciously extend the negotiation to reap greater rewards. Adopt a contingency-based fee arrangement similar to those advertised by personal injury attorneys and he or she might negotiate the best deal possible. He or she might also reject offers that you find perfectly acceptable or take greater risks than you would prefer to secure an even better deal. This is even more likely if the representative believes the compensation package includes an opportunity to create or maintain a reputation as a strong negotiator who achieves great outcomes for clients. Even if you are comfortable with the risks he or she assumes, how will you factor terms or interests that cannot be quantified into the contingency equation?

Managing Relationships Between Representatives and Principals

To reap the benefits of using representatives while minimizing the risks they introduce, the relationship must be managed carefully. This begins when representatives are selected. Interviews, investigations of their negotiation experiences, background investigations, including reference checks, and otherwise getting to know each other should enable principals to carefully assess representatives' qualifications. Both of them should also assess their compatibility and determine whether any differences are irreconcilable.

The Traditional Approach

Despite the aforementioned problems, some argue that specifying exactly what authority representatives have from the start establishes clear expectations about the process to be followed and the outcome to be achieved. This includes clarifying when and how information should be shared with the principal, what information can be shared with the other side, which tactics are acceptable to use and what constitutes an acceptable agreement. Aligning rewards with what the principals expect will also help with this. If principals fail to do this, representatives should seek clarification of these matters. Since negotiations are often not visible to the principals, these limitations should protect them against dishonest representatives, and representatives against accusations of dishonesty (Fassina, 2004; Cutcher-Gershenfeld & Watkins, 1999).

An Alternative Approach

Instead of asking, "How much authority should I grant the representative?" a more appropriate question is, "How should I adjust the commitment authority level of the representative over the course of the negotiation?" Advocates of this interest-based approach argue that initially representatives should not be authorized to make binding commitments on substantive issues. This is because negotiators who possess commitment authority, whether principals or representatives, naturally frame their communications in terms of what would or would not be an acceptable offer. They also vigilantly attend to the other party's words or deeds to assess the shape of a possible offer. This is not conducive to the development of an effective working relationship between the parties and an environment in which flexibility and creative problem solving occur (Fisher & Davis, 1999).

Since productive negotiations are predicated upon the occurrence of considerable learning, this approach further argues that representatives should use their latitude and professional judgment to design a process that evolves through a series of stages appropriate to the nature and complexity of the subject matter. Premature commitment to specified acceptable or unacceptable tactics or outcomes should be avoided because this misdirects the representatives' attention and inhibits creative problem solving. The principal's substantive instructions, instead, should emphasize his or her own interests, priorities and alternatives, and these should be discussed with the representative to ensure clarity and understanding (Fisher & Davis, 1999).

To avoid the aforementioned problems about sharing too much information too early and too little too late, communication between the principal and the representative should not reflect the typical focus on offers and counteroffers that have been exchanged. Instead, it should emphasize what the representative learns about the other party's interests, the alternatives that have been discussed and any other information that might cause the principal to reconsider his or her interests, BATNA, options and objective criteria. The representative's thoughts about how much authority would be useful for the next segment of the negotiation should also be discussed. As the negotiation evolves and the principal and representative gain additional insight, the representative's authority to disclose information to the other party and to make binding commitments should gradually expand. This focus on learning and interests mitigates some of the concerns about sharing too much information about bottom lines or resistance points too early. Multi-issue negotiations also limit these concerns because there is usually no single bottom line that is or is not acceptable. What is acceptable for one issue often depends on what is achieved on other issues. Simply put, as the negotiation evolves and you gain confidence in, comfort with and information from the representative, granting additional authority to disclose information and make binding commitments should be easier (Fisher & Davis, 1999).

MULTIPARTY NEGOTIATIONS

As noted at the beginning of this chapter, multiparty negotiations are common, they assume different forms, and they encompass many challenges. Hopefully, the previous section clarified the nature of agents or representatives and the roles they assume in negotiations because they are an important challenge encompassed by multiparty negotiations. Audiences and audience effects, coalitions, and the dynamics of involving more people at the table are also important challenges that will be discussed in this section. Organizations are increasingly using team-based work processes that require members to negotiate a variety of decisions. Some are formed to perform a specific task such as finding a better way to manage inventory (see Negotiation in Action 10.1). Others are created to focus on innovation or to produce goods or services. Some teams include members from the same department or functional specialty; others are cross-functional – people with different professional orientations must work together to complete their assignments.

NEGOTIATION IN ACTION 10.1

The Blood Glucose Meter (BGM) Inventory Team was formed at a large medical clinic to find a way to combat rising BGM inventory costs and the dramatic decline of the inventory turn ratio – an efficiency measure of usage relative to available inventory. More specifically, the turn ratio in 2008 was the second best of the clinic's 23-year history; a year later, it was the worst. This inefficiency was causing the clinic to experience excessive costs, so representatives from the units that significantly and independently affect the turn ratio were asked to join the team. The leader shared her perspective of the problem and

(Continued)

(Continued)

asked the members if they saw the problem differently. A few shared different perspectives and they were incorporated to create a more complete definition of the problem. She also established ground rules for the meeting – all suggestions for addressing the problem, no matter how wild they seemed, were encouraged; individuals were not to criticize any of the suggestions; questions could be asked to gain clarification of the suggestions; and anyone could build upon others' ideas.

During the brainstorming session, a lot of information was shared by all of the participants and numerous viable suggestions surfaced and were built upon. This was facilitated by sharing additional information that was deemed relevant – projections for the number of BGMs that would be needed in the next six months compared to existing inventory levels, the consequences that would result if purchases from BGM manufacturers were canceled, the availability and viability of buying used meters, the possibility of selling or trading excess meters in this clinic to other clinics and hospitals, and the possibility of giving or selling them to patients (generally diabetics and their caregivers) were provided. The team then negotiated which three were best and action plans for implementing them. These plans included accountabilities and time limits. An objective criterion was also negotiated for evaluating and monitoring the effectiveness of each of these options. Negotiating these issues enabled the clinic to cancel $100,000 worth of meter purchases, transfer $10,000 worth of meters to other clinics, hospitals and physicians' offices and sell $15,000 worth of meters to patients and their caregivers.

Some groups of negotiators look and act like teams, but the members actually represent different organizations. The negotiations pertaining to the expansion of the Big Ten and Pac 10 conferences that were discussed earlier are examples because the member universities sent representatives to negotiate these decisions. Whichever form these multiparty negotiations take, each party undoubtedly has a vested interest in the outcome but different ideas about what they want or need and how to achieve it. Some groups have formal leaders with decision-making authority; others do not. Either way, managing multiple parties can be challenging. **Readings 10.1** and **10.2** provide additional insights and guidance.

Preparation for multiparty negotiations is more complex than it is for dyadic negotiations, largely because there are more people involved. Members want to reach a common solution, but they have different interests and preferences. If you are not able to identify each member's issues and interests, and how they prioritize them, consider postponing the negotiation until you can. This will help you build a strong foundation for your negotiation – it will be even stronger if you can develop a shared and complete understanding of the situation, understand each person's goals, strategies, target and resistance points and BATNAs.

Decision Making

How these groups make decisions is another difficulty beyond those already discussed. Using objective criteria can be very useful, but the complexity of the process often requires additional decision-making rules. Voting is common because requiring majority support is democratic and simple. If most parties support a proposal, it is approved. This seems reasonable, but securing 51% support means that 49% may oppose the idea. This may seriously jeopardize implementation. Voting also fails to account for the strength of a party's preferences. One party may feel very strongly about an issue and another may not care much, but their votes count the same. Voting on one issue at a time, which is typical, further diminishes efforts to find integrative tradeoffs or other creative solutions. If enough interests remain unsatisfied, the solution may be rejected (Beersma & de Dreu, 2002).

Majority rule presents an additional problem if the parties are deciding among multiple alternatives. As illustrated in Negotiation in Action 10.2, winners change as a function of the order in which the alternatives are proposed.

NEGOTIATION IN ACTION 10.2

Assume that three possible solutions are created by three different negotiators. After arguing for hours about which one they should adopt, they agree to vote. The initial vote between #1 and #2 favors #1, so #2 is eliminated. The next vote between #1 and #3 favors #3, so it wins.

Assume that the architect of one of the 'losers' objects and demands another vote. This time, they vote for the alternatives in a different order. The first vote between #2 and #3 favors #2. The next vote between #1 and #2 favors #1, so it wins. Changing the order in which the options are voted on often changes the outcome: it isn't possible to combine parties' preferences in a way that guarantees maximum team preferences when there are three or more members choosing among three or more options. This is even more problematic if votes misrepresent true preferences. Strategic complexity suggests that a party could vote "against" the most competitive alternative to increase his or her chances of winning (May, 1982; Arrow, 1963).

Requiring unanimity enables the parties to overcome the difficulties of majority rule voting, but finding tradeoffs or other creative alternatives that will expand the "pie" enough to satisfy all parties' interests and account for the strength of their preferences can be very difficult (Mannix, Thompson & Bazerman, 1989).

Additional problems may also plague multiparty negotiations.

- Participants often fail to develop a clear and shared understanding of what their task is, and what is expected of them. They may even fail to understand or accept that each party has legitimate interests. As noted in Chapter 7, ignoring others' cognitions leads to poor decision making and interferes with efforts to create value. Participants may also fail to recognize that multiple approaches exist for finding creative solutions and that multiple solutions may work for everyone. There is rarely one best or worst solution.
- There may be a few people who do all of the talking. The participants with domineering personalities often fail to give up the 'floor.'
- Participants who are very shy or quiet may be reluctant to contribute.
- Participants often focus most of their attention on commonly held information rather than unique information. This is problematic because unique information may force people to think differently about the issues or otherwise help them find better solutions.
- Interpersonally, members may not trust or respect each other or afford others the respect they deserve. This often leads to incompatibility and disharmony among the parties.

Six Thinking Hats

Rather than clarifying the purpose and establishing objectives and sub-objectives, suggestions, criticisms, emotions, information and judgment are commonly mixed together in a sort of thinking stew until someone stumbles upon some approach that seems to achieve what is desired. **Six Thinking Hats** techniques provide an effective approach for eliminating or minimizing reliance on the narrow, biased or haphazard exploration that often plagues teams and multiparty negotiations. This is a structured approach that encourages forward-focused and creative thinking that leads to consensus by asking team members to wear different hats to accomplish their objectives (de Bono, 1985). The six hats are summarized in Table 10.1.

What does this mean for negotiators?

Video 10.1

Six Thinking Hats

White Hat thinking requires each party to present the facts, figures and other relevant information they have to the other group members. This data, which should be verifiable and verified if there are doubts, helps negotiators create a clear and shared definition of the situation. As noted in Chapter 2, it is very difficult to effectively solve problems or capitalize on new opportunities if different negotiators define the situation differently. When wearing the white hat, a party's presentations of and requests for information must be framed neutrally and objectively, independent of his or her values and beliefs – it should not be presented or requested in a way that promotes or denigrates an argument or a proposal. Parties should be wary of efforts to evaluate this information when it is presented, and of efforts to snowball others with it by presenting so much information that processing it becomes impracticable.

Green Hat thinking is required for negotiators to invent the types of integrative options – bridging solutions, nonspecific compensation, logrolling or other new solutions that satisfy all parties' interests. This requires the deliberate creation of new ideas, concepts and perceptions, and finding new ways to do things because we think they could be done in a simpler or better way. When looking for solutions, we usually stop thinking once we identify one possibility. The green hat, though, does not settle for just one possible solution.

We generally want to be secure and 'right,' but this hat requires us to create new ideas and take risks. It requires us to leave current patterns of thinking behind and adopt new ones. This is challenging because our brains are set up to use patterns of thinking and to condemn things that do not fit them. We typically evaluate new ideas by comparing them to what we know, or to our normal patterns of experience. We often reject new ideas that do not fit our knowledge structures or our patterns of thinking because we do not know if they are correct. Moreover, as noted in Chapter 7, it is often difficult for us to consider and understand another person's perspective when we have already thought about something in our own way. To escape our habitual patterns of thinking or perceiving, we must question our ideas or proposals. Where will they get us? What is interesting or different in these ideas? What do these ideas suggest that is new? How will they satisfy each party's interests? We can also focus on ideas we do not like to determine how they could be modified to make them more suitable. Finally, we can opt for a different starting point from which we begin deliberations. Creative thinking is also encouraged by considering the suggestions discussed in Chapter 4. These suggestions and wearing the green hat will not make us creative, but they may help us escape from old ideas and facilitate our search for new ones.

Yellow Hat thinking requires us to assess the positive qualities of ideas, arguments or proposals. These positive assessments must be based on your experience, available information such as trends, or at least a logical deduction. If it leads to some action that is in the chosen direction or helps you

Table 10.1   Six Thinking Hats: Awareness of the Thinking

Blue Hat
Managing the Process
"Control" Hat
Organizes the thinking
Sets the agenda and the focus
Summarizes and concludes
Ensures that rules and processes are observed

White Hat
Information
What is the information we know?
What information do we need to know?
How do we get that information?
Determines accuracy and relevance
Looks at other people's views

Red Hat
Feelings, Intuition, Gut Instinct
Permission to express feelings and hunches
No need to justify or explain
Represents feelings right now
Keep it short
A key ingredient in decision making

Yellow Hat
Benefits and Feasibility
The optimistic view
Reasons must be given
Need more effort than the black hat
Finds the benefits, values and advantages
Consider both short-term and long-term perspectives

Black Hat
Risks, Difficulties and Problems
The skeptical view
Reasons must be given
Points out thinking that does not fit the facts,
experience, regulations, strategy, values
Points out potential problems

Green Hat
New Ideas, Possibilities
Creative thinking
Seeks alternatives and possibilities
Removes faults
Doesn't have to be logical
Generates new concepts

(Adapted from de Bono, 1985.)

make progress, for example, it probably has value. Optimism based merely on hope is misplaced – it reflects Red hat thinking. Yellow hat thinking is speculative because it is about looking forward at the likely benefits of the solution or method if it is implemented. This speculation turns some people off, but the benefits of an idea that is new and has not been implemented cannot be known with certainty. Yellow hat thinking is worth the effort – entrepreneurs are adept yellow hat thinkers because they commonly see value in an opportunity that others cannot or have not yet seen. This thinking is difficult, especially for those raised in Western culture, because we are taught to argue, to think critically rather than constructively, and to determine why something will not work rather than why it will work. This negativity is valuable, but it reflects red or black hat thinking.

Black Hat thinking is the opposite of yellow hat thinking because it is about negative assessments. It might include pointing out the risks, dangers, shortfalls and potential problems that could arise if the solutions or ideas are adopted. It is useful because it protects us from excessive risk, danger and making mistakes. Though negative, black hat thinking is logical and truthful – there must be reasons given indicating why an idea will not work, and these reasons must be sound and justified. Unsupported assertions or criticisms reflect red hat thinking.

Hunches, intuitions, impressions, emotions and feelings about information, ideas or options reflect *Red Hat* thinking. Reasons, justifications and bases for these thoughts or reactions are unnecessary. Traditionally, people argued that emotions muck up thinking so they should be avoided. In actuality, emotions give relevance to our thinking and help explain our needs. We react emotionally because actions and decisions affect our values. Emotions that remain hidden or suppressed will affect other aspects of our thinking (emotions are discussed in more detail in Chapter 13). When wearing the red hat, our focus should be placed on whether a particular course of action satisfies our desires and, if so, if it does so at the expense of other desires.

Blue Hat thinking is about leadership and control – it organizes the thinking process. This includes asking the right questions to define the situation and move the negotiation in the desired direction. It includes setting thinking tasks and inserting different thinking hats into the discussion to complete essential tasks. Wearing this hat may also require participants to establish norms of respectful and productive interaction, and norms of meaningful participation. The latter is required to ensure that everyone contributes information that is consistent with the hat being worn, unique relevant information is shared, and that everyone is listening with an open mind. (de Bono, 1985).

Implementing Six Hats Thinking When Negotiating

Implementing this consensus-seeking approach requires all participants to wear the same color hat at the same time. The sequencing of the hats may also be important, although there is no one sequence that is appropriate for all situations. It may not even be necessary to wear each hat. Negotiators might consider engaging in white hat thinking first to gather the information that is required to develop a clear and shared definition of the situation, surface the issues that are included in it and identify the parties' interests. Green hat thinking might follow so the parties can begin creating new solutions that will satisfy these interests. Yellow hat thinking might follow to assess the positive qualities of the ideas or options that are invented. Black hat thinking could follow to identify the negatives and any components that need to be modified. Meritorious criticisms will then require more green hat thinking to overcome the black hat objections or problems. Blue hat thinking is required at different times to summarize what has been accomplished and where the group stands. Red hat thinking might conclude the process because decisions are at least partially evaluated by how we feel about them. Beginning with red hat thinking also makes sense if the negotiation is about highly emotional or sensitive topics because emotions must often be addressed before meaningful progress can be made on substantive concerns.

Audiences and Audience Effects

There are always audiences when you negotiate, even in a dyadic negotiation. Anyone who is at the table with you is an audience. If you are representing others, your constituents are an audience, as are the other negotiators' constituents. If you negotiate an agreement with a supplier for your company, bystanders such as other suppliers and your firm's competitors may be indirectly affected by the terms you agree to so they are also audiences. The media is often an audience, and it makes the larger population an audience. This happens in labor-management and merger/acquisition negotiations. It also happens when owners of professional sports teams negotiate with star players or coaches. To illustrate, think about how the fans in Cleveland initially tried to help the Cavaliers persuade LeBron James to stay, and then joined with the owner in denigrating him after he announced that he was joining the Miami Heat.

Audience effects are particularly important for negotiators to be aware of because they tend to change negotiator's behaviors. They raise our aspirations and cause us to try harder. We negotiate tougher, using tactics that may be ethically questionable and damage relationships (e.g., threats, misrepresentations, intimidation). Audiences also make time pressures more salient, thus leading to the use of more competitive tactics. How much tougher we negotiate depends upon several factors – the more visible the audience is and the more dependent they are on the outcome, the more competitively we will negotiate (Mosterd & Rutte, 2000; Druckman, 1994; Carnevale, Pruitt & Britton, 1979). We do this because we want them to accept the agreement we reach with the other party, and we want them to evaluate us favorably.

Coalitions

A coalition is a subset of a larger social group. In multiparty negotiations, coalitions may form. Those who join together will merge their resources to exert greater influence on outcomes (Komorita & Parks, 1995). **Coalitions** are informal groups of two or more interacting parties that are deliberately constructed to advance explicit purposes or issues. They take concerted actions to persuade others to consider certain information, interests, or proposals more carefully (Polzer, Mannix & Neale, 1998; Murnighan, 1986; Pearce, Stevenson & Porter, 1986). The idea is that if multiple parties join together to advocate for something, others must pay more attention. The example in Negotiation in Action 10.3 illustrates how coalitions can work.

NEGOTIATION IN ACTION 10.3

Wind-energy developers typically build wind farms by leasing large blocks of land from different land-owners. In 2006, these developers began knocking on the doors of Wyoming ranchers to lease their land to build wind farms. At first, the ranchers began signing leases without knowing the true value of the wind sweeping across their land. Grant Stumbough of the U.S. Department of Agriculture heard

(Continued)

(Continued)

about the wind developers crisscrossing Wyoming and had a brainstorm – by working together, the ranchers might be able to get better deals. He formed 'wind associations' or coalitions of ranchers and farmers who pooled as much as 100,000 acres of their land, negotiated leasing rights with wind developers as a group and divided the profits. Eight wind associations now exist in Wyoming, and they are catching on in other western states.

These associations now market their land rights to dozens of companies, sometimes triggering bidding wars in the process. Royalties from a wind project could potentially generate hundreds of thousands of dollars annually for a rancher – a gold mine for those who are struggling to stay afloat in a depressed cattle market (Program on Negotiation, 2009a).

Coalitions are not unusual or uncommon. They reflect the interpersonal networks that determine informal structures of organizations. They are often less formal than those illustrated in Box 10.3. Two executive vice presidents might coordinate their budget recommendations to ensure acceptance of their proposals or to sabotage those of a third vice president, or several team members might combine to ensure that the procedures they prefer are accepted by their team leader or their remaining teammates (Murnighan, 1986).

We join coalitions to avoid being coerced into accepting undesirable offers. Rather than 'going it alone' or hiring representatives to negotiate for us, several weaker parties can join together to negotiate in a collective, organized manner with stronger parties. Absent the coalition, the wind developers in Box 10.3 could have walked next door to a neighbor and negotiated with him or her if one rancher or farmer rejected its offer. In addition to enhancing power and ability by pooling their resources, forming coalitions reduces or eliminates destructive competition among and between the members because the other party can no longer pit one against another. Coalitions may benefit everyone. The wind developers might have to pay a higher price per acre to lease land from an association, but they will have to negotiate fewer contracts. This reduces their negotiation costs and they prefer negotiating with landowners who understand their contracts (Program on Negotiation, 2009a).

Coalitions usually begin forming when a party decides that he or she is unable to accomplish a desired outcome alone. Determining who you should join with is easy if you know you will work together effectively to accomplish your goals. If it is not this easy, make contacts early and spend time getting to know the members of the coalition you are thinking about joining, or the members you are thinking about inviting to join yours. Weigh the pros and cons carefully and talk about the costs and benefits of joining with them. Explicitly discussing each of your interests will help you build stronger and more stable relationships with the other members – shared and compatible interests unify members' demands and strengthen coalitions (Polzer et al., 1998; Bottom, Eavey & Miller, 1996). Making these assessments early can be valuable because once people express interest or join, they are more likely to join, and once they join they are less likely to leave.

Consider the resources you and the other members or potential members will bring to the coalition as well. Coalitions will be stronger if a member brings more resources, or a greater variety of resources (Polzer et al., 1998). The downside, however, is that parties bringing more resources to the coalition may demand a greater share of whatever value is eventually created. Simply put, adding more members with more resources or a larger variety of resources increases the power of the coalition, but it also limits how much each member will receive when the outcome is allocated. Rather than forming or joining the largest possible coalition, therefore, it might be better to form or join one that is just large enough to achieve the desired outcome. Having alternative members available to ensure that it remains large enough is advised in case a member leaves because he or she is no longer willing or able to support the coalition.

These and other considerations are summarized in the following questions.

- Is the coalition organized well enough to negotiate with the other side? Does it understand the value of collaborative negotiation?
- What resources will be allocated to these efforts?
- What are your interests, and how are they prioritized? Are they compatible with those of the people with whom you may join?
- If it is not new, does the coalition have a good ethical reputation and record of success?
- If the coalition succeeds, how will the value it creates be allocated, and do these benefits outweigh the risks?
- How much will have to be paid, if anything, to join and remain a member? What costs might be incurred by members in the future? What other consequences might be faced if a negotiation does not go well? (Program on Negotiation, 2009a)?

The added complexity that typifies multiparty negotiations applies to coalitions because they often include more than two parties. This means a coalition must engage in its own internal negotiation before it can negotiate with the larger group.

INTER-TEAM NEGOTIATIONS

Inter-team negotiations happen when two or more people from your party negotiate against two or more people from the other side. One of the most common examples already alluded to is when people representing a labor union negotiate a new contract with people representing management. These are challenging because they introduce additional variables to consider that alter the dynamics.

If you have a choice, consider how many people and who you want on your team. Some argue that four or five is optimal (Latane`, 1981). A larger team helps to ensure that the requisite expertise is present, but it introduces greater coordination and communication complexities that may undermine your efforts. Members with good negotiation skills and abilities are essential to simplify preparation, help you craft appropriate solutions and avoid escalating conflict. Members with the requisite technical expertise are also necessary to help you clarify your interests, ensure that your proposals are appropriate and that those crafted by the other side are evaluated properly.

Cohesive groups – those that have unified members with good interpersonal relationships – pool or share information effectively and tend to work well together. Teams of friends, though, are not always as vigilant about sharing information or claiming value. There is also a bias toward like-mindedness that inhibits creative thinking (Phillips, Mannix, Neale & Gruenfeld, 2004; Peterson & Thompson, 1997; Gruenfeld, Mannix, Williams & Neale, 1996). This is particularly important when your team prepares to negotiate with the other side because intra-team preparation is essentially a multiparty negotiation. Simply put, you must reach an agreement with your teammates regarding the definition of the situation, goals, issues, interests, target and resistance points, BATNAs, your analysis of the other party and so on. To facilitate your efforts to reach this consensus, consider using Six Hats Thinking techniques. In addition to the items discussed in Chapter 2 and earlier in this chapter regarding preparation for a multiparty negotiations, assess the extent to which your team-mates are accountable to others outside of the team – some evidence demonstrates that negotiators who are accountable to people who are not on the team negotiate more effectively than when they are negotiating only for themselves (Peterson & Thompson, 1997). And, when you analyze the other team, test your assumptions to determine whether each member fully embraces their team's defini-tion of the situation, goals, issues, target and resistance points, BATNA, interests, priorities and other important aspects of the negotiation.

When you engage in an inter-team negotiation, plan to caucus occasionally, especially if your negotiation is tough or lengthy. Stepping away will enable you and your teammates to verify that you are still together on a particular argument, issue or option, and allow you to relax or blow off steam. Integrative agreements are more likely when teams are involved especially if the members are trained and experienced. Teams may create value more effectively because they are better at gathering and exchanging information than individual negotiators (Polzer, 1996; Thompson, Peterson & Brodt, 1996). Teams also seem to be more adept at claiming value than solo negotiators – because they have, or are perceived as having, more power than individuals, or perhaps because larger audiences are present (Mosterd & Rutte, 2000; Thompson et al., 1996; Druckman, 1994).

CONCLUSION AND IMPLICATIONS FOR PRACTICE

Potentially, teams are more effective than individuals. Adding people, information, conversations, relationships, strategies and tactics, coalitions, audiences and procedural complexity, however, requires careful preparation and effective management for this potential to be realized. The process of managing much of this complexity can be simplified if Six Hats Thinking techniques are used to structure the consensus-seeking process. If agents are used to secure better outcomes or preserve relationships, they must be selected and managed carefully. The following suggestions should help you manage multiparty negotiations.

1. Identify non-negotiating stakeholders who can make the negotiations go awry. If you believe that there are people who are not at the table who might scuttle the deal, take appropriate steps to involve them more actively in the negotiation.

2. Negotiate with your principals to find out what they want and need, and their priorities, before you meet with the other side. Surveys and interviews usually work better than voting if you are unable to secure unanimity. Clarify what information you can and cannot share with the other side, what information you must share with them, and what terms you can and cannot agree to without securing their approval. Seeking latitude pursuant to the interest-based approach discussed in this chapter will effectively serve your needs and your principals' needs. If the other side has not attempted to clarify its authority, encourage him or her to do so (Program on Negotiation, 2010b).

3. Making the negotiator for the other side look bad to his or her constituents will seriously inhibit your efforts to secure a favorable agreement because saving face is often as important as the substantive terms in a negotiation. You may even have to help the other negotiators save face to

ensure that an agreement can be reached. Paying attention to the other negotiator's words and actions will help you understand their situation. Conveying appreciation and respect for it will begin to help them save face. If they find themselves backed into a corner after making a strong commitment, enable them to retreat gracefully to eliminate the sense of weakness and loss of face that will exist if they must retreat. This, or ignoring their commitment, may preclude them from having to dig their heels in (Program on Negotiation, 2010a; Kolb & Williams, 2003).

4. If your boss is involved, try to move the negotiation to a private setting and report back when you are finished. This strategy prevents succumbing to the inhibition and tension that exists when bosses are present, and damaging your relationship with your boss and teammates. For example, we often freeze up or use inappropriate strategies such as being defensive or ingratiating, both of which are debilitating to the negotiation, team relationships and productivity. If moving the setting is not possible, remember that failing to negotiate successfully will eventually harm your work situation, so remain focused on the process. Whether your audience includes allies or enemies, try to neutralize their presence by privately acknowledging your feelings and separating your emotions from the task at hand. (Program on Negotiation, 2007).

5. Know when and how to form a coalition. If a stronger party is pitting you against other weaker parties, perhaps to take advantage of you, it may be time to form a coalition. Good coalitions improve the quality of the offers you receive and make talks more efficient. They also enhance effectiveness because weaker parties gain information and confidence. When joining or forming a coalition, therefore, seek members with common interests and resources because they will strengthen it (Program on Negotiation, 2009a).

6. Spend ample time brainstorming about and debating substantive matters such as issues, interests, priorities and goals. Resolving issue conflicts prior to the negotiation often leads to better outcomes, Consider bringing in experts to help if you are having trouble agreeing on important facts. Caucuses and even secret signals can also be adopted before the negotiation begins to signal when someone is off track.

7. Choose roles for team members that reflect their strengths. A diversity of knowledge and experience is needed to solve difficult problems or tackle complex negotiations. Keep in mind, however, that friendship networks spring up based on similar interests and skills. Familiarity among members enables them to engage in better exchanges of information and constructive conflict, both of which facilitate effective problem solving. Resolve conflicts within your team before you meet with the other team, or else you may be vulnerable to the other side's efforts to exploit the chinks in your team's armor (Program on Negotiation, 2009b).

8. When multiparty negotiations become too procedurally complex, negotiate the process. For example, **negotiauctions** are increasingly being used in multiparty negotiations for high-value items. If there are multiple buyers, the auction begins with each party submitting its bid. Bidders are eliminated until the three highest remain. The seller negotiates with each one to determine what they can work out to finalize the deal. Another tool for managing the process is to include deal protection provisions. They allow the parties to capitalize on better offers being made or received. Assume you are buying an expensive piece of property and are indifferent between two buildings. You make an offer on one, which is accepted. Shortly thereafter, the seller receives a better offer. You are protected, but the seller loses out on the higher offer. If you had negotiated a deal protection clause that allowed the seller to pay a sizable breakup fee to you if he

Video 10.2

Concept of
Negotiauctions

or she received a better offer before the deal closed, you could have pursued the other property and pocketed the breakup fee, and the seller could have sold the building for more money. Sophisticated deal structures such as these create value by capitalizing on differing beliefs while protecting both the buyer and the seller (Program on Negotiation, 2008, 2010c).

STUDENT STUDY SITE

Visit the Student Study Site at **www.sagepub.com/hames** for additional learning tools.

KEY TERMS

Agent

Audience

Audience effects

Coalitions

Deal Protection Provisions

Informational Complexity

Inter-team negotiations

Intra-team negotiations

Multiparty negotiations

Negotiauctions

Procedural Complexity

Representative

Six Hat Thinking

Social Complexity

Strategic Complexity

REFERENCES

Arrow, K. J. (1963). *Social choice and individual values.* New Haven, CT: Yale University Press.

Beersma, B. & de Dreu, C. K. W. (2002). Integative and distributive negotiation in small groups: Effect of task structure, decision rule, and social motive, *Organizational Behavior and Human Decision Processes*, 87(2), 227-252.

Bottom, W. P., Eavey, C. L. & Miller, G. J. (1996). Getting to the core: Coalitional integrity as a constraint on the power of agenda setters, *Journal of Conflict Resolution*, 40(2), 298-319.

Brown, B. R. (1968). The effects of need to maintain face on interpersonal bargaining, *Journal of Experimental Social Psychology*, 4, 107-122.

Carnevale, P. J. D., Pruitt, D. G. & Britton, S. D. (1979). Looking tough: The negotiator under constituent surveillance, *Personality and Social Psychology Bulletin*, 5, 118-121.

Cutcher-Gershenfeld, J. & Watkins, M. (1999). Toward a theory of representation in negotiation. In R. H. Mnookin & L. E. Susskind (Eds.), *Negotiating on behalf of others*, Thousand Oaks, CA: Sage, 23-51.

de Bono, E. (1985). *Six thinking hats.* Boston: Little, Brown.

Druckman, D. (1994). Determinants of compromising behavior in negotiation, A meta-analysis, *Journal of Conflict Resolution*, 38(3), 507-557.

Fassina, N. E. (2004). Constraining a principal's choice: Outcome vs. behavior contingent agency contracts in representative negotiations, *Negotiation Journal*, July, 435-459.

Fisher, R. & Davis, W. (1999). Authority of an agent: When less is better. In R. H. Mnookin & L. E. Susskind (Eds.), *Negotiating on behalf of others*, Thousand Oaks, CA: Sage, 59-80.

Gruenfeld, D. H., Mannix, E. A., Williams, K. & Neale, M. A. (1996). Group composition and decision making: How member familiarity and information distribution affect process and performance, *Organizational Behavior and Human Decision Processes*, 67(1), 1-15.

Kolb, D. G. & Williams, J. (2003). *Everyday negotiations: Navigating the hidden agendas in bargaining*. San Francisco: Jossey-Bass.

Komorita, S. S. & Parks, C. D. (1995). Interpersonal relations: Mixed-motive interactions, *Annual Review of Psychology*, 46, 183-207.

Latane`, B. (1981). The psychology of social impact, *American Psychologist*, 36, 343-356.

Lax, D. & Sebenius, J. (1986). *The manager as negotiator: Bargaining for cooperation and competitive gain*. New York: The Free Press.

Mannix, E. A., Thompson, L. & Bazerman, M. H. (1989). Negotiation in small groups, *Journal of Applied Psychology*, 74(3), 508-517.

May, K. (1982). A set of independent, necessary and sufficient conditions for simple majority decisions. In B. Barry & R. Hardin (Eds.), *Rational man and irrational society*. Beverly Hills, CA: Sage.

Mosterd, I. & Rutte, C. G. (2000). Effects of time pressure and accountability to constituents on negotiation, *International Journal of Conflict Management*, 11(3), 227-247.

Murnighan, J. K. (1986). Organizational coalitions: Structured contingencies and the formation process. In R. J. Lewicki, B. H. Sheppard & M. H. Bazerman (Eds.), *Research on negotiations in organizations, Vol 1*. Greenwich, CT: JAI Press, 155-173.

Pearce, J. L., Stevenson, W. B. & Porter, L. W. (1986). Coalitions in the organizational context. In R. J. Lewicki, B. H. Sheppard & M. H. Bazerman (Eds.), *Research on negotiations in organizations, Vol 1*. Greenwich, CT: JAI Press, 97-115.

Peterson, E. & Thompson, L. (1997). Negotiation teamwork: The impact of information distribution and accountability on performance depends on the relationship among team members, *Organizational Behavior and Human Decision Processes*, 72(3), 364-383.

Phillips, K. W., Mannix, E. A., Neale, M. A. & Gruenfeld, D. H. (2004). Diverse groups and information sharing: The effects of congruent ties, *Journal of Experimental Social Psychology*, 40(4), 497-510.

Polzer, J. T. (1996). Intergroup negotiations: The effects of negotiating teams, *Journal of Conflict Resolution*, 40, 678-698.

Polzer, J. T., Mannix, E. A. & Neale, M. A. (1998). Interest alignment and coalitions in multiparty negotiation, *Academy of Management Journal*, 41(1), 42-54.

Program on Negotiation (2007). Who's watching? How onlookers affect team talks, *Program on Negotiation Newsletter*, 10(7), 1-4.

Program on Negotiation (2008). What to do when the table gets crowded, *Program on Negotiation Newsletter*, 11(5), 6-7.

Program on Negotiation (2009a). Can't beat them? Then join a coalition, *Program on Negotiation Newsletter*, 12(3)

Program on Negotiation (2009b). The surprising benefits of conflict in negotiating teams, *Program on Negotiation Newsletter*, 12(2), 5-7.

Program on Negotiation (2010a). How to help your counterpart save face, *Program on Negotiation Newsletter*, 13(7), 5-6.

Program on Negotiation (2010b). Dealing with backstage negotiators, *Program on Negotiation Newsletter*, 13(2), 4-6.

Program on Negotiation (2010c). Pull ahead of the pack with a "negotiauction," *Program on Negotiation Newsletter*, 13(1), 1-5.

Ross, S. A. (1973). On the economic theory of agency: The principal's problem, *American Economic Review*, 53, 134-139.

Rubin, J. Z. & Sander, F. E. A. (1988). When should we use agents? Direct vs. representative negotiation, *Negotiation Journal*, 4(4), 395-401.

Thompson, L., Peterson, E. & Brodt, S. (1996). Team negotiation: An examination of integrative and distributive bargaining, *Journal of Personality and Social Psychology*, 70(1), 66-78.

Weingart, L. R., Bennett, R. J. & Brett, J. M. (1993). The impact of consideration of issues and motivational orientation on group negotiation process and outcome, *Journal of Applied Psychology*, 78(3), 504-517.

Reading 10.1

HOW TO MANAGE YOUR NEGOTIATING TEAM

Jeanne M. Brett, Ray Friedman
and Kristin Behfar

The Biggest Challenge May Lie on Your Side of the Table.

You are leading a negotiating team for your company, facing off with a major client to work out a price increase. You think you're on solid footing—you've done your homework, and you know the terms you're looking for. But after some opening niceties, one of your team members blurts out: "Just tell us—what do we need to do get more of your business?" And in that moment, you know you've lost the upper hand.

Gaffes like this are more common than most businesspeople would care to admit. Team members, often unwittingly, routinely undermine one another and thus their team's across-the-table strategies. We studied 45 negotiating teams from a wide array of organizations, including ones in the finance, health care, publishing, manufacturing, telecom, and non-profit sectors. And they told us their biggest challenges came from their own side of the table.

Drawing on the lessons from the experiences of these teams, we offer advice on how to manage the two major obstacles to a negotiating teams' success: aligning the conflicting interests held by members of your own team and implementing a disciplined strategy at the bargaining table.

Aligning Your Own Team's Interests

It's not surprising that negotiating teams wrestle with internal conflicts. After all, companies send teams to the negotiating table only when issues are political or complex and require input from various technical experts, functional groups, or geographic regions. Even though team members are all technically on the same side, they often have different priorities and imagine different ideal outcomes: Business development just wants to close the deal. Finance is most concerned about costs. The Legal department is focused on patents and intellectual property. Teams that ignore or fail to resolve their differences over negotiation targets, trade-offs, concessions, and tactics will not come to the table with a coherent negotiation strategy. They risk ending up with an agreement that's good for one part of the company but bad for another. On the basis of our research, we recommend four techniques for managing conflicts of interest within the team.

Plot out the conflicts. Confronting diverging interests helps clarify team goals, uncover personality conflicts, and ultimately build unity of purpose. Many managers examine competing interests by creating a matrix of the issues that need to be addressed. For each issue, they plot out their own priorities and position, as well as what they think are the priorities and positions of each of the other team members.

Consider the team whose conflicts of interest are represented in the exhibit "What Does This Team Want?" The general manager would like her company to earn more profit. The product manager is concerned that a price increase will erode market share. The sales representative is bent on preserving his account relationship no matter what the cost is. And the business

Source: Jeanne M. Brett, Ray Friedman, and Kristin Behfar, "How to Manage Your Negotiating Team," Harvard Business Review, September 2009, 105–109. Used by permission of Harvard Business School Publishing.

manager wants to increase customer support so that his department will get more work. By plotting out each element up for negotiation, team members can recognize the internal trade-offs they must make before they can coalesce around the highest-margin proposal.

Work with constituents. Underlying many conflicts of interest is the simple fact that members represent different constituencies within the organization. People don't want to let their departments down, so they dig in on an issue important to their constituents that might not be in the best interest of the whole company. If constituents are presented with all the facts, however, they might be willing to concede more ground because they'll also see the bigger picture.

To help get everyone on board with a single negotiation strategy, some leaders deliberately assemble teams that contain only individuals good at forming relationships across constituencies. Managers who don't have the luxury of choosing their team term members, though, might have to go an extra mile to engage those constituencies themselves. One way is to invite important opinion leaders or decision makers to attend team planning sessions. Alternatively, team managers might have to embark on multiple rounds of bargaining with constituent departments. One manager described the many times he went back and forth between the customer service department, the program managers, and the engineers. He'd say, "O.K, we need you to move a little bit more and get your number down a little bit more. We are close—just come this little extra bit."

If those approaches fail, you can engage in reality testing (dubbed "the nuclear scenario" by one manager). To illustrate the dangers of not working together to make a deal happen, for instance, one leader sent his team members back to their own departments with the worst-case outcome for the company and individual units. This sobering hypothetical softened up

hard liners and allowed members to align their interests. Finally, some companies have a formal structure in place to support negotiating teams: If deals involve strategic decisions that affect multiple divisions, a corporate coordinator (often a C-level executive) who has the formal power to get constituencies to fall in line joins the team.

Whatever tactics you choose, know that you cannot skip this step. If your team's members lack the authority or political clout to unilaterally commit their part of the organization to the negotiating strategy, you must somehow get all constituencies on board before you get to the table.

Mediate conflicts of interest. If, despite best efforts, the team cannot reconcile its differences, the best approach may be mediation, led by either a team member or an outside facilitator. The mediator acts as a buffer of sorts. One manager described his team's experience like this: "You've got team members who are extremely competitive, who want to win and are afraid to show weakness." The team member acting as mediator explained that he heard their concerns and their goals, told them where other teammates were coming from, and asked questions like, "Can you just kind of talk through this a little bit? Why do you guys need to be here, and why are you afraid to have that dialogue?" In other words, he applied the classic across-the-table negotiation strategy of asking "why" and "why not" questions to the negotiating team itself.

Persuade with data. The fact that team members don't have access to the same data is often the root of conflicts of interest. In our research, leaders found that their members were understandably unwilling to commit time and resources to the negotiating team until they saw facts and figures that clearly demonstrated the effect their efforts would have on their departments.

Unfortunately, the obvious solution—give people more data—is not as easy as it sounds. Individuals are likely to distrust data that come from other departments, suspecting the information to be biased and self-serving. One company solved that problem by assigning a small task force from within the team to jointly analyze the data provided by each department.

Other companies brought in an outside consultant to gather and analyze the data. An experienced consultant told us how explicit details relating to the purchase of hospital equipment helped one team decide on a strategy. "Physicians feel like they're generating revenue for the hospital, and therefore the hospital should be able to provide the equipment and products that the physician wants," the consultant explained. "What they're surprised to see is that a lot of times the hospital actually loses money on every procedure that's done in their group. Sharing that information with the physician is an eye-opener. So when we put the whole package together for the physicians across groups, they were more likely to understand and be willing to work with the hospital." A body of data, especially if it's provided in a way that emphasizes its objectivity, can align team interests because it offers members the opportunity to save face by making concessions for the greater good.

We found that when teams took the time to resolve their conflicts of interest, members discovered one another's strengths and weaknesses along the way. Thus, their efforts to manage internal conflicts also helped them identify the best roles for each member to play in the next phase of team negotiation: across-the-table bargaining.

Implementing a Shared Strategy

Gaffes made at the bargaining table are usually the result of genuine differences in participant's negotiation styles, a lack of preparation, or frustration. Although rarely intentional, breakdowns in discipline sabotage a team's strategy in ways that are almost impossible to recover from. Such breakdowns reveal fissures that the other party eagerly exploits.

Our interviews uncovered many examples of undisciplined behavior. Sometimes team members get emotional and become irrationally intransigent toward the other side, revealing information that jeopardizes a position or exposes a weakness. Sometimes the reverse happens, and an overeager team member says, "We can do that" – without asking for a reciprocal concession.

Interpersonal conflicts can contribute to these problems. We heard of many teams that struggled internally with defensive posturing, perceived arrogance, and clashes about appropriate negotiation styles. Emotional and personal differences can make people unpredictable and difficult to align with the agreed upon strategy. Drawing on our research, we recommend three tactics to avoid breakdown at the negotiating table.

Simulate the negotiation. To head off surprises at the table, savvy teams role-play ahead of time aspects of the negotiation that they expect to be contentious. Team members who have prior negotiation experience with the other party can be especially valuable. One manager asks his teammates "to throw out objections, so that you're able to figure out, 'OK, if they throw that one at me, who is going to respond to it, and what is the response going to be?'"

Rehearsals Enable Individuals to Determine When to Contribute and When to Keep Silent.

Rehearsals like that enable individuals to determine when they should contribute and when they should keep silent. They help people anticipate their own and others' likeliest emotional responses, predict where team discipline might break down, and clarify who has authority to make concessions and decisions. Role playing takes time, however, and requires extensive knowledge of the other side in order to make accurate predictions. If your team lacks either of those requirements, focus instead on the next two negotiating tactics.

Assign Roles to Capitalize on Team Members' Strengths and Interests.

Most people are familiar with the good cop-bad cop routine as a way to whipsaw an opponent. In a variation of that theme, you can help individual members feel comfortable with the team strategy by giving them specific roles. For example, one team protected the member ultimately responsible for long-term client care by "keeping the bullets away from him." His teammates were the ones who directly confronted the client about pricing.

Team members with particular expertise should, of course, be prepared to speak when their input is needed. But our interviews revealed that experts frequently offer too much information or chime in at inopportune moments. Experts need to be prepped: how much to say, when to speak up, and when not to. We found that teams also ran into trouble at the table when experts were unavailable. Well-prepared teams plan for the possibility that a key decision maker or expert might for some reason be prohibited from attending a session.

Negotiation teams need to have a leader, but sometimes, when a team lacks hierarchy, it's not obvious who that leader should be. Hence, team leadership itself can be the subject of intrateam negotiation. And although someone must take the reins-managing preparation logistics, making sure the team's strategy has been vetted by higher-level management or even the board, and finalizing roles and responsibilities for the bargaining session itself, the most effective team leaders we studied did not try to do everything themselves. You've got a team, managers told us, so use it!

One offered this example: "Even if I can handle all the technical issues myself, if at all possible I'm going to take another specialist with me, preferably someone who has negotiated before.

That way, I don't have to be sitting there thinking, 'I've got to understand their point. I've got to figure out how to respond to it and then negotiate it.' Nobody's brain works that fast."

Research by psychologists Leigh Thompson and Susan Brodt found that negotiating teams achieve higher quality outcomes than solo negotiators. Teams are able to learn more about the other party's priorities than one person can. Having a lead negotiator who does most of the talking and a lead strategist who does most of the listening and is responsible for strategy adjustment makes maximum use of team resources.

Establish a plan for intrateam communication. This sounds like obvious advice, but it's often overlooked. Although caucusing is always an option, managers told us they tried to avoid it because they didn't want to signal a need to adjust strategy. Instead, they established creative ways to communicate with one another, which ranged from the explicit to the implicit and from low to high tech. Said one manager, "At one point Jim was going down the path I didn't want him to talk about, and I just put both my hands on the table and did my stretch thing. That was our code to change the subject." Other teams arrange the seating so members can nudge one another and pass notes discreetly.

Managers did say that it was better to caucus about critical issues than risk a major mishap. In one team we studied, only the lead negotiator was allowed to speak, but if a team member had critical input, she needed only to speak the leader's name, and he would stop, even in the middle of a sentence, for a quick recess.

There are higher-tech solutions for sidebar communications. Teams we studied whose members were geographically dispersed found text messaging to be particularly useful and more subtle than calling one another on cell phones. Text messaging also works well for teammates in the same room who send messages to discuss what's happening without distracting the lead negotiator. Large teams using text messaging or chat technology often had a gatekeeper decide when the lead negotiator needed to be alerted about new ideas bubbling up during the course of the talks. One team we interviewed believed that having an intrateam communication link via online chat was a strategic competency. The team also negotiated a contract with a vendor using computer-based document-sharing and conference call technology to talk across the table, while team members (spread across two continents) kept in touch and updated the strategy using chat. Although complex, this system allowed them to decide in real time when to move ahead in discussing an issue, when to reveal new information, and when to make offers and concessions.

The payoff from negotiating as a team is clear. With access to greater expertise and the ability to assign members to specialized roles, teams can implement more complex strategies than a solo negotiator can ever pull off. But negotiating as a team also clearly presents challenges. How well a team resolves internal conflicts of interest is closely related to how well it performs at the negotiating table: A lack of internal alignment increases the probability that team discipline will break down. A lack of discipline increases the odds that a team's strategy will break down. Either deficiency can push the team into a spiral that is hard to reverse—one the other party will certainly capitalize on. That's why it's critical to engage in internal negotiations *before* your team sits down at the table.

Thinking Further 10.1

1. List and describe the advantages and disadvantages of team versus individual negotiations.

2. Would you prefer to negotiate in a team or as an individual? Why?

Reading 10.2

THE SURPRISING BENEFITS OF CONFLICT IN NEGOTIATING TEAMS

Program on Negotiation

In December 2008, incoming U.S. president Barack Obama created a stir by appointing Senator Hillary Clinton, his bitter opponent for the Democratic nomination, to be his secretary of state. Could Obama expect loyalty from someone he had traded barbs with for months? Would the risky choice be vindicated, or would it backfire?

Some compared Obama's choice to Abraham Lincoln's decision, following his hard-fought election in 1860, to appoint all three of his rivals for the Republican nomination to his cabinet. In her book Team of Rivals: The political Genius of Abraham Lincoln (Simon & Schuster, 2005), Doris Kearns Goodwin maintains that Lincoln was largely able to inspire his former opponents to overcome their differences and rally around him. But in an op-ed piece in the New York Times, historian James Oakes argues that Lincoln was a successful president despite the "contentious, envious and often dysfunctional collection of prima donnas" in his cabinet, not because of them.

Source: Program on Negotiation, 2009. The surprising benefits of conflict in negotiating teams, *Program on Negotiation Newsletter*, 12(2), 5–7.

Note: This article first appeared in *Negotiation,* a monthly newsletter published by the Program on Negotiation at Harvard Law School, www.pon.harvard.edu. Copyright 2006–2011 Harvard University.

In the realm of negotiation, the question as to whether rivalries and differences of opinion harm or help teams is a critical one. Here we examine what negotiation research reveals about team harmony and cohesion.

The Pros and Cons of Teamwork

When a negotiation is a complex one that requires a broad set of knowledge, skills, and experience, gathering a team can be a smarter choice than trying to go it alone, according to Professor Elizabeth Mannix of Cornell University.

Negotiation research supports the notion that teams are more effective than individuals in many situations. Yet without adequate coordination and planning, teams are unlikely to meet their full potential, and the results can be disappointing.

What determines whether team negotiations succeed or fail? In interview with experienced team negotiators, Kristin Behfar (University of California, Irvine), Ray Friedman (Vanderbilt University), and Jeanne Brett (Northwestern University) found that the degree to which teams effectively meet their unique challenges with appropriate strategies depends on how well they manage their internal dynamics.

Notably, the researchers found that the type of disputes that occur within teams can have very different effects on performance. When teams face disagreements that center on substantive issues related to the negotiation tasks, such as those related to interests, priorities, and goals, the resolution of such conflicts can actually spur better outcomes. By contrast, when conflicts get personal—deteriorating into bitter denunciations and criticism, for example—team performance may suffer.

How Your Team Can Thrive Amid Conflict

The following three suggestions can help you foster productive rather than debilitating conflict within your negotiating team:

1. Seek Familiarity, not Friendship.

In their research, Deborah Gruenfeld and Margaret Neale of Stanford University, Katherine Philips of Northwestern University, and Elizabeth Mannix found that team members who had not worked together before were unable to pool the information necessary to solve a problem. By contrast, teams of individuals who were familiar with one another easily pooled information and solved the same problem. Familiarity enables team members to share information and engage in the constructive conflict needed to find a solution, according to Mannix.

This doesn't mean that teams should be built around close friendships. On the contrary, because friendship networks tend to spring up based on similar interests and skills, teams of friends may lack the diversity of knowledge and experience that's needed to tackle a difficult negotiation. Thus, the best team may be one made up of people with diverse skills who have worked together before (and even clashed from time to time), rather than teams of close, like-minded individuals.

2. Discuss Differences in Advance.

To prevent conflicts among diverse, strong-minded team members from overshadowing group goals, Mannix advises negotiation teams to spend at least twice as much time preparing for upcoming talks as they expect to spend at the table. Because the other side will be ready and willing to exploit any chinks in your team's armor, it's important to hash out your differences in advance.

Start by encouraging the team to brainstorm and debate the issues to be discussed during talks. Spend time debating goals, the team's best alternatives to the present agreement, and your reservation point—the worst outcome you, as a team, will accept. Then, spend just as much time exploring the other side's likely goals, background, alternatives, and reservation point.

Having trouble coming to agreement on the facts? Teams sometimes resolve substantive differences by bringing in experts for guidance on areas of confusion, Behfar and colleagues found in their research.

What about personality conflicts? In the Behfar study, some negotiators described the particular problem of coping with highly confrontational or emotional group members. Teams that overcame this difficulty did so by practicing their negotiation script in advance with the goal of directing and controlling the behavior of volatile members. To avoid conveying weakness to the other side, rather than calling for a break at the first sign of trouble some teams devised secret signals they could use to bring wayward members in line—for instance, someone might stretch out her arms to communicate to another member that he's getting off track.

3. Assign Roles and Responsibilities.

Before negotiating, teams should also discuss how to take advantage of members' different skills, suggests Mannix. Which member has the best listening skills? This person could be put in charge of watching and reading members of the other team and reporting his observations to his own team members. Which member has the most negotiation experience? This person could be appointed the team leader—the chief decision maker who corrals the rest of the group. Who is the best communicator? The team spokesperson should be a calm articulate individual who is willing to follow the leader and the team's negotiation plan.

In addition to brainstorming different scenarios that could occur at the table and role-playing how you will respond, your team should discuss the decision rules you will use when you confer privately to weigh the various offers on the table. Because unanimity can be difficult to achieve, you might opt for a majority-decision rule that allows most parties to get what they need from a deal.

By dividing up key responsibilities, debating differences of opinion before negotiating, and keeping talks respectful, your team will be in a strong position to capitalize on its differences.

As for the Obama administration, can Hillary Clinton and other cabinet members look beyond their individual interests and negotiate effectively on behalf of the president and the American people? Stay tuned.

Thinking Further 10.2

1. The author of the article recommends three preparatory steps that help foster productive conflict within a negotiating team. What other types of preparation would you recommend for team negotiations? Why?

2. Although negotiating as a team involves greater complexities, in what ways might it simplify the individual negotiator's roles and responsibilities?

CHAPTER 11

Individual Differences

How Our Unique Qualities Affect Negotiations

Previous chapters have not yet addressed the unique qualities we possess that shape all aspects of our lives. These qualities are important because they make us different from one another, and they may influence how we negotiate. This chapter examines the effects of gender, personality, negotiation styles and emotions on negotiation processes and outcomes.

INTENDED BENEFITS OF THIS CHAPTER

When you finish reading this chapter, you should be able to:

1. Discuss gender differences, emotions and emotional intelligence, and how they affect negotiation processes and outcomes.
2. Recognize important aspects of personality and how they affect negotiation processes and outcomes.
3. Describe different negotiation styles and how they affect negotiation processes and outcomes.

THE ESSENCE OF INDIVIDUAL DIFFERENCES

Most of us expect or assume that individual differences matter when we negotiate because they make such a difference whenever we interact with others. Men and women are socialized to behave differently, so we expect them to negotiate differently. If we have to negotiate with coworkers who get angry whenever someone questions their ideas, we expect them to try to win by bullying us. We expect people who are really smart to "wow" us with how quickly they comprehend complex ideas and how easily they interject their ideas into conversations. We generally believe that emotions and feelings muck up our thinking, but that people who are "emotionally intelligent" are relatively unencumbered by them because they deal with their own and others' emotions so effectively.

Do these and other individual differences really affect negotiation processes and outcomes? Examining the evidence from the 1960s and 1970s tells us that the answer is "no." Qualities like gender, age, race and personality exerted only modest effects, and they were inconsistent – they affected negotiations in some investigations, but not others. Moreover, these investigations revealed that characteristics of the situation, like the nature of the problem being negotiated, the parties' relative power and the presence or absence of constituents, affect negotiations far more than individual differences (Thompson, 1998; Rubin & Brown, 1975).

This seems odd, counterintuitive, even nonsensical. From our own experiences, qualities like gender, personality, intelligence, and emotions shape the nature of our interpersonal relationships, and these relationships are an essential component of our negotiations. This chapter examines the influence of these qualities on negotiation processes and outcomes to help us reconcile what we think we know with what the evidence tells us.

GENDER

Most of the evidence demonstrates that men outperform women in both distributive and integrative negotiations. The difference is small, but the consequences are not. Relative to men, small differences in starting salaries may cost women as much as $1 million during their careers (Babcock & Laschever, 2007; Kray & Thompson, 2005). One way to learn why these gender effects occur in negotiation is to examine the "origins" of gender differences. These include the gender of the negotiator, the gender expectations of the negotiator's opponent, differences attributed to the situation, and how the negotiator's gender combines or interacts with the situation to influence negotiations. The common theme underlying each of these origins is that gender effects emanate, to some degree, from gender stereotypes. The stereotypic traits associated with how men and women behave are listed in Table 11.1. The qualities that people often attribute to effective and ineffective negotiators are listed in Table 11.2. The redundancy is obvious: stereotypic masculine qualities are more valuable at the bargaining table than stereotypic feminine qualities.

Table 11.1 Stereotypes of How Men and Women Behave

Stereotypic Male Attributes	Stereotypic Female Attributes
Strong	Weak
Dominant	Submissive
Assertive	Accommodating
Rational	Emotional

Table 11.2   **Qualities of Effective and Ineffective Negotiators**

Effective Negotiators	Ineffective Negotiators
Strong	Weak
Dominant	Submissive
Assertive	Accommodating
Rational	Emotional

(Kray & Thompson, 2005.)

Gender Differences and Their Origins

The Gender of the Negotiator. This orientation argues that psychological and biological differences between men and women affect their performance. These performance differences are attributed to how we are socialized, our self-construals, and our moral values.

Socialization. From a very early age, boys are socialized to be less verbal, more aggressive, more quantitative and more visual-spatial than girls. When they do speak, they use argument, persuasion and debate to convince others that their ideas should prevail. Girls are socialized to understand that dialogue is central to how they solve problems. They frame, consider and resolve problems through communication and interaction with others because this enables joint exploration of ideas (Kolb & Coolidge, 1991; Tannen, 1990). These differences exist even in those households that try to negate them because the boys' and girls' friends, schools, televisions and other environmental forces teach and reinforce them. This suggests that males negotiate more competitively than females.

Self-Construals. These reflect how men and women see themselves – their self-concepts. Women define themselves in terms of their relationships. They consistently show sensitivity to others' needs and points of view, and incorporate them in their judgments. Seeking intimacy and consensus, women attempt to solve problems by discussing them with others. They also try to create positive impressions. Men, on the other hand, seek independence through their discussions with others. They negotiate more confrontationally than women (Kray & Thompson, 2005; Kolb & Coolidge, 1991).

Moral Values. When settling disputes, women prefer to preserve their own personal integrity and satisfy both parties' interests to preserve relationships. Since they generally understand events contextually, the boundaries between themselves and others, and between events, are often blurred. Understanding women's interests, therefore, requires viewing the context from which they emerge and how they evolve. Men prefer to rely on abstract principles and fundamental rights. They try to hash out what is right and wrong, with a clear winner and loser. They also view events as bounded by task and structure, so each negotiation is viewed as a separate "game" with its own set of rules (Kray & Thompson, 2005; Kolb & Coolidge, 1991; Ury, Brett & Goldberg, 1988).

The evidence suggests that men generally negotiate more competitively than women, and that women are generally more concerned with relationships than men. It also suggests the following:

- Women lack self confidence at the table. They seem to discount or discredit their own ability and worth, and succumb to the stereotypic belief that negotiation is a masculine task – you must be strong, dominant and assertive.
- Men set higher goals before they begin a negotiation, expect to be compensated more highly and are less apprehensive about negotiating.
- Women adhere to stricter standards of what they think is fair and appropriate negotiating behavior (Kray & Babcock, 2006; Walters, Stuhlmacher & Meyer, 1998).

Gender Expectations of the Negotiator's Opponent. This framework argues that men and women behave differently because their opponents expect them to, not because they are fundamentally different (Kray & Thompson, 2005). Simply put, the values and behaviors expected of effective negotiators are highly correlated with stereotypic masculine characteristics such as independence, assertiveness, self-reliance and power, but not with stereotypic feminine characteristics such as communality, caring and helpfulness. This often causes people to assume that women lack the competencies required for success (Tinsley, Cheldelin, Schneider & Amanatullah, 2009; Eagly & Karau, 2002). Even worse, women who act in stereotypically masculine ways may be viewed as competent, but they typically suffer financial and social *backlash*. This inhibits their independence and assertiveness (Davies, Spencer & Steele, 2005; Barron, 2003).

Women are stuck between a rock and a hard place when they negotiate because of this conundrum. They must choose between being perceived as likable but incompetent because they behave in stereotypically feminine ways, or as unlikable but competent because they behave in stereotypically masculine ways (Tinsley et al., 2009; Bowles, Babcock & Lai, 2007). In job negotiations, for example, interviewers judge self-promoting women to be more competent but socially unattractive and less desirable (Heilman, 2001; Janoff-Bulman & Wade, 1996). Women who ask for more compensation are similarly judged as being more demanding and less "nice" than males who engage in the same behavior. Finally, people who negotiate salaries against assertive women desire less interaction with them than with males who negotiate the same way – inside and outside of the workplace. One related finding is particularly compelling: these negative reactions happen whether the evaluator is male or female (Bowles et al., 2007). Reading 11.1 discusses backlash, and how it can be avoided or managed.

The Situation. The underlying premise of this source of gender differences is that men and women are inherently alike, but situational variables such as power, structural positions and experience precipitate differences at the bargaining table (Kray & Thompson, 2005).

Power and Status. Having "power over" others may feel alien to women because it leads away from connection. They prefer to secure "power with" others because mutual empowerment encourages and supports information sharing and joint action, both of which are required for creating value. Having "power over" others is more comfortable and familiar for men because they are socialized to be competitive (Kolb & Coolidge, 1991),

Men and women who have equal power should negotiate similarly. Men, however, usually have more, so they have more latitude when making demands. This enables them to push harder to satisfy their own interests. When women have more power and status, they use their advantage to promote joint outcomes because of their greater concern for the relationship (Kray & Thompson, 2005; Kolb & Coolidge, 1991).

Structural position. Women hold fewer positions of power and engage in fewer negotiations than men do, so they may be viewed as numerical minorities or "tokens" when they do hold these positions or negotiate. Being a "token" usually affects self-concepts and expectations, and others' perceptions and expectations of them. So this, rather than gender, may place them at a disadvantage. These differences should be more pronounced when men and women negotiate against each other than when they negotiate against members of the same gender. As tokens, women face additional problems at the table. People tend to see tokens in more stereotypical terms, and this causes them to be misunderstood more than their male counterparts. It also polarizes and exaggerates gender differences – perceptions are distorted to fit the feminine stereotype, needlessly inducing more contentious behavior and more impasses (Kray & Thompson, 2005; Inzlicht & Ben-Zeev, 2000; Kanter, 1977).

Experience. Just as women tend to have less power and status than men, they also have less experience at the table. Differences between men and women at the table, therefore, reflect experience differences. They may suffer from not being mentored as often or as well as their male counterparts, thus limiting how much information they gain about the implicit norms that govern the negotiation process (Babcock & Laschever, 2007; Kray & Thompson, 2005).

The evidence seems to support these assertions:

- When men and women have equal power, their behavior is comparable (Watson & Hoffman, 1996; Watson, 1994).
- Women negotiate more submissively with men than they do with other women unless explicit norms have been set that override their tendency to behave consistently with gender stereotypes (Kray & Thompson, 2005; Eagly & Wood, 1991).
- Men are more attuned to power asymmetries than women. They exploit them more when negotiating with members of the same gender (Wolfe, 2004).
- Women initiate negotiations less frequently than men – they report that more time has passed since their last negotiation and they anticipate more time will pass before their next one. They negotiate employment packages less frequently and ask for additional compensation less often when they complete a task than men. This is true even when they evaluate their performance on the task comparably. Men and women negotiate at a comparable rate, however, when norms exist that encourage negotiation (Babcock & Laschever, 2007; Small, Babcock, Gelfand & Gettman, 2007).

The Combination of the Negotiator's Gender and the Situation. This orientation argues that gender and characteristics of the situation combine or interact to influence negotiating behavior. That is, men and women experience the bargaining table differently even if the circumstances are identical. Gender effects should be small in strong situations – those with clear guidelines specifying what behaviors are appropriate. They should be more pronounced in weak situations – those without these guidelines. More specifically, gender effects are minimized when guidelines specify that negotiation is appropriate and that particular issues are negotiable. Gender effects are greater when these parameters are absent or not understood (Kray & Thompson, 2005; Deaux & Major, 1987).

The evidence is supportive. When bargaining parameters such as the zone of possible agreement are unambiguous, gender does not affect performance measures like bargaining aspirations, intended first offers and agreements. When the bargaining parameters are ambiguous, these performance measures favor males. Women who represent others at the table, are more assertive and fare better than when they negotiate for themselves. Pushing harder for their constituents is consistent with their relationship orientations and with their desire to avoid appearing greedy. Somewhat more tenuously, gender differences emerge more in work settings than in non-work settings. Relative to men in these settings, women initiate negotiations less, they are more benevolent when making allocation decisions, and their performance suffers more when they are being monitored. These differences disappear in contexts outside of the workplace (Babcock, Gelfand, Small & Stayn, 2004; Bowles, Babcock & McGinn, 2004; Major, Bylsma & Cozzarrelli, 1989).

PERSONALITY

If you have negotiated or interacted with people who are stubborn, risk averse, opportunistic, short-tempered, shy or cocky, you know how important personalities are in determining how the negotiation or interaction unfolds. Personality reflects patterns in individuals' behavior that are stable and enduring, and that reappear in different situations. They predispose us to respond in characteristic ways. A person who is "aggressive," for example, is likely to behave aggressively at work, when driving and when playing games with friends. Personality traits are the labels we use to summarize these patterns. Understanding these traits will help us formulate appropriate strategies and tactics. Learning about the other negotiator's personality will help us know what to expect and make necessary adjustments (Gilkey & Greenhalgh, 1991).

The early evidence pertaining to how personality influences negotiations was not very supportive. At best, findings were modest and inconsistent. Some of the traits that have demonstrated some explanatory power include the following:

Personality Traits

Face Threat Sensitivity. This trait reflects how sensitive people are to losing face – their good name, image or reputation. Highly sensitive negotiators are more likely to compete and less likely to create value that will benefit all parties because they perceive the other party's actions as a threat (White, Tynan, Galinsky & Thompson, 2004).

Machiavellianism pertains to how cynical we are about others' motives (Christie & Geis, 1970). High "Machs" are unsympathetic and opportunistic – they use whatever means are available to accomplish their goals, including deception and violations of social norms, if they think it will help them (Barry, Fulmer & Long, 2000). Low Machs, but not when negotiating distributively, high Machs achieve more than low Machs (Fry, 1985).

Self-efficacy. This trait reflects a person's assessment of how well he or she can perform in a particular situation (Gist, Stevens & Bavetta, 1991). Negotiators who have high self-efficacy are more apt to initiate negotiations and set higher goals (Arnold & O'Connor, 2006; Brett, Pinkley & Jacofsky, 1996; Gist et al., 1991). They also engage in collaborative problem solving and achieve larger outcomes – whether negotiating distributively or integratively (Sullivan, O'Connor & Burris, 2006; Alexander, Schul & McCorkle, 1994).

Self-monitoring reflects a person's sensitivity to the social cues that emanate from the social environment (Snyder, 1974). High self-monitors are attentive to these social cues and use them to decide what constitutes appropriate behavior and how they should adapt to it. Negotiators who are high self-monitors work harder to plan the impressions they want to make on the other party, consider a wider range of strategies and achieve better outcomes than low self-monitors (Jordan & Roloff, 1997).

Social Value Orientation. Individuals' preferences for their own outcomes relative to others' outcomes is the essence of **social value orientation** (Kuhlman & Marsbello, 1975). **Proselfs** choose options that maximize their own gain and, when preparing, they ask more competitive questions. **Prosocials** choose options that maximize joint gain. When preparing, they ask more questions about cooperative tendencies because they value cooperation, equality and desirable outcomes for themselves and the other party. They are also more responsive than proselfs to reciprocity (Van Kleef & de Dreu, 2002; Van Lange & Visser, 1999).

High and Low Trust. This is partly attitudinal because it shifts with changing relationships and changing situations. It is also a personality trait because people are more or less predisposed to trust (Rotter, 1980). *High trusters* believe that others are trustworthy, and their behavior signals that they should be trusted. *Low trusters* do not believe that others are trustworthy, and their behavior signals that they are not trustworthy. This limits disclosure and encourages dishonesty and deception. Low trusters may, however, feign trusting behavior to exploit the other side (Chaudhuri, Khan, Lakshmiratan, Py & Shah, 2003).

Despite these modestly encouraging findings, most personality traits seem to be too narrow and weak to make meaningful differences in how we negotiate or what we achieve (Bazerman, Curhan, Moore & Valley, 2009). A more promising approach for examining what we think we know – that personality affects the nature of our interpersonal interactions, including our negotiations – requires us to look at the relationship between broader categories or related groups of personality traits and negotiating behavior.

The Five-Factor Model

Most of the important personality traits seem to fall into one of five categories (Antonioni, 1998; Barrick & Mount, 1991). This model of personality, typically called the "Big 5" has gained substantial attention in many different domains. These five factors are summarized in Table 11.3.

The relationship between these five dimensions of personality and negotiation has not been investigated extensively. Since these dimensions reflect categories of traits rather than individual traits, they should enhance our understanding of how personality influences negotiation processes and outcomes. The limited evidence that does exist demonstrates that extraversion and agreeableness are liabilities in distributive negotiations. The adverse effects of extraversion are more pronounced in the early stages of negotiating because it makes negotiators more susceptible to anchoring effects. It may benefit negotiators later in the process, however, when they are trying to secure commitments. Agreeable negotiators are also susceptible to anchoring effects. But the adverse effects persist throughout the negotiation, especially if they have low aspirations. This is consistent with other evidence demonstrating that the effects of individual difference variables such as gender are greater when behaviors are not driven by strong contextual factors or clear behavioral norms (Barry & Friedman, 1998; Deaux & Major, 1987).

Table 11.3   The Big-Five Factors

Categories or Factors	Description
Introversion-Extraversion	*Introverted* people are reserved, timid and quiet. Those who are extraverted are outgoing, sociable, gregarious and assertive.
Agreeableness-Antagonism	*Agreeableness* reflects the degree to which people are cooperative, understanding, trusting and sympathetic. *Antagonists* are harsh, insincere, untrusting and unsympathetic.
Conscientiousness-Undisciplined	*Conscientious* people are achievement-oriented, hardworking, organized, dependable and firm. Those who are *undisciplined* are lazy, disorganized, unreliable and indecisive.
Openness-Closeness	People are *open* if they are reflective, creative, imaginative, curious, broad-minded and comfortable with theory. They are *closed* if they are conservative in their opinions, set in their ways, narrow-minded and practical.
Emotional Stability-Neuroticism	*Emotional stability* describes people who are calm, self-confident, secure and patient. *Neuroticism* describes people who are tense, anxious, insecure and irritable.

(Antonioni, 1998; Barrick & Mount, 1991).

Some evidence suggests that extraversion, conscientiousness, openness and agreeableness are positively related to integrative negotiation (Ma & Jaeger, 2005; Nauta & Sanders, 2000; Antonioni, 1998). Other evidence, however, indicates that cognitive ability or "intelligence," not extraversion and agreeableness, influences outcomes when integrative potential exists. In these more complex negotiations, the "smarter" negotiators seem to understand the other party's interests better and this enhances their ability to make better deals. Although "smarter" negotiators create more value without increasing their own costs, they do not extract better deals for themselves. Conscientious negotiators do claim more value for themselves, so maybe it pays to be smart and conscientious (Barry & Friedman, 1998).

Myers-Briggs Type Inventory

Video 11.1
Four Facets of
Personality

Another promising approach for examining how categories of traits influence negotiation processes and outcomes involves the Myers-Briggs Type Inventory. Technically, these "types" are not personality traits. Recognizing that we fluctuate up and down each continuum at different times, they reflect the behavior we tend toward and are most comfortable with in most situations. The "types" are summarized in Table 11.4.

The limited evidence that exists regarding these types and relevant behaviors suggests that:

- Ss perceive and process concrete stimuli and information, while Ns favor abstract information and perceptual processes.

- Ts tend to be assertive in resolving conflicts, while Fs are more inclined to cooperate.
- SFs perceive relatively low levels of risk and are extremely risk tolerant, especially when they anticipate sharing the risk with others, but STs perceive high levels of risk and are highly risk averse.
- NTs and NFs perceive and tolerate risk at moderate levels.
- ETJs favor competition as a conflict management strategy while all other Ts are inclined to compromise.
- EFJs tend to collaborate in resolving conflict, while all other Fs prefer accommodation (Gardner & Martinko, 1996).

Table 11.4 The Myers-Briggs Types

Types	Description
Introvert (I)-Extravert (E)	This reflects how people are energized, or from where they get and direct their energy. Es are energized or charge their batteries by interacting with others, and they focus most of their energy on people and things. They are likely to initiate interactions with others. Is are energized by being alone, and they focus most of their energy on thoughts and ideas. They are less likely to initiate contact with others.
Sensor (S)-Intuitor (N)	This pertains to the kind of information to which we naturally gravitate. Ss pay attention to facts and details. They are linear thinkers and sensible. They like new ideas only if they have practical value and prefer new applications for things that are already established. Ss trust their direct experiences and their 5 senses. Ns try to understand meanings, connections and implications. They are imaginative and like new ideas for their own sake. Ns see and do things differently than what's been done before. They trust their gut instincts.
Thinker (T)-Feeler (F)	How we make decisions or come to conclusions is at the core of this continuum. Ts make decisions objectively, carefully weighing the pros and cons. Persuaded most often by logical arguments, they are analytical. Fs make decisions based on how they feel about an issue and how they and the other party will be affected by it. They are sensitive, empathetic, and usually find strong emotional appeals to be persuasive.
Judger (J)-Perceiver (P)	This is about how we organize our worlds. Ps continue to take in more information because making decisions makes them uneasy and uncertain. They would rather leave options open in case something unexpected arises. They are flexible, spontaneous and see all sides of issues. They may hear firm plans as merely options, and they are comfortable letting others call the shots. Js make decisions quickly and easily. They are organized, goal-oriented and punctual. They want things settled and they usually want to be in control. They are more definitive and require less information to make decisions.

Source: William L. Gardner, Mark J. Martinko, "Using the Myers-Briggs Type Indicator to Study Managers: A Literature Review and Research Agenda," Journal of Management, Spring 1996. Reprinted by permission of SAGE Publications.

NEGOTIATION STYLES

The Dual Concerns Model was introduced in Chapter 1. It argues that there are five different conflict management styles – collaboration, competition, compromising, accommodation and avoidance. Some have tried to translate these into negotiation styles. Others have described them as dispositions – we are predisposed to manage conflict or negotiate in one of these ways. Negotiation styles, however, are more complex than this. These styles, or learned patterns of behavior that can be recognized and managed, are determined by and chosen because of individual differences and characteristics of the situation. (Ogilvie & Kidder, 2008).

More specifically, a variety of individual differences combine to determine negotiators' styles - integrating/collaborating, dominating/competing, compromising, obliging/accommodating or avoiding. These include gender, personality and types, culture, emotional intelligence, attitudes toward negotiating, motivational orientation (cooperative or competitive) and characteristics of the situation (relative power, status of the other negotiators, expected style of the other negotiators, time constraints, importance of the relationship importance of the outcome, format of the negotiation (electronic or face-to-face), number of parties and nature of the negotiation (trade, dispute, team decision, whether integrative potential exists or not). These styles then manifest themselves in different behaviors (e.g., information seeking, concession making, issuing threats, making demands, emotions). These and other behaviors of the negotiators combine to determine the perceived performance or outcome of the negotiation (Ogilvie & Kidder, 2008; Olekalns & Smith, 2005).

EMOTIONS AND EMOTIONAL INTELLIGENCE

Emotions influence interpersonal interactions, including negotiations. An emotion is a "felt response" – not just something you think about, but something you feel.  They are contagious and the impact of strong emotions lingers long after the emotion has passed (Fisher & Shapiro, 2006). Table 11.5 lists a small sample of emotions that may exist when you negotiate. Negative emotions can divert your attention away from substantive matters, damage relationships and be used to exploit you. Unless they are too extreme, positive emotions can make it easier to satisfy your substantive interests and enhance relationships (Ariely & Lowenstein, 2006; Fisher & Shapiro, 2006).

Negative emotions are sometimes so problematic that people try to ignore or suppress them. Unfortunately, we cannot stop having them or turn them on and off. Nor can we ignore them because they engender physiological responses like smiling, crying or turning beet red, and they affect our thinking – they "clog" our heads with negative thoughts. Negative emotions also motivate us to act on them. If we become angry, for example, we may feel like hitting the other person. We usually stop ourselves from engaging in these regrettable actions, but thinking about this instead of the substantive issues and how to solve them inhibits effective negotiating.

Even if we think we are good at it, we are often mistaken when we try to recognize emotions. This may be particularly true in the middle of a negotiation when we are thinking about substantive issues, the relationship and the process we are trying to execute. Trying to identify emotions and the specific cause is, at best, unlikely. The challenge, therefore, is how we deal with and attempt to

Video 11.2
Theories of
Emotional Intelligence

Table 11.5 Examples of Positive and Negative Emotions

Positive Emotions	Negative Emotions
Calm	Angry
Comfortable	Anxious
Content	Disgusted
Enthusiastic	Envious
Excited	Embarrassed
Grateful	Hopeless
Happy	Humiliated
Guilty	Impatient
Humbled	Intimidated
Patient	Irritated
Respectful	Panicked
Relieved	Regretful
Sad	Resentful

transform situations that produce negative emotions into situations that produce positive emotions – those that reduce or eliminate our anxiety about being exploited, lead to thinking that is open, creative and flexible, and facilitate inventing workable solutions instead of rejecting them (Fisher & Shapiro, 2006).

Emotional Intelligence

Some people are *emotionally intelligent* – they have the ability to use and understand emotions adaptively in everyday life (Mayer & Salovey, 1997). Emotional intelligence encompasses several abilities.

- *Perceiving* emotions – detecting and identifying emotions in oneself and others
- *Facilitating* emotions – using emotions productively in the context of various cognitive processes, including creativity, problem solving and reasoning;
- *Understanding* emotions – comprehending how they combine, progress or transition from one to the other; and
- *Managing* emotions – coping with and regulating them in oneself and others in adaptive ways (Mayer, Salovey & Caruso, 2000).

Emotionally intelligent negotiators enjoy a more positive experience and induce positive mood/affect and satisfaction in the other party. These other parties are more willing to negotiate with the emotionally intelligent negotiator again in the future. They also create value, but they do not claim it as well as their counterparts (Kong & Bottom, 2010; Mueller & Curhan, 2006; Foo, Elfenbein, Tan & Aik, 2004).

Addressing Underlying Concerns

Another approach for managing emotions requires us to change our focus from identifying individual emotions to identifying the concerns underlying them. Positive and negative emotions generally emanate from one or more of five concerns – appreciation, affiliation, autonomy, roles or status

(Fisher & Shapiro, 2006). Negotiators, therefore, must manage these factors to induce positive rather than negative emotions.

Appreciation. Though some claim they do not care what others think about them, most people want and need to be appreciated. Feeling appreciated induces positive emotions, while feeling unappreciated gives rise to negative emotions. Appreciating the other negotiator's situation, ideas, feelings and face – the appreciative moves from the shadow negotiation (see Chapter 13), engender positive emotions. Conversely, failing to understand a negotiator's feelings, perspectives ideas, arguments, proposals or actions, and failing to communicate your understanding of their merits, inhibits appreciation and induces negative emotions (Fisher & Shapiro, 2006).

Affiliation. Assuming the person with whom you are negotiating is an adversary is common. Unfortunately, this creates negative emotions and hinders efforts to achieve beneficial outcomes. It is also somewhat nonsensical. We negotiate with others to create satisfactory outcomes, and waste as little time and other resources as possible. Working together requires us to feel affiliation or connectedness with the other negotiator, and this connection is required for creating value. Structural connectedness and personal connectedness are both components of affiliation.

Structural connection exists when your roles place you in a common group. A sincere conversation about your family if you both have children, shared athletic interests, shared membership in professional organizations and graduating from the same university are examples. Treating the other negotiator as a colleague rather than a foe, using first names, emphasizing the shared nature of your task, and meeting with the other negotiator and his or her team in a less formal social setting such as a restaurant for lunch will also help. Be sure to include each team member – exclusion from team activities undermines affiliation and creates negative emotions that are extremely hard to fix (Fisher & Shapiro, 2006).

Meeting in person rather than electronically, discussing things you find personally important, asking for advice on how to deal with work issues and staying in contact as time passes will help you create *personal connections* that also promote affiliation. Rather than developing a close friendship with the other party, your purpose is to establish enough of a connection for you to work together to solve problems jointly and effectively (Fisher & Shapiro, 2006).

Failing to establish these connections, and the negative emotions that result, often inhibits listening and makes you question the other negotiator's honesty. Too much connection, however, makes you vulnerable to being manipulated by the other party. When we feel too close to another person, we tend to rely on our gut feelings and our perceptions of his or her feelings when we decide how to respond to his or her requests. To protect yourself, consult your head and your gut before making a commitment. Consulting your head requires you to use objective criteria, your BATNA and your interests to evaluate proposals. You might also want to consult trusted advisors or colleagues to ensure you are making good decisions. Consulting your gut requires you to ask yourself how you feel about it now, and how you think you will feel about it tomorrow. Also ask yourself how you will feel if you say yes, and how you will feel if you say no (Fisher & Shapiro, 2006).

Autonomy. Emotions emanate from our feeling of autonomy. We enjoy having choices and the freedom to make them. Even if we do not have final decision-making authority, we can expand our autonomy by making recommendations or brainstorming, with or without the other side, to invent options. We can invent without deciding, which is useful in all negotiations.

If we do have decision-making authority, exercising too much autonomy may lead the other negotiator to believe that we are impinging on his or her autonomy. This will be particularly problematic if he or she did not agree to something, was not consulted or was not informed. We do not like being told what to do because it impinges on our autonomy, so avoid excluding a negotiator from the process if he or she will be impacted by it. Some decisions are so small that you may only need to inform the other negotiator that you are making them. At the very least, this will give him or her a chance to be heard. More significant matters require you to consult with the other side before making decisions. Big decisions, those that will impact either side appreciably, must be negotiated (Fisher & Shapiro, 2006).

Status. Status refers to your standing relative to where others stand. It is not a zero sum phenomenon – if one negotiator has it, the other does not lose it. For the same reason, trying to raise your own by reducing the other negotiator's does not make sense. Having status is beneficial because it raises our self-esteem and the esteem with which others view us – everyone wants to "feel like someone." It also enhances our credibility and our ability to influence others. Treating the other negotiator respectfully and courteously enhances his or her status, thereby inducing positive emotions. Listening carefully to how the other negotiator describes him- or herself, including the level of formality to which he or she is comfortable, will enable you to match this preference, thereby making him or her feel respected.

A person's high standing in a specific domain such as education, computers, business, athletics, morals, emotional intelligence or with particular subject-matter reflects one's *particular status*. Since we all have different forms of this status, often more or less than others, we should remind ourselves of our own expertise, and explicitly acknowledge the other negotiator's expertise, to enhance each negotiator's status and trigger positive emotions. Appreciating his or her status, particularly that which is pertinent to your discussion, can be accomplished by weighing his or her opinions more heavily than others. Be cautious, however, to avoid according undeserved weight to a negotiator's opinion because he or she is of high status in an area that is not pertinent to the issue you are discussing. The opinion of a celebrity, for example, may be weighted heavily because of his or her celebrity status, not because he or she has relevant expertise. When deciding whether to accept a proposal or not, rely on your objective criteria, BATNA, interests or trusted advisors' assessments, not the other party's irrelevant status or expertise (Fisher & Shapiro, 2006).

Roles. Negotiators perform conventional and temporary **roles** during the negotiation process. Fulfilling roles, those that have a clear purpose and are meaningful, induce positive emotions. Conversely, negative emotions emanate from unfulfilling roles, including role conflict – when different roles you assume cannot be satisfied simultaneously. Awareness of and understanding your normal roles is essential because it enables you to reconfigure them to incorporate more meaningful activities, and modify or eliminate those that are unfulfilling. Acknowledging and explicitly appreciating the other negotiator's important roles enhances his or her identity, thereby conferring status and affiliation. Losing these roles compromises his or her identity and triggers negative emotions (Fisher & Shapiro, 2006).

In addition to our conventional roles, we assume temporary roles. Sometimes we allow others to choose or define them for us. If the other party negotiates adversarially, for example, we may respond in kind or try to prove him or her wrong. If we do this, our role is probably not fulfilling. We must be aware of our temporary roles, just as we must be aware of our conventional roles. Consider adopting temporary roles that foster collaboration if you want to create value and such roles are fulfilling. Also consider appreciating the other party's temporary roles and suggesting others that are mutually beneficial (Fisher & Shapiro, 2006).

The scenario in Negotiation in Action 11.1 illustrates each of these concerns and offers suggestions for managing them.

NEGOTIATION IN ACTION 11.1

Ryan nervously walked into his boss's office for his performance review. His annual bonus was riding on a successful review, and his ego couldn't handle too much abuse. He said hello to his boss, John, and sat in the chair on the opposite side of the desk. He tried to assess John's mood to decide whether this was going to be easy or painful. Ryan didn't like his somber and serious expression. John began, "Obviously, this meeting is to talk about your performance evaluation. Generally, your performance over the past twelve months has been acceptable. There are some aspects that need improvement, but let's start with the good news. . . . " He went over a list of things Ryan had done well, but Ryan wasn't listening. He was worrying about what areas would 'need improvement.' When John moved to the topic of improvement, Ryan sat up straight in his seat. And that's when things got tense. John began, "For starters, you need to follow through better. You forgot to write up that memo last month for our biggest client. We're lucky they stayed on board." Ryan responded, "But that memo was not my responsibility. And there are at least ten other memos that I sent out ahead of schedule." John replied, "Fine, but that's what I saw." Ryan sat quietly, his heart beating rapidly. He was trying to stop himself from arguing. "I did not want to give him the satisfaction of rattling my nerves, but I also wanted him to have an accurate impression of who I am." John continued, "You need better availability. I know you have a family. But there is work to be done. We have customers to serve. If you have to pick up the kids, bring your cell phone." Ryan tried to explain by saying, "I try my hardest to be available. But I can't be available twenty-four hours a day." "Fine, but that's what I've observed," said John. "He continued to point our mistakes I had made, and I tried not to take his critique personally, but I was not successful. I rebutted many of his criticisms with little effect. Thirty minutes later, I walked out of his office emotionally exhausted, angry and with no indication that I would receive a bonus."

Ryan enjoys many parts of his job, but his *conventional role* is not as fulfilling as it could be. Rather than passively accepting this role, he could seek advice from his boss about different activities that he could try – to gain the kind of managerial experience he needs to prepare for a high-level management position, which is his long-term goal. Since his wife gets home early from work on Tuesdays, he might also ask if he could work later on Tuesdays so that he could spend more time with his kids on Wednesdays. Instead of assuming the *temporary role* of victim and awaiting punishment from his boss, he could choose to assume other temporary roles. While preparing for his review, he could think of different ways that he sincerely *appreciated* John and the organization, and share one or two of them at the start of the meeting. He could also find a way to convey his appreciation for the time and effort John devoted to preparing his evaluation. He cannot force John to appreciate him, but he can listen actively to the review. Once John feels heard, he may be more willing to listen to Ryan. Ryan may also feel appreciated if he listens actively to the positive aspects of his evaluation. Appreciation is also likely if he models the behavior John desires or if he devotes his energy to making him look good to his superiors.

Affiliation was missing because Ryan began the meeting with his defenses up. He was unwilling to listen and prepared to counter whatever his boss told him. To convert this into more of a learning conversation, Ryan could reframe John's feedback in a way that builds affiliation. He could, for example, encourage a brainstorming session to help him learn how to balance his work and nonwork obligations. He could also establish a personal connection by asking John how he managed working and raising kids. Ryan also impinged on his own autonomy. He can pick and choose which issues to contest. He could have listened to his boss's feedback, treated it as a hypothesis and discussed it with his spouse at home or contemplated it alone in his office instead of regarding it as the truth. Or he could have discussed it with his boss after thinking about it for a while. Given that he anticipated difficulty before his review began, he could have conducted a self-appraisal and sent a memo to his boss outlining the things he thought he did well and those areas where he needed improvement. He could have made recommendations or asked for advice on how to improve. Taking these kinds of actions rather than becoming defensive would help him preserve his autonomy. Finally, John outranks Ryan, has more managerial experience and more decision-making experience. Ryan should respect and acknowledge John's particular status. He should also recognize his own. He outranks John in terms of ground-level understanding of what goes on in their organization. He should use this to trigger his own positive emotions (adapted from Fisher & Shapiro, 2006).

CONCLUSION AND IMPLICATIONS FOR PRACTICE

Many people believe that individual differences (gender, personality, emotions) influence our interactions, including our negotiations. Although the evidence is only modestly supportive, it does suggest that these qualities combine with characteristics of the situation (power, position, experience, behavioral norms or guidelines) to influence negotiation processes by shaping our negotiation styles. Emotions can get in the way of rationality, but they are unavoidable. They reflect our values, impart substantial meaning about what is or is not important and influence our decision making. For those who are less adept at identifying and managing emotions, it is possible to cultivate emotional intelligence. It is also possible to manage the concerns that underlie most emotions and trigger emotional responses. The remainder of this chapter discusses tactical suggestions for understanding and managing individual differences.

1. Women may need to work harder to hone negotiation skills than men. Negotiating comes more naturally to men. They create and claim more value than women, in part because they seem to set higher goals, engage in negotiations more often and have more confidence in their abilities and the process. Whether you are a woman or a man, thorough preparation and practice, and cultivating status to enhance your self-esteem and help you set your aspirations higher, should help

you develop positive attitudes about the process and enhance your performance at the table (Elfenbein, Curhan, Eisenkraft, Shirako & Baccaro, 2008; Barry, Fulmer & Van Kleef, 2004).

2. If you're a woman who is reluctant to negotiate, consider why. Studies show that women negotiate less frequently than men. If confidence is the reason, the suggestions mentioned in #1 should help. If fear of backlash is the cause, behaving assertively within the core feminine stereotype (e.g, framing demands in a manner that reflects how other individuals, your department or your organization will benefit rather than how you will benefit), and the other suggestions included in **Reading 11.1**, should enable you to minimize or eliminate backlash. If an inability to recognize or take advantage of power asymmetries is the reason, you can think in terms of the power you have "with" the other side rather than the power you have "over" the other side. Cultivating power and using it in this way should enhance your ability to create value. It should also reduce backlash because it is more consistent with the feminine stereotype.

3. Remember that individual difference variables are not things you can change for a particular negotiation. Being aware of them, and of important situational variables like behavioral norms and customs, power, experience, whether issues are negotiable, the ZOPA and other elements of the negotiation should help you anticipate the other party's negotiation style and manage your own. Clarifying these behavioral norms and guidelines should also create a "strong situation," thereby minimizing the influence of face threats, low self efficacy, low self monitoring, proself orientations, gender and perhaps introversion, antagonism and closeness. This may also help you move him or her to the "feeling" and "intuitor" ends of these Myers-Briggs spectrums, both of which are more conducive to creative problem solving. Thorough preparation is essential for this.

4. Consider the evidence that suggests gender and personality do not explain much variance in negotiated outcomes cautiously. These conclusions are due, in part, to the limitations of the research that is used to derive them – most of it is conducted in laboratory settings rather than in the "real world." As indicated in #3, these qualities may also combine with characteristics of the situation to determine our negotiation styles. Consistent with the discussion of "strong situations" (see the discussion of gender differences and #4), how people negotiate may reflect their professional role or the culture of their organization more than their gender or their personality. Managers, for example, may negotiate like managers, regardless of their gender or their personality traits. Employees who work in very competitive organizations may negotiate very competitively because this is encouraged or even rewarded by their organization.

5. Remember that both negative and positive emotions are integral to the negotiation. While it is true that negative emotions can and do adversely affect our thinking, and even motivate us to engage in regrettable actions, we would lose valuable information if we tried to silence them. If you are sufficiently emotionally intelligent, you have the advantage of being able to naturally perceive, facilitate, understand and manage them. If you are not able to do these things as well as you would like, consider cultivating your emotional intelligence. In addition, you can manage emotions for yourself and others by addressing the concerns that typically trigger them. Inducing appreciation, affiliation, autonomy and status, and creating fulfilling roles, trigger positive emotions that facilitate productive negotiations. Ignoring or detracting from these qualities triggers negative emotions that facilitate unproductive negotiations. **Reading 11.2** provides additional guidance for managing emotions.

6. Keep in mind that agreements should be based on objective criteria, interests, your BATNA and perhaps consultations with trusted advisors. Some evidence suggests that emotional intelligence and cognitive abilities (intelligence) enable negotiators to create value, but these qualities do not necessarily help individuals claim it. Considering these factors should enhance your ability to claim a fair amount of the value you created.

STUDENT STUDY SITE

Visit the Student Study Site at **www.sagepub.com/hames** for additional learning tools.

KEY TERMS

Affiliation

Autonomy

Emotional intelligence

Face Threat sensitivity

Five-Factor Model

Gender stereotypes

High and low trust

Individual differences

Machiavellianism

Meyers-Briggs Type Inventory

Motivational orientation

Personal Connection

Prosocials

Proselfs

Roles

Self-efficacy

Self-monitoring

Social value orientation

Status

Structural connection

REFERENCES

Alexander, J. F., Schul, P. L. & McCorkle, D. E. (1994). An assessment of selected relationships in a model of the industrial marketing negotiation process, *Journal of Personal Selling & Sales Management*, 14(3), 25-41.

Antonioni, D. (1998). Relationship between the big five personality factors and conflict management styles, *International Journal of Conflict Management*, 9, 336-355.

Arnold, J. A. & O'Connor, K. M. (2006). How negotiator self-efficacy drives decisions to pursue mediation, *Journal of Applied Social Psychology*, 36, 2649-2669.

Babcock, L., Gelfand, M. J., Small, D. A. & Stayn, H. (2004). *Propensity to initiate negotiations: Toward a broader understanding of negotiation behavior.* Unpublished manuscript cited in Kray & Babcock (2006).

Babcock, L. & Laschever, S. (2007). *Women don't ask.* Princeton, NJ: Princeton University Press.

Barrick, M. R. & Mount, M. K. (1991). The Big Five personality dimensions and job performance: A meta-analysis, *Personnel Psychology*, 44, 1-26.

Barron, L. A. (2003). Gender differences in negotiators' beliefs, *Human Relations*, 56, 635-662.

Barry, B. & Friedman, R. (1998). Bargainer characteristics in distributive and integrative negotiation, *Journal of Personality and Social Psychology*, 74, 345-359.

Barry, B., Fulmer, I. S. & Long, A. (2000). *Ethically marginal bargaining tactics: Sanction, efficacy, and performance,* Presented at the annual meeting of the Academy of Management, Toronto.

Barry, B., Fulmer, I. S. & Van Kleef, G. (2004). I laughed, I cried, I settled. In M. J. Gelfand & J. M. Brett (Eds.), *The handbook of negotiation and culture.* Stanford, CA: Stanford Business Books, 71-113.

Bazerman, M. H., Curhan, J. R., Moore, D. A. & Valley, K. L. (2009). Negotiation, *Annual Review of Psychology*, 51, 279-314.

Bowles, H. R., Babcock, L. & Lai, L. (2007). Social incentives for gender differences in the propensity to initiate negotiations: Sometimes it does hurt to ask. *Organizational Behavior and Human Decision Processes,* 103(1): 84–103.

Bowles, H. R., Babcock, L. & McGinn, K. (2004). *Gender as a situational phenomenon in negotiation.* Unpublished manuscript cited in Kray, L. J. & Babcock, L. (2006).

Brett, J. F., Pinkley, R. L. & Jacofsky, E. F. (1996). Alternatives to having BATNA in dyadic negotiation: The influence of goals, self-efficacy, and alternatives on negotiated outcomes, *International Journal of Conflict Management*, 7, 121-138.

Briggs, K. C. & Myers, I. B. (1983). *Myers-Briggs type indicator test booklet (abbreviated version),* Palo Alto, CA: Consulting Psychologists Press.

Chaudhuri, A., Khan, S. A., Lakshmiratan, A., Py, A. & Shah, L. (2003). Trust and trustworthiness in a sequential bargaining game, *Journal of Behavioral Decision Making*, 16, 331-340.

Christie, R. & Geis, F. L. (1970). *Studies in Machiavellianism.* New York: Academic Press.

Davies, P. G., Spencer, S. J. & Steele, C. M. 2005. Clearing the air: Identity safety moderates the effects of stereotype threat on women's leadership aspirations. *Journal of Personality and Social Psychology,* 88(2): 276–287.

Deaux, K., & Major, B. (1987). Putting gender into context: An interactive model of gender related behavior, *Psychological Review*, 94 (3): 369-389.

Eagly, A. H. & Karau, S. J. (2002). Role congruity theory of prejudice toward female leaders. *Psychological Review,* 109(3): 573–598.

Eagly, A. H., & Wood, W. Explaining sex differences in social behavior: A meta-analytic perspective, *Personality and Social Psychology Bulletin*, 17(3): 306-315.

Elfenbein, H. A., Curhan, J. R., Eisenkraft, N., Shirako, A. & Baccaro, L. (2008). Are some negotiators better than others? Individual differences in bargaining outcomes, *Journal of Research in Personality*, 42(6), 1463-1475.

Fisher, R. & Shapiro, D. (2006). *Beyond reason: Using emotions as you negotiate.* New York: Penguin.

Foo, M. D., Elfenbein, H. A., Tan, H. H. & Aik, V. C. (2004). Emotional intelligence and negotiation: The tension between creating and claiming value, *International Journal of Conflict Management*, 15, 411-429.

Fry, W. R. (1985). The effect of dyad Machiavellianism and visual access on integrative bargaining outcomes, *Personality and Social Psychology Bulletin*, 11, 51-62.

Gardner, W. L. & Martinko, M. J. (1996). Using the Myers-Briggs type indicator to study managers: A literature review and research agenda, *Journal of Management,* 22(1), 45-83.

Gilkey, R. W. & Greenhalgh, L. (1991). The role of personality in successful negotiating. In J. W. Breslin & J. Z. Rubin (Eds.), *Negotiation theory and practice.* Cambridge, MA: The Program on Negotiation, 279-290.

Gist, M. E., Stevens, C. K. & Bavetta, A. G. (1991). Effects of self-efficacy and post-training intervention on the acquisition of complex interpersonal skills, *Personnel Psychology*, 44, 837-861.

Heilman, M. E. (2001). Description and prescription: How gender stereotypes prevent women's ascent up the organizational ladder. *Journal of Social Issues* 57(4): 657–674.

Heilman, M. E. & Okimoto, T. G. (2007). Why are women penalized for success at male tasks? The implied communality deficit. *Journal of Applied Psychology* 92(1): 81–92.

Inzlicht, M., & Ben-Zeev, T. (2000). A threatening intellectual environment: Why females are susceptible to experiencing problem-solving deficits in the presence of males, *Psychologica Science, 11*, 365–371.

Janoff-Bulman, R. & Wade, M. B. (1996). The dilemma of self-advocacy for women: Another case of blaming the victim? *Journal of Social and Clinical Psychology* 15(2): 143–152.

Jordan, J. M. & Roloff, M. E. (1997). Planning skills and negotiator goal accomplishment, *Communication Research*, 24, 31-63.

Kanter, R. M. (1977). *Men and women of the corporation*. New York: Basic Books.

Kolb, D. & Coolidge, G. G. (1991). Her place at the table: A consideration of gender issues in negotiation. In J. W. Breslin & J. Z. Rubin (Eds.), *Negotiation theory and practice*. Cambridge, MA: Harvard Program on Negotiation, 261-277.

Kong, D. T. & Bottom, W. P. (2010). *Emotional intelligence, negotiation outcome and negotiation behavior,* Manuscript presented at the annual meeting of the Academy of Management, Montreal.

Kray, L. J. & Babcock, L. (2006). Gender in negotiations: A motivated social cognitive analysis. In L. L. Thompson (Ed.), *Negotiation theory and research*. New York: Psychology Press, 203-224.

Kray, L. J. & Thompson, L. (2005). Gender stereotypes and negotiation performance: An examination of theory and research. In B. Staw & R. Kramer (Eds.), *Research in Organizational Behavior*, 26, New York: Elsevier, 103-182.

Kray, L. J., Thompson, L. & Galinsky, A. D. (2001). Battle of the sexes: Gender stereotype confirmation and reactance in negotiation, *Journal of Personality and Social Psychology*, 80, 942-958.

Kuhlman, M. D. & Marsbello, A. F. J. (1975). Individual differences in game motivation as moderators of preprogrammed strategic effects in prisoner's dilema, *Journal of Personality and Social Psychology*, 32, 922-931.

Ma, Z. & Jaeger, A. (2005). Getting to yes in China: Exploring personality effects in Chinese negotiation styles, *Group Decision and Negotiation*, 14, 4 5-437.

Major, B., Bylsma, W. H. & Cozzarrelli, C. (1989). Gender differences in distributive justice preferences: The impact of domain, *Sex Roles*, 21, 497-497.

Mayer, J. D. & Salovey, P. (1997). What is emotional intelligence? In P. Salovey & D. J. Sluyter (Eds.), *Emotional development and emotional intelligence: Educational implications*. New York: Basic Books, 3-31.

Mayer, J. D., Salovey, P. & Caruso, (2000). Emotional intelligence. In R. Sternberg (Ed.), *Intelligence*. Cambridge: Cambridge University Press, 396-420.

Mueller, J. S. & Curhan, J. R. (2006). Emotional intelligence and counterpart mood induction in a negotiation, *International Journal of Conflict Management*, 17, 110-128.

Nauta, A. & Sanders, K. (2000). Interdepartmental negotiation behavior in manufacturing organizations, *International Journal of Conflict Management*, 11, 135-161.

Ogilvie, J. R. & Kidder, D. L. (2008). What about negotiator styles? *International Journal of Conflict Management*, 19(2), 132-147.

Olekalns, M. & Smith, P. L. (2005). Cognitive Representations of Negotiation, *Australian Journal of Management,* 30(1), 57-76.

Rotter, J. B. (1980). Interpersonal trust, trustworthiness and gullibility, *American Psychologist*, 35, 1–7.

Rubin, J. Z. & Brown, B. R. (1975). *The social psychology of bargaining and negotiation*. New York: Academic Press.

Small, D. A., Babcock, L., Gelfand, M. & Gettman, H. (2007). Who goes to the bargaining table? The influence of gender and framing on the initiation of negotiation. *Journal of Personality and Social Psychology,* 93(4): 600–613.

Snyder, M. (1974). Self-monitoring of expressive behavior, *Journal of Personality and Social Psychology*, 30, 526-537.

Sullivan, B. A., O'Connor, K. M. & Burris, E. R. (2006). Negotiator confidence: The impact of self-efficacy on tactics and outcomes, *Journal of Experimental Social Psychology*, 42, 567-581.

Tannen, D. (1990). *You just don't understand: Women and men in conversation*. New York: Ballantine Books.

Thompson, L. (1998). *The mind and heart of the negotiator*. Upper Saddle River, NJ: Prentice Hall.

Tinsley, C. H., Cheldelin, S. I., Schneider, A. K. & Amanatullah, E. T. (2009). Women at the bargaining table: Pitfalls and prospects, *Negotiation Journal*, 25(2), 233-247.

Ury, W. L., Brett, J. M. & Goldberg, S. B. (1988). *Getting disputes resolved*. San Francisco: Jossey-Bass.

Van Kleef, G. A. & de Dreu, K. W. (2002). Social value orientation and impression formation: A test of two competing hypotheses about information search in negotiation, *International Journal of Conflict Management*, 13, 59-77.

Van Lange, P. A. M. & Visser, K. (1999). Locomotion in social dilemmas: How people adapt to cooperative, tit-for-tat and noncooperative partners, *Journal of Personality and Social Psychology*, 77, 762-773.

Walters, A. E., Stuhlmacher, A. F. & Meyer, L. L. (1998). Gender and negotiator competitiveness: A meta-analysis, *Organizational Behavior and Human Decision Processes*, 76, 1-29.

Watson, C. (1994). Gender differences in negotiating outcomes: Fact or fiction? In A. Taylor &

J. Bernstein-Miller (Eds.), *Conflict and gender*. Cresskill, NJ: Hampton Press, 191-210.

Watson, C., & Hoffman, L. R. (1996). Managers as negotiators: A test of power versus gender as predictors of success, *Leadership Quarterly*, 7, 63-85.

White, J. B., Tynan, R., Galinsky, A. D. & Thompson, L. (2004). Face threat sensitivity in negotiation: Roadblock to agreement and joint gain, *Organizational Behavior and Human Decision Processes*, 94, 101-124.

Wolfe, R. J. (2004). *Effects of power asymmetries and gender on negotiation outcomes*. Unpublished Manuscript cited in Kray & Thompson (2005).

READINGS

Reading 11.1

WHAT HAPPENS WHEN WOMEN DON'T ASK?

Program on Negotiation

Stereotypes and the threat of backlash sometimes hold back women negotiators. Tailored strategies can motivate them to ask for what they need.

About 10 years ago, a group of female graduate students appeared in the office of their program's director, professor Linda Babcock, at Carnegie Mellon University's Heinz School of Public Policy and Management, with a complaint. Their male counterparts in the program would all be teaching their own courses in an upcoming semester, the women said, while they were left serving as mere teaching assistants. Why had they been passed over?

As Babcock recounts in her new book with Sara Laschever, *Ask for It: How Women Can Use the Power of Negotiation to Get What They Really Want* (Bantam, 2008), she took the students' concerns to the associate dean in charge of

teaching assignments. He explained that he sought out opportunities for students who approached him about teaching courses. The gender difference was simple to explain, he said: "More men ask. The women don't ask."

Babcock recalled other situations in which male students had negotiated for what they wanted, and female students had waited for career opportunities to come to them. Was there a larger trend? To find out, Babcock started a research program with several colleagues. Their laboratory findings confirmed her observations: in general, men initiate negotiations to advance their interests about four times more often than women do.

At the same time, research by Babcock, professor Deborah Kolb of the Simmons School of Management, and others has revealed that women negotiate just as often as men in certain circumstances. Moreover, many successful women show no difficulty identifying and asking for what they need. When do women pass up opportunities to negotiate, and at what cost?

Source: Tinsley, C. H., Cheldelin, S. I., Schneider, A. K. & Amanatullah, E. T. (2009). Women at the bargaining table: Pitfalls and prospects, *Negotiation Journal*, 25(2), 233–247.

Note: This article first appeared in *Negotiation*, a monthly newsletter published by the Program on Negotiation at Harvard Law School, www.pon.harvard.edu. Copyright 2006–2011 Harvard University.

What strategies can women adopt to ensure that their appeals are well received? How can organizations better support women negotiators? Current research on gender and negotiation offers answers to these pressing questions.

The Hidden Costs of Not Asking

Over the course of a woman's career, the costs of overlooking opportunities to negotiate for her own interests can be staggering. As an example, Babcock and her colleagues found that only 12.5% of women graduating with master's degrees from the Heinz School in 2002 had negotiated their starting salaries, as compared with 51.5% of male graduates. Babcock calculated that students who did not negotiate their starting salaries would forfeit at least $1 million in income over their lifetimes.

Salary aside, Babcock says that men are more likely than women to negotiate for resources, training, and other factors that boost job satisfaction and success. It stands to reason that men who seek out career opportunities will advance more quickly in their organizations than equally qualified women who do not. In reaction to such inequities, women may grow frustrated and decide to quit. Given that turnover costs American companies billions of dollars each year, Babcock and Laschever argue that organizations suffer significantly from the fact that women ask for what they need less often than men do.

How Stereotypes Hold Women Back

Why do women sometimes pass up opportunities to negotiate? One factor may be *gender schemas,* or stereotyped assumptions about sex differences that shape our expectations and behaviors, says Kolb.

One persistent gender schema is the belief that women are worse negotiators than men, write researchers Laura Kray of the University of Arizona and Leigh Thompson and Adam Galinsky of Northwestern University. The stereotype of women as cooperative and men as competitive leads many people to expect that men will negotiate better deals than women.

Of course, we all know that women can be competitive, just as men can be cooperative. But women understand that acting contrary to gender schemas can carry a high price. Suppose that a woman has misgivings about the travel demands of a work assignment she's been offered. The fear of seeming pushy or demanding— too "masculine"—might lead her to accept the assignment without negotiating a better fit.

A Second Generation of Bias

Although overt gender discrimination in the American workplace is largely a thing of the past, a more subtle form of inequity persists, according to Kolb and Kathleen McGinn of Harvard Business School. Rather than intentional acts of bias, *second-generation gender biases* reflect the continuing dominance of traditionally masculine values in the workplace.

Consider subtle discrimination practices such as these:

- A woman's boss assumes she won't want a promotion because she is pregnant and hires a less-qualified man instead.

- A manager chooses a man to conduct a negotiation in which "toughness" is needed, rather than a woman who has more experience with the client.

- A department head routinely assigns women rather than men to administrative tasks that attract little attention.

These "micro-inequities" don't just slow a woman's career, according to Kolb. They also require her to negotiate over issues that many of her male colleagues do not have to face. Moreover, a woman may find herself confronting cultural norms, such as the notion of an "ideal worker" who is on call 24/7. Challenging the status quo can be a risky move.

A Very Real Backlash

A recent series of experiments shows that women do face a significant backlash when they assert themselves in negotiations. Babcock and colleagues Hannah Riley Bowles of Harvard and Lei Lai of Carnegie Mellon had male and female participants imagine that they were senior managers evaluating an internal candidate for a position within their firms. Next, participants watched videotaped interviews of pairs of actors carrying out the job negotiation.

In evaluations of the candidates, both male and female participants (whose average age was 29) were significantly less willing to work with a female candidate who attempted to negotiate her salary than with a female candidate who did not try to negotiate salary. Female participants also penalized male negotiators who asked for more money, but male evaluators did not. Participants of both sexes viewed women who asked for more to be less nice and more demanding than women who didn't ask.

The stark truth: Women who asked for more money were disliked—and penalized accordingly. Women's reluctance to negotiate may actually be a reasonable choice in such instances.

Having achieved significant gains in the workplace, women now face a double bind. To advance and succeed, they need to advocate for their interests—yet when they do so, they may be punished for being unfeminine.

Advice for Women Negotiators

How can women ask for what they need without triggering a backlash? Here are three pieces of advice:

1. **Collaborate to be liked.** In *Negotiation,* we stress the importance of using collaborative techniques to get what you want. When you explore the other side's interests, engage in joint problem solving, and use influence strategies rather than coercion and demands, you'll be in a better position not only to create value for both sides but also to claim greater value for yourself.

Although a collaborative approach obviously benefits all negotiators, it may be crucial for women. Why? Because women need to make an extra effort to be liked during negotiation, write Babcock and Laschever, or risk a backlash.

That doesn't mean pasting on a permanent smile when asking for a higher salary. Rather, it means expressing appreciation for the other side's perspective, supporting arguments with objective criteria, and framing comments in positive terms—"I'm ready for a new challenge" rather than "I'm really tired of my job." (Babcock and Laschever offer a refresher course on mutual-gains negotiation for women in *Ask for It.*)

2. **Connect your goals to the organization's.** Despite research showing that many women are reluctant to ask for what they need, evidence also suggests that women who do negotiate are likely to thrive. That's the conclusion Kolb and her Simmons colleague Jill Kickul drew from a 2005 survey of 470 professional women attending a leadership conference.

These women recognized the value of negotiation as a tool for career success; 53% of them showed a strong proclivity to negotiate. Attesting to the power of negotiation, this group was much more satisfied with their jobs than those who asked less regularly for what they needed (74% versus 26%).

How did these women negotiate effectively for their success without triggering a backlash? By identifying pressing concerns within their groups, they were able to lobby for resources and responsibilities. These "small wins" in turn attracted positive attention. Connecting their individual interests to the good of their organizations helped these leaders avoid appearing aggressive and established a formula for success.

3. **Navigate the shadow negotiation.** Suppose that a manager named Gwen makes a case for a significant raise following a year of excellent

performance. To her surprise, her usually supportive boss responds by downplaying her achievements: "That request is way out of line with what I've seen from you." Gwen is tempted to back down, though she knows a male colleague was recently awarded a hefty raise for meeting similar targets.

When Women *Do Ask*

Researchers have identified certain contexts in which women routinely negotiate and achieve outcomes that match or exceed those of men:

- **When issues matter to them.** In a survey of investment-bank employees, Iris Bohnet and Fiona Greig of Harvard's Kennedy School of Government found that women professionals were ready and willing to negotiate career issues of particular importance to them, most notably their work-related travel and daily schedules. This could be in part because women feel it is socially acceptable for them to negotiate issues that directly affect their families.
- **When they negotiate on behalf of others.** Although some studies have found that men excel in competitive negotiations, women negotiators in one study achieved better outcomes than men when bargaining on behalf of someone else. In an experiment involving graduating MBAs, researchers Hannah Riley Bowles, Linda Babcock, and Kathleen McGinn found that acting as someone's agent seemed to motivate female participants to work extra hard, perhaps because they expected that assertiveness would be better tolerated than if they were lobbying on their own behalf.
- **When they have good information.** In highly ambiguous situations, gender stereotypes are more likely to emerge, putting women at a disadvantage. In their study,

Bowles, Babcock, and McGinn found that men negotiated higher salaries than women in fields where starting salaries were ambiguous, including telecommunications, real estate, health services, and media. Yet women performed just as well as men when negotiating for jobs in industries where compensation was fairly clear, including investment banking, consulting, and high technology.

5 Take-Aways for Women Negotiators

1. You may be passing up opportunities to negotiate on your own behalf.
2. Avoid a backlash by meshing your interests with those of your organization.
3. Set high negotiation goals for yourself—and reap dramatic results.
4. Be on the lookout for power tactics, and turn them to your advantage.
5. Start a movement in your organization by encouraging other women to ask for what they need.

Old Gender Roles Die Hard

If you think you are immune to gender schemas, consider the results of a popular online test.

The computerized Implicit Association Test (IAT) developed by Anthony Greenwald of the University of Washington, Mahzarin R. Banaji of Harvard University, and Brian Nosek of the University of Virginia reveals deep-seated biases by requiring test takers to make connections quickly, without time for conscious thought.

In one IAT, thousands of men and women have proved much more adept at linking words associated with work (such as *salary* and *office*) with men's names than with women's names. At the same time, people are much better at linking words associated with home (*parents, children,* etc.) with women's names than with men's names.

As open-minded as we strive to be, we may still find the image of a woman leading a work team or a man cooking dinner for his family to be unnatural at a subconscious level. That's all the more reason to be vigilant about double standards at the office and at home.

When you negotiate issues that challenge people's deeply seated beliefs about gender, they may respond with moves that question your credibility and competence, according to Kolb. In their book *Everyday Negotiation: Navigating the Hidden Agendas in Bargaining* (Jossey-Bass, 2003), Kolb and Judith Williams write that such moves are part of a "shadow negotiation" that goes deeper than the issues at stake. Your shadow negotiation with someone encompasses how you treat each other, who gets heard, and how cooperative and open you are.

Women can counter demeaning, critical, and threatening moves by turning the conversation in a more productive direction. Rather than backing down or becoming defensive, Gwen might ask her boss about his reasoning: "Can you explain why you feel that way?" She could also reference data showing the cost savings she has achieved. When you recognize a move as a power tactic, you gain the ability to respond strategically and effectively.

Advice for Concerned Leaders

Without support from higher-ups, even women who negotiate regularly will advance only so far. To ensure that your organization takes greater advantage of women's talents and skills, follow these three tips from Babcock and Laschever:

1. **Audit your assignments.** Reflect back on the work assignments you made in the past year. How often did male or female employees approach you about taking on a new opportunity? Were female employees less likely to initiate such negotiations? If so, pause the next time a man asks you for a plum assignment and consider whether he is truly the best candidate.

2. **Serve as a mentor.** If you've noticed that certain talented female employees are working behind the scenes, talk to them about opportunities that might attract more attention. Simply telling someone that "everything is negotiable" can have a big impact. After Babcock took steps to encourage women graduate students at the Heinz School to negotiate their starting salaries, the percentage of women who did so rose from 12.5% to 68% within three years, matching the negotiation rates and starting salaries of male students.

3. **Raise awareness.** Organizational policies may subtly discourage women from negotiating and advancing. If administrative staff can work flexible hours but managers cannot, some women may have trouble getting ahead, and men striving for a greater work-life balance may be at a disadvantage as well. Examine your organization's culture for such hints of bias, and institute more gender-neutral practices.

When Negotiation is *Not* the Answer

Before wasting your time and money on unproductive talks, do a cost-benefit analysis.

You may be surprised to read it here, but negotiation isn't always the best way to resolve conflicts and achieve your goals. Here are three cases in which the decision to negotiate got people into trouble, as described in *Negotiation Genius: How to Overcome Obstacles and Achieve Brilliant Results at the Bargaining Table and Beyond* (Bantam, 2007) by Harvard Business School professors Deepak Malhotra and Max H. Bazerman:

1. A Harvard economics professor developed the habit of stealing manure for his garden from a nearby farm. Upon being caught by a farmhand, the professor offered $20 for the load of manure already in his truck—and upped the price to $40 when the farmhand turned him down. Infuriated,

the farmhand called the police. The professor was charged with trespassing, larceny, and malicious destruction—and briefly became the laughingstock of late-night television.

2. While teaching a negotiation course in Bangkok, Thailand, Bazerman learned that he could impress his students with his real-world negotiating skills by haggling with taxi drivers each day for a low fare back to the faculty dorms. Then Bazerman's wife arrived in Thailand. At the end of her first night in town, Bazerman turned away two taxis after being unable to negotiate a low fare. Exhausted by her travels, his wife offered to give him the 40 cents he needed to impress his class the next morning.

3. A couple purchased a plot of land and negotiated with eight builders for a contract to build their dream house. After receiving a rock-bottom bid, they haggled with the builder to lower the price further. Reluctantly, the builder came down another 3%. The house was completed late and over budget, and when the couple moved in, they found the workmanship was shoddy. The contractor was belligerent with them on the phone and slow to make repairs. Ultimately, they wished they had never built their dream house.

Anecdotal evidence suggests that, generally, people are more likely to overlook opportunities to negotiate than to dive into the wrong negotiation. Yet when you negotiate without first analyzing the costs and benefits, the results can range from mildly annoying to disastrous.

When Negotiation Is a Bad Idea

In *Negotiation Genius,* Malhotra and Bazerman identify a number of broad categories in which the decision to negotiate may be a mistake. Here are four of them:

When trivial issues are at stake. Have you ever found yourself obsessing about an eBay auction for an item you could live without? As Bazerman's

spouse reminded him in Thailand, focusing on getting a good deal in every transaction wastes valuable time on deals that don't matter in the long run. Before spending hours on trivial negotiations, think about how you might better spend your time.

When everyone knows you have no good alternatives. Graduating Harvard MBA students often approach their negotiation professors for advice about negotiating job offers. What if a student has only one good offer, and the recruiter knows this? In this case, a professor might encourage the student *not* to try to negotiate a higher salary before acceptance, but instead to raise the possibility of a salary increase after accepting the job.

In negotiation, your greatest form of power is a strong outside alternative to agreement. Therefore, if you already have a good offer, trying to bargain further with someone who knows you have nowhere else to go may not be the best strategy. Accepting the offer on the table and *then* asking for more may be the most effective route when you're at a power disadvantage.

When negotiating would send the wrong signal. Why was it a mistake for the economics professor to offer the farmhand $20 for the stolen manure? Certainly the farmhand could spare the manure, and he could have found ways to spend the $20.

This rational analysis failed to account for the farmhand's emotions. Rather than risk offending the farm hand with a cash offer that looked and smelled like a bribe, the professor should have apologized for stealing the manure and then asked how he could make amends, say Malhotra and Bazerman. It pays to think twice before initiating a negotiation that might convey that you don't care about the other side's interests.

When relationships would be harmed. What about the couple who bargained with the contractor for the thinnest profit margin possible? They ended up with a disgruntled contractor and a terrible house. They might have done better by negotiating "friendlier" issues, such as timeliness bonuses and lateness penalties, rather than focusing exclusively on price. When you look at negotiation as the start of a long-term relationship rather than a one-off transaction, you can save everyone a great deal of stress.

6 Questions to Ask Before You Begin

How can you reduce the risks of launching the wrong negotiation? By conducting a cost-benefit analysis before you begin, advise Harvard Law School professors Gabriella Blum and Robert H. Mnookin in their chapter "When *Not* to Negotiate" in *The Negotiator's Fieldbook: The Desk Reference for the Experienced Negotiator* (American Bar Association, 2006). In particular, Blum and Mnookin advise you to ask yourself the following six questions:

1. "Can we meet each other's interests?" Identifying and prioritizing your interests in a potential negotiation will help you determine whether it's worth the time and effort. Moreover, thinking about what the other party might want from a deal with you should also lend crucial insights.

If the couple planning their dream house had paused to think this question through before negotiating with contractors, they would have recognized that ending up with a well-made house was more important than getting the lowest price possible. Similarly, they would have realized that any contractor would need to make a respectable profit for the deal to be worthwhile to him.

2. "What are our alternatives to negotiating?" If you're involved in a dispute with another party, alternative dispute-resolution techniques such as mediation and arbitration may offer appealing alternatives to negotiation. Although negotiation is often the lowest-cost

option, the input of disinterested experts can reduce tension and prompt mutually agreeable solutions. In a similar vein, the farmhand apparently conducted a quick cost-benefit analysis and decided that handing the Harvard professor over to the authorities was a better option than negotiating with him over the price of manure.

3. "What are my alternatives to this negotiation, and what are my counterpart's?" As Malhotra and Bazerman have noted, pressing someone for a better offer could be the wrong move if she's aware that you have no better alternative to the current deal. If you both know you'll take the offer, consider appealing to her sense of fairness *after* acceptance rather than negotiating details up front. On the flip side, what if you're the one with an abundance of power? Suppose that you tell a salesperson, truthfully, that you have a better offer from another company. If he's unable to match or beat that deal, negotiating with him further would be a waste of time.

4. "How likely are we to reach and implement a deal?" It's not enough that a potential negotiation might create tremendous gains for you and a potential counterpart. You also need to assess whether the potential benefits of agreement outweigh the risks of deal failure. Will your counterpart be able to uphold her end of the bargain? If not, it would make little sense to negotiate with her.

On a similar note, consider whether constituencies on both sides of the deal will support an agreement. Bazerman valued his trivial negotiations with Bangkok taxi drivers for the interactions they provided with his students. However, when these negotiations inconvenienced his wife, it was time to stop haggling.

5. "What are the direct and indirect costs of the negotiation?" Virtually any negotiation has *transaction costs*—investments of time, money, labor, and other resources. Retailers set prices because haggling with customers over

the cost of every sweater or bottle of water would impose enormous transaction costs on the company. Seizing every opportunity to negotiate that comes your way would quickly exhaust your patience and time.

Negotiations can also have indirect costs. A physician who chooses to settle a baseless malpractice claim rather than go to court may find her reputation irreparably damaged, write Blum and Mnookin, while a firm that negotiates with striking workers might convey weakness to other unions. Concerns about outside parties need not dominate your decision, but you should at least factor them into your analysis.

6. **"What are the ethical implications of the negotiation?"** When you invite a party to negotiate with you (or agree to negotiate with her), say Blum and Mnookin, you implicitly acknowledge the legitimacy of her interests and claims and put your own ethics on the line. In the realm of global politics, many governments have a policy against negotiating with terrorists and insurgent groups for fear of conferring legitimacy upon them and sanctioning their unlawful acts.

That said, negotiators often commit the error of attributing people's behavior to their character rather than the situation. As a result, we're biased toward dismissing potential negotiating partners as "evil" or labeling certain issues as sacred and thus nonnegotiable. This may be especially true when issues of identity are at stake, according to Blum and Mnookin. Beware the "us versus them" mentality that can infect close-knit groups. Sometimes negotiation truly is the best way to bridge differences and find common ground.

Does Your Reputation Precede You?

Seasoned negotiators are familiar with arguments in favor of networking and reputation building. When you're well regarded in the realms in which you negotiate, such as your organization, your industry, or your neighborhood, it stands to reason that potential partners will flock to you, offering you abundant opportunities to reach your goals.

Yet gossip, rumors, stereotypes, and fleeting impressions can lead your negotiating partners to construct inaccurate opinions about you that infect your network like a virus. We have only so much control over how other parties perceive us.

To what degree does actual negotiating behavior shape reputation? In a recent series of studies, Cameron Anderson and Aiwa Shirako of the Haas School of Business at the University of California at Berkeley examined this question by looking at a breeding ground for reputations: MBA negotiation classes. By watching how students behaved in negotiation simulations over the course of a semester, Anderson and Shirako were able to monitor how reputations developed within the class. They looked not only at negotiators' *firsthand reputations,* or those based on direct interactions between negotiators, but also the *secondhand reputations* that formed when students shared their opinions about their negotiating partners with others in the class.

A number of interesting findings emerged. First, and somewhat surprisingly, individuals' distributive outcomes, or the amount of resources they claimed in single-issue negotiations, did not influence their reputations. Why? Anderson and Shirako speculate that especially assertive negotiators may have avoided a reputation for selfishness because they were seen as fair, even if aggressive.

Second, in integrative tasks (where it was possible to both claim and create value), individuals' negotiating behavior had a mild effect on the reputations they developed. Those who acted cooperatively during such negotiation simulations gained a reputation for being cooperative, and those who behaved selfishly became known for being selfish.

Overall, the link between behavior and reputation was not very strong. It was stronger, however, for a subgroup of the students: those with many social ties.

In two of the studies, on the first day of class, students were asked to rate how well they knew every other student in the room. As you might expect, some of the students were better known and had more connections in their MBA community than others. By the time the course ended, these socially connected individuals were more likely to have developed reputations for being either cooperative or selfish (depending on their behavior) than their lesser-known classmates.

Prominent individuals made stronger impressions on their counterparts than other negotiators, and these impressions in turn were more likely to spread through the class. This was true despite the fact that socially connected students behaved no more cooperatively or selfishly than other negotiators.

The bottom line: If you're negotiating in a realm in which you receive a great deal of social attention, be aware that your behavior may attract added scrutiny. Your cooperative moves are likely to be appreciated, but news of behavior that suggests a lack of concern for the other party's outcomes could spread quickly through your social network.

On the other hand, when you negotiate with prominent individuals, recognize that you may find yourself forming conclusions about their behavior, whether positive or negative, while letting the self-interested or cooperative behavior of lesser-known counterparts slip beneath your radar.

Resource: "Are Individuals' Reputations Related to Their History of Behavior?" by C. Anderson and A. Shirako. *Journal of Personality and Social Psychology, Vol. 94, 2008.*

Thinking Further 11.1

1. Do you believe women have a harder time negotiating effectively than men do? Does it matter if they are attractive or unattractive?

2. Do you agree that 'working within the core feminine stereotype' will help women negotiate more effectively or will it simply compound the problem and reinforce the stereotype? Why?

Reading 11.2

WILL YOUR EMOTIONS GET THE UPPER HAND?

Program on Negotiation

New research shows that emotions affect our judgment in different ways.

Anticipate how you might act on feelings that arise – and negotiate more rationally.

Imagine yourself in each of these three negotiation scenarios:

A. You purchase a plot of land and hire an architect to draw up plans for your new home. He presents plans for a house that is larger and more luxurious than you originally discussed. Though the plans are beyond your budget, you find yourself swept up a desire to make the dream home a reality.

B. Talks with a longtime negotiating counterpart are proceeding smoothly until you

Source: Program on Negotiation (2008). Will emotions get the upper hand? *Program on Negotiation Newsletter*, 11(3), 1–5.

Note: This article first appeared in *Negotiation*, a monthly newsletter published by the Program on Negotiation at Harvard Law School, www.pon.harvard.edu. Copyright 2006–2011 Harvard University.

raise the possibility of extending a delivery deadline during the winter holidays. "You left us in the lurch last year," the buyer's rep says, pushing aside your sales proposal. "You're going to have to get your act together." His outburst makes you furious. After all, you were only trying to give him fair warning.

C. You're meeting a negotiating counterpart for the first time. To your surprise, she physically resembles a college friend of yours who passed away suddenly a number of years ago. As you begin to chat with the woman, sorrowful memories of your old friend flood your mind.

What do these scenarios have in common? In each case, you find yourself experiencing a strong emotion – excitement, anger, and sadness, respectively – during the course of a negotiation. New research suggests that these different emotions will predispose you to act and react in very different ways during the talks that follow, regardless of the relevance of these feelings to the issues at hand.

For many years, research on judgment and decision making centered on cognition, identifying the ways in which our intuition leads us astray. More recently, researchers have begun to explore the impact of emotion on our judgments, including the decisions we make during negotiations. This research is supported by findings from neuroscience showing that our immediate reactions to a situation, a person, or some other stimuli are often emotional.

While emotions provide negotiators with valuable feedback about each other's preferences and interests, they can be detrimental when unaccompanied by rational decision making. Yet whether we realize it or not, we often base our decisions on passing moods. New findings on how emotions affect decisions can help you anticipate how certain feelings may influence your negotiations and adjust your strategies accordingly.

A Tighter Focus on Emotions

Early research on the effects of emotions on judgment and decision making failed to distinguish between specific emotions. Rather, researchers compared how people in a "good" mood performed various tasks as compared to people in a "bad" mood.

Perhaps not surprisingly, this broad categorization of emotions reached contradictory conclusions. We can all think of instances in which two different emotions, such as fear and anger, caused us to behave in very different ways.

Recently, Harvard Kennedy School of Government professor Jennifer Lerner and her colleagues have zeroed in on the impact of specific emotions, including anger, sadness, fear, and disgust, on our judgments. According to this research, specific emotions trigger a specific set of appraisal tendencies – goals, typically unconscious, that lead us to view and respond to the world in certain predictable ways. For example, fear motivates the desire to flee a situation, and sadness causes us to turn inward. Although these tendencies were adaptive to human evolution, protecting us from predators and illness, in today's society they sometimes work against us.

Different Emotions, Different Results

Our fleeting emotions affect our financial transactions in different ways. In the article "Why Your Selling Price May Be Too High" in our October 2007 issue, we describe the *endowment effect* or the tendency for sellers to place an irrationally high value on items they own, a phenomenon identified by psychologists Daniel Kahneman, Jack Knetsch, and Richard Thaler. In a study conducted by these researchers, participants overvalued items they owned briefly, such as inexpensive mugs given to them during the experiment. This type of overvaluation can lead to disappointment for sellers when buyers refuse to pay their inflated asking prices.

Might different emotional states influence the endowment effect? In a 2004 study, Lerner, Deborah Small of the Wharton School of Business, and George Lowenstein of Carnegie Mellon University considered this question. Prior to having participants engage in a buying-and-selling task similar to Kahnemen, Knetsch, and Thaler's, the researchers primed some participants to feel disgust by showing them a graphic, disgusting scene from the movie *Trainspotting*. Other participants were shown a neutral clip from a nature film. Participants primed to feel disgust seemed to feel an "urge to purge" during the financial task that followed. Relative to participants in the neutral condition, disgusted seller reduced their selling prices and disgusted "choosers" (those choosing between a commodity and money) were less willing to acquire new items. Disgust eliminated the endowment effect.

In a related experiment, the researchers primed participants by showing a sad scene from the movie *The Champ*. These "sad" participants seemed motivated to change their circumstances in the financial task. As compared to participants in a neutral condition, sad sellers reduced their prices, similar to disgusted sellers. However, sad choosers were willing to pay more for an item, the opposite of the effect found with disgusted choosers. Thus, sadness produced a reverse endowment effect, or what Lerner and colleagues termed the "misery is not miserly" effect.

Let's return to the scenario in which a fellow negotiator's resemblance to a deceased friend makes you feel sad. The desire to change your emotional state could make you more receptive to extreme proposals from your counterpart, regardless of whether such changes would benefit you.

Unrelated Emotions Matter

According to Jennifer Lerner, no one is surprised when integral emotions—those triggered by the negotiation itself—affect negotiated outcomes. If your counterpart shows up an hour late, makes an offensive joke, and issues careless threats, you are likely to feel furious, and your anger will influence how talks unfold. (For more on how anger affects judgment, see the sidebar, page 4.)

What's more surprising is the finding that incidental emotions, or feelings unrelated to the task at hand, can have an impact on talks. The participants in the Lerner, Small, and Loewenstein study insisted that the emotions generated by the sad or disgusting film clips did not affect the prices they set in the financial task, yet the emotions they experienced—sadness and disgust—had significant and differing effects on their behavior.

Managing Emotions in Negotiation

Too often, write professors Maz H. Bazerman of Harvard Business School and Don Moore of Carnegie Mellon University in their forthcoming book, *Judgment in Managerial Decision Making, Seventh Edition* (Wiley, 2008), people view themselves as slaves to their emotions. In fact, the following five steps can help minimize the negative impact of your emotions on your negotiations.

1. Take a time-out. Loewenstein has noted that when people are feeling angry or upset, they incorrectly predict what they want when they feel more calm and rational. Unfortunately, anger often prompts us to make immediate, emotional decisions that we may later regret when we feel calmer, such as punishing the other side or seeking revenge for a perceived wrong.

To avoid committing such errors, call for a time-out whenever you are feeling upset during a negotiation, advises Lerner. Letting a hot emotion cool helps you realize that seeking punishment or revenge is not in your interest. And if you sense that your negotiating counterpart is in a foul mood, reschedule the rest of your session for another day. On a related note, keep in mind that we're most likely to make emotional snap judgments when we're pressed for time. For this reason, allot ample time to negotiate.

2. Acknowlege your feelings.

Simply being aware that your mood is likely to affect your judgments is an important step. When you label your feelings, you begin to reduce their influence.

Thinking about the source of your emotions and moods (or gently guiding your counterpart to do the same) can help as well. In one study of this phenomenon, researchers Norbert Schwarz of the University of Michigan and Gerald Clore of the University of Virginia found that participants surveyed by phone on cloudy days reported feeling less satisfied with their lives than those surveyed on sunny days. But consider what happened when pollsters asked this question before beginning the survey: "By the way, how is the weather down there?" This subtle cue about a fleeting condition led cloudy-day participants to report being just as satisfied with their lives as sunny-day participants.

3. Reappraise rather than suppress. In her February 2005 Negotiation article, "Emotional Strategy," Stanford University professor Margaret A. Neale writes that it would be a mistake for negotiators to try to suppress emotions that crop up during negotiation. Not only can it be impossible to suppress a strong feeling, but our emotions often offer valuable information about the negotiation.

Consider the case of a counterpart who berates you for bringing up a potential deadline extension. Rather than trying to suppress the anger his remarks trigger, Neale advises you to reappraise the way you view the situation. The negotiator's outburst suggests that you have old business to discuss. By listening to his concerns about how your company let him down in the past, you pave the way for a better relationship and a more constructive agreement.

4. Institute accountability. Making negotiators accountable to others for their decisions is another proven way of managing the harmful impact of certain emotions. In one study, Lerner and Philip Tetlock of the University of California at Berkeley found that participants who had to justify their decisions to an audience learned to control their emotions and engage in more systematic thinking.

You can introduce effective accountability into an upcoming negotiation by agreeing with the other party in advance that you will each be responsible for privately justifying your decisions to an impartial audience, such as a mutually trusted adviser or mediator. For accountability to be effective, negotiators should be accountable not only for their outcomes, but for the negotiation process they outline in advance. Furthermore, they should avoid finding out the opinions of the adviser to whom they are accountable about the issues at stake.

5. Present multiple proposals. The timing of the presentation of options influences our susceptibility to harmful emotions, Bazerman, Ann Tenbrunsel of Notre Dame University, and Kimberly Wade-Benzoni of Duke University have found. Specifically, we tend to act on our emotional preference when evaluating options one at a time, but we become more capable of engaging in reasoned analysis when evaluating options jointly.

If your architect simultaneously presented you with two very different plans for a house—one modest and affordable, the other luxurious and expensive—you would be better equipped to choose the more logical option over the more "affectively arousing" one. Better yet, having two or more options enables you to choose the best qualities of both. Whenever possible, present multiple proposals to your counterparts and ask them to do the same.

Researchers are only just beginning to understand the effect of different emotions on our judgments and negotiations. In the meantime, encouraging with greater rationality will help generate better outcomes for everyone involved.

Thinking Further 11.2

1. Do you believe displaying anger could benefit someone who is negotiating distributively? Would you recommend this tactic? Why or why not?

2. Since preparation is the key to successful negotiation, how might you prepare yourself emotionally prior to negotiating?

CHAPTER 12

International Negotiations

Managing Culture and Other Complexities

Operating across national borders and interacting with people who are not governed by the same national culture present significant challenges because negotiating internationally is more complex than negotiating domestically. This chapter examines these additional challenges and their impact on the negotiation process. This chapter will help you understand how to modify your preparation, and choose and execute your strategy and tactics, so that you can negotiate successfully in the international arena. It will not prepare you to negotiate and close deals, settle disputes or make team decisions in a particular country.

INTENDED BENEFITS OF THIS CHAPTER

When you finish reading this chapter, you should be able to:

1. Describe the elements of international negotiations that make them more complex than domestic negotiations and discuss the tools that are available for managing them.

2. Recognize important aspects of national cultures and how they influence preparation for international negotiations, and explain how to accommodate these challenges.

3. Recognize important aspects of national cultures and how they influence your choice and execution of strategies and tactics when negotiating in this arena.

355

THE ESSENCE OF INTERNATIONAL NEGOTIATIONS

When negotiating domestically, deal making, the settlement of disputes and team decision making is guided by a single ideological backdrop – the negotiators make similar assumptions about social interactions, legal requirements, the role of the government and economic concerns. When negotiators are from different countries are governed by different cultures, they operate with and are guided by different ideological backdrops. Whether purchasing or selling, forming joint ventures, partnering with companies of different nationalities to share distribution channels in a third country or acquiring a foreign company, the negotiators' ideological backdrops must be understood.

HOW DOMESTIC AND INTERNATIONAL NEGOTIATIONS DIFFER

The foregoing suggests that a variety of factors change when negotiating internationally rather than domestically. These factors are interdependent, but each will be discussed independently for the sake of clarity. **Reading 12.1** provides additional insights into these differences and the added complexity that must be managed when negotiating internationally.

International Monetary Factors

Negotiating with people from countries using a different currency requires us to understand currency exchange rates and fluctuations because they can change the value of the deal, perhaps significantly. The nearly 32 percent appreciation of the Euro relative to the U.S. dollar between 2000 and 2010, for example, altered the value of negotiated agreements appreciably if adequate protections were not incorporated. Alternatively, the Mexican peso lost 43 percent of its value relative to the U.S. dollar in 1994. Agreements negotiated between businesses from Mexico and the United States that year experienced precipitous declines in value or windfall gains if adequate protections were not incorporated (Phatak & Habib, 1996).

These protections might include basing the deal on 'most likely' exchange rates from reliable sources such as international banks and currency futures markets, or contingency clauses that would protect both sides from wild swings in the exchange rates for their respective currencies (Phatak & Habib, 1996). Absent these provisions, the "new" value of the agreement may no longer be acceptable.

Foreign exchange controls imposed by many governments also influence international negotiations. The ability of a foreign company to pay for imported raw materials, or to repatriate profits or dividends, depends on the willingness of the host government to make the necessary foreign exchange available. These agreements, therefore, must include provisions to avoid or blunt the effects of any blockages the host government imposes. Foreign exchange restrictions, for example, could be circumvented by exchanging goods or services rather than cash (Phatak & Habib, 1996; Salacuse, 1991).

Legal Pluralism

When negotiating internationally, each country has a different legal system, and your agreement must comply with each set of legal requirements or rules. These rules constrain both the process of the negotiation and the outcome. Examples of legal pluralism constraints abound. Legislation in the United States, for example, prohibits the exportation of various technologies, especially those with potential military applications. To illustrate Cray Computer was not allowed to sell a supercomputer to the Indian government because it raised national security questions. Some countries limit wholly-owned foreign investments in certain industries (e.g., telecommunications, automobile manufacturing). Companies such as Ford, General Motors, Volkswagen and Daimler AG (Mercedes) were required to form joint ventures with indigenous companies to enter the Indian and Chinese markets (Phatak & Habib, 1996; Salacuse, 1991). Whether doing business in the United States or in other countries, U.S. firms are prohibited from issuing or taking bribes to facilitate negotiation processes or achieve desired outcomes. Businesses in countries located along the Indian Ocean rim, however, expect bribes from companies desiring to transact with them (Pedigo & Marshall, 2009).

International merger and acquisition agreements have also been thwarted by differing legal requirements. When Australia's BHP Billiton initiated a $40 billion hostile takeover of Saskatchewan, Canada's Potash, Corp. in November 2010, the Canadian government blocked it but gave BHP thirty days to make additional representations before making its 'final decision.' Saskatchewan's provincial government then threatened legal action if BHP was allowed to take over Potash. In response to these actions, BHP withdrew its bid (English.news.cn).

The challenges of enforcing compliance when international agreements are negotiated also raise concerns. If you are not confident the other company will fully execute or comply with the terms you have agreed upon, or that international law affords adequate protection, seek alternative enforcement mechanisms rather than abandoning the deal. Negotiating a clause in the agreement that requires the parties to submit disputes to international arbitration, for example, allows you to avoid the legal arena and maintain confidence that the deal will be enforced.

Political Pluralism

Just as negotiators must now deal with at least two different legal systems, they must also deal with at least two different political systems, or **political pluralism**. All democracies do not operate in the same way, and some governments are socialistic or communistic. Policies also differ. For example, an American executive running a French subsidiary of a U.S. company must be aware of both French and American foreign policies as they apply to engaging in a business relationship with Cuba or China. An agreement that is in the political and economic interests of France may run counter to those of the United States. An oft cited example of the challenges imposed by political pluralism involves the construction of the Trans-Siberian pipeline in the former Soviet Union in the 1980s. Several European subsidiaries of American companies had negotiated contracts to supply equipment and services necessary for constructing the pipeline. When the Soviets invaded Afghanistan, American foreign policy turned quite hostile toward the Soviet Union. The U.S. government demanded that American firms and their subsidiaries cease doing business with the Soviets. The European governments, however, demanded that the European subsidiaries of American companies be allowed to fulfill their contractual obligations because the pipeline served the national interests of the European countries. Only high-level diplomacy finally resolved the problem (Phatak & Habib, 1996).

Role of Foreign Governments

Government policies and practices in other countries may differ from what negotiators are used to in their home country, and this may influence the processes and the outcomes of negotiations.

Governments may control the total output of an industry and grant or deny permits that would allow companies to expand their production capacity. They may exercise monopoly power, subsidize businesses or be actively involved in imports, exports and other business activities. They may prohibit private enterprise from operating in certain industries such as telecommunications, oil and gas, shipping and airlines, or these businesses may have to compete with government enterprises (Phatak & Habib, 1996). Businesses are owned or operated by the state in some countries. When negotiating deals with these governments or state-owned businesses, the welfare of its citizens or other social and political concerns may be more salient for them than profit.

The nature and role of governments must be considered when preparing for negotiations. In addition to different goals and interests, governments are generally more bureaucratic than businesses. They may adhere rigidly to standard contracts and standard payment terms, neither of which is customary for you or your business. While preparing, you must determine how or if you will adapt to these practices. It is also important to recognize that government policies and practices change. In the United States, for instance, government subsidies and intervention were once quite rare in unregulated industries. In 2009, however, the government intervened to save the banks, Chrysler and General Motors. And, when Fiat attempted to purchase Chrysler assets in 2009, the deal was struck, subject to the approval of the U.S. government. Moreover, the governments of the United States and Canada both bought stakes in the combined company (de la Merced & Maynard, 2009).

Instability and Change

We have witnessed substantial changes in the world since the 1980s – the fall of the Soviet Union, the unification of Germany, the Gulf Wars, the opening of markets in China, India and Russia and the saber rattling in the Koreas. These events and others like them introduce tremendous opportunities, and enormous risks. Negotiators must prepare for war, social, political and military coups and other forms of social unrest, changing government policies, the closure of international trade routes and other opportunities and risks that occur. Negotiation in Action 12.1 illustrates what negotiators may encounter and must be prepared to manage.

NEGOTIATION IN ACTION 12.1

In February 2007, Venezuelan President Hugo Chavez announced the government's planned takeover of the Orinoco Belt oil fields. He outlined plans for Petroeos de Venezuela SA, Venezuela's state oil company, to become the majority stakeholder in four projects in these oil fields with a minimum stake of 60%. He expressed his hope that the five foreign firms operating in these fields would remain minority partners – Exxon Mobil, Chevron, British Petroleum PLC, Total SA and Statoil ASA. While Chavez expressed his hope that these companies would cooperate, his Minister for Energy and Mines announced that the oil fields would be seized if no agreement was reached with the international oil companies. "We're going to take control as of May 1 . . . " (Adapted from Figueroa-Clark, 2007).

One way to cope with such challenges is to include sophisticated political and risk analyses in your preparations. These could include consultations with relevant experts and the acquisition of pertinent knowledge and expertise about the opportunities and risks for your products and services in the global business environment. These analyses should help you evaluate the desirability of conducting business in certain regions. If you decide to move forward and negotiate agreements, consider including cancellation clauses and arbitration clauses to settle any disputes that arise over the execution of the agreement. Purchasing foreign investment insurance to finance the risks you assume may also help (Phatak & Habib, 1996; Salacuse, 1991).

Ideological Differences

The body of ideas upon which the political, economic and social system is based constitutes a country's ideology. The challenge for international negotiators is to avoid taking this foundation for granted and to realize that all countries have **ideological differences** and that our ideologies differ from those of other countries. Political freedoms may vary. Equality among the sexes, and the right to own property or engage in all segments of business may or may not exist. Foreign investment is not always fully embraced and may be viewed as another form of foreign domination. When preparing, negotiators must develop a more complete understanding of these differences. Finding a reasonable middle ground, and framing the language and the content of the negotiation in acceptable patterns is also necessary (Phatak & Habib, 1996).

Video 12.1

New Rules of
International Negotiation

CULTURE

Culture could be treated as an individual difference because most countries have culturally diverse populations. It could also be treated as one other element differentiating domestic and international negotiations. It is so robust and critical, however, that it warrants treatment as a separate section and it deserves additional discussion. Negotiation in Action 12.2 illustrates what some might consider a cultural deal breaker in a negotiation.

NEGOTIATION IN ACTION 12.2

Joe Romano, a partner in a U.S. technology-marketing company, found out on a business trip to Taiwan how close a slip of the tongue can come to ruining a deal. He had been traveling to Asia for 10 years and considered himself to be fluent in Mandarin and Taiwanese. When he met the CEO of a major Taiwanese manufacturer, he meant to say, "Au-ban," which means, "Hello No. 1 Boss." But he slipped and said, "Lau-ban ya," which means "Hello wife of the boss." Simply put, he called this man a woman in front of 20 senior Taiwanese executives. The others all laughed, but the CEO looked at Joe like he was going to kill him. As Joe recounted, "In Asia, guys are hung up on being seen as very manly." Joe had to keep asking them to forgive 'the stupid American' before the CEO would accept his apology (adapted from Garfinkel, 2004).

Cultural Deal Breakers

Language mistakes and violations of local protocol are difficult to avoid and overcome when negotiating internationally, but they are rarely deal breakers. A sincere apology can go a long way toward mending relationships. The real cultural deal breakers are embedded in two critical components of the negotiation process: when planning the negotiation and when choosing which strategy to use (Brett, 2007). Negotiation in Action 12.3 illustrates how both of these problems can undermine your efforts.

NEGOTIATION IN ACTION 12.3

Lafarge, a large and successful building materials company in France, was trying to acquire a state-owned cement operation in China. While planning to enter China by acquiring this operation, Lafarge assumed that China would sell the cement operation if an acceptable price was offered. As logical as this might sound, China was less interested in money than it was in having access to Lafarge's state-of-the-art cement manufacturing processes. Adequate preparation would have informed Lafarge that China had plenty of foreign capital. What it needed was a means to upgrade its inefficient construction manufacturing industry, preserve jobs and ensure a steady supply of construction materials. It also would have learned that the government preferred to transfer state-owned entities to local entities because this would be viewed more favorably by the Chinese people.

Strategically, Lafarge mistakenly sent two fairly junior members of its investment team to talk to the heads of the two state-owned cement companies. It was simply engaging in some due diligence research to find out if either or both of these companies were the right ones to acquire. The Chinese, however, were very unhappy that two analysts were sent to talk to business directors. The due diligence process in China is different than in the West – you need to develop a solid relationship before embarking on due diligence research (adapted from Brett, 2007).

How Culture Influences Our Conception of a Negotiation

Fundamentally, culture influences our conception of what constitutes a negotiation. A few examples are illustrative. People from the United States view it as a competitive exchange of offers and counteroffers while the Japanese consider it to be an opportunity for information sharing. Negotiation is an informal process for Americans, but quite formal for the English, French and Germans (Foster, 1992). Sensitivity to time varies across cultures. People from the United States show up at the scheduled time, try not to waste it and act as if being Change to: "faster" is better because productivity is so highly valued. In China and Latin America, negotiators focus on the task rather than time per se (MacDuff, 2006). Orientations toward risk vary. Relative to Asians and some Europeans, who are risk averse, Americans are risk-takers (Foster, 1992). Finally, agreements differ and mean different things. Americans think memorandums of agreement conclude the negotiation process; the Chinese think they establish a relationship so that negotiations can begin (Foster, 1992). These diverse conceptions influence how negotiators from different cultures frame negotiations. If these frames are sufficiently different or incompatible, they probably lead to misunderstandings, misinterpretations or impasses.

What Is Culture?

Culture is the distinct character of a social group (Lytle, Brett, Barsness, Tinsley & Janssens, 1995). It reflects that group's patterned responses when interacting socially. Culture can be described, metaphorically, as an 'iceberg.' The behaviors and institutions of the group are visible, like the part of the iceberg that rises above the water's surface. Beneath the water line are the values, beliefs, norms, assumptions and knowledge structures of the group – the components that support the visible parts of the 'iceberg.'

The Visible Components

The characteristic behavior patterns of the group include, for example, differences in how people greet others, their physical closeness and their expressiveness. In Japan, people greet by bowing. People in the United States shake hands. In Spain and Italy, people exchange 'dos besos' or kisses on each cheek. It is helpful, of course, to observe these protocols. As cultural outsiders, however, errors will not be deal breakers. Bowing in Japan, for example, is so complex that outsiders will probably never master the appropriate degrees of inclination – the appropriate incline depends upon the other person's status. Interpreting these behaviors is more important than mastering them. Misinterpretations, though, often happen because we view them through the lens of our own culture. This creates confusion, misunderstanding and other problems because we decode the messages differently than they were encoded.

The institutional portions of culture reflect the components of the process discussed previously – the economic, social, political and legal elements, and religion. Culture is manifested in institutional choices (e.g., whether there is a free-market economy, the form of government) and it is embedded in the institutions' ideologies – the principles and precepts underlying institutional choices (Brett, 2007). In Box 12.2, for example, China desired foreign investment, but also wanted to maintain some local ownership, preserve jobs, maintain sufficient supplies of building materials and acquire state-of-the-art technology. These institutions, therefore, may help negotiators identify the other party's interests and priorities.

The Invisible Components

Supporting these behavior patterns and institutions are the parts of the iceberg that are beneath the water line – the group's values, beliefs, norms, assumptions and knowledge structures. These help us understand what and how people of a certain culture negotiate. Cultural *values* are shared judgments about what is important. They differentiate national cultures (Trompenaars, 1993; Hofstede, 1980). Cultural *beliefs* are expectations about how people of that group interact with themselves and with others. Knowing what to expect from others makes it easier to function effectively in our daily activities. They also help us understand the other party's priorities, willingness to trust, power and strategic choices (Brett, 2007).

Together, values and beliefs tell us which issues will be the most salient, how behavior will be interpreted, whether the other negotiator is likely to begin trusting us quickly or not, the importance of building rapport, the relative importance of the relationship and the substantive terms being negotiated, whether contracts will include detailed provisions or general principles, and attitudes toward winning and losing (Meyerson, Weick & Kramer, 1996).

Cultural *norms* are standards of appropriate and inappropriate conduct. Since they tell us how to behave in a particular context, including how we should negotiate, they limit the choices we have.

These norms tell us how people are likely to execute their negotiations, including the pace of the negotiation, whether they communicate directly or indirectly, how confrontational they are likely to be and whether decisions are made by consensus or autocratically. *Knowledge structures* integrate values, beliefs, norms and assumptions to shape how we construct our mental models or scripts. They guide our judgments and decisions and tell us how we should behave in different situations. When negotiating globally, they guide our behavior by having us examine the situation through our cultural lens. *Assumptions*, or unproven suppositions, form the broad base of the cultural iceberg. They are linked to knowledge structures and the ideological backdrop underlying cultural institutions. They are widely held by members of a culture and they govern our actions, yet we are often unaware of them – we recognize them only when we encounter people operating with very different assumptions than our own (Brett, 2007).

The role of culture in international business has garnered substantial attention (Trompenaars, 1996; Schwartz, 1992; Hofstede, 1980). Most of the evidence pertaining to the relationship between culture and negotiation examines the relationship between various cultural dimensions and negotiation processes and outcomes.

Dimensions of Culture

Examining the dimensions of culture allows us to focus on the degree to which individuals possess different traits rather than relying on broad country stereotypes. Three of these dimensions have commanded virtually all of investigators' attention.

Individualism-Collectivism

This continuum differentiates cultures based on the extent to which they focus on individual or collective interests. Social, economic and legal institutions promote and protect individuals' autonomy, accomplishments and rights in **individualistic cultures** (e.g., the United States, Israel). In **collectivistic cultures** (e.g., Japan, Mexico), these institutions promote individuals' interdependencies with others in their families, at work and in their communities. Individual achievements reflect back on those with whom a person is interdependent. Collective interests are also supported above individual interests by legal institutions. For negotiators, this continuum should differentiate the goals, issues, targets and resistance points that are most salient. The focus on autonomy in individualistic cultures also suggests that direct confrontation and distributive negotiation should be more prevalent than in collectivistic cultures where indirect confrontation and collaboration prevail.

Power Distance

People are more accepting of unequal distributions of power in **high power distance** or **hierarchical cultures** (e.g., China, Egypt). Social status determines social power and it generally transfers across situations. Social ranks in these cultures are usually more closed and inflexible as well. In **low power distance** or **egalitarian cultures** (e.g., Australia, Austria), social boundaries are more permeable and social status may be more short-lived and variable across situations. A negotiator's power is largely derived from his or her BATNA. Confronting a higher-status negotiator or team member is less likely in a hierarchical culture than in an egalitarian culture. In fact, a lower status individual is more likely to ask a high status other to intervene in a dispute than he or she is to confront the other person. These value differences limit the strategic choices of negotiators.

Context

This dimension of culture reflects how directly people communicate. People in **low context cultures** (e.g., Canada, Norway) communicate directly. Meaning is communicated explicitly, largely from the words used. Understanding is achieved because people share a vocabulary. Low context cultures tend to be individualistic. In high context cultures (e.g., Brazil, Russia), people communicate indirectly. Meaning is determined from the words used and from the context in which the conversation takes place – from prior interactions, the physical context and nonverbals. In fact, the same words may take on different meaning in different contexts. Understanding is achieved because people share the social context. These cultures tend to be more collectivistic.

Talking around issues without getting directly to the point and interpreting messages differently than what the words suggest reflect the patterned responses of a high context culture. People in these cultures are reluctant to say 'no.' Communicating too directly in high context cultures may cause the other party to lose face; that which is not sufficiently direct in low context cultures may cause the speaker to lose face.

Additional dimensions of culture have been identified, but how they influence negotiations has not been investigated. This is surprising and unfortunate. They might fill some of the voids in our understanding of how culture influences negotiations by enhancing our understanding of international negotiators' interests, priorities and strategic choices.

Culture and Negotiated Outcomes

Video 12.2
Criss-cultural
Negotiations

There is some evidence that culture affects negotiated outcomes. For example, negotiators from collectivistic cultures achieve greater joint gains than negotiators from individualistic cultures (Brett, Adair, Lempereur, Okumura, Shihkirev, Tinsley & Lytle, 1998; Lituchy, 1997). In addition, cross-cultural negotiations produce more modest outcomes than intracultural negotiation (Brett & Okumura, 1998; Lituchy, 1997; Adler & Graham, 1989).

Culture and Negotiation Processes

Most of the evidence argues that the differences in negotiated outcomes are not directly attributable to culture. Instead, people of different cultures negotiate differently and these process differences lead to different outcomes. How culture influences negotiation processes draws heavily on the aforementioned cultural dimensions, especially individualism-collectivism and context. **Reading 12.2** offers additional guidance.

One of the more compelling findings pertaining to how culture influences negotiation processes involves context and individualism-collectivism. These two dimensions impact negotiation processes similarly because, as noted previously, low context cultures are usually individualistic and high context cultures are usually collectivistic. Negotiators from low context/individualistic cultures adopt a **reciprocal questioning approach**. They ask questions about interests and priorities, assume the other party is telling the truth and then reciprocate with information about their own interests and priorities. Information is also exchanged about mutual interests and differences, as is feedback about the correctness of the other party's inferences. This happens during the first two-thirds of the negotiation and enables the parties to identify possible trade-offs. This information is later used to make offers that capture these trade-offs (Brett, 2007; Adair & Brett, 2005).

Negotiators from high context/collectivistic cultures adopt a more indirect approach. They do not like sharing information directly and they often do not believe the other party's answers. They seem to be asking, "Why should I bother asking questions if I'm not going to believe what I'm told?" To gain information about the other party's interests and priorities, therefore, they engage in a *reciprocal offering strategy*. They make single- and multi-issue offers, and the information about interests and priorities is inferred from the sequence of offers and counteroffers that are exchanged. In other words, understanding the other negotiator's interests and priorities is derived from how the offers and counteroffers change as they are exchanged. One of the critical factors that differentiates these two approaches is the rate at which offers are extended, and when. In all cultures, the rate at which offers are exchanged increases over time and it is about the same in the fourth quarter of the negotiation. But negotiators from high context/collectivistic cultures begin reciprocating offers at a much higher rate, much earlier in the negotiation, than negotiators from low context/individualistic cultures (Adair & Brett, 2005; Adair et al., 2004; Adair, Okumura & Brett, 2001).

If these cultural dimensions influence negotiation approaches this dramatically, what happens when people from low and high context cultures or from individualistic and collectivistic cultures negotiate with each other? Undoubtedly, the reciprocal questioning and the reciprocal offering strategies are both available to all negotiators. Those who are from high context or collectivistic cultures are able to share information directly, and they are able to understand the direct communications they receive when they negotiate with someone from a low context or individualistic culture. They seem to have a mental map or script for adapting to the questioning strategy, and it is activated when negotiating with people from low context or individualistic cultures (Brett, 2007; Adair & Brett, 2005).

The reverse does not seem be true. Negotiators from low context or individualistic cultures do not seem to be able to draw accurate inferences of the other negotiator's interests and priorities from the patterns of offers and counteroffers that are exchanged, especially if they are reciprocated one at a time. Pairs of negotiators from low context or individualistic cultures who use the reciprocal offering strategy also achieve lower joint gains if they exchange explicit offers early in the negotiation. They treat these offers as anchors and adjust from there instead of using them to search for information, and this limits their ability to find integrative outcomes (Brett, 2007; Adair & Brett, 2005).

Additional evidence, some of which supports the foregoing, demonstrates that:

- Negotiators from collectivist cultures spend more time planning for long-term goals. Individualists spend more time planning for short-term goals, and they make more extreme offers than negotiators from collectivist cultures (Gelfand & Christakopoulou, 1999; Cai, 1998).
- Collectivistic (Japanese) negotiators frame some conflicts as breaches of social position, a frame not used by the individualistic (U.S.) negotiators (Gelfand et al., 2001).
- Accountability to constituents leads to more competition among individualists but to more cooperation among collectivists. Before negotiating, the individualists also possess more competitive behavioral intentions and thoughts (Gelfand & Realo, 1999).
- In intracultural negotiations, individualistic negotiators engage in direct information exchange about preferences and priorities and comment more about the similarities and differences between the negotiators than do those from collectivistic cultures. Collectivistic negotiators engage in indirect information exchange and infer the preferences of the other negotiator by comparing several different offers and

counteroffers. They also justify tradeoffs with persuasive arguments (Adair et al., 2004; Adair et al., 2001).

- In cross-cultural negotiations, collectivist (Japanese) negotiators adapt to individualist (U.S.) behaviors and are more willing to share information directly than they do in intracultural negotiation (Adair et al., 2001).
- When negotiating via e-mail, collectivistic (Hong Kong) negotiators achieve higher joint gains than in face-to-face negotiations. The higher joint gains result because they issue more extreme opening offers and make more multiple-issue offers when negotiating via e-mail. There is no difference in the joint gains achieved by individualistic (U.S.) negotiators when negotiating electronically or face-to-face. In cross-cultural e-mail negotiations, the negotiators from Hong Kong achieve greater individual gains than those from the United States because they make more aggressive opening offers (Rosette, Brett, Barsness & Lytle, 2004).
- Individualist negotiators are more susceptible to mythical fixed pie perceptionism and fundamental attribution errors than collectivist negotiators (Valenzuela, Srivastava & Lee, 2005; Gelfand et al., 2002; Wade-Benzoni, Okumura, Brett, Moore, Tenbrunsel & Bazerman, 2002; Gelfand & Christakopoulou, 1999).

CONCLUSION AND IMPLICATIONS FOR PRACTICE

International negotiations are more complex than domestic negotiations because you have to deal with fluctuating currency exchange rates, two or more legal and political systems, different governmental roles, sudden change or instability and different ideological backdrops. You must also learn about the other negotiator's culture because this will shape his or her issues and interests and how they are prioritized, the relative importance of the relationship and the substantive terms of the negotiation, how he or she negotiates and whether the final outcome will contain specific terms and conditions or general principles of agreement. This requires you to determine how you will adapt your preparation, and your strategy and tactics, to Change to: "fit" these differences. Some tactical suggestions follow.

1. Learn as much as possible about the other party's language, culture and interests. Consider enlisting the services of an interpreter. He or she may be able to help you understand the other party's culture and ideological backdrop as well as the language. This information should be used to develop a prototype – you must still explore once you meet with the other party because individuals differ within cultures. You run the risk of inappropriately stereotyping the other party if you assume that he or she Change to: "fits" the general precepts of the culture perfectly. As in all negotiations, understanding interests, validating accurate assumptions and modifying unfounded ones about what will or will not be helpful or good for the other party must be accomplished before you begin inventing options. This will also help you decide how or if you must adapt your practices.

2. Understand the relationship between your own currency and the other party's currency, and what factors might cause the exchange rate to fluctuate. Consult respected international banks, currency futures markets or other financial institutions to understand what the exchange rate is predicted to be when payment is required. If the delay between the agreement date and the execution

date is expected to be lengthy, you might also want to incorporate payment contingencies to protect against precipitous increases or decreases in the value of the deal for each party. Contingent arrangements may also help you counter any move by the government to impose disadvantageous foreign exchange controls. This might include agreeing to exchange goods or services instead of money.

3. Clarify the role of the other government during the preparation stage. If you are negotiating with the government, explore very carefully to understand its true interests. Social, political, infrastructure and technological concerns, for example, may be more important than profit. It may also have standardized contracts, payment terms or other practices that do not comply with how you or your company prefers to conduct business. You must decide if you are willing and able to adapt or if this is a deal breaker. Understanding the culture and the practices of the government will also enable you to avoid critical mistakes like the one Lafarge made when it sent analysts to conduct due diligence before establishing relationships with the business directors in China (Box 12.3).

4. Determine whether your own government, or the other country's government, will allow you to conduct business with the other company before you begin negotiating. Your preparation must assess the legal and political viability of conducting business or using desired practices with companies from the other country. If you are not confident about the international legal system enforcing any agreement that you are able to secure, consider incorporating a provision that requires international arbitration to settle disputes about the execution of your agreement.

5. Enlist experts to perform a thorough risk analysis to help you determine if the potential gain of negotiating with parties from another country is worth the political risk. Military, political and social coups, government takeovers of foreign assets or operations in their country, and other instances of instability or sudden change are extremely difficult to anticipate and manage. Even the U.S. government intervenes in business operations to cope with economic calamities, as illustrated in the first decade of this century. International arbitration and cancellation clauses should help you exit if that becomes necessary. And foreign investment insurance should help you finance the risk of engaging in these risky ventures.

6. Adapt your negotiating style. If you are collectivistic or high context and encounter someone using the reciprocal questioning strategy, ask questions about issues, interests and priorities. Focus on matters that you are willing to share because he or she will stop sharing if you are unwilling to do so. Consider sharing some information about your own issues, interests and priorities before you ask him or her to share to help you build trust and the relationship. If you cannot share this information, explain why, honestly, and share other information. Also share honest feedback about why something does or does not work for you (Brett, 2007). If you are individualistic or low context and encounter someone using the reciprocal offering strategy, change your mental map. Rather than using early offers as anchors, use them as information about interests and priorities. Wait for a sequence of offers to be extended to draw inferences, based upon how they change as time passes. Facilitate your understanding of this information by maintaining a log of the other party's offers and counteroffers (Brett, 2007).

7. Do not automatically trust the other party and reveal sensitive information and priorities, especially if you are concerned about the party's trustworthiness. Make multi-issue offers. This reduces the need for trust and eliminates any need to share sensitive information about individual issues. Nor do you have to worry about whether you should believe the other negotiator's answers to your questions (Brett, 2007).

STUDENT STUDY SITE

Visit the Student Study Site at **www.sagepub.com/hames** for additional learning tools.

KEY TERMS

Approach	Individualistic cultures
Collectivistic cultures	Legal pluralism
Culture	Low context cultures
Currency fluctuations	Low power distance (egalitarian) cultures
High context cultures	Political pluralism
High power distance (hierarchical) cultures	Reciprocal offering
Ideological differences	Reciprocal questioning approach

REFERENCES

Adair W. L. & Brett, J. M. (2005). The negotiation dance: Time, culture, and behavioral sequences in negotiation, *Organizational Science*, 16(1), 33-51.

Adair, W., Brett, J., Lempereur, A., Okumura, T. P., Tinsley, C. & Lytle, A. (2004). Culture and negotiation strategy, *Negotiation Journal*, 20(1), 87-111.

Adair, W., Okumura, T. & Brett, J. M. (2001). Negotiation behavior when cultures collide: The United States and Japan, *Journal of Applied Psychology*, 86(3), 371-385.

Adler, N. J. & Graham, J. L. (1989). Cross-cultural interactions: The international comparison fallacy? *Journal of International Business Studies*, 20, 515-537

Brett, J. M. (2007). *Negotiating globally: How to negotiate deals, resolve disputes, and make decisions across cultural boundaries,* 2nd. San Francisco: Jossey-Bass.

Brett, J. M., Adair, W., Lempereur, A., Okumura, T., Shihkirev, P., Tinsley, C. & Lytle, A. (1998). Culture and joint gains in negotiation, *Negotiation Journal*, 14(1), 61-86.

Brett, J. M. & Okumura, T. (1998). Inter- and intra-cultural negotiation: U.S. and Japanese negotiators, *Academy of Management Journal*, 41, 495-510.

Cai, D. A. (1998). Culture, plans, and the pursuit of negotiation goals, *Journal of Asian Pacific Communication*, 8, 103-123.

de la Merced, M. J. (2010). BHP withdraws Potash takeover offer, *New York Times*, November 4, www.dealbook.nytimes.com/.

de la Merced, M. J. & Maynard, M. (2009). Fiat deal with Chrysler seals swift 42-day overhaul, *New York Times*, June 10, www.nytimes.com/2009/06/11.

Figueroa-Clark, L. (2004). Venezuela's Chavez sets oil fields takeover for may, says Bush should resign, Venezuelanalysis.com.

Foster, D. A. (1992). *Bargaining across borders: How to negotiate business successfully anywhere in the world.* New York: McGraw-Hill.

Garfinkel, P. (2004). On keeping your foot safely out of your mouth, *New York Times*, July 13, C7.

Gelfand, M. J. & Christakopoulou, S. (1999). Culture and negotiator cognition: Judgment accuracy and negotiation processes in individualistic and collectivistic cultures, *Organizational Behavior and Human Decision Processes*, 79, 248-269.

Gelfand, M. J., Higgins, M., Nishii, L. H., Raver, J. L., Dominguez, A., Murakami, F., Yamaguchi, S. & Toyama, M. (2002). Culture and egocentric perceptions of fairness in conflict and negotiation, *Journal of Applied Psychology*, 87(5), 383-845.

Gelfand, M. J., Nishii, L. H., Holcomb, K. M., Dyer, N., Ohbuchi, K. & Fukamo, M. (2001). Cultural influences on cognitive representations of conflict: Interpretations of cognitive episodes in the United States and Japan, *Journal of Applied Psychology*, 86, 1059-1074.

Gelfand, M. J. & Realo, A. (1999). Individualism-collectivism and accountability in intergroup negotiations, *Journal of Applied Psychology*, 84, 721-736.

Hofstede, G. (1980). *Culture's consequences: International differences in work-related values.* Thousand Oaks, CA: Sage.

Lituchy, T. R. (1997). Negotiations between Japanese and Americans: The effects of **collectivism on integrative** outcomes, *Canadian Journal of Administrative Sciences,* 14(4), 386-395.

Lytle, A. L., Brett, J. M., Barsness, Z. I., Tinsley, C. H. & Janssens, M. (1995). A paradigm for confirmatory cross-cultural research in organizational behavior. In L. L. Cummings & B. M. Staw (Eds.), *Research in Organizational Behavior* 17. Greenwich, CT: JAI Press, 167-214.

MacDuff, I. (2006). Your pace or mine? Culture, time, and negotiation, *Negotiation Journal*, 22(1), 31-45.

Meyerson, D., Weick, K. E. & Kramer, R. M. (1996). Swift trust and temporary groups. In R. M. Kramer & T. R. Tyler (Eds.*), Trust in organizations: Frontiers of theory and research*. Thousand Oaks, CA: Sage, 166-195.

Pedigo, K. L. & Marshall, V. (2009). Bribery: Australian managers' experiences and responses when operating in international markets, *Journal of Business Ethics*, 87, 59-74.

Phatak, A. V. & Habib, M. H. (1996). The dynamics of international business negotiations, *Business Horizons*, 39, 30-38.

Rosette, A. S., Brett, J. M., Barsness, Z. I. & Lytle, A. L. (2004). *When cultures clash electronically: The impact of e-mail and culture on negotiation behavior,* DRRC Working Paper No. 302. (Cited in Brett, 2007).

Salacuse, J. (1991). Making deals in strange places: A beginner's guide to international business negotiation. In J. W. Breslin & J. Z. Rubin (Eds.), *Negotiation Theory and Practice*. Cambridge, MA: Program on Negotiation Books, 251-259.

Salacuse, J. (2004). Negotiating: The top ten ways that culture can affect your negotiation, *Ivey Business Journal Online,* September/October, www.iveybusinessjournal.com/article.asp?intArticle_ID=514.

Schwartz, S. H. (1992). Universals in the content and structure of values: Theoretical advances and empirical tests in 20 countries. In M. Zanna (Ed.), *Advances in experimental social psychology* 25. Orlando, FL: Academic Press, 1-65.

Sebenius, J. K. (2002). The hidden challenge of cross-border negotiations, *Harvard Business Review*, March, 76-85.

Trompenaars, F. (1993). *Riding the waves of culture: Understanding diversity in global business.* London: The Economist Books.

Trompenaars, F. (1996). Resolving international conflict: Culture and business strategy, *Business Strategy Review*, 7(3), 51-68.

Valenzuela, A., Srivastava, J. & Lee, S. (2005). The role of cultural orientation in bargaining under incomplete information: Differences in causal attributions, *Organizational Behavior and Human Decision Processes*, 96, 72-88.

Wade-Benzoni, K. A., Okumura, T., Brett, J. M., Moore, D. A., Tenbrunsel, A. E. & Bazerman, M. H. (2002). Cognitions and behavior in asymmetric social dilemmas: A comparison of two cultures, *Journal of Applied Social Psychology*, 87, 87-95.

READINGS

Reading 12.1

THE HIDDEN CHALLENGE OF CROSS-BORDER NEGOTIATIONS

James K. Sebenius

International deal makers have long bowed to local traditions and etiquette. But new research suggests they also need to understand something deeper the subtle yet potent ways that national culture shapes the governance and decision-making process.

Source: James K. Sebenius, "The Hidden Challenge of Cross-Border Negotiations," Harvard Business Review, March 2002, pp. 76–85. Used by permission of Harvard Business School Publishing.

CULTURAL DIFFERENCES can influence business negotiation in significant and unexpected ways, as many a hapless deal maker has learned. In some cases, it's a matter of ignorance or blatant disrespect, as with the American salesman who presented a potential Saudi Arabian client with a multimillion-dollar proposal in a pigskin binder, considered vile in many Muslim cultures. He was unceremoniously tossed out and his company blacklisted from working with Saudi businesses. But the differences can be much more subtle, arising from deep-seated cultural tendencies that influence how people interact—everything from how people view the role of the individual versus the group to their attitudes, say, about the importance of time or relationships. In response to these challenges, a great body of literature has emerged to help executives navigate differences not only in protocol and deportment but in deeper cultural tendencies as well.

But my research shows that there's another, equally treacherous, aspect to cross-border negotiation that's been largely overlooked in the literature: the ways that people from different regions come to an agreement, or the processes involved in negotiations. Decision making and governance processes, which determine either a "yes" or "no", can differ widely from culture to culture, not just in terms of legal technicalities but also in terms of behaviors and core beliefs. In my experience observing and participating in scores of international negotiations, I've seen numerous promising deals fail because people ignored or underestimated the powerful difference in processes across cultures. In these pages, I will examine how systematic differences in governance and decision making can disrupt cross-border negotiations, and I will offer advice on how to anticipate and overcome possible barriers on the road to yes.

Map the Player and the Process

In any negotiation, you are always interacting with individuals, but your real purpose is to influence a larger organization—representing a diverse set interests—to produce a meaningful yes. In an international deal, just as at home, you need to know exactly who's involved in that larger decision process and what roles they play. But in unfamiliar territory, the answers might surprise you. Indeed, applying "home" views of corporate governance and decision making to international deals may seriously hinder the negotiation process. I find it's useful to break down the decision-making process into several constituent parts: Who are the players? Who decides what? What are the informal influences that can make or break a deal? Let's look at each of these factors, which can vary dramatically when you cross national borders.

Who are the Players? If you're accustomed to deal making in the United States, you know that extra players beyond those representing the two companies may influence the deal: SEC, the Federal Trade Commission, and the Justice Department, among others. In his book *Master of the Universe,* Daniel J. Kadlec writes that when Travelers and Citicorp were contemplating a merger, the heads of both companies together visited Federal Reserve Chairman Alan Greenspan to get a reading on the Fed's likely attitude.

Abroad, you'll of course find extra players as well, but they will be different and often less obvious. For those executives experienced in North American shareholder-based corporate governance, it may come as a surprise to discover that in Germany, labor has virtually equal representation on many supervisory boards of directors. It will probably be less surprising, though no less discomfiting, to discover that local party officials play an integral part in Chinese negotiating teams in the People's Republic, even when the Chinese company is nominally "private." In the European Union, various Brussels commissions may get involved in business negotiations. If an acquisition target has foreign subsidiaries, the skein of negotiating partners may grow even more tangled. All these constituencies bring their own interests to the table, as well as varying abilities to block or foster negotiations. Even GE, one of the most experienced acquirers, suffered a humiliating defeat in its attempted merger with Honeywell, in part because GE's management underestimated the nature and seriousness of European concerns about competitiveness and the potential for these concerns—and GE's European competitors—to obstruct the deal.

Another example is drawn from the research of my colleagues William A. Sahlman and Burton C. Hurlock: Near the time of the collapse of the Soviet Union, California-based venture capital firm Sierra Ventures was negotiating with the director of the Institute for Protein Research in Russia, hoping to get the rights to an apparently revolutionary biotechnology process. Marathon negotiations with the institute's management team—heroically bridging huge gaps between East and West, business and science, bureaucracy and venture capital—seemed as if they would finally culminate in an acceptable deal for both sides. Although the deal ultimately succeeded, nearing the finish line it suddenly became clear that several Moscow ministries, each with its own point of view and agenda, also had to approve the agreement. This posed a potentially fatal set of obstacles that could have been anticipated had the Sierra team made more than a perfunctory effort early on to learn about the real decision process.

Who decides what? Even if you know who's playing, a failure to understand each player's role—and who owns which decision—can be very costly. For example, when Italian tire maker Pirelli sought to acquire its German rival, Continental Gummiwerke, Pirelli claimed control of a majority of Continental's shares and received tactic backing from Deutsche Bank and support from Gerhard Schröder, then Prime Minister of Lower Saxony, where Continental is based. In a U.S. transaction, merely owning enough equity often allows the acquirer to control the target. But not in this setting.

Unfortunately for Pirelli, German corporate governance provides a structure in which other key players can block the will of even a majority of shareholders. While the management board in most large German companies has day-to-day management responsibilities, it is only one of four sets of players—along with shareholders, a supervisory board, and labor—that can play a significant role in any major decision. What's more, under union codetermination, labor elects fully half of the members of the supervisory board, which in turn elects the management board. And the management board can prevent any single shareholder, no matter how large his or her holdings, from voting more than 5% of the total company shares. Thus, having failed to gain real buy-in from all the players, especially labor and key managers, Pirelli couldn't complete the transaction, even though it claimed effective control over Continental's shares and had powerful allies—a humiliating defeat that cost the Italian company nearly half a billion dollars.

There are some impressive stories of executives deftly navigating these potential barriers—U.K. based Vodafone's successful acquisition of Germany's Mannesmann is a notable recent example—and such cases might seem to herald major changes in German law and governance. But the circumstances and tactics in Vodafone's case were highly specific to the deal, and the general implications for Euro-governance seem limited. Deeply entrenched structures continue to blindside many a corporate suitor and not just in Germany. In fact, versions of this cautionary tale could be repeated in locales as distinct as Switzerland and Japan, where boards of directors representing constituencies other than shareholders may exert powers unfamiliar to those accustomed to Anglo Saxon-style governance, including voting of outside equity holders.

Cultural assumptions can sometimes make it very difficult to recognize or acknowledge who has formal decision rights. For example, when Honda invested heavily in an extensive relationship with British automaker Rover, workers and managers at the two companies developed very positive working relationships for more than a decade. The partnership intensified after the government sold Rover to British Aerospace (BAe), but as Rover continued to lose money, BAe decided to discard the relationship, abruptly selling Rover to BMW through a secretive deal that caught Honda completely unaware. The Japanese automaker considered its connection with Rover a long-term one, much like a marriage, and it had shared advanced product and process technology with Rover well beyond its effective contractual ability to protect these assets. Honda's leaders were dumbfounded and outraged that BAe could sell—and to a competitor, no less. Yet while Honda's prized relationship was at the level of the operating company (Rover), the Japanese company had not taken seriously enough the fact that the decision rights over a Rover sale are vested at the parent (BAe) level. From a financial standpoint, the move made sense for BAe, and it was perfectly legal. Yet Honda's cultural blinders made the sale seem inconceivable, and its disproportionate investments in Rover in effect created a major economic opportunity for BAe. The bottom line: Understanding both formal decision rights and cultural assumptions in less familiar settings can be vital.

A final note identifying decision rights: Even the experts may stumble over their assumptions. U.S. attorneys apparently told Bernard Arnault's French Luxury conglomerate LVMH that companies traded on the New York Stock Exchange could not increase their share base by a significant amount without shareholder approval. With this understanding, LVMH acquired almost 35% of Gucci in a takeover bid. However, it turns out that different stock rules apply to companies based outside the United States—Gucci, for instance, traded in New York

but was chartered in the Netherlands and is headquartered in Florence. Gucci's defense team discovered this loophole and used it to shut down the deal. The company first issued 20% new shares to its employees in an ESOP-like transaction and then offered 42% additional new shares to a group controlled by Francois Pinault, Arnault's French rival. LVMH's massively diluted position in effect handed ultimate control to Pinault, leaving LVMH trapped as a relatively powerless minority shareholder in Gucci.

What are the informal influences that can make or break a deal? It's important to understand which people must sign the contract to finalize a deal, but that's often not enough. Many countries have webs of influence that are more powerful than the actual parties making the deal, even though those webs don't have the formal standing of, say, government agencies. In Japan, it may be the keiretsu—industrial groups that are linked by a web of business ties, lending, and cross-shareholdings. In Germany's financial sector, it might be the insurance giant Allianz. In Italy, it may be a set of powerful families. In Russia, it can be the Russian mafia and other protection rackets. Outsiders need to understand these webs and factor them into their negotiating approach. It's a lesson many companies have learned the hard way.

And influence on negotiations need not be driven by an informal, underlying power structure, as U.S. Stone Container Corporation learned. While negotiating the terms of a major forest project in Honduras, Stone Container's executives assumed that the Honduran president and his relevant ministries had the power to decide whether to allow the project and therefore dealt primarily with the president. But while the president did have the legal authority to make the deal and ultimately approved it, the company's proposal and negotiating strategy seemed to signal a possibly corrupt deal among elites. This inadvertently triggered the involvement of the Honduran Congress, labor unions, political parties, potential business competitors, indigenous people in the affected region, and domestic and international environmental groups. Had Stone taken into account the history of strained relationships between Honduras and the U.S. government and multinationals, as well as the fragile status of the presidency in this fledgling democracy, it could have developed a strategy that accommodated this informal web of potential influences. Instead, Stone's lack of foresight caused it to become enmeshed in an adversarial, multiparty process that ultimately failed. When interviewed for a Harvard Business School case, Stone executive Jerry Freeman likened the experience to being "caught in a drive-by shooting with no place to hide."

U.S. companies like Stone—and others from cultures with strong legal systems—frequently underestimate the power of informal influences because they assume that foreign legal systems will enforce formal contracts just as they are expected to at home. What they may ultimately learn is that dispute resolution can look very different in different cultures. In Japan, which has a relatively small legal system and few lawyers, companies rely on relationships and negotiation to sort through most commercial disputes. Present-day Russia has practically no functioning judiciary. Many countries' legal systems are corrupt or controlled by local political powers.

The fact is there can be a great gulf between the laws on the books and how things really work, as one U.S electrical goods manufacturer learned after it entered a joint venture with a Chinese company and hired a local manager to run the Chinese operation. As described in Charles Olivier's 1996 *WorldLink* article, "Investing in China: 12 Hard Lessons," the company tried to expand its product line, but the Chinese manager balked, insisting there was no demand for the additional products. The U.S. management team tried to resolve the dispute through negotiation, and when the Chinese manager wouldn't budge, the team fired him—but he wouldn't leave. The local labor bureau refused to back the U.S. team, and when U.S. executives tried to dissolve the venture, they discovered they couldn't recover their capital because Chinese law dictates that both sides need to approve dissolution. A foreign law firm, hired at great expense, made no headway. It took some behind-the-scenes negotiation on the part of a local law firm to finally overcome the need for dual approval—an outcome that demanded local counsel well versed in the intricacies of Chinese culture.

In short, successful cross-border negotiators begin by discarding home-market presumptions and developing a clear map of the players who are likely to influence the formal and informal decision process. Only when you know exactly who these players are can you develop strategy that targets their interests.

Adapt Your Approach

Unfortunately, however, knowing who's involved in the process is only half the battle. While you negotiate with people, you are typically seeking to influence the outcome of an organizational process. That process can look different in different cultures, and different processes may call for radically different negotiation strategies and tactics. Even seasoned executives often fail to adapt their approaches to those different processes, with costly consequences. While it's difficult to generalize, such processes tend to take one of several forms: top down, consensus, and multistage coalition building.

Top Down. In some cases, you will deal with a "real boss," a top-down authority who won't delegate in any meaningful way and will ultimately make the decision unilaterally. When there is the local equivalent of a very much in charge Admiral Rickover, Harold Geneon, or Robert Moses, revealing key information or making premature concessions to those not genuinely in the decision loop can work to your disadvantage. The most effective negotiators avoid making deals with relatively powerless agents who function as important messengers or emissaries but not as powers in their own right. Instead, these negotiators find ways to interact directly with the boss—or, if that's not possible, to connect with people outside the process who have close ties to or influence over the boss.

In some cultures, even if the boss delegates authority, going directly to the top can sometimes be more effective. For example, when one Italian industrial products firm wished to acquire a large division of a French conglomerate, it first made friendly overtures to the target unit. But as it became clear that unit management wouldn't even consider discussions about a possible sale, the Italian chief went quietly to the top. He eventually closed the deal with the boss, who—consistent with that company's top-down culture and, in fact, much of French corporate governance—simply "crammed it down" on the division, softening the blow somewhat by offering any reluctant managers a chance to be absorbed into the French parent. This strategy must be used cautiously, however. It can easily backfire when subordinate players have opportunities to sabotage the deal or erode its effectiveness.

What's more, it can be risky to impute omnipotence even to apparently powerful bosses. U.S. executives almost reflexively ask, "Who is the real decision maker?" But the answer can be misleading, as Stone Container learned in its negotiations with the Honduran president. This is not a problem limited to less-developed countries. Even in negotiating with U.S. presidents, parties such as the Shah of Iran or South Vietnamese leaders have made deals or reached critical understandings, only to learn later that limits on presidential power would prevent the deal from transpiring as expected. And even in one-party, relatively authoritarian countries, deals at the top may not translate into action on the ground.

The case of Armand Hammer's protracted negotiations to form, and later manage, a joint venture between Hammer's Occidental Petroleum (Oxy) and the state-run China National Coal Development Corporation (CNCDC) reveals how even the highest-level backing can be insufficient. Hammer and China's then-paramount leader Deng Xiaoping, who met in person about the project, both expressed their serious commitment to making the venture work, despite signals during preliminary negotiations that the deal would not succeed. As Roderick MacLeod recounts in his book, *China, Inc.: How to Do Business With the Chinese*, Hammer saw the project as the crowning achievement of his career: the largest-scale foreign investment in China in history. Deng, for his part, was anxious to show the world that his market reforms were transforming China into an economy ripe for investment. The two ordered their subordinates to reach an agreement, and the Oxy-CNCDC project became a highly visible test case. Yet because of bureaucratic conflicts, clashing expectations and interpretations, and escalating antagonisms, the formal negotiations dragged on for years, and Oxy ultimately pulled out after more than a decade of frustration.

Consensus. If top-down authority is at one end of the decision-making spectrum, then consensus is at the other. The consensus process can have many variations and is especially common in Asia. It sometimes requires agreement among the members of the other side's negotiating team; at other times, it requires agreement from the broader enterprise and can include external stakeholders and governments.

When a consortium of U.S. companies submitted a proposal to assist in building a dam in the Three Gorges section of China's Yangtze River—a project debated by the consensus process—the consortium's negotiating team largely directed its efforts at a single agency, the Yangtze Valley Planning Office (YVPO). But in

China, bureaucratic units like the YVPO are explicitly ranked, and no one unit has authority over another of the same rank: permission from above is required if there is disagreement. As a result, decisions are pushed up to the highest authority possible, overloading the top levels of bureaucracy. The only practical solution is consensus, which has become a cornerstone of the modern Chinese bureaucracy.

To move a process along, each affected unit must engage in a complex bargaining system to establish compatible goals and to protect interests. By failing to appreciate the involvement of these other units, the U.S. team didn't anticipate enemies or, even more important, help potential allies back its plan. (Hampered by U.S. government opposition to the project—driven by environmental and human rights concerns—the U.S. team also made some classic negotiation errors, such as failing to understand the other side's interests. For example, the team's proposal emphasized efficient machinery and a lean labor force, while maximum employment is one of China's top priorities. With a little more thought, the U.S. group might have placed greater stress on elements such as technology transfer, training, and foreign investment, rather than cost cutting and speed.

The need for consensus among players on the other side will affect your negotiating strategy in other ways as well. First, since consensus cultures often focus on relationships rather than deals, the parties involved will often want to take substantial amounts of time to learn about you and forge a deeper relationship before talking about the deal. In consensus cultures, relationship building is critical not only to reaching an agreement but also to making it work. The lengthy timetable may be very frustrating to teams from decisive, top-down cultures; unfortunately, there's usually little they can do to hurry the process unless the other side is desperate for a deal—which generally means the consensus is already there—or the other side wants a deal and you're

credibly engaged in parallel conversations with one of their serious rivals.

Second, since consensus processes often go hand-in-hand with near-inexhaustible demands for information, you should be prepared to provide it—many different forms, in great detail, and repeatedly. Third, to the extent that you can and should design your approach to help your proponents on the other side convert the doubters, giving them the data they need and supplying them with arguments they can use internally to address specific concerns.

Fourth, you may need to shift your focus away from the bargaining table and instead interact extensively and informally with the other side as it tries to reach a position internally. With some bitterness, U.S. trade negotiators dealing with seemingly immovable Japanese counterparts have puzzled, "Before the Japanese have reached a consensus, they can't negotiate; after consensus is attained on the other side, there is nothing to negotiate." Your objective is to get your interests, point of view, and plans incorporated into their consensus process. If you wait to do this until you are at the bargaining table, you will have to pry open their now-fixed position, reached before the players officially sit down to negotiate. As John Graham and Yoshihiro Sano, authors of *Doing Business With the New Japan*, explain, "In Japan what goes on at the negotiation table is really a ritual approval of what has already been decided through numerous individual conversations in restaurants, bathhouses, and offices. In Japan, the negotiating table is not a place for changing minds. Persuasive appeals are not appropriate or effectual." Often, breaking apart a previously settled mind-set requires near-collusion between you and their bargaining team returns home with a powerful argument to reopen the process.

And finally, you'll need to adjust your own expectations—and your organization's—of how long the deal will take. Failure to do so can put you into a bargaining vise, with your home management team pressuring you for quick results and the relaxed other side exploiting your own side's impatience. Caught in the middle, you may feel as though your choices are limited: You can walk away (and undermine your effectiveness and waste resources), or you can make major concessions (and dilute the value of the deal). In general, if you think your side cannot handle a lengthy negotiation, you may be better off avoiding the negotiation altogether.

As frustrating as the need for consensus may be to those from fast-moving cultures, there can be offsetting advantages. A slow and painstaking negotiation process may lead to a decision that has more staying power. What's more, actual implementation may occur more quickly than with a top-down agreement. People may also be more attached to the deal after investing so much in it. In one case, a U.S. firm negotiated for two years with a major Japanese company to create a large-scale joint venture under Japanese control. During this excruciatingly detailed process, the negotiations were halted several times due to what the Japanese team described as a breakdown in its consensus process. Each time, however, the Japanese company resumed negotiations with a stronger consensus on the central role of the deal to its long-term global strategy.

When a European firm unexpectedly made a tender offer for the entire U.S. business, the Japanese company had to decide whether to drop out of the process or seek to acquire the whole firm. After years of negotiations and mentally integrating the U.S. operations into its long-term strategy during its exhaustive consensus process, the Japanese company had essentially fallen in love with its target. Rather than face the internal organizational costs of "losing," it was willing to pay an extraordinarily high price for the U.S. firm—far more than it would have paid had it not been part of the frustratingly long consensus process.

In short, you should not be blindsided by the need for consensus. It may require more time, relationship building and information than expected. Dealing with a consensus process effectively requires facilitating it while doing what you can—with real external deadlines and competitors—to speed it up, but also recognizing what you can't do and setting realistic expectations.

Coalition Building. Decision processes don't always come in pure forms such as top down or consensus. Sometimes, they're less defined and don't require the agreement of every player but rather the support of a sufficient subset of players—a "winning coalition" that can effectively pressure, sidestep, or override dissenters. At other times, a "blocking coalition" that has interests no one can ultimately overrule can bring a proposal to a halt. Pirelli's failure to win over Continental Gummiwerke's all-important management board and labor force in its failed takeover foray into Germany left a blocking entity in control. Stone Container in its negotiations with the Honduran president, and Armand Hammer in his attempts at an agreement with Deng Xiaoping both fell victim to ad-hoc blocking coalitions. Navigating such coalitions requires an understanding of the likely interests and options of the players who will be needed as allies in a winning coalition or who may seek to form a blocking entity.

Governance processes often drive these considerations, so taking a close look at the key players and how they work together can help you anticipate opportunities and obstacles as well as appropriately sequence your approach. For example, one foreign would-be acquirer of a German company first approached the supervisory board and obtained agreement in principle to go forward. Then, to the surprise of the board, the acquirer suddenly put the deal on hold. The acquirer had delayed the negotiations in order to approach the German company's management board, lay out the terms it had proposed, and offer it total veto power over the transaction. In reality, the management board already had the ability to obstruct the deal, but the move felt like a concession because the board was not accustomed to being incorporated into the process in this way. Finally, after spending a great deal of time working out the strategy with the management board, the acquirer went back to the shareholders on the supervisory board to conclude what became a very successful transaction.

In closing, it's worth noting that cultural allegiances are often not as simple as they appear. While national culture can tell you a lot about the person sitting across the table from you, every individual represents a number of cultures, each of which can affect negotiation style. Beyond her French citizenship, an ABB executive may well be from Alsace, have a Danish parent, feel staunchly European, have studied electrical engineering, and earned an MBA from the University of Chicago. Gender, ethnicity, and profession all play a role. But along with assessing

the person across the table is figuring out the intricacies of the larger organization behind her. And to do that, you need to diligently map the governance and decision-making processes, which can take devilishly unexpected forms across borders. Then, you must design your strategy and tactics so that you're reaching the right people, with the right arguments, in a way that allows you maximum impact on the process to yield a sustainable deal.

1. Razeen Sally, "A French Insurance Firm And 'Fortress Germany'; The Case of AGF and AMB," and The Associated "Appendix," Instead Cases 394-052-1 and 394-052-5, 1994.

2. Bryan Burroughs, "Gucci and Goliath," *Vanity Fair,* July 1999.

Thinking Further 12.1

1. What, in your opinion, is the most critical preparation step when you are planning an international negotiation? Why?

2. If the other negotiating party and you agree that the goal is to negotiate collaboratively, do you believe a multi-national negotiation would be more successful if each party negotiates one on one or as a team? Explain why.

Reading 12.2

NEGOTIATING: THE TOP TEN WAYS THAT CULTURE CAN AFFECT YOUR NEGOTIATION

Jeswald W. Salacuse.

Ten particular elements consistently arise to complicate intercultural negotiations. These "top ten" elements of negotiating behavior constitute a basic framework for identifying cultural differences that may arise during the negotiation process. This article discusses this

framework and when to apply it. The top ten elements are: 1. Negotiating goal: Contract or relationship? 2. Negotiating attitude: Win-Lose or Win-Win. 3. Personal style: Informal or formal. 4. Communication: Direct or indirect. 5. Sensitivity to time: High or low. 6. Emotionalism: High or low. 7. Form of agreement: General or specific. 8. Building an agreement: Bottom up or top down. 9. Team organization: One leader or group consensus. 10. Risk taking: High or low. With

Source: Jeswald W. Salacuse, Negotiating: The top ten ways that culture can affect your negotiation," Ivey Business Journal Online, Sep/Oct 2004. Used by permission of Ivey Publishing.

this knowledge, you may be better able to understand the negotiating styles and approaches of counterparts from other cultures. Equally important, it may help you to determine how your own negotiating style appears to those same counterparts.

When Enron was still—and only—a pipeline company, it lost a major contract in India because local authorities felt that it was pushing negotiations too fast. In fact, the loss of the contract underlines the important role that cultural differences play in international negotiation. For one country's negotiators, time is money; for another's, the slower the negotiations, the better and more trust in the other side. This author's advice will help negotiators bridge the cultural differences in international negotiation.

International business deals not only cross borders, they also cross cultures. Culture profoundly influences how people think, communicate, and behave. It also affects the kinds of transactions they make and the way they negotiate them. Differences in culture between business executives—for example, between a Chinese public sector plant manager in Shanghai and a Canadian division head of a family company in Toronto—can create barriers that impede or completely stymie the negotiating process.

The great diversity of the world's cultures makes it impossible for any negotiator, no matter how skilled and experienced, to understand fully all the cultures that may be encountered. How then should an executive prepare to cope with culture in making deals in Singapore this week and Seoul the next? In researching my book *The Global Negotiator: Making, Managing, and Mending Deals Around the World in the Twenty-First Century* (Palgrave Macmillan, 2003), I found that ten particular elements consistently arise to complicate intercultural negotiations. These "top ten" elements of negotiating behavior constitute a basic framework for identifying cultural differences that may arise during the negotiation process. Applying this framework in your international

business negotiations may enable you to understand your counterpart better and to anticipate possible misunderstandings. This article discusses this framework and how to apply it.

1. Negotiating Goal: Contract or Relationship?

Negotiators from different cultures may tend to view the purpose of a negotiation differently. For deal makers from some cultures, the goal of a business negotiation, first and foremost, is a signed contract between the parties. Other cultures tend to consider that the goal of a negotiation is not a signed contract but rather the creation of a relationship between the two sides. Although the written contact expresses the relationship, the essence of the deal is the relationship itself. For example in my survey of over 400 persons from twelve nationalities, reported fully in *The Global Negotiator*, I found that whereas 74 percent of the Spanish respondents claimed their goal in a negotiation was a contract, only 33 percent of the Indian executives had a similar view. The difference in approach may explain why certain Asian negotiators, whose negotiating goal is often the creation of a relationship, tend to give more time and effort to negotiation preliminaries, while North Americans often want to rush through this first phase of deal making. The preliminaries of negotiation, in which the parties seek to get to know one another thoroughly, are a crucial foundation for a good business relationship. They may seem less important when the goal is merely a contract.

It is therefore important to determine how your counterparts view the purpose of your negotiation. If relationship negotiators sit on the other side of the table, merely convincing them of your ability to deliver on a low-cost contract may not be enough to land you the deal. You may also have to persuade them, from the very first meeting, that your two organizations have the potential to build a rewarding relationship over the long term. On the other hand, if the other side is basically a contract deal maker, trying to build a relationship may be a waste of time and energy.

2. Negotiating Attitude: Win-Lose or Win-Win?

Because of differences in culture, personality, or both, business persons appear to approach deal making with one of two basic attitudes: that a negotiation is either a process in which both can gain (win-win) or a struggle in which, of necessity, one side wins and the other side loses (win-lose). Win-win negotiators see deal making as a collaborative, problem-solving process; win-lose negotiators view it as confrontational. As you enter negotiations, it is important to know which type of negotiator is sitting across the table from you. Here too, my survey revealed significant differences among cultures. For example, whereas 100 percent of the Japanese respondents claimed that they approached negotiations as a win-win process, only 33% of the Spanish executives took that view

3. Personal Style: Informal or Formal?

Personal style concerns the way a negotiator talks to others, uses titles, dresses, speaks, and interacts with other persons. Culture strongly influences the personal style of negotiators. It has been observed, for example, that Germans have a more formal style than Americans. A negotiator with a formal style insists on addressing counterparts by their titles, avoids personal anecdotes, and refrains from questions touching on the private or family life of members of the other negotiating team. A negotiator with an informal style tries to start the discussion on a first-name basis, quickly seeks to develop a personal, friendly relationship with the other team, and may take off his jacket and roll up his sleeves when deal making begins in earnest. Each culture has its own formalities with their own special meanings.

They are another means of communication among the persons sharing that culture, another form of adhesive that binds them together as a community. For an American, calling someone by the first name is an act of friendship and therefore a good thing. For a Japanese, the use of the first name at a first meeting is an act of disrespect and therefore bad.

Negotiators in foreign cultures must respect appropriate formalities. As a general rule, it is always safer to adopt a formal posture and move to an informal stance, if the situation warrants it, than to assume an informal style too quickly.

4. Communication: Direct or Indirect?

Methods of communication vary among cultures. Some emphasize direct and simple methods of communication; others rely heavily on indirect and complex methods. The latter may use circumlocutions, figurative forms of speech, facial expressions, gestures and other kinds of body language. In a culture that values directness, such as the American or the Israeli, you can expect to receive a clear and definite response to your proposals and questions. In cultures that rely on indirect communication, such as the Japanese, reaction to your proposals may be gained by interpreting seemingly vague comments, gestures, and other signs. What you will not receive at a first meeting is a definite commitment or rejection.

The confrontation of these styles of communication in the same negotiation can lead to friction. For example, the indirect ways Japanese negotiators express disapproval have often led foreign business executives to believe that their proposals were still under consideration when in fact the Japanese side had rejected them. In the Camp David negotiations that led to a peace treaty between Egypt and Israel, the Israeli preference for direct forms of communication and the Egyptian tendency to favor indirect forms sometimes exacerbated relations between the two sides. The Egyptians interpreted Israeli directness as aggressiveness and, therefore, an insult. The Israelis viewed Egyptian indirectness with impatience and suspected them of insincerity, of not saying what they meant.

5. Sensitivity to Time: High or Low?

Discussions of national negotiating styles invariably treat a particular culture's attitudes toward time. It is said that Germans are always punctual, Latins are habitually late, Japanese negotiate slowly, and Americans are quick to make a deal. Commentators sometimes claim that some cultures value time more than others, but this observation may not be an accurate characterization of the situation. Rather, negotiators may value differently the amount of time devoted to and measured against the goal pursued. For Americans, the deal is a signed contract and time is money, so they want to make a deal quickly. Americans therefore try to reduce formalities to a minimum and get down to business quickly. Japanese and other Asians, whose goal is to create a relationship rather than simply sign a contract, need to invest time in the negotiating process so that the parties can get to know one another well and determine whether they wish to embark on a long-term relationship. They may consider aggressive attempts to shorten the negotiating time as efforts to hide something. For example, in one case that received significant media attention in the mid-1990's, a long-term electricity supply contract between an ENRON subsidiary, the Dabhol Power Company, and the Maharashtra state government in India, was subject to significant challenge and was ultimately cancelled on the grounds that it was concluded in "unseemly haste" and had been subject to "fast track procedures" that circumvented established practice for developing such projects in the past. Important segments of the Indian public automatically assumed that the government had failed to protect the public interest because the negotiations were so quick. In the company's

defense, Rebecca Mark, chairman and CEO of Enron International, pointed out to the press: "We were extremely concerned with time, because time is money for us." (Enron's Rebecca Mark: "You Have to be Pushy and Aggressive" *Business Week*, February 24, 1997, http://www.businessweek.com/1997/08/b351586.htm.)

This difference between the Indian and U.S. attitudes toward time was clearly revealed in my survey. Among the twelve nationalities surveyed, the Indians had the largest percentage of persons who considered themselves to have a low sensitivity to time

6. Emotionalism: High or Low?

Accounts of negotiating behavior in other cultures almost always point to a particular group's tendency to act emotionally. According to the stereotype, Latin Americans show their emotions at the negotiating table, while the Japanese and many other Asians hide their feelings. Obviously, individual personality plays a role here. There are passive Latins and hot-headed Japanese. Nonetheless, various cultures have different rules as to the appropriateness and form of displaying emotions, and these rules are brought to the negotiating table as well. Deal makers should seek to learn them.

In the author's survey, Latin Americans and the Spanish were the cultural groups that ranked themselves highest with respect to emotionalism in a clearly statistically significant fashion. Among Europeans, the Germans and English ranked as least emotional, while among Asians the Japanese held that position, but to a lesser degree.

7. Form of Agreement: General or Specific?

Whether a negotiator's goal is a contract or a relationship, the negotiated transaction in almost all cases will be encapsulated in some sort of written agreement. Cultural factors influence the form of the written agreement that the parties make. Generally, Americans prefer very detailed contracts that attempt to anticipate all possible circumstances and eventualities, no matter how unlikely. Why? Because the deal is the contract itself, and one must refer to the contract to handle new situations that may arise. Other cultures, such as the Chinese, prefer a contract in the form of general principles rather than detailed rules. Why? Because, it is claimed, that the essence of the deal is the relationship between the parties. If unexpected circumstances arise, the parties should look primarily to their relationship, not the contract, to solve the problem. So, in some cases, a Chinese negotiator may interpret the American drive to stipulate all contingencies as evidence of a lack of confidence in the stability of the underlying relationship.

Among all respondents in my survey, 78 percent preferred specific agreements, while only 22 percent preferred general agreements. On the other hand, the degree of intensity of responses on the question varied considerably among cultural groups. While only 11 percent of the English favored general agreements, 45.5 percent of the Japanese and of the Germans claimed to do so.

Some experienced executives argue that differences over the form of an agreement are caused more by unequal bargaining power between the parties than by culture. In a situation of unequal bargaining power, the stronger party always seeks a detailed agreement to "lock up the deal" in all its possible dimensions, while the weaker party prefers a general agreement to give it room to "wiggle out" of adverse circumstances that are bound to occur. According to this view, it is context, not culture that determines this negotiating trait.

8. Building An Agreement: Bottom Up or Top Down?

Related to the form of the agreement is the question of whether negotiating a business deal is an inductive or a deductive process. Does it start from an agreement on general principles and proceed to specific items, or does it begin with an agreement on specifics, such as price, delivery date, and product quality, the sum total of which becomes the contract? Different cultures tend to emphasize one approach over the other. Some observers believe that the French prefer to begin with agreement on general principles, while Americans tend to seek agreement first on specifics. For Americans, negotiating a deal is basically making a series of compromises and trade-offs on a long list of particulars. For the French, the essence is to agree on basic principles that will guide and indeed determine the negotiation process afterward. The agreed-upon general principles become the framework, the skeleton, upon which the contract is built.

My survey of negotiating styles found that the French, the Argentineans, and the Indians tended to view deal making as a top down (deductive process); while the Japanese, the Mexicans and the Brazilians tended to see it as a bottom up (inductive) process. A further difference in negotiating style is seen in the dichotomy between the "building-down" approach and the "building-up approach." In the building down approach, the negotiator begins by presenting the maximum deal if the other side accepts all the stated conditions. In the building-up approach, one side begins by proposing a minimum deal that can be broadened and increased as the other party accepts additional conditions. According to many observers, Americans tend to favor the building-down approach, while the Japanese tend to prefer the building-up style of negotiating a contract.

9. Team Organization: One Leader or Group Consensus?

In any negotiation, it is important to know how the other side is organized, who has the authority to make commitments, and how decisions are made. Culture is one important factor that affects how executives organize themselves to negotiate a deal. Some cultures emphasize the individual while others stress the group. These values may influence the organization of each side in a negotiation.

One extreme is the negotiating team with a supreme leader who has complete authority to decide all matters. Many American teams tend to follow this approach. Other cultures, notably the Japanese and the Chinese, stress team negotiation and consensus decision making. When you negotiate with such a team, it may not be apparent who the leader is and who has the authority to commit the side. In the first type, the negotiating team is usually small; in the second it is often large. For example, in negotiations in China on a major deal, it would not be uncommon for the Americans to arrive at the table with three people and for the Chinese to show up with ten. Similarly, the one-leader team is usually prepared to make commitments more quickly than a negotiating team organized on the basis of consensus. As a result, the consensus type of organization usually takes more time to negotiate a deal.

Among all respondents in my survey, 59 percent tended to prefer one leader while 41 percent preferred a more consensual form of organization. On the other hand, the various cultural groups showed a wide variety of preferences on the question of team organization. The group with the strongest preference for consensus organization was the French. Many studies have noted French individualism. (Edward T. Hall and M. Reed Hall, *Understanding Cultural Difference*, Yarmouth, Maine: Intercultural Press, 1990.)

Perhaps a consensual arrangement in the individual French person's eyes is the best way to protect that individualism. Despite the Japanese reputation for consensus arrangements, only 45 percent of the Japanese respondents claimed to prefer a negotiating team based on consensus. The Brazilians, the Chinese, and the Mexicans to a far greater degree than any other groups preferred one-person leadership, a reflection perhaps of the political traditions of those countries.

10. Risk Taking: High or Low?

Research supports the conclusion that certain cultures are more risk averse than others. (Geert Hofstede, *Culture's Consequences: International Differences in Work-related Values* (Newbury Park, CA: Sage Publications, 1980)

In deal making, the negotiators' cultures can affect the willingness of one side to take risks—to divulge information, try new approaches, and tolerate uncertainties in a proposed course of action. The Japanese, with their emphasis on requiring a large amount of information and their intricate group decision-making process, tend to be risk averse. Americans, by comparison, are risk takers.

Among all respondents in the author's survey, approximately 70 percent claimed a tendency toward risk taking while only 30 percent characterized themselves as low risk takers. Among cultures, the responses to this question showed significant variations. The Japanese are said to be highly risk averse in negotiations, and this tendency was affirmed by the survey which found Japanese respondents to be the most risk averse of the twelve cultures. Americans in the survey, by comparison, considered themselves to be risk takers, but an even higher percentage of the French, the British, and the Indians claimed to be risk takers.

Faced with a risk-averse counterpart, how should a deal maker proceed? The following are a few steps to consider:

1. Don't rush the negotiating process. A negotiation that is moving too fast for one of the parties only heightens that person's perception of the risks in the proposed deal.

2. Devote attention to proposing rules and mechanisms that will reduce the apparent risks in the deal for the other side.

3. Make sure that your counterpart has sufficient information about you, your company, and the proposed deal.

4. Focus your efforts on building a relationship and fostering trust between the parties.

5. Consider restructuring the deal so that the deal proceeds step by step in a series of increments, rather than all at once.

Negotiating styles, like personalities, have a wide range of variation. The ten negotiating traits discussed above can be placed on a spectrum or continuum, as illustrated in the chart below. Its purpose is to identify specific negotiating traits affected by culture and to show the possible variation that each trait or factor may take. With this knowledge, you may be better able to understand the negotiating styles and approaches of counterparts from other cultures. Equally important, it may help you to determine how your own negotiating style appears to those same counterparts.

As a general rule, it is always safer to adopt a formal posture and move to an informal stance, if the situation warrants it, than to assume an informal style too quickly.

In the building down approach, the negotiator begins by presenting the maximum deal if the other side accepts all the stated conditions. In the building-up approach, one side begins by proposing a minimum deal that can be broadened and increased as the other party accepts additional conditions. According to many observers, Americans tend to favor the building-down approach, while the Japanese tend to prefer the building-up style of negotiating a contract.

Thinking Further 12.2

1. In what ways, if any, might negotiating via e-mail improve multicultural negotiations? Explain why.

2. Do you believe the three tips for avoiding a culture clash also pertain to intracultural negotiations? Why or why not?

CHAPTER 13

Difficult Negotiations

Managing Others Who Play Dirty and Saying No to Those Who Play Nice

This chapter examines effective but underutilized approaches for moving the negotiation forward without breaking the bank or losing face when you must break an impasse, counter dirty tricks or difficult tactics and persuade reluctant negotiators to negotiate with you. It also examines different approaches for changing the nature of the "game" if you think the other negotiator's approach is misguided, how you can say "no" to someone who is important to you without letting him or her down, and how you can manage conversations and negotiations that make you anxious and uncomfortable.

INTENDED BENEFITS OF THIS CHAPTER

When you finish reading this chapter, you should be able to:

1. Discuss the influence of impasses, dirty tricks and other difficult tactics on negotiation processes and outcomes.

2. Explain how the shadow negotiation can be used to break impasses, manage difficult tactics, get reluctant negotiators to the table and move difficult negotiations in a more productive direction, and execute it effectively for these purposes.

3. Change the nature of the game to move difficult negotiations in a more productive direction, and say "no" to people who are important to you without jeopardizing your relationship with them.

THE ESSENCE OF DIFFICULT NEGOTIATIONS

If you and the other party become deadlocked after you have been negotiating for quite some time, the impasse may be breakable only if you change course. Particularly aggressive tactics or dirty tricks like intimidation require you to reframe the negotiation in a more productive direction to facilitate reaching an acceptable agreement. If, for example, a large customer with whom your company has had a long and rewarding relationship recently became unusually combative and threatened to take his business to one of your competitors unless you offered him a much better deal, it may be tempting to accept the abuse and cave in to the threats because losing such an important customer would hurt your business. But what happens if giving him a better deal will also hurt your business? There are techniques available for unlocking impasses, countering difficult tactics and changing the nature of the game that preserve relationships and produce good outcomes for both parties. There are also effective techniques available for getting reluctant negotiators to the table. These techniques are useful if they use reluctance as a tactic, it reflects their preference for avoidance, or they always seem too busy or unwilling to meet with you to discuss important matters like your promotion or pay increase.

Difficult negotiations do not end with impasses, difficult tactics and reluctant negotiators. You may be required to jointly find a solution to correct a teammate's performance because it is holding your team back, terminate a problem employee or tell your boss, who has been very supportive, that you are quitting. If you are a purchasing professional, you may have to inform production professionals that certain parts were not available from your supplier, or that the ones you received were defective. You may also have to tell your boss or other people you like, respect or depend on that you are unwilling or unable to do something. These conversations and negotiations are never easy and they make many people anxious and uncomfortable. But there are ways to do this without letting them down and without looking like a slacker.

IMPASSES

For a variety of reasons, negotiators reach impasses even when obviously available solutions exist.

Why They Happen

Incompatible frames. The words chosen, the tone of voice or how parts of messages are emphasized establish frames that are unacceptable to the other party. An impasse may result if, for example, one negotiator adopts a "power" frame and uses threats or manipulative language to coerce you to agree, and you respond using a "rights" frame by emphasizing what you are entitled to receive.

Incompatible negotiation styles. Impasses are likely if negotiators use incompatible styles. If both use very dominating styles, for example, neither will give in without a fight.

Unrealistic expectations. Negotiators' expectations and goals, or those of their constituents, may be so out of line or extreme that that neither one is willing to back down. This may preclude them from finding an acceptable solution.

Dirty tricks. The most obvious example of difficult tactics leading to an impasse is when both negotiators play "chicken" and neither one backs down. Disenchantment with the other negotiator's persistent use of dirty tricks also causes stalemates.

How to Break Them

Traditional thinking about breaking impasses argues that *making small concessions* should induce some movement. These might include sharing small amounts of additional information or making small substantive moves. *Acknowledging the other party's concerns* helps because people sometimes merely need to feel like they have been heard and understood. Since frustrations and negative emotions are common when negotiators reach impasses, you may have to deal with emotions before you can find good solutions. Establishing ground rules that allow negotiators to *vent* or release their frustrations without eliciting a reaction from the other side usually helps with this. Calling a *caucus* also serves this purpose because stepping away from the other party allows both of you to cool down, relax and reconsider what is being demanded or offered. This break may enable you and the other party to *reframe your arguments* and view the situation from a different perspective. Taking sufficient time away from each other and the negotiation may also restore your ability to generate better options.

If an impasse arises because a party has "backed him- or herself into a corner" with a really strong commitment or ultimatum, offering new information that has not yet been dismissed or rejected should facilitate movement because it was not part of the initial commitment or ultimatum. This enables the negotiator to concede *without losing face.* New justifications, new frames and new solutions serve this purpose for the same reasons. *Enhancing your own power* and increasing your aspirations by, for example, cultivating credible alternatives and marshalling resources that the other negotiator needs should induce movement away from the impasse. Conversely, sharing information that raises legitimate questions about the viability or value of the other party's BATNA will induce movement away from the impasses by reducing his or her power and aspirations.

DIRTY TRICKS

What Are They?

Bogey, chicken, good cop-bad cop, intimidation, lowball-highball, nibble, and *snow job* are all examples of dirty tricks or tactics. As indicated in Chapter 3, dirty tricks and tactics are often used aggressively, in a winner-take-all manner, and they involve deception. This makes them difficult to counter. It is tempting to "respond in kind" to protect yourself when they are used against you.

Rather than help, however, responding in kind is likely to escalate the conflict. At best, this leads to impasses.

How to Manage Them

Traditional thinking argues that you should call out or name the other negotiator's use of these tactics. He or she will probably stop using these tactics once you establish your awareness of them because they will no longer have their desired effect. Also consider *negotiating the process.* Before you begin discussing the substantive issues, explicitly discuss how you want to negotiate with the other party and why this would be more appropriate or beneficial for everyone. This includes establishing an appropriate framework for creative and productive problem solving, specifying the information that must be shared and the tactics that should or should not be used.

Video 13.1

Managing Difficult Negotiations

ALTERNATIVE APPROACHES FOR MANAGING DIFFICULT NEGOTIATIONS

The *shadow negotiation* and *changing the nature of the game* are alternative approaches for managing difficult negotiations. Thus far, this book has emphasized negotiating the substantive issues the transaction. The *shadow negotiation* underlies all aspects of these negotiations, and provides useful guidance for dealing with impasses, countering dirty tricks, getting reluctant negotiators to the table and changing how the other party negotiates. *Changing the nature of the game* provides valuable insights into many aspects of the negotiation process, but is mostly about transforming others' attacks, threats, dirty tricks and rigid adherence to positions into joint problem solving.

The Shadow Negotiation

The traditional approach discussed earlier for dealing with impasses, dirty tricks and other counterproductive tactics makes sense and works. The **shadow negotiation** provides a more comprehensive approach that will also help you get reluctant negotiators to the table and change the other party's misguided tactics. Rather than focusing on transactions such as buying-selling or acquiring-disposing of resources, this examines the relational aspects that underlie all negotiated transactions.

Since full disclosure is rare or nonexistent, negotiators must make assumptions about the other party – what he or she wants, weaknesses and likely behaviors. Making assumptions about ourselves is also common – how much leverage we have, what we can legitimately demand and probably others. We then size each other up, poke here and there to find out where the give is, test for flexibility to gauge how strongly the other negotiator feels about a certain point and how strongly we feel about that point. Simply put, this exploration is about jockeying for position to test our assumptions, ensuring that our ideas, interests and proposals receive a fair hearing, and persuading the other negotiator to cooperate in resolving the issues. It is also about ensuring that we understand the other party's issues, interests and proposals (Kolb & Williams, 2003).

There is no place for passive observers in this part of the process. You can maneuver to put yourself in a good position or let others create a position for you. Your action, or inaction, determines what takes place in the substantive negotiation. In other words, you can build a platform from which you effectively advocate for your interests, reframe the negotiation and establish connection with the other negotiators to develop the clear and shared understanding of the real issues, all of which are necessary for effective joint problem solving, or you can observe the other party do this – to your detriment.

Informally, we build the platform from which we can effectively advocate for our interests by touting our positive qualities and achievements. This might include highlighting our strengths, emphasizing the quality of our products or services and discussing how effectively we have worked together in the past. More formally, we use *strategic moves* and *strategic turns*. We also use *appreciative moves* to help with this, but mostly to establish connection with the other negotiator (Kolb & Williams, 2003).

Strategic Moves

Strategic moves include giving the other party **incentives** to listen, consider and negotiate our ideas. Understanding that we have something the other negotiator needs will encourage him or her to come to the table to negotiate with us, and carefully consider our arguments and proposals. **Pressure moves**

raise the stakes for not dealing with us by making the status quo unattractive or raising the cost of "business as usual." **Enlisting support** involves using allies who are respected by the other negotiator to ensure that we gain a favorable hearing and credibility. Allies may also be able to use tactics that are unavailable to us or that we are not comfortable using in a particular situation. The scenarios presented in Negotiation in Action 13.1 illustrate how each of these strategic moves are used.

NEGOTIATION IN ACTION 13.1

Toni is a partner in a growing architecture firm. She gradually assumed responsibility for managing the office, including finances. Her partner discounted this responsibility and gave her no credit for it. As she was preparing to leave for a conference in London, she asked if he had questions. He said he'd be fine. When she had been gone for only a few days, he was forced to make emergency runs to the bank to transfer funds and handle other things that didn't go well. These challenges enabled him to gain appreciation for her added responsibilities, and their importance to the firm. When Toni returned from London, her was very willing to negotiate the division of responsibilities with her.

Cory had always accepted extra work because resources were tight and everyone was stretched. Now, though, taking on more work without help would undermine the quality of the finished product and this would be a disservice to the firm's clients. But he did not want to be viewed or labeled as a partner slacker. He listed all of his projects and their due dates on the white board in his office. When his supervisor approached and asked him to manage another assignment, Cory said he'd be happy to take on another client. But, while pointing at his white board, he asked, "Which of my current projects should I drop or delay?" His supervisor was now willing to negotiate and hired him an assistant.

Ana is the Executive Director of a nonprofit community health agency. She was becoming increasingly frustrated by her agency's dependence on the United Way and waning state monies for funding. She wanted to expand her agency's financial base so that she could grow the agency, but private foundations were not very receptive to her requests. They questioned whether she and her agency could handle the large budget required for the planned growth. Rather than arguing with them, she recruited the head of the School of Public Health at a local university, who was also a prominent surgeon in town, to join her board of directors. She also recruited two prominent business leaders to her board to head the finance and budget committees. The three new board members then accompanied her to foundation presentations. They enhanced her credibility so much that the foundations listened more attentively and they began helping her prepare her grant applications (these scenarios are adapted from Kolb & Williams, 2003).

Strategic Turns

If the other negotiator questions your abilities or motives, threatens you, devalues your proposals or otherwise tries to put you in a "one-down" (inferior) position, resistance is warranted. How we resist is critical. Even if we think it will make us feel good, responding in kind or using other aggressive tactics usually escalates the conflict or creates impasses that can be very hard to break, and it damages relationships. A more productive approach, using *strategic turns*, helps us reframe the negotiation (Kolb & Williams, 2003).

If the other negotiator surprises you by making unexpected comments or offering unexpected challenges, it is tempting to respond immediately. But knee-jerk reactions or responses that are devoid of careful thought and preparation often jeopardize all that you have worked to achieve. Instead, **interrupt the move** by taking a break or changing the pace. This will slow the momentum and give you time to think about how you want to respond. Excusing yourself to get a drink, make a phone call, use the restroom or caucus provides such a break.

Naming the move or calling out the other negotiator's use of unproductive actions (e.g., dirty tricks) serves two important purposes. First, it clarifies that you understand what he or she is doing. Second, and perhaps more important, your awareness signals that the tactic or action is not working or that you think it is inappropriate. If a tactic is not having its desired effect, negotiators usually stop using it. Negotiators who question or raise doubts about anything that supports your perspective, or challenge the underpinnings of your demands and the merits of your arguments, are trying to make you question whether your own motives, views, arguments and demands are worthy of consideration. They may even be trying to make you question your own worthiness. Unmasking these can be accomplished using **corrective turns** – revising or reframing the other negotiator's distortions and misinterpretations by shifting the focus to the positive (Kolb & Williams, 2003). The scenarios presented in Negotiation in Action 13.2 illustrate how each of these strategic turns are used.

NEGOTIATION IN ACTION 13.2

Carla had just been appointed head of her company's market review committee. To get started on a positive note, she invited all members to a get-together session. They were in the middle of discussing how to proceed when Ellen rushed in. Ellen is a member of this committee who actively campaigned for Carla's job. She was angry she didn't get it and bad feelings remained. Ellen apologized for being late and began to pass out copies of a four-page memo. Skimming the pages, Carla saw the outlines of a market-review strategy. She smiled at Ellen and said, "What a lot of work." She then picked up her mug and asked, "Anyone else want a refill?" The committee members all got up and began to congregate by the coffeepot. When they sat back down, Carla told Ellen, "The committee has not made as much progress as you have. We have yet to identify the approach we want to take, or our priorities. Perhaps it would be better to consider your memo when ideas have been discussed a bit more." Carla's interruption gave her time to collect her thoughts and think about a response. It enabled her to resist being rude to a member who had obviously put in a lot of effort, without allowing that work to dominate the discussion. Nor did she cut Ellen off. Instead, Carla tabled the discussion and signaled to all members that no single person would control the sessions. Absent her interruption, the committee would have been locked on Ellen's memo.

Gloria is a media executive who was trying to negotiate television rights to a hot property. After trying for several days, she finally reached the elusive literary agent on the telephone. Before she could say hello, the agent started screaming at her, attacking her competence and her experience. She was shocked that he would jeopardize a lucrative deal for his client, but whatever his motivation, she could not let his approach go unchecked. "I called to start talking deal points," she interrupted. "You are obviously having a bad day. Why don't I get back to you?" Gloria soon learned that the agent attacked to buy himself time – he had gone on the offensive to stall because he did not yet control the television rights to the property. Her naming of the situation ensured that when they did talk again, she would not be doing so from a defensive position. Naming his move put the conversation back on track.

Leonard was the Vice President of Human Resources at a large bank. During one particularly memorable interview while he was job hunting, he barely had a chance to introduce himself before the chairman of the board began firing questions at him about how he handled problem employees. When the chairman ran out of questions, he praised Leonard on his 'people skills' but argued that, "Unfortunately, the demands of this bank require more expertise from its human resources managers than the ability to work with difficult people." Taken aback that he drew only this conclusion, Leonard began answering the questions he should have been asked by the chairman. "As soon as I could get a word in edgewise, I told him how I reduced teller turnover from 82 percent to 15 percent and explained how I saved the bank $50,000 the first year and over a million the second when I renegotiated the health insurance package with the carriers." Leonard went from being dismissed to being desired by correcting the banker's misguided impressions. His answers to his own questions piqued the chairman's interest in him (these scenarios are adapted from Kolb & Williams, 2003).

If the other side questions your motives, correct his or her negative explanation for your actions or decisions by creating new ideas. If, for example, you are accused of being unyielding or uncooperative when you tell someone that he or she cannot do something, jointly discuss other ways to accomplish the desired outcome. Any options you are able to invent should correct the flawed impression of your motives and preclude him or her from casting negative aspersions about you. If the other negotiator questions your ability or willingness to fulfill your promises, discuss your prior successes with similar problems (see Box 5.3 In Chapter 5).

Inappropriate comments that are demeaning might involve intimidation, efforts to exploit vulnerabilities or tired stereotypes about demographic or ethnic groups. Instead of ignoring these comments and hoping they go away, turn them - quickly. Negotiation in Action 13.3 demonstrates how this can be done.

NEGOTIATION IN ACTION 13.3

Grace, an intellectual property attorney who could easily pass as a model, went into a meeting to finish up the last details of a contract. Both men in the room, one of whom she had not met, immediately referred to her appearance. "First, Jack tells me how stunning I look. Then this new guy, Frank, turns to Jack and says he understands why the negotiations have taken so long. He then looks at me and gives me an exaggerated wink." Grace continued, "You get jerks like this from time to time. I never let that nonsense go. As soon as the words were out of Frank's mouth, I turned a cold shoulder on him." Addressing Jack, I said, "He's a real charmer." She silenced Frank, indirectly – by cutting him out of the conversation and addressing his partner. The exclusion was calculated. She took the papers out of her briefcase and began discussing them with Jack. If Frank wanted to deal with her, he had to stop his 'charming' observations and start talking about the contract (adapted from Kolb & Williams, 2003).

Appreciative Moves

Strategic moves and turns are clearly needed for true problem solving, but they are not sufficient. Finding solutions other than trade-offs and packages requires all parties to develop a complete and shared understanding of the situation. **Appreciative moves** facilitate this process by helping us develop a complete and shared understanding of the other negotiators' perspectives, and linkages between these perspectives and our own. Stated differently, appreciative moves enable negotiators to capture the applicable synergies and move beyond what anyone thought was possible by overcoming the lack of candor, incomplete sharing of ideas, hidden agendas and failure to truly hear ideas that are shared, all of which plague many negotiations.

The other party obviously understands his or her situation better than you do. You can openly *appreciate it* by soliciting his or her views, perceptions and thoughts, encouraging him or her to elaborate on them, and respecting his or her objections. This includes steering the conversation toward perceptions and away from blame and personalities. This should enhance your understanding, validate his or her thoughts and perceptions, and show that they are important to you. (Kolb & Williams, 2003).

Some argue that emotions and feelings should be ignored or suppressed because they muck up our thinking. As discussed in Chapter 11, this is not possible. Nor is it desirable. Emotions and feelings are an important element of our thinking. Our concerns and interests emanate from them (and from our perception or definition of the situation), and we communicate valuable insights about our experiences and expectations through them. Instead of trying to separate feelings from perspectives, it makes more sense to *appreciate the other party's feelings* because this will facilitate dialogue about important matters. Whether they are expressed nonverbally or using other signals, you can openly appreciate the other negotiator's feelings by attending to them and asking the other party for the reasons why they are important to him or her. This should help you build rapport and connection different from that built from shared ideas, and it can take mutual understanding to a new level that will facilitate finding better solutions (Kolb & Williams, 2003).

Discarding, rejecting or otherwise eliminating the other party's ideas, even if they are merely casual ones, may shut down the conversation and even be taken as a personal affront. *Appreciating the other party's ideas* will help you keep the dialogue flowing, spark the creation of new ideas, or suggest different ways to jointly revise ideas that are already under consideration to create better ones (Kolb & Williams, 2003).

As noted throughout this book, image and saving face are major concerns for negotiators. How we look to ourselves and to others often counts as much as the terms of the deals we negotiate. To enhance connection with the other side, therefore, we must *appreciate his or her face*. This will help you and the other party build trust and invent solutions, and inhibit resistance to them. If the other negotiator backs him- or herself into a corner, digs in his or her heels or finds other ways to stubbornly adhere to positions, your task is to make it easier for him or her to retreat. As noted earlier, different frames, different information and different proposals should help with this. An example of how appreciative moves could help build connection is presented in Negotiation in Action 13.4.

NEGOTIATION IN ACTION 13.4

After six years as the moving force behind public radio's *The Connection,* host Christopher Lydon and senior producer Mary McGrath were put on a disciplinary two-week paid leave and escorted from the building. The next day, in a show of unity, the rest of *The Connection* staff quit. Lydon soon made the break permanent stating, "We're angered . . . knocked out . . . stunned. . . . It's a lockout and a shock. WBUR broke "*The Connection*" today instead of negotiating the future of the program with the people who created it. . . . We were willing to return. . . . Unilateralism and bad faith have marked the station's performance with us for many months culminating in the lockout . . . and the announcement that they did not want to talk with us anymore."

Publicly blaming Jane Christo, the station manager, was probably not the best approach because both sides had much to lose by not agreeing. WBUR endangered a signature program if it forced out the host so closely identified with the show's image, and Lydon risked a large salary and a platform that showcased his talents. The deal-breaker in the negotiation was Lydon's demand to share, fifty-fifty, the show's syndication revenues. He demanded this because he viewed the show largely as his personal creation. He frequently cited *Car Talk* as a relevant precedent. Christo, however, was determined not to follow that precedent because the circumstances were entirely different. *Car Talk* was the brainchild of two WBUR volunteers who formed a for-profit company that funded all development costs. Only subsequently did they enter into a contractual arrangement with WBUR to co-produce the show. Half of the funds for developing *The Connection* came from individual supporters while none came from Lydon. Christo didn't mind paying him handsomely, but she considered turning over ownership rights to the show a violation of the public trust. Contrary to public television, public radio had not yet adopted the model of on-air hosts with ownership control and she and WBUR resisted it strenuously. Preoccupied with his 'rights,' Lydon ignored Christo's concerns. Asking her why she preferred a stellar salary offer over a revenue-sharing arrangement would have enhanced his understanding of why she took such a hard line with him.

They both questioned the other's intentions and otherwise escalated tensions. They conducted the negotiation in either/or terms. He wanted ownership; she opposed it. But there were shadings between these two positions. WBUR was unwilling to form or fund Lydon and McGrath's for-profit company, but they never told them they could not form their own company. Christo also suggested that arrangements could be fluid within certain boundaries, but this fluidity and these boundaries were not explored. If outright ownership would not work, what would? Just how flexible was she? This exploration would have cost him nothing and might have gone a long way toward restoring the trust and good faith that were missing. He could have appreciated her ideas and feelings by exploring her objections to revenue sharing and why it was a deal-breaker. Had he connected with her real concerns, it might have been possible to come up with solutions that served both their needs. Furthermore, Lydon believed that he made the show a success and felt slighted, but she probably believed that her efforts were unappreciated. She went to bat for Lydon for an unprecedented salary, only to see him portray her as an unfeeling martinet. Rather than treat the salary offer as inconsequential, essentially a slap in her face, he

(Continued)

(Continued)

could have acknowledged that she had gone out of her way to find a solution. A sincere apology also would have helped get the negotiation back on track.

Finally, he could have appreciated her face. When he rebuffed Christo's offer of a large pay raise, he undercut her with management at NPR by attacking her management style. He backed her into a corner by circulating e-mails and memos that embarrassed both WBUR and NPR. In his letter on the failed contract talks to NPR, he characterized WBUR as having a "system of harassment that calls itself man-agement. He should have demonstrated that he appreciated the public embarrassment he was causing, toned down the rhetoric and resisted the urge to rally the troops – the press corps and his audience – to his cause. Simply put, Lydon's actions gave Christo no room to maneuver. Any accommodation she might have entertained carried substantial and public loss of face (Kolb & Williams, 2003; Jurkowitz, 2001).

Changing the Nature of the Game

There may be times when you think the other party's approach is misguided. If integrative potential exists but he or she insists on employing aggressive or demeaning distributive tactics, for example, you may want to **change the nature of the game** so that both of you can reap greater gains. When we are confronted with a fait accompli, threats and attacks, or rigid adherence to positions, we typically respond in kind, give in or quit. Responding in kind rarely makes us feel better or accomplishes much that is beneficial. Giving in because his or her aggressive tactics make us uncomfortable, or believe that failing to reach an agreement is our fault, similarly fails to produce an agreement that is satisfying. Terminating relationships with clients or quitting our jobs because we cannot resolve our differences when these kinds of tactics are used is also unsatisfactory in most cases (Ury, 1993).

In addition to negotiating the process and implementing the shadow negotiation's moves and turns, another approach for transforming threats, attacks and rigid adherence to positions into joint problem solving argues that we must begin with ourselves because we often lose sight of our interests and our objectivity when we encounter these tactics.

Go to the Balcony

Retaining our objectivity and maintaining our focus on interests, both of which are required for creating value, can be accomplished by "**going to the balcony**." Metaphorically, this allows us to objectively observe the stage where the negotiation is taking place. We can distance ourselves from the stresses and unproductive emotions of the negotiation that may cause us to react impulsively and lose sight of what we really want to accomplish. Simply put, going to the balcony allows us to step back, collect our thoughts and see the situation objectively. It also allows us to recognize the move or tactic the other side is using and name it. For the reasons discussed earlier, conveying your awareness of the difficult tactics being used should diminish their effectiveness (Kolb & Williams, 2003; Ury, 1993).

Manage Your Own Emotions

Video 13.2

Managing Emotions During a Negotiation

Neutralizing the effects of these difficult tactics also requires us to recognize how they make us feel. We all have certain emotional susceptibilities or "hot buttons" that are difficult to manage. If the other negotiator elicits anger, fear, guilt or other negative emotional responses by pushing our hot buttons with these kinds of tactics, we will not be able to negotiate as effectively as we otherwise would.

Consider strategically turning the negotiation by **interrupting the move**. Taking a short break, caucusing or simply pausing and saying nothing for a few minutes will allow us to "go to the balcony." Since it is only possible to pause for so long in the middle of a negotiation, we can also slow down the conversation by playing it back. Paraphrasing what has been said thus far and checking for understanding, or asking the other party to review what has transpired, may allow us to "go to the balcony" to collect our thoughts, realize what the other side is doing and how we are reacting to it, and respond thoughtfully rather than emotionally. Finally, avoid making an important decision on the spot. Sleep on it and make it the next day or, if that is not possible, 'go to the balcony' and make it there. Avoiding the tensions of the negotiation will facilitate better decision making (Kolb & Williams, 2003; Ury, 1993).

Create a Climate That Is Conducive to Problem Solving

Creating this climate requires us to manage our own emotions and those of the other party. We cannot reason with someone who is unreceptive because our arguments and proposals will fall on deaf ears. Some advocate ignoring the other party's emotions, but this is not truly possible. Nor will it help because they are a significant part of the negotiation and they add richness to the conversation. A more feasible and beneficial approach involves disarming the other party by defusing his or her emotions. Restating or paraphrasing, and checking for understanding, will help because people want and need to be heard and understood. Acknowledging and *appreciating his or her ideas and feelings* should reduce the anger that often underlies attacks, and the fear that often underlies stonewalling. An apology will also help because people who have been wronged need this recognition, even if we are not responsible for it. This does not require us to agree – it simply means we must recognize and understand his or her perceptions.

Emphasizing what has already been agreed upon, agreeing to additional items without conceding, mirroring the other negotiator's positive verbal and nonverbal behaviors, but not those that are negative, using "I" statements rather than "You" statements (e.g., "I feel frustrated when this happens" rather than "You frustrate me when you do this"), using strategic turns and other appreciative moves will also facilitate productive communication and encourage reasonable and safe negotiations that are devoid of threats, attacks and intransigence (Kolb & Williams, 2003; Ury, 1993). Negotiation in Action 13.5 is illustrative.

NEGOTIATION IN ACTION 13.5

A salesperson from AT&T was trying to sell Boeing a $150 million telecommunications system. After making a persuasive pitch on the kind of service to be delivered, the company's prompt response to problems and the speed of their repairs, Boeing responded, "Fine. Now put each one of your promises in writing and guarantee that if each problem isn't fixed on time you'll pay damages." Caught off guard, the AT&T sales representative said, "The company will make its best efforts to resolve any problems that arise, but we can't be held liable for all the things that might go wrong. Lightning can strike." After going back and forth for a while, the Boeing negotiator got mad and claimed, "You're fooling around with us. If you're going to make these promises, why are you unwilling to commit to them? You're negotiating in bad faith. We can't deal with you."

(Continued)

(Continued)

The AT&T sales manager later intervened to save the sale. He listened, didn't try to refute Boeing's arguments or defend his own. When he acknowledged that he understood Boeing's views and that they were correct, the Boeing representative's anger subsided and he became more receptive. After stepping to the Boeing manager's side in this way, the sales manager was invited to offer his explanation. He explained what the situation looked like from his perspective. "AT&T would, of course, put its promises in writing. Damages are an issue we have trouble with, but we will discuss it with you. It seems to me that Boeing has an engineering culture – there's no tolerance for ambiguity or error when people's lives are at stake. So if you promise a certain safety specification, you'd better be sure you're on target. And, of course, everything has to be clearly specified in writing." When he asked if he was making any sense, the Boeing manager said, "Yes, but I don't see what it has to do with our problem." The AT&T sales manager responded, "If you'll bear with me, I'll try to explain. At AT&T, we also have engineers, but we're primarily in the business of providing a service. We have more of a relationship culture – relationships with our clients are of the utmost importance. If the client's not happy, we're not either. That's why people call us 'Ma Bell.' When your mom tells you she's going to make your lunch and drive you to school, you don't say to her, 'Now, mom, put it in writing and I'm going to hold you liable for damages,' do you? Of course not. You just expect that she'll do the best she can. Now, obviously, there's a big difference between a household and a business, but this should give you a sense of where we're coming from. We make oral promises and fully expect to deliver on them. Our track record, you'll have to admit, is very good. It's a new experience for us to meet with a lot of skepticism and a demand for damages from a client. That's why we collided with each other at the last meeting – we were coming from very different places. You were right from your perspective, and we were right from our perspective."

When he finished, the negotiation began to get back on track and, soon thereafter, AT&T and Boeing reached an agreement on the sale (adapted from Ury, 1993).

Problem Solve

After creating this favorable climate for the negotiation, it is time to change the nature of the game to joint problem solving. Recast any threats or attacks on you as an attack on the problem. This may require patience, self-control and even some wordsmithing, but it should help you refocus his or her attention on the problem. If he or she remains focused on positions, explore them in more detail. Ask why a particular position is important, or how it will help, or what purpose it will serve for him or her? If your proposal is rejected, ask why it will not work, or what problems it will cause for him or her? If the other party's offer fails to solve your problem, you can also ask for advice. "If you were in my situation, how would you handle this?" Another approach involves asking, "What if . . . ?" questions. For example, if the other side cannot afford your asking price, you could ask, "What if we stretched out the project so that some would be paid out of your current budget and the rest out of next year's budget? Even if these questions do not elicit solutions or outcomes that create value for both parties, they may elicit more information that helps you understand his or her interests more fully and suggest other plausible solutions. In short, reframe the negotiation to be about interests rather than positions.

Even if you have created solutions that you think work for all parties, there may be some reluctance to agree. As noted in Chapter 5, making a mistake and being taken advantage of are the two primary reasons negotiators are hesitant to say yes. Overcoming these fears can be accomplished by ensuring that the other party understands that the value he or she will gain is greater than the cost he or she will incur, that all of his or her interests are satisfied, that saying yes will not cause him or her to lose face, and that his or her constituents will attribute the positive outcome to his or her efforts (Ury, 1993). **Reading 13.1** provides additional suggestions for managing difficult people when they seem to be the problem, and for salvaging otherwise difficult negotiations. **Reading 13.2** provides suggestions for salvaging negotiations when litigation seems like it is inevitable.

MANAGING DIFFICULT CONVERSATIONS

Conversations, including negotiations, help us build relationships. Some, however, are difficult and test our effectiveness as communicators because we must talk about something that elicits anxiety. Changing the nature of the game, disciplining a subordinate, disagreeing with a majority of your teammates or with a coworker who is a friend, interviewing for a promotion or a job, and severing our employment, especially with a supervisor who has been a good ally or mentor, are but a few examples. We may prefer to avoid these conversations, but that is rarely wise or effective, and sometimes it is not possible.

Structurally, difficult conversations entail three separate conversations.

The Conversations Within a Difficult Conversation

In many instances, your story of what happened and the other person's story of what happened differ. We usually respond to this by asserting, harder and harder, that our story is right and his or hers is wrong. This frequently escalates the argument. Moreover, it is rarely as simple as, "I'm right and you're wrong." Our stories usually differ because our backgrounds, mental models or scripts, decision-making errors and personality traits influence our choices of what information we take in and use. Even if we are using the same information, our interpretations of it differ because our diverse backgrounds shape the lenses we use to encode and decode it. Our diverse backgrounds also shape the rules that implicitly or explicitly govern our lives – how the world is supposed to work and how people are supposed to act are examples. These rules, especially if they conflict, will lead us to different information or different interpretations of it, and this will also produce different stories (Scott, 2004; Stone, Patton & Heen, 2000).

Difficulties also arise because we assume, often incorrectly, that we know what the other person intended to do. Unfortunately, intentions are invisible so our assumptions are commonly based on how the other person's actions impact us. We then act consistently with the intentions we attribute to him or her. This reinforces that behavior, and the intentions we assumed become true. Blaming the other party for having malevolent intentions inhibits our ability to find out what really caused the problem and to correct it. Even if it is legally sanctioned, blame makes the accused less forthcoming, less willing to apologize and less effective at problem solving. Blame also looks backward, and we cannot fix or prevent things that have already happened – problem solving requires us to look forward (Scott, 2004; Stone et al., 2000).

The Feelings Conversation

This conversation is not whether we should or should not have feelings because we do. Instead, it is about how we deal with them. Feelings and emotions are at the heart of difficult conversations because they are at the heart of what is wrong. Although they are intricately involved with many substantive problems, and it is not possible to separate them, we usually frame issues in substantive terms without addressing feelings. This is problematic because ignoring feelings precludes us from learning important things about each other such as likes, dislikes, hot buttons, attributions, accusations, judgments and perceptions of what happened. Moreover, unexpressed feelings will be expressed in unproductive ways if we wait for them to leak into the conversation, and this may jeopardize the conversation even more (Scott, 2004; Adler, Rosen & Silverstein, 1998).

The Identity Conversation

Perhaps the most challenging, and subtle, of the three conversations is about our identities. This is challenging because it requires us to look inward to find out what the difficult conversation is saying about ourselves (Stone et al., 2000). It makes us anxious because we must face the other person and our self. Simply put, difficult conversations threaten our identities because they potentially disrupt our sense of who we are. If you recently accepted a new job and you do not need references or any other assistance from your current employer, resigning should be easy. For example, assume your father worked his entire career for a single company and you admired his loyalty. If you believe in doing the right thing, this includes sticking by the important people around you, telling your boss that you are leaving may raise this loyalty issue directly, making the identity conversation difficult (Stone et al., 2000).

Identity issues make us anxious because we tend to consider our self-concepts in 'all-or-nothing' terms. If you are conversing with someone who challenges your purely positive loyalty identity, you will probably respond by either denying the challenge or by exaggerating the negative feedback and flipping your self-concept. The former happens because there is no room for negative feedback so we must deny the challenges and create other explanations for why we are leaving. The latter happens because we allow others' feedback to define who we are – rather than adjusting our self-concepts, we exaggerate the negative feedback. This may sound odd, but if you are not 'purely loyal,' you may flip your self-concept and conclude that you are not loyal and that you will never become an important senior executive (Stone et al., 2000).

How to Manage Them

Negotiators engage in difficult conversations often enough that learning how to manage them, effectively, is beneficial. Being aware of their structure should help, but additional steps should help even more (Scott, 2004; Stone et al., 2000).

1. Prepare for a difficult conversation by walking through these three conversations. Listen to your instincts and avoid discounting them. Recognizing that your intentions are so complex that you are probably never purely anything is essential.

2. Instead of blaming the other party, think about and accept what you might have done to contribute to the problem. Even if you did nothing explicitly, did you contribute in other ways? For example, did you avoid discussing the issues? Did you appear to be unapproachable (you may not intend this or be aware that it is happening, but the personal rules that govern our lives, our communication styles and our background experiences may cause others to perceive us this way)?

3. The relationship between our identities and what we are discussing may not be obvious. Effectively managing the identity conversation requires us to understand those qualities and concerns to which we are particularly sensitive – our own hot buttons.

4. Understand the purpose of the conversation and what must be accomplished. This will clarify whether you really need to raise the issue and how you can make the conversation meaningful.

5. Share this purpose and begin the conversation by asking the other person to partner with you to figure out what really happened and how you can solve it. Recognize that your stories of what happened are different, not right or wrong, and, begin by exploring the difference between them. Ask open-ended questions. Active listening will enhance your understanding, allow the other person to feel heard, and encourage him or her to listen when you share your perspective. Speak clearly so that the other person does not have to draw inferences or guess. Use powerful language, and distinguish facts from perceptions, accusations from feelings and blame from contribution.

6. Distinguish blame from contribution by asking questions like, "What did I do that helped cause this situation?" Stand in the other person's shoes to enhance your understanding of his or her perceptions of your contribution, or view the situation from the perspective of a disinterested observer to understand how others would explain what happened. Use "I" statements to convey your feelings because they cannot be refuted by the other side, and avoid "You" statements because they suggest that you are blaming him or her for what happened.

7. Appreciate the other party's feelings by framing them into the problem, and refrain from evaluating them. If the other person claims to have been hurt, do not argue that he or she is overreacting.

8. When perceptions are clarified and a shared understanding of the situation has been developed, begin problem solving. As discussed in several locations throughout the book, this means inventing options that are designed to satisfy all parties' interests.

SAYING 'NO' TO PEOPLE WHO ARE IMPORTANT TO YOU

Another difficult conversation or negotiation happens when we must say "No" to someone who is important to us or upon whom we depend. "No" is a very powerful word, but it creates a tension between asserting power and preserving relationships – we fear it will undermine deal-making, harm the relationship or engender retaliation. Conversely, we think that saying "yes" makes us attentive to the relationship but weak if we really do not want to comply (Ury, 2007).

How We Usually Say 'No'

Negotiators typically respond to this dilemma by accommodating, attacking or avoiding. We *accommodate* by saying yes when we really want to say no – we tend to the relationship even if it requires us to sacrifice our true interests. This often leads to resentment if we keep saying yes and rarely get anything of value in return. Even worse, it may lead us into a vicious cycle – we continue saying yes so the other negotiator continues to make demands. Instead of accommodating, sometimes we *attack* by saying "no" in a way that is hurtful and undermines relationships. Asserting power in this way often leads to impasses and makes the other person reluctant or unwilling to engage with us again. If we do not want to offend the other person or jeopardize the relationship, we engage in *avoidance* by saying nothing. Though unlikely, we hope the problem will go away on its own (Ury, 2007).

Saying 'No' Positively

Tending to the relationship and using power are not mutually exclusive, so we can escape this conundrum by saying "No" positively. To protect what is important, say "Yes" to your own interests, assert your power by respectfully saying "No" to the other side's demand, and further the relationship by inviting him or her to reach a mutually beneficial agreement with you. In short, avoid accommodation by holding firm to your interests. Avoid attacking by saying "No" to the other party's demand, not to him or her. And reaffirm the relationship by being respectful and inviting him or her to find an outcome that satisfies his or her interests and your own (Ury, 2007). Negotiation in Action 13.6 illustrates how we can say "No" positively.

NEGOTIATION IN ACTION 13.6

John worked for his father in the family business by putting in long hours that kept him away from his wife and kids, even during holidays. Although his workload and responsibilities far exceeded those of his coworkers – his three brothers-in-law – his father paid everyone the same salary to avoid perceptions of favoritism. Fearful of confronting his father and incurring his disapproval, John had never complained. Privately, however, he fumed about the time commitments and the inequity. At a family dinner, when John had finally decided that something had to change, he told his father that he wanted to speak with him, alone. In private, he respectfully told his dad that he wanted to be with his family during the upcoming holidays, that he was not working overtime anymore and that he wanted to be compensated proportionately for his work. Instead of arguing, his dad said okay to the holidays and the overtime, and agreed to talk more about the salary issue.

John discovered that it is possible to simultaneously use power, even with his father who is his boss, and preserve the relationship. He said 'yes' to his self-respect, his primary interest, because it would allow him to spend more time with his family, he stood on his own two feet without standing on his father's toes – he asserted his power by respectfully informing his father that he would no longer be working on weekends or holidays, and he invited his father to jointly search for an arrangement that would satisfy each of their interests – getting the work done in the office, spending the time he needed with his family and being paid equitably (adapted from Ury, 2007).

CONCLUSION AND IMPLICATIONS FOR PRACTICE

The material examined in this chapter pertains to aspects of the negotiation process that make us anxious or uncomfortable. The shadow negotiation and changing the nature of the "game" are underutilized approaches for dealing with impasses, managing difficult tactics and encouraging reluctant negotiators to join us at the table. Understanding the structure of difficult conversations and why it is so hard to say "no" to important people will help us manage them and avoid the anxiety and discomfort that accompanies them.

1.   Use strategic moves to build a platform from which you can effectively advocate for your interests and ensure that they receive a fair hearing. This approach is more productive than exercising your power advantage, which is often perceived as force, manipulation or intimidation, because these perceptions do not enhance relationships or encourage honest and open exchanges of information. Merely touting your relevant accomplishments can help build this platform, but true strategic moves will help you build a stronger one even if you have less power than the other party.

2.   Use strategic turns to reframe the conversation when it turns in an unproductive direction. This is particularly effective when dealing with the more difficult and important issues, when countering dirty tricks, if the other side starts "blaming" you for what happened or if you have less power.

3.   Use appreciative moves to create an environment that will enable you to merge ideas and capitalize on any synergies that exist. These moves will help you develop a complete and shared understanding of the situation, manage the other party's emotions and make the other party more receptive to your ideas and arguments, which should help you create even better solutions.

4.   Interrupt the move and 'go to the balcony' whenever you need a chance to think or make decisions objectively. Being in an environment that is free of the tensions and pressures of the negotiation will give you the opportunity to choose how to proceed to bring the negotiation back on track.

5.   Do not automatically blame the other party when negotiations go awry. Although your stories of what happened are probably different, this does not mean that one is right and the other one is wrong. It simply means they are different. Look for how each party contributed, explore each version of what happened by asking open-ended and probing questions, and merge the versions to create a shared understanding of what happened. This is essential if you want to avoid defensiveness and find solutions that create value.

6.   Explore your own feelings and hot buttons and appreciate those of the other party. Feelings contain valuable information about what happened, and they will influence decisions to accept or reject solutions. Feelings and emotions will also find other, far less productive ways to surface, if they are not raised explicitly. And this may undermine problem-solving efforts. When hot buttons get triggered, 'go to the balcony' to calm down and regain your composure before you proceed.

7.   Say "no" respectfully. To avoid letting someone down by saying "no" to his or her request or demand, focus on saying "yes" to your own interests as the reason you must say 'no.' At the very least, this will reinforce that your decision is right for you. Say "no" respectfully and invite the other party to find mutually beneficial solutions with you. Together, these steps should ease your discomfort and lead to an optimal outcome for both sides.

STUDENT STUDY SITE

Visit the Student Study Site at www.sagepub.com/hames for additional learning tools.

KEY TERMS

Appreciative moves

Changing the nature of the game

Corrective turns

Difficult tactics

Enlisting support

Feeling conversation

Going to the balcony

Identity conversation

Incentives

Interrupting the move

Impasses

Managing emotions

Naming the move

Pressure moves

Problem solving

Shadow negotiation

Strategic moves

Strategic turns

What happened conversation

REFERENCES

Adler, R. S., Rosen, B. & Silverstein, E. M. (1998). Emotions in negotiation: How to manage fear and anger, *Negotiation Journal*, 14(2), 161-179.

Jurkowitz, M. (2001). WBUR suspends 2 in fight over 'Connection,' *Boston Globe*, February 16, A1.

Kolb, D. (2004). Staying in the game or changing it: An analysis of moves and turns in negotiation, *Negotiation Journal*, 20(2), 253-268.

Kolb, D. & Williams, J. (2003). *Everyday negotiation*. San Francisco: Jossey-Bass.

Scott, S. (2004). *Fierce conversations: Achieving success at work & in life, one conversation at a time*. New York: Berkley Books.

Stone, D., Patton, B. & Heen, S. (2000). *Difficult conversations: How to discuss what matters most*. London: Penguin Books.

Ury, W. (1993). *Getting past no: Negotiating your way from confrontation to cooperation*. New York: Bantam Books.

Ury, W. (2007). *The power of a positive no: How to say no and still get to yes*. New York: Bantam Books.

Weeks, H. (2001). Taking the stress out of stressful conversations, *Harvard Business Review*, July-August, 112-119.

READINGS

Reading 13.1

BRING YOUR DEAL BACK FROM THE BRINK

Program on Negotiation

What to do when a difficult person is the main obstacle between you and your goals.

Source: Program on Negotiation (2008). Bring your deal back from the brink, *Program on Negotiation Newsletter*, 11(8), 1-4.

Note: This article first appeared in *Negotiation*, a monthly newsletter published by the Program on Negotiation at Harvard Law School, www.pon.harvard.edu. Copyright 2006–2011 Harvard University.

Jessica tried to stifle her joy. Charlie, the majority owner of the boutique hotel she managed in Miami, had just told her he wanted to sell the business to her. "I'm ready for a new challenge," he said from his usual seat at the bar, where he had spent the evening drinking wine and doing Sudoku puzzles. "Can we make a deal?"

After acquiring the hotel from his ex-wife during their divorce, Charlie had put himself on salary as the marketing manager. Since he hired Jessica to manage the hotel six years ago, its reputation and bookings had steadily climbed. Charlie was nice enough, but Jessica had grown increasingly frustrated with his habit of blocking key improvements and neglecting his duties. He was holding the business back, she believed.

Jessica knew the deal was possibly a once-in-a-lifetime opportunity. Charlie offered to be bought out at a bargain price, stressing that she was the only person he'd entrust with the hotel. Nervous and excited, Jessica spent the next month lining up an investor. Lawyers wrangled over the details for another month.

The night before the deal was to be inked, Charlie called Jessica over to his bar stool. "I have a bad feeling about your investor," he said. "I'm withdrawing my offer. I'm going to rededicate myself to the business. Shall we pop open some champagne?"

Infuriated and crushed, Jessica stopped just short of quitting on the spot. She knew she needed to think through the situation before making any rash decisions.

We've all faced the unpleasant task of negotiating with people we view as irrational, incompetent, and downright aggravating. When such individuals say no to a beneficial deal, walking away may be the path of least resistance. Yet giving up could mean accepting a less desirable outcome.

What can you do when a difficult person is the main obstacle to a promising deal? There are a number of strategies you can use to bring a negotiation back from the brink of failure. We present 10 suggestions here, in an order that you can alter according to the nature of your negotiation.

1. Set Standards of Behavior.

Discuss acceptable norms of behavior with a potentially difficult counterpart before you negotiate, advises Stanford University Professor Stephen John Stedman, who has studied "deal spoilers" in the context of global peacemaking initiatives.

Such norms can help you judge the legitimacy of the other party's demands and behaviors. If you think tempers could rise, for example, you might agree to listen respectfully to each other and to not raise your voices. Or if you suspect someone could get cold feet at the last moment, you might pledge to discuss ways to save the deal before walking away from the negotiating table.

By suggesting to Charlie that they confer with each other regularly while dealing individually with third parties, such as lawyers and potential investors, Jessica might have headed off his last-minute surprise.

2. Avoid Dismissive Labels.

Too often, we label anyone standing in the way of our goals as irrational, stubborn, or worse. Such judgments can limit our options and result in costly strategic errors.

Even if you feel certain that someone's behavior is foolish, destructive, or downright crazy, acknowledge that he is acting out of very human concerns and emotions. It's your job to find out what they are.

After Charlie rescinded his offer, Jessica was tempted to dismiss him as capricious and selfish. But she knew Charlie to be lazy, not flighty. She wondered if perhaps there was more to the story.

3. Take the Pressure Off.

Time pressure can cause negotiators to say no to a deal when it would be in their best interest to say yes. For this reason, be sure all parties to an agreement have ample opportunity to consider proposals and contract drafts. Calling for a break gives everyone time to make smart decisions and can head off an escalating war of words.

Jessica speculated that Charlie was trying to revoke their deal because he was nervous about signing the contract the next day. She considered the possibility that he needed more time to get used to the idea of leaving the hotel.

"I can't stop you if you want to call off the deal," she said to him, "but remember that decisions have consequences. How about if we meet tomorrow—just the two of us, no lawyers—and talk about what's best for us and for the hotel."

This suggestion had a calming effect on Charlie, who agreed to meet the next day to discuss his sudden reversal.

4. Probe the Other Side's Point of View.

How can you figure out the motives behind someone's seemingly stubborn position? Begin by questioning her about the problem she is trying to solve. Deal blockers may be held back by financial, legal, personal, or other constraints you don't know about, according to Harvard Business School professor Deepak Malhotra. A tough stance could also communicate a psychological need that isn't being satisfied.

At their meeting the next day, Jessica asked Charlie to explain the "bad feeling" he had about her financier, an investment banker who was a longtime customer at the hotel's restaurant.

As it turned out, Charlie had been offended by the banker's hard-bargaining style. "He wouldn't return my calls, and his lawyer kept trying to lowball me," he said. "I refuse to do business with someone who doesn't take me seriously."

Jessica knew Charlie had held lingering grudges against others for far lesser slights. Instead of trying to persuade him to accept her investor, she decided to examine Charlie's change of heart about his own role in the hotel. "You told me you were ready for a new challenge," she said. "But now you say you're ready to work hard here. What's going on?"

Charlie hedged a bit and then admitted he was no more enthusiastic about fulfilling his marketing duties than he had been before. "I just want to make sure you stay in charge." He said. "And, frankly, I'm not really sure what I want to do next. It's little scary to think of leaving this place."

5. Put Forth Multiple Proposals.

Jessica was gaining a clearer picture of Charlie's reason for canceling the sale. After their meeting, she drew up three proposals:

- Together, they could meet with her investor to talk through his and Charlie's differences in negotiating style and assess whether a deal was still possible.
- Jessica could try to find another investor to buy out Charlie, though he would have to agree to some ground rules on timing and selection criteria before she agreed to this option.
- Jessica would stay on at the hotel with Charlie as owner if he would agree to let her farm out his duties to outside firms and give her a stake in the business, with annual percentage increases based on performance.

Sometimes people will block deals simply to get your attention. By developing several proposals that meet your interests well and that also address the other side's needs, you convey the important message that you've been listening.

6. Be Ready to Walk.

Note that Jessica's package of proposals contained an implicit threat: she would quit her job if nothing changed. She was tired of working for someone who blocked progress.

Threats and punishment may be necessary when you're negotiating with people who rigidly adhere to all their demands, according to Stanford's Stephen John Stedman. You must be prepared to follow through on your threats, of course. That's why it's crucial to research your best alternative to a negotiated agreement, or BATNA, at the same time you're negotiating your preferred deal.

For Jessica, this meant quietly putting out feelers with her industry contacts during the time she was negotiating with Charlie. She became confident that she would be able to find a comparable job without too much trouble, though it would be difficult to match the day-to-day decision-making power that Charlie gave her.

7. Share Your Feelings.

When someone calls off a deal at the last minute, don't assume she's deliberately trying to hurt you. It could very well be that she's preoccupied with her own interests and hasn't thought about how her decision will affect you.

For this reason, not only do you need to give potential deal spoilers a chance to vent, but you also need to articulate your own frustrations constructively. By doing so, you can encourage the other party to understand your perspective and guide her toward more collaborative behavior.

"Your decision about the investor was a huge letdown for me," Jessica said to Charlie before presenting her proposals. "Running my own hotel is my dream, as you know, and I feel as if you haven't thought about how changing your mind affects me."

Charlie apologized for putting Jessica through the wringer and promised to work with her toward a mutually beneficial solution. "I guess we're both feeling disrespected," he said. "I'll try to do better."

8. Weigh the Benefits of a Concession.

Another option for dealing with difficult negotiators is to craft what Harvard Law School professor Robert C. Bordone calls a "workaround"—a strategy for meeting your current goals without the involvement or support of your adversary.

You might be able to induce a yes with a tempting concession on a key issue, according to Bordone. Offering a concession can be a dangerous strategy, as it may only encourage someone to push for more. But if a concession would allow you to move beyond that person once and for all, it may be your best option.

Jessica, for instance, might try to convince Charlie to get past his bad feeling about her investor by raising more money, whether from the same investor or other sources, and offering Charlie a higher price for his shares. Running the hotel without Charlie's interference might be worth the short-term cost of securing extra funds.

9. Build a Coalition.

Another workaround technique is to build coalitions that will influence the deal blocker in your favor. By enticing a recalcitrant party to follow influential others on a particular course, coalitions exploit *pattern of deference,* according to Harvard Business School professor James Sebenius.

To build a coalition in support of your desired outcome, make a list of those who have an interest in a potential deal, and consider how they might influence the spoiler. Next, figure out the best sequence in which to approach these parties. Finally, present your case to these key individuals.

Jessica contacted two people who had invested in the hotel in the early days and still owned a small stake: a cousin of Charlie's ex-wife and the hotel's first manager. Both were interested in selling their shares to Jessica for the right price. Jessica hoped that showing Charlie that other buyers saw value in selling their shares would convince him to join them.

10. Accept No for An Answer.

Badgering someone into accepting a deal is never a good idea, even if you're sure it would be in her best interest. Not only can coercion be unethical and even illegal, but also a dissatisfied counterpart could sabotage the deal during implementation. If you've exhausted the strategies above and the other party still won't say yes, it's time to move on.

In the end, Charlie continued to balk at selling all his shares in the hotel to Jessica. However, he was receptive to one of her other proposals. He agreed to give her 15% ownership of the hotel, a percentage that would increase over time based on her job performance. He also promised to grant her even more decision-making authority, to turn over his marketing duties to outside professionals, and to cut his salary.

After talking through the offer with several trusted advisers, Jessica decided it was her best option at this point in her career. She and Charlie drew up a new contract, and she began looking at him as a partner rather than an obstacle.

Thinking Further 13.1

1. Which, if any, of the nine strategies for managing people who say no would you recommend that negotiators prepare for *prior* to a negotiation? Would being prepared with these strategies in advance help reduce the possibility that the other party will say no? Why or why not?

2. Would calling out the other party's lack of willingness to come to an agreement be productive or counterproductive to a negotiation? Might it depend on the situation? Explain why.

Reading 13.2

WILL YOU NEGOTIATE OR LITIGATE?

Deepak Malhotra

When a legal battle looms, negotiating with your opponent might seem impossible. But it's never too late to find common ground.

The owner of a manhattan co-op apartment spent $909 to install childproof window guards on windows in his unit and presented the building's co-op board with the bill. Immediately, a dispute arose over who should cover the cost of the project. The unit's owner argued that the cost should be divided among the building's residents, while the board believed that the owner of the unit should pay the bill in its entirety. The law was unclear on the matter, and neither party was willing to compromise.

Whenever a dispute flares up, the parties involved must ask themselves which course of action will yield the best outcome. Should they negotiate, litigate, or simply walk away and accept the status quo? In this true story, the co-op board decided to take the matter to court. Given that $909 was not a trivial expense, it seemed like a reasonable decision at the time.

Six years and $100,000 in legal fees later, the two sides were still fighting in the courts. The co-op board eventually "won" the dispute, but in truth, there were no winners—except, of course, for the lawyers. All of this was brought on by a dispute over $909 in which neither

Source: Malhotra, D. (2004). Will you negotiate or litigate? *Program on Negotiation Newsletter,* 7(10), 1–3.

Note: This article first appeared in *Negotiation,* a monthly newsletter published by the Program on Negotiation at Harvard Law School, www.pon.harvard.edu. Copyright 2006–2011 Harvard University.

party was willing to make concessions or to consider the possibility of negotiation.

There are several reasons to pursue litigation rather than negotiation. When the dispute is complex, the stakes are high, legal rights are unclear, and the parties are entrenched in extreme positions and making seemingly irreconcilable claims, it makes sense to obtain legal representation. But litigation is costly; furthermore, it removes control of the dispute resolution process from the disputants and puts it in the hands of lawyers, judges, and juries who have very little, if any stake in the outcome.

The costs of a lawsuit are often worth the benefit of a legal victory. Before taking on these costs, however, you need to evaluate some important considerations. I'll introduce you to some of the often-overlooked drawbacks of litigation and explain why you should remain open to the possibility of negotiation even after you've gone to court.

The Hidden Costs of Litigation

When considering whether to resolve a dispute through legal action, most people do some comparison-shopping among lawyers to try to get a sense of the fees involved. Unfortunately, many critical costs associated with litigation are not visible or salient when you're deciding whether to pursue legal action. Here are some that are often overlooked:

1. The Number of Billable Hours.

How long will litigation last, and how many billable hours are likely to accrue in pursuit of a victory? You should find out what hourly fee you'll be charged, and ask lawyers to estimate how many hours you're likely to be billed.

2. The Possibility and Cost of Further Litigation.

What will happen after the dispute is "resolved" in court? What if you or the other side wants to appeal the decision or pursue further litigation?

In the window childproofing case, more than 80% of the $100,000 in legal fees accrued *after* the courts had ruled that the unit owner was responsible for the $909 cost. Amazingly, roughly half of the legal fees mounted up from litigation that took place even after an appellate court ruled to uphold the initial ruling, when the co-op board sued to have the unit owner pay its legal fees. Before pursuing any legal action, you should work with your lawyer to assess what each party is likely to do under every potential outcome of the lawsuit and calculate the costs associated with these possibilities.

3. The Effect of Litigation on Relationships.

How will litigation affect your relationships with the other side and with anyone else who may be involved? The way in which people handle and resolve conflict says a lot about the strength of their relationship. When deciding whether to litigate or negotiate, be sure to consider the effects of legal action on future interactions, business transactions, and relationships. Disputes may strain relationships, but litigation tends to destroy them. Just imagine the stony silences in the elevator after the unit owner and the building's other residents took their dispute to court. The long-term emotional and financial repercussions are even worse when you're battling with business partners or family members.

4. Time Spent Pursuing Legal Action.

How many months or years can you expect to devote to litigation? The hours billed by your legal team hardly compare to the hours you'll spend preparing; worrying; working with lawyers; and traveling to and from meetings, hearings, and depositions. Looking back, you may wish you'd spent that time with your family or working to bring home a bigger paycheck. In the childproofing case, litigation lasted six years. Legal fees aside, it's hard to imagine that any of the disputants would have committed themselves up front to spending six years fighting over $909.

It's Never too Late to Negotiate

One year after their legal dispute began, the unit owner's and co-op board's combined legal bills slightly exceeded $1,000. At this point the parties could have chosen to negotiate to settle their difference, but they didn't. After another year passed, the parties had invested more than $10,000. Again they could have fired their lawyers and hired a mediator to help them negotiate but they didn't. Four years later, their bills totaled $100,000. At every moment in this escalating conflict, the parties faced a choice among backing down, walking away, or proposing to settle the dispute out of court. Any of these options would have saved them tens of thousands of dollars.

In the heat of battle, it's easy to escalate commitment to one's chosen course of action. Staying the course is psychologically comforting, socially justifiable, and politically defensible. It can also be strategically disastrous. Effective negotiators learn from the past but are not its prisoners. They understand that it's never too late to negotiate. When a dispute goes from bad to worse, that's all the more reason to consider the possibility of negotiation or mediation.

Negotiate *and* Litigate

One of the drawbacks of pursuing legal action is that once litigation begins, interaction between the disputants becomes rare. Any interaction that does occur is constrained and formal, as attorneys advise their clients to refuse comment and eschew conversation. Such tactics aid litigation but hinder negotiation.

In fact, litigation and negotiation are not mutually exclusive. Both can—and often should—be pursued simultaneously. Speaking with regard to the Middle East conflict (and paraphrasing David Ben-Gurion's famous quotation),

former Israeli Prime Minister Yitzhak Rabin often remarked that he would fight terror as if there were no peace process and make peace as if there were no terror. In other words, he would give up neither negotiation nor the use of military force. Although clearly controversial in the realm of global politics, Rabin's two-pronged strategy illustrates the fact that dispute resolution sometimes requires both a *power-based* and an *interest-based* approach, such as the simultaneous pursuit of litigation (the use of legal power) and negotiation (attempts to reconcile each party's interests).

Here are some strategies that can help disputants keep interest-based bargaining alive even after legal action has been initiated:

1. Keep Communication Lines Open.

If you and the other party have a preexisting relationship (as business partners, family members, or friends), it's important to communicate regularly regarding alternative ways to resolve your dispute. As legal bills accumulate, disputants often begin to soften their positions, and new openings for agreement can emerge. In addition, if the dispute was due in part to miscommunication or misinformation, keep working to clarify your perspective and understand the other side's point of view. Just because legal action was pursued prematurely doesn't mean it must be seen through to the bitter end. While it's not easy to negotiate in the midst of legal maneuvers, you should at least leave open the possibility.

2. Ask Other Parties to Mediate.

When communication with the opposing side is strained or difficult, consider bringing in a mutually trusted third party to serve as a go-between. Mediators can facilitate information exchange, vouch for good-faith efforts, and propose ways to resolve the dispute. Third parties can also help provide a reality check by reminding disputants of the costs and likely repercussions of litigation.

3. Don't Lose Sight of Your Underlying Interests.

Far too many people view negotiation as a battle in which the goal is to win, a misperception that's accentuated by litigation. When you think you're in the right, both morally and legally, the desire to win can distract you from pursuing your true underlying interests. As the child-proofing case shows, however, it's possible to win the lawsuit and still lose. With this in mind, revisit the following questions often during your dispute: What are my true underlying interests? How can I best achieve them? How much am I willing to pay just to be able to say that I won? It's important to recognize that when you lose sight of your interests, you lose the possibility of negotiation.

4. Understand Your Lawyer's Role and Perspective.

Your lawyer's job is to educate you and advocate for you. He or she is not – and should not

be – the primary decision maker on your behalf. As the disputant, you must understand not only your rights but also your options – especially your non-litigation options. The best lawyers will help you comprehend all of those alternatives. But the fact remains that lawyers make their living by giving legal advice and pursuing litigation. As a result, your incentives will never be completely aligned with those of your lawyer. Furthermore, your lawyer's expertise is probably restricted to the domain of law. It's incumbent to negotiation. One way to do this is by getting second opinions from legal experts who have no financial stake in the case.

The decision to litigate should not be taken lightly, and the power of negotiation should not be taken lightly, and the power of negotiation should not be underestimated. You should pursue litigation only as a last resort, staying focused on the pursuit of negotiation, underlying interests, and the goal of preserving and strengthening relationships.

Thinking Further 13.2

1. Why, in your opinion, do so many people litigate without first attempting to negotiate? What might incentivize them to negotiate before attempting to litigate?

2. List and describe the advantages and disadvantages of litigation. Name some circumstances in which you believe litigation could be preferable to negotiation.

CHAPTER 14

Third-Party Intervention

Recourse When Negotiations Sputter or Fail?

Despite your formidable efforts to manage difficult negotiations, they sometimes collapse, and finding an acceptable solution seems to be impossible. If the approaches suggested in Chapter 13 fail to help you circumvent or overcome the obstacles and produce a satisfactory outcome, you do not have to walk away and settle for no agreement, or pursue a legal settlement. Several alternatives to the legal system exist. This chapter examines the nature of alternative dispute resolution and the two approaches that are most commonly used by businesses. It also examines the factors managers should consider when deciding how to intervene in intra-organizational conflicts.

INTENDED BENEFITS OF THIS CHAPTER

When you finish reading this chapter, you should be able to:

1. Explain why alternative dispute resolution is a growth industry.
2. Explain the difference between mediation and arbitration, and their respective processes.
3. Discuss the criteria managers should consider when deciding how to intervene in intra-organizational disputes, the intervention strategies that are available and the relationship between the criteria and strategies.

409

THE ESSENCE OF THIRD-PARTY INTERVENTION

Whether you are trying to close deals, settle disputes or make team decisions, some negotiations are inherently tough. Differences in substantive expectations may be too substantial to overcome. Emotional hurdles may be insurmountable. Other obstacles may undermine your efforts. At times, these challenges preclude negotiators from finding acceptable solutions or even looking for them. They seem to think it is better to give up and walk away, or to pursue legal remedies by suing the other side. This may not be wise. You initially engaged in the negotiation process because you thought you could do better with the other party than you could on your own, so walking away does not make sense unless you have improved your BATNA. Nor does suing the other side make much sense – it is time consuming and costly, and the person who will be telling you what to do probably has little or no expertise with your issues, and little or no concern for your interests. In other words, these approaches may resolve the problem, at least in the short run, but neither one is likely to yield beneficial outcomes.

ALTERNATIVE DISPUTE RESOLUTION (ADR)

Civil litigation costs $200-300 billion per year in the United States (Naimark, 2004). That, coupled with the backlog of cases and the excessive amount of time required to resolve them, has caused many to seek alternatives to the legal system. Organizations have bought into alternative dispute resolution (ADR) for many reasons, but mostly because it is faster and less expensive than the legal system, and because it often yields solutions that are more beneficial for you than walking away without an agreement or settling for a court-imposed solution. The most common forms of ADR are mediation and arbitration – usually to help with commercial and employment problems.

Dispute-Wise Organizations

An American Arbitration Association survey of businesses found that some companies have adopted a strong risk-management focus that enables them to avoid or minimize litigation, and resolve disputes quickly and inexpensively. This has also enhanced their relationships with customers, suppliers, partners and employees. These companies are 'dispute-wise' (Naimark, 2004). The relevant practices that characterize these companies include top management support for risk management, with a strong focus on preserving important business relationships rather than simply winning cases; developing organizational cultures that value resolving conflicts quickly and efficiently, without litigation; and integrating legal departments into the planning process. Arbitration and mediation are both used if negotiations fail, but mediation is preferred because it affords outcome control to the negotiators – they, rather than the third party, create the solution (Naimark, 2004). These organizations have also reaped benefits from resolving conflicts quickly and privately, so training managers how to intervene to manage conflict and find good solutions has assumed greater importance.

When ADR Is Likely to Be Used

Negotiators are most likely to seek third-party assistance when emotions preclude them from finding acceptable solutions, they are unable to correct poor communication without assistance, misperceptions or stereotypes hinder productive information exchanges, repeated negative behaviors such as blaming and name-calling create barriers, there are serious disagreements about data – its importance, how it should be collected, and how it should be analyzed and interpreted— real or perceived interests are incompatible, they are unable to get past impasses, or they are unable to get the other party to the table (Naimark, 2004).

Different forms of ADR such as mini-trials (informal, unofficial trials, commonly conducted by a judge who is not acting in his or her official judicial capacity) are available, but they are not widely used. Mediation and arbitration are used far more often by dispute-wise companies and other business organizations. These two processes, both of which have their roots in labor-management relations but have expanded into many other arenas, involve neutral third parties. How neutral or unbiased mediators and arbitrators are is frequently debated, but they do not have a vested interest in the outcome. Mediation is an extension or elaboration of the negotiation process. Mediators lack direct outcome control, but they influence outcomes appreciably by facilitating communication and problem solving, and otherwise shaping the process. Arbitration is not directly linked to the negotiation process. In this informal judicial process, disputants organize and present information to persuade the arbitrator to decide in their favor. Arbitrators have outcome control because they impose solutions on disputants that are, in most cases, final and binding. There are some constraints on what information is presented and how, but they are more relaxed than in judicial proceedings. Simply put, mediators facilitate negotiations by managing the process. Arbitrators listen to the information presented by the parties, apply it to their interpretations of the pertinent legal, contractual or policy provisions, and then render decisions that are usually final and binding.

Video 14.1
Parties Can Solve
Their Own Problems

MEDIATION

Mediation is an extension or elaboration of the negotiation process. A person who is acceptable to the negotiators intervenes to help them voluntarily reach a mutually acceptable solution to their problem. Mediators have no authority to make final outcome decisions – that is left to the negotiators. They do manage or facilitate the process, however, and that includes making process-oriented decisions (Moore, 1996). There are different models or approaches used by mediators. One of the key variables differentiating these approaches is how directive the mediators are, or how much control they exercise over the process. Mediators, in other words, vary in how much they emphasize the negotiators' substantive, process and relationship interests. "*Orchestrators*" empower negotiators to solve their own problems and make their own decisions. They focus on developing better relationships between the negotiators, assisting with the process, and enhancing negotiators' abilities to solve future problems and manage difficult negotiations without assistance. "*Dealmakers*" are more directive on both substantive and process interests. They delineate the problem-solving steps to be followed, determine who talks and when, decide whether the parties meet jointly or separately, voice their opinions about the issues and assume a much more active role in inventing options with or for the parties. Relatively speaking, orchestrators are more relationship-oriented while dealmakers are more outcome-oriented (Moore, 1996; Bush & Folger, 1994; Kolb, 1983).

When Mediation is Most Appropriate and Effective

Mediation is most appropriate when the conflict is moderately intense, the parties are receptive to assistance and motivated to settle (i.e., the conflict is ripe or ready to be addressed), they believe in the mediation process and are committed to it, the issues are not limited to those involving severely limited resources, the parties are relatively equal in power, and the problem is more about creating terms of a new contract or policy than interpreting an existing one (Greig, 2001; Coleman, 2000, 1997; Lewicki & Sheppard, 1985).

Mediators help negotiators save face, enhance relationships, remove or reduce obstacles to agreement and produce outcomes the negotiators desire and value. They may also help the parties solve the true cause of the problem rather than symptoms or the surface issues (van Ginkel, 2004; Rubin, 1980). The evidence suggests that mediators' success rates range between 20% and 80%, and that overall they are successful about 60% of the time (Wall, Stark & Standifer, 2001; Kressel & Pruitt, 1989).

Mediators are most likely to enjoy this success if they gain the negotiators' acceptance, trust and confidence, and the conflict is ripe (Goldberg & Shaw, 2007; Goldberg, 2005; Esser & Marriott, 1995). Acceptability is established by demonstrating empathy, trustworthiness and flexibility, and by remaining calm and friendly. *Ripeness* or readiness means that the conflict has induced enough discomfort to motivate the parties to settle, but not so much that they are unable to do so. Mediators' success also depends upon how effectively they structure discussions, follow an explicit agenda, help the negotiators set their priorities, control the process, and avoid criticizing or embarrassing the negotiators (Grieg, 2001; Zubek, Pruitt, Pierce, McGillicuddy & Syna, 1992). Difficulties may arise if the mediator is inflexible or too closely aligned with one of the parties. The alignment problem can be overcome if the mediator mediates evenhandedly and treats the parties fairly. Insurmountable difficulties are more likely if he or she provides greater support to one of the parties than the other (Wall & Stark, 1996; Botes & Mitchell, 1995; Conlon & Ross, 1993).

How the Mediation Process Works

Negotiators are generally more satisfied with mediation than arbitration and the legal system because it is less costly and time consuming, and because they participate directly in creating the outcome (Brett, Barsness & Goldberg, 1996). Since there are different models, and no two mediators will execute even the same model the same way, it is not possible to give a definitive description or explanation of how all mediations work. One of the most common frameworks, however, is sufficiently representative to give you a reasonable approximation of how mediations unfold. In general, mediators attempt to identify the issues or problems to be addressed, determine what is causing them and their consequences, and then formulate plausible solutions. Simply put, they attempt to develop a picture of the conflict and what the solution will look like when it's implemented. Negotiation in Action 14.1 outlines one of the more common mediation models – an interest-based approach. This, coupled with the following discussion of the elements of the process, should demonstrate why or how mediation is an extension of the integrative negotiation process. In essence, it's facilitates separating the person from the problem, focusing on interests rather than positions, inventing options and using objective criteria to evaluate the options that are invented.

Opening Remarks

Mediators begin by *introducing* themselves, the negotiators and their representatives (if they are present in addition to or instead of the negotiators). They explain that the process is *voluntary* – the negotiators may accept or reject whatever solutions are proposed, and they may leave the session if they decide it is not working well enough for them. They also explain that the *goal* of the mediation

NEGOTIATION IN ACTION 14.1

The Mediation Process

I. Opening Remarks

- Introduce self, negotiators, representatives
- Voluntariness of the process
- The goal of the process – to achieve a mutually satisfactory solution
- Roles – of the mediator and of the negotiators
- Confidentiality for the mediator and for the negotiators
- Outline the process
- Share perspectives on issues and concerns/interests
- Mediator's summary of the issues to be addressed
- Joint problem solving by the negotiators
- Prepare a written agreement if an agreement is reached
- Caucus – as needed
- Ground Rules – no interruptions, respond honestly, respectfully

II. Parties Share Perspectives

- Clarify issues, interests

III. Mediator's Summary of Issues, Interests

- Creates agenda for problem solving

IV. Problem Solving

- Select issue to begin with and explore for underlying interests
- Seek acceptance of interests and frame issues/interests as joint problem-solving tasks
- Invent options for mutual gain and evaluate using interests and objective criteria
- Repeat for other issues

V. Write an Agreement

is to find a mutually acceptable solution. To accomplish this goal, they discuss the *roles* that will be assumed by each of the participants.

The mediator's role is to facilitate the negotiation to help the parties create an acceptable solution. The role of the negotiators is to create the solution. In these opening remarks, the *confidentiality* of the process is discussed. The negotiators are informed that mediators cannot be required to testify or give depositions if this matter should go to court. For their safety and security, the parties are also encouraged to maintain the confidentiality of the process. Mediators explain what *caucuses* are and why they might be called. Then they outline the process – the parties will share their perspectives of the situation, the issues and interests revealed will be summarized to create an agenda, joint problem solving will follow, and a *written agreement* will be prepared if an agreement is reached. Mediators close their opening remarks by setting *ground rules*. This typically includes asking the negotiators to be respectful and to avoid interrupting others when they are speaking. They may also set other guidelines that have facilitated previous mediations.

These opening remarks are valuable because they help to clarify expectations and reduce uncertainty or fear about what will happen. Clarifying expectations is particularly important if the negotiators have never mediated. Opening remarks allow mediators to begin earning the negotiators' trust and confidence, both of which enhance the effectiveness of the process. Establishing behavioral guidelines or ground rules helps mediators manage emotions and other obstacles that may be elicited by tensions or frustrations. Opening remarks are largely presented by the mediator. He or she should keep this brief so the parties do not get bored or overwhelmed. It is important to ask the parties to contribute when it is appropriate. This works well, for example, when setting behavioral guidelines or ground rules because the negotiators may have unique insights into how they do and do not work well together, and what kinds of limits or boundaries may facilitate the process. Involving the negotiators may also enhance their trust of and confidence in the mediator.

Sharing Perspectives

This stage of the process begins when the mediator asks neutrally-framed, open-ended questions such as: What are the important issues we need to address? Why are we here? Will you tell us about the events leading up to this meeting? But not: What did the other side do that made you so angry? Mediators encourage the parties to share their "story" of what happened.

This helps him or her begin to understand the situation and identify the parties' issues and interests. More important, it allows the negotiators to express themselves productively and feel heard – this may be the first time the negotiators have been able to fully and productively share their stories. It may also be the first time the negotiators have really listened to what the other person is saying. Creating value requires the negotiators to understand and respect the other party's perspective, so facilitating a productive exchange is essential.

The mediator may ask probing and clarifying questions about the negotiators' answers, summarize key points, paraphrase or restate what is said and check for understanding. This allows him or her to flesh out the negotiators' issues and interests. It allows the negotiators to feel heard, and to understand the situation from the other side's perspective. Some mediators conduct this part of the process by caucusing. They may get the parties to share information more openly in this manner, but it precludes the negotiators from hearing and understanding the other party's story, and it precludes them from feeling heard by the other party. Both of the latter consequences may be detrimental to the process.

Mediator's Summary

Summarizing what he or she learned while the parties shared their perspectives enables the mediator to create a "final" list of issues and interests to be addressed. This establishes the agenda for problem solving. Framing the issues neutrally is essential. Using the negotiators' language, after removing any blame or other biased language, is best because it avoids arousing negative emotions that may undermine the process. Framing them as joint or shared problems specifies, at least symbolically, that the parties must work together to find solutions that work for each of them.

Problem Solving

Mediators select an issue to begin with, frame it as a shared problem, neutrally, and remind the negotiators of the interests that are associated with it. They seek clarification and acceptance of these interests, and ask questions to determine if there are others that have been overlooked. The negotiators are then asked to begin brainstorming mutually beneficial solutions. When a sufficient number have been invented, the mediator and the negotiators will evaluate them relative to the parties' interests and the objective criteria they identify. If solutions do not meet these standards, the negotiators will resume their efforts to invent options or modify those that have been invented to make them better. If the negotiators are unwilling or unable to invent acceptable solutions, the mediator may encourage them to invent multi-issue options or multiple equivalent offers. He or she may caucus with each negotiator independently. They may be more willing to share their thoughts or invent options alone than they are with the other party present. The mediator may also create 'what if' solutions and ask each of the negotiators if they would accept it if the other side agreed. If these do not work, or if the parties lack conviction, pressure may be applied. The mediator may become more directive by assuming a greater role in inventing options. He or she may even threaten to leave by saying something like, "If you are unwilling to invent adequate solutions, call me when you are ready."

The Written Agreement

If an agreement is reached, it must be reduced to writing. Leaving it to a verbal agreement or memory may lead to numerous misunderstandings, misinterpretations or misapplications. The written document must be written clearly and accurately to avoid these problems. This is particularly important because these agreements are usually legally enforceable.

ARBITRATION

While mediation is an extension, elaboration or continuation of the negotiation process, arbitration is a method for resolving failed negotiations by having a third party impose a decision on the negotiators. It is usually used to settle disputes – violations of legal, contractual or policy provisions.

Video 14.2
The Arbitration
Process

To a lesser degree, it is used to finish negotiations that fail to produce a new contract. A person who has no vested interest in the outcome listens to the evidence and testimony presented by the negotiators, applies it to his or her interpretation of the legal, contractual or policy provision at issue (if it is a dispute), and renders a decision that is usually binding – legally enforceable. Arbitrators exert limited control over what information is presented and how. Witnesses take an oath so they cannot perjure themselves. Parties may object to allowing the presentation of certain information because they believe it is impertinent. Arbitrators can sustain them and delete the material from the record, or overrule them and allow it. Reflecting the relative informality of the process, arbitrators tend to be more lenient than judges when deciding whether evidence and testimony are admissible. They evaluate it when they make their decisions and weigh it accordingly. Some arbitrators assume a more active role in managing the process by asking the witnesses questions to gather additional information or clarify that which has been presented.

When Arbitration Is Most Appropriate and Effective

Arbitration is most appropriate when the conflict is highly intense, the parties are not motivated to settle (perhaps because it is unripe), the issues are limited to those involving severely limited resources, special expertise is required or the problem is more about interpreting a legal principle or the provisions of an existing contract or policy than creating a new one (Greig, 2001; Coleman, 2000, 1997). The primary advantages of arbitration are that it provides a definitive resolution to the problem, and it is simpler, faster and less costly than litigation (Devinatz & Budd, 1997; Brett & Goldberg, 1983).

This is a high profile form of ADR because of its use in labor-management relations and in professional athletes' salary disputes. It also has a long history in disputes between investors and investment companies and in international disputes. In most of these arenas, it is used to settle disputes. In labor disputes, it is most commonly used to resolve grievances (alleged breaches of collective bargaining agreements). It is also used in the public sector to finalize the terms of collective bargaining agreements when the negotiations stall or fail because strikes are legally impermissible for many public sector employees. Despite this awareness and popularity, several criticisms have been levied against the process.

Problems With Arbitration

The biasing effect. Arbitrators must maintain an image of fairness and impartiality. Even if the facts warrant their decisions, a pattern that systematically favors one side or the other creates the perception that they are biased. This inhibits acceptance of and compliance with their decisions, and diminishes their acceptability to at least one the parties (Conlon & Ross, 1993).

The chilling effect. Disputants who believe that achieving an acceptable solution is unlikely and that the arbitrator will simply split the difference between their final offers are not likely to compromise or negotiate seriously to find solutions. Since maintaining an extreme position will benefit them if the arbitrator does split the difference, this is understandable (Kritikos, 2006; Kochan, 1980). The evidence demonstrates that arbitrators rarely split the difference (Keer & Naimark, 2001). Nevertheless, our perceptions are often our reality. If educating the disputants does not help, adopting **final offer arbitration** might. Rather than creating an appropriate solution or splitting the difference, arbitrators must select the party's final offer that he or she thinks is best or closest to the most appropriate solution. This gives the disputants a powerful incentive to continue negotiating seriously, especially if they are fearful that the arbitrator will not accept their extreme offer (Hanany, Kilgour & Gerchak, 2007). **Reading 14.2** explains why or how final offer arbitration motivates negotiators to find acceptable outcomes.

The decision-acceptance effect. Compliance with unsatisfactory decisions that are imposed on us will wane. People do not like to be told what to do. They are more likely to accept and commit to decisions they help create. Thus, compliance with mediated outcomes is often greater than compliance with arbitrated outcomes (Leavitt & Bahrami, 1988).

The half-life effect. The more arbitration is used, the less satisfaction the parties derive from both the process and the outcomes produced. This disenchantment drives many to find alternative approaches for resolving failed negotiations (Anderson & Kochan, 1977).

The narcotic effect. Agreement is not guaranteed when parties negotiate, and the process can be difficult and time-consuming. To avoid what they expect will be an inefficient use of their time, disputants defer to the arbitration option too quickly. Just as people rely on narcotics, disputants rely on arbitration. This is especially true if they are representing constituents because maintaining tough, unyielding positions may be lauded by the people they represent and they can defer blame to the arbitrator for "bad" outcomes. **Reading 14.2** discusses a form of arbitration that overcomes some of these problems and encourages disputing parties to negotiate with greater commitment to reaching an acceptable outcome.

Mandatory Arbitration

Mandatory arbitration has gained considerable attention in recent years. This highly controversial and heavily criticized practice requires clients, customers and employees to arbitrate all disputes rather than pursue legal action. Negotiation in Action 14.2 discusses this controversy.

NEGOTIATION IN ACTION 14.2

In the 1980s, when the courts began to recognize exceptions to the doctrine of employment at will that allowed employers and employees to sever their employment relationships at any time for any reason, be it good cause, no cause or a morally wrong cause, judges and juries began awarding substantial damages to employees who were wrongfully discharged – plaintiffs won about 68% of the discharge cases that went to juries and the damages they collected averaged about $450,000. Some awards were closer to $20 million. Even in the cases they won, employers paid $100,000-200,000 in legal fees and expenses (St. Antoine, 2010). In response, employers began seeking alternatives that were simpler, faster and less expensive. One of the most controversial responses involves mandatory arbitration of employment disputes. More than 6 million employees have been forced to waive legal claims against their employers in favor of binding arbitration (Colvin, 2004; Hill, 2003). In Gilmer v. Johnson/Lane Corp. (1991), and 14 Penn Plaza, LLC v. Pyett, (2009), the U.S. Supreme court ruled that these mandatory arbitration requirements are legally valid and enforceable. Mandatory arbitration has become prevalent in many other domains as well. It is getting harder and harder to open a software program, buy any major goods or services or open a bank account without agreeing to binding arbitration of any dispute you have with the other party (Hoffman, 2006).

The Gilmer decision initially outraged many people. They argued it was a grave affront to public policy, and that employers who were repeat players and a major source of arbitrators' future business would overwhelm employees who were one-time players in this 'game.' There is some evidence that repeat players enjoy more success – but it is due to their experience, not to arbitrator bias (Sherwyn, Estreicher & Heise, 2005). Some have also argued that this is a union deterrent or union busting tactic because many regard grievance procedures and arbitration as one of the principal benefits of unionization. This may or may not be a valid criticism, since union membership in the U.S. has been declining since 1947 (St. Antoine, 2010). Claiming that this development reduces or eliminates access to the legal system and that arbitration outcomes will unduly favor employers may also be unfounded. The cost of litigation inhibits access – the median income in the U.S. is approximately $41,000/year, and people making less than $60,000 typically cannot afford to sue. Because of its lower costs, twice as many people can

(Continued)

(Continued)

afford arbitration (Colvin, 2004; Hill, 2003; Maltby, 2003). Regarding outcomes, higher paid employees filing complaints pursuant to their individual employment contracts prevail in 40-69% of arbitration cases; lower paid employees filing complaints pursuant to their employee handbooks prevail in 21-40% of their arbitrations. In court, employees (probably those who are more highly paid) win 12-57% of their lawsuits. Overall, the differences in outcomes for employees in litigation and arbitration appear to be negligible (Sherwyn et al., 2005). Finally, subsequent to the Gilmer decision, the courts have required arbitrators to be neutral, the process of selecting them to be fair, at least minimal discovery (evidence gathering), written awards, the same types of relief that are available under the statute, and employees to pay no more than reasonable costs or fees for these mandatory arbitration provisions to be enforceable (McMullen v Meijer, Inc., 2004; Hooters of America v Phillips, 1999; Cole v Burns International Security Services, 1997).

How the Arbitration Process Works

Arbitration is most commonly invoked when parties believe that a legal, contractual or policy provision has been violated. It may also be used when an employer and one of its labor unions are unable to negotiate a new contract. Although it does not have to be, this 'interest arbitration' is largely unique to the public sector – many government labor laws in the United States prohibit unions from striking the government, so arbitration is used to complete the negotiation of new contracts. Two of the most critical components of the arbitration process are how hearings are conducted and how arbitrators decide cases.

The Arbitration Hearing

Arbitration hearings usually begin with the claimant, and then the defendant, presenting their opening statements. Rather than introducing facts and evidence, the parties take this opportunity to briefly explain what they intend to prove during the hearing – why they are right and why the other party is wrong.

Witnesses, who must take an oath, are called to present evidence and testimony in the second part of the hearing. They are examined, and then cross examined, by the people who are representing the parties (usually attorneys). Arguments and rebuttal arguments, all of which are orchestrated to persuade the arbitrator to decide in their favor, are presented.

The hearing concludes with each party presenting its closing statement – they draw conclusions indicating what the evidence and testimony proves. The most beneficial arguments, evidence and testimony are highlighted and emphasized, again to persuade the arbitrator to decide in their favor.

Arbitrator Decision Making

Arbitrators are generally required to determine what a legal, contractual or policy provision means when they are deciding disputes. Using the information presented in the hearing, they must then decide whether it was violated. If there is a provision requiring 'just cause' for terminating contractual relationships (they usually pertain to employment and commercial relationships), they may be asked to decide what just cause entails and whether it existed for terminating the relationship. Some cases involve elements of both – the arbitrator must initially interpret the focal provision to decide whether the individual violated it, and then determine whether that violation constitutes just cause for the disciplinary action. The criteria arbitrators use to interpret these provisions and determine whether just cause exists are summarized below.

Interpretation Cases

Custom and Past Practice. Past practices are well established habits of action or methods of doing things that are unequivocal, clearly enunciated (albeit not in the contract or policy statement) and acted upon, and readily ascertainable over a reasonable period of time as a fixed and established practice accepted by both parties (Elkouri & Elkouri, 1985; Celanese Corp of America, 1954). These will be considered if they are pertinent to the claim because they clarify what the parties intended.

Precedent Cases and Decisions. Published cases are examined to learn how other arbitrators have interpreted them. More weight will be accorded to these precedents if the contract/policy language, situation and parties are similar to those in the focal complaint.

Other Provisions of the Contract or Policy Manual. Arbitrators view documents in their entirety, not in isolated parts. The language of one part of the document, therefore, will be interpreted in the same way that similar language in other parts of the document is interpreted. This also means that specific language outweighs general language.

Negotiating History. Arbitrators will consider the minutes or notes collected when the provision at issue was written or negotiated. They will not, however, consider these minutes or notes if they are inconsistent with the clear meaning of a provision.

Industry Practice. Arbitrators' interpretations reflect industry practice. Silent or ambiguous provisions, therefore, are clarified by determining the usual or customary manner the industry deals with the focal issue.

The Ordinary Meaning of Words. If the language is unclear and the other provisions of the document do not clarify its meaning, arbitrators will resort to the dictionary and related sources. Their interpretations reflect dictionary definitions or the ordinary meaning of words.

Terminations for Just Cause

Disciplining employees and terminating contractual relationships generally requires *just cause*. Simplistically, this means there is a legitimate reason for taking this action. The criteria established by labor arbitrators have been applied consistently in labor and employment cases for decades. They are summarized below. Some are obviously not applicable and must be modified to determine whether there is just cause for terminating other kinds of contractual relationships.

Does a Rule (or Performance Standard) Exist? There must be a specific rule against a particular act, or a clear performance standard. Disciplining someone for violating a nonexistent rule or performance standard is unjust.

Is the Rule Reasonable? A rule is reasonable if it serves a legitimate business purpose, and it is an appropriate means for achieving this purpose. If, for instance, a company prohibits smoking in an area that contains flammable materials, the rule is reasonable – it serves a legitimate safety purpose and is an effective means for achieving this purpose. If the rule prohibits smoking anywhere on the company premises for this purpose, however, it is overbroad. It is an ineffective means for achieving this safety purpose so it is unjust.

Was the Rule Communicated to the Other Party? Was the other party aware of the rule, or should he or she have been aware of it? Disciplining an employee for 'excessive absenteeism' when the attendance policy has not been communicated or made available is unjust. If, however, the rule is published in the employee handbook that is distributed to all employees when they are hired, an employee cannot claim that it was not communicated because he or she failed to read the handbook. He or she should have been aware of it – ignorance is not always bliss.

Has the Rule Been Consistently Enforced? Assume that a forklift operator was terminated because he 'snuck up' behind his supervisor who was waiting for an elevator in a golf cart. The forklift operator lifted the cart on the forks, with his supervisor in it, but dropped it. The cart was damaged, but his supervisor was not hurt. The employer maintains a 'no-horseplay' rule and the employee violated it. If one of his coworkers did the same thing a year earlier and was suspended for two weeks without pay, this termination would be deemed unjust and overturned by an arbitrator because the rule was inconsistently enforced.

Did the Party Actually Violate the Rule? A fair and adequate investigation of the charges or allegations must be conducted to determine whether the party actually violated the rule. This requires the accusing party to inform the accused of the charges or allegations, interview him or her and the accuser, interview witnesses, conduct a hearing to allow both sides to present their supporting arguments and counter those presented by the other disputants. There must be sufficient credible evidence that the accused party did what he or she is accused of doing to support the disciplinary penalty. In employment cases, "sufficient" means 'beyond a reasonable doubt' if the employee is being terminated or if the offense involves a criminal or immoral act such as theft. The charge must be supported by a 'preponderance of the evidence' if the charge involves a lesser offense.

Was Progressive Discipline Administered to the Accused Party? Immediate discipline is warranted if the investigation reveals that the party's action threatened the safety of people or property. Otherwise, this usually requires companies to issue a verbal warning, a written warning if the verbal warning does not correct the problem, suspension or probation if the written warning fails to correct the problem, and termination if the suspension or probation fails to correct it.

Is the Penalty Reasonably Related to Seriousness of the Offense? The penalty must not exceed that which is necessary to correct the problem. When evaluating the appropriateness of the penalty, arbitrators consider the party's record – previous infractions or mitigating circumstances.

MANAGERS AS THIRD PARTIES

In a 2007 survey, practicing managers were asked to identify the top five problems, challenges or critical issues they faced. The most frequently cited: 'dealing with employee conflict' (Brotheridge &

Long, 2007; also see Mintzberg, 1975). This, coupled with dispute-wise companies' preference for solving problems quickly and privately, suggests that knowing how to intervene to help employees or other managers solve problems is an important managerial competency.

How Managers Should Intervene

Intervention Strategies

Using outcome control (high or low) and process control (high or low) as the two determinants of how managers should intervene (Thibault & Walker, 1975) produces the four strategies depicted in Figure 14.1. Inquisitors exert high outcome and high process control – this is how most managers intervene and it is typical of the legal system in European countries (Elangovan, 1995; Lewicki & Sheppard, 1985). Arbitrators exert high outcome control but little process control. Mediators exert little outcome control but high process control. Motivators exert little outcome or process control.

Determinants of Which Strategy Is Most Appropriate

Before deciding which of these strategies is most appropriate, managers must consider a variety of contingencies or criteria. These include:

Goals of the Manager

- Effectiveness – the solution must address all issues and be congruent with the organization's goals.
- Efficiency – the solution must be found in a timely manner to avoid consuming excessive resources (time, money, materials).
- Compliance – this includes satisfaction with and acceptance of the solution by the manager and the disputants, fairness, ease of implementation and the durability of the solution or adherence to it over time.

Characteristics of the Conflict

- The intensity of the conflict.
- Time pressures for finding a solution to the conflict.
- Importance of the conflict to the organization.

Characteristics of the Parties

- The power of the third party.
- The relative power of the disputants/negotiators.
- The abilities of the disputants/negotiators to create good solutions (Elangovan, 1995; Sheppard, 1984).

Linking the Determinants and the Intervention Strategies

The evidence suggests the following linkages between these contingencies and the four intervention strategies.

Figure 14.1   Intervention Strategies for Managers

		Outcome Control	
		High	**Low**
Process Control	Low	Arbitrator	Motivator
	High	Inquisitor	Mediator

Inquisitor. Managers should control the process and the outcome if the solution must be acceptable to him or her and the disputants are unable to produce such a solution; it must be fair to the disputants; serious time pressures exist so efficiency matters; the conflict is intense; and it is important to the organization so the solution must be effective.

Mediation. Managers should intervene in this manner when the outcome must be effective, fair and acceptable to the disputants; satisfaction, compliance and durability matter because they are engaged in an ongoing relationship; the conflict is not overly intense; it is important to the organization and the manager believes the disputants are able to create an effective solution; and it involves the creation or modification of a policy rather than the interpretation or execution of it. **Reading 14.1** at the end of this chapter provides additional reasons why managers should consider intervening in this manner.

Arbitration. Managers should adopt this strategy when serious time pressures make efficiency important; the conflict involves the interpretation or execution of an existing contract or policy rather than creating or modifying one; and the manager does not believe the disputants can create effective solutions.

Motivation. This strategy calls for managers to encourage the disputants to find a solution so that they can move on. It is most appropriate if the other three approaches do not apply (Elangovan, 1995; Lewicki & Sheppard, 1985; Sheppard, 1984).

CONCLUSION AND IMPLICATIONS FOR PRACTICE

When negotiators are unable to reach an agreement, involving third parties can be an effective and efficient way to reach an acceptable outcome. Third-party interventions are often preferred to relying on the legal system because they are private, faster, cheaper and simpler, and because the negotiators and select third parties possess relevant and necessary expertise. This enables them to create more effective solutions. The two most common forms of third-party intervention are mediation and arbitration. Both are appropriate and can be effective, albeit under different circumstances. Many organizations, especially those that are 'dispute-wise,' have recognized that managers spend a substantial amount of their time dealing with conflict, and that addressing it quickly and effectively is important. In addition to using formal mediators and arbitrators, they are training managers how to intervene as informal third parties. The following suggestions should facilitate your efforts to effectively deal with conflict, formally or informally.

1. Save money and time, and enjoy better relationships with employees, customers and business partners by being 'dispute wise.' 'Dispute-wise' companies focus their risk management efforts on preserving important business relationships rather than simply winning cases, and developing organizational cultures that value resolving conflicts efficiently and effectively, without litigation. They seek third-party assistance when emotions, communication breakdowns, repeated negative behaviors or disagreements about data preclude them from finding acceptable solutions through negotiation.

2. Choose mediation when the negotiators believe in the process, the conflict is moderately intense and ripe and integrative potential exists. Mediators extend the negotiation process by managing it and helping the parties create solutions that satisfy their respective interests. Mediated outcomes are preferable to arbitrated outcomes because the negotiators create them – they own that which they create and they are not told what to do by the third party.

3. Choose arbitration when the conflict is highly intense, the parties are not motivated to settle, integrative potential does not exist and special expertise is required. Arbitrators decide cases to settle disputes or, occasionally, to complete failed negotiations. Having arbitrators make decisions and impose them on the disputants provides a definitive resolution to the problem, and it is private, simpler, faster, less costly and often more effective than litigation.

4. Choose mandatory arbitration when you want to minimize costs, time and potentially negative publicity, and when you want to preserve important relationships. It may be a wise choice for employees and individual customers because it is more accessible, financially, than litigation. Approximately 6 million employees and managers in the United States are subject to mandatory arbitration requirements. Clients, consumers and business partners are also required to mediate or arbitrate disputes rather than litigate them. The U.S. Supreme Court has upheld mandatory arbitration requirements even though it seems to deny people 'their day in court.' It is not clear, however, if these rulings will last, because Congress is now debating whether the Federal Arbitration Act should be amended to limit employers' abilities to force this dispute resolution process on employees and perhaps others.

5. Know how to prepare for mediation. Remember the elements of your preparation, especially the resistance points you set, your BATNA and your interests. Remain flexible in case innovative solutions are created that cannot be evaluated using your target or resistance points. A common model of the mediation process was presented in this chapter. It is, however, important to remember that different mediators follow different models and execute even the same model differently. They may, for example meet with each side jointly or separately, and be more or less actively involved in managing (or controlling) the process and encouraging solutions.

6. Know how to prepare for arbitration. Consider the criteria the arbitrator will use to interpret your legal, contractual or policy provision and/or determine if just cause existed for the disciplinary action or termination. When you understand these criteria and their relevance to your dispute, configure the evidence and testimony you are presenting to effectively and persuasively address those that should be the most influential.

7. Choose a dispute resolution method that will offer you the greatest advantages. To enhance your effectiveness, consider your goals and how you want to achieve them, and consider characteristics of the conflict and the parties before deciding how much you want to control the process and the outcome. Intervening as an inquisitor, arbitrator, mediator or motivator can be effective. But each is likely to be most effective when the circumstances are appropriate.

STUDENT STUDY SITE

Visit the Student Study Site at **www.sagepub.com/hames** for additional learning tools.

KEY TERMS

Alternate dispute resolution

Arbitration

Decision-acceptance effect

Final offer arbitration

Half-life effect

Inquisitor

Mandatory arbitration

Mediation

Mini-trials

Motivator

Narcotic effect

The biasing effect

The chilling effect

REFERENCES

Anderson, J. C. & Kochan, T. A. (1977). Impasse procedures in the Canadian Federal Service: Effects on the bargaining process, *Industrial & Labor Relations Review*, 30(3), 283-301.

Botes, J. & Mitchell, C. (1995). Constraints on third-party flexibility, *Annals of the American Academy of Political and Social Science*, 542, 168-184.

Brett, J. M., Barsness, Z. I. & Goldberg, S. B. (1996). The effectiveness of mediation: An independent analysis of cases handled by four major service providers, *Negotiation Journal*, 12(3), 259-269.

Brett, J. M. & Goldberg, S. B. (1983). Grievance mediation in the coal industry: A field experiment, *Industrial & Labor Relations Review*, 37(1), 49-69.

Brotheridge, C. M. & Long, S. (2007). "The 'real-world' challenges of managers: Implications for management education", *Journal of Management Development*, 26(9), 832-842.

Bush, R. A. B. & Folger, J. P. (1994). *The promise of mediation: Responding to conflict through empowerment and recognition*. San Francisco: Jossey-Bass.

Carver, T. B. & Vondra, A. A. (1994). Alternative dispute resolution: Why it doesn't work and why it does, *Harvard Business Review*, 72(3), 120-130.

Celanese Corp. of America, 24 LA 168 (1954).

Cole v Burns International Security Services, 105 F.3d 1465 (D.C. Cir. 1997).

Coleman, P. (2000). Fostering ripeness in seemingly intractable conflict: An experimental study, *International Journal of Conflict Management*, 11, 300-317.

Coleman, P. (1997). Refining ripeness: A social-psychological perspective, *Peace and Conflict: Journal of Peace Psychology*, 3, 81-103.

Colvin, A. J. S. (2004). From Supreme Court to shop floor: Mandatory arbitration and the reconfiguration of workplace dispute resolution, *Cornell Journal of Law & Public Policy*, 13, 581-597.

Conlon, D. E. & Ross, W. H. (1993). The effects of partisan third parties on negotiator behavior and outcome perceptions, *Journal of Applied Psychology*, 78(2), 280-290.

Devinatz, V. G. & Budd, J. W. (1997). Third-party dispute resolution: Interest disputes. In D. Lewin, D. J. R. Mitchell & M. A. Zaida (Eds.), *The Human Resource Management Handbook* 1. Greenwich, CT: JAI Press, 95-135.

Elangovan, A. R. (1995). Managerial third-party dispute intervention: A prescriptive model of strategy selection, *The Academy of Management Review*, 20(4), 800-830.

Elkouri, F. & Elkouri, E. A. (1985). *How arbitration works*, 4th. Washington, D.C.: The Bureau of National Affairs.

Esser, J. & Marriott, R. (1995). Mediation tactics: A comparison of field and laboratory research, *Journal of Applied Social Psychology*, 25(17), 1530-1546.

Gilmer v Johnson/Lane Corp., 500 U.S. 20 (1991).

Goldberg, S. B. (2005). The secrets of successful mediators, *Negotiation Journal*, 21(3), 365-376.

Goldberg, S. B. & Shaw, M. L. (2007). The secrets of successful (and unsuccessful) mediators continued: Studies two and three, *Negotiation Journal*, 23(4), 393-418.

Greig, J. M. (2001). Recognizing conditions of ripeness for international mediation between enduring rivals, *Journal of Conflict Resolution*, 45, 691-718.

Hanany, E., Kilgour, D. M. & Gerchak, Y. (2007). Final-offer arbitration and risk aversion in bargaining, *Management Science*, 53(11), 1785-1792.

Hill, E. (2003). AAA employment arbitration: A fair forum at low cost, *Dispute Resolution Journal*, 58(2), 8-17.

Hoffman, D. A. (2006). The future of ADR practice: Three hopes, three fears and three predictions, *Negotiation Journal*, 22(4), 467-473.

Hooters of America, Inc. v. Phillips, 173 F.3d 933 (4th Cir. 1999).

Keer, S. & Naimark, R. W. (2001). Arbitrators do not "split the baby": Empirical evidence from international business arbitration, *Journal of International Arbitration*, 18(5), 573-578.

Kochan, T. A. (1980). *Collective bargaining and industrial relations*. Homewood, IL: Irwin.

Kolb, D. M. (1983). *The mediators*. Cambridge, MA: MIT Press.

Kressel, K. & Pruitt, D. (1989). *Mediation Research: The process and effectiveness of third-party intervention*. San Francisco: Jossey-Bass.

Kritikos, A. S. (2006). The impact of compulsory arbitration on bargaining behavior: An experimental study, *Economics of Governance*, 7, 293-315.

Leavitt, H. J. & Bahrami, H. (1988). *Managerial psychology: Managing behavior in organizations*, 5th. Chicago: University of Chicago Press.

Lewicki, R. J. & Sheppard, B. M. (1985). Choosing how to intervene: Factors affecting the use of process and outcome control in third party dispute resolution, *Journal of Occupational Behaviour*, 6, 49-64.

Maltby, L. L. (2003). Employment arbitration and workplace justice, *University of San Francisco Law Review*, 38, 105-118.

McMullen v. Meijer, Inc., 355 F.3d 485 (6th Cir. 2004).

Mintzberg, H. (1975). The manager's job: Fact or folklore, *Harvard Business Review*, 53, 49-61.

Moore, C. W. (1986). *The mediation process: Practical strategies for resolving conflict*. San Francisco: Jossey-Bass.

Naimark, R. (2004). Getting dispute wise, *Dispute Resolution Journal*, 59(1), 56-57.

14 Penn Plaza, LLC v. Pyett, 129 S. Ct. 1456 (2009).

Rubin, J. Z. (1980). Experimental research on third party intervention in conflict: Toward some generalizations, *Psychological Bulletin*, 87, 379-391.

Sheppard, B. H. (1984). Third party conflict intervention: A procedural framework. In B. M. Staw & L. L. Cummings (Eds.), *Research in Organizational Behavior* 6. Greenwich, CT: JAI Press, 141-190.

Sherwyn, D., Estreicher, S. & Heise, M. (2005). Assessing the case for employment arbitration: A new path for empirical research, 57. *Stanford Law Review* 1557-1571.

St. Antoine, T. S. (2010). ADR in labor and employment law during the past quarter century, *ABA Journal of Labor & Employment Law*, 25(3), 411-447.

Thibault, J. & Walker, L. (1975). *Procedural justice: A psychological analysis*. Hillsdale, NJ: Lawrence Erlbaum.

van Ginkel, E. (2004). The mediator as face-giver, *Negotiation Journal*, 20(4), 475-587.

Wall, J. A. & Stark, J. B. (1996). Techniques and sequences in mediation strategies: A proposed model for research, *Negotiation Journal*, 12(3), 231-239.

Wall, J. A., Stark, J. B. & Standifer, R. L. (2001). Mediation: A current review and theory development, *Journal of Conflict Resolution*, 45(3), 370-391.

Zubek, J., Pruitt, D., Pierce, R., McGillicuddy, N. & Syna, H. (1992). Disputant and mediator behaviors affecting short-term success in mediation, *Journal of Conflict Resolution*, 36, 546-572.

READINGS

Reading 14.1

RESOLVE EMPLOYEE CONFLICTS WITH MEDIATION TECHNIQUES

Program on Negotiation

Alternative dispute resolution offers solutions for bringing your people together.

If you manage people, disputes will show up at your door. The marketing VP protests that the budget cap you and your new finance VP proposed is hindering a research initiative you supported. Two young sales representatives are embroiled in a turf war. Your administrative assistant is upset because the HR director won't approve the extra week of paid maternity leave you promised her.

Fail to address such employee concerns and you've failed as a leader. But it can be difficult to know how to respond, especially when you have a stake in the problem. Sometimes third-party intervention can make matters worse.

In recent years, managers have begun to adopt the proven skills of professional mediators and arbitrators to resolve workplace conflict. In his book *Leading Leaders: How to Manage Smart, Talented, Rich, and Powerful People* (Amacom, 2006), Tufts University professor Jeswald Salacuse shows how alternative dispute-resolutions techniques can defuse tensions and get everyone back to work.

Using Mediation Skills as a Leader

Rather than imposing a decision, a trained mediator applies communication skills, objectively, and creativity to help disputants reach their own voluntary solution to the conflict. As a leader, your role can be more complicated. Unlike an actual mediator, you'll have to live with the outcome of the dispute on a daily basis. Your personal allegiances and objectives may lead you to have strong opinions about the best result. In addition, the negotiated solution must satisfy the interests of the broader organization as well as those of the disputants.

For those reasons, leaders need to adapt mediation skills to their purposes. As long as the disputants respect your authority, you should feel empowered to try to change the behavior of one or both sides to serve the organization's best interests, writes Salacuse. He has identified six bases of social power that will give you the leverage you need.

1. **Rewards.** As a leader, you have access to resources you can use to reward disputants for changing their behavior. Suppose you have been so impressed by your marketing VP's achievements that you're committed to funding the research initiative despite the budget cap that your finance VP wants to enforce. As CEO, you may be able to tap special funds for the project without requiring an exception to the rule. Anticipate, however, that some in your organization may view such special arrangements and rewards as a sign of weakness or as a bad precedent.

2. **Coercion.** Leaders can punish as well as reward, notes Salacuse. If you are tired of your sales reps' constant bickering over who poached whose client, you could threaten to take away key accounts from both if they can't work out a solution. But be careful not to be too heavy-handed

Source: Program on Negotiation, Resolve employee conflict with mediation techniques, *Program on Negotiation Newsletter*, 10(2), 6–7.

Note: This article first appeared in *Negotiation*, a monthly newsletter published by the Program on Negotiation at Harvard Law School, www.pon.harvard.edu. Copyright 2006–2011 Harvard University.

with coercion tactics, lest you drive the conflict deeper and close to home.

3. **Expertise.** Often, subordinates bring their disputes to their bosses because they expect them to apply specialized expertise to a problem. Your managerial smarts should convince your finance VP to accept your support of the marketing VP's new initiative. Lawyers, doctors, and other professionals bring unique knowledge and skills to the conflicts in their office. Salacuse warns, however, that disputants may be dismissive of your recommendations if they perceive your expertise to be no greater than theirs.

4. **Legitimacy.** A leader's legitimacy varies by organization and by the nature of the dispute. In a top-down organization, employees will be more likely to accept the guidance of an authority figure than employees of a less-hierarchical firm will be. If your HR director is used to having a great deal of autonomy, he may fight back if you lobby for your assistant to receive an extra week's maternity leave.

5. **Relationships.** The degree to which you can influence a disputant also depends on the nature and strength of your relationship with that person. Suppose you decide that you erred in offering your assistant a longer maternity leave than other employees. You should have a better chance of persuading her to accept this view if she has worked closely with you for 10 years than if she only joined the organization a year ago. The desire to preserve the relationship can be sufficient motivation for a disputant to follow your advice.

6. **Coalitions and networks.** Sometimes outside help is required to effectively resolve a dispute. By building coalitions and capitalizing on existing social networks, you can gain support for your proposal, Salacuse writes. For instance, if you are relatively new to your organization, you might ask a senior partner who has worked closely with at least one of the two warring sales reps to help you resolve the conflict.

Thinking Further 14.1

1. In what ways are the six mediation skills in the article related to types of power and influence? Explain your answer.

2. Do you believe employee disputes should be settled by their manager or by a third party, such as an organizational ombudsman? Explain why.

Reading 14.2

Borrowing From Baseball: The Surprising Benefits of Final-Offer Arbitration

Stephen B. Goldberg

It's a satisfying paradox: agreeing to final-offer arbitration boosts the likelihood of a negotiated resolution – and actually decreases the chances that you'll need to hire an arbitrator.

Imagine that you're a young, ambitious divisional sales manager at a Fortune 500 company. During your three years in this post, sales in your division have more than doubled. You think you can do

Source: Goldberg, S. B. (2005). Borrowing from baseball: The surprising benefits of final-offer arbitration, *Program on Negotiation Newsletter*, 8(8), 4–6.

Note: This article first appeared in *Negotiation,* a monthly newsletter published by the Program on Negotiation at Harvard Law School, www.pon.harvard.edu. Copyright 2006–2011 Harvard University.

even better and would like to stay with the company. What's more, the CEO appreciated your results and doesn't want to lose you. The only problem? Your salary. Having shown what you can accomplish, you believe you're entitled to a significant raise, from $80,000 to $200,000 annually; the company has offered $125,000. Both you and the CEO think your offers are fair, and neither side wants to compromise. How can you resolve this dispute?

If you were a major league baseball player, the answer would be obvious. Major League Baseball (MLB) and the MLB Player's Association have agreed that if a club and a player with more than three but less than six years of major league service cannot agree on the player's salary, they must submit their dispute to binding, *final-offer arbitration*. If the player has more than six year's service, he can seek a position with another team, or he and the club can agree to have their dispute arbitrated. In Major League Baseball, a neutral arbitrator determines, based on the player's performance statistics and the statistics and salaries of other players in his position, what his salary should be.

The strategy of agreeing to final-offer arbitration in the case of impasse can be used to resolve all types of disputes over contract terms. What's more, as I'll show, such an agreement is likely to result in a negotiated resolution and, paradoxically, help you *avoid* the need for arbitration.

Using the Risk of Arbitration to Break Impasse

Suppose that both you and your CEO agreed before beginning salary negotiations that, if you could not reach agreement, you would each simultaneously submit a final offer to a neutral arbitrator for a binding decision. You also agreed that the arbitration couldn't reach a compromise decision; he would have to select either your final proposed salary offer or the company's final offer. Such an agreement describes the

process of final-offer arbitration used in Major League Baseball.

Now you and your CEO are deadlocked on the salary question. You haven't given up hope of reaching a negotiated agreement but are preparing for the first step in the arbitration procedure: the simultaneous exchange of final offers. How should you decide what your final offer should be?

If you're like most people, you'll reason that the arbitrator, faced with selecting one of two offers, will choose the more reasonable of the two. Accordingly, your goal should be to submit a final offer that is more reasonable than your company's. But how?

Remember that you asked your CEO for a raise from $80,000 to $200,000; he offered $125,000. While you still think that you are entitled to $200,000, you decide that a demand of $175,000 may be more persuasive to the arbitrator. The CEO is likely to follow the same strategy, raising his offer from $125,000 to $140,000.

The gap of $75,000 between your $200,000 demand and the company's $125,000 offer now has shrunk to $35,000 between your $175,000 final offer and the company's $140,000 final offer. Now assume that you and the CEO, like most people, would prefer to resolve the salary dispute yourselves rather than having an outsider make the decision and that your prenegotiation agreement provides that you can continue to negotiate even after you exchange final offers. You're likely to agree on a salary that falls between $140,000 and $175,000, thus avoiding the need for arbitration.

Evidence from Major League Baseball supports the theory that providing for final-offer arbitration in the event of impasse tends to lead to agreement, not to arbitration. From 1974, when final-offer arbitration was adopted, through 2005, 2,741 Major League Baseball players who could not reach agreement with their teams filed a demand for salary arbitration. Of those players, 83% reached agreement with their team prior to arbitration;

only 17% had their salaries determined by an arbitrator.

The Opt-Out Option

Final-offer arbitration does not always lead to agreement. When you agree to arbitration, you run the risk that the other side will make an extreme final offer that the arbitration will select – a risk that the other side runs as well. Suppose that your CEO made a final offer of only $90,000 and that you demanded $300,000. The arbitrator would be required to choose between one of these unreasonable offers, and one side would be very unhappy.

If the risk of unreasonable final offers were troubling to you and your CEO (though it is not to Major League Baseball and the Player's Association), you might modify the normal procedure such that if either party believes that the other side's final offer is wholly unreasonable, that party is free to withdraw from arbitration. With this opt-out modification, each of you safely agree to final-offer arbitration in the event of impasse.

Admittedly, the right to opt out of arbitration after seeing the other party's final offer might reduce the frequency with which disputes are resolved, whether by arbitration or by negotiation. On the other hand, it might not. If both parties genuinely want an agreement, each will seek to avoid making an extreme final offer that will cause the other side to withdraw from arbitration. The party's doing so may not only encourage arbitration but also encourage a negotiated agreement.

What If You Have to Arbitrate?

The likelihood that a provision for final-offer arbitration in the event of impasse will actually result in arbitration is slim. However, as a prediction, you and your counterpart should agree on an arbitrator before you start negotiating. (It's easier to choose an arbitrator when both sides view arbitration as unlikely than arbitration is imminent and feelings are running high.) You need not engage (or pay) the arbitrator at this time, since you probably won't need her services.

The potential arbitrator should be in the same business as you are or at least know the business well, such as an attorney who represents parties in the industry. Another option would be to seek out a professional arbitrator through provider organizations such as the American Arbitration Association or the CPR Institute for Dispute Resolution, both based in New York City.

Arbitration proceedings, when necessary, should be neither complex nor lengthy. The arbitrator's responsibility is to decide which final offer is fairer and more reasonable under the circumstances and should include such criteria as industry practice and prior dealings between the parties. Each party will have presented arguments on many of these issues during negotiations and should present these arguments, perhaps supplemented by factual material, to the arbitrator. The parties may limit the length of the arbitration hearing and require the arbitrator to decide the matter within a specified number of days.

Beyond Salary Disputes

Consider a royalty dispute between an author and a publishing firm. The author has published previous books with the company, and the two sides have a solid working relationship. The publisher offers an increase in the author's royalty rate from 10% to 12% and refuses to go higher; the author proposes a 22% royalty rate and will go no lower. The parties could bridge their differences if the publisher were motivated to increase its offer to 15% (to appeal to an arbitrator) and if the author reduced her demand to 19% for the same reason. An agreement in the neighborhood of 17% thus would be likely.

So far, I've discussed disputes that resolve around a single monetary issue. But a provision for final-offer arbitration in the event of impasse also has been used to encourage agreement (and avoid strikes) in multi-issue contract negotiations between public-sector employers, such as schools and fire and police departments, and their employees. In this context, too, there is evidence that the very risk of arbitration breaks impasse and avoids the need for an arbitrator's services.

What's Wrong With Traditional Arbitration?

You may wonder why I'm promoting final-offer arbitration over traditional arbitration for the resolutions of contract formation disputes. The fact is, in such cases, traditional arbitration tends to discourage rather than encourage agreement. Traditionally, the arbitrator is not limited to selecting one of the parties' contract proposals but may determine the contract terms on his own. If negotiators know that impasse will lead to traditional arbitration, they typically assume that the arbitrator will reach a decision that's an approximate midpoint between their final offers. To move the midpoint as close as possible to a preferred outcome, each side will propose the most extreme final offer it can justify, thus reducing the likelihood of a negotiated agreement.

As an illustration, let's return to the salary negotiations between you and your CEO, in which you demanded $200,000 and the company offered $125,000. If you assume that the arbitrator will split the difference, her decision is likely to be about $162,500. You are also likely to assume that if you increase your final offer to $250,000, and the company remains at $125,000, the midway point would move to $187,500, thus motivating you to submit $250,000 as your final offer.

Following the same reasoning, your CEO is more likely to submit a final offer of $90,000, rather than the $125,000 he proposed in negotiations. Now agreement is even less likely, with both parties separated by a vast gulf of $160,000. A provision for traditional arbitration as the endpoint of negotiations thus can be expected to have a chilling effect on the likelihood of the two sides reaching agreement.

If, however, the negotiating parties have given up hope of reaching a voluntary agreement and would rather have any agreement than none at all, traditional arbitration will achieve that goal. Most recently, the New York Metropolitan Transit Authority and the New York Jets, unable to reach agreement on the price the Jets should pay for the West Side rail yards, agreed to submit the issue to traditional arbitration. (That agreement was subsequently undone when a second potential buyer, Cablevision, made a better offer than the Jets, and the Port Authority resumed negotiations with both parties.)

Arbitration is not appropriate for the resolution of all disputes about contract terms. Sometimes the differences separating the parties' position on key issues may be so great that neither would agree to allow an arbitrator to select the other side's final offer. Other times, so many issues may separate the two sides that arbitration is impractical. Still, in many cases, particularly when agreement is blocked by disagreement on just one or two issues, you'd do well to consider a provision for final-offer arbitration, perhaps with an opt-out clause, in the event of impasse.

Thinking Further 14.2

1. What are the benefits of final-offer arbitration? What are its drawbacks?
2. Compared to conventional arbitration, what are the advantages and disadvantages of final-offer arbitration?
3. Do you believe agreeing on final-offer arbitration is likelier to result in distributive or collaborative negotiation between parties? Why?
4. Is final-offer arbitration likelier to result from distributive or integrative negotiation? Why?

Part II Cases

CASE 3

Musical Operating Room A + B

By Raymond Friedman

Questions

1. What is this conflict about?

   Typical answers include: authority, who has power, access to a scarce resource, and the hospital's priorities

2. Why is there a conflict over these issues?

   Some answers include: tradition, norms, changes in market competitions the need to grow, separation between departments.

3. How are each of the doctors doing now at managing the conflict?

   At this point, I list the doctors' names and their key complaint. Then I ask: What was this doctor's strategy for managing conflict? What should they have done? Would you do what they did?

4. As Dr. Wilkins, who is asked to resolve this dispute, what source of leverage do you have?

   What options are possible? What impact would each option have? What are your overall goals?

5. Hand over or read the "B" case to let them know what happened.

Musical Operating Rooms (A)

Dr. John Wilkins sat staring at the phone message in front of him. Dr. Peter Mikelson, Chief of Orthopedics,

had called again wanting to discuss the current system used to schedule operating room times. As Chief of Medicine, technically, Dr. Wilkins had the power to dictate who would use the operating resources and when. Up to now he had been reluctant to use that power, relying instead on scheduling administrators to handle the schedule for operating room use. Perhaps the time had come to review that system and implement changes if necessary.

Mercy Hospital, a not-for-profit hospital located in the Northeast, employed 1,000 doctors in 30 different departments. The facility had an outstanding reputation as a teaching hospital. About 40% of its doctors were full-time faculty while the remaining 60% were volunteer staff (those doctors who, while not employees of the hospital, worked with residents and had access to hospital resources). The hospital currently had 25 operating rooms located throughout the hospital. Operating rooms were not assigned to any particular department but doctors tried to use the rooms closest in proximity to their department wing. In some more extreme cases, it was simply understood that the operating rooms in certain wings were to be used only by certain departments.

Dr. Wilkins decided to have some informal discussions with different department chairs to gauge how dire the situation really was. His first stop was with Dr. Steve Daly, Chief of Urology. "You know John," Dr. Daly explained, "I understand urology is not a high profile glamour specialty but I am having a very difficult time attracting both volunteer staff and the best residents because of the trouble I have scheduling procedures. We have 20 doctors in 3 different departments sharing 4 operating rooms. I know to you this may sound like an inability on my part to plan but let me put this to you in terms that may mean something to you. The operating room is where we make our money. If my doctors and I can't easily schedule time in the OR we can't continue to build the department. I have already seen a decline in the number of referrals from primary care physicians. If this keeps up, this hospital will have a hard time maintaining this specialty at a competitive level."

Next on Dr. Wilkin's list was Dr. Jack Palmer, Chief of Neurosurgery. Jack Palmer was a bit of a legend in the region. This was due to a combination of the high profile nature of his specialty, his long tenure at the hospital, and his impressive client list that included many of the people who sat on Mercy Hospital's Board of Directors as well as their families and friends. As John walked through the department, he noticed that all 3 of the ORs in the Neurosurgery wing were not in use. When he mentioned this to the department secretary she replied that this was always the case on Friday mornings. For as long as she could remember Neurosurgery held a weekly teaching conference from 7-12 every Friday. The secretary then informed John that Jack could not free up any time to speak with him but she did relay the message that all was fine in Neurosurgery as far as OR time.

Dr. Wilkins next spent some time with Dr. Sheehan, Chief of Ophthalmology. After reviewing the OR schedule for the next month, Dr. Wilkins was astounded at the number of procedures Dr. Sheehan and members of her department were scheduled to perform. Dr. Sheehan explained, "Well John, I've actually put a little cushion in there to make sure I have the time I need. At the beginning of the month I sign up those surgeries I am sure we will perform as well as some "phantom" patients. That way, if surgery runs over because I'm teaching the procedure to a resident or if a patient shows up in a condition under which I can not operate I can easily reschedule him. Patients get quickly rescheduled, doctors office hours aren't disrupted and everyone is happy.

The name of the game is customer service. Peter [Dr. Mikelson] is new and will learn the system like everyone else did. I'm feeling particularly charitable today. Send Peter my way and we'll see if we can't negotiate for some of my scheduled time."

Dr. Wilkins spoke with Dr. Mikelson last. "John, I know I'm the new kid on the block but this system is simply unacceptable. Six months ago when I took this position you and the board made it very clear to me the importance of building the practice. I've done as much as I can but my capacity analysis shows that if my growth continues I'll need four operating rooms instead of the one I am currently allocated. The bottom line is the bottom line and you and I both know the money Orthopedics brings in to the hospital. If I have to beg and plead with Susan Sheehan every time an unexpected change in my schedule pops up or rely on the grapevine to figure out when the OR is available, I can't keep my patients happy. The game has changed, John. Unhappy patients simply go elsewhere for surgery."

Dr. Wilkins knew Dr. Mikelson was right. *How would he fix the situation in a way that made everyone happy including patients, doctors, administrators and the Board of Directors? What was the proper criteria to use: longevity, political clout, fiscal impact? How was he going to allow for emergency surgeries? How much control did he really want to take away from the physicians in scheduling their procedures?*

Musical Operating Rooms (B)

Dr. Wilkins decided to keep control of the operating room schedule in the hands of the doctors. He set up a committee made up of representatives from each department. Because a committee of 30 would be too unwieldy, ten department representatives sat on the committee for six months. At the end of six months, 10 new departments put representatives on the committee. Every month, these doctors divided up the time available in the operating rooms among all 30 departments. All operating rooms were in the pool including those that had informally become the exclusive domain of certain departments over time.

Every attempt was made to allocate rooms in a manner that was logistically convenient for doctors.

The criteria used to determine how much time each department would receive was based on historical data from the last six months including the number of procedures performed and revenue generated for the hospital. The data was reviewed every six months and OR time was adjusted accordingly. For example, if a department only used 60% of the time that had been allocated to it, its share of the time was lowered by half a room a day.

In the event that a procedure was canceled, the department could reallocate the time to another doctor in the department. If the department did not think it would need the time, it then was put back into the pool and reallocated to those departments running over capacity. A certain percentage of the operating room time was always set aside for emergency procedures.

Because the allocations were based on statistics, most of the doctors on staff found this new procedure to be an equitable solution. The physicians who disliked the system tended to be those like Dr. Palmer who had built up power over the course of their long tenures and argued that they had earned the right to schedule procedures when and where they saw fit. Their arguments gained little support because the actual time their departments were allocated was equal to the time they had before. Operating rooms were now running at a higher capacity which meant more procedures were being performed. More operations meant more doctors' fees, more time to teach residents, more opportunities to schedule patients and more revenue generated for the hospital.

Reference

Ury. W. L., Brett, J. M., & Goldberg, S. B. (1988). *Getting disputes resolved; Designing systems to cut the costs of conflict.* San Francisco: Jossey-Bass.

Thinking Further—Case 3

Musical Operating Rooms (A)

1. What is this conflict about? Why is there a conflict over these issues?

2. How is each of the doctors doing now at managing the conflict? If you were asked to resolve this dispute, what source of leverage would you have?

Musical Operating Rooms (B)

1. Do you believe Dr. Wilkins's handling of the conflict was appropriate? Was it effective? Why, or why not?

2. What would you have done to resolve the conflict if you were Mary Jones? Explain why.

CASE 4

At long last, Petrolink's founders have the start-up capital they need. The VC's check is in hand—but so is news that the investor may have breached the founder's trust. Now what?

Take the Money- or Run

By John W. Mullins

IT WAS NEARLY 9 PM. Robert Jameson, Karl Fenstermann, and Nigel Ritson of Petrolink Transport Technologies had been huddled since early morning with their lawyers and with BRX Capital's Lech Wojtalik and Walter Cronbach and their two lawyers. They were in the final, exhausting stages of negotiating a 4 million investment that would give Petrolink the cash it needed to build a natural gas pipeline in the Baltic Sea. The check lay on the table.

After working all day and taking only a short break for supper, they were back at the table. There were only six items in the shareholder's agreement

Source: John Mullins, "Take the Money—or Run," Harvard Business Review, November 2004, pp. 35–47. Used by permission of Harvard Business School Publishing.

to work out; everything else was already settled. Robert and Karl knew they could give in on these points if they had to, though they were prepared to negotiate to get the best deal they could.

The BRX lawyers provided a fresh draft of the documents that included the agreed-upon changes from earlier in the day. "Just look at the high-lighted passages," said Walter. "They're the only ones that we need to reach agreement on. Everything else is OK. We should have this wrapped up very soon."

With a sigh, Robert picked up the newest draft. Despite Walter's recommendation, he read carefully through the whole document, wanting to be sure he had not overlooked anything that he or Karl would later regret. The financing was his responsibility, and he knew that the Petrolink team was relying on his expertise to ensure that this part of the deal would be well managed.

As he read the antidilution clause, something caught his eye. He reread it, then read it once more. A quick check against an earlier, predinner version of the shareholder's agreement confirmed his suspicions. The clause had been changed to language far more onerous to management. "What is this?" asked Robert. "This antidilution clause is not the same as the one in the previous versions."

The Opportunity

The story had begun some 15 months earlier, on a cold and blustery Baltic night. Karl was then the managing director of the Eastern European division of Beckman Engineering, the world's largest devel-oper and builder of rigs and pipelines for the oil and gas industry. Given the opportunity, he loved getting out of the office and out to sea. So when the president of Balto Gas & Oil invited him to visit the company's new Beckman-built rig on its first day of operations in the recently developed Helmark field in the Baltic Sea, Karl jumped at the opportunity.

Once the Gas Started Flowing, Whoever Operated the Pipeline Would Be Drowning in Cash.

The weather turned nasty as the helicopter carrying Karl and Balto's president, Per Persson, approached the rig. It took the pilot three attempts to set down the aircraft. "We may have to spend the night here," he shouted to the passengers.

The wind and spray hit them full in the face as they scurried under the still revolving blades. It was a relief to get indoors. "I'm sorry to get you out on a day like this," Per. "We didn't expect this weather. I don't think we'll be doing anything today unless it calms down soon. But we can put you up, and the radio operator can get you in touch with your family."

Karl didn't mind. A night on board offered him a perfect opportunity to get to know Per, a smart move in light of Balto's interest in purchasing more rigs down the line. And he felt a certain pleasure in being warm and safe inside while the wind and sea battered the rig outside.

Despite a brief flash of sunshine, the wind stayed strong, and at 3:00 PM, Per announced that the start of operations would be postponed until the morning. Following a tour to inspect some of Beckman's latest innovations in rig design, the two men joined the rig's senior management in the mess for dinner, and they spend a lively evening swapping war stories. Per and the production superintendent went way back, and Karl's presence didn't inhibit them.

After dinner, although the rig was officially dry, the production superintendent invited Per and Karl to his quarters for a nightcap. Per produced a bottle of Polish vodka from his coat pocket. He said, "Bet we'll get better use out of it now."

Over drinks, the production superintendent asked Per how negotiations were going with Gazprom, the Russian oil and gas giant, which currently operated the only available pipeline for shipping gas from Helmark to the mainland. Per grimaced and took a shot from his glass before answering. "Well, we've agreed to access," he said. "And they swear that they'll put in safeguards to keep the flow data confidential. But I don't trust them."

Per's concern was understandable. Like all independent gas producers, he was unhappy at having to rely on an arch competitor to take his gas to market. No one wanted Gazprom to know exactly how much gas each portion of the field would be producing, which is exactly what Gazprom would know from its flow meters if its pipeline were used. The information would give the deep-pocked competitor an edge as additional leases were auctioned.

"Anyway," he continued, "it's only a temporary solution. That 16-inch pipeline won't have the capacity to handle Helmark's output. The independents will need their own—one twice the size—if the field's as rich as I think it is."

Karl leaned forward. Was this an opportunity for Beckman?

"Have you thought of building your own pipeline?" he asked. "Obviously not by yourselves; you couldn't afford it. But you could get together with the other independents."

"They won't bite," replied Per. "Everyone wants to save their money for the new leases. Anyway, none of us has any experience in managing a pipeline. And we'd probably still have trouble keeping the flow data under wraps. Why would we trust each other any more than we trust Gazprom? No, we really need a third party to do it for us. Do you think Beckman might be interested?"

Karl didn't think so. "We'd love to build it," he said. "But I doubt we'd be interested in operating it. I'll make some noises."

The conversation moved on, and Karl reckoned it was time to leave the others to it. Besides, he needed to clear his head, and the wind had eased a little, so he could stay on deck. The talk had put a crazy idea

in his head that he needed to think through. Beckman, he knew, wouldn't bite. The company had turned down this kind of business before.

But what if he, Karl Fenstermann, were to operate the pipeline? As a vendor, Beckman could finance some of the construction, and if he could get commitments from Per and the other independent producers that they would use the pipeline, why shouldn't he be able to raise more money? Once the gas started flowing, whoever operated the pipeline would be drowning in cash. He looked up, and for a moment the clouds parted and he saw a brilliant full moon, high in the sky.

The Team

Karl knew he would need help. In spite of having built his division from nothing onto Beckman's fastest-growing unit in five years, he had never been a real entrepreneur. Besides, he was not about to walk away from Beckman without being more certain that his idea would work. What if he built the pipeline and the independent producers decided to use Gazprom's existing pipeline instead? What if someone else beat him to market with a competing pipeline? What if, despite the projections, Helmark didn't play out?

His first call was to Robert Jameson, an entrepreneur whom Karl had met in the 1980s, when both were working for Siemens's railway engine business in Germany. Although the two men had kept in touch, their careers had diverged, with Karl eventually joining Beckman and successfully selling four ventures, three of which served Eastern European markets.

To Karl's delight, Robert was immediately sold on the idea: "We're perfectly matched. I've got the experience raising money and setting up a new business from scratch. You know the people in government and business we'll have to deal with, and you're well placed to find someone with operational experience. Once we've got our candidate, we can go to the VCs."

"I already know the person," said Karl. "My number two, Nigel Ritson, spent ten year at Transco, the company that runs Britain's gas grid. He's in his thirties and hungry. I think he'd jump at the chance."

The Backers: Part 1

With the team in place, the Petrolink project moved forward quickly. Nigel and Karl negotiated a draft contract for the pipeline construction with Beckman and secured letters of intent from Balto and three other large independent producers, accounting for half of the potential independent gas production in the Helmark field.

Robert brought in Philip Calthorepe, a former senior vice president of a large London-based investment bank, as a financial adviser. He felt that a deal could be struck with a capital structure of approximately one-third equity, one-third debt, and one-third vendor finance, which Beckman would provide. Philip estimated the funding requirements at nearly $42 million (of which $37 million was capital expenditure), phased over several rounds of equity and debt. He suggested they offer the first-round equity investors a 28th stake for an initial $4 million.

Unfortunately, venture capital investors had grown very cautious following the dot-com bust, the downturn in technology company valuations, and the recent dearth of IPOs. After six weeks of knocking on doors in various European financial capitals without success, the Petrolink team members were introduced to Charles Jackson-Poole, a managing partner at London Development Partners, a large, well-established venture capital firm.

LDP's roots were in private equity investing, and over the past 20 years it had built a portfolio of early-stage investments in companies that were mostly, but not exclusively, technology based. LDP typically would provide a relatively small early round of investment to enable the founders to prove the viability of their concept, build prototypes, and attract beta customers, and then follow with additional rounds of investment to help the company develop. It was common for LDP to bring additional

investors into syndicates to fund these later rounds, both to share the risk and to provide the sometimes large amounts of capital that were necessary to fully take advantage of the opportunity as it developed.

Robert was delighted that LDP was interested in investing in Petrolink. He viewed LDP's interest as validation of the project. "If they think we have a viable business here," crowed Robert over beer and kielbasa one night in Warsaw, "then we probably do!"

LDP was certainly serious. Over the next several weeks, Robert and Karl made numerous visits to London to answer what seemed a never-ending array of questions from Charles and his associates. Why would the independent oil producers do business with a start-up instead of with Gazprom, and on what terms? How would Petrolink's competitive advantage be sustained? Could a price war be avoided? Could Petrolink really fend off Gazprom in the market-place? How important was Gazprom's political and market clout? Did the Petrolink team have what it would take to successfully build the business?

Karl was impressed with this professionalism. "They ask great questions," he said to Robert after one of the meetings. "Charles would be a great person to have on our board, even though he doesn't know all that much about the oil and gas business. I really like his approach in dealing with us. He tells us what his concerns are and trusts us to figure out the solutions."

After six weeks, LDP finally came to the point. "It's good to see you chaps again," said Charles, welcoming them in LDP's oak-paneled office in oak-paneled offices in London Wall. "The material you sent last week has eased our concerns about the Gazprom situation, so we'd like to talk today about what sort of deal might be possible for us."

"Great!" replied Robert. "We look forward to hearing the terms."

But Karl and Robert's enthusiasm was short-lived. The package Charles outlined was far from

> The biggest sticking point was that LDP—despite its lack of experience in the oil and gas business—expected to have de facto veto power over most important decisions.

what they'd been hoping for. Instead of $4 million, LDP would commit a mere $1.5 million for the first round, for which it would receive a 20th stake, and would make no tangible commitments to future rounds. What's more management's 80th stake would stake vest over a three-year period and would be diluted in future rounds, though it was not clear by how much.

But the biggest sticking point was that LDP—despite its lack of experience in the oil and gas business—expected to have de facto veto power over most important decisions, through board control and a detailed set of shareholders' agreements to be negotiated to align with LDP's "standard" terms.

Robert thought it best to put their cards on the table. "Karl and I really appreciate your interest, Charles, and we've really benefited from all of the tough questions that you've raised about our business plan. I think you should know, though, that we've been in discussions with another prospective investor, and we're meeting later this week. We want to hear what the company has to say before making any commitments. We'll be in touch next Monday with our response."

The Backers: Part 2

Shortly after their second meeting with LDP, Robert and Karl had been introduced by their financial adviser to a Polish venture capital firm, BRX Capital. Although BRX had been in business fewer than five years, it had already made several investments in infrastructure deals in Eastern Europe, including two in the oil and gas industry, one of which was with an independent producer that had signed a letter of intent with Petrolink.

> "Doing business with people we can't trust isn't my idea of fun. If they're trying to screw us before our deal is even done, what will they try to do to us in the future?"

Karl and Robert hit it off well with BRX's senior partners. Karl in particular got on well with Lech Wojtalik, one of the firm's founders, whose background was in the oil industry. Robert, for his part, developed an easy camaraderie with Walter, a former entrepreneur whose career mirrored Robert's own.

Nigel was more skeptical. "Do you trust these chaps?" he asked one day over lunch with Robert and Karl. "It all seems a bit too friendly. I'd be happier if they asked more questions. And these guys don't have the track record of LDP—they've only been going five years. And I'm sure Lech used to be a party member."

"Don't worry," said Karl. "It's easier because they know our business. The reason LDP was all over us was because they were new to the gas business. Lech's a real oil and gas man, and Walter has the entrepreneurial background. And don't be worried about the party thing—anyone who wanted to be anything joined back then. Of course, we should keep an eye on them, but BRX really wants to be in this business, and they're much more likely to give us the deal we want."

Karl's optimism seemed to be justified. BRX not only agreed to the capital structure that Robert had proposed, but it also agreed to invest both the first- and second-round equity amounts, totaling $8 million. On completion of the first two rounds, management would hold 55th of the equity and BRX 45th The funding would come in as convertible loans that would convert to equity upon certain management milestones, which were also tied to a management share option scheme.

BRX, however, was not interested in participating in the third round of equity or the debt financing. The proposed arrangement met Karl and Robert's main objectives in several important ways. Not only would both the first- and second-round funding be in place, but the third-round funding from a different investor would ensure that no one investor would wield too much clout over Petrolink.

The deal was irresistible. Karl called LDP's Charles Jackson-Poole to tell him of their decision. "I'm disappointed," said Charles. "We like your team, and we like your business. I'm sorry we cannot meet the terms proposed by your other investor, but if things don't work out, we'll still be here." Robert then called Walter Crobach and said, "Let's wrap up our deal."

And so, after a hectic three weeks of due diligence and drafting, there they were with their prospective investors, BRX Capital, in the offices of BRX's lawyers in Warsaw on a stormy October night.

The Dilemma

"What's the story here, Walter?" asked Robert. Walter's face went red. His body language made it plain that the changes in the antidilution clause had been intentional. The lawyers, however, were much smoother, blaming the discrepancy on a typing error made by a junior staff member. They left the room, ostensibly to find out what had gone wrong. "We've worked with them for years," said Lech. "It must be a clerical error." Lech and Walter then left the room as well. In a few minutes, they returned, and Lech said, "It's no problem; we're putting the earlier language back in."

Robert asked for a recess. He, Karl, and Nigel want next door to discuss what to do. "Doing business with people we can't trust isn't my idea of fun," said Robert. "If they're trying to screw us before our deal is even done, what will they try to do to us in the future? Can we expect them to help us if we get into trouble, or will they try and steal the business? Even if this this a better deal now, I'm not sure we won't regret it later."

> Even if the altered contract had been legally enforceable, it is still morally damaged. Morality and the law do differ.

"I don't think we have a choice," said Karl. "We've spent almost six months getting here. Maybe LDP will still do a deal with us, but we already know it won't be anything like this. And we don't know how long LDP's due diligence will take and whether its deal will actually come through at the end of the day. What if someone else is working on a Helmark pipeline? There isn't room for two of us. I think we still have to go with these guys, even though we'll have to watch them."

"I don't like this any more than you do," added Nigel. "But remember, Karl and I are planning to leave Beckman at the end of this month. We don't have the cash to pay our salaries yet, and both of us will need to be working full time soon."

Commentary:

Robert Jameson, Karl Fenstermann, and Nigel Ritson are facing a problem: what to do about BRX's deceptive alteration of the antidilution clause in the contract offered to them. But they are also confronting difficulties because of their desires and decisions concerning the BRX contract.

If the legal circumstances surrounding this contract are unclear, the ethical circumstances are not. It is hard to imagine any plausible ethical system that would condone what BRX did. Even if the altered contract had been legally enforceable, it is still morally damaged. Morality and the law do differ.

In these situations, managers should consider not only their own best interests but also their responsibilities to others. If Robert, Karl, and Nigel sign the contract with BRX, they will hire employees, make agreements with suppliers and customers, and eventually seek other investors. These groups will be Petrolink's stakeholders. If BRX acts again as it has acted in this instance, it is plausible that these stakeholders will be harmed. One way to discharge the responsibilities is to protect stakeholders from any future malfeasance by BRX. Another way would be to advise the stakeholders of the risks of being involved with BRX. If Robert, Karl, and Nigel are uncertain whether they can do the former and are not prepared to do the latter, they should consider pulling out of the deal. Part of looking at matters ethically is considering the consequences for all affected parties. Informed choice is crucial both to ethics and to economics.

Finally, trust (or distrust) is a theme that runs throughout the case. Because of the change in the contract, Robert, Karl, and Nigel do not trust BRX. This lack of trust will impel them to write a tighter contract, to monitor BRX's behavior more closely, and to protect important Petrolink information. This will be costly and may have a negative snowball effect on the relationship. Even the best-constructed contract will not give scruples to scoundrels.

It's easy to see how the team got into this mess. Sometimes we want things so bad we don't see the warning signs. And if they are brought to our attention, we dismiss them with facile explanations. BRX, we are told, wasn't asking many questions. The Petrolink team chose to think it must have been because the company knew all the answers. Furthermore, BRX was ready to make a seemingly irresistible deal, but no one else would make a similar offer. The team members should be alert to the possibility that they are treading in treacherous territory, their judgment clouded by their own desires and aims.

There is also the problem of psychological commitment. We often get so bound up in projects that it is difficult to back away. The psychologist John Darley, a professor at Princeton University, has discussed the problems to which committing to a course of action may lead. One need only think of the space shuttle *Challenger*, the Ford Pinto, and the brakes B. F. Goodrich initially manufactured for the Air Force's A7D aircraft. In all these cases, individuals and organizations committed themselves to certain projects and then sought excuses, explanations, and evasions when bad news cropped up so as to permit these troubled projects to go ahead. The

Petrolink team seems headed down a similar road in its relationship with BRX.

What should the team do? If it can meet its responsibilities to other stakeholders, it might go ahead with the present deal. But it is a perilous course and should be taken only after the team has looked closely at BRX and its past dealings with other ventures. Absent a better explanation of BRX's behavior than we currently have, Petrolink should explore how far LPD might go to improve its offer. Even if the team does not get a better offer, Petrolink would be working with a solid, reputable firm that it can trust. Once committed to this project, LDP might well help Petrolink to find other sources of funding. If this is not possible, it may be a sign that the project is fraught with so many difficulties that, both personally and morally, the risks outweigh the advantages of going ahead.

In my career as an entrepreneur and an adviser to entrepreneurs, I have faced this dilemma before, and I would recommend that Petrolink take BRX's money. Robert is correct that accepting funding from potentially untrustworthy investors is very risky, but Petrolink's management can mitigate this risk by meeting the plan's targets; bringing in a strong second investor quickly; continuing to control the majority of the company; basing the company in a jurisdiction where the rule of law is powerful; and controlling the local operations.

At the same time, the team needs to go back to LDP and ask what terms the firm might want in order to be the second-round investor and what structures it would consider unacceptable. Many of the corporate governance control measures that LDP seems to be insisting upon now may be moot by the time a second round is needed. (For example, the team will have met its plan or the business will need serious thinking "outside the box," LDP's key strength).

If the team really feels BRX can't be trusted or managed, I would return to LDP, ask the firm to lead the round, and then bring BRX to the table as part of a syndicate. Petrolink should also insist on the full $4 million. The team can also argue that if LDP can't indicate its commitment to further rounds of funding, then the VC needs to remove clauses from the terms that later round investors will find unacceptable. Petrolink will need to ask its financial adviser to conduct research into second-round financing term sheets. If LDP is as experienced as the case indicates, the firm will appreciate this argument.

The members of the team have only themselves to blame for this situation. They gave notice to Beckman without securing the cash to fund themselves after their departure. Now their idea is in the market, and a team with comparable knowledge and capital could very easily take their opportunity. They also should have continued the LDP process in parallel with the BRX one—there's no evidence that either VC had requested Petrolink to enter an exclusive negotiation. If the team had moved LDP along to a point where it and BRX both had checks on the table, and then mentioned to LDP that someone else had offered better terms, Petrolink's negotiating position would have been stronger. Now, if the team returns, LDP will realize that something has gone wrong with Petrolink's other potential funder and perhaps lighten the terms.

Is Petrolink willing to say no to both BRX and LDP and go back to the venture capital markets looking for a new investor?

Before making any decisions, however, they need to ask themselves some hard questions. Are they willing to say no to both BRX and LDP and go back to the venture capital markets looking for a new investor? How long are they willing to continue the search for capital? They also need to get a better grip on the competitive situation. With such a large infrastructure opportunity, it's odd that the team wouldn't know whether there is someone else looking

to build a pipeline. What do they want from their investing partner: industrial expertise (BRX) or analytical expertise (LDP). Most venture capitalists place themselves in one of these two camps, and many entrepreneurs won't take funding from what they consider "dump" money. Who really is the dump money here?

Finally, Petrolink's founders need to reconsider their financing structure to see whether they can build any more wiggle room into the deal. Can they spread out the financing rounds at all? Can they afford to spend time looking for money as well as developing the venture? There is a trade-off between the comfort of having one investor cover two rounds and having the kind of control they seem to want, and they need to revisit that issue.

In these situations, the first and foremost issue is one of trust. Whenever you take VC money, you are simultaneously paying for it and hiring a partner.

This situation is not uncommon. I've seen at least a dozen cases where lawyers have come back with very different documents than the entrepreneurs thought they had agreed to. In these situations, the first and foremost issue is one of trust. someone who's going to help you succeed. Given the harshness of the VC's terms, you're paying a lot; you should get a partner who will help rather than harm you.

There are many ways in which VC's can quite legally make life miserable for entrepreneurs. As in the case of Petrolink, VCs stage their capital commitment, which means that the venture is guaranteed to need more money. First-round VCs have a huge impact on the pricing and availability of that new money. If they are supportive, new capital can be obtained on fair terms from helpful investors. If not, the process can be messy and expensive. Moreover, because the VCs have seats on the board, they can be helpful—in tasks like hiring, setting strategy, framing partnerships, and raising money—or they can be difficult. Bad directors often meddle in operations and make obstreperous or self-interested financial decisions. Some VCs have hidden agendas. They back another horse in the same race or have secret plans to replace management soon after the deal is consummated.

I should point out that the dilution clause is only about sixth or seventh on the list of things an entrepreneur should care about. There's a distinct possibility that there are other agreed-upon terms in the contract that are more damaging than the new dilution clause. Karl and Robert need to begin by reviewing what they did agree to as well as checking the document for changes.

They must also assess how these VCs behave when the chips are down. There's a wonderful description of the due diligence carried out by LDP. They asked a ton of questions, called lots of people, and checked references. There's no evidence that the entrepreneurs have done the same kind of due diligence on their potential investor. They need to find venture-founding CEOs who have worked with BRX—ones who were fired and ones who lasted the course. Because BRX has already committed a breach of trust, the due diligence will need to be especially thorough. If Karl and Robert find any indication that BRX has behaved badly toward other entrepreneurs, they should walk away.

LDP made much more sense as a partner. Of course, there was less money on offer, and Karl and Robert were quite reasonably worried about running out of money before producing enough information to justify a second round. But for all Karl and Robert knew, LDP might have a good history of supporting their companies by helping them raise money elsewhere or by providing interim funding themselves. Perhaps they routinely lowball their first offer to see how the entrepreneurs react and are actually quite open to bargaining. Choosing so quickly between

LDP and BRX is further evidence of these entrepreneurs' inexperience.

This project is much riskier than Robert, Karl, and Nigel seem to realize. In Eastern Europe, the gas pipeline industry is politically sensitive, and Gazprom, the dominant player, is rich and immensely well connected. Although Poland is changing, it retains much of the mentality and work habits imposed by 50 years of Soviet rule; I would not want to rely on Polish officials or courts to protect me against Gazprom. For that very reason, my company has always avoided investing in raw materials businesses. A gas pipeline attracts more attention from governments than a chocolate factory. Last, but not least, Petrolink's partners have never operated as a management team.

There are many imponderables to a new venture in Eastern Europe. Institutions are still fragile, business environments unstable, and courts inexperienced in dealing with complex business agreements. These considerations make trust crucial. Because each party has a certain measure of control, the VC-entrepreneur relationship is inevitably interdependent. The VCs may hold the purse strings, but they usually need the entrepreneurs to run the company and for information, expertise, and local networks. Unless each side feels that it can trust the other not to abuse its power, the relationship will not produce a win-win outcome.

BRX has blatantly proved its untrustworthiness. Lech Wojtalik and Walter Cronbach's crude attempt to swindle Karl and Robert by changing the dilution clause is typical of the apparatchiks (if indeed Lech was a party member) whose networks still have clout in the raw materials industries in Eastern Europe. The move also suggests that BRX wants control of Petrolink—certainly in terms of ownership and probably also in terms of managerial decision making. Robert is right to worry about what BRX might do down the road. With 45% ownership already agreed to, it doesn't have far to go.

LDP would make a much better partner. It is large and well established, and it has a long track record in investing and helping successful ventures. Both Karl and Robert were engaged in and positive about the due diligence process, which suggests that LDP's questions were to the point. LDP's limited expertise in oil and gas is actually an advantage; it means LDP needs management's expertise more than BRX would. LDP also has a much healthier approach to control. It simply wants to mitigate the high risks of this investment.

Karl and Robert's real dilemma is not about taking BRX's money—they absolutely should not—but whether they should go back to LDP or abandon the deal all together. If they go back to LDP, they should focus on understanding the logic behind the deal structure LDP proposed. Perhaps its stringent terms reflect a history of investing in businesses that are not capital intensive or a sense of not knowing enough about the industry. If so, it may be that Karl and Robert can persuade LDP to put in more money.

To do this, though, they need to work harder at winning LDP's trust. Greater trust will also make LDP more relaxed about the control issues that clearly worry the Petrolink team and will make the VCs more likely to give the team latitude.

If the team members cannot reach a compromise with LDP, they should go back to their old jobs. None of them will have lost more than six months or their time over the deal, and Karl and Nigel will not find going back to Beckman as hard as they seem to think. Beckman was willing to support them in the venture, so it clearly values them. What they have already gained in terms of experience in dealing with VCs will stand each of them in good stead in any future venture.

If the team members cannot reach a compromise with LDP, they should go back to their old jobs.

Robert also needs to ask himself whether he, Karl, and Nigel can function as a management team. His reaction to BRX's move is quite measured; the others are a little hysterical and lacking in business instincts.

Thinking Further—Case 4

Take the Money or Run

1. How might Petrolink have prepared more strategically prior to starting the negotiation to prevent BRX from engaging in dirty tricks? Give examples.

2. Which of the commentators do you agree with most? Why? Would you have gone through with the deal with BRX? Why, or why not?

CASE 5

Collective Bargaining At Magic Carpet Airlines: A Union's Perspective

By Peggy Briggs and William Ross

History of Magic Carpet Air

Magic Carpet Air (MCA) began operations in 1961 serving two cities and grew to serve eighteen cities by 1987. River City Airlines (RCA) began in 1969 with service to four cities and grew to serve twelve cities by 1987. In January 1987, Magic Carpet Air purchased River City Airlines and merged the two operations. The joining of these two regional airlines created a "national" airline (defined as a carrier with sales between one hundred million dollars and one billion dollars).

Source: Peggy Briggs and William Ross, "Collective Bargaining at Magic Carpet Airlines: A Union Perspective," Midwest Society for Case Research, 1991. Used by permission of Midwest Society for Case Research.

With the joining of these two regional airlines, by definition Magic Carpet Air became a national carrier with sales of $140,265,000 in 1987.

In May 1988, Magic Carpet Air entered into a marketing agreement with a major carrier (e.g., American, United) and became a "feeder" airline for that carrier (e.g., American Eagle, United Express). That is, MCA delivered passengers from small airports to larger ones, where passengers could make connections using that airline. Subsequently, no more reservations were given to the public as Magic Carpet Air; passengers believed that they bought tickets for the major carrier. The company also repainted all aircraft to make the public believe Magic Carpet Air was part of the major carrier.

Prior to 1987, the flight attendants at neither company were unionized. However, both MCA and RCA flight attendants worried about what they perceived as the arbitrary way that MCA management resolved personnel issues such as merging seniority lists. Such fears led several workers to contact the League of Flight Attendants (LFA), a union whose membership consisted solely of flight attendants. Despite opposition to unionization from MCA, the LFA won a union certification election with 82% of the vote.

Negotiations

Negotiations for the first MCA-LFA contract began in November of 1987 and negotiators from both sides cooperated effectively. The committee borrowed language from other airline contracts (e.g., Piedmont Airlines). The committee also incorporated the past practices and working conditions that were used at River City Airlines. These rules had not been written down but had been mutually acceptable past practices. Negotiators signed the final contract in August of 1988. The contract was effective until midnight, August 31, 1991.

What follows is a synopsis of the second contract negotiations from a union negotiator's perspective.

League of Flight Attendants (LFA) Negotiating Team

Whenever an LFA carrier began negotiations, the National Office of LFA sent a National Bargaining Representative (NBR) to the scene. Dixie Lee, the NBR assigned to the MCA negotiations, met with the flight attendants' Master Executive Council (MEC) to select a negotiating team. The negotiating team prepared for negotiations and conducted the actual bargaining sessions. Once at the table, Dixie spoke for the committee. Using an NBR as the spokesperson lessened the likelihood that a flight attendant who was emotionally involved with an issue might say something inappropriate while trying to negotiate. Dixie had fourteen years experience and had also assisted with the 1987 MCA contract negotiations. Although Dixie was the spokesperson, the negotiating team was formally chaired by Ruth Boaz, LFA MEC President at Magic Carpet Air. Other members of the team included local LFA Union Presidents Peggy Hardy, Marie Phillips, and Jody Rogers.

Determining the Union's Bargaining Objectives

The LFA negotiating committee members first identified their bargaining objectives. For the 1991 contract, the LFA negotiating committee devised an opening offer based on the average working conditions and wage rates offered by other national carriers. The committee members knew the financial history of MCA and kept their proposals within financial reach of the company. They also used other employee groups (e.g., pilots) within MCA as a guide—many of the proposals were items that these unions already had in their contracts. The LFA negotiating committee hoped to bring wages and work rules in line with the company's financial performance and industry standards (see Table 1 on p. 454).

Committee members also considered the wishes of the rank-and-file members. To do this, the committee mailed a survey to the 115 LFA members asking questions regarding wages, working conditions, and issues of concern to flight attendants. They received a 75% response rate; results are shown in Table 2 on p. 455.

After tallying the responses, negotiating team members discovered that the flight attendants' major concern was wage determination. MCA currently paid flight attendants for the time they were in the aircraft with it moving under its own power—they were not paid for the time spent sitting in airports waiting for flights. Union members wanted MCA to implement "duty rigs." A duty rig paid the attendant a fixed percentage of the period of time he or she was on duty with the company.

For example, suppose an attendant worked a fifteen-hour day, but worked in moving aircraft for only six hours. Under the current system, MCA paid wages for six hours, plus one hour for preparation time ("duty time") at the beginning of the day. However, if the duty rig pay rate was 67%, MCA would pay that attendant for ten hours of work, plus one hour for duty time. Thus, duty rigs would require the airline to pay a percentage of the wage for all time at work, whether flying or sitting.

Flight attendants also voiced concern over job security and working conditions. When they analyzed the job security issue, team members found that in the event of any merger or buyout of MCA, the flight attendants wanted their seniority with the carrier to be continued by any new company. Second, flight attendants sought protection from layoffs in the event of a merger or acquisition.

The survey also had a section for employee comments. The area that members most frequently relayed as a concern was their current sick leave program. Many flight attendants complained that they were not allowed to use their accrued sick time when they were sick. Others complained that they had to give management a five-day notice whenever they wanted to swap routes with other MCA attendants.

From this information, union negotiating committee members identified two broad objectives: increased wages via a duty rig provision, and increased job security. They also decided that their initial package would be very close to their final objectives. The committee members proposed a duty rig clause with the same standards as the pilots, although the dollar amount was less important than just obtaining the provision itself. They also devised a "successorship clause" allowing attendants to arbitrate their seniority rights in the event someone bought MCA. In order to obtain these clauses, the union also proposed two "throwaway" clauses: an expensive health care package, and "double time" wages for working holidays.

Strategies of the Union

During planning sessions, the negotiating committee identified four strategies for achieving its objectives through bargaining. These strategies were:

1. keeping union members informed of negotiation progress;

2. getting union members involved;

3. convincing the company that the union's demands were serious; and,

4. settling an issue only with the unanimous consent of the negotiating committee.

Informing Union Members

The first strategy attempted to keep the union members informed. The negotiating committee mailed a short letter after each bargaining session, explaining the issues discussed and the general content of any agreed-upon sections. Members were also sent Negotiation Update newsletters every two weeks, telling flight attendants of their progress. These newsletters did not reveal any initial proposals because committee members knew that members would be disappointed if the union did not receive what was initially requested.

Involving Union Member

The second strategy sought to get the union members involved. The negotiating committee printed the slogan, "We make the Difference and they make the Money" on pens, buttons, and T-shirts. These were distributed to all members. The union also invited any member in good standing to attend any negotiation session.

Convincing Company

The third strategy attempted to convince the company to take the LFA seriously. In a widely-publicized move, negotiation team members did extensive research on both economic picketing and informational picketing, inquiring at all of their domicile cities as to what permits would be needed to picket. The union mailed their Negotiations Updates Newsletters to each manager's home address, informing them of the LFA's preparations in the event a future strike occurred. Committee members hoped these actions would convince management that the LFA made serious proposals and would strike if they were not met.

Settling Issues

The fourth strategy was that the team would not proceed with an item without the entire team being in total agreement. All planning meetings and caucuses (meetings without the company team members present) during negotiations would involve every committee member.

Company Negotiating Team

The company negotiating team consisted of the following people:

- Bill Orleans, Director of Labor Relations
- Ross Irving, Director of Human Resource
- Kristine Lamb, Director of Inflight Services
- Christian Andrew, Executive Vice-President
- Willie Sanders, Senior Vice-President of Operations
- Tom Windham, Chief Executive Officer (CEO) & President.

The company team was in a state of transition, and, consequently, suffered from much confusion.

Bill Orleans, had recently been demoted from Director of Human Resources to that of Director of Labor Relations-- a move he resented. Ross Irving, the new Director of Human Resources hired from another firm, avoided the sessions; he seemed uncomfortable sitting next to his predecessor, particularly since Mr. Orleans had negotiated most union contracts at MCA. Finally, Mrs. Lamb, who was used to giving orders to flight attendants, acted as if the negotiations reflected a lack of loyalty on the part of the workers and interference with her job on the part of management. Tom Windham was grooming Willie Sanders to take over upon Windham's retirement.

The Negotiating Process: Initial Positions

Airlines are governed under the Railway Labor Act of 1926, as amended. This act states that labor contracts never expire, but may be amended on their amendable dates. When the amendable date comes near, a letter is mailed by the party requesting changes in the contract to the counter party in the contract. This letter allows contract talks to begin. Dixie mailed MCA such a letter on March 31, giving a full sixty days notice of the flight attendants' intent to open talks for amending their current contract before September 1.

Inasmuch as the company would not meet in a neutral city, LFA negotiators agreed to an MCA proposal to meet at a hotel located near corporate headquarters. MCA paid for the meeting room. The first negotiation session was scheduled for May 31, 1991.

Everyone on the LFA committee had the jitters. It was the first time in negotiations for Marie, Jody, and Peggy. Dixie gave them some last-minute instructions:

I don't want y'all to speak or use any facial expressions at the table. Instead, I want all of y'all to silently take notes. Draw a vertical line down the middle of each note page. Write whatever the managers say on the left side of the page and write whatever I say on the right-hand side of the page. Is it OK with y'all if I do the negotiating? I've found things go best if only one person talks at the bargaining table.

As the LFA negotiators filed into the conference room, they saw it was empty. Each of the managers arrived late. Twenty minutes later, Mr. Orleans still had not come. As everyone waited, CEO Tom Windham arrived. Small talk began as Mr. Windham glanced over his notes and spoke:

You know that as a feeder airline we do not have full control over our own destiny; the marketing agreement with the major carrier restricts our flexibility. Even so, I am willing to give your flight attendant group a modest increase. I am not looking for any concessions. Also, my philosophy is that all the groups (pilots, agents, office personnel) should be treated equally. However, your union does have a good agreement right now—say, why don't we just agree to continue the present contract for another six years? It could save a lot of time!

As everyone chuckled at Mr. Windham's joke, Mr. Orleans arrived. The union negotiators could tell by the expression on his face that he was surprised and embarrassed to see Tom Windham there. Mr. Windham stood up, wished everyone good luck, and left.

The Union's Initial Position

Dixie spent the first day describing problems with the current contract. At 4:15 p.m., the union presented the Company with its neatly typed contract proposal. Dixie had written "change," "new," "clarification," etc. in the margin next to each paragraph that had been changed in any way from the 1987 contract.

ORLEANS: This is a 'wish book!' Do I look like Santa Claus?

LEE: Stop fidgeting, Mr. Orleans. Let me explain why we are insisting on these changes.

Dixie read only about one-third of the provisions in the union's contract proposal. Two additional sessions were necessary to read through the entire proposal. The major changes are summarized in Table 3 on p. 456.

Management's Initial Position

On the fourth day, company representatives presented their initial offer to the union. Mr. Orleans handed each of the LFA committee members a book in a binder. As they leafed through the book, members were puzzled. They did not see any notations indicating changes from the current contract. Mr. Orleans talked quickly, summarizing the provisions in the contract; most of the proposed provisions included some type of union concessions, but he did not highlight these.

LEE: Is this a serious proposal? The union presented a realistic proposal using industry standards, and your opener (opening offer) is totally unreasonable.

ORLEANS: Don't get your panties in a wad. The party has just begun and there is lots of time to dance.

Why, we didn't even list any wages in our proposal—we were hoping you would work for free, ha ha.

Mr. Orleans then gave a long, patronizing, sermon regarding MCA's poor financial health and how the company could be bankrupt at any time. However, in the history of Magic Carpet Air, the company had never shown a loss on its financial statement.

A recess was called for lunch. As the union members caucused, Peggy looked depressed. Marie sat with fists clenched.

MARIE: I can't eat anything! I am furious at Mr. Orleans—he has some nerve!

JODY: The others were not much better. Did you hear their snide remarks when they went to lunch?

PEGGY: What are we going to do? They have asked for concessions on everything! And Mr. Windham promised us just the opposite.

DIXIE: Now girls, just relax. It is still the first week of negotiations. I suggest that we just work from our initial contract proposal and ignore theirs. It can't be taken seriously, anyway, in my opinion.

MARIE: Well, you'll have to carry on without me tomorrow; I have to work. Management won't let me rearrange my schedule to negotiate. At least I won't have to watch Mr. Orleans chain smoke!

Talks resumed after lunch break. Dixie summarized each section of the LFA proposal. Mr. Orleans fidgeted and kept saying, "No." Nothing was settled that day.

By noon the next day, it became obvious that not much was getting accomplished. Finally, the union moved to sections where it did not propose any changes and the managers tentatively agreed to keep those intact. It seemed like a mountain had been climbed, just to get the company to agree to those "no changes." Negotiations were adjourned for the day.

LEE: When can we meet? Monday, at 8:30?

SANDERS: No good for me. I have important meetings that day.

LEE: How about Tuesday?

ANDREW: I can't make it. Every day next week is bad.

ORLEANS: The following week I will be out of town. Sorry!

LEE: OK, y'all tell us when y'all's schedules are free.

ORLEANS: We'll have to caucus. We'll get back to you.

Instead of caucusing and deciding when they could next meet, the managers simply went home, leaving the union negotiating team to wonder when—or if—bargaining would continue.

Round Two

On Wednesday, July 17th, Ruth Boaz got a letter from management asking for a meeting two days later. Ruth quickly scheduled a planning session for Thursday night, where the LFA team members reviewed their objectives and the progress to date. Negotiations with MCA resumed Friday.

July 19: Grievances and Uniforms

Mr. Irving proposed using the same language for a revised grievance procedure as printed in the pilot's contract. The union caucused. Ruth telephoned the pilot's union, and, once she was satisfied that the pilots were happy with their grievance procedure, convinced the union negotiating team to agree.

The discussion moved to the section on uniforms. After some countering back and forth on various issues, a winter coat was added as an optional item; however, who would pay the cost was still an issue. The union wanted MCA to pay the total cost.

ORLEANS: Unacceptable. You'll have to buy your own coats. We already give $16.00 per month for uniform cleaning.

LEE: But a winter coat is expensive. Surely y'all recognize that a poor little ol' flight attendant couldn't be expected to shoulder the entire cost of a new coat. Mr. Orleans, have a heart.

ORLEANS: I do have a heart; fortunately, it is not attached to my wallet, ha ha. OK, we will allow $40 every five years to buy a coat.

LEE: According to my research, a new coat costs $120. And it costs $10.00 per month to clean.

ORLEANS: How often does someone dry clean a coat she only wears three months of the year? She doesn't clean it twelve times! (pause) OK, if you drop this silly request for free shoes, then we'll raise the combined uniform and coat maintenance allowance to $16.50 per month.

LEE: But, Mr. Orleans, shoes are a part of our uniform, too. You expect us to all wear the same type of shoes, don't you? You pay for the other parts of our uniforms. So, it is only reasonable that MCA should also pay for shoes. Our research shows that two pair of standard shoes cost, on average, $100.00.

ORLEANS: However, you can wear the shoes when you are not on duty, too. You

probably wouldn't do that with other parts of your uniforms. So we're not paying for shoes you can wear other places.

BOAZ: Mr. Orleans, I can assure you that we don't wear our uniform shoes when we go dancing on the week-ends. (Everyone laughed.)

ORLEANS: If we pay $25.00 for shoes and $45.00 for a coat, then we will pay $17.50 per month for uniform maintenance.

LEE: Good, but not good enough. (Both sides sat in silence for nearly four minutes. Mr. Orleans was obviously uncomfortable with this period of silence.)

ORLEANS: Let's see . . . (fumbling with a pen and paper) we'll split the costs of the new coat, so that is $60.00 and we'll pay $25.00 for shoes. Good enough now?

LEE: Raise the combined uniform and coat maintenance to $18.00 per month and you have a deal.

LEE: (As they were writing the agreed-upon section) Why don't we make it one new coat for the life of the three-year contract, instead of one new coat every five years? That makes it so much easier for everyone to keep track of.

Mr. Orleans rolled his eyes and nodded in acquiescence. The meeting then adjourned for the weekend.

July 22: Seniority and Fringe Benefits

On Monday, Mr. Irving was absent, so Mr. Orleans continued as chief MCA negotiator. He brought in a typed version of the agreed-upon sections. As the LFA negotiating committee reviewed them, they grew perplexed.

HARDY: Mr. Orleans, I know we agreed not to change several clauses in the contract, but as I look through this, it appears to me that nothing is changed! In fact, the uniform clause is your initial, concessionary, contract proposal! Mr. Orleans, are you trying to pull a 'fast one' on us? Because if you are . . .

ORLEANS: Oh, I must have given the wrong pages to my secretary to type. Sorry. It won't happen again.

But it did happen again. Whenever his secretary typed any provisions, Mr. Orleans brought in a retyped version of MCA's initial concessionary contract provisions for one or more contract clauses. Repeatedly, Dixie sent it back to be retyped according to what they had actually agreed. Interestingly, this only occurred at meetings where Ross Irving and Tom Windham were absent.

LEE: I propose that laid-off (or "furloughed") flight attendants continue to accrue seniority even while laid off. Also, flight attendants who had transferred out of flight attendant positions or into management positions should be stricken from the seniority list.

LAMB: I like your furlough proposal, but not your seniority proposal. Instead, I propose that people hired in these other positions be added to the seniority lists.

LEE: Mrs. Lamb, I understand that you do not want your staff to lose their seniority rights. But those employees do not have the same concerns as our active LFA members. They should not get this benefit.

LAMB: It was acceptable in the last contract, what's different now? You have to look out for the interests of your employees and I have to look out for the interests of mine. I'm sure you understand.

After much wrangling, it was obvious that the two sides could not agree. So they recessed for lunch. During lunch, Mr. Sanders found the LFA group in the hotel restaurant.

SANDERS: I have an idea that might resolve this issue. Consider the following: Flight attendants transferring into other jobs will continue to accrue seniority, but if they want to return to flight attendant positions, they cannot "bump" existing attendants. Rather, they must wait until there is an opening and "bid" on that opening. In return for accepting that proposal, management will agree to the following: (1) flight attendants will be officially recognized as Safety Professionals, (2) two flight attendants will be allowed to attend each domicile's bi-monthly Safety Committee meeting, (3) two union officers can meet monthly with domicile managers to discuss flight attendants' working conditions and (4) union officers can have one paid day off each month to conduct union business.

LEE: Let us caucus.

HARDY: What is he up to, coming to us at lunch like this? I am real suspicious of this 'all-or-nothing' proposal. Besides, it sounds like he is trying to 'buy us off' with added benefits for union officials.

BOAZ: These types of 'package deals' are common; it is OK.

LEE: Let's work up a counterproposal while we eat lunch.

After their lunchtime caucus, Dixie offered a counterproposal:

LEE: We'll accept Mr. Sanders' offer, provided you give LFA officers three paid days off each month (plus free travel passes) for union business, and give all LFA attendants paid days off for jury duty or funerals.

Mrs. Lamb frowned. Mr. Sanders stroked his chin. It was now management's turn to caucus. Upon returning, Mr. Orleans offered the group's response.

ORLEANS: Let's compromise on one day with free travel for union business. As for your other two suggestions, my first response is: 'why pay people for not working?' Besides, people will abuse the funeral leave. Every week, some step-nephew-twice-removed will pass away!

LEE: Well then, what do you propose?

ORLEANS: Jury duty at half-pay. And one extra 'personal leave' day per year. If they want to use it to go to a funeral, they can. They can go fishing if they like. Just so they give us two days advance notice.

LEE: Make it two personal leave days and we'll accept it.

ORLEANS: Done.

With that, the parties agreed to adjourn until the next morning.

July 23: Ladies in Waiting

LFA negotiators met at a nearby coffee shop and then proceeded as a group to the scheduled 8:00 a.m. meeting. The MCA managers did not arrive until 8:45 a.m.

LEE: Now for the tough one—wages. Wages should increase for starting flight attendants from $11.00 to $13.45 per hour, and from $18.20 to $23.55 per hour for attendants with five or more years of seniority. Further, we want the minimum pay increased from 65 hours to 70 hours per trip, because we are away several days on each trip. Finally, our attendants want guaranteed pay of 4.5 hours per day for showing up (in case weather cancelled the flight).

ORLEANS: We'll have to caucus on this proposal.

Seven hours later, the LFA team members still sat in the negotiation room, waiting. Gradually, they realized that the managers were not caucusing at all, but had probably returned to their normal work activities. At 5:00 p.m., a secretary appeared at the door to announce that the MCA managers had decided that they would prefer to continue negotiations another day. Further, no manager could meet the following day—or any day until August 21st.

That evening, Dixie called Tom Windham at home to complain about the delay. Mr. Windham promised to investigate. The next day, a very cordial Ross Irving called to ask if the union could meet earlier—Monday, August 5th.

LEE: I'm sorry, but that day, we'll be counting ballots from the LFA strike authorization vote. But I could squeeze y'all in on Tuesday.

Round Three

Before the Tuesday meeting, the union faced a decision. Dixie had become ill and could not attend. Marie and Jody had to work. Only Peggy and Ruth were available to negotiate. Although neither felt competent to serve as spokesperson, they agreed to meet anyway. By a toss of a coin, Peggy Hardy was chosen as spokesperson.

August 7: Arbitration Rulings, Health Care, and Sick Leave

The negotiators devoted the morning to modifying contract clauses in ways that incorporated previous arbitrator's rulings. They devoted the afternoon to arguing about the LFA proposal to increase health care coverage by 25%. Nothing was accomplished. The two sides agreed to move to other issues.

HARDY: We are offering a fair sick leave proposal. Under this plan, workers receive pay for all time missed due to illness for the first month and then one-third pay for any days beyond one month.

IRVING: Peggy, this is unacceptable. I'm sorry. MCA already pays seven days off for illness and we agreed to give you two personal leave days. The industry average is only to pay for 78 hours due to illness.

HARDY: OK, increase the paid time off for illness from 56 hours (seven days) to 78 hours at full pay and then the remainder can be at half-pay.

ORLEANS: You girls are dreaming. Tell you what: I know that your flight attendants complain whenever they show up for work and their flights are cancelled. That's why we guarantee 3.25 hours of pay—just for showing up. We'll

increase your minimum daily guaranteed hours, if you agree to drop your sick leave proposal.

HARDY: Now, you're dreaming!

Taking a page from Dixie's book, Peggy sat silently staring at him. After some fidgeting and a few calculations, Mr. Orleans paused and lit his tenth cigarette of the day.

ORLEANS: We'll increase your daily guarantee to 3.50 hours and we'll increase your paid sick leave to 78 hours. Total. That's the best we can do.

HARDY: Agreed.

BOAZ: Now, I think we should discuss wages—and no 'running away' this time!

ORLEANS: I was looking at your proposal and I saw you wanted duty rigs. No-can-do. Duty rigs are too costly!

IRVING: Your minimum guaranteed pay demand of 4.5 hours would bankrupt the company. That simply isn't feasible!

ORLEANS: And your demands are outrageous—what do you think we are flying—gold-plated aircraft? The trouble with you union types is you only know one word—gimme.

BOAZ: Do you want to discuss our proposal? Or would you rather spend your time thinking up clever insults?

ORLEANS: We are willing to negotiate, but negotiations can't be all one way; we've got to see more "give" and less "take" on your part—especially in the area of wages.

BOAZ: Mr. Orleans, look at how MCA compares to other airlines! Our attendants earn less than those working for other national carriers of similar size.

ORLEANS: There are reasons for that. We are smaller. We make less profit. We have to keep costs low, to keep our "feeder" contract. To put it simply, we can't afford to give you what you are asking for. We've been generous up to this point, but we've given about all we can give—that is true for wages and for health care. No more concessions! Sorry!

BOAZ: (Standing) Then we have nothing further to discuss.

IRVING: Wait, Ruth. Would you like me to call the government and request a Federal Mediator?

BOAZ: Fine. (Glancing at Mr. Orleans) Just pick someone who doesn't smoke. With that, the meeting was adjourned.

August 27: Mediation

On Tuesday, August 27, the mediator arrived. Dixie, who had recovered from her illness, led the LFA team. The mediator, Cal Crenshaw, told of his fifteen years experience at handling airline negotiations. He also asked the negotiators if they had seen a recent issue of Monthly Labor Reports containing airline worker wage and benefit averages. Everyone nodded.

Mr. Crenshaw then reviewed all areas of the contract that had been agreed upon and all sections still outstanding. Each side explained its positions on the provisions in question. Mr. Irving tried to show the mediator that MCA could not afford the LFA requests. Dixie tried to show the mediator that the requests matched industry averages. This process took the entire day.

Tuesday, Mr. Crenshaw separated the two sides and met extensively with each side. He met with MCA first and then with the union.

CRENSHAW: First, I want to assure you that everything said here is confidential, Now, Dixie, can you accept anything else instead of your duty rig request?

LEE: No.

CRENSHAW: Can we lump the wage items together into one dollar amount? MCA thinks in terms of total labor costs and you'd be presenting the information in their lingo.

LEE: No, each issue is important in its own right and should be considered separately.

CRENSHAW: Well, tell me, what do you really want in the area of wages? What is your bottom line?

LEE: Sir, other flight attendants have duty rig provisions. We want them too. Also our wage proposal calls for a modest wage increase and the company's proposal offers nothing. Now which is more reasonable to you?

CRENSHAW: What offer could you give me to discuss with the other side? What concession could you make?

LEE: The principle of the duty rig is more important than the specific pay level. So we are flexible on our demand for one hour's pay for every two hours of duty. We'll come down on health benefits too.

The remainder of the day was spent in such caucuses with the mediator, discussing wage and benefit issues. By the end of the day, the union had softened its duty rig demand to one hour's pay for every 2.5 hours of service and MCA management had agreed in principle to the concept, but not to any pay level. Finally, Mr. Crenshaw realized that progress was unlikely and adjourned negotiations until 9:00 a.m. the following morning.

August 28: Working Conditions and Job Security

To the union leaders, the morning of August 28th seemed wasted. The mediator caucused with each side. When with the union, he asked, "What if…" questions. He then presented hypothetical scenarios and observed Dixie's reaction.

CRENSHAW: If you gave up your demand for eight paid holidays at double time—holiday periods are big travel days for flight crews—what would you expect in return?

LEE: Currently, if an attendant wants to trade routes with another attendant, he or she has to give a five-day notice to the company. What difference does it make to MCA who flies what routes? As long as all of them are covered, what do they care? We think a 24-hour advance notice is sufficient.

Mr. Crenshaw left. Two hours later, the mediator returned.

CRENSHAW: They accepted the compromise. They wouldn't have bought the 24-hour proposal if they had believed you had thought of it, so I told them it was my idea. I also kept pointing out that this would not cost them any money. Clever, eh?

That afternoon, discussion turned to job security. Mr. Crenshaw continued to caucus with the union.

CRENSHAW: As I understand it, you want two things: (1) the contract will remain binding in the event of any change in ownership and, (2) arbitration will be used to protect the seniority rights of all on the flight attendant seniority list.

LEE: Right.

CRENSHAW: Let me offer a proposal: Have you ever heard of a 'me-too' clause? That is where one group's contract determines the terms for another group.

ROGERS: I don't follow. What's your idea?

CRENSHAW: My sense is that MCA will never agree to your proposal because of who you are—flight attendants. However, clauses that are virtually identical to what you are requesting are found in both the pilots' and the mechanics' contracts. So, I suggest you negotiate a clause that says that your group will be treated the same as those two unions.

BOAZ: I don't like the idea of leaving our fate to others.

CRENSHAW: Think about it. Planes can easily fly with scab flight attendants. Planes can't fly without the unionized pilots or mechanics. So, you are allowing more powerful unions than your own to negotiate for you!

LEE: What makes you think MCA will go for it?

CRENSHAW: Three factors. First, the costs are remote. I know that MCA is not planning any airline acquisitions or mergers within the next three years, so this doesn't cost management anything. Second, they don't have to renegotiate this clause with you in the future. Whatever they negotiate with the other unions covers you too. Third, if you let them pick the more favorable (to their side) of the two contracts—the mechanics or the pilots—they still feel like they are 'managing.' Either is better than what you can get on your own.

LEE: I like it. We'll agree if they will.

But MCA did not agree. And the managers requested more joint meetings and fewer private caucuses. The joint meetings produced nothing but bickering. This continued throughout the week. By Friday afternoon, Mr. Crenshaw had had enough.

CRENSHAW: As you know, tomorrow is your last day to bargain before the present contract expires. It has become increasingly clear that I am no longer an asset to the negotiation process, but a liability. Each side seems to be trying to make the other look bad in front of me. You are not far from an agreement and you can conclude these talks successfully, but you all have to want to settle. I've arranged to go back to Washington, so when you resume tomorrow, you must agree on your own.

As the meeting adjourned, the union members sat in stunned silence. Peggy looked at her notes, containing a chart of the issues (Table 4). She saw that the union was so close1—and yet so far—from agreement. She wondered what would happen next.

Table 1   1989–90 Airline Industry Comparisons

	Starting Wage/Hour	Days Off/Per Month	Duty Rig* as Airline Percent of Time
Air Wisconsin	$12.50	10	33%
Atlantic SE	$12.00	10	none
Aloha Airline	$13.00	12	62%
Hawaiian Air	$12.00	13	none
Magic Carpet	$11.00	10	none
Midway Air	$13.00	12	none
Aspen	$15.00	11	60%

*__Duty Rig__ is a pay calculation that is a certain percentage of the period of time which a flight attendant is on duty with the company. Duty Time normally begins 45 minutes prior to first scheduled trip departure time and ends 15 minutes after arrival time at the end of the day.

Table 2   Results of the Flight Attendant Survey

Questionnaires Mailed	115	Questionnaires Returned	86
Question : What was the flight attendant's top priority for the new contract?			
direct wages	40%		
job security	31%		
working conditions	26%		
other	3%		
Question: How did the flight attendant want to receive her/his direct wages?			
duty rigs	47%		
hourly rate	34%		
holiday pay	15%		
other	4%		
Question: How did the flight attendant want her/his job security?			
seniority protection	60%		
protection from layoffs	28%		
protection of contract	12%		

Table 3 Changes in the Magic Carpet Air League of Flight Attendants Contract

	Contract Provision	1988–1991 Contract	Union Proposal
Compensation			
Base Wage	$11.00	$13.45	none
Wage after five years	$18.20	$23.55	none
Duty rig pay	none per 2 hr duty (50%)	1 hr. pay	none
Daily guarantee hours	3.25 hours	4.5 hours	3.5 hours
Holiday pay		8 holidays at "double time" rate	Two paid (regular rate) personal holidays
Job Security			
Successorship	none	Contract will still be binding	none
Protection of seniority rights in the event of merger	none	Arbitrator combines MCA seniority list with that of the other airline	none
Working Conditions			
Trip trading lead time hours prior	5 days	24 hours	24 hours
Shoe allowance $25/year	none	$100/year	
Winter Coat $60/three years	none	Total cost	
Uniform maintenance $18/month	$16/month	$20/month	

Table 4 Changes in the Magic Carpet Air League of Flight Attendants Contract as of August 30, 1991

Contract Provision Compensation	1988–1991 Contract	Initial Union Proposal	Settlement to Date
Base Wage	$11.00	$13.45	none
Wage after five years	$18.20	$23.55	none
Duty rig pay	none	1 hr. pay per 2 hr. duty (50%)	
Daily guarantee hours	3.25 hours	4.5 hours	3.5 hours
Holiday pay	none	8 holidays at "double time" rate	Two paid (regular rate) personal holidays.
Job Security			
Successorship	none	Contract will still be binding	None
Protection of seniority rights in the event of a merger	none	arbitrator combines MCA seniority list with that of other airline	
Working Conditions			
Trip trading lead time 24 hours prior	5 days	24 hours	
Shoe allowance $25/year	none	$100/year	
Winter Coat years	none	Total cost	$60/three
Uniform maintenance	$16/month	$20/month	$18/month

Thinking Further—Case 5

1. What did the union negotiators do, neglect to do, or do incorrectly to cause the negotiation to result in a stalemate the evening before the contract would expire? Think in terms of preparation, strategies and tactics.

2. Did the mediator appear to be biased in favor of one side, or equally fair to both sides? Explain why.

3. Say that the union negotiators decided to bring in a new negotiator for the last day of negotiating. If you were that new negotiator, what strategies and tactics would you use on that last day to reach an agreement with management? What is it about these strategies and tactics that would make them more likely to be effective than those that the union negotiators already tried?

Appendix

THE CULTURAL INTELLIGENCE SCALE (CQS)

Read each statement and select the response that best describes your capabilities. Select the answer that BEST describes you AS YOU REALLY ARE.

(1 = strongly disagree; 7 = strongly agree)

	Strongly Disagree						Strongly Agree
1. I am conscious of the cultural knowledge I use when interacting with people with different cultural backgrounds.	1	2	3	4	5	6	7
2. I adjust my cultural knowledge as I interact with people from a culture that is unfamiliar to me.	1	2	3	4	5	6	7
3. I am conscious of the cultural knowledge I apply to cross-cultural interactions.	1	2	3	4	5	6	7
4. I check the accuracy of my cultural knowledge as I interact with people from different cultures.	1	2	3	4	5	6	7
5. I know the legal and economic systems of other cultures.	1	2	3	4	5	6	7
6. I know the rules (e.g., vocabulary, grammar) of other languages.	1	2	3	4	5	6	7
7. I know the cultural values and religious beliefs of other cultures.	1	2	3	4	5	6	7
8. I know the marriage systems of other cultures.	1	2	3	4	5	6	7
9. I know the arts and crafts of other cultures.	1	2	3	4	5	6	7

(Continued)

(Continued)

	Strongly Disagree						Strongly Agree
10. I know the rules for expressing nonverbal behaviors in other cultures.	1	2	3	4	5	6	7
11. I enjoy interacting with people from different cultures.	1	2	3	4	5	6	7
12. I am confident that I can socialize with locals in a culture that is unfamiliar to me.	1	2	3	4	5	6	7
13. I am sure I can deal with the stresses of adjusting to a culture that is new to me.	1	2	3	4	5	6	7
14. I enjoy living in cultures that are unfamiliar to me.	1	2	3	4	5	6	7
15. I am confident that I can get accustomed to the shopping conditions in a different culture.	1	2	3	4	5	6	7
16. I change my verbal behavior (e.g., accent, tone) when a cross-cultural interaction requires it.	1	2	3	4	5	6	7
17. I use pause and silence differently to suit different cross-cultural situations.	1	2	3	4	5	6	7
18. I vary the rate of my speaking when a cross-cultural situation requires it.	1	2	3	4	5	6	7
19. I change my nonverbal behavior when a cross-cultural situation requires it.	1	2	3	4	5	6	7
20. I alter my facial expressions when a cross-cultural interaction requires it.	1	2	3	4	5	6	7

Source: © Cultural Intelligence Center 2005. Used by permission of the Cultural Intelligence Center.

Scoring

Items 1–4 reflect the strategic dimension of one's cultural IQ (CQ).

Items 5–10 reflect the knowledge dimension of one's CQ.

Items 11–15 reflect the motivational dimension of one's CQ.

Items 16–20 reflect the behavioral dimension of one's CQ.

To assess each dimension, average the scores using the 1–7 ratings. To determine your overall cultural IQ, average the dimension averages. Each dimension is explained below. These explanations/interpretations are excerpted and adapted from Ang, VanDyne, Koh, Ng, Templer, Tay & Chandrasekar (2007). References have been omitted.

Metacognitive or Strategic CQ reflects mental processes that people use to acquire and understand cultural knowledge, including knowledge of and control over individual thought processes relating to culture. High scores on this dimension indicate that people plan, monitor and revise mental models of cultural norms for countries or groups of people These people are consciously aware of others' cultural preferences before and during interactions. They also question cultural assumptions and adjust their mental models during and after interactions.

Knowledge or Cognitive CQ reflects one's knowledge of the norms, practices and conventions in different cultures. This includes knowledge of the economic, legal and social systems of different cultures and subcultures, and knowledge of basic frameworks of cultural values. Those with high cognitive CQ understand similarities and differences across cultures

Motivational CQ reflects the capability to direct attention and energy toward learning about and functioning in situations characterized by cultural differences. Those with high motivational CQ direct attention and energy toward cross-cultural situations based on intrinsic interest and confidence in their cross-cultural effectiveness.

Behavioral CQ reflects the capability to exhibit appropriate verbal and nonverbal actions when interacting with people from different cultures. Mental capabilities for cultural understanding and motivation must be complemented with the ability to exhibit appropriate verbal and nonverbal actions, based on cultural values of specific settings. This includes having a wide and flexible repertoire of behaviors. Those with high behavioral CQ exhibit situationally-appropriate behaviors based on their broad range of verbal and nonverbal capabilities. Examples include exhibiting culturally appropriate words, tone, gestures and facial expressions.

REFERENCES

Ackerman, P. L. 1996. A theory of adult intellectual development: Process, personality, interests, and knowledge. *Intelligence,* 22: 227–257.

Ang, S., Van Dyne, L., & Koh, S. K. 2006. Personality correlates of the four-factor model of cultural intelligence. *Group and Organization Management,* 31: 100–123.

INCIDENTS IN NEGOTIATION SCALE

Use the scale provided to rate the appropriateness of each of these tactics for negotiating something that is important to you. Be as candid as you can about what you think is appropriate and acceptable to do.

(If you have any need to explain your rating on a tactic, please do so in the margin or at the end/back of the questionnaire.)

	Not Appropriate				Very Appropriate		
1. Promise that good things will happen to your opponent if he/she gives you what you want, even if you know that you can't (or won't) deliver these things when the other's cooperation is obtained.	1	2	3	4	5	6	7
2. Intentionally misrepresent information to your opponent in order to strengthen your negotiating arguments or position.	1	2	3	4	5	6	7
3. Attempt to get your opponent fired from his/her position so that a new person will take his/her place.	1	2	3	4	5	6	7
4. Intentionally misrepresent the nature of negotiations to your constituency in order to protect delicate discussions that have occurred.	1	2	3	4	5	6	7
5. Gain information about an opponent's negotiating position by paying your friends, associates, and contacts to get this information for you.	1	2	3	4	5	6	7
6. Make an opening demand that is far greater than what you really hope to settle for.	1	2	3	4	5	6	7
7. Convey a false impression that you are in absolutely no hurry to come to a negotiated agreement, thereby trying to put time pressure on your opponent to concede quickly.	1	2	3	4	5	6	7
8. In return for concessions from your opponent now, offer to make future concessions which you know you will not follow through on.	1	2	3	4	5	6	7
9. Threaten to make your opponent look weak or foolish in front of a boss or others to whom he/she is accountable, even if you know that you won't actually carry out the threat.	1	2	3	4	5	6	7
10. Deny the validity of information which your opponent has that weakens your negotiating positon, even though that information is true and valid.	1	2	3	4	5	6	7

(© Robinson, Lewicki, and Donahue, 1997)

	Not Appropriate				Very Appropriate		
11. Intentionally misrepresent the progress of negotiations to your constituency in order to make your own position appear stronger.	1	2	3	4	5	6	7
12. Talk directly to the people who your opponent reports to, or is accountable to, and tell them things that will undermine their confidence in your opponent as a negotiator.	1	2	3	4	5	6	7
13. Gain information about an opponent's negotiating position by cultivating his/her friendship through expensive gifts, entertaining or "personal favors."	1	2	3	4	5	6	7
14. Make an opening demand so high/low that it seriously undermines your opponent's confidence in his/her ability to negotiate a satisfactory settlement.	1	2	3	4	5	6	7
15. Guarantee that your constituency will uphold the settlement reached, although you know that they will likely violate the agreement later.	1	2	3	4	5	6	7
16. Gain information about an opponent's negotiating position by trying to recruit or hire one of your opponent's teammates (on the condition that the teammate bring confidential information with him/her).	1	2	3	4	5	6	7

Use the scale to compute averages for the following Dimensions of the Ethics Scale from Chapter 9.

Traditional Competitive Bargaining – #6, 7, 14

Attacking Opponent's Network – #3, 9, 12

False Promises – #1, 8, 15

Misrepresentation – #2, 4, 10, 11

Inappropriate Information Gathering – #5, 13, 16

COMMUNICATION STYLE SURVEY

Carefully consider each of the following statements; then circle the answer that best describes you. If you are torn between two answers, go with your initial reaction. It is more likely to reflect your personal style. When you are finished, use the Scoring Summary sheets to compute your score. Be as honest as you can in your responses, as no one else will need to see them.

You will be using the following key: For each question circle the letter that best represents your response.

A   Not at all like me

B   Not much like me

C   Somewhat like me

D   A lot like me

E   Completely like me

1.	I am not very precise	A	B	C	D	E
2.	I am reserved around strangers	A	B	C	D	E
3.	I like envisioning big projects	A	B	C	D	E
4.	I do not promote an atmosphere of harmony	A	B	C	D	E
5.	I do not follow instructions	A	B	C	D	E
6.	I am courageous	A	B	C	D	E
7.	I lack attention to detail	A	B	C	D	E
8.	I mix easily with new people	A	B	C	D	E
9.	I feel calm and relaxed most of the time	A	B	C	D	E
10.	I am not talkative	A	B	C	D	E
11.	I like big challenges	A	B	C	D	E
12.	I analyze situations carefully	A	B	C	D	E
13.	I maintain a cheerful disposition	A	B	C	D	E
14.	I am shy with new people	A	B	C	D	E
15.	I am persistent	A	B	C	D	E
16.	I am soft-spoken	A	B	C	D	E
17.	I pay attention to detail	A	B	C	D	E

18.	I am quick to challenge the views of others	A	B	C	D	E
19.	I enjoy talking in front of a group	A	B	C	D	E
20.	I am careful and deliberate in making a decision	A	B	C	D	E
21.	I am not peaceful in my inner self	A	B	C	D	E
22.	I am not confident in my abilities	A	B	C	D	E
23.	I am a good team player	A	B	C	D	E
24.	I am daring	A	B	C	D	E
25.	I am focused on getting things done right	A	B	C	D	E
26.	I am even-tempered under most circumstances	A	B	C	D	E
27.	I do not like taking risks	A	B	C	D	E
28.	I am not generous with my time	A	B	C	D	E
29.	I make new friends easily	A	B	C	D	E
30.	I am very cautious	A	B	C	D	E
31.	I am trusting of others	A	B	C	D	E
32.	I am not outgoing	A	B	C	D	E

Source: Adapted from Douglas, E. (1998). *Straight talk: Turning communication upside down for strategic results.* Davies-Black Publishing, Palo Alto, CA. Used by permission of the author.

Glossary

Accommodation approach to negotiation: Adoption of a lose-win strategy because the relationship is more important than the substantive terms of the deal

Active listening: Tools and skills that listeners use to help interpret the speaker's message accurately

Affiliation: The degree of connectedness that one negotiator feels toward the other

Agent: A person who negotiates for others

*Allies: Supporters who are respected by the other party or who possess resources the other party needs

Alternative dispute resolution: A third-party method of resolving differences that does not involve the legal system

Alternatives: A closing tactic in which one party offers multiple choices to the other party

Anchoring and adjustment: Opening offers and other positions set anchors from which adjustments or concessions are made

Anger: An emotional decision-making error in which intense negative feelings are directed at the other party and interfere with our ability to think logically and accurately

Appreciative moves: A strategy that negotiators use to capture applicable synergies and thereby overcome non-productive negotiation tactics and irrelevant issues

Arbitration: An informal judicial process in which disputants organize and present information to persuade neutral third party to decide in their favor

Aspiration levels (a.k.a. target points): What you realistically hope to achieve for each issue

Assuming the close: A closing tactic in which one party assumes the other party has agreed to the deal, even though the other party has not done so

Attitudes: General evaluations people hold about themselves, others, objects and issues

Attribution error: The tendency to attribute others' successes externally and failures internally, and our own successes internally and failures externally

Audience effects: Adopting stronger tactics when others watch us negotiate

Autonomy: A person's freedom to make recommendations and decisions

Availability of information: How easily information is retrieved from memory

Avoidance: A hands-off approach to conflict management

Balance sheet (a.k.a. cost-benefit) closing tactic: One party lists the benefits of their own proposal on one side of a piece of paper and then asks the other party to list their costs on the other side in order to demonstrate that the first party's benefits outweigh the second party's costs

Bargaining mix: The issues to be negotiated

467

Bargaining power: The ability to bring about desired outcomes (Salancik & Pfeffer, 1977)

Best Alternative To a Negotiated Agreement: (BATNA): The best alternative outcome available to you without the other negotiator

Body language (a.k.a. nonverbal communications): The transfer of messages using any means other than the spoken word

Bridging solution: An integrative solution that bridges the gap between incompatible positions

Building rapport: Creating the sense that you and the other party are in sync

Changing the nature of the game: for managing difficult negotiations by responding constructively to the other party's non-constructive approach

Chicken: A tactic that leads to an impasse because neither negotiator will back down

Closing tactics: Tactics that a negotiating party uses to persuade the other party to say yes

Coalitions: A subgroup of the larger social group in multiparty negotiations

Coercive power: The ability to punish, credibly threaten or withhold positive outcomes that the other party wants or needs

Cognitive decision-making errors: Errors that are usually caused by using faulty information-processing shortcuts

Collaborative approach to negotiation (a.k.a. integrative, principled, interest-based, mutual gains and win-win approach): Substantial importance is attached to both the relationship and the substantive terms of the outcome for both parties

Collectivistic cultures: Cultures that promote and protect individuals' interdependencies with their families, social and work groups and communities

Commitment: A strong position combined with a pledge of a specific course of action that can sometimes be perceived as threats

Communication channel: The medium through which messages are sent

Comparison closing tactic: One negotiating party delineates and compares the benefits and/or costs that the other party will derive from different proposals proposal in order to demonstrate the advantages of the desired proposal

Competitive approach to negotiation: Adoption of a win-lose strategy because the substantive terms of the outcome are more important than the relationship

Competitive arousal: An adrenaline-fueled decision-making error in which emotions interfere with our ability to think logically and accurately

Compromise (a.k.a. split the difference) closing tactic: The parties divide in half the difference between each of their last offers

Compromising: A negotiation outcome in which both parties get something they wanted but neither is fully satisfied with the result

Concessions: Reductions in demands made to opening offers

Confirmation trap: The tendency to look for information that supports or justifies our hypotheses and decisions

Contrast principle (a.k.a. relativity): We exaggerate the difference between offers or objects when we make decisions

Corrective turns: Revising or reframing the other negotiator's distortions and misinterpretations by shifting the focus to the positive

Cost-benefit (a.k.a. balance sheet) closing tactic: One party lists the benefits of their own proposal on one side of a piece of paper and then asks the other party to list their costs on the other side in order to demonstrate that the first party's benefits outweigh the second party's costs

Creating value: Expanding the pool of available resources by creating solutions that satisfy all parties' interests

Culture: A country's (or social group's) distinct set of values and norms that govern attitudes and behavior

Cutting the costs for compliance: One party's costs are minimized in return for agreeing to allow the other party to satisfy its interests

Dealcrafting: Creating solutions that help you make deals is unnecessary

Deception: Not telling the truth in order to save face or put the other negotiating party at a disadvantage

Decision-acceptance effect: Compliance with unsatisfactory decisions imposed on us by arbitrators wanes because we do not like being told what to do

Default option: People are more concerned about the risk of change than the benefits of changing, so proposals persuade people to say yes if they preserve the status quo and do not require them to change

Dilemma of honesty: The other party may take advantage of you if you share too much information, but you may not be able to reach an agreement if you share too little (Rubin & Brown, 1975)

Dilemma of trust: The other party may take advantage of you if you believe too much of what he or she tells you, but you may not be able to reach an agreement if you believe too little (Rubin & Brown, 1975)

Dirty Tricks (a.k.a. hardball tactics): Aggressive distributive bargaining tactics in which one party pressures the opposing party into doing something it otherwise would not do

Distributive bargaining: A competitive process for determining how to distribute or allocate scarce resources

Distributive tactics: Tactics that are used to implement the distributive bargaining strategy

Dual Concerns Model: Posits five approaches for handling conflict and negotiation: competition, accommodation, avoidance, compromising and collaboration

Emotional decision-making errors: Biases that are rooted in inconsistencies between feelings and actions, feelings and the judgments we make about them, and feelings that arise at different times during a negotiation

Emotional intelligence: A person's ability to use and understand emotions adaptively in everyday life

Enlisting support: Using allies who are respected by or who possess resources needed by the other negotiating party to ensure receiving a favorable hearing and credibility

Expectations: A perceptual decision-making error in which our experiences match our assumptions: if we think something will be good or bad, it usually is

Expert power: Power derived from a negotiator's special expertise, knowledge, understanding, skills, competencies or technical know-how

Explanations (a.k.a. social accounts): Reasons given for decisions or offers. Explanations are especially important when communicating bad news or negative consequences

Exploding offers: Attempting to close deals using time pressure

Extremism: A perceptual decision-making error in which we believe our own perception map onto objective reality—when others differ we view them as extremists

Fairness and justice: An ethical framework that argues similarly situated people should be treated similarly in terms of the allocation of rewards and burdens, and in terms of the process that is used to determine the allocation

Feedback: Verbal and nonverbal responses to messages that are received

Final offer: A point in the negotiation beyond which a negotiator is unwilling or unable to go

Final offer arbitration: A form of arbitration in which arbitrators must select the party's final offer that he or she thinks is best or closest to the most appropriate solution

Final stage of a negotiation: Typically includes implementing agreements as intended

First impressions: Implicit assumptions that we make about people almost instantaneously upon meeting them, and sometimes even after before we meet them

Five-Factor Model: A personality model that divides personality traits into five categories

Fixed pie: Fixed or limited resources

Flinching: Feigning shock or surprise when the other party extends an offer

Focalism: A tendency to overestimate how much we will think about an event in the future and to underestimate the extent to which other events will influence our thoughts and feelings

Framing: How we say something, not what we say. How a negotiator defines the situation

Gender stereotypes: This often reflects expectations about how members of certain groups behave

Going to the balcony: A strategy that negotiators use to retain objectivity and maintain focus on interests after the other party uses distracting tactics

Good cop-bad cop: A hardball negotiation tactic in which two negotiators in the same party pretend to take different approaches: one opens with a very tough position and the other follows this by playing nice

Half-life effect: People tend to become less satisfied with arbitration the more it is used

Hardball tactics (a.k.a. dirty tricks): Aggressive distributive bargaining tactics in which one party pressures the opposing party into doing something it otherwise would not do

High context cultures: People communicate indirectly; meaning is determined by the words used and by the context in which the conversation takes place

High power distance (hierarchical) cultures: People are more accepting of unequal power distributions; social power is derived from social status, and it usually transfers across situations

Ideological differences: The body of ideas upon which the political, economic and social system is based

Ignoring other's cognitions: A perceptual decision-making error in which we are unable or unwilling to assess another's thoughts, concerns or perspectives

Impact bias: An emotional decision-making error in which we mispredict the intensity or duration of the pleasure or pain that future events will bring

Impression management: A desire to positively manage other's impressions of us

Individual differences: Our unique qualities - gender, personality, emotions and negotiation styles.

Individualistic culture: Cultures that promote and protect individuals' interests

Influence: A process of changing another's attitudes, beliefs and/or behaviors

Informational power: Grounded in substantial differences in the knowledge of two individuals on particular subjects, this reflects the negotiator's ability to control the availability and accuracy of information

Initial stage of a negotiation: Typically includes pre-negotiation preparation, rapport building and additional information gathering (testing assumptions)

Instrumental interests: Something a negotiating party needs or values because it will help him or her in the future

Integrative approach to negotiation (a.k.a. collaborative, principled, interest-based, mutual gains or win-win approach): A collaborate process for creating value to help the parties satisfy their interests

Inter-team negotiations: Negotiations between teams of negotiators

Interest-based approach to negotiation (a.k.a. collaborative, integrative, principled, mutual gains or win-win approach): Substantial importance is attached to both the relationship and the substantive terms of the outcome for both parties

Interests: The motives underlying your positions, your reasons for wanting them or the purposes they will serve for you

Interrupting the move: A tactic in which negotiators pause the negotiation process to counteract non-productive tactics that the other party uses

Intimidation: A form of aggressive behavior, such as anger, guilt, threats, insults, attacks, pushiness, impatience, intransigence and hard-nosed demands, used to make the negotiators appear more powerful in order to impose their position on the other party

Intra-team negotiations: Negotiations between the members of the same team

Intrinsic interests: Something a negotiator needs or values because it will help him or her now

Irrational escalation of commitment: The continuation of a previously selected course of action beyond what rational analysis would recommend

Issues: The specific components or dimensions of the situation that must be addressed

Legal pluralism: Dealing with more than one country's laws when participating in an international negotiation

Legitimate power: Authority derived from a negotiator's age, social status, caste, or rights derived from his or her position, role or title in an organization

Logrolling: A solution process in which parties maximize joint gain by finding trades that capitalize on their differences

Losing face: A loss of image or status in the eyes of others

Lose-win approach to negotiation (aka accomodation): Negotiating party cares more about preserving the relationship with the other party than winning

Low context cultures: People communicate directly; meaning is determined by the words used

Low power distance (egalitarian) cultures: People are less accepting of unequal power distributions; Power is largely derived from negotiators' BATNAs

Lowball-highball: An aggressive distributive bargaining tactic in which negotiators begin with an extremely high or low opening offer in order to convince the other negotiators to temper their demands

Machiavellianism: A cynical, unsympathetic and opportunistic attitude toward others

Mandatory arbitration: Clients, customers and employees are required to arbitrate all disputes rather than pursue legal action

Mediation: An extension or elaboration of the negotiation process in which a neutral third party facilitates communication between the negotiating parties to help them reach an agreement

Message decoding: How attitudes, beliefs, values, work experiences, culture, desires, needs and knowledge influence how receivers interpret messages

Message encoding: How attitudes, beliefs, values, work experiences, culture, desires, needs and knowledge influence what senders of messages say and how they say it

Meyers-Briggs Type Inventory: A continuum of dispositions that reflects the behavior we tend toward and are most comfortable with in most situations

Middle stage of a negotiation: Typically includes formulating arguments and counterarguments, exchanging offers and counteroffers and closing the deal

Mixed-motive negotiation: Negotiators must cooperate enough to reach an agreement and compete enough to claim sufficient value for themselves

Mood: An emotional decision-making error in which we allow our emotional state to influence our decisions

Motivational orientation: A person's tendency to negotiate more cooperatively or competitively

Multiparty negotiations: Negotiations involving more than two parties

Multiple equivalent offers: A closing tactic in which one party offers more than one choice to the other party, and all of the offers are nearly equivalent

Mutual gains approach to negotiation (a.k.a. collaborative, integrative, principled, interest-based and win-win approach): A collaborate process for creating value to help the parties satisfy their interests

Naming the move: Calling attention to the other negotiator's use of unproductive tactics

Narcotic effect: The tendency to choose arbitration over negotiation too quickly because the latter can be difficult and agreements are not guaranteed

Negotiation: A social process by which interdependent people with conflicting interests determine how they will allocate resources or work together in the future

Negotiauctions: To simplify procedural complexity when multiple bidders exist for goods or services, conduct auctions to eliminate the lowest bidders on price and then negotiate with the highest bidders to determine which bidder prevails and to work out the details on other issues

Nibble: After negotiating for some time, in which a negotiator asks for a small concession on an issue that has not yet been discussed to close the deal

Noise: Any disturbance that interferes with the transmission of a message

Nonspecific compensation: A solution in which one party is paid off for allowing the other to satisfy its interests

Nonverbal communication (a.k.a. body language): The transfer of messages using any means other than the spoken word

Outcome bias: People tend to overlook ethically questionable behavior unless the outcome is harmful

Overconfidence/overoptimism: A decision-making error in which negotiators overestimate their abilities or the occurrence of positive events, and underestimate the occurrence of negative events

Perceptual decision-making errors: Interpersonal biases that have their roots in faulty perceptions of social entities and situations

Perspective taking: The ability to consider the situation from another's point of view

Political pluralism: Dealing with more than one country's politics when participating in an international negotiation

Position: Commonly an offer or a counteroffer, it is one possible outcome

Positional negotiation (a.k.a. distributive, zero-sum and win-lose negotiation): A competitive process for determining how to distribute or allocate scarce resources

Power: The ability to effect desired outcomes or to work effectively with the other party

Pressure moves: Tactics that make the status quo unattractive or raise the cost of business as usual

Principle interests: Intangible interests that pertain to strongly held beliefs (e.g., what is right and wrong)

Principled approach to negotiation (a.k.a. collaborative, integrative, interest-based, mutual gains and win-win approach): A collaborate process for creating value to help the parties satisfy their interests

Prosocials: People with this personality trait prefer options that maximize joint gain

Process interests: Interests pertaining to how a deal is made or how a dispute is settled

Proselfs: People with this personality trait prefer options that maximize their own gain

Reactive devaluation: A perceptual decision-making error in which we discount offers or concessions because of who made them

Reciprocal questioning approach: Negotiators ask questions about interests and priorities, assume the other party is telling the truth and then reciprocate with their own information

Reciprocity: The act of returning a favor, even when the favor was unsolicited or unwanted

Reference points: Points or values against which you compare offers

Referent power: Power derived from being liked, because the other negotiator can identify with you or because he or she wants to be like you – all because you have integrity, because of your personality, or because you are attractive, charismatic, credible and trustworthy

Reject then retreat: When one negotiating party makes an extreme demand that is rejected by the other party, and then comes back with a smaller demand

Relationship interests: Interests pertaining to the nature of the relationship you want to have with the other party

Relativity (a.k.a. contrast principle): We exaggerate the difference between offers or objects when we make decisions

Representative: A person who negotiates for others

Reservation price (a.k.a. resistance point or walk away price): Your breakeven point or the worst acceptable outcome for each issue. You would rather walk away without an agreement if you cannot achieve terms that are better than or equal to this point

Resistance point (a.k.a. reservation price or walk away price): Your breakeven point or the worst acceptable outcome for each issue. You would rather walk away without an agreement if you cannot achieve terms that are better than or equal to this point

Reward power: The ability to give the other negotiator items that he or she values, or to credibly promise these items – money, information, tangible resources, approval or other items that he or she wants or needs

Rights and duties: An ethical framework that argues people are governed by certain universal rights and that these rights impose upon themselves and others a corresponding duty

Selective attention: The tendency to notice information that supports or justifies our hypotheses and decisions and to not notice information that contradicts them

Self-efficacy: A person's assessment of how well he or she can perform in a particular situation

Self-monitoring: A person's sensitivity to the social cues that emanate from the social environment

Sequential questions: A closing tactic that uses a sequence of questions which begins with a question that is sure to elicit a yes response and continues with questions that lead logically and incrementally from the first question

Shadow negotiation: The subtle games negotiators play that underlie the substantive aspects of the negotiation, including strategic movies, strategic turns and appreciative moves

Six Hat Thinking: A structured approach to multiparty negotiations that encourages forward-focused and creative thinking that leads to beneficial solutions and consensus

Snow job: An aggressive negotiation tactic in which one party inundates the other with so much information that it is not possible to determine what is accurate or relevant

Social accounts (a.k.a. explanations): Reasons given for decisions or offers. Explanations are especially important when communicating bad news or negative consequences

Social contract: An ethical framework that argues an action is ethical if it is consistent with or is grounded in a community's social norms that govern the interaction

Social value orientation: A personality trait that reflects an individuals' preferences for their own outcomes relative to others' outcomes

Split the difference (a.k.a. compromise) closing tactic: The parties divide in half the difference between each of their last offers

Status: A person's standing relative to where others stand

Status quo bias: People are more concerned about the risk of change than the benefits of changing, so proposals persuade people to say yes if they preserve the status quo and do not require them to change

Stereotypes: A perceptual decision-making error in which our expectations influence our perceptions of members of a particular group

Strategic moves: Tactics that persuade the other party to come to the bargaining table and to give your interests and arguments a fair hearing

Strategic turns: Tactics that help reframe the negotiation when it moves in an unproductive direction

Strategy: The plan or process by which negotiators attempt to achieve their goals

Structural connection: Affiliation increases when you and the other negotiator are members of a common group

Structuring conversations: Determining who speaks, when, to whom and for how long

Substantive interests: Interests pertaining to the tangible issues being negotiated

Substantive negotiation terms: The tangible items you negotiate.

Sweeteners (a.k.a. sweeting the deal): A closing tactic in which one party offers a final concession if the other party accepts their offer

Tactics: The specific, short-term actions that serve to implement the broader strategy

Target points (a.k.a. aspiration levels): What you realistically hope to achieve for each issue

The biasing effect: A potential problem with arbitration in which it appears that the arbitrator systematically favors one side over the other

The chilling effect: A potential problem with arbitration in which disputants believe that achieving an acceptable solution is unlikely and as a result they do not adopt strategies that will lead to compromise or finding mutually beneficial solutions

Face Threat Sensitivity: How sensitive people are to losing face

Two-sided messages: Messages that acknowledge the other negotiator's argument and then refute it

Utilitarianism: An ethical framework that argues an action is ethical if it produces the greatest good for the greatest number of people affected by it

Walk away price (a.k.a. reservation price or resistance point): Your breakeven point or the worst acceptable outcome for each issue. You would rather walk away without an agreement if you cannot achieve terms that are better than or equal to this point

Win-lose (a.k.a. distributive, positional and zero-sum negotiating): A competitive process for determining how to distribute or allocate scarce resources

Win-win approach to negotiation (a.k.a. collaborative, integrative, principled, interest-based, mutual gains approach): A collaborate process for creating value to help the parties satisfy their interests

Winner's curse: Getting what you want too easily and being unhappy with it

Wise agreement: One that satisfies your interests and, perhaps, the other party's (Fisher et al., 1991)

Zero-sum negotiation (a.k.a. distributive, positional and win-lose negotiation): A competitive process for determining how to distribute or allocate scarce resources

Zone of possible agreement (ZOPA): The range between your resistance points

Index

Note: In page references, f indicates figures and t indicates tables

Accommodation approach to negotiations:
  communications and, 166
  definition of, 465
  dual concerns model and, 8–9
Accountability:
  e-mail communications and, 185
  emotional issues and, 353
  ethics and, 273
  international negotiations and, 364
Active listening:
  communications and, 89, 168
  definition of, 465
Adjustment, 211–212
  decision-making and, 213t
  definition of, 465
Affiliation:
  closing deals and, 120
  concessions, 164
  emotional issues and, 334
Aggressive behaviors:
  communications and, 169
  hardball tactics/dirty tricks and, 69
  integrative negotiations and, 87
  See also Behavior
Allies:
  definition of, 465
  difficult negotiations and, 387
  international negotiations and, 375
  power/influence and, 240t, 241, 252
  social proof and, 247
Alternative Dispute Resolution (ADR), 410–411
  arbitration and, 416
  definition of, 465
Alternatives:
  BATNAs and, 61

closing deals and, 125
  communications and, 165
  decision-making and, 208–209
  definition of, 465
  difficult negotiations and, 385
  distributive bargaining and, 60
Ambiguity:
  commitments and, 71
  e-mail negotiations and, 184
  ethics and, 282
  integrative negotiations and, 105
American arbitration association, 410, 427
Anchors:
  decision-making and, 211–212, 211t, 213t, 222
  definition of, 465
  distributive bargaining and, 72
  first offers and, 64
  international negotiations and, 364, 366
  opening offers and, 63
Anger:
  definition of, 465
  difficult negotiations and, 392–393
  emotional decision-making errors and, 221t
  emotional issues and, 218, 351, 352
  hardball tactics/dirty tricks and, 69
Anonymity, 14, 16, 185, 191, 194
Anxiety:
  difficult negotiations and, 395, 399
  e-mail communications and, 189–190
Appreciative moves, 11
  definition of, 465
  difficult negotiations and, 390–392, 399
  emotional issues and, 334
  multiparty negotiations and, 313

Arbitration:
  ADR and, 411
  definition of, 465
  third-party interventions and, 415–420
Ariely, D., 207
Aspiration levels, 31–32
  definition of, 465
  distributive bargaining and, 59
Assertiveness:
  empathy and, 20–21
  gender issues and, 326, 345
Assumptions:
  building/testing, 36–37
  challenging, 55–56
  closing deals and, 120, 127, 465
  culture and, 361
  decision-making and, 207, 212, 217
  difficult negotiations and, 386
  distributive bargaining and, 72
  e-mail communications and, 188–189
  estimating the other party's resistance points
    and, 61
  ethics and, 283
  hardball tactics/dirty tricks and, 69
  international negotiations and, 361, 362, 363,
    365, 370–371
  inter-team negotiations and, 312
  multiparty negotiations and, 299, 300
  mythical fixed pie and, 213–214
  opening offers and, 63
  power/influence and, 237–238
  testing, 10
Attitudes:
  communications and, 161
  culture and, 378
  definition of, 465
  ethics and, 271, 275
  harnessing the science of persuasion and,
    260, 261
  power/influence and, 237, 239, 241, 243,
    244–245, 252–253
Attribution error:
  definition of, 465
  perceptual decision-making errors
    and, 217t
Audience effects:
  competitive arousal and, 218
  multiparty negotiations and, 308, 309
  strategic complexity and, 300

Autonomy:
  closing deals and, 120
  definition of, 465
  structural connection and, 334–335
Availability biases:
  decision-making and, 211
  ethics and, 277
  See also Biases
Availability of information:
  cognitive decision-making errors and, 210, 213t
  definition of, 465
Avoidance approach to negotiations:
  definition of, 465
  dual concerns model and, 8–9

Background investigations, 302
Backward mapping, 114–115
Balance sheets:
  closing deals and, 125
  definition of, 466
Bargaining mix, 38
  issues and, 30–31
Bargaining power, 35, 466
  See also Power
Bazerman, M. H., 225
Behavior:
  arbitrary anchors and, 211t
  communications and, 169
  contentious, 185–186
  culture and, 361
  ethics and, 268, 269, 270, 271t, 272, 277, 283
    See also Ethics
  gender issues and, 326, 327
  goals and, 30
  harnessing the science of persuasion and,
    259, 261
  international negotiations and, 361, 369
  mirroring other party's, 174
  personality issues and, 328
  power/influence and, 237, 241, 243, 244–245
  See also Aggressive behaviors
Beliefs:
  communications and, 161
  culture and, 361
  ethics and, 269
  international negotiations and,
    361, 362, 369
  multiparty negotiations and, 299, 306
  power/influence and, 241, 243, 244–245

Best Alternative To A Negotiated Agreement
    (BATNA), 22, 32–33
  arbitration and, 423
  bargaining power and, 35
  communications and, 165
  deadlines and, 67
  decision-making and, 212
  definition of, 466
  difficult negotiations and, 385, 403
  distributive bargaining and, 60, 63, 72, 73
  3-D negotiations and, 108, 109, 110, 111, 114
  estimating the other party's resistance points
    and, 61
  ethics and, 282
  first offers and, 64
  haggling and, 79, 80, 81
  hardball tactics/dirty tricks and, 69
  impact biases and, 219
  individual differences and, 339
  integrative negotiations and, 87, 92
  international negotiations and, 362
  inter-team negotiations and, 312
  multiparty negotiations and, 303, 304
  negotiating with inferior powers and,
    250–251
  power/influence and, 239, 240, 240t, 249, 252,
    253, 256, 257, 258
  preparations and, 39
  quantifying a, 34
  status and, 335
  structural connection and, 334
  third-party interventions and, 410
  understanding/improving, 61–62
  understanding your opponent and, 202
  walk aways and, 68
Bhappu, A. D., 182
Biases:
  arbitration and, 416
  availability, 211, 277
  cognitive, 207, 208–212
  decision-making errors and, 207–208
  e-mail communications and, 186, 188
  ethics and, 275, 288
  impact, 219–220, 221t, 468
  inter-team negotiations and, 311
  managing negotiation teams and, 318
  outcome, 274
  overconfidence, 212
  perceptual, 207

  status quo, 126, 472
  women and, 343
Biasing effect:
  arbitration and, 416
  definition of, 473
  See also Biases
Black hat thinking, 307t, 308
Blame, 438, 440
  ADR and, 411
  arbitration and, 417
  closing deals and, 128
  communications and, 165
  difficult negotiations and, 390, 396, 397, 399
  e-mail communications and, 190
  integrative negotiations and, 90
  mediation and, 414
Blue hat thinking, 307t, 308
Bluffing, 21
  analyzing the other party and, 35
  ethics and, 270, 275, 276, 292, 293
  hardball tactics/dirty tricks and, 69, 70
Body language, 438
  communications and, 162t, 172–176
  culture and, 378
  definition of, 466
  e-mail communications and, 183, 184
  testing assumptions and, 37
  See also Nonverbal communications
Bogey, 69
  definition of, 466
  difficult negotiations and, 385
Booth, B., 103
Bribery:
  ethics and, 276, 278, 280
  international negotiations and, 357
Bridging solution:
  dealcrafting and, 100
  green hat thinking and, 306
  integrative negotiations and, 94
Brown, J. G., 182
Building rapport *See* Rapport

Caucuses:
  mediation and, 413
  multiparty negotiations and, 313
  third-party intervention and, 445, 453
Change, 7
  closing deals and, 118–119, 126, 128
  harnessing the science of persuasion and, 259

international negotiations and, 358–359
power/influence and, 244, 252–253
Changing the nature of the game:
definition of, 466
difficult negotiations and, 384, 386, 392, 395
Chicken:
definition of, 466
difficult negotiations and, 385
take-it-or-leave-it offers and, 21
Chilling effect:
arbitration and, 416
definition of, 473
special challenges and, 428
Chugh, D., 225
Closing deals, 117–129
Coalitions:
difficult negotiations and, 403
multiparty negotiations and, 300, 309–311, 312
negotiating with inferior powers and, 251
Coercive power, 239–240, 240t, 252
definition of, 466
See also Power
Cognitive biases, 207, 208–212
See also Biases
Cognitive decision-making errors, 231t, 466
Cognitive frames, 209
See also Frames
Collaboration, 466
communications and, 165, 166
culture and, 378
distributive bargaining and, 58
dual concerns model and, 8–9
integrative negotiations and, 83
multiparty negotiations and, 311
power/influence and, 238
roles and, 336
strategies and, 30
women and, 344
Collectivistic cultures:
definition of, 466
international negotiations and, 362, 363, 364, 365
See also Culture
Collectivist negotiators, 365
Commitment, 71–72
definition of, 466
difficult negotiations and, 385
hardball tactics/dirty tricks and, 70
multiparty negotiations and, 303
power/influence and, 247–248

Communications, 159–178
arbitration and, 423
channel, 161, 466
closing deals and, 120–121
culture and, 377, 378–379
difficult negotiations and, 390, 395–397, 406
3-D negotiations and, 108
elements of, 160f
ethics and, 270
integrative negotiations and, 88, 89–90, 100
international negotiations and, 362, 363
managing negotiation teams and, 319–320
multiparty negotiations and, 300, 303
negotiating with inferior powers and, 251
negotiations and, 163–168
nonverbal, 172–176, 185, 471
patterns of, 166
power/influence and, 253
styles, 163
third-party interventions and, 410, 411
See also E-mail communications
Comparison closing tactic, 124–125, 466
Competitive arousal:
definition of, 466
emotional biases and, 218–219
emotional decision-making errors and, 221t
Competitive negotiations, 440
communications and, 164
definition of, 466
distributive bargaining and, 57–58
dual concerns model and, 8–9
e-mail communications and, 185, 186–187
ethics and, 276, 282
goals and, 29–30
international negotiations and, 364, 370
investigative negotiations and, 56
mythical fixed pie and, 213–214
negotiations and, 11
power/influence and, 238, 239
strategies and, 30
women and, 343
Compromise, 75–77
closing deals and, 124
definition of, 466
distributive bargaining and, 72
dual concerns model and, 8–9
integrative negotiations and, 87, 98
Computer-mediated communicators, 13–18
See also E-mail communications

Concessions, 81, 447
  closing deals and, 120, 124, 126
  communications and, 163, 164–165
Confidence:
  closing deals and, 122, 125
  culture and, 380
  decision-making and, 212
  first impressions and, 173
  gender issues and, 338
  mediation and, 412, 414
  multiparty negotiations and, 303, 313
  negotiation places and, 37–38
  online dispute resolutions and, 14
Confidentiality, 134, 135, 294
  mediation and, 413
Confirmation trap, 208, 210, 231t
  definition of, 466
Conflict:
  managing negotiation teams and, 316–317, 318
  negotiating teams and, 320–322
Conflicts of interest, 272, 289
  managing negotiation teams and, 316, 317,
    318, 320
Consensus-seeking:
  international negotiations and, 373–375
  multiparty negotiations and, 308, 312
Consistency:
  closing deals and, 128
  decision-making and, 208
  power/influence and, 247–248
  principle for, 261–263
Constraints:
  explanations and, 165
  legal pluralism and, 356
  motivational orientation and, 332
  preparations and, 53, 55
  strategic planning and, 28
  third-party interventions and, 411
Contrast principle:
  definition of, 467
  power/influence and, 245–246, 247
Cooperation, 443
  communications and, 170t
  dual concerns model and, 8–9
  e-mail communications and,
    185, 186–187, 188
  goals and, 29–30
  harnessing the science of persuasion and, 261
  international negotiations and, 364
  negotiations and, 11

Corrective turns, 388–389, 467
Cost-benefits, 125, 467
Costs See Economic issues
Counterarguments, 10, 88, 120
  closing deals and, 120
  procedural complexities and, 299–300
Counteroffers:
  closing deals and, 118
  communications and, 161, 163, 169
  distributive bargaining and, 72
  3-D negotiations and, 108
  haggling and, 81
  international negotiations and, 364–365, 366
  multiparty negotiations and, 303
  positions and, 31
Creating value, 56
  affiliation and, 334
  closing deals and, 131
  dual concerns model and, 8–9
  ethics and, 283
  at the expense of outsiders, 287–288
  integrative negotiations and, 111–113
  power/status and, 326
  sharing perspectives and, 414
  strategy for, 30, 83–100
Creative thinking:
  factors that increase, 93t
  inter-team negotiations and, 311
  multiparty negotiations and, 306
  suggestions for increasing, 94–96
Credibility:
  difficult negotiations and, 387
  first impressions and, 173
Cues:
  e-mail communications and, 183, 184, 188
  negotiation places and, 37–38
  nonverbal communications and,
    172, 173, 178
  online dispute resolutions and, 14–15
  social, 185
  visual, 37–38
  vocal, 174
Culture:
  collectivistic, 362, 363, 364, 365, 466
  communications and, 161, 162t
  definition of, 361, 467
  e-mail communications and, 184
  high context/collectivistic,
    363, 364, 468
  individualistic, 362, 363, 364, 365, 366, 469

international negotiations and, 355, 356,
    359–365, 369, 372, 373, 374, 375,
    376–382
low context/individualistic, 363, 364, 366, 469
low/high context, 363
multiparty negotiations and, 308
women and, 343
See also Customs
Currency issues, 356, 365–366
Customs:
    ethics and, 279–280
    individual differences and, 338
    integrative negotiations and, 96
    See also Culture
Cutting compliance costs, 95, 467

Deadlines:
    distributive bargaining and, 66–67
    3-D negotiations and, 108
    integrative negotiations and, 88
    See also Time issues
Dealcrafting, 100, 218
Deception:
    alternatives to, 284t
    behavioral cues and, 177t
    definition of, 467
    detecting, 175–176
    difficult negotiations and, 385
    ethics and, 276, 282, 283
    nonverbal communications and, 172, 173
    See also Honesty
Decision-acceptance effect, 416, 467
Decision biases, 250
    See also Biases
Decision-making, 205–222
    alternatives to, 284
    arbitration and, 416, 418–419
    autonomy and, 335
    closing deals and, 122
    culture and, 380, 381
    difficult negotiations and, 403, 404
    emotional issues and, 351
    ethics and, 272, 274, 277, 279, 280
    international negotiations and, 362, 368, 369,
        370, 371, 372, 373, 374, 375, 376
    mediation and, 411
    multiparty negotiations and, 304–305
Decision-making errors:
    emotional, 221t
    ethics and, 283

multiparty negotiations and, 299
perceptual, 217t
power/influence and, 245, 250, 253
summary of cognitive, 213t
Default options, 126, 467
Defining the situation:
    integrative negotiations and, 84
    preparations and, 38
    strategic planning and, 25–26
Demands:
    communications and, 167
    ethics and, 282
Democracy:
    international negotiations and, 357, 372
    multiparty negotiations and, 304–305
Difficult negotiations, 383–399
    alternatives and, 385
    anger and, 392–393
    anxiety and, 395, 399
    appreciative moves and, 390–392, 399
    assumptions and, 386
    BATNAs and, 385, 403
    blame and, 390, 396, 397, 399
    bogey and, 385
    changing the nature of the game and, 384, 386,
        392, 395
    chicken and, 385
    coalitions and, 403
    commitment and, 385
    communications and, 390, 395–397, 406
    corrective turns and, 388–389
    credibility and, 387
    deception and, 385
    decision-making and, 403, 404
    dirty tricks and, 384, 385, 386, 399
    e-mail communications and, 392
    emotional issues and, 385, 390, 396, 399, 401
    enlisting support and, 387
    expectations and, 384, 390
    feedback and, 396
    frames and, 384, 385, 390
    frustrations and, 385
    goals and, 384
    going to the balcony and, 392
    good cop-bad cop and, 385
    identity issues and, 396, 397
    impasses and, 384–385, 386
    interests and, 386, 398, 399, 407
    interrupting the move and, 393
    intimidation and, 384

issues and, 386
legal issues and, 407
losing face and, 385
naming the move and, 388
needs and, 391
norms and, 401
open-ended questions and, 397, 399
personality issues and, 390
positions and, 390
power and, 385, 397–398, 399
pressure moves and, 386–387
problem solving and, 385, 386, 393–395, 396, 397
proposals and, 386
rapport and, 390
relationship interests and, 384, 392, 397–398, 399
resources and, 385
respect and, 390, 399
rhetoric and, 392
rules and, 385
saving face and, 390
shadow negotiations and, 386, 392
snow jobs and, 385
status quo and, 387
strategic moves and, 386–387
strategic turns and, 387–389, 399
time issues and, 385
ultimatums and, 385
walk aways and, 404
Dilemma of honesty, 35, 467
See also Honesty
Dirty tricks, 68–71
definition of, 467
difficult negotiations and, 384, 385, 386, 399
distributive bargaining and, 72–73
3-D negotiations and, 108
Dishonesty, 265, 302, 329
See also Deception; Distrust; Honesty; Truth
Dispute resolutions, online, 13–18
Disrespect:
closing deals and, 127
culture and, 378
international negotiations and, 369
See also Respect
Distributive negotiations, 57–73, 72
bargaining power and, 35
definition of, 467
dual concerns model and, 8–9
hardball tactics/dirty tricks and, 68–71

integrative negotiations and, 83
preparations and, 59–60
strategies and, 30
Distrust, 439
e-mail communications and, 185, 189
ethics and, 270
integrative negotiations and, 98
See also Dishonesty; Honesty; Trust
3-D negotiations, 107–116
BATNAs and, 108, 109, 110, 111, 114
communications and, 108
counteroffers and, 108
deadlines and, 108
dirty tricks and, 108
personality issues and, 108
trust and, 108
walk aways and, 108
Dual concerns model, 8–9, 9f
communications and, 166
definition of, 467
distributive bargaining and, 57–58
integrative negotiations and, 84
negotiation styles and, 332
Duties:
ethics and, 271, 277–278, 280t

Ebner, N., 182
Economic issues:
arbitration and, 423
civil litigation and, 410
closing deals and, 128
international negotiations and, 356, 365–366
legal actions and, 405–406
multiparty negotiations and, 310
objections and, 121
strategic planning and, 29
Effective/ineffective negotiators, 325t
Egocentrism:
decision-making and, 215
decision-making errors and, 217t
illusion of transparency and, 216
integrative negotiations and, 93–94
E-mail communications, 5, 15, 16, 17, 38
communications and, 169, 170t, 182–196
difficult negotiations and, 392
emotional issues and, 88
international negotiations and, 365
See also Communications; Technology
Emotional decision-making errors, 221t, 467

Emotional intelligence, 337
definition of, 467
individual differences and, 333
negotiation styles and, 332
Emotional issues, 350–353
biases and, 207–208, 218–220
communications and, 167, 169
culture and, 379
decision-making and, 213t
detecting deceptions and, 175–176
difficult negotiations and, 385, 390, 396,
399, 401
e-mail communications and, 184, 185, 190
ethics and, 276
individual differences and, 332–339
integrative negotiations and, 88–89, 100
managing, 392–393
managing negotiation teams and, 318
mediation and, 414
multiparty negotiations and, 301, 306,
308–309, 313
negotiating team conflict and, 322
positive/negative, 332–334, 333t, 338
third-party interventions and, 410
Empathy:
assertiveness and, 20–21
distributive bargaining and, 72
e-mail communications and, 192, 195–196
mediation and, 412
Endowment effect:
decision-making and, 211–212
emotional issues and, 351–352
Enlisting support, 387, 467
Equality:
of fairness, 67, 68t
ideological differences and, 359
social value orientation and, 329
Equity:
of fairness, 67, 68t
second generation of biases and, 343
Ethics, 267–284
guidelines for, 290
hardball tactics/dirty tricks and, 69, 70
integrative negotiations and, 87
negotiation tactics and, 280t
questionable tactics and, 276t
schools of bargaining, 291–295
European countries, 51, 52, 109, 126
arbitration and, 421
culture and, 360

international negotiations and, 369, 370, 375,
376, 379
political pluralism and, 357
third-party intervention and, 421, 434, 435, 436
Exaggeration, 275
Exchange rates, 356, 365
Expectations:
decision-making and, 214
definition of, 467
difficult negotiations and, 384, 390
first offers and, 63
integrative negotiations and, 98
perceptual decision-making errors and, 217t
Expert power, 240t, 467
See also Power
Explanations:
communications and, 165–166
definition of, 468
integrative negotiations and, 97
power/influence and, 245
Exploding offers, 127, 468
Extremism:
biases and, 216
definition of, 468
perceptual decision-making errors and, 217t
Eye contact:
communications and, 174
e-mail communications and, 195
turn taking behaviors and, 175t

Face-to-face negotiations:
communications and, 169, 170t
decision-making and, 216
e-mail communications and, 184, 185, 186,
188, 189, 191, 192, 193, 194, 195
international negotiations and, 365
Facial expressions:
behavioral cues suggesting deceit and, 177t
communications and, 174
detecting deceptions and, 175–176
e-mail communications and, 183
Fairness:
definition of, 468
distributive bargaining and, 67, 68t
ethics and, 271, 278–279, 280t
integrative negotiations and, 96, 97
False promises, 276t
Favoritism:
ethics and, 275
in-group, 288

Fear:
    objections and, 122–123
    power/influence and, 243
Federal arbitration act, 423
Feedback:
    closing deals and, 119
    communications and, 161, 169
    difficult negotiations and, 396
    e-mail communications and, 183, 188
    international negotiations and, 366
    nonverbal communications and, 173
Final offer arbitration, 416, 426–429
    definition of, 468
Final offers:
    chilling effect and, 416
    definition of, 468
    risk of arbitration and, 426, 427
    traditional arbitration and, 428
Final outcomes:
    first offers and, 63
    international negotiations and, 365
    mediation and, 411
    reservation prices and, 33, 59
Final stage of negotiations, 10f, 12, 468
First impressions:
    communications and, 173
    definition of, 468
    determinants of positive/negative, 174t
    nonverbal communications and, 173
    testing assumptions and, 37
First offers:
    distributive bargaining and,
        63–65, 66, 72
    haggling and, 80, 81
    understanding your opponent and, 202
Five-factor model:
    definition of, 468
    personality issues and, 329–330, 330t
Fixed pie:
    definition of, 468
    integrative negotiations and, 87
    mythical, 93, 120, 213–214, 216, 217t, 365
Flinching, 67, 72, 468
Focalism:
    decision-making errors and, 219
    definition of, 468
    emotional decision-making errors and, 221t
    managing emotional biases and, 220
Frames:
    cognitive, 209

    decision-making and, 209–210, 212–213, 213t,
        233–236
    definition of, 468
    difficult negotiations and, 384, 385, 390
    e-mail communications and, 193
    international negotiations and, 360, 364
    managing emotional biases and, 220
    mediation and, 414
Fraud:
    ethics and, 268, 274
    legal issues and, 282
    management-level, 211
    poker school and, 292
Fundamental attribution error, 188, 270, 365
    decision-making and, 215

Gazing patterns, 176
Gender issues:
    deeply seated beliefs about, 346
    ethics and, 271t, 275, 288
    individual differences and, 324–328, 324t,
        337–339
    women and, 342–346
Gender schemas, 343
Gender stereotypes, 324
Gestures:
    behavioral cues suggesting deceit and, 177t
    communications and, 174, 175t
    culture and, 378
Globalization:
    ethics and, 280
    strategic planning and, 29
Goals:
    analyzing the other party and, 35
    arbitration and, 421, 424
    collectivistic cultures and, 362
    culture and, 377
    decision-making and, 212
    difficult negotiations and, 384
    distributive bargaining and, 58, 72
    emotional issues and, 351
    ethics and, 272
    fairness norms and, 68t
    gender issues and, 326
    hardball tactics/dirty tricks and, 69
    integrative negotiations and, 84
    international negotiations and, 364, 374
    inter-team negotiations and, 312
    managing negotiation teams and, 316, 317
    mediation and, 412–413

multiparty negotiations and, 299, 304, 310, 313
negotiating team conflict and, 321
negotiating with inferior powers and, 251
personality issues and, 328
power/influence and, 252
preparations and, 24, 38
strategic planning and, 25, 29–30
substantive, 29, 30
women and, 344, 345
Going to the balcony:
definition of, 468
difficult negotiations and, 392, 393, 399
Good cop-bad cop:
definition of, 468
difficult negotiations and, 385
hardball tactics/dirty tricks and, 69
Greed:
detecting deception and, 175
ethics and, 287
Green hat thinking, 306, 307t, 308
Guilt:
distributive bargaining and, 75
hardball tactics/dirty tricks and, 69
managing, 392
positive/negative emotions and, 333t

Haggling, 78–81
Half-life effect, 416, 468
Hardball tactics, 68–71, 468
Harm:
communications and, 165
ethics and, 273, 274, 278, 283
Harmonizers, 163
Highball, 69, 470
High context cultures, 363, 364, 468
High power distance cultures, 362, 468
Honesty:
analyzing the other party and, 35
detecting deceptions and, 175–176
e-mail communications and, 192
ethics and, 275, 277, 283
integrative negotiations and, 98
international negotiations and, 366
power/influence and, 250
structural connection and, 334
See also Deception; Distrust; Truth

Ideological differences, 359, 468
Ignoring others' cognitions, 215, 468
Illusion of transparency, 216, 217t

Impact biases:
decision-making errors and, 219–220, 221t
definition of, 468
See also Biases
Impasses:
closing deals and, 133
communications and, 165
culture and, 360
decision-making and, 217, 219
difficult negotiations and, 384–385, 386, 387, 397, 398
integrative bargaining and, 88
structural positions and, 327
successful negotiations and, 5
third-party interventions and, 411
Implicit Association Test (IAT), 37, 288, 345
Impression management, 208, 213t, 469
Indirect route, 244–245
Individual differences, 323–339
BATNAs and, 339
customs and, 338
emotional issues and, 332–339
gender issues and, 324–328, 324t, 337–339
negotiation styles and, 332
norms and, 338
personality issues and, 328–331, 337–339
power and, 338
ZOPA and, 338
Individualistic culture, 362, 363, 364, 365, 366
definition of, 469
See also Culture
Individualist negotiators, 365
Influence, 237–253, 469
See also Power
Informational power, 240t, 469
See also Power
Information gathering, 10, 250, 276
Initial stage of negotiations, 10f, 469
Institutions:
culture and, 361
international negotiations and, 362
Instrumental interests, 91, 469
Insults, personal, 21, 69, 185
Integrative negotiations, 83–100
definition of, 469
dual concerns model and, 8–9
strategies and, 30
Integrative solutions:
closing deals and, 120
communications and, 187, 188

integrative negotiations and, 92, 97–98
negotiating with inferior powers and, 251
types of, 94
Interest-based negotiations:
    authority and, 302
    decision-making and, 213
    definition of, 469
    dual concerns model and, 8–9
    integrative bargaining and, 84
    legal issues and, 406
    perspective taking and, 202
Interests:
    analyzing the other party and, 35
    closing deals and, 118, 119–120, 123, 128
    communications and, 160, 167
    component parts of the situation and, 31
    definition of, 469
    different combinations of, 72
    difficult negotiations and, 386, 398, 399, 407
    distributive bargaining and, 73
    e-mail communications and, 186
    ethics and, 269, 283
    first impressions and, 173
    gender issues and, 325
    haggling and, 81
    integrative negotiations and, 84, 85, 87, 88,
        90–92, 95, 98, 100
    international negotiations and, 361, 363, 364,
        365, 366, 374, 375
    inter-team negotiations and, 311, 312
    managing negotiation teams and, 316, 319
    mediation and, 414, 415
    multiparty negotiations and, 299, 300, 301,
        302–303, 306, 309, 310, 311, 313
    negotiating team conflict and, 321
    negotiating with inferior powers and, 251
    power/influence and, 250, 252, 253
    preparations and, 38
International negotiations, 355–366
    currency and, 356, 365–366
    hidden challenges of, 368–376
Internet:
    e-mail communications and, 185 .See also
        E-mail communications
    negotiation places and, 38
    online dispute resolutions and, 13–18
Interrupting the move, 393, 469
Inter-team negotiations, 297, 298, 311–312
Interviews:
    multiparty negotiations and, 302, 312, 318, 319

power/influence and, 264
    preparations and, 36
Intimacy:
    gender issues and, 325
    online dispute resolutions and, 14–16
Intimidation:
    definition of, 469
    difficult negotiations and, 384
    dual concerns model and, 8–9
    hardball tactics/dirty tricks and, 69
Intraorganizational negotiations, 36
Intra-team negotiations, 297, 298, 311
Intrinsic interests, 91, 469
Investigative negotiations, 51–56
Irrational escalation of commitment, 208, 469
Issues:
    analyzing the other party and, 35, 36
    collectivistic cultures and, 362
    communications and, 160
    component parts of the situation and,
        30–31
    definition of, 469
    difficult negotiations and, 386
    integrative negotiations and, 97–98
    international negotiations and, 365, 366
    inter-team negotiations and, 312
    mediation and, 414
    multiparty negotiations and, 299, 313
    testing assumptions and, 36–37

Just cause, 418–419, 423
Justice, 271, 278–279, 279, 280t

Knowledge structures, 245
    culture and, 361
    international negotiations and, 362
    thinking hats and, 306
Kovach, K. K., 182

Labor-management negotiations, 309
Labor unions:
    arbitration and, 416, 418
    international negotiations and, 371–372
    inter-team negotiations and, 311
    strategic planning and, 28
    See also Union negotiations
Language:
    international negotiations and, 365
    power/influence and, 244
Larson, D. A., 13

Leadership:
  culture and, 381
  managing negotiation teams and, 319
Legal issues:
  arbitration and, 415–420, 423
  difficult negotiations and, 407
  ethics and, 280, 282, 283
  integrative negotiations and, 96
  international negotiations and, 372
  third-party interventions and, 410
Legal pluralism, 356–357, 469
Legitimate power, 240, 240t, 469
  See also Power
Listening:
  integrative negotiations and, 89
  negotiating with inferior powers and, 251
Litigation *See* Legal issues
Logrolling:
  definition of, 469
  integrative negotiations and, 94–95, 100
Lose-win approach to negotiations, 8, 469
Losing face:
  closing deals and, 120, 122–123, 128
  concessions and, 65
  definition of, 469
  difficult negotiations and, 385
  international negotiations and, 363
  personality issues and, 328
Lowball, 402, 441
  definition of, 470
  hardball tactics/dirty tricks and, 69, 385
Low context cultures:
  definition of, 469
  international negotiations and, 363, 364, 366
Low power distance cultures, 362, 469
Lying *See* Deception

Machiavellianism:
  definition of, 470
  detecting deceptions and, 176
  personality issues and, 328
Malevolent motives, 169, 214, 395
Mandatory arbitration, 417, 470
McCredie, M., 103
Mediation, 452–453
  ADR and, 411
  blame and, 414
  caucuses and, 413
  confidence and, 412, 414
  confidentiality and, 413

decision-making and, 411
definition of, 470
emotional issues and, 414
empathy and, 412
final outcomes and, 411
frames and, 414
goals and, 412–413
interests and, 414, 415
issues and, 414
open-ended questions and, 414
orchestrators and, 411
power and, 412
problem solving and, 411, 413, 414–415
relationship interests and, 411, 412
resources and, 412
ripeness and, 412
saving face and, 412
skills, 429–430 and
time issues and, 412
trust and, 412, 414
Merger/acquisition negotiations, 28–29, 309
Message decoding, 161, 470
Message scope, 243, 470
Message sidedness, 243
Middle stage of negotiations, 10f, 12, 118, 470
Mini-trials, 411, 422
Misrepresentations, 268, 276t, 282
Miswanting, 219–220, 221t
Mixed-motive negotiations, 9, 470
Mnookin, R. H., 22
Mood:
  definition of, 470
  emotional biases and, 218
  emotional decision-making errors
    and, 221t
  negotiating with inferior powers and, 251
Moral values:
  ethics and, 268
  gender issues and, 325–326
  See also Values
Motivational orientations:
  definition of, 470
  negotiation styles and, 332
  power/influence and, 242, 245
Multi-issue negotiations:
  integrative negotiation and, 113
  international negotiations and, 364, 366
  multiparty negotiations and, 303
  power/influence and, 257
  third-party intervention and, 415, 428

Multiparty negotiations and, 297–314, 301
    managing, 316–320
Multiple equivalent offers:
    closing deals and, 125
    definition of, 470
    integrative negotiations and, 98
Multiple-issue offers, 217, 365
Mutual gains negotiations:
    dual concerns model and, 8–9
    integrative negotiations and, 103
Myers-briggs type inventory, 330–331, 331t, 338
    definition of, 470
Mythical fixed pie, 120, 213–214, 365
    decision-making and, 216
    integrative negotiations and, 93
    perceptual decision-making errors and, 217t
Myths:
    integrative negotiations and, 86–87
    power/influence and, 239

Naming the move, 388, 470
Narcotic effect, 416–417, 470
Needs:
    communications and, 161
    difficult negotiations and, 391
    e-mail communications and, 186
    integrative negotiations and, 84
    interests and, 31
    power/influence and, 245, 253
    understanding your opponent's, 202
Negotiating teams, 297–314, 444, 445, 447
    culture and, 381
    inter-teams, 297, 298, 311–312
    intra-teams, 297, 298, 311
    managing, 316–320
Negotiation styles:
    incompatible, 384
    individual differences and, 332, 337, 338
    multiparty negotiations and, 318
Nibble:
    definition of, 470
    hardball tactics/dirty tricks and, 69–70, 385
No-agreement alternatives, 32, 94
Noise:
    communications and, 161, 162t, 177
    definition of, 471
    negotiating with inferior powers and, 251
Nonspecific compensation, 95–96, 100, 306
    definition of, 471
    integrative negotiations and, 95–96

Nonverbal communications, 172–176
    definition of, 471
    e-mail communications and, 185
    nonverbal cues and, 13, 14, 15, 177, 178.
        See also Cues
    types of, 172t
    See also Body language
Norms:
    communications and, 165, 170t
    culture and, 361–362
    difficult negotiations and, 401
    ethics and, 279–280
    of fairness, 67, 68t
    gender issues and, 327
    individual differences and, 338
    international negotiations and, 361, 362
    multiparty negotiations and, 301
    personality issues and, 329
    women and, 343

Objections:
    appreciative moves and, 390
    black hat thinking and, 308
    closing deals and, 118–123, 128
    distributive bargaining and, 71–72
    preparations and, 118–123
Objective criteria:
    distributive bargaining and, 65–66
    integrative negotiations and, 96–97, 100
    preparations and, 24
Offers:
    closing deals and, 118
    communications and, 169
    international negotiations and, 364–365, 366
    multiparty negotiations and, 299–300
Online dispute resolutions, 13–18
    See also E-mail communications; Internet
Open-ended questions:
    closing deals and, 123
    communications and, 167, 170
    difficult negotiations and, 397, 399
    integrative negotiations and, 89
    mediation and, 414
    See also Questions
Opening offers:
    closing deals and, 124
    communications and, 163
    concessions and, 65
    decision-making and, 212
    distributive bargaining and, 59, 63–65, 72

ethics and, 282
hardball tactics/dirty tricks and, 69
international negotiations and, 365
optimistic, 62–63
Orchestrators, 411
Outcome biases, 274
Overconfidence biases, 212
Overconfidence/overoptimism:
　decision-making and, 212, 213t
　definition of, 471

Peppet, S. R., 22
Perceptions:
　communications and, 161–163
　decision-making and, 217
　integrative negotiations and, 88, 89
Perceptual biases, 207
Perceptual decision-making errors:
　decision-making and, 212–217
　definition of, 471
Peripheral route, 244–245, 250, 251
Personal insults, 21, 69, 185
Personality:
　culture and, 378, 379, 382
　decision-making and, 215
　difficult negotiations and, 390
　3-D negotiations and, 108
　ethics and, 271t
　individual differences and, 328–331,
　　337–339
　integrative negotiations and, 98
　negotiating team conflict and, 322
Personal relevance, 242, 243
Perspective taking, 201–203
　decision-making and, 215
　definition of, 471
　perceptual decision-making errors and, 217t
Persuasion:
　harnessing the science of, 258–266
　negotiating with inferior powers and, 251
　power/influence and, 252
Planned offers, 63
Planning:
　international negotiations and, 364
　negotiating team conflict and, 321
　strategic, 25–30
　See also Preparations
Political issues:
　analyzing the other party and, 36
　culture and, 361

international negotiations and, 358, 359, 365,
　366, 371–372
　power/influence and, 238
Political pluralism, 357, 471
Positional negotiations:
　definition of, 471
　distributive bargaining and, 59
　dual concerns model and, 8–9
Positions:
　component parts of the situation and, 31
　difficult negotiations and, 390
　distributive bargaining and, 59, 73
　ethics and, 282
　integrative negotiations and, 90–92
Power, 237–253, 441
　bargaining, 35, 466
　BATNAs and, 61
　coercive, 239–240, 240t, 252, 466
　communications and, 164
　different combinations of, 72
　difficult negotiations and, 385, 397–398, 399
　distributive bargaining and, 72
　e-mail communications and, 188
　ethics and, 269–270
　expert, 240t, 467
　gender issues and, 326–327, 338
　increasing, 252
　individual differences and, 338
　informational, 240t, 469
　international negotiations and,
　　361, 362, 371, 373
　legitimate, 240, 240t, 469
　mediation and, 412
　multiparty negotiations and, 298, 310, 311
　negotiating with inferior, 250–251
　power/influence and, 244
　referent, 240, 240t, 471
　rewards and, 239–240, 240t, 472
　securing, 201
　sources of, 240t
　strategic planning and, 28
　women and, 344
Praise, 259, 260
Premature judgment, 92
Pre-negotiations, 10
　BATNAs and, 33
　e-mail communications and, 191–192
　power/influence and, 249
Preparations, 23–24, 38–39
　BATNAs and, 33

building/testing assumptions and, 36–37
closing deals and, 128
decision-making and, 212, 216–217, 221
distributive bargaining and, 59–60, 72
hardball tactics/dirty tricks and, 70
integrative negotiations and, 84–86
international negotiations and, 355, 359, 365
inter-team negotiations and, 311
managing negotiation teams and, 318, 319
multiparty negotiations and, 304, 312
negotiating with inferior powers and, 251
operationalizing the plan and, 30–36
power/influence and, 249–250, 252, 253
strategic planning and, 25–30
See also Planning
Pressure moves, 386–387, 471
Prestige, 164
Principled approach to negotiations, 8–9, 471
Principle interests, 91, 471
Priorities:
    integrative negotiations and, 91–92
    international negotiations and, 363, 364, 366
    inter-team negotiations and, 312
    negotiating with inferior powers and, 251
Prior negotiations, 35–36, 270
Private negotiations, 28
Probing questions, 89, 119, 122, 399
    See also Questions
Problem analyzing, 42–50
Problem solving:
    communications and, 166–168
    culture and, 378
    decision-making and, 217
    difficult negotiations and, 385, 386, 393–395,
        396, 397
    e-mail communications and, 188
    integrative negotiations and, 89
    mediation and, 411, 413, 414–415
    multiparty negotiations and, 302, 313
    negotiation places and, 38
    online dispute resolutions and, 13–18
    personality issues and, 328
    third-party interventions and, 411
Process interests:
    ADR and, 411
    definition of, 471
    integrative negotiations and, 91
Proposals:
    BATNAs and, 32
    decision-making and, 216

difficult negotiations and, 386
multiparty negotiations and, 309
negotiating with inferior powers and, 251
power/influence and, 247, 252, 253
Proselfs, 329, 471
Pro socials, 329, 471

Questions:
    assumptive, 127
    communications and, 166–168, 178
    international negotiations and, 363, 364, 366
    probing, 89, 119, 122, 399
    reciprocal, 363, 364, 366, 471
    sequential, 127–128, 472
    targeted, 167
    See also Open-ended questions

Race issues, 275, 288
Rapport, 36–37
    building, 36–37
    communications and, 169, 170t, 173–174, 175
    definition of, 466
    difficult negotiations and, 390
    e-mail communications and, 184, 185, 188,
        189, 191–192, 195
    ethics and, 283
    first impressions and, 173
    integrative negotiations and, 84, 86, 88
    international negotiations and, 361
    multiparty negotiations and, 300
    nonverbal communications and, 173
Reactive devaluation:
    decision-making and, 216
    definition of, 471
    perceptual decision-making errors and, 217t
Reciprocal offering strategy, 364, 366
Reciprocal questioning approach, 363, 364, 366
    definition of, 471
    See also Questions
Reciprocation, 81
Reciprocity:
    communications and, 170t
    definition of, 471
    power/influence and, 246
    principle of, 260–261
Recognition, 31, 86, 91, 119
    building rapport and, 191
    closing deals and, 120
    communication and, 197
    problem solving and, 393

Red hat thinking, 307t, 308–309
Reference points:
    decision-making and, 210
    power/influence and, 248
Referent power, 240, 240t, 471
    See also Power
Reject then retreat, 246, 471
Relationship interests, 11, 441
    analyzing the other party and, 35–36
    arbitration and, 418–419, 423
    closing deals and, 127, 128
    communications and, 166
    compromise and, 76
    culture and, 377–378, 380
    definition of, 471
    difficult negotiations and, 384, 392,
        397–398, 399
    dual concerns model and, 8–9
    effect of litigation of, 405
    e-mail communications and, 190–191
    emotions and, 332–337
    ethics and, 294, 295
    fairness norms and, 68t
    first impressions and, 37
    gender issues and, 325, 326–327, 328
    goals and, 29–30
    hardball tactics/dirty tricks and, 68
    harming, 72
    harnessing the science of persuasion and,
        260, 261
    integrative negotiations and, 86, 88, 91, 98,
        99, 100
    international negotiations and, 360, 361, 362,
        365, 366, 369, 370–371, 372, 374, 375
    inter-team negotiations and, 311
    litigation and, 410
    managing negotiation teams and, 316–317
    mediation and, 411, 412
    multiparty negotiations and, 299, 300, 301,
        302, 309, 310, 312, 313
    nature of interactions and, 28
    negotiation styles and, 332
    online dispute resolutions and, 13–18
    personality issues and, 329
    power/influence and, 238, 252
    third-party interventions and, 430
Relativity, 245–246, 471
Representatives, 300–303
Reputation, 349–350
    alternatives to, 284

communications and, 164
ethics and, 269, 276, 283, 295
hardball tactics/dirty tricks and, 68
harming, 72, 73
unethical negotiating behavior and, 281
Reservation prices, 33–34
    definition of, 471
    distributive bargaining and, 59
    haggling and, 79
Resistance points, 33–34
    arbitration and, 423
    collectivistic cultures and, 362
    concessions and, 65
    decision-making and, 212, 221
    definition of, 472
    distributive bargaining and, 59, 60f, 72
    estimating the other party's, 61
    ethics and, 282
    first offers and, 66
    integrative negotiations and, 92
    inter-team negotiations and, 312
    multiparty negotiations and, 303, 304
    power/influence and, 250
    revealing, 70
    See also Target points
Resources:
    arbitration and, 415–416
    difficult negotiations and, 385
    distributive bargaining and, 58, 59, 60
    ethics and, 279
    fixed, 213
    mediation and, 412
    multiparty negotiations and, 310–311, 313
    negotiating with inferior powers and, 251
    negotiation places and, 37–38
    power/influence and, 239, 252
    strategic planning and, 28
Respect:
    building rapport and, 36, 173
    closing deals and, 120, 127
    culture and, 378
    decision-making and, 209, 221
    difficult negotiations and, 390, 399
    ethics and, 278
    multiparty negotiations and, 305, 308, 313
    power/influence and, 250
    preparations and, 39
Responsibilities:
    international negotiations and, 370
    negotiating team conflict and, 322

Retribution, 281
Revenge:
    ethics and, 270
    hardball tactics/dirty tricks and, 68
Reward power, 239–240, 240t, 472
    See also Power
Rewards:
    ethics and, 271, 278–279
    multiparty negotiations and, 302
    negotiating with inferior powers and, 251
    power/influence and, 247–248
Rhetoric, 392
Rights:
    different combinations of, 72
    duties and, 472
    ethics and, 271, 277–278, 278, 280t
Ripeness, 412
Risk taking, 439
    culture and, 381–382
    different attitudes towards, 95
    international negotiations and, 358, 359, 360,
        366, 373
    multiparty negotiations and, 308, 311
Roles:
    definition of, 472
    emotional issues and, 335–336
Rules:
    arbitration and, 420
    culture and, 381
    difficult negotiations and, 385
    ethics and, 280
    international negotiations and, 356–357

Saving face:
    closing deals and, 120
    difficult negotiations and, 390
    managing negotiation teams and, 318
    mediation and, 412
    multiparty negotiations and, 312–313
Scarcity:
    power/influence and, 247
    principle of, 264–265
Schemata:
    communications and, 162–163, 177
    power/influence and, 241–242, 245
    stereotypes and, 214
Schneider, A. K., 182
Scope, message, 243
Sebenius, J. K., 368
Secrecy, 70, 116, 134

Selective attention, 208, 213t, 472
Self-construals, 325
Self-efficacy, 328, 472
Self-esteem, 335, 337–338
Self-monitoring, 329, 472
Sequential questions, 127–128, 472
    See also Questions
Shadow negotiations, 10–11
    definition of, 472
    difficult negotiations and, 386, 392
Shared strategy, 318
Silence:
    communications and, 161, 169
    distributive bargaining and, 66, 72
    managing negotiation teams and, 318–319
Sincerity, 99t
    building rapport and, 173–174
    first impressions and, 173
Sinister attribution, 202
    e-mail communications and, 188–189,
        190, 192
Six hat thinking:
    definition of, 472
    inter-team negotiations and, 312
    multiparty negotiations and, 306–309, 307t
Skills:
    communication, 195
    e-mail communications and, 189
    integrative negotiations and, 92
    inter-team negotiations and, 311
    mediation, 429–430
    multiparty negotiations and, 301
    negotiations and, 11
Snow jobs, 70
    definition of, 472
    difficult negotiations and, 385
Social accounts, 165, 472
Social awareness, 169, 186, 187
Social comparisons, 247
Social contracts, 270, 279–280, 280t
    definition of, 472
Social cues, 185, 329
    See also Cues
Social heuristics, 76, 77
Social informational processing theory, 14
Social interactions:
    gender issues and, 325
    nonverbal communications and, 172
Social norms:
    communications and, 170t

ethics and, 270
See also Norms
Social proof:
  power/influence and, 247
  principle of, 261
Social status *See* Status
Social value orientation, 329, 472
Splitting the difference, 124, 472
Status:
  closing deals and, 120
  communications and, 161
  culture and, 361
  definition of, 472
  emotional issues and, 335
  ethics and, 279
  first impressions and, 173
  gender issues and, 326–327
  international negotiations and, 362
Status quo:
  closing deals and, 126
  difficult negotiations and, 387
  women and, 343
Status quo biases:
  closing deals and, 126
  definition of, 472
  See also Biases
Stereotyping:
  ADR and, 410
  culture and, 362
  decision-making and, 214–215
  definition of, 472
  ethics and, 275, 288
  gender issues and, 324, 326, 327, 338, 345
  international negotiations and, 365
  perceptual decision-making errors and, 217t
  testing assumptions and, 37
  women and, 343
Strategic moves, 11
  definition of, 472
  difficult negotiations and, 386–387
Strategic planning, 25–30
  See also Planning; Preparations
Strategic turns, 11
  definition of, 472
  difficult negotiations and, 387–389, 399
Strategies:
  definition of, 473
  distributive bargaining and, 58, 59t
  goals and, 30
  multiparty negotiations and, 304

Structural connection, 334
Structural position, 327
Structuring conversations, 174–175, 473
Substantive interests, 29, 30
  definition of, 473
  dual concerns model and, 8–9
  integrative negotiations and, 91
Surveys, 312, 444, 455t
Sweeteners, 126, 473
Synchronicity, 184, 185
  communications and, 169
  utilizing, 190

Tactics:
  closing deals and, 127–128
  definition of, 473
  distributive bargaining and, 60–68
  ethical questions and, 275–276
  hard bargaining, 21–22
  integrative bargaining and, 87–94
  strategies and, 30
Targeted questions, 167
  See also Questions
Target points, 31–32
  arbitration and, 423
  decision-making and, 212, 222
  definition of, 473
  distributive bargaining and, 59, 60f, 62
  ethics and, 282
  first offers and, 63–64, 66
  integrative negotiations and, 92
  inter-team negotiations and, 312
  multiparty negotiations and, 304
  opening offers and, 62
  revealing, 70
  See also Resistance points
Targets:
  collectivistic cultures and, 362
  distributive bargaining and, 62, 72
  international negotiations and, 375
  power/influence and, 252
Team negotiations, 297–314
  culture and, 381
  managing, 316–320
Technology, 5–6
  communications and, 169
  international negotiations and,
    356–357
  managing negotiation teams and, 319–320
  negotiation places and, 38

Text messaging, 38
  communications and, 169, 170t
  managing negotiation teams and, 319–320
  See also E-mail communications; Technology
Third-party interventions, 409–424, 435
  closing deals and, 120
Threats:
  hardball tactics/dirty tricks and, 69
  integrative negotiations and, 88
Threat sensitivity, 328
  definition of, 473
Time issues:
  arbitration and, 416, 422, 423
  building rapport/testing assumptions and,
    36–37
  civil litigation and, 410
  closing deals and, 120, 128
  culture and, 379
  difficult negotiations and, 385
  distributive bargaining and, 66–67
  e-mail communications and, 190
  international negotiations and, 360, 364, 366,
    369, 374
  legal actions and, 405–406
  mediation and, 412
  multiparty negotiations and, 298, 309
  preparations and, 39
  See also Deadlines
Tradeoffs:
  closing deals and, 120
  communications and, 165
  decision making and, 235
  distributive bargaining and, 75, 76
  integrative negotiations and, 91, 95, 98
  international negotiations and, 365
  multiparty negotiations and, 305
  preparation and, 31, 35
Transparency:
  good cop-bad cop and, 69
  illusion of, 216, 217t
Trust, 439, 440, 441
  analyzing the other party and, 35
  building rapport and, 10, 36, 173
  closing deals and, 122
  communications and, 170t
  culture and, 382
  decision-making and, 209, 221
  detecting deceptions and, 176
  3-D negotiations and, 108
  dual concerns model and, 8–9

  e-mail communications and, 185, 188,
    190–191, 195
  ethics and, 270, 275, 283, 293
  harnessing the science of persuasion
    and, 261
  increasing/repairing, 99t
  integrative negotiations and,
    86, 98–99, 100
  international negotiations and, 361, 366
  lacking, 72
  mediation and, 412, 414
  multiparty negotiations and, 299
  online dispute resolutions and, 13–15
  personality issues and, 329
  power/influence and, 250
  preparations and, 39
  See also Distrust
Truth:
  detecting deceptions and, 175–176
  ethics and, 268, 270, 275–276, 277, 282, 294
  international negotiations and, 363
  multiparty negotiations and, 308
Tulumello, A. S., 22
Two-sided messages, 243, 473

Ultimatums:
  diffcult negotiations and, 385
  integrative negotiations and, 88
Union negotiations, 444–457, 454t
  multiparty negotiations and, 300
  strategic planning and, 28
  See also Labor unions
U.S. Supreme Court, 423
Utilitarianism:
  definition of, 473
  ethics and, 270, 277, 279, 280t

Values, 20
  communications and, 161
  culture and, 361, 381
  ethics and, 268, 269, 272, 287–288
  gender issues and, 325, 326
  international negotiations and, 361, 362
  multiparty negotiations and, 299, 306
  See also Moral values
Visual cues, 37–38
Vocal cues, 174

Walk aways, 33–34, 435, 441
  closing deals and, 124

commitments and, 71–72
decision-making and, 208–209
definition of, 473
difficult negotiations and, 404
distributive bargaining and,
 62, 68, 72, 73
3-D negotiations and, 108
ethics and, 282
haggling and, 81
international negotiations and, 375
opening offers and, 63
power/influence and, 240, 252
third-party interventions and, 410
White hat thinking, 306, 307t, 308
Win-lose negotiations, 376, 378
definition of, 473
dual concerns model and, 8–9
Winner's curse:
communications and, 161
definition of, 473
distributive bargaining and, 62
first offers and, 66

Win-win negotiations, 37, 133, 376, 378, 441
definition of, 473
dual concerns model and, 8–9
Wise agreements, 72, 89, 99
definition of, 473
preparations and, 38

Yellow hat thinking, 306–308, 307t, 308

Zero-sum negotiations:
definition of, 473
dual concerns model and, 8–9
fixed pie and, 87
mythical fixed pie and, 93, 213
Zone Of Possible Agreement (ZOPA), 35
decision-making and, 207
definition of, 473
distributive bargaining and, 59, 60
first offers and, 64
haggling and, 80–81
individual differences and, 338
opening offers and, 63

About the Author

David S. Hames earned his PhD in Organizational Behavior at the Kenan-Flagler School of Business, University of North Carolina at Chapel Hill. He teaches courses in Negotiation and Alternative Dispute Resolution, Human Resources Management and Labor-Management Relations. His research has been published in journals such as *Group and Organization Management*, *Human Resource Management Review*, *Leadership and Organization Development Journal*, *Employee Responsibilities &* *Rights Journal*, and *Labor Law Journal*. He is a member of the editorial board of the *Decision Sciences Journal of Innovative Education*. He has served as a labor arbitrator and as a mediator of employment disputes. Before becoming an academic, Dr. Hames served as the Human Resources Director at the Clinton Memorial Hospital, and as a professional recruiter in the Human Resources Department at Standard Oil of Indiana (now BP Amoco).

SAGE Research Methods Online
The essential tool for researchers

**Sign up now at
www.sagepub.com/srmo
for more information.**

An expert research tool

- An **expertly designed taxonomy** with more than 1,400 unique terms for social and behavioral science research methods
- **Visual and hierarchical search tools** to help you discover material and link to related methods

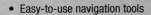

- Easy-to-use navigation tools
- Content organized by complexity
- Tools for citing, printing, and downloading content with ease
- Regularly updated content and features

A wealth of essential content

- The most comprehensive picture of quantitative, qualitative, and mixed methods available today
- More than **100,000 pages of SAGE book and reference material** on research methods as well as editorially selected material from SAGE journals
- More than **600 books** available in their entirety online

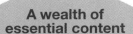

Launching 2011!

$SAGE research methods online